D1338498

FASCISM TODAY

Angelo Del Boca
and Mario Giovana

FASCISM TODAY
A World Survey

Translated by
R. H. BOOTHROYD

HEINEMANN : LONDON

William Heinemann Ltd

LONDON MELBOURNE TORONTO

CAPE TOWN AUCKLAND

Printed in Great Britain by
Clarke, Doble & Brendon Ltd
Plymouth

Contents

Contents

Acknowledgements

We feel that we must first of all express our sincere thanks to the Editor and Directors of the *Gazzetta del Popolo* of Turin, who have kindly allowed us to reproduce extracts from interviews and articles written for that journal by Angelo Del Boca and have shown that they fully appreciate the importance of the subject with which our book deals.

We also owe a debt of gratitude to the directors and archivists of the *Fédération Internationale des Résistants* (FIR), Vienna; to Simon Wiesenthal of the *Dokumentationszentrum des Bundes jüdischer Verfolgter des Naziregimes*, Vienna; to Hubert Halin of the *Union de la Résistance et de la Déportation* (UIRD), Brussels; to the *Commission Internationale des Juristes*, Geneva; to Mrs Moira Field, Head of Library Research, *Encyclopaedia Britannica*; to the Librarian and staff of the *Biblioteca Civica*, Turin; to the *Centro Studi Pietro Gobetti,* Turin, and in particular to our friend Signora Carla Gobetti; and to the Editors of the periodical *Resistenza*. We have also to thank Signorine Mariangela Rosolen and Consolina Vigliero for their assistance in translating certain texts, and our colleagues Eugenio Galvano, Michele Pavissich, Ugo Ronfani, Bruno Tedeschi and Stelio Tomei for their collaboration.

We are also grateful for information, suggestions and statements received from numerous sources, and in particular we would like to mention the following: in ITALY: Professor Riccardo Bauer; Senator General Raffaele Cadorna; Senator Pietro Caleffi; Deputies Carlo Donat-Cattin, Vittorio Foa, Giorgio La Pira and Achille Marazza; the writer Primo Levi; Dr Lucio Libertini; Senator Emilio Lussu; Professor Giulio Mazzon of the national secretariat of the ANPI (National Association of Italian Partisans); Dr Lamberto Mercuri of the *Comitato Anticoloniale Italiano*; Deputy Fausto Nitti, Senator Ferruccio Parri, Professor Luigi Rostagni of the UTET publishing firm in Turin; the writer Ignazio Silone; Professor Leo Valiani; in FRANCE: Maître Pierre Stibbe, of the Paris Bar; Georges Montaron, editor of *Témoignage Chrétien*; Jean-Marie Domenach, editor of *Esprit*; Françoise Giroud, co-editor

vii

Acknowledgements

of *L'Express*; André Delcroix, of *France-Observateur*; our friends
Robert Paris, Raffaele Coraluppi and Luciano Bolis; in GERMANY:
Kron Brandeburg, spokesman in Bonn for the Social-Democratic
Party; the writer and journalist Heinz Abosch; Willy Höhn of the
Vereinigung der Verfolgten des Naziregimes (VVN), Frankfurt·
in AUSTRIA: the Under-Secretary for Internal Affairs, Otto Kranzl·
mayr; in BELGIUM: the journalist Michel Géoris-Reitshof; the
secretary-general of the *Front de l'Indépendance*, Georges Dewamme;
in YUGOSLAVIA: M. Božidar Gorjan, of the Slovene Republic's
Information Service; in SPAIN: the writers Marcos Ana, José
Agustín Goytisolo, Dionisio Ridruejo, López Salinas, García Horte-
lano, Jesús López Pacheco; the publisher José Martínez; the former
Prime Minister Gil Robles; in PORTUGAL and ANGOLA: the poets
Costa Andrade and Mario de Andrade; in JAPAN: the Italian diplomat Antonio Widmar; the secretary-general of the Liberal-Demo-
cratic Party, Deputy Schigeo Maeo; the Socialist Deputy Shimpei
Fujimaki, head of the political secretariat; Akira Iwai, secretary-
general of the *Sōhyō* trade unions; Tomio Nishizawa, of the
Communist Party's central committee; Deputy Sasaki, vice-
secretary of the Social Democratic Party; Joji Onoda, secretary-
general of the *Zengakuren* student movement; the writers
Sawako Ariyoshi, Tatzuo Ishikawa and Jiro Osaragi; in
SOUTH VIETNAM: Simon Michau, correspondent in Saigon of the
Agence France-Presse; Nguyen Van Huan, director of the Informa-
tion and Press Service; in the UNITED STATES OF AMERICA: the
journalist Mauro Calamandrei; the editors and archivists of the
New York Herald Tribune; in SOUTH AFRICA: Albert John Luthuli,
winner of the Nobel Peace Prize; the writer Alan Paton; in AFRICA:
Ferhat Abbas, former head of the provisional government in
Algeria; Mohammed Boudiaf, ex-member of the provisional government in Algeria; Allal el-Fassi, leader of the *Istiqlal*; Aberrahim
Bouabid and Abderrahman Yusufi, leaders of the *Union Nationale
des Forces Populaires* (UNFP); Léopold Sédar Senghor, President
of Senegal; Sékou Touré, President of Guinea; the Ghanaian opposition leaders Kofi Busia and the late Joseph Danquah, who died
in prison at Accra in February 1965.

Lastly, we have to acknowledge statements and information received from Maître Tixier-Vignancour, Sir Oswald Mosley, Fred
Borth, Akao Bin and Salvatore Francia.

Foreword

When we started to write this book, our idea was to provide our readers with a preliminary review, as coherent and objective as possible, of neo-Fascism and neo-Nazism as they exist today, including all kindred movements. But on thinking the matter over, we felt that it was essential, and only right, that such a review should be preceded by a brief retrospective study. In other words, it was incumbent upon us to take a step backward in time in order to relate the neo-Fascism and neo-Nazism of the 1960s, the kindred trends existing in many countries and the surviving régimes of the Fascist type to their remote and original sources, these being imperialistic nationalism, racialism, and the various dictatorships which sprang up in Europe and elsewhere between the two wars— in short, all movements which were quasi-Fascist, or at all events nationalistic in their aggressive tendencies, wherever they were to be found with an organization of their own and with specific plans of action.

There were two ways of approaching this task of reviewing the tendencies and activities of right-wing totalitarian movements. One was to take each country in turn and give a brief account of the movements or forms of government which existed in each of them before the 1939–45 war, or in some cases even survived it. The other was to make only a brief mention of these historical factors and to concentrate on the conditions which enabled them to exist and sometimes to succeed, while at the same time to avoid seeing Fascists hiding behind every bush and taking good care to distinguish between the varying results.

We discarded the first solution, because it would have meant limiting ourselves to a series of 'handbooks' on the vicissitudes of too many countries, reduced to such a generic form as to constitute little more than a chronological table interspersed with a few hasty comments. We therefore turned to the second solution and set ourselves the task of defining the nature of the phenomena we were studying, trying at the same time to give an accurate classification,

A*

and to establish certain distinctive features, of the movements with which we were dealing.

Naturally, we were far from thinking that we would be able to produce a complete history of the various forms of Fascism, Nazism and other right-wing movements, nor did we flatter ourselves that our efforts could provide an exhaustive and definitive analysis of each of these trends. What we have tried to do is to give the reader information well supported by documents, but without pretensions to historical completeness, and thus to provide a reasonably ample panorama of the subject together with a tentative judgement as to the causes and nature of the events with which we were dealing. Consequently, in the first part of this volume our criterion has been to give a rapid account of the antecedents of neo-Fascism and neo-Nazism as well as of any other right-wing movements which have a certain importance in the world of today. The second part of the book, dealing with the present situation, or rather with the events of the last twenty years, contains a greater number of documentary references and items of information that are the result of long and laborious research. For obvious reasons our attention has been concentrated mainly on those phenomena which to us seemed most important, and we have devoted less space to those of minor interest.

In our approach to the subject it has been our constant aim to report events as fairly as possible and to discard all preconceptions when analysing them. That, of course, does not mean that we have no convictions of our own or that we do not, in general, support the ideals of anti-Fascism, or that we have not based our interpretation on our own ideological standpoint, of which we make no secret. This will, we trust, be made sufficiently clear to our readers in the pages that follow, thus rendering any further mention of the question superfluous. In other words we make no claim to a 'neutrality' which we do not feel, and we shall raise no objections if we are accused of having written about Fascism and National Socialism from a standpoint based on a particular method of historical analysis, since in doing so we are merely claiming the right to exercise our own critical faculties.

Awareness of the past and a knowledge of the present can help the generation of today to guard against the allurements and deceits of the enemies of its future, which were once the cause of such monstrous disasters and have not been entirely destroyed by the flames that reduced Adolf Hitler's bunker to ashes or by the inglorious end of Benito Mussolini. The collapse of Fascism and Nazism has not removed those aspirations and temptations from which reactionary dictatorships draw their nourishment. That is why we must study them and be on our guard.

ANGELO DEL BOCA
MARIO GIOVANA

1965

1 What is Fascism?

A note on definition of terms

In October 1944 accusations of 'Fascism' were being bandied about
between the various political parties in Italy, and this prompted
Benedetto Croce to write his famous article *Who is a Fascist?*
The Neapolitan philosopher's primary aim was to give his own
ideas on the nature of the phenomenon, which to his way of thinking was akin to Nazism in its origins, in the inconsistencies of its
doctrines and in its aims. In this he was deliberately following the
assumption of Drucker, who denied that there was any historical
or logical foundation for the theory that these two forms of totalitarianism had their roots in the class struggle, and on the contrary
emphasized the heterogeneous nature of the consensus that was
their life-blood, from which he concluded that they were historical
episodes, due mainly to the prevalence of a wave of aberration in
the nations which had the misfortune to be the protagonists of
these movements. 'Because,' says Croce, in support of the thesis
put forward by Drucker in *The End of Economic Man*, 'Fascism,
Nazism, was a factor, or an intellectual and moral disease, not
confined to one class, but pervading the minds and imaginations
and wills of men in general, a crisis born of the loss of faith not
only in rational Liberalism, but also in Marxism, which in its
own way, despite its materialism, was rational, though it had failed
to achieve that free society of equal men which it had promised,
and instead paved the way for forms of absolute rule under a
privileged class of bureaucrats.' For the philosopher, the conditions
which favoured the success of the two forms of totalitarianism
created by Mussolini and Hitler must be sought 'in the void which
had opened in the souls of men and in the decline of their will-
power', in a suspension of men's ability to distinguish spiritual and
rational values; this culminated in 'a sudden impulse; since they had
faith in nothing and no positive system of ideas, they rejected the
past and declined to justify the seizure of power by totalitarian
régimes; all of which attracted and fascinated the masses despite

the fact that few people believed what the Fascists and Nazis asserted.'[1] For this reason Croce returned to the theory of a 'temporary indisposition' which afflicted the collective souls of the Italians and Germans (Wilhelm Röpke subsequently described Nazism as a 'sickness of the German soul')—a kind of accidental and transient aberration from the paths of reason which could be cured only by a deliberate act of will and a return to rationality, a return, in other words, to the lost rational dimensions of human thought and action.

In his *Storia d'Italia*, when discussing the genesis of Italian nationalistic feeling, Croce had already given a striking description of a similar crisis of bewilderment, of abandonment to the delusions of a diseased imagination:

> . . . Bismarckism and industrialism, their repercussions and internal antitheses, which could not be transformed into a new and more serene religion, had created a confused state of mind, hovering between avidity for life, the spirit of adventure and conquest, and a frantic hankering for power . . .'[2]

The Neapolitan philosopher thus confirmed the doctrines of the Liberal historians when faced with the complex realities of Fascism and Nazism, and this just before the close of the war which the régimes symbolized by the fasces and the swastika had let loose upon Europe and the world—at a time, that is to say, when the problem of a profound and exhaustive study was beginning to take shape, the problem of discovering the causes of these phenomena which had threatened to overwhelm mankind, of laying bare their intimate essence, their real sources, and the reasons for their success. For such a task Croce's analysis did not seem very helpful. It merely cast a pallid gleam on the outlines of the problem, a feeble light which illuminated only some of the broader implications and did not get at the crux of the matter. The theory of a crisis of the 'rational soul' relegated to the darkness of the inscrutable and the casual a question which was complicated, but—as was soon to become more and more evident—was intrinsically related to actual events and contained the key to a rational explanation of their passage from embryonic trends and influences to complete systems of government. If the question were to be put in the way Croce suggested, the causes of Fascism and Nazism, together with the real nature of the two movements, would be consigned to a species of limbo, over which there hovered the sin of the irrationality of nations and the mysterious, still prevalent, faith in an unrealized surge of contrition which would suffice to cancel the error and relegate it to the recesses of a past that could never repeat itself. Moreover, in this way Fascism and Nazism become fabulous figurations of the spirit of evil, capable of bewitching a whole generation of human beings who, be it said to their credit, are normally good and rational, but are exposed to the dangers of temptation to such a degree that they are prone to collective madness.

These were but fragile answers to the question all the world was asking after the tragic experiences of those years. It was not enough to say in reply that a kind of 'landslide' had led to a decline in rational responsibility, thus identifying Fascism with a lapse into the irrational. It was not enough, and unsatisfactory for everybody, to be told that every form of Fascism is due to a lack of true faith, to a lack of any effective policy, or that it is an experiment in violence, an improvisation based on violence. Nor was it enough to be told that Fascism had triumphed because of the decline of intellectual and moral restraining influences, excited by rhetoric and by the delusive tricks of imagination, and that it had imposed itself thanks to a faith extorted from the masses and by claiming that the solutions it offered were novelties. All these things had been vaguely perceived by those who had lived through it—the crisis of bewilderment, the intellectual and moral subjection and the distortion of values had undoubtedly been among the causes of the great tragedy. What was lacking was, one might say, a stratigraphic description of the concrete historical factors from which these régimes sprang. No answer had been found to two crucial questions: to what extent Fascism and Nazism were favoured or directly helped by the conditions prevailing at the time when they first appeared; and why they were successful not only in the sphere of intellectual or intellectualistic speculation, in one sector of public opinion, but also as forms of government which to a certain extent supplanted the former ruling class and became régimes after destroying the traditional existing order of things, obviously with the consent, either active or passive, of the forces which were part of that order.

The real point was, whether and by what means the wave of irrationality first aroused by nationalism and subsequently heightened by the subversive ideas of Fascism, Nazism and kindred ideologies received its first impulse from prevailing conditions, from elements already latent in the individual social structures, or

whether it was the outcome of a more general phase of the upheavals then taking place all over the world, of demands coherently
and objectively expressed by forces and systems which were themselves developing along recognized historical lines, and not as a
result of emotional outbursts capable of upsetting the logic of
history.

By denying that there was any class element in Fascism and
Nazism, and solemnly asserting that specified social impulses had
contributed to their success and given them a quantitative content,
Croce was confusing causes with results. This was a step backwards
compared with the contributions to the study of Fascism made by
the young Turinese Liberal Gobetti, by Salvatorelli and by the
leading exponents of *Rivoluzione liberale*, during the early years of
the Mussolini era. Gobetti showed a far more acute appreciation
of the fact that Fascism had its roots in a profound and remote
crisis of the unified Italian State, the rapid decline and patent
imperfections of which had produced a ruling class incapable of
'coming to terms' with the workers, incapable of finding any truly
Liberal solution, narrow-mindedly absorbed in its function of pre-
serving, and consequently ready to entrust its destiny and that of
the country to subversive reactionary movements, to which it
bequeathed the glorious inheritance of the *Risorgimento*, the prerogative of government and its own role as trustee of democratic
institutions.

Salvatorelli gave a brilliant exposition of the close relationship
between nationalism and Fascism, and in discussing 'National
Fascism' (a term which from the political and historical point of
view had a far deeper significance than perhaps even the author
himself imagined when he coined it) he revealed all the dismal
truth underlying this *petit-bourgeois* movement exploited by reactionary interests. In it he discerned, in penetrating fashion, all the
frustrated ambitions of the 'office-workers', a provincial and angry
Bismarckism, a militarism exasperated by defeats, the cult of a
'semi-culture' crammed with doctrinaire eclecticisms and pseudo-
ideas, ready to swallow the most absurd myths imported from
France along with 'Maurrasism', and the manipulation of certain
themes drawn from French and German philosophy and from the
teachings of Sorel.[3]

Croce's intervention in the debate on this highly controversial
question was thus hardly one of the happiest episodes in the study
of Fascism by Italian Liberal historians. In any case it was easy

to foresee what would be the insuperable limitations of any contribution from such a source. The Liberal school of thought had obviously reached the zenith of its own possibilities and, with a growing feeling of resignation and impotence, was preparing to yield to the new and original ideas to be found in the writings and analyses of historians with a Marxist background, whose rediscovery of Gramsci had represented a fundamental stage in the process. In his *La Germania nazista* Enzo Collotti summarized his opinion of the contribution made by German historians of the Liberal school to the study of Nazism by pointing out that the 'most valid aspect' of the works of the leading exponents of this trend—Röpke, Meinecke, Hofer, Kohn—was that they all agreed in tracing the origins of Hitlerism back to 'the historical and cultural trajectory marked by the names of Father Jahn, Fichte, Nietzsche, Houston Stewart Chamberlain, Wagner, the pan-Germanism of William II's reign and Prussian militarism'; although, as Collotti adds, 'this agreement was expressed in a great variety of nuances and with varying degrees of polemical stress'.[4] Something very similar might be said of the contributions made by Italian Liberal historians. Their 'most valid aspect' was the series of analyses ascribing the origins of nationalism and Fascism to the shortcomings of the *Risorgimento* State, to the dominating influence in Italy of certain imported cultural trends, and to the authoritarian attitude, particularly noticeable during the Crispi era, of the *bourgeoisie* as ruling class.

In short, in Italy and elsewhere, by the end of the Second World War, the weapons needed for a fundamental study of Fascism had already been sharpened by Marxist historiographers, whereas the Liberal school were still intent on finishing off the outlines of the sketch they had already made, and were willing to concede, in tones very different from those of the past, that the 'class' factor had had greater importance than they had believed. Even before the war Daniel Guérin provided food for thought by making the first serious attempt to produce a book on Fascism and Nazism which emphasized their 'class' elements, and the emergence of phenomena of a 'universal character', which, however, did not mature everywhere. Nevertheless, as the French historian pointed out, they did 'at least appear in embryonic form', precisely because they were phenomena bound up with a more general phase in the evolutionary process of imperialistic capitalism.[5] The labours of this Marxist historian revealed in particular (thanks to his com-

parative study of the movements) how the class factor was at the
root of all these excrescences, and how their success or failure
depended entirely on the presence of determining factors connected
with objective circumstances in the development of capitalism.

Guérin naturally saw that the elements which contributed to the
growth and spread of Fascist and Nazi notions were very
numerous and could not be automatically reduced to a simple
unified form. Nevertheless, what was indisputable was that these
movements originally sprang from reactionary impulses (although
in their early phases they might contain and express other impulses
of an almost directly opposite kind, gaining the approval of the
masses outside those social groups which had a vested interest in
reactionary or conservative solutions), whereas their success as
forces of political hegemony was inextricably bound up with the
support they received from such sectors as the rich landowners and
industrialists, the monopolistic middle class, the military castes,
civil servants, etc., etc. In other words, Guérin clearly demonstrated
the relationship between the objective trends of capitalism and the
social categories tied to it, and the increasing opportunities offered
to extreme right-wing movements with a Fascist or near-Fascist
colouring, until eventually they came to power. At the same time
he emphasized that none of the solutions put forward had a
character of its own or appeared in circumstances traceable to the
cultural climate, the economic and social structure, the traditions
and behaviour of the political forces in each of the countries
concerned.[6]

In recent years the diligence of Marxist historians has increased
and has led to a more exact definition of a number of terms in the
discussion regarding the origins and causes of Fascism. First and
foremost, historians have rejected the bald statement that it was
the product of one phase of the class struggle on an international
scale and of the imperialistic process. This, according to Paolo
Alatri, has dissipated 'the impression created by many Marxist
historical works that the Fascist phenomenon did not originate in
post-war Italy with characteristics peculiar to that country, but in a
hypothetical setting far removed from any definite location in space
and time'.[7] Guérin made a contribution of the highest importance
to this revised theory, and Gramsci's studies have provided ample
material and starting-points for a reconsideration of Italian history
during that period, based on direct and indirect factors in the
crisis of the Liberal State.

Alatri himself, when criticizing those theories of Federico Chabod which reasserted the fallacy in works by Liberal historians of a class interpretation of the Fascist phenomenon, reverted in a most striking way to the idea of a 'preventive counter-revolution', aimed at checking the rise of the working classes, and pointed out that it could not be grasped in its essence without a complete understanding of 'the relationship, not direct and automatic, but indirect and dialectic, which supporters of the idea of a class origin of Fascism have established between economics and politics'.[8] This made it all the more essential 'to reconstruct the origins and early development' of the Fascist movement and the attitude towards it of the Italian ruling class on a more concrete basis which, 'while not ignoring the class theory, or even accepting it, pays due attention to the antecedents and the situation in Italy, thus achieving a compromise between the two theses of the historians', i.e., the rigid formula of a 'class struggle', which ignores the complexity and ramifications of the historical process, and the other thesis which with equal rigidity denies the decisive importance of that factor. 'It is absurd to suppose', Alatri continues, 'that anyone would be ready to uphold an historical interpretation of Fascism in which Mussolini figures merely as the material executor of orders issued by the Italian industrialists . . .' And he goes on to say:

The class nature of Fascism . . . does not exclude the possibility that it may have come into being and flourished thanks to support received from certain political quarters, even if these were the normal channels and to a certain extent inevitable in view of its character and aims. Undoubtedly it is the historian's duty to identify and explain these mediating influences, but the identification of them, far from constituting an obstacle to a synthetic explanation of historical phenomena—in this case Fascism—is an indispensable condition and provides us with the necessary data for a reconstruction which the historian is under an obligation to make when explaining the fundamental driving forces of the historical process. In this particular case, that Fascism received its first impulse and encouragement from those who wrongly imagined that they could use it as an instrument in their struggle against the masses (the *Partito Popolare*, and above all the Socialists and after them the Communists) and later bring it back to the current of Liberal tradition, that this idea proved to be an illusion, that Fascism brought about a complete substitution of a new ruling class and thus satisfied its own appetite for prestige and power—all these things do not alter the fact that it was in substance a capitalist revival, due to new factors in the political and social struggle during the post-war years,

quite different from those prevailing in the Giolitti era and during
the war (though born of the premises which were posed in the
course of those two periods and especially during the latter).[9]

This strengthens the view that Fascism was not, in the strict
sense of the term, just 'reaction', but a specific form of reaction
bound up with certain factors in the historical and political situation which developed over a fairly long period. In the work we
have just quoted Collotti emphasizes that the genesis of National
Socialism as a 'reaction to the democratic experiment' started in
the atmosphere of post-war Germany and contained all the elements
of a moral, political and intellectual crisis which were already
present in German tradition and came to the surface as a result
of the tragedy of the war, but within the framework of a clearly-
defined political and economic structure already existing in that
country, and 'more especially in the Third Reich'.[10] Similarly,
Collotti raises certain objections, which in our opinion help to
clear up any misunderstanding that might arise if we were to
interpret Fascism by sociological, psychological, or even psycho-
analytical methods. In all such cases, it is not a matter of analysing
a phenomenon as such, but of inquiring into the behaviour of
certain social groups, or, still more often,

> of making an exhaustive analysis of authoritarian trends within
> the State and contemporary society, in which certain collective
> tendencies (in the first place the development of mass propaganda
> and of the techniques for influencing public opinion) offer a
> fruitful field for this kind of research. The importance of such
> analyses of totalitarian psychology lies in the fact that they
> emphasize the new relationship between the individual and the com-
> munity as a whole, and consequently the undoubted influence of
> suggestion and collective psychological brainwashing in the manifesta-
> tion of the political will of individuals or of the masses, even if
> we obviously cannot accept the easy and automatic transposition
> of psycho-analytical theory into the field of social studies.[11]

Collotti concludes by observing that we are thus brought face to
face with subsidiary factors, which can be utilized in historical
research within limits and with the 'necessary caution'. And we
must also reject the explanation of, for example, Nazism, 'as a new
technique for exploiting the political myth (Cassirer) or as a re-
assessment of symbols or new religious myths'. If such methods
are used, the problem of power is reduced to the 'formation of
a new type of élite', which covers only 'the external, and one might

say ritual, aspects of the Nazi phenomenon', and the result is thus no longer an analysis of National Socialism, but a catalogue of 'the evidence provided by a cultural background permeated with intellectualism and the crisis of a society, out of which Fascism and Nazism emerged as forms of imperialistic reaction'.[12]

The question is thus confined within narrower limits. A careful analysis of movements and régimes which may be included in the lengthy list of extreme right-wing movements will give an exact idea of the amplitude and nature of these phenomena only if we bear these premisses in mind and develop them coherently. That is why it is difficult to accept the facile suggestion put forward, for example by Touchard, that we should not, when discussing the doctrines of Nazism, abandon the custom of describing it, too, as 'Fascist' (though Touchard hastened to add that this custom is 'very questionable' because it 'places on the same plane two systems —National Socialism and Fascism—which, though in some respects similar, developed in a different context and to a varying degree').[13] Moreover, in such cases it is essential to avoid drawing the conclusion that because of certain analogies one system is a 'true copy' of another, or being content with careless approximations (for example, describing as 'Fascist' *tout court* the régime of General Franco), since to avoid this is not only a precept of historical scholarship, but also an indispensable rule if we are to avoid creating pernicious confusion and making highly arbitrary deductions. Political propaganda may encourage and make a perfectly legitimate use of such approximations, but they are liberties which, when transferred to the field of historical research, distort our view of events, sometimes with serious consequences.

Right-wing reaction produces Fascism, Nazism and variations of them which *are* variations, not because they contain certain external characteristics differing from those of their Italian and German models, but because they belong, as we have said, to different forms and stages of development in the history of each nation, dependent on the problems which at any given moment the governing class had to solve if it were to survive and strengthen its own position. In such cases right-wing reaction resorts to reactionary solutions which are more or less copied from the classical models—the régimes of Mussolini and Hitler—but each solution is, one might say, in direct proportion to the existing possibilities or the prevailing needs of the groups which make the final decision.

Similarly, there are right-wing authoritarian régimes which, although they tend to model the practical application of their ideas on the usual Fascist lines, nevertheless invariably adapt themselves to the type of 'inevitable solution' that determined their advent, using methods which are not only not 'Fascist' in the real sense of the term, but on the contrary in certain respects often engulf and even discredit their allies of the same way of thinking. Lastly, there are forms of authoritarianism which are still the subject of lively discussion, because, although born in circumstances quite different from those which witnessed the advent of the Mussolini and Hitler régimes, they have rejected the grotesque and brutal trappings of their formulation and application and appear to be following in the tracks of several Fascist solutions just when these are disappearing below the horizon of history. Here, too, discussion has to be based on the only real foundation possible, that is, on a concrete comparison of the problems of development inherent in the new trend and in the new demands of a capitalistic society, on the extent to which capitalism can make use of democratic institutions and methods in keeping with the hegemonic prerogatives of the *bourgeoisie* and the overall aspect assumed by crises within the State under pressure from conflicting class interests.

The most striking factor at the present time, and one which provides ample scope for the prophecies of politicians and for the interpretative efforts of historians, is Gaullism. France of the 1960s presents us with an authoritarian régime with marked characteristics of its own—a nationalism aspiring to a *'Europe des Patries'*, a reduction of the elected legislative bodies to the mere function of offices which ratify the decisions of the executive power, militarism, and a form of economic planning aiming at the expansion and consolidation of monopolistic private undertakings by means of a State control subordinated to their plans, etc., etc. As a result, there is much talk of Gaullist 'Fascism' or of Gaullism as a variant of Fascism. Charles de Gaulle's 'Caesarism' undoubtedly has its roots in Bonapartism and Boulangism, and in some ways is a kind of Vendean reprisal against the France of the Revolution, since its conceits of *grandeur* are a synthesis of all the urges of French traditionalism deriving from the legends of Joan of Arc and the 'role of the French nation'. The General is likewise the embodiment, one might say, of aspirations and dreams which might have been taken direct from the programme of Maurras and inserted—

anachronistically, but not without deliberation—into the context of a France torn by a crisis of the old ideals and a lack of confidence in her own ability to achieve new goals. Nevertheless, the composite nature of Gaullism as a political programme and an ideology must not blind us to the fact that it owes its success to the fact that it is fighting not only against the workers' movement, but also against the old middle-class trend and against movements with an undisguised Nazi-Fascist colouring. In this respect, Maurras might have approved the realization of his hopes, despite the failure to restore the monarchy. But Gaullism has nothing to do with the precapitalistic ideals of the *Action Française* and can justifiably claim that it is completely anti-Fascist. As a movement that has already achieved power, it represents in reality a tentative solution which is authoritarian, or tendentially so, in its attitude to the new impulses and complex demands of the more dynamic sectors of French capitalism. The myths of French traditionalism and memories of Napoleon form a kind of halo round a system which, amid innumerable difficulties and contradictions, is still trying to achieve a democracy under the wing of the demiurge of Colombey-les-Deux-Églises, a democracy deprived of all vigour and significance by the fact that monopolistic interests have taken complete possession of the State. That is why De Gaulle has come into conflict with the old and genuinely Nazi-Fascist extreme Right, which advocated solutions dangerous for the whole system and supported a retrograde colonialism concerned only with the problem of exploiting the territories under French occupation.

The régime the General has set up corresponds to the stage at which, in questions fundamental to the hegemony of the class system, the power of decision is transferred to those sectors which control the country's finances and productivity. Consequently the Chamber of Deputies has been reduced to the status of a ratifying organ and democracy survives only below a certain level, above which all its demands and protests are atomized in the rarefied atmosphere surrounding De Gaulle and his technocrats. Gaullist colonialism has consigned to oblivion the colonialism of the Salans and the *pieds-noirs*, for which it has substituted the technical know-how offered to (and imposed upon) colonial exploitation by the policies of aid and economic blackmail from outside the underdeveloped areas. For all that, it is highly unlikely that De Gaulle would ever be the 'agent', in the popular sense of the term, of anyone, and he pursues his own visionary aims of political power.

By putting forward such a solution, however, Gaullism becomes, objectively speaking, the most suitable 'vehicle' for the setting-up in France of a régime of that modern authoritarian type which relies in practice on 'human relations', on the restriction of liberty by means of a 'planning' which is not confined to the fields of economy and productivity, on the expansionary trend of the great monopolies, and on the maintenance of a democratic middle-class structure as a mere shadow of representative government. The projects of this dynamic French capitalism may well fail, while the dissensions within the Gaullist ranks and the selfish aspirations of the monopolistic middle class are so many and of such a kind, even against the background of the ever greater expansion of capitalism on an international scale, that they make any forecast hazardous. The outlines of Gaullist 'Caesarism' must therefore be viewed against the background of the trends we have just mentioned, as a mass phenomenon useful for solving the problems of the transition, in the qualitative as well as in the quantitative sense, of French capitalism to a higher and different plane of stability.

'Classical' Fascism, and with it the claims of the heirs of 'Maurrasistic' dogma, the wild ideas of Colonel La Rocque and all those who throughout a whole century fanned the embers of myths dear to Burke, Taine, Renan and neo-traditionalism (though Péguy and Barrès did not reject the heritage of the French Revolution), is moving steadily away from Charles de Gaulle, even if the Fascists may imagine that in him they have a more or less faithful exponent of some of their theories. The General remains in the rut of traditionalism, in so far as he is the prisoner of 'providentialistic' notions reminiscent of De Maistre. But in the political world of the 'sixties he has the look of an open-minded statesman, who has learned the lesson of his times and is well aware of the forces to which he owes his power and on which the perhaps illusory future of his experiment depends.

2 The 'Dark Valley' Years

In a book entitled *Les fascismes français*—in many respects an admirable work—Jean Plumyène and Raymond Lasierra claim that Italian Fascism 'was an attempt to bring about a transition from Liberal capitalism to industrialism, in a country torn by social upheavals and economically still backward'. The two young historians go on to say that 'from this point of view Mussolini's movement was the ideal type of Fascism. Other capitalistic countries had to face the same problem, but they found other solutions to it'.[1] A definition of this kind is, generally speaking, acceptable, though it is formulated in terms too vague to satisfy those who wish to make an exhaustive study of Fascism and Nazism and the crisis of the Liberal State. It is nevertheless true that, quite apart from the nature of the support it received at the start, the movement founded by Benito Mussolini became a mass organization and rose to power within the framework of the crisis which followed upon the 1914–18 war. The economic situation and the accompanying problems which capitalism had to face during those post-war years, were the mainsprings of a whole series of *coups de main* in Europe during the 1920s and 1930s, and favoured the growth of extreme right-wing reactionary movements. Nazism, too, came to power against the background of this formidable European surge towards 'preventive counter-revolution', in which every reactionary solution aimed at paving the way for a totalitarian conquest of the State. This happened all over continental Europe, as a result of the war and because capitalism was becoming more and more monopolistic in character, but similar situations arose in Latin America and Japan, though the causes obviously depended on the stage of development reached by each particular country and its specific conflicts.

In countries where the capitalist system and the Liberal State succeeded in tackling and solving the problems of the post-war period and the transition to a more advanced stage of industrialism (either because their greater resources enabled them to

maintain a better social equilibrium, or else because certain historical factors in their evolution strengthened the traditional forms
of government), the tendency towards Fascism and similar movements was confined to scattered groups, or came up against insuperable obstacles. A typical case occurred in Great Britain, where
the 'British Fascists' (afterwards known as the 'British Union of
Fascists'), founded in 1923 by Sir Oswald Mosley, Bt., at first
aroused some interest, heightened by the eulogies of Italian Fascism
which soon began to pour in from certain by no means negligible
Conservative quarters. But the attraction of Fascism for such
people and for certain sectors of British public opinion was essentially due to the fact that in the eyes of many Tories the Mussolini
régime had raised the banner of the anti-Bolshevik crusade and
seemed to have restored an atmosphere of concord in an Italy which
a short time before had been the scene of grave disturbances, with
the right-wing parties proclaiming the danger of a new version of
the Soviet revolution. Despite this, from the very beginning the
British Fascists, like the 'Blueshirts' founded in 1931 by Oliver
Locker-Lampson, who was known as the 'British Hitler', had to
struggle to exist and were forced to content themselves with ridiculous parodies of the 'oceanic' rallies of Mussolini's Blackshirts
and with singing the '*Horst Wessel Lied*'. Mosley was a very active
man but his followers never amounted to more than a group of initiates
who found little support in British public opinion as a whole. Great
Britain, which according to Sir Oswald urgently needed a solution
of the Fascist type (adapted, as he himself hastened to add, to
British requirements and customs), had taken rapid and technically
speaking modern measures to meet the worldwide crisis, measures
akin to those later formulated by John Maynard Keynes which
became the capitalist gospel at the time of the New Deal. Victorious
in the war and with a prosperous empire which could bear the cost
of post-war reconstruction and recovery and survive the upset in
the financial world caused by the 1929 crisis, 'perfidious Albion'
managed to weather the storm and the Conservative ruling class, with
the tacit support of the Labour Party, did not have to ask themselves
any awkward questions regarding the stability of their own system.
Against a political and historical background so unfavourable for
his aspirations, Mosley had to be content to play a minor role
which (despite all the noisy propaganda) had no real political significance. Later, the increasingly anti-British attitude of Fascism

and National Socialism shattered his last hopes of success and he and his followers were relegated to the wilderness.

In France the situation was more dangerous and for a brief space right-wing reaction asserted itself. During the crisis the demands of the masses caused some anxiety, while the Liberal State seemed to be weak and doubtful as to which course to take in response to the claims of the more reactionary conservative elements and of the powerful trusts whose influence had increased enormously as a result of the profits made during the war. This afforded a loophole for the extreme Right, which enjoyed the consistent support of the traditional elements and accordingly began to levy a kind of blackmail by exploiting the bogey of a *coup de force*. The *Action Française* under the leadership of Maurras and Léon Daudet, the *Camelots du roi*, Colonel de la Rocque's *Croix-de-Feu* and the various nationalistic organizations gravitating in the orbit of the patriotic *ligues* entered the lists at a time when the first nuclei of a really Fascist trend (the *Faisceau* founded by Georges Valois in 1925, forerunner of Marcel Bouchard's *Francisme* of 1933) were coming into being. But this attempt to force the pace ended with the defeat of the right-wing elements on 6 February 1934 and the consequent advent of the *Front Populaire*. Gaston Doumergue and his cabinet contaminated by radical nationalism (Pétain was Deputy Premier and Minister of Defence; Barthou, a rabid nationalist, was Minister for Foreign Affairs) fell, notwithstanding the outcry raised by the reactionary organizations, and were replaced by exponents of the old clan who, having exhausted the possibilities of the *Front Populaire*, steered the ship of the Liberal State until they had to hand over the helm to the 'Caesarism' of Daladier, thus providing an intermediate solution lying between an authoritarian government and a cabinet of the normal parliamentary and democratic type. In any case it was a solution which was not determined either by the extreme nationlistic elements or by Jacques Doriot's *Parti Populaire Français*, which made its appearance in 1935 with a definitely Fascist programme. However reactionary the political 'strata' behind Daladier might be, their dominant feature was the prevalence within their ranks of that sector of the traditional ruling class which was unwilling to risk a showdown with the workers and preferred to govern a democracy shorn of all real significance but nominally still attached to its institutions. It was these men of the conservative Right who were to lead France to the disasters of 1940, and it was left to the Vichy government to sanction the handing over of ephemeral power to Fascists and nationalists of the Pétain type (whose ideas were more consonant with those of the *Action Française* than with those of the Doriot movement). They, however, played the sorry role of servile collaborators of the Nazis, either because they were fanatically convinced of the soundness of Nazism and certain that it would win, or else because they despaired of obtaining from a victorious Germany the freedom to build that *douce France* which Giraudoux continued to extol mournfully through the microphones of a broadcasting service controlled by the Gestapo.[2] And at the same moment came the eruption of that delirium which during the long years of waiting had been nourished by the 'Fascism of the literary men' and by Doriotism. Nevertheless, there is nothing more lacking in political consequence than the frenzied utterances and oratorical exercises of Louis-Ferdinand Céline, Drieu La Rochelle, Marcel Déat and Robert Brasillach.

In Holland the crisis brought about a rather serious economic setback and in 1922 this drove the Socialist masses to protest against a régime which expected the proletariat and the middle classes to bear the cost of economic recovery. The Liberal and clerical right-wing elements joined forces and returned the leader of the 'anti-revolutionaries', Colijn, to power, thus creating a conservative front that embraced extremists with openly avowed pro-Nazi sympathies who were useful in restraining the Socialists and Communists. Here too, the resources provided by the colonies and the stability of the country were sufficient to check the advance of the pro-Fascist trends, though the latter were by no means negligible. In 1931 Anton Adriaan Mussert founded a National Socialist Party (NSB), which received financial support from Rome and was viewed with favour by some of the *bourgeoisie*, while Arnold Mejier created his 'Black Front', a collection of groups resembling the Italian action squads and with a policy not unlike that of the Italian Fascist Party. Two journals—*De Bezem* and *Fascistisch Studiebaad*, the latter being the organ of the youth organizations—were the mouth-pieces of the *Fascisten Bond* founded by the journalist Jan A. Baars. Utrecht was more or less the focal point of these Blackshirt bands,[3] whose political effectiveness was due mainly to the fact that they gradually paved the way for a *rapprochement* between the Dutch *petite bourgeoisie* and German Nazism, the fruits of which were to become apparent after the occupation, when the phenomenon of collaboration assumed notable proportions in Holland.

In Sweden, the Socialists, who stayed in power nearly all the time, kept the two most active pro-Nazi movements, the *Sveriges Nationella Förbund* and the *Riksförbund det uya Sverige*, in a state of semi-legality. Like their Dutch counterparts, neither of these movements was very important, but they paved the way for a certain amount of collaboration with the Nazis. In Finland, the Socialists were equally severe, though here the necessity—which involved all parties—of maintaining amicable relations with the Soviet Union acted as an effective brake on any connivance between the Conservatives and the extremist right wing. Nevertheless, in 1930 the anti-Communist offensive headed by the landowners, whose shock troops were provided by Vihtori Kosola's 'Lapua' movement, nearly led to an authoritarian régime. The Diet was dissolved because the Conservative government failed to obtain the two-thirds majority prescribed by the constitution for passing the laws against Communist propaganda proposed by the 'Lapuists', and the composition of the house after the general election made it possible to pass these laws, the new Prime Minister being Svinhufvud, an Agrarian and one of the supporters of Marshal Mannerheim. In 1932, however, the Socialists returned to power, dissolved the 'Lapua' movement, arrested the ringleaders, Walenius and Kosola, and prohibited the parades and military uniforms of all right-wing movements.[4] Later on, when the Soviet Union attacked Finland in 1939, the nationalists again came to the fore, while Mannerheim was destined to become the symbol of the struggle against the Communists and of the preservation of the State and national independence. But this counter-offensive was one of the results of the Second World War, when the situation was quite different from that which led to the development of extreme nationalism elsewhere in Europe between 1930 and the outbreak of hostilities.

In Belgium, post-war difficulties and an epidemic of scandals in the democratic middle-class parties caused much discontent, and about 1930 the hostility between Flemings and Walloons flared up again, with the result that right-wing reaction became bound up with this nationalistic revival and soon assumed a pro-Fascist and Nazi hue. In 1933 Gustave De Clercq organized the pro-German Flemish national movement, transforming the 'Frontist Party' into the 'Flemish National League' (*Vlaamsch National Verbond* = VNV), of which he became the leader, and advocating a corporative, racial and anti-Communist policy at meetings which were frequently noisy. 'We are not Latins, we are Germans,' the VNV proclaimed in its leaflets and in the columns of its newspaper, *Volk en Staat*. 'Flanders must seek protection against invasion from the South' (i.e. from France).[5] The movement was subsidized by the Germans and in 1936 was flanked by the *Rex* party under Léon Degrelle, a university graduate who had previously been head of the Catholic *Christus Rex* organization, which had aspects reminiscent of Fascist mysticism. Degrelle found supporters among the Walloon nationalists and advocated a policy akin to that of Italian Fascism, from which he soon received considerable sums of money (19 million francs in 1936–7, according to some sources),[6] but he did not spurn the advances of Hitler's agents, and in reality his policy was based on National Socialism. Eighteen months after the birth of their movement the Rexists obtained 275,000 votes in the general election of 1936, with twenty-seven seats in the lower house and seven in the Senate. The youthful head of the Rexists was the first to be surprised by this unexpected success, but he was wrong in his interpretation of it. He believed that there were large numbers of people in Belgium ready to embark on an authoritarian experiment of the Fascist type, but the truth was that the electorate was protesting primarily against the traditional parties and the series of financial scandals involving their leading figures. The extreme Right certainly wanted an anti-parliamentary solution, but the ruling class was able to keep control of the situation. For this reason the Rexists and nationalists remained a force to be reckoned with, but they were unable to obtain control of the country. After the German occupation the fortunes of Degrelle and his party revived, whereas the VNV had to be content with a subordinate role, in the shadow of a new movement of a strictly Nazi type, *De Vlag* (*Duitsch-Vlaamsche Arbeidsgemeenschaf* = organization for German-Flemish collaboration), of which we shall have occasion to speak when discussing events after 1940.

In European countries where the consequences of the First World War had to be borne by fragile economic systems which were subjected to a still greater strain by the 1929 crisis on Wall Street, the landowners and industrialists viewed with evident distaste the troubles and contradictions of the Liberal State and tried, whenever opportunity offered, to give it the *coup de grâce*. After the Bolshevik revolution of 1917, fear of a rising of the masses became a nightmare. On the other hand, Maximalism and reformism split many of the Socialist parties and gave rise to paralysing internal dissensions which revealed all the weaknesses of leadership in the workers' parties and the extent to which, despite their undaunted fighting spirit, they were exposed to the danger of a crushing defeat should their opponents be in a position to deal sudden and decisive blows. In Spain, for example, the long-standing conspiracy between the right-wing parties and the army was still on the alert and in 1923 succeeded in bringing General Miguel Primo de Rivera to power.

The De Rivera régime exalted the reactionary and feudal traditions and opened the dykes to the flood-waters of nationalism. In fact, under the General's government, Giménez Caballero, Ramiro Ledesma Ramos and Onésimo Redondo laid the foundations of Fascism a good many years before the advent of José Antonio Primo de Rivera's *Falange* and Albiñana's *Partido Nacionalista Español*, which was formed after the death of the dictator as a nationalist party ready to accept the nationalistic principles of Fascism and to use the methods of the Italian *squadristi*. De Rivera's dictatorship collapsed in 1930, but from then on, despite the abolition of the monarchy and the proclamation of the 'Second Republic', reactionary and clerical Spain gradually closed its ranks and formed a united front determined to take its revenge by crushing democracy. The moderate 'professors' who governed the Republic without ever attempting to come to grips with the problem of a drastic and organic reform of the country's antiquated structure, and gave top-level responsible posts to anti-Republican military men, soon found themselves being attacked from within. The 1936 rebellion united the nationalistic 'traditionalists' of the army and civil service, the 'Carlists', who were its 'medieval' element, and the groups with a definitely Fascist colouring led by Albiñana and José Antonio (in addition, of course, to the ecclesiastical hierarchies and those sectors of the economic right wing which had an interest in bringing the republic down). The contributions made by Italian Fascism and German Nazism gave a veneer of authority to this alliance between the Spanish right-wing elements and the Falange.

The 'Falangists' and 'Albiñānists' embraced the obscure ideology of Fascism, which in the case of José Antonio de Rivera comprised a 'social' trend that was as loud as it was abstract in its implications. 'The State the Falange wants,' asserted the young son of the dead dictator, 'will be based on the real trinomial of the organic, living and vital elements in the human race. On the family. On the community. On the trades and professions . . .'[7] Work was to be the best qualification for civic office. The trade unions and co-operative societies which 'hitherto have been prevented from participating in the life of the nation, must break down the artificial barriers raised by parliament and the political parties and raise themselves to the rank of *direct organs of the State*.'[8] 'The new national State must uphold the integrity of the family, which is the cradle of social unity; it must safeguard the autonomy of the community, which is the cradle of territorial unity; it must support the trades and professions, their trade unions and co-operatives, which are the elements and organs of the nation's totalitarian framework.'[9] There was much in these obscure postulates and in the anti-capitalistic emphasis to be found in certain parts of José Antonio's doctrines and programme that was bound to be viewed with distaste by Francisco Franco and, in general, by the powerful monarchical-traditionalistic *bloc* which was the real backbone of the anti-Republican revolt. Franco realized that he could become dictator if he succeeded in liquidating, coolly and with Levantine astuteness, his most direct competitors in the *entourage* of army generals, but also, and more especially, if he showed that he could fulfil the expectations of those wider circles which gave motive power to the anti-Republican restoration. These circles cherished no dreams, however remote, of achieving 'social reforms' of the type that obsessed the soul of José Antonio and disturbed the minds of the young men who followed him. Moreover, the suspicion that the real aim of the Falange was to harness the fate of Spain to the destinies of the Fascist and Nazi régimes, was distasteful to the cautious empiricism of the ex-commander of the *Tercio Extranjero* and to the no less cautious and far-seeing ideas of the ecclesiastical hierarchies, who wanted a Spain freed from all political squabbles, on which a régime of the Mussolini type might easily be grafted. Money and weapons, the bureaucratic set-up and the influence of the clergy and aristocracy, were things which weighed the balance on the side of Franco. 'Falangism', which, like Albiñana's movement, soon lost its leader, never grew up, and the crisis of the Republic was exploited by the stronger elements of the extreme and traditionalist right wing, which flourished and operated in a country where the adjective 'right' denotes the ensemble of the predominant feudal cliques, or a retrograde capitalism still in its infancy as regards its constituent parts. Hence the defeat of the Falange and its replacement by nationalism *tout court*, which gradually absorbed the De Rivera movement, accepting it as part of the 'new order', but limiting its functions to those of a mere framework or decoration, or at the most allowing it to play only an auxiliary role; with the result that it soon lost all its political significance in the Spain governed by the *Caudillo*. Thus the revolt which the Falangists believed to be the first stage in the installation of the kind of régime they wanted, was reduced to the level of a military *pronunciamiento* and led to the establishment of a reactionary State which from Fascism borrowed only a few institutions as subsidiary instruments of a savage dictatorial system closer to the traditions of Iberian authoritarianism than to its Mussolinian prototype.

Halfway between a dictatorship of this kind and the stern paternalism of certain South American governments lies the régime established by Professor Oliveira Salazar, Prime Minister of Portugal since 1932. Seven years before, the army had destroyed the country's tottering democratic structure by making General Carmona President of the Republic. Salazar, a former member of the so-called 'Catholic Centre', agreed to accept office only after he had been assured that he would be allowed to take any measures he liked in order to rescue the Portuguese economy from its difficulties, and resorted to a solution of a definitely reactionary type with the support of the landowners and the military. In this way the *União Nacional* was born, which from now on was to be the only Portuguese political party, the alpha and omega of the nation's political life. Concerning the Carmona régime Italian Fascist writers had said that '. . . it was not a question of an idea finding the bayonets, but of the bayonets finding an idea, and before they found the idea, they found the man'.[10] The reserved and austere professor of Coimbra University was asked whether he thought the Fascist régime could be 'adapted' to meet Portuguese requirements, and he replied: 'Our dictatorship has points of contact . . . with the Fascist dictatorship . . . because: a) it strengthens the authority of the government; b) it has declared war on certain democratic principles; c) it is definitely nationalistic in character; d) it intends to bring about social reforms.' It differs from Fascism, Salazar continued, 'in the methods it uses. The Fascist dictatorship is tending towards a pagan Caesarism, towards a new kind of State which recognizes no limitations of a juridical or moral nature, which is marching without let or hindrance towards its goals. Mussolini . . . is a marvellous opportunist when it comes to action; he leans first to the right, and then to the left.'[11]

The head of the *Estado Novo* postponed until a later date any further discussion of the differences between the two régimes, but in a speech which he made on 23 November 1932 he gave an interesting interpretation of certain principles of the Portuguese dictatorship which had 'risen against the disorder in the country' brought about by 'parliamentarism' and the 'excesses of the parties'. 'We have a creed and we are a power,' said Salazar,

> and since we are a power, it is our duty to govern; we were given our mandate by a triumphant revolution [i.e. the *coup d'état* of 1926], without opposition and with the full consent of the country . . . In such circumstances no pacts or transitions or transactions are possible. Those who accept our programme are acting as patriots by declaring their consent and openly helping us; those who do not agree may be equally sincere and equally worthy men so long as they merely proclaim their disagreement, but if they should undertake any political action, we shall see to it that they do not hinder us too much.

To this ominous warning the dictator added a scathing condemnation of all forms of class struggle and any form of left-wing agitation which—in his opinion—might be aiming at the 'complete overthrow of the established order' with a view to creating 'a new society without a fatherland, without the family, without property, and without a moral code'. This, the Coimbra professor asserted, would be contrary to Portuguese principles, and the government would accordingly 'co-ordinate' the demands of the workers and 'integrate them into the complex of the national economy'.[12] From every citizen the dictatorship would demand 'discipline, homogeneity and purity of ideals'; parliamentary democracy was in the grips of 'a universal crisis' and the 'national revolution' had merely taken time by the forelock when it dissolved the parties; the 'whirlwind of revolution which is sweeping across the world and shaking the very foundations of the social order . . . makes it a prime necessity that we should take over power, conquer the State and defend without flinching the public peace'.[13]

These are concepts all too familiar to anyone who has the slightest acquaintance with the vocabulary of the authoritarian right wing —discipline, homogeneity, the public peace, safeguarding the interests of the workers integrated into the national economy, etc., etc., were the stock phrases of Miguel Primo de Rivera and Mussolini, of De Clercq and Hitler. And in fact the Portugal of Salazar's *Estado Novo* was plunged into the deep and troubled sleep of a police State completely dominated by the landowners, with a flimsy superstructure of the Fascist type provided by the 'Greenshirt' organizations. The country was ruled by the PIDE—the police of the régime—and became a haven for conspirators against the Spanish republic, while the Nazis established their espionage bases there and hatched their plots against all the four quarters of the world.

The return of the generals

During the 1930s the generals who had been more or less victorious in the various phases of the First World War were able to devote themselves to the congenial task of 'restoring order' whenever the so-called 'national forces' in the countries concerned called upon them to demolish the parliamentary régimes. In 1920 the Habsburg admiral Miklós Horthy dealt with Bela Kun's attempted revolution and became head of the State. At that time Hungary was governed by the landowners and the aristocrats who were still in mourning for the collapse of the Austro-Hungarian Empire. In 1932, Horthy appointed as his Prime Minister General Jákfa Gömbös, who in 1923 had founded the 'National Union Party' (later merged into the 'Unity Party' headed by the great landowner Count Bethlen). Alignment with Hitler's Germany and Fascist Italy followed almost immediately, and before Gömbös had been a year in power Hungary had half-a-dozen organizations modelled on their Fascist counterparts, whose aims were the 'fight against Communism' and 'revisionism', in other words a radical revision of the Treaty of Versailles. Horthy's régime was thus a dictatorship with a tame parliament in which the various Fascist and nationalist organizations were represented and in reality were the only political bodies that were allowed to operate.

In Greece, in October 1934, General Kondylis restored the monarchy after a lapse of eleven years and was appointed Prime Minister by the generals who had been his accomplices in the *coup d'état*. Among them was the former chief of the general staff of the Greek army during the 1914–18 war, Ioannis Metaxas, who in 1920 had founded the 'Free Opinion' monarchical party and was the brain behind the legitimist counter-revolution. Kondylis remained in office until August 1936, when he handed over the reins of government to Metaxas, who had no doubts about the best way to exploit the reactionary tendency of the Greek State. To this end he established friendly relations with Rome and Berlin, while in Greece itself he behaved like a dictator, backed by the King and the army. His counterpart in Yugoslavia, Premier Milan Stojadino-vich, went even further in his enthusiasm for Fascism, an enthusiasm shared by the restricted circle of Serbian agrarians and aristocrats whose representative he was. According to Galeazzo Ciano, Stojadinovich was a faithful supporter of the 'Anti-Communist Pact', so much so that, Ciano says, he would have liked to go 'even further', in other words to establish in Yugoslavia a régime on the Fascist model.[14] The regent, Prince Paul, prevented him from doing this on the eve of the Second World War, and he was re-placed—as a precautionary measure—by General Simovich, who in the eyes of the Yugoslav monarchists and conservatives had at least the merit of not being prepared to sell them wholesale to Mussolini without getting anything in return.

Further north, the general trend of the reactionary elements was exemplified by the situation in Poland. The republic which arose after the First World War, with a coalition government of Christian Democrats and exponents of the right-wing Peasants' Party, had made a bad start by carrying on a continuous battle against the working-class masses. 'A self-satisfied Poland of bankers and country gentry', said Stanislaw Thugutt, one of the peasant leaders, 'from the very beginning established a shameful political system, in which calumny, corruption and violence were legal tender.'[15] The Socialists fought this reactionary coalition, but fell into a trap when they supported a *coup d'état* organized by the army and Marshal Jozef Pilsudski, former commander of the 'Polish Legion' which had been raised abroad to fight in the war against Russia. Pilsudski was a renegade Socialist. As soon as the *coup d'état* was over he had a meeting, in May 1926, with the leading exponents of the agrarian reactionary movement, among them being Prince Eustace Sapieha, who in 1918 had led the offensive of Polish notables against the Socialist government. This meeting resulted in the formation of Pilsudski's party, the 'non-party *bloc* for collaboration with the government' (BBWR). Ex-officers of the 'Legion' were the backbone of the marshal's political staff. Bartel, one of Pilsudski's henchmen, was appointed head of the government; Pilsudski himself took over the Defence Ministry and, when he was elected President of the Republic, retired in favour of his friend Ignacy Moscicki, a leading industrialist and trusted adviser of the group controlling the production of synthetic nitrogen. In 1930, when the left wing again began to threaten action, the marshal repeated the operation by placing at the head of the government Colonel Beck, another trusted disciple of the 'national hero', whose instructions Beck followed even after Pilsudski's death. The BBWR was a reactionary coalition of the purest water, though it objected to being called a para-Fascist organization, like Pilsudski himself, who distrusted the Fascists and preferred to use authoritarian methods handed down by Habsburg and Tsarist tradition. In 1932 the secretary of the BBWR, Dolanowski, hastened to refute the statements of Italian Fascist journalists who had praised the coalition because it seemed to them to be a Polish version of Fascism. To Dolanowski's denials the Fascists replied: 'We do not wish to argue. The ideas and the way they are put into practice are the important thing. The aim of the Polish organization is a strong government and a national policy, and we maintain that this bears the stamp of Fascism.'[16] And they were not altogether wrong. Poland was, in fact, under the yoke of a government representing the most retrograde elements of the landowning aristocracy and the army, and the BBWR had buried any prospect of democracy in the name of nationalism and anti-Communism.

In Rumania, too, the 'thirties were the golden age of military men who restored 'public order' in the interests of the economic and political extreme right. In the reign of Carol II the 'Iron Guard', otherwise known as the 'Legion of the Archangel Michael', had been founded by Corneliu Codreanu on Nazi lines (it proclaimed the 'historical role of the Rumanian people' and demanded from its followers a mystical adherence to the racial, corporative and authoritarian ideals of its policy), but it was nevertheless a source of anxiety to the compact group of reactionary bureaucrats and military men who surrounded the sovereign. In fact the 'legionaries' blamed the ruling class for not being bold enough in their fight against Communism and in anti-Semitic discrimination. They wanted a government of the Nazi type, and above all they wanted to get rid of the political figures then in office. They therefore went over to 'direct action', and when the Prime Minister, Duca, ordered their movement to be dissolved, they murdered him and then indulged in a series of crimes designed to weed out their adversaries on both the right and the left wings. The monarchical circles took fright, and with the connivance of the King evolved a plan to eliminate Codreanu, who was in fact murdered by Armand Calinescu on 30 November 1938. Hitler swore vengeance for the murder of the leader of the Iron Guard, who on his mother's side actually had 'German blood in his veins'.[17] As it happened, however, vengeance was taken by that very ruling class which had suppressed Codreanu. His successor as head of the Iron Guard was Mihail Antonescu, ex-chief of staff of the army, who had distinguished himself at Budapest in 1919 during the suppression of the revolutionary pro-Soviet movement. Antonescu, who had been Minister of Defence in 1933, became Prime Minister a year after Codreanu's death, thus paving the way, in agreement with Hitler, with whom he was on very friendly terms, for the removal of the King. Carol II abdicated in favour of his son Michael and left Rumania in the company of his mistress, Maria Lupescu, in a ten-coach train full of 'personal effects', handing the country over to his ex-general, who was on the point of announcing the birth of a 'Legionary State' in which he was to be the *Conducadore*, i.e., Duce. This régime was a mixture of military dictatorial power and Nazi State organization, with all the relative implications and all the defects of a bad copy of the original.

In Bulgaria, on the other hand, it was the King himself who provided the authoritarian solution. In 1934 King Boris took an unfavourable view of the agitation among the workers and peasants, and at the same time distrusted the activities of the nationalistic pro-Nazis. An important factor in the country was the *Rodna Zactita* (National Defence) under the leadership of General Skoinoff, who had given the movement a Fascist stamp, including the usual lugubrious uniforms (black shirts and black trousers). There was also a Bulgarian Fascist party led by Alexander Staliysky, which had been founded in 1931. These two organizations (the latter wanted a corporative State on the Fascist lines) were insistent in their demands that the monarchy and the ruling class should put an end to the feeble democratic régime, and above all to the activities of the left wing. If this were not done, they threatened to start seditious activities which would strike at the crown and all its faithful adherents. King Boris silenced them by means of a *coup d'état* organized by the army, and appointed the ex-colonel Kimon Giorgiev Prime Minister. The political parties were dissolved and a general election was ordered, as a result of which the King had a puppet government directly under his control. The remnants of Bulgarian democracy were broken up one by one, until the law of October 1937 was passed, which modified the electoral system and assigned to parliament the mere function of controlling the executive power, while all political parties were definitely banned. The despot who had thus made a clean sweep of the opponents of his right-wing allies now had to deal with the Nazi agents and those who sympathized with Hitler's ideas. He wrongly imagined that he would be able to resist their demands by ignoring the claims of the workers and destroying the semblance of democracy that was still tolerated, but Hitler's war aims swept him aside when he made his last and blindest mistake by appointing the pro-Nazi Filov to be Prime Minister in 1940.

By more tortuous paths the reactionary tidal wave of the 'thirties sealed the fate of the Catholic Chancellor Engelbert Dollfuss as well as that of his country, Austria. The Dollfuss cabinet of May 1932 was the prelude to a counter-offensive of the Austrian right-wing parties against the spread of Socialism. The inflation crisis which afflicted Austria as a result of difficulties common to most of the countries defeated in the war gave birth to a right-wing coalition of which the diminutive and frigid chancellor was undoubtedly the spearhead (his apologists tell us edifying stories of his religious fervour).[18] On 4 March in the year after he became Prime Minister Dollfuss dissolved parliament; after this he dissolved the Communist Party and the workers' organizations, and started a policy of systematic rejection of all wage demands, while, conversely, he gave *carte blanche* to the pro-Nazi *Heimwehren* led by Major Pabst and Prince Starhemberg and allowed them to augment their semi-military forces, which were paid from Berlin.[19] On 12 February the populace in Vienna and other Austrian cities revolted against the brutal methods of the police and the wave of reaction which the government had let loose. Dollfuss had workmen mown down by machine-gun fire and took advantage of the opportunity to inflict the last mortal blows on their organizations. The 'preventive counter-revolution' undertaken by the Catholic chancellor was the prelude to the entry into the cabinet of Schuschnigg, who later put his trust in Arthur Seyss-Inquart, the 'first of the Quislings', because he was favourably impressed by the fact that he was 'a diligent churchgoer'.[20] In this way Dollfuss destroyed the barriers erected by Austrian democracy against the swashbuckling Nazis. Hitler's hired assassins killed him in his office, and it was left to Schuschnigg to drag into the presence of the German dictator the mere shadow of a government which was powerless to reject the Nazi ultimatums because, since the days of the pious Dollfuss, it had been the prisoner of that reactionary logic from which the Braunau house-painter was to draw the ultimate advantage. The chancellor's last anguished appeal, on the eve of the *Anschluss,* was made to the working classes, when he implored them to defend the independence of the country. But the workers had been vanquished in February 1934 by those same 'national' elements who now realized that they in their turn would be thrown out by the Nazis. The *bourgeoisie* triumphed over the 'subversives' in the suburbs of Vienna, only to pave the way for the soldiers of the Führer.

Fascism as an 'export'

The consolidation of the Fascist régime and the advent of Hitler as chancellor of Germany thus took place in a Europe torn by reactionary movements without precedent since the days of the Holy Alliance. The rising tide of 'preventive revolutions' with a more or less authoritarian colouring and the successes which Fascism and Nazism seemed to be achieving played the role of obstetricians in assisting the birth of extreme nationalist movements, even in countries where conditions appeared to be least favourable. Neither of these régimes had the slightest scruples in exploiting for their own ends both the anti-Communist and the anti-democratic fury of the right-wing parties already in power, as well as the desire for expansion of semi- or pro-Fascist and Nazi organizations which were cropping up more or less everywhere, either by spontaneous generation or else thanks to the determined efforts of agents from Rome or Berlin. The Mussolini government played a notorious role in the organization and financing of the *Cagoule,* officially known as the CSAR *(Comité secret d'action révolutionnaire),* a terrorist organization started by Eugène Deloncle which had armed squads all over France whose task it was to raise a 'prestigious' military leader to power, to carry out acts of terrorism and try to persuade the army to support a *coup d'état.* In 1937 the Fascist régime commissioned these forerunners of the OAS to carry out a double assassination according to all the rules of the art—the killing of the leader of the anti-Fascist movement known as 'Justice and Liberty', Carlo Rosselli, and of his brother Nello. These two adversaries of the Duce (Carlo Rosselli was particularly obnoxious to the régime because he was a skilful polemicist and organizer) were stabbed to death in the forest of Bagnoles-sur-l'Orne. It was later ascertained that the crime had been prepared by the counter-

Intelligence department of Italian Military Intelligence (SIM) in conjunction with some of Mussolini's closest collaborators, who had entrusted the actual execution of the murders to the *cagoulards* and had supplied them with weapons and money.

In 1932 the Italian Fascists extended their protection to the bands of the *Ustaše* terrorist organization, founded in that same year by two Croat exiles, Ante Pavelich and Vanca Mihailovich. The aim of Pavelich and the *Ustaše* was the creation of an' independent Croatia governed on Nazi-Fascist lines. The Italian government supplied them with all they needed in order to foment unrest in Yugoslavia and to carry out more or less everywhere those acts of terrorism of which the Croat nationalists were so fond. Moreover, the Fascists offered hospitality to the *Ustaše* in the training-camps they had set up in Southern Italy, where their agents received instructions and the first contingents of the future militia units were trained. Pavelich himself had a marked propensity to crime, and thanks to this paternal assistance was able to work out the plan for the assassination, at Marseilles in October 1934, of the French Premier, Barthou, and King Alexander of Yugoslavia.

Certain analogies in their fanatical mentalities linked the leader of the Croat Fascists with the Norwegian Vidkun Quisling, a former army officer and Minister of Defence, who in 1933 founded the 'Norwegian National Party' *(Nasjonal Samling)*. In his early years Quisling was a brilliant young officer, but a term in Russia as military attaché induced him to leave the army and take to politics. Having failed in his attempt to persuade the Norwegian Labour Party to let him raise a 'Red Guard' on the lines of the Soviet revolutionary militia, he turned with a certain nonchalance to the Nazis. Rosenberg, one of whose projects was the foundation of a 'Nordic Empire', cleansed of Jews and other impure races and destined to prosper under Nazi guidance, became interested in this young Norwegian disciple, but Quisling was trying to sow his seeds in a country most reluctant to accept the philosophy of the author of *The Myth of the Twentieth Century* and most unlikely to provide large numbers of members for any Hitlerian party. Consequently, prior to the outbreak of war, Quisling had to go round begging for support less platonic than that which Rosenberg offered him. Only after the war had started did the German General Staff and Secret Services think of using this ex-officer and entrusting him with tasks connected with their project for the invasion of Norway. Quisling's functions were subsequently reduced to those of a mere

B*

tool for the execution of Nazi orders, to such an extent that his name became a synonym for treason and collaborationism.

In Switzerland, too, spasmodic outbursts of nationalism and para-Fascism attracted the attention of the two totalitarian régimes. These were for the most part very modest enterprises, of a purely local character, often without any specifically Fascist or Nazi characteristics, and merely reflecting the claims of the various cantons, though with a marked nationalistic colouring. Some of these groups had more clearly defined trends towards Fascism and Nazism, but their followers were limited to a few students and intellectuals. Among these, tendencies akin to those of Nazism and Fascism were displayed by the groups known as *Ordre et Tradition*, *Ordre National Neuchâtelois*, the *Cercle fédéraliste de Fribourg*, and the *Neue Front*. On the other hand, the *Helvétisme* movement at La Chaux-de-Fonds was definitely Fascist in its programme and ritual. The two most important groups with a totalitarian stamp were the 'National Union', founded at Geneva in 1931 by Georges Oltremare, and Tobler's 'National Front' in Zürich. Both these movements proclaimed Fascist and Nazi principles, paid lip-service to the régimes in Rome and Berlin and, although they were not large parties, had a certain influence on the middle classes in the two Swiss cities; especially Tobler's 'Front' in Zürich, where pro-German feeling was a natural product of the ethnical origins of the population. In Canton Ticino, Italian Fascists created the *Lega Nazionale*, which received direct support from Mussolini's government. Generally speaking, these Swiss movements were little more than modest bridgeheads suitable for nuisance and propaganda purposes, when they were not just organizations for camouflaging the activities of German and Italian agents. The embassies supplied them with funds, while the Fascist and Nazi parties placed printed matter at their disposal for further distribution.

Of far greater significance was the penetration of these ideas into Czechoslovakia after the advent of Hitler in 1933. The republic was fruitful soil for the Nazis because of the presence in the Sudetenland—in the north-west and south-west of the country—of a large German minority. So long as Germany remained a democratic republic, the claims of this minority had been limited to requests for greater autonomy and the safeguarding of their rights. The rise to power of the Nazis unleashed the forces of nationalism, this being mainly due to a physical-training instructor, Konrad Henlein, who in that same year 1933 founded the 'Patriotic Front of the Sudeten Germans'. The pro-Nazi and subversive nature of this movement became obvious at once, but the wavering government in Prague did not dare to resort to drastic measures, and when the activities of these irredentists became more insistent and arrogant, the authorities merely demanded that the name of the 'Front' should be changed to 'Sudeten German Party' (SDP). Two years after its foundation the party was receiving regular financial aid from the German Foreign Office. Henlein was paid 15,000 marks a month for organizing in the republic a kind of mighty Trojan horse, which Hitler would be able to utilize when he put into execution the so-called 'Green Plan', the cover-word in the German General Staff's secret code for the projected invasion of Czechoslovakia.

In a speech which he made on 3 March 1928 Mussolini had declared in his usual categorical fashion: 'Fascism is not an article for export.' Two years later in his 'message for the year IX' the Duce seemed to think that the situation had changed: 'The struggle is now being carried on all over the world,' he told his Blackshirts, 'and that is why Fascism is the topic of discussion in every country; it is feared by some, it is the object of the implacable hatred of others, and elsewhere it is ardently desired. I never said that Fascism is not for export. That is far too commonplace.' The fact of the matter was that the régime had changed its tone and, having consigned to oblivion the peaceful utterances of its early days, it was now indulging the more aggressive flights of Mussolini's foreign policy. Starting from the years 1930–3, this question of 'export' became for Rome and Berlin a worldwide undertaking. The Fascists founded their *Fasci italiani all'estero*, which acted as foreign branches of the party, enabled them to keep a check on Italians living abroad and were also used to spread information among foreigners about the 'realizations' of the régime. At the same time they opened 'Houses of Fascist Culture', which likewise served as propaganda offices, but were also useful as cover for the work of subsidizing and encouraging the activities of para-Fascist or extreme right-wing organizations in the various countries, on which the régime spent considerable sums. More detailed and more fruitful was the work of the Nazis, one reason being that the Germans brought to it a thoroughness and efficiency which the Fascists never possessed.

One of the most promising fields for the Nazis was Latin America, and three factors contributed to make this huge area a fruitful theatre of operations. The first was the spread, among the lower and middle *bourgeoisie* of the Latin-American countries, of the tendency to rebel against the oppressive and predatory economic hegemony of the great United States trusts, which controlled and exploited the agricultural and mineral resources of the various countries (and in particular oil) in an arbitrary way reminiscent of colonialism. Such feelings, which had spread, though for other reasons, even to certain sectors of the 'landowning aristocracy' that had come into being as a result of decades of pioneer colonization, were indirectly linked with the instinctive urge to revolt prevailing among the countless masses of hungry subproletarians. This tended to give them a nationalistic flavour, in which the desire to free their native soil from foreign influence was mingled with demands for social progress and freedom from the heavier burdens imposed by the all-powerful monopolies. The political hub of such movements was often the army, thanks to a very special assimilation of Liberal and progressivist claims, a process which made itself felt owing to the social provenance and degree of culture of the army cadres in extremely backward countries. In his study of the causes and nature of this phenomenon, Giorgio Galli quotes the explanations of it given by the sociologist Raymond Aron and by Professor Charles Moraze of the Sorbonne, both of whom, in our opinion, have grasped the essence of the problem. According to Aron:

> The South American armies were politically split because the various currents to be found in them represented groups which, under a democratic régime, would have found expression through the parties. One day I asked the editor of a Brazilian daily why it was that South American revolutions were always organized by army officers. His answer was: 'Because our officers are the equivalent of your intellectuals.' This, of course, was a witticism, but it is nevertheless significant. The officers are drawn from the middle classes or from the upper strata of the lower classes, and the same applies to the business executives. The schools give them a modern education, and some of them are uprooted from their social milieu and feel the impatient longings for political and economic progress which are usually attributed to European intellectuals. Hostile to a parliamentarism which is sometimes monopolized by the upper middle class and at other times anarchical, they are inclined to support despotic régimes, some of which are essentially conservative, while others are authoritarian and socially progressive.[21]

And Moraze, in his turn:

> When I asked Santiago Dantas, one of the ablest advisers of President Vargas, for an explanation in broad terms which would

help me to understand the frequent intervention of the armed forces in Latin-American politics . . . he said: 'If you want to understand the function of the army in our countries, compare it with that of the Radical-Socialist Party in France.' And in fact, in the countries of which Santiago Dantas was thinking, the army represents the middle class, above all because we have historical proof that it has played an essential rôle in the technical education of those peoples. The war in Paraguay showed that many of the Latin-American countries, although they have had faculties of law and medicine for a long time, have no technical schools except those of the army, these being indispensable for the training of artillery and signals officers, etc. The army has thus become a training college for technicians and engineers, and it is therefore not surprising to see colonels or generals becoming heads of important administrative departments or business executives. Moreover, an army of this kind affords opportunities for social advancement; lying between the big landowners who form the aristocracy and the workmen and poor peasants, the middle class joins the army and receives its further education there. To the middle class and to ambitious men of the lower classes who choose to join it, the army offers possibilities of social advancement which they could not possibly find anywhere else.[22]

It was thus among the cadres of the small South American armies that the Nazis found numbers of men who were ready to listen not only to advice of a technical or military character, but also to tirades against the imperialism of the United States, all forming part of a more elaborate exposition of National Socialist ideology. At the same time the Nazis provided an opportunity to raise the standard of professional military training and technical knowledge, to create national movements whose aim was the freeing of the country from the grip of foreign exploitation, and to ensure that a type of government would emerge which would be authoritarian, but at the same time 'social', anti-democratic but administratively capable—in so far as its intentions were concerned—of bringing about a prosperity which would ultimately be extended even to the poorest classes. Such ideas inevitably attracted those military men who had a genuine desire to reconcile the ideals of caste with the interests of society in general—even if they had no idea how this was to be done—as well as those who cherished authoritarian ambitions and saw that it would be easier to win the support of the masses by diluting the aims of despotism with a dose of 'plebeianism' which would arouse the enthusiasm of millions of sub-proletarians who had never experienced any other destiny than a total disregard for their lot. In plain words the 'stick and carrot' method might comprise something far better than the outdated hotchpotch of the *pronuciamientos*, still in vogue among the dictators and those who aspired to imitate them, and on whom the United States trusts generally relied to maintain their satrapies.

The penetration of Nazism into the South American continent was helped by a second factor—the presence of very active German communities, some of whose members had settled there many years before the 1914 war. These Germans were often the heads of important industrial and commercial concerns, for example in Bolivia, where 'a dozen German firms practically controlled the market'.[23] And lastly, a third factor was the fact that, even before the advent of Nazism, the German military missions had made a reputation for themselves in South American military circles, especially among those who were fervent admirers of Prussian organization and of the *Wehrmacht's* operational techniques.

When Ernst Röhm, the future head of the SA, visited Bolivia and other South American countries in 1925, he tried to enrol as many military men as possible in the Nazi ranks. This tentative ideological 'capture' of officers produced good results, so good that in the early years of the Nazi régime the general staffs of South American armies were packed with supporters of National Socialism and nourished in their bosoms groups of believers in Hitlerian ideology (adjusted, of course, to meet the needs of each particular case and the ideas of the most ardent admirers). Though each organization went its own way and often came into conflict with the others, this task of spinning the web of pro-Nazi feeling and German influence in the armies and in radical political parties was furthered by Rosenberg's foreign policy department (APA), by the organization set up by Rudolf Hess to control the activities of Germans abroad (AO=*Auslands-Organisation*), and by the military intelligence department *(Abwehr)* of the OKW (*Oberkommando der Wehrmacht*=Supreme Headquarters Armed Forces) under Admiral Canaris. These three organizations were the hubs of an extensive and highly complex network dealing with military and political matters, espionage, provocation, and all manoeuvres likely to influence the situation, but their activities were interwoven to such an extent that no layman, not even some of the leading figures in the Third Reich, could unravel the inextricable skein.

In three South American countries this Nazi enterprise met with considerable success in military and political circles—in Bolivia, Brazil and Argentina. In the first two it was probably a contributory element in the conspiracies which culminated in the dictatorships of Gualberto Villaroel and Getulio Vargas; in the third, it managed to spread a feeling of solidarity with Hitlerian Germany, and in particular to appeal to an officer like Juan Domingo Perón and a student like Juan Queralta, founder of the notorious *Tacuara*, the most formidable Fascist and racialist organization in South America.

The 1943 dictatorship of Villaroel in Bolivia and the Vargas régime in Brazil both belonged to that category of ideas which we have just mentioned as being the heritage of the nebulous political paraphernalia of 'populism' set against a corporative background and mixed with a strong dose of authoritarianism. 'Getulism' in particular, during its twenty-five years of power in Brazil, combined drastic measures for the partial relief of the masses with a police system strongly reminiscent of the dictatorships of Fulgencio Batista in Cuba and Leónidas Trujillo in the Dominican Republic. Vargas came to power by exploiting all possible means and alliances, but he owed his success primarily to the army and to Plinio Salgado's 'Greenshirts', formed in 1933 with the unmistakable physiognomy of a 'South American version of European Fascism'. Salgado's aim was the creation of a Corporative State, which at the same time was to be demagogically 'social', nationalist and 'integralist', this last term being extremely vague but borrowed directly from the vocabulary of Fascism. The Nazis—as would now seem to be proved by documents—had chosen Brazil as the launching-site for their invasion of the continent from within, and Salgado and his 'integralists' were to be the tools for this first experiment. But while there was still time, Vargas realized that his own personal fate depended on his making a final sprint and beating his adversaries in the last few yards, and in November 1937 he suddenly announced the birth of an *Estado Novo*, with a programme which was bound to give the 'integralists' grounds for satisfaction. 'Getulist' opportunism thus jumped the last hurdle represented by Salgado, and placed its reliance entirely on the army and on the trade unionism *sui generis* which the watchwords of Vargas had called into being. Nevertheless, the mortgage on the army held by the conservative groups would have paralysed any tendency on the part of the dictator to introduce reforms of a truly revolutionary type, and the régime therefore owed its continued existence to the carefully tended cult of the man who was its head, giving the Brazilian masses certain guarantees in matters of social legislation, but leaving the feudal structure of the country unchanged. That the granting of these guarantees was itself a novelty and a harbinger of further developments in the recognition of the Brazilian proletariat, is undoubtedly true; but the problem concerned the dialectic process of history and only partially involved the dictator's personal intentions, while it had no connexion whatsoever with the aims pursued by the Nazis when they helped to achieve the 'Getulist' victory, or by the military men when they provided the pillars on which the régime rested.

The 'School of the Imperial Way'

The Japanese often give the name *kurai tanima*—'dark valley'—to the period between 1931 and 1941, the decade immediately preceding the outbreak of the Pacific War. For during these years the still delicate plant of liberalism and personal freedom that had sprouted during the twenties was effectively killed.[24]

It is with these words that Richard Storry evokes the period of the explosion of Japanese nationalism and imperialism, at a time when Europe was passing through a similar 'dark valley' leading up to the moment when the paths of her tragedy would cross those of the drama of the land of cherry-blossom.

The 1914–18 war had enabled Japan to achieve a commercial monopoly in the Far East. The war itself cost the Mikado's government very little (about 40 million gold dollars), and on the other hand had brought about an almost complete suspension of European exports to Asia and a considerable reduction of those from North America. This meant an enormous boost for Japanese industry and trade, accompanied in certain sectors by a process of rapid monopolistic concentration and by a phase of wild speculation (dividends rose from 50 per cent to 200 or 300 per cent, and in the case of the shipbuilding industry even 600 per cent). The incredibly low level of industrial wages contributed to this astronomical rise in profits; during the war wages had shown a slight improvement, but it had been a fractional and at all events a very slow rise compared with the increase in the cost-of-living index. The wages of agricultural labourers—representing more than two-thirds of the nation's total wage-bill—rose at an absurdly low rate, and the consequent impoverishment of the countryside went steadily on. The Japanese middle class experienced its 'golden age' and seized with greedy hands the incessant flow of benefits it received, thanks to the complete freedom of action which it enjoyed on the markets, the near-slavery nature of its relationship with the workers, and the acquiescence of successive governments. The cost of creating these huge concentrations of financial and industrial power, controlled by the old clans who had dominated the economic and commercial structure of Japan since the beginning, was an accentuation of the already very marked social inequalities. Consequently, the wretched condition of the peasantry and the working-class proletariat formed a sharp contrast to the boundless wealth of the business undertakings, in a society in which a middle class virtually did not exist.

Once the war was over and foreign competition made its reappearance on the markets of the Far East and the archipelagos, all those injustices came to light which had been concealed beneath a semblance of prosperity due to rapid expansion during the war years. Agriculture had lagged behind, and the various branches of industry had developed in an uneven and chaotic way, one of the reasons being the inadequacy of the technical set-up, coupled with the ephemeral character of many of the new enterprises; these had been born and flourished on the crest of the boom, but could not stand up to normal competition either at home or abroad. In other words, the economic and industrial structure of Japan experienced those shocks which every capitalistic economy naturally has to bear when a gigantic and artificial expansion has been grafted on to a body unprepared for it and beset by backwardness and such great discrepancies between one sector and another that it is liable to go bankrupt at the first even temporary change in the course of events. Add to this the fact that Japanese expansion was of very recent date and had been experienced by a country burdened with feudal institutions and an inherited sluggishness. The consequences could only be stagnation, followed by a crisis that struck at the very heart of the whole complex mechanism. Japanese capitalism was faced with a problem which was not exactly a novelty—the problem of solving its contradictions in the only way that the logic of the system demanded; that is, by throwing the burden of the crisis on the shoulders of the working classes and the peasantry, and finding outlets on the international markets by means of a determined policy of imperialistic expansion. All the more so because the lower classes, under the pinch of hunger, were becoming restive and the incipient class organizations found no lack of followers.

The poverty of the urban proletariat formed a link between their claims and the renewed demands of the peasants, who in the past had always been averse to mass violence, which had invariably misfired owing to the lack of political leadership. From 1919 on these claims gave rise to more labour disputes than Japan had ever known before, which is not surprising in view of the increasing trend towards the left. In 1920 the first 'Socialist League' was founded, followed in 1921 by the formation of the first Japanese Communist Party. In that same year the sporadic outbreaks in the country districts became more organized thanks to the guidance offered by the association known as the *Nihon-Nomin Koumai* (in 1920 there were 2,100 agrarian disputes involving more than 12,000 landowners and about 50,000 concerns).[25] Parallel to this was the growth of the campaign for universal suffrage, with the consequent formation of a 'National League'; this, with the support of the Radicals and Communists of the *Katayama*, demanded the abolition of electoral discrimination on a property basis and encountered the stubborn opposition of all the conservative elements, of the army and of the so-called Liberal *bourgeoisie*, whose Liberal principles and democratic ideals were of an extremely pallid hue. In short, Japan, which had not entered the arena of the modern world until the end of the nineteenth century, was suddenly, owing to a process of industrialization which started a hundred years later than was the case with her European and American competitors, plunged into the midst of social struggles. Violating as they did the ancient code of passive 'behaviour' in the presence of authority and the 'lords' and all those customs which were so firmly established that they seemed to be invulnerable, these outbreaks of unrest among the proletariat and the class movement of the workers' advance-guards conjured up before the anxious eyes of the startled and scandalized custodians of imperial power terrifying visions of an uprising which by sheer force might sweep away centuries of religious precepts cleverly transformed into an ethical policy of slavery. It is true that the powerful remnants of feudalism and obedience to the canons of the 'Toguwaka code', a gospel of social meekness, still contrived to keep thousands of peasants yoked to the myths of the divine nature of monarchy and the unquestionable supremacy of those whom a mysterious supernatural will had placed at the head of affairs in the empire of the Rising Sun, but notwithstanding this, the pinch of hunger and the growth of class feeling brought into the streets behind red flags thousands of ragged and undernourished men, exploited beyond the limits of endurance by the usurers, who were often their own employers.

To the military and financial oligarchy in whose hands the real power lay, these rebellious outbursts, which were no longer disorganized demonstrations of a feeble peasant *jacquerie*, brought a sense of imminent peril, not only because of the demands for a reform of the State (democratic and constitutional only on paper), but also because of the advanced measures of a social character which were put forward at the same time. In the country districts the instigators of the famous 'rice revolt' of 1918 were still active; on that occasion 10 million peasants had risen on two-thirds of the national territory, burning chambers of commerce, barns and landowners' houses and killing speculators with an uncontrollable fury. The government had arrested 80,000 people and the revolt had petered out. But now it had the appearance of an ominous volcanic eruption, spewing forth enough boiling lava to melt all the myths, all the restraining prejudices and archaisms which hitherto had kept the people tied to the ecstatic contemplation of the divinely ordered social distinctions. To make things worse, the drying-up of commercial outlets became more acute and the rich pastures of the Chinese market were threatened by the competition of the American and British trusts, which drove out the Japanese businessmen or relegated them to marginal areas.

In 1915 Baron Okuma, one of the exponents of Japan's economic oligarchy, had said without mincing words: 'We must hasten to take advantage of the chance that has been offered us to become the guiding spirit in Asiatic affairs. No other great power is in such a favourable position as our youthful and vigorous empire when it comes to illuminating and civilizing the Chinese people.'[26] For at least fifty years past China and Manchuria had been the favourite objectives of Japanese businessmen and also of the 'colonial' aims of the military, who, in their descents on the mainland, had shown what they meant by 'civilization' of the Chinese, the Manchurians and the Koreans. The *zaibatsu* (financial cliques) felt that it was their mission to rescue their neighbours, the archipelagos of the Pacific and the rest of the Asiatic continent from barbarity. But the outlet that attracted them more than any other was China, partly because it offered them a huge market within easy reach, and partly because many businessmen, and many generals as well, looked upon it as the gateway to the Siberian regions on the one side and the Indies on the other (the history of the invasion of Korea in

1910 is an interesting example of the cordial unanimity which existed among the warlords and the more practical executives of big trusts like the *Mitsui*).

Projects for expansion were thus a matter of the utmost urgency. In 1920 the Western powers were helping the remnants of the Tsarist armies to fight the Soviets, and this provided Japan with an excuse for intervening in Siberia. The Mikado's troops were not withdrawn until 1922, after the Washington conference and insistent pressure from the United States; but meanwhile the forward march of Japanese expansion had begun and nobody could stop it. At home, this imperialism had its counterpart in the increasing reluctance to make any democratic concessions and a trend towards an unbridled nationalism. In 1925 the government was at last compelled to introduce universal suffrage (excluding, however, soldiers, students, paupers, women, and all citizens under twenty-five). Shortly after this a law was passed against 'dangerous ideas', secret societies and agitation against private ownership. The paragraph dealing with secret societies remained a dead letter in so far as the innumerable military and extreme right-wing associations were concerned, but it was rigidly enforced against the workers' organizations and left-wing movements. Meanwhile the economic crisis was becoming more and more acute. In 1927 the issuing bank in Formosa failed and this brought about the collapse of the Suzuki trust controlling the production of rice, camphor and sugar-cane. A chain reaction set in and the other institutions controlled by the Bank of Japan suspended payment. A three months' moratorium was ordered and in one week the monetary circulation rose from 1,226 to 2,239 million yen. Thirty banks closed their doors, with a total capital of 908 millions. This forerunner of the Wall Street crash two years later had repercussions all over the world; it put the capitalists on their guard and inspired the militarists with a holy zeal for the 'security of the country', undermined by a parliamentary system which was in truth torn by devastating scandals. The protagonists of these scandals were, however, none other than the henchmen of the economic right wing and of the bewildered and paralysed liberal *bourgeoisie*, who for that matter were quite ready to flock to the support of their nominal adversaries. 'They were ready', says Storry, 'to respond to a strong appeal from some force outside the elected Diet. By virtue of the nature of Japanese state education this kind of appeal would be much more effective than that of Marxism.'[27] And it was obvious that the task of drawing up plans for 'saving the country' would fall in the first place to the generals.

In that same year, 1927, after the fall of the Wakatsuki government (guilty of having shown too much tolerance towards certain liberal tendencies), Giichi Tanaka, the new Prime Minister and Foreign Secretary, submitted to the Mikado a plan of vast proportions covering the conquest of Manchuria and Northern China, and subsequently of Soviet Siberia and the Indies, after which military operations were to be extended to any zone where it might be necessary to oppose and defeat the imperialism of the United States. The Tanaka memorandum, which was published for the first time in September 1931 by the Shanghai periodical *China Critic* and subsequently reproduced by left-wing European journals, caused an uproar. The Japanese did not dispute its authenticity, but they cast doubts on the accuracy of the version published in the Chinese press; but, as Chassague points out, the 'facts' were destined to *'démentir le démenti'*.[28] Tanaka had not minced words when outlining his plan:

> In the interests of her own safety and that of other countries,' he wrote in his memorandum, 'Japan can settle her own troubles in Eastern Asia only by adopting a policy of blood and iron. If, after we have done that, we want to take control of China, we must first defeat the United States. In other words, we must deal with them as we dealt with Russia at the time of the Russo-Japanese war. To conquer China, we must first conquer Manchuria and Mongolia. Once all the resources of China are at our disposal, we shall undertake the conquest of the Indies, of Asia Minor, Central Asia and even Europe . . . Manchuria and Mongolia are the Belgium of the Far East. In our war against Russia and the United States, Manchuria and Mongolia will have to suffer all the horrors of war.[29]

The 1929 crisis had less serious effects in Japan and lasted a shorter time than in the other countries involved. But the troubles of the Japanese capitalistic economy were chronic. It was struggling with the insoluble difficulties of a monopolistic industrial set-up dependent on foreign countries for its raw materials, which had achieved very considerable dimensions on the eve of the recession in the international markets and in home consumption. Capital was employed for purely speculative purposes and agriculture was a deadweight on the shoulders of the other more progressive sectors. Only a wartime economy, and the prospect of acquiring new resources by depriving other countries of them, could save Japanese capitalism from the morass in which it was floundering. In 1931, taking advantage of the difficulties the United States had to face as a result of the depression which followed the 1929 crisis, the troops of His Majesty the Tenno occupied Manchuria and a year later proclaimed it an independent State, under a satellite government within easy reach of Japanese 'advice' backed up by Japanese bayonets. The Tanaka plan had played its first card, by means of a thrust which, although at first sight it might seem to be merely a tentative sounding of the reactions of Japan's adversaries, was in reality the prelude to the grand offensive of Japanese pan-Asiatic imperialism. After this passage of the Rubicon, the attack on parliamentary institutions and the domestic liberties of the country burst forth in all its fury, and was carried on in the style of a local version of Italian *squadrismo*, tinged with the medieval traditions so jealously cultivated by the Japanese army. Political assassinations and military *coups de main* became everyday occurrences. Minister Hamaguchi, guilty of having accepted, at the naval conference in London, a quota of only six cruisers for Japan against the ten each assigned to Great Britain and the United States, was murdered; Baron Dan, managing director of the Mitsui holding company, the Finance Minister, Inouye, and Premier Inukai met with the same fate. The last-named fell to the revolvers of some young officers who announced that they were members of an association comprising 2,000 of their colleagues, 280 in the district of Tokyo alone.

The secret societies and factions set up by officers of the armed forces became more and more numerous; most of them were sinister organizations membership of which could only be obtained after a ritual initiation, but there were other groups which pursued their activities openly and admitted non-military members, though their aims were unmistakably pro-Fascist or National Socialist. Among the officers' associations the most important was the *Kōdō-ha*, or 'School of the Imperial Way'. It was important not only because some of its members were high-ranking officers of the army general staff, but because it also included followers of the ideas, conventionally known as 'informative concepts', of the 'Showa Restoration' *(Shōwa Ishiu)*.[30] The essence of this vaguely Nazi doctrine had been excogitated by Kita Ikki, a fiery fanatic with a touch of genius, who immediately after the First World War put his ideas into writing in a volume entitled *Nihon Kaizō Hōan Taikō* ('Plan for the Reconstruction of Japan') which met with a favourable reception. According to Kita Ikki, the task for the younger generation in Japan was the creation of a State governed by the armed forces, with the Emperor at the apex of the pyramid and a highly-centralized administrative superstructure which would control a planned society. The 'reconstruction' of Japan could be achieved, according to this writer, only by means of a military *coup d'état*, which would inaugurate a new era of 'State Socialism' and a policy of imperial expansion.

According to Richard Storry, during the 'Meiji Restoration' (the latter half of the nineteenth century and first decade of the twentieth) 'the great lords had surrendered their fiefs to the Emperor, thus nominally "restoring" to the sovereign the lands that his family had owned and governed in ancient times. In the "Showa Restoration" the capitalists would have to surrender, or "restore" their riches; and the political parties, too, would be called upon to surrender their powers to the Emperor.'[31] On closer examination, Kita Ikki's ideas look very like the type of National Socialism which, as we have seen, was current among the officers of South American armies during the 'thirties—the army as an expression of the national conscience, faithful to tradition, but at the same time standard-bearer of an expansionist policy which would not be imperialist in the normal acceptance of the term, since it was the policy of an 'anti-capitalist nation' and its aim was the redemption of all Asiatics and the inauguration of a 'new order'. The synthesis is in substance the same as that of all doctrines of the Fascist and National Socialist type, with the necessary adaptations to Japanese tradition—the roles of the army and the Emperor, the cult of the mission handed down by ancestors, etc., etc.

Sadao Araki, a general of the authoritarian type, was a member of the *Kōdō-ha*, which had a right wing that was purely and simply imperialistic and xenophobic and did not accept the ultimate aims of the 'Showa Restoration'. After the death of Inukai in 1932, Araki became Minister of War in the government formed by Admiral Saitō. The admiral's régime was a somewhat colourless one, this being partly due to the insipid personality of its leader, who was a Conservative of moderate views and a practical man, but weak, and partly to the improvised and composite character of the government itself. The only man who knew exactly what he wanted was Araki, and many believed that he and General Mazaki were the leaders of the *Kōdō-ha*. Araki and his followers were engaged in a bitter struggle with another extremist military faction called the

Tōsei-ha or 'Control School', which repudiated many of the points in the programme of the 'Showa Restoration' and looked upon the occupation of Manchuria as the first step towards an attack on China, whereas for the *Kōdō-ha* it was to be the jumping-off ground for the invasion of Russia. At first sight these differences of opinion would appear to be merely a question of priorities within the same overall plan, but in reality they reflected the hidden interests and aspirations of the big business 'clans' and the dissension between the army and the navy. In any case Araki, like Tanaka, must be given the credit for putting his views down in black and white, for in August 1932, only two months after he became Minister of War, he wrote an article for the review *Kaikosha* in which he said:

> Our country is determined to propagate its national idea on all the Seven Seas, to spread it throughout the five continents, even if we have to use force. We are descendants of the gods and are destined to rule the world.[32]

Araki's programme was thus identical with the memorandum compiled by his colleague in 1931 and submitted to the benevolent attention of the Mikado, but he was at pains to make his views even clearer, as is plain in this passage regarding Mongolia:

> Japan cannot tolerate the existence of such an ambiguous territory as Mongolia which is immediately adjacent to her sphere of influence. At all costs the Mongolian territory must be joined to the East . . . It must be made quite clear that any enemy who opposes the propagation of the imperial idea will be destroyed![33]

This reveille sounded by the imperial trumpets from the government benches electrified the extreme right wing. The already-operating nationalistic and para-Fascist organizations redoubled their efforts, while others sprang into being in a flash. The shock troops with which a radical nationalism sought to impose these policies on the nation were by no means negligible, even outside the ranks of the army. For example, the 'Reservists' Association', under the control of the War Ministry and therefore inclined to extremist views, had 3 million members; the 'Retired Officers' Association' had tens of thousands of members who sympathized with Araki's ideas or with movements reflecting them. Most important of all was the 'River Amur Society' *(Ko Kuryu Kai)*, better known as the 'Black Dragon', a powerful and sinister organization founded in 1901 and counting among its members many officers of the general staff and leaders of the financial cliques. For thirty years past the 'Black Dragon' had been a kind of freemasonry which evolved expansionist plans and determined the fate of the adversaries of nationalism, often even arranging for their physical removal from this world. Then there was the 'Society of the Cherry-tree Blossom', another very powerful faction consisting mainly of junior officers who cherished the usual hopes of strengthening the imperial power with the aid of the army. Offshoots of these societies were a number of minor organizations, whose official aims were often of a cultural nature, and the initiates of the larger sects were at the same time members of these branches. In addition there was the 'National Foundation Society' (founded by Inamoura, one of the Mikado's privy councillors), of which Araki was a member; the 'Ardent World Society' *(Génoschia)*; the 'National League of the New Japan' *(Shin Nihon Kokumin Dōmēi)*, whose aim was the establishment of a 'unified anti-capitalist economy' by means of an 'equal distribution of the world's natural resources' (naturally according to the geopolitical concepts of Japanese nationalism); the 'Women's Fascist League' *(Nihon Foujn Dōmēi)*; the 'Greater Imperial Japan Association', one of whose leaders was Akao Bin, a lawyer who later became famous as a determined advocate of a Fascist-type State; and the pro-Nazi 'Party for the Creation of a Greater Japan', which numbered among its organizers another eminent extremist, Katsumaro Akamatsu, an ex-Communist, ex-leader of the right wing of the Social Democratic Party and now a convert to the teachings of Hitler. On various levels of Japanese society were the 'Pan-Japanese Labour Party', the 'National Defence Society', the 'Japanese National Party', the 'Local Patriotism Association', etc., etc.

There was thus a whole galaxy of associations, sects and parties, with numerous offshoots and different political functions, but hardly any of them had a firm foothold among the masses, except the ex-soldiers' organizations and the women's leagues, which recruited their members mainly from the lower middle class. Nevertheless, despite their limited memberships, these associations formed a background and a by no means negligible recruiting pool for the factions which were the real spearheads of the nationalist offensive; that is to say, the armed forces and the cliques which controlled the economic power of the great monopolistic trusts.

But even between these two solar systems of the authoritarian trend there was a sharp divergence of views and attitudes, and the process of involution which they were bringing about did not develop along straightforward lines without violent controversies within each movement. Among the Service elements, the rivalry between army and navy made itself felt at every moment and pro-voked a dour struggle for supremacy when opinions differed as to the priority to be given to the various objectives of imperialist expansion—objectives which were bound up with the role that each of the two Services was to play in the future development of the plans for foreign conquest. In high financial and industrial circles, the sudden aggressiveness of the armed forces following upon the entry of Araki into the government and the demands of those sectors which wanted war at any price, at once caused apprehension among the representatives of the more moderate elements, who were afraid of a popular reaction if they supported these demands and also had their misgivings about the expansion towards Russia advocated by the *Kōdō-ha*. Moreover, these lukewarm supporters of the military programme had doubts of another kind, which were a consequence of the open dissension between the capitalistic factions; that is to say, between the interests of the traditional con-cerns to which they themselves belonged and those of the new and more dynamic trusts (e.g. *Mori, Konhara, Noguti*), who sided with Araki's extremists because of the short-term advantages they believed would accrue from a phase of rapid military conquests. It is thus evident that the differences of opinion between military circles and the ruling economic class were confined to questions of tactics and the way the imperialistic programme should be carried out, and did not involve the principles or the strategic sound-ness of the programme itself.

The nationalistic demagogy of the followers of the 'Showa Restoration', together with the trend towards National Socialism, weakened and split the Socialist front. In the minds of many naïve leaders of the left wing there was a feeling that the military 'anti-capitalists' were in a position to put into effect the plans they advocated, even at the cost of bloodshed, and it was believed that they were the key personages in the plot that was being hatched by the general staff and the army cadres. In 1934, a conspiracy organized by officers, who even contemplated the massacre of the entire government by means of an aerial bombardment, failed by pure chance, but paved the way for the revolt of 1936 which shattered the 'social' aspirations of the paladins of the 'Showa Restoration'. In 1934 Araki resigned for health reasons, and that meant the end of *Kōdō-ha* supremacy in the government. The generals who succeeded him belonged to the *Tōsei-ha*, or were under its influence, and they accordingly removed their rivals from all key positions. The *Kōdō-ha* then organized a plot and whole regiments mutinied. Nagata, the Minister for War, was cut down by the sword of a lieutenant-colonel. For four days government forces faced the rebels, each side poised to attack the other, but the rebels gave in as soon as they realized that the element of surprise was lacking. Thirteen of the ringleaders were sentenced by courts martial to be shot, among them being Kita Ikki, the theorist of the 'Showa Restoration'. The National Socialist wing of the military front collapsed and the *Tōsei-ha* were the victors—the supporters of an integral nationalism based on the old authoritarian and expansionist models, without any infiltration of 'socialistic' ideas or complicated ideologies imported from abroad. The *Tōsei-ha* took a firm hold of the reins of government and installed Hirota as Premier, but he was 'little more than its tool'.[34]

This brings us to the last chapter in Japan's constitutional crisis. In December 1936 Hirota signed the Anti-Comintern Pact with Germany, thus safeguarding the Japanese north-western flank in the event of an attack on China, which was the *Tōsei-ha*'s choice, as we pointed out above. The wheels of war had been well oiled. No one could now halt the authoritarian drive of the Japanese State, which the militarists quickened while arranging their pawns for the attack on China in July 1937. The resistance which they encountered as they proceeded with their work of destruction grew weaker and weaker. Even the right-wing nationalist elements whose plans conflicted with those of the *Tōsei-ha*, finally decided to bury the hatchet and give their whole-hearted support to a policy which, when all was said and done, was in harmony with their own aspirations (and in fact Araki and the survivors of the *Kōdō-ha* allowed things to run their course).

In the Second World War Japan remained a spectator until 1941, but in 1940 the constitution was amended to sanction the abolition of the existing parties, and the only political organization which retained its right of citizenship was Prince Konoye's, known as 'Assistance to the Imperial Throne'. This creature of one of the Mikado's ultra-nationalist courtiers sounded the death-knell of the democratic State, which in reality had ceased to exist many years before, and marked the transition to a totalitarian form of government that had no 'Duce', but in which the imperial court, the army and the navy were the nerve-centres of a collective authoritarianism, under the watery eyes of the imperial sphinx, who to all appearances remained true to his traditional function of counting for nothing in the decisions of his henchmen in the government, but in substance presumably welcomed a system which guaranteed the perpetuation of the privileges of the crown in the most congenial way. The Japanese Fascists and Nazis aligned themselves with the 'Assistance to the Imperial Throne', renouncing their demands for 'social reform' and their special brand of anti-capitalism. 'The idea of the Nation', wrote Tagore, 'is one of the most powerful anaesthetics that man has invented.'[35] Under the effects of this narcotic, administered in shock doses by capitalism and by militarist reaction, the dreams of a compromise between imperialism, tradition and progress, which had matured in the chaotic ideological minds of men like Kita Ikki, vanished into thin air. A similar disillusionment was reserved everywhere for the Fascist and National Socialist ideals of those who were fond of describing themselves as 'children of the sun'.

3 The 'New Order' Myth

Towards the conquest of the world

Both in Europe and overseas, the progress achieved by Nazi and Fascist ideas between 1933 and 1939 was indisputable. The area covered by more or less authoritarian extreme right-wing movements that had overcome their teething troubles and had often survived political upheavals of some moment, had become immeasurably larger. Some of them had organized themselves so efficiently and acquired such influence that they were in a position to seize power, or at all events to pull the strings of government. This had been the case, to quote only one example, with the Rumanian 'Iron Guards', who, after their organization had been dissolved by a law passed in 1938, had transformed themselves into the 'All for the Fatherland' party, and with the connivance of the army were undermining the monarchy and the government. In Spain, thanks to the substantial aid of Nazi and Fascist arms, General Franco and the 'traditionalist' and Fascist forces under his command were destroying the Republic and establishing a clerico-military dictatorship steeped in Fascist ideas. Other movements, in different circumstances, had strengthened their positions by cannibalizing minor organizations or assuming a more dynamic attitude, in order to gain prestige as the pivots of anti-Communist and 'patriotic' fronts.

In the fierce onslaught on Socialism during the post-war years and the economic crisis, the Liberal and Catholic leaders everywhere had relegated, or tried to relegate, the workers' parties to the fringes of the political sphere, or else had endeavoured to deprive the masses of the weapons they needed to carry on the struggle and thus make it impossible for them to storm the capitalist citadel. The extreme right-wing parties had drawn sustenance from this pitched battle between the Liberal democracies and the popular fronts; they had raised the banner of the anti-Marxist crusade and had tried to push their way into the crisis of the *bourgeois* state and put forward their own solutions. The task

of extricating the Liberal State from the problems threatening its
very existence was accomplished by strengthening the functions of
the executive power and depriving the legislature of much of its
concrete significance. The State organism had been riddled by
speculation and corruption, this being due not to abstract mal-
practices or to an unforeseeable decline in the morality of the
individual, but to the rifts which had been opened by a dynamic
force that tended to deprive democracy of its significance and allow
every kind of intrigue to creep in; while the subversive right-wing
movements had seized the opportunity to launch their 'moral
reform' campaigns, which led to the negation of democracy and an
urge to 'restore order' with the aid of 'strong governments'. On the
one hand the Liberal State tried to save itself by resorting to a
violent repression of popular movements; on the other it strove
to lessen the risk represented by its inconvenient right-wing allies
in the battle against Socialism, by adopting parliamentary tactics
and precautionary half-measures. The only result of this was that
it hastened its own decline and left the Fascist or extreme nationalist
trends ample room to manœuvre. The not unnatural sympathies of
the militarists for such movements induced them to break away
from the rest of the ruling class, while the Church and the ecclesiastical hierarchies, once the fears, dating from the days when the
reactionary and anti-socialist aspects of Fascism and Nazism were
less evident, had been stilled, hailed as saviours not only the men
behind movements of this kind, but the whole complex of systems
claiming to be bulwarks of 'Christian values' against 'Bolshevik
atheism'. In countries where democratic institutions were of more
recent date and were barely tolerated by the reigning houses, right-
wing authoritarianism was able to impose itself with comparative
ease, often contriving to avoid replacing the ruling class by the
extreme right wing of Nazi or Fascist persuasion, but in reality
paving the way for such a substitution.

Pressure exerted by the Nazi and Fascist régimes with their arms
at the ready emboldened the extremist elements. Once the masses
had been disarmed, the traditional governments were prisoners of
their own isolation, of their fear that they might have to rely on
those very forces which previously they had brutally suppressed,
and they therefore took the only way out they could see; that is
to say, an approach to the Germany of Hitler or the Italy of
Mussolini, and they were prepared to oblige the dictators by
appointing to responsible posts men whom these dictators trusted.

The post-war upheaval had laid bare the mean and narrow-minded aspects of the Liberal democracies, and had discredited the parliamentary system and the practices of governments entangled in a mesh of Machiavellian inter-party compromises, personal antipathies and sinister lobbying, which the man in the street attributed —and often rightly—to petty factional interests. The price of doing away with the most glaring inequalities due to the lack of balance in the capitalistic economies had been borne not only by the workers and peasants, but also by the middle classes, who, however, had been led to believe that Europe, with each of its individual countries, was on the brink of ruin owing to the claims of the proletariat and the tempest of revolutionary myths raised by Soviet Russia. The *petit-bourgeois* moralism of these sectors of society, and their obvious need to find an authoritarian outlet from the gloom of their own horizons, made them an easily manœuvrable mass ready to respond to the irrational appeals of the Fascist crusade. Where the 'Left' had already been in power, for example in France with the *Front Populaire*, the experience had been merely a delusion, apt to frighten both the upper and the lower middle class, without demolishing any of the old ruling structures and thus exposing the State and the lower classes to the perils of an even more rabid reaction.

From this depressing atmosphere the Fascists and Nazis drew all the oxygen they needed. Moreover, from 1930 on there entered the political arena a generation which had not experienced the difficulties of the post-war years and now saw only the decay of the State system or the withering of every democratic ideal in sterile and incomprehensible struggles between inept and decrepit forces and individuals, the symbols in the eyes of the younger generation of a past characterized by errors and impotence. The Nazis and Fascists swore that they would devote all their energies to getting rid of these 'politicians' corroded by inertia and ignorance, in order to pave the way for a revolution of the young, whose aims might be vague and contradictory, but who would banish all selfishness, ennoble labour, preserve, by renovating it, social progress without undermining the traditional institution of the family, and be 'internationalistic' while at the same time extolling the spiritual values of the nation. They held out the prospect of a crude 'vitalistic' myth, the protagonists of which would be devotees of a kind of pagan religion whose gods of violence would set the world ablaze in order to purify corrupt mankind in the flames, and at the same time would defend certain abstract ideal concepts and certain traditions. 'In reality,' Maurice Bardèche wrote many years later, thus confirming that he was indeed a 'Fascist writer', 'man, as the Fascists conceived him, was a young savage believing only in those qualities which were necessary in order to live in the steppes or on an ice-floe. He repudiated civilization, because in it he saw only hypocrisy and fraud. He believed in pioneers, in builders, in the warriors of his tribe.'[1] And what was Fascism in the eyes of the millions of people who were ready to fight for it? 'It is the party of the angry nation,' says Bardèche, 'it is above all the party of that sector of society which normally relaxes amidst the comforts of *bourgeois* life, but which in times of crisis is jolted out of its class, is irritated and infuriated by upheavals, and then intervenes violently in political affairs with purely passional reflexes—in other words, the middle class. But for Fascism this anger of the nation is indispensable. It is the very blood that irrigates Fascism. Without it Fascism would beat its flanks in vain, creating eddies which would impress nobody, and it would exalt in vain the image of the hero who ought to exist in an age which does not understand the need for heroism.'[2] There are a number of truths in this postmortem analysis. Disappointment and irrational anger, when directed into certain channels at moments of crisis, give the *petite bourgeoisie* the impression that they can transform into facts that 'fantastic world of abstract idealism' which, as Salvatorelli points out, 'knows nothing of the real values of the modern world' and 'clasps to its bosom the bloodless and shapeless manikin' of the national myth, convinced that 'all those who do not conform with its a-political moral code are evil and corrupt, and enemies of their country'.[3] For the younger generation, the Fascist and Nazi message, stuffed with distorted concepts and cultural blandishments, had the terrible, but real, fascination of an appeal to cleanse the face of every country with sponges of iron, because otherwise this process of purification could not possibly be successful, and because that was the only way, or so the Fascists maintained, to establish an order freed from capitalist bloodsuckers and also from Marxism—which was represented in the grotesque caricatured form of a Moloch insatiably devouring all spiritual values.

Amid all the paraphernalia of Nazi and Fascist doctrines and programmes, and precisely because each one of them exhausted itself in proclaiming principles and lived on an absolute empiricism, we often come across certain postulates which were calculated to satisfy the most disparate demands; the whole was bundled together or left in the liquid state, so that anyone could extract a twig or take a sip and believe that he had discovered the truth. The pagan myths of the vitality of the race and the supremacy of brute force went side by side with claims to be the saviours of the integrity of Western Christian traditions; revolutionary aspirations shot through with muddled socialistic ideals were grafted on to the cult of tribal traditions and an accentuated nationalistic individualism; anti-capitalism went arm-in-arm with a negation of the class struggle; 'Europeanism' was mingled with xenophobia; hatred of culture and of ideologies had its Freudian counterpart in a seeking after a cultural and ideological dignity, which plundered the intellectual heritage of many centuries in its efforts to achieve impossible syntheses.

In the glittering heyday of their fame Germany and Italy contrived to harness the national and nationalistic movements of the Arab world to the policies of Nazism and Fascism, just as they had sought to influence similar trends in South America. Ahmed Hussein and his Egyptian 'Greenshirts' of the 'Young Egypt' party, Fathi Radouan and Nour Eddine Tarraf, the leaders of the 'New National Party', got into touch with the Nazis; the Grand Mufti of Jerusalem, Amin el Hussein, entered into relations—at first clandestine and, for reasons of prudence, purely formal—with Mussolini's government; with the utmost caution and taking care not to compromise themselves in their public utterances, the leaders of the Tunisian and Algerian liberation movements weighed the advantages of accepting the help of the two régimes in their struggle against French colonialism. Such approaches were not unnatural, and only in the case of the Egyptians and the Mufti did they assume the proportions of a definite alignment with Nazi-Fascist policies, whereas for the other groups they never got beyond the stage of sporadic contacts which did not assume the character of an open political alliance. The middle class and the military men who controlled the Arab nationalistic organizations were anti-British owing to the nature of their claims, but this tactical necessity was supplemented by a definite leaning towards the methods and principles of National Socialism, the teachings of which were put to good use by Egyptian officers and were destined to leave a lasting mark. In the radical wing of the Indian nationalist movement, too, the attractions of Nazism and Fascism induced the Deputy Chandra Subhàs Bose to secede from the Congress Party

c

in 1943 and become the head of a government in exile at Singapore and the commander of a 'national army'.

Anti-Semitism naturally played an important part in these sympathies of the Arab world for the Nazis and Fascists. Arab nationalism welcomed the theory of a 'worldwide Jewish conspiracy' against the nations, not so much because it fitted into the general anti-Communist scheme, but rather because it was the quintessence of the spirit of the anti-Jewish crusade, which certain elements made the keystone of their campaign to mobilize the masses in the religious field in keeping with the programme of the 'Muslim Brotherhood'. Similarly, the racial motive was undoubtedly a dominating factor in the popularity which Hitler and National Socialism achieved among certain sectors of the ruling class in South Africa. For twenty years past the Afrikaners, descendants of the Boer colonizers, had been using the Bible as the gospel of a nationalism and racialism which to Rosenberg seemed to be the quintessence of his own theories. From the distant extremity of the Dark Continent they applauded the exploits of the Nazis, who had formulated doctrines which would serve to justify, from a legal point of view as well, the discriminatory measures against the Negroes in the Union. For them Hitler was the symbol of the 'leader' whose coming—according to their own interpretation of Biblical prophecies—had been foretold, a leader who would redeem the world in accordance with the theory of the 'chosen people'. The Afrikaners believed that they were an integral part of this chosen people; they accordingly misused their power over the Coloured races, at the same time pocketing the enormous profits made by exploiting the native labourers for the benefit of the white minority in the country, while the condition of the labourers themselves was practically one of slavery.

The outbreak of war in 1939 and the sensational sequence of victories achieved by the Germans on every front raised to fever point the enthusiasm of the fanatical believers in the 'new order', scattered all over the world. There seemed to be no human force that could stand up to the might of Hitler; during the *Blitzkrieg* the German tanks crushed the democracies beneath their tracks and paved the way for the Pharaonic car of the Nazi system—a miracle of chronometrical exactitude in the way it controlled civilians in the occupied territories and rooted out its hidden enemies, who were liquidated *en masse*. Was the 'new order' about to begin? Hitler had said that 'to subjugate an independent country with the intention of restoring its liberty afterwards is absurd. The blood that has been shed confers the right of property.'[4] And in fact the sole purpose of his plans was to make the occupied countries marches of the Nazi empire; Britain, France and the Soviet Union must be destroyed. 'Against these powers,' we read in *Mein Kampf,* 'no methods must be deemed too harsh, no sacrifice must seem impossible, until we are finally in a position to crush the enemy who hates us so bitterly.'[5]

The 'new order' had a dogma which the leading Nazi jurist, Karl Schmitt, had been ordered to formulate. This Nazi ideologist did his best to justify, from the standpoint of international law, the geo-political concept of *Grossraumordnung,* a kind of new Monroe doctrine, starting from the principle whereby—to quote Collotti— 'the powers which are racially and geographically extraneous to a given area' have no right to 'interfere in what goes on inside that area *(Grossraum)*,' such things being the prerogative of the great power which is master of the *Grossraum*. This meant that the German hegemony would be a kind of 'pluralistic commonwealth of free peoples'.[6] Racial uniformity was to be the basis of this community of homogeneous groups, and within this sphere each component of the political set-up would be expected to serve the common 'cause' by adapting its own economy in accordance with an overall plan of reciprocal integration to be drawn up and controlled by the 'guiding country'. This concept is nothing but a cunning disguise devised by the Nazi insurance magnate to camouflage the policy of German aggression as a mission of redemption in the occupied countries. The putting into practice of Schmitt's postulates involved a large-scale plundering of the subjugated economies, a process which Goering's technical departments refined with a truly Teutonic diligence. But the ideological and juridical framework was the last straw for those who had indulged in the dreams of the 'new order' which Fascist and Nazi myths had conjured up in every country. Here the Mussolini régime lost its last chance of making an experiment which might have served as a guide; the supremacy of Nazism had already been a humiliation, and now the concept of a 'pluralistic commonwealth of free peoples' shifted the centre of gravity definitely to the German side, as regards the 'revolutionary' hopes which had nourished the myth of a more genuinely international Fascism.

Italian Fascism could not compete with its ally when it came to exporting the 'new order' by force of arms, or even exporting the finished product, if we may call it so, which the Nazis were offering to their admirers. The best that Rome could do was to harness to the car of its 'imperial' dreams auxiliaries such as Albanian Fascism or the *Ustaše* of Pavelich, on whom she conferred the title of *Poglavnik* (i.e. Duce) of a kingdom in which the sovereign-designate [Aimone Duke of Spoleto] took good care never to set foot. The sole aims of the Croat collaborationists were to take vengeance on the Serbs and to gratify a savage, almost tribal, desire for independence, which was to cost the people of Yugoslavia, as the result of Fascist massacres, 800,000 victims out of a total population of 5 millions in the so-called 'Free State of Croatia'. The guiding motive of Croat nationalism was extraneous to the problems of the 'new order', and Pavelich's militia murdered Serbs and Croats, Jews and gipsies, under the pretext that they were converting the infidels to Catholicism.[7]

After the first phases of the war Mussolini's Italy hardly had sufficient prestige to control phenomena of such proportions in its own sphere. Nazism, on the other hand, now appeared as the main force behind the realization of those 'revolutionary' ideas and pseudo-solutions for which the large and small groups composing the international galaxy of the extreme right wing had been fighting for years. What actually happened was that the collaborationists were drawn towards National Socialism by a kind of centrifugal force, not only because it recruited most of the Nazis and Fascists in the occupied countries into the ranks of the SS and the army, but also because it was towards the Nazi ideological programme that, almost without knowing it, the Italian Fascists of certain 'left-wing' trends, the theorists and the blind believers in the 'new order' were tending. Mussolini and his régime never got further than a vague and useless plan for 'Europaism' or the 'Romanity' resuscitated by the creation of the new Italian 'empire', and they never succeeded in evolving a 'planned' programme of political solutions such as the barbaric majesty of National Socialism possessed.

For this reason the conversion of the fanatics transferred the honour of the burden of the 'revolutionary' task to Germany. In Belgium, the occupation enabled Degrelle to organize his *Formations de combat Rex*, and later on his *Gardes wallones*, subsequently incorporated into the *Légion Wallonie*, which in its turn became the *Freiwilligenbrigade SS Wallonie*, while the Rex militia collaborated with the Gestapo in repressing the internal resistance movement. De Clercq, the leader of the *Vlaamsch Nationaal Ver-*

bond (Flemish National League), raised the *Légion Flandre*, and later the 'Black Brigade of the Germanic Militia' (which in 1942 numbered 12,000 men, almost as many as the members of the movement). But the greatest attraction and the widest influence were exercised by the group known as *De Vlag* (The Flag), modelled on the National Socialist party, which demanded annexation to Germany and incorporation in the Third Reich. In Norway and Sweden collaboration took the form of Nazism pure and simple. The Falangists of the Spanish 'Blue Division', which fought in the Russian campaign, were fascinated by German military efficiency and anti-Communism, and also by the belief that a victorious Germany would transform Europe in accordance with the principles of Karl Schmitt, in which they thought to discern the elements of the Falangist 'social' doctrine that had been thrown overboard by General Franco's régime. A Nazi of the purest water was Josef Tiso, head of the government in the Slovak Republic, while fanatical followers of Hitler were the members of the quasi-military formation called 'Hlinka Guards', who terrorized the areas of Czechoslovakia which they controlled. Mussert's Dutch collaborationists supplied Hitler's armed forces with a larger number of volunteers, in proportion to the population, than any other European country, because they saw in the National Socialist 'new order' the keystone of their own desires for a radical transformation of society.

Lastly, there was a movement on Nazi lines in the anti-Pétain sector of French Fascism. This was the *Légion des Volontaires Français*, nominally an offshoot of four Fascist organizations—*Francisme*, Doriot's *Parti Populaire Français*, Costantini's *Ligue Française*, Marcel Déat's *Rassemblement National Populaire*—but in reality a creation of Doriot's, and in 1942 Joseph Darnand founded his *Milice Française*, which was inspired by the teachings of Maurras and preserved the tone of a traditional nationalist organization, though with National Socialist leanings which became more and more evident as time went on. In France this trend of Fascism towards Nazism occurred under a régime which, according to the Fascists, did not satisfy their ideals, and Bardèche mentions this point in a very significant passage:

> To those who wanted a *national revolution* in accordance with Fascist principles the régime of the *French State* seemed like a return to the authoritarian republic of MacMahon . . . To me the motto of the *French State*—so wise, so patriarchal, so reassuring—

seems to be a species of tranquillizer of a somewhat suspect kind. I cannot help thinking that *Work, Family, Fatherland* is a motto which would be more appropriate for Switzerland . . . *Work* means submission to the rich; *Family*, obedience to the moral code; *Fatherland*, submission to the policeman.[8]

In the columns of *Œuvre,* Marcel Déat, who had given his *Rassemblement* the character of a 'left-wing' Fascist organization, accused Vichy of being the capital of 'reaction' and of clerical obscurantism, a preserve of the hated disciples of 'Maurrasism', and he demanded a revolution which he conceived as a 'continuation of 1789'. To the crazy mind of Déat, Hitler's troops were engaged in the same revolutionary task as the republican armies of those days. 'Is not the Nazi *Weltanschauung* anti-capitalist, anticlerical and Socialist?'[9] On 5 July 1940 Déat wrote: 'We are not going to construct a new kind of France; we are going to build up a France which will be integrated into the new Europe and will have its own important and legitimate role, but for this very reason will change its political methods and its social aims.'[10] Pétain's 'national revolution', which was nationalistic and 'individualistic', claimed to be 'national in its foreign policy, hierarchical in home affairs, co-ordinated and controlled in its economy, and above all social in spirit',[11] but in these things the French National Socialists saw only the imprint of old-fashioned *Action Française* ideas and the survival of the old anti-republican notions which for more than a century had held together all those reactionaries who favoured a restoration of the *ancien régime* without any qualifying adjectives. In short, it was 'a counter-revolution that called itself a revolution'.[12] In reality, the 'left-wing' Fascists were caught in the web of their daydreams of a 'new order' and believed that the German armies would do away with capitalistic privileges and the Bolshevik 'materialism' of the class struggle, making a Europe united in a peaceful commonwealth of nations the hub of a society which at one and the same time would safeguard the liberty of individuals and social equality, the cult of pioneers and heroes, and the full spiritual affirmation of what they called 'Christian civilization'.

Those whose minds were completely absorbed in this attempt to reconcile nationalist doctrines with Socialist aspirations, in whatever part of the area dominated by the Nazis they might be, thus found themselves up against a mass of insoluble contradictions resulting from arguments of this kind. *Giovane Europa,* the organ of the 'Young Combatants in European Universities', published in

1942 a number of articles on the subject, written by Italian and foreign contributors. Professor Ugo Inchio of Rome maintained that the Corporative State could not possibly represent a *quid medium* between capitalism and Socialism, because the *basic function* of history is that of *work*. 'In the new civilization which the Corporative State and National Socialism are ushering in,' he wrote, 'we intend to create a world in which men will recover the human sense of life, with the freedom, and also the obligation, to work; we want everything to be restored to its *natural value*, starting with capital—which is a means, not an end—and we do not wish that mankind should continue to be the prey of the blind forces of materialism, and cease to be enlightened and guided by the mind.'[13]

Vidkun Quisling declared:

> We are living at a time when the countries of the world are uniting to form world empires. In the struggle for supremacy now being waged the smaller States have no prospect of continuing to live alone. Even Europe, with its impotence and divisions, is in danger of being crushed by the great impowers which have grown up on either side. This danger has been averted thanks to the intervention of Germany, and with Germany as its pivot Europe is fast becoming the fifth great power in the world.[14]

From Holland Mussert wrote:

> Although today we are living in a country—our own—which is passing through a transitional phase, we all share the same faith. That is why we form a solid block, so that from it there may be born a *future* infinitely richer and more manifold [*sic*] than in the past . . . I am . . . convinced that National Socialism will develop within us a remarkable multiplicity of faculties and that it will have fulfilled its mission only when this multiplicity has brought about a new evolution which today we can hardly imagine. That is why we foresee a Europe which will be far *better*, and consequently far *stronger*.

And Degrelle maintained that the Belgian Rexists were in the front line in the struggle between the 'Europe of corruption' and the 'Europe of the united nations'. Belgium, he declared, 'is the historical battlefield of Europe. The demo-plutocratic *bloc* made up of France and Britain wanted to be sure that Belgium would remain the jumping-off ground for an attack against Hitler's Germany.' That plan had failed and now the Rexists were fighting side by side with the Nazis; and 'animated by the spirit of honour, by the will to work, they and the Belgian people are striving to further the European projects of our Führer Adolf Hitler.'[15]

The Führer himself contributed a few pages to this review in explanation of the European problem, but he returned to the theme of Germany's duty to liberate the continental peoples from the Anglo-American schemes to subjugate them by, for example, forcing them to accept American art and culture, products which—Hitler remarked—might seem admirable in the eyes of a 'Judaic medley of races', but for Europe were merely 'a symptom of decadence' and 'a legacy of Jewry or of the negroid races'. 'The struggle which has gradually become inevitable,' the author of *Mein Kampf* goes on to say,

> and in which the German Reich is now called upon to intervene, goes *even beyond* the interests of our own people. Just as at one time the Greeks fought the Persians, but not for Greece, while the Romans fought the Carthaginians, but not for Rome, the Romans and Germans fought the Huns, but not for the West, the German emperors fought the Mongols, but not for Germany, and the Spanish heroes fought Africa, but not for Spain, *so today Germany is fighting, not for herself alone, but for the whole of our Continent.*[16]

And lastly, when the end of Hitler's Germany was looming on the horizon in 1943, Josef Goebbels appealed to the Europeans who were taking part in the 'battle between the Steppes and our Continent', warning them that:

> the West is in danger. Whether their governments and their intellectuals understand that or not, is not important [*sic*]. Here we see once more international Jewry, like a diabolical, decomposing leaven, cynically enjoying being able to plunge the world into chaos, and bringing about the decline of millenary civilizations in which they have never really had a share . . . Two thousand years of Western humanity's work is in danger.[17]

Even in the midst of his invective against the Judaic and plutocratic machinations of the Anglo-Americans, the Reich's Propaganda Minister could not let the opportunity slip of offering a bait to the 'enemies of the West': 'What would Britain and America do if the European mainland were to fall into the hands of Bolshevism?' was the rhetorical question which Hitler's 'propaganda genius' asked. 'Will somebody come over from London to tell Europe that such a contingency could never get across the English Channel?'[18] With wild statements of this kind and appeals to anti-Bolshevik feeling, it is clear that the cyclone let loose by the Nazis was blowing itself out.

One by one, the Nazis had to offer hospitality to all the Quislings of Europe as they were driven back by the advance of the Western Allies and the Soviet forces, but in reality they and their last disciples had already been isolated for a long time, since the imminence of a German defeat had reduced Nazism and Fascism in the various countries to scattered groups of men who no longer enjoyed even the tacit support of their former *bourgeois* admirers. In Japan, the Mikado's ministers, who in the years preceding the war had buried the remains of democracy, were worried because they feared that an eventual defeat might result in the removal of the Emperor from the throne. 'A Japan without an emperor was inconceivable,' says Richard Storry, but a few lines below he adds: 'Furthermore, it was feared that among the people at large, revolutionary sentiment might spread once foreign troops began to fight their way into Japan. In the last resort the rulers of Japan feared revolution much more than defeat.'[19] Like Victor Emmanuel and Marshal Badoglio in Italy, to quote Salvemini's caustic remark, the 'warlords' of the Rising Sun were ready to fight only one more battle—against a rising of the people. In Nazi Germany, caught in the throes of convulsion, plots and attempts to overthrow the régime were in the main confined to the army general staff; some of these were nipped in the bud, while others were more extensive and even included some of the leading figures at Hitler's Supreme Headquarters. But no subversive movement in the conservative opposition or in the ranks of the military could formulate the problem of a new German government in terms other than authoritarian, and they never repudiated the 'objective bases' on which the foundations of Nazism rested. The dilemmas facing these conspirators, torn as they were between adhesion to the ideas which had been the régime's life-blood (repudiation of the Versailles Treaty, aggressive anti-Communism, Prussian-type nationalism) and the feeling that they were compromising the future of their country and the whole system, had such a paralysing effect that their plots came to nothing or were limited to the possibilities of success of individual acts of heroism. The *coup de main* of 20 July 1944, planned by von Stauffenberg with the aim of eliminating Hitler and assuming control, wanted to replace the Führer by Field-Marshal Rommel, to negotiate an honourable peace with the Allies and to 'maintain order in the country'. The generals taking part in the

c*

conspiracy were to make no move until the death of the dictator had been confirmed and Berlin isolated. Apart from his qualities of exceptional moral courage and intelligence, von Stauffenberg was a broad-minded aristocrat who shared the opinion of his 'Prussian' colleagues that the only alternative was a conservative government virtually under military control; his fellow-conspirators probably made this condition a *sine qua non;* including Rommel, who for that matter was a somewhat unusual figure in the sinister and murky atmosphere of the *Wehrmacht's* Supreme Headquarters.

In this motley world of European conservatives and right-wingers, rambling talk of a 'new order' had never aroused much enthusiasm, or even qualified approval. For them the 'new order' was just a barricade against the Communists, a form of political authoritarianism under which the iron fist of the police state would crush all opposition and popular demands, and at the same time safeguard the capitalist system and the hegemony of the traditional castes. Everything else was accepted and endured as so much junk, or else caused a certain amount of alarm with its vague prophecies of a 'revolutionary' future, which, however, was relegated to a future so remote and nebulous that it was not worth worrying about unduly. But when the crude Nazi and Fascist régimes began to decline, the allies, accomplices or beneficiaries of the system were brought face to face with a question couched in the most elementary terms: they had to separate their responsibilities from those of the vanquished deities and get ready to pose as 'saviours of the country', once more entrusted with the task of identifying the national interests with their own. Their aim was to join the opposition on the other bank, severing all links with the past and working for a restoration which would authorize them to review certain deeds and factors of that past, but with one insuperable barrier— the integrity of the old class privileges and the legal right to become once again the trustees of democracy after having been the guarantors of authoritarianism.

The chimerical 'new order's' last line of defence was thus entrusted to the survivors of the Nazi-Fascist action squads and to those members of the younger generation who were still chasing an absurd mirage or trying to prove their consistency at all costs. Round the deathbeds of the two régimes in the last and grimmest phase of Nazism and Fascism this marginal fringe of the last twenty years gave vent to their thirst for vengeance and their moral frustration, products in some cases of the genuine tragedy in the lives of these young men who had failed to grasp the real import of the National Socialist mystifications. The 'Italian Social Republic' was on the whole a faithful reflexion, in an organic form, of this final curve in the parabola of the totalitarian experiment and of the state of mind which it had conjured up. The supporters of the golden age of the anti-Bolshevik crusade slunk out by the back door. The Fascists of Salò fought on only to air their old grievances, for their own physical preservation and for an idea which had died in the wombs of the régimes that conceived it.

National Fascism and National Socialism

After the armistice of 8 September 1943, various factors induced a multitude of people to support the Italian Social Republic—temporary reasons due to the collapse of the army, the determination 'not to betray' the alliance with the Germans, the abandonment of which at the very last moment was thought to be 'dishonourable', together with every kind of opportunism, ill-conceived notions of 'military honour', and so on. Even if we take these reasons with a pinch of salt, there remains the fact, which it would be foolish to ignore, that some of them had an undeniable value as proofs of good faith. Such motives, however, do not concern us here, if we want to get as clear an idea as possible of the real nature of this experiment and what it meant for the genuine Fascists who supported it. The watchword of the new Republic, born at the Verona congress where it proclaimed its programme of 'socialization', was 'back to the beginning'. It was the only expedient to which Mussolini and the Germans could resort in order to gather together a nucleus of men ready to give their services to a power which was already in a state of coma. The Duce devoted himself to this task with all that propagandist ardour which he undoubtedly possessed. As Frederick William Deakin points out:

> . . . he tried to hold out hopes of realizing that ideal world which the preceding twenty years had not been able to create . . .[20]
> The early compromises of Fascism with the Italian monarchy were at one blow outdated. The new Republic could begin with a *tabula rasa,* and most important of all, in psychological terms, the treason of the Italian surrender became the exclusive guilt of the Sovereign. The Republic of Salò was to start its existence without a history, and unburdened by all the errors of the previous régime . . .
> The new régime was republican, but also socialist and revolutionary. It would conduct this central task, which it had abandoned in the compromise with the monarchy in 1922 and failed to press

at the time of setting up the machinery of the Corporate State. Here was the great opportunity, and round this subject was fought the main battle of words in the few months during which the régime was permitted by events to survive.[21]

Benito Mussolini—that 'marvellous opportunist', as Salazar called him—now proceeded to give a good example of his ability as a quick-change artist untroubled by principles or questions of political consistency. With one wave of his magic wand he resuscitated the programme of the 'first hour', proclaimed on 23 March 1919 at the meeting in Piazza San Sepolcro at Milan. It was the programme of the 'Fighting Italian Fasces', the hub of the turbulent, revolutionary provincial action squads bent on lawless rebellion, despite the fact that they were subsidized by the landowners of the Lombard plain; and it was also the programme of the 'left-wing' elements inspired by the anarchical trade unionism of Sorel and, to a lesser degree, by the nationalism of the Fiume legionaries intoxicated by the 'Charter of the Carnaro', which Giolitti had described as 'his [Gabriele d'Annunzio's] worst literary work'. On that day Mussolini declared that Fascism would demand:

> universal suffrage on a regional basis, with proportional representation; women to be eligible to vote and stand as candidates; lowering of the minimum age for voters and candidates; abolition of the upper chamber; a constituent assembly which would decide the form to be given to the State; workers' technical councils in industry, transport, communications, etc., to be elected by the professional bodies and the trades, endowed with legislative powers and the right to appoint special commissions with ministerial powers; legislation on labour questions; an eight-hour day; a minimum wage and the participation of the workers in the management of industrial undertakings and public services; the eventual handing-over of the management of industries and public utilities to the workers' organizations if they proved to be worthy of it; a short-service national militia, whose tasks would be purely defensive; the nationalization of armament factories; a foreign policy which by means of peaceful competition would ensure that the Italian nation took its place in the world; a crushing capital levy which would take the form of a partial expropriation of existing riches; confiscation of the property of religious bodies and the abolition of the bishops' mensal revenues; revision of all contracts for supplies to the armed forces and confiscation of 85 per cent of the profits made thereon.[22]

Measures of these proportions, bundled together in a programme which in so many respects was ambiguous, sounded very much like demagogy, but they at least served as a useful means of obtaining the support of the motley band of 'left-wingers' whom the Fascists had gathered into their ranks. For his part Mussolini soon took care to limit and water down the 'Socialist' content of a programme which had been thrust upon him by circumstances. His adjustments were set in the nationalistic key. The Fascists, he declared, were ready 'to oppose the imperialistic ambitions of other nations if they might prove harmful to Italy', but would accept the decisions of, for example, the League of Nations, provided Italy's right to annex Fiume and Dalmatia was recognized. 'Imperialism', he was at pains to make clear, 'is the basis of life for every nation which is tending towards economic and spiritual expansion . . . We want to take our place in the world because we have a right to it.'[23] In October 1919, at the congress which ratified the Piazza San Sepolcro programme, the future Duce swept aside the assertion that the Fascist doctrine was rigid and immutable, or that Fascism had any doctrine. 'We have no preconceived doctrines,' he said; 'our doctrine is what has been done.' On 23 March he had been even more explicit: 'We shall permit ourselves the luxury of being both aristocratic and democratic, conservative and progressive, reactionary and revolutionary, legal and illegal, according to the circumstances of time, place and background in which we have to live and act.' And on 19 April, in the *Giornale d'Italia*, he repeated his statement that opportunism would be the only principle of his policy. 'Preliminary issues,' he wrote, 'are links in a chain which may be made either of iron or of tin. We have no republican or monarchical prejudices; we are neither Catholic nor anti-Catholic, neither Socialist nor anti-Socialist. We are problem-solvers, activists, realizers!'[24] That ambiguity which, as Tasca has pointed out, is so typical of the ideology and propaganda of all Fascist movements, here has the practical value of an appeal to the country's conservative and reactionary right wing.

Beaten at the 1919 general election by the 'Popular' and Socialist parties, Fascism accentuated the demagogic and maximalist character of its appeals to the masses and at the same time its function as pacemaker in the repression of the workers. Mussolini paved the way for his accession to power by a compromise which he stipulated behind the backs of the 'left wing' of his movement. At the Rome congress in 1921, the 1919 programme was pigeon-holed. The unity of the movement was restored and it became a party on the only basis which could hold together the hybrid bands of Blackshirts and ensure that it would cease to be a minority. This was the method of a violent seizure of power, the secret aim of which was to achieve a reactionary solution. The only course for the Fascists, Mussolini repeated, was to be 'relativists *par excellence*', in other words to stick to their policies only if they suited the purpose. Tasca has given a shrewd explanation of the reasons which led to the settling of the dispute between Mussolini and Grandi, leader of the 'agrarian Fascists'. He writes:

> The controversy regarding policy was distorted by a medley of formulas and facts which made it impossible to reduce it to a more precise and coherent form. The 'conservative' Mussolini had been thinking for some weeks of collaborating with the Socialists, who the real conservatives hoped would be liquidated once and for all thanks to the Fascist truncheons. Grandi, who talked of a new *Risorgimento*, who wanted to meet the masses halfway and raise the Quarnaro Republic to the status of an Italian question, relied on the Fascists of the Po Valley, inspired and led by the landowners, the most despicable of all the castes and the one most hostile to the workers. Mussolini did not conceal his distrust of Fascist trade unions, especially when there was talk of making them the foundations of a 'trade-union State', but Grandi, who wanted to be both a revolutionary and a trade-unionist, was the leader of the Fascism of the 'punitive expeditions', which were extirpating the trade unions in one third of Italian territory . . . On neither side was there any cohesion between formulas and facts, between 'principles' and the forces which were to put them into practice, and this 'comedy of errors' finally brought about a fusion of the two trends. Mussolini's reactionary ideology was bound to spread to Grandi's reactionary henchmen, and from that moment unity was restored.[25]

This restoration of unity in reality marked the defeat of the action squads led by Farinacci, Balbo and Grandi, and also led to a clarification of Fascism as a movement which—to quote Gioacchino Volpe, one of the régime's historians—could be accepted by all those who understood that it was a 'movement of authoritarian democracy [*sic*] and national', which was 'in spiritual contact with the monarchy and the papacy and more and more convinced of the function in the life of the nation these two institutions have exercised and can still exercise', which was organizing 'the new "autonomous" or "economic" or national trade-unionism', or in other words preparing to destroy every kind of trade-unionism.[26] Volpe thus attributes to Mussolini the merit of having taken up his position on 'historical ground' because he was grafting Fascism on to the 'legality' of the State; and he gives a long though somewhat halting description of this process:

. . . the government of the State, once it had become Fascist, began what is called the 'Fascistization' of the State itself, the creation of an intrinsically 'national' State, above all parties, and even above the Fascist party.

Nevertheless, despite these innovations, no one detected in the institutional order that subversive element which is bound up with the ordinary meaning of the word revolution. And there were some who, whether they were Fascists or anti-Fascists, blamed or derided Mussolini because he had nipped the revolution in the bud. The reason is that Mussolini's 'revolution' was not subversive, was not 'Russia' [*sic*]. He no longer believed in a revolution of that kind, although at one time he may have done so. He had taken his stand on historic ground; that is to say, he had set himself limits, these being in particular the 'four pillars' of the State and Italian society— the monarchy, which Mussolini declared he wanted to 'fortify and make more august', the Church, the army and the constitution, or in other words the representative institutions (*cf.* his speeches of 28 October 1923 and 4 October 1924). He intended to make a profound change, but also to 'insert the revolution into the Con- stitution', 'to graft it on to the not yet withered trunk of the old legality', to harmonize the old with the new, what was sacred in the past with what will be sacred and mighty in the future ('the second phase', *cf. Gerarchia*, January 1923); in short, to utilize elements which already existed and were still alive and vital . . . Then again, there was one immediate and pressing task, which would have absorbed the energies of the most vigorous government . . . a task which was a technical rather than a party matter. This was to pull the State and the country off the sandbanks on which they had run aground, to steer them clear of the fickle currents which were making it impossible to set a given course; in short, to give both the accelerator and the brakes a thorough overhaul.[27]

In the accomplishment of this twofold task of grafting Fascism on to a 'not yet withered trunk' and dealing with a 'technical matter', Mussolini had the full support of the 'elements which al- ready existed', that is to say of the monarchy, the army, industrial and agrarian capitalism and the Vatican hierarchies; and so the 'revolution' was postponed *sine die*, but remained an instrument of blackmail in the Duce's hands and a lure which could be flour- ished before the eyes of simpletons. The Fascist State carried out its nationalistic programme and succeeded where Corradini's nat- ionalists had failed, i.e. in making full use of a nation-wide political party. 'For Fascism,' Alatri points out, 'this was a victory over nationalism, as regards party organization and mass-psychology; but at the same time it was a victory of nationalism over Fascism as regards ideology and because it involved a definite renunciation

on the part of Fascism of its primitive, nebulous and turbid socialistic ideas and an acceptance of the dynamic, nationalistic type of
conservatism which, as Salvatorelli rightly says, "tended not to
maintain, as the lesser of two evils, the existing relationships between political forces, but to revolutionize them, to the detriment
of the left-wing parties." '[28] The 'revolutionary' longings were banished to the outlying districts of Italy, where the régime allowed
the provincial bosses to gnash their teeth and keep alive the notion
of a 'left-wing' agitation which in reality was merely a reflexion
of the disappointment and resentment felt by the action squads
who now found themselves out in the cold. The Fascist State was
created with the aid of nationalist elements, the 'technicians' whom
the action squads were unable to supply, but who abounded in
the ranks of the old reactionary currents. Men like Rocco, Forges-
Davanzati and Gentile were useful because of the reputation they
enjoyed in upper-middle-class circles and because their presence
put an end to any fears which might still exist as to whether the
régime still cherished certain radical ambitions distasteful to those
who had helped it to seize power. When, in 1930, Augusto Turati
offered for the second time to resign the secretaryship of the Fascist
party, because he disagreed with the tendency of the régime, he
declared—according to Tamaro, another Fascist historian—that in
the Fascist ranks 'there were too many Dantons and Robespierres
who wanted to run the party', too many 'stuffed shirts' who might
well be the cause of its decline. The Corporative State, Turati wrote
to Mussolini, instead of being a revolutionary achievement, was in
danger of becoming a mere bureaucratic reform, a laboratory for
economic and social experiments, or perhaps a university. 'If things
go on like this,' Turati continued, 'the structures of the old economic world will remain in full working order; Pirelli, Donegani and
the other capitalists will become the managing directors of the
Corporations.'[29] In September 1928 Arnaldo Mussolini had already
said that Fascism had granted 'extremely favourable conditions to
the capitalist economy'.[30] Turati had not noticed it, but the Duce's
brother had.

The 'revolutionary' theme remained in favour as a decorative
element, as a means of levying blackmail or as a political tactic
useful for depriving the 'left-wing' action squads of a weapon
against the régime. But above all it was on these lines that Fascism
modelled its ideological mystifications. Since it was fulfilling its
function of policing capitalism and creating a social order based on

the cast-iron precepts of self-preservation and reaction, the régime relegated to a distant future the hopes and watchwords which the second generation of Fascists discussed so eagerly, building up an idealistic explanation of the struggle and concentrating its energies. A day would come—the party leaders asserted—when the urgent 'technical tasks' of re-establishing order and 'national harmony' would have been accomplished, and then Fascism would resume its forward march and achieve the promised revolution on behalf not only of 'proletarian Italy', but also of the other 'proletarian nations'; on that day, the temporary and unavoidable truce with the old forces of the historical State would be broken by this desire for renewal, which was part of the problem of creating for the nation new and 'revolutionary' loyalties beyond its frontiers. This was more or less the tone of all the arguments which attracted to Fascism a host of young people who attained their majority in the 1930s. And whatever we, with the wisdom of hindsight, may think of it, the mirage of a 'second phase' which would succeed where Socialism had failed and Communism—according to the Fascists—had offered a solution that was unacceptable because of its 'materialism', its anti-Christian bias and its denial of all the 'values of Western civilization'—this mirage, distorted by cultural misrepresentations, secured the spontaneous and heartfelt support of many sectors of the *petit-bourgeois* younger generation—a support which was not confined to those who were able to engage in the kind of discussion and political research urged upon them by the régime.

Let us listen to what one of the protagonists of these discussions says:

> In those days politics meant Fascism. And the young found themselves face to face with it, unarmed and alone. It is true that they were torn between a spontaneous, generous, even enthusiastic admiration for it and a shrewd suspicion (or merely an instinctive feeling) that there was something not quite right about it all. But it was something they could not identify, and for the more far-seeing and daring it was something *inside* Fascism, like a flaw or a wormhole, which had to be eliminated . . . That is why they felt it was incumbent upon them to take part, a feeling which between 1933 and 1935 gradually spread, because it served to underline the critical aspect or 'contribution' which the younger generation imagined it could make to the development of the 'revolution'.[31]

There thus existed, amidst torments and confusion, a 'Left' made up of states of mind, which became ever more critical and began to question the value and validity of the Fascist experiment, ready to follow the path, at first of a rebelliousness still fostered by 'illusions' of revisionism, and later that of anti-Fascism pure and simple. Others—and they were probably the majority—were impressed by the bracing and active atmosphere of the régime, and by the 'mysticism' in which it shrouded itself. They had no links with the pre-Fascist past; on the contrary they had a firm conviction that the past had been a long and obscure era of cowardice, treachery and poverty of ideas—a state of affairs that must be energetically combated. Fascism offered them outlines and titbits of philosophical, literary and political notions culled at random from every source and enframed in a formal logic or in a sequence of rhetorical images which it was claimed were the dogma of a 'revolutionary religion' that must be implicitly obeyed. Even those whose critical faculties were more acute or who were in contact with the everyday realities of the régime, and felt the repercussion of its moral and idealistic shabbiness, found it hard to free themselves from the shackles of the system. 'Fascism,' says Zangrandi, 'was a reality too overwhelming, too complex and obsessive (and also too stimulating) to enable young men of our limited experience to rid themselves of it without help from outside.'[32]

Zangrandi himself, when discussing the years 1933–35, reminds us how, in its domestic policy, the régime was lavish with its references to the 'crisis of capitalism' and the need for 'social justice', and how, in its foreign policy, it steered a zigzag course between bouts of aggressiveness and attempts to ease the political tension; how it signed the 'four-power pact' with Germany, France and Britain; the treaty of non-aggression with the Soviet Union; and finally the Stresa agreement, which bound Italy to the two greatest democracies in Europe, Britain and France. 'Thanks to these precedents,' says Zangrandi, 'the Abyssinian enterprise, when it loomed on the horizon between the spring and autumn of 1935, did not seem to be a mere colonial adventure, but was viewed as a legitimate attempt to provide a young and prolific nation with room for expansion and at the same time to raise Italy to the level of the great European powers.'[33] This attitude was due to the prevailing belief that Fascism represented a 'revolutionary conquest achieved by the human mind, filtered through the political experiments of the past, to the "survivals" of which the Fascist stood in the same relation as the new to the old'.[34]

The controversies, the criticisms, and even the hints of a struggle to restore Fascism to the 'integrity of its original aims' or to give it a new desire for change which it was believed had been temporarily blocked by impediments that could be easily overcome, became the distinctive trait of these 'left-wing' ferments, which were sometimes mixed up with the old, impatient and futilely destructive *squadrismo*, but more often were just attempts to further individual demands, such as we can find among the more clearly defined and pathetic actors in this tragedy of lost illusions. When faced with the concrete reality of the régime, many left-wing Fascists withdrew or tended towards anti-Fascism; some prepared to throw themselves headlong into the struggle, with a reasoning which was puerile, but at the same time sincere and inspired by their crisis of revolt against the reality of Fascism; they felt that it was necessary to fight in order to force the régime's corrupt and opportunist hierarchies either to change their ways or to resign. The war assumed the dimensions of a biblical washing-away of guilt; it would eliminate all the ugly features of the system, separate the dross by a kind of ineluctable process and pave the way for the emergence of a Fascism of the 'pure' and 'uncorrupted', i.e., the revolutionaries. Guido Pallotta, head of the Fascist Youth Movement and editor of *Lambello*, one of the best-known publications for the younger generation of Fascists, pursued this vain hope, and when he realized that the régime and Fascism itself continued to exist because they formed part of a sphere of political expedients a thousand miles removed from the ideal image he had forged, he obeyed his conscience and went to his death on the battlefields of Russia.[35]

The two basic currents which were frankly inspired by Fascism and National Socialism, and combined in the programme of the 'Italian Social Republic', thus derived their ideal content and their motive force from the action squads which had been overthrown by Mussolini's 'legalization' of the régime and by the process of 'captivation' of the younger generation that Fascism had introduced in its heyday. In its criteria and in the mentality underlying it, the 'revolutionary' edifice of the Republic of Salò had a purely instrumental value. The anti-capitalist and 'socializing' programme of Mussolini's government did not make the slightest impression on those who were in danger of being overwhelmed by such a cataclysm. Replying to the German ambassador, who had told him that it was absolutely necessary to accept 'socialization' in its entirety, the chairman of Fiat, Italy's biggest industrial enterprise, said: 'The Duce's law on socialization will meet with the approval of all those who, rising above private interests, see in the social programme of Fascism not only the safeguarding of an orderly symbiosis of capital and labour, but also the possibility of asserting the personality and the initiative of the individual.'[36] An admission of this kind coming from Professor Vittorio Valletta enables us to understand how the industrialists made light of a law dictated *in articulo mortis* by a régime which was at its last gasp. Nevertheless, many young men believed in the sincerity of the 'return to the origins', because they had long been waiting anxiously for the 'second phase' in the evolution of the régime's ideas and policy.

The Italian Social Republic and its Nazi gaolers exploited these misunderstandings shamelessly. When the new régime was already nearing its end, Edmondo Cione, who had been a pupil of Croce and was considered to be one of the 'philosophers' of 'left-wing' Fascism, organized a self-styled opposition party called the *Raggruppamento Nazionale Repubblicano Socialista*, which wanted to come to an agreement with the Socialists and their partisan bands in order to create a united anti-Communist front. Cione also founded a weekly paper called *L'Italia del Popolo*, and in its columns he launched an appeal to 'reawaken the sense of Italian pride, oppose any attempt to restore the monarchy and capitalism, support socialization, and control, by means of constructive criticism, the actions of the government and the civil administration'.[37] Cione's party was officially approved by Mussolini, who explained to Rahn, the German ambassador, the Machiavellian idea that had induced him to authorize it:

> Professor Cione is no great brain, and will have no success. But the people who are now seeking an alibi will gather around him, and will therefore be lost to the much more dangerous Liberation Committee.[38]

Machinations of this sort did not further the Duce's schemes in any way, nor did they weaken the Italian resistance movement, but on the other hand they did help to poison the minds of those disappointed men who were relying with renewed confidence on the mystifications of the régime. The hopeless war the Republic of Salò was waging was for them a matter of national honour and embodied their hopes of a social recovery. There had been a transition from National Fascism to National Socialism. Adolf Hitler had checked the 'anti-clockwise' ramifications of his movement by the operation known as the 'night of the long knives', after which the dogma of Nazism had been fused completely with the myths of *Volk*, 'soil and blood', the mission of the German race and a planned society on the Prussian model, with all the country's energies concentrated on a resuscitation of the old German Empire. Mussolini could not follow the same line. In his revolution the arms were wielded by those who were opposed to the attempt to 'legalize' Fascism by means of a compromise with the existing institutions and their traditional and nationalistic political figures. To defeat these forces, the Duce allied himself with the politicians and in this way, although he could not completely eliminate the discontent among the action squads (which would not have suited his purpose, because, as we have said, he could use them as a bogey and as a means of blackmailing the middle classes), he at least managed to relegate it to the marginal areas, and achieve power by the only course open to him. In a régime which was not based on a mythology or on the complex feelings of resentment rooted in the minds of the Germans, the themes of social revolution and European unity could be used to obtain the approval of the masses. Consequently, the Fascist régime had, through its propaganda organs, developed an array of ideal notions which made a great impression on the younger generation. Now, after the advent of the Social Republic, the fruits of the expectation aroused by the hopes of a 'second phase' of Fascism ripened into a complete acceptance of the 'Socialist' swindle excogitated by Mussolini. The action squads of the 'first hour', however, remained the most bitter opponents of this policy. The only logical definition of what they wanted or meant by Fascism was a perpetuation of arbitrary control by the Blackshirts, violence and revenge. They were against the monarchy, against the army and the people who had helped Mussolini to come to power, but they were equally, and perhaps even more, hostile to any 'social' projects, and this despite the fact that they had greeted the 'Manifesto of Verona' with the jubilation of men who, after keeping a close watch on Mussolini and the Fascist 'right wing' for so many years, now saw them admit at last that the previous experiment had been a complete failure.

The Social Republic was above all an incarnation of their desire to avenge the humiliation they had suffered at the time of the Duce's flirtation with the monarchy, the army and the ecclesiastical hierarchies, coupled with a desire to get their own back and their almost hysterical admiration for the Nazis. Farinacci was on the

breach, full of resentment against those comrades who had compromised themselves during the past twenty years and hurling fiery
darts at the 'left-wingers' who were busily looking for proletarian
allies. After the emergence of Cione's *Raggruppamento* he became
the mouthpiece of the distrust which the action squads felt for
such initiatives:

> It is true that some of our men are trying to make contact with
> these youthful groups [i.e. the 'republican' elements who were trying
> to create a 'national movement' based on Cione's ideas] in the hope
> of making them face up to the national emergency, which at this
> moment demands fighting and bloodshed; but it is a vain hope.
> Similarly, those other comrades are wasting their time when they
> wave aloft our social programme in the hope of winning over to our
> cause a few Communists, a few Socialists and members of the
> defunct Popular Party. But what they are really doing is creating
> such confusion that, while they discourage those Fascists who are
> ready for any sacrifice in order to save the honour and liberty of
> Italy, no advantage can possibly accrue to our party. That is why
> we continue to appeal to those who have remained faithful to the
> infallible ideals of the eve [of the Fascist accession to power].
> Then there was no need for enticements, and those who flocked to
> our standards knew that they were fighting solely to free the nation
> from anarchy and to rout all the parties who today, through our
> fault and because of our generosity, have emerged once again in
> the invaded territories. What we would have liked to see done after
> the armistice of 8 September was this: appeal to all Italians—
> employers and workers, artisans, middle class, peasants, students and
> intellectuals—to rally to the flag of the Fascist Republic with one
> immediate purpose—to take up arms again and drive the enemy
> out of our country. Once victory is achieved, all those who have
> earned the right to speak in the name of an Italy risen from the
> ashes, should decide the fate of the nation and guide it towards
> bolder social reforms. When, as at the present time, some people
> maintain that an indispensable premiss for the continuation of
> Fascism is a policy in the interests of one class only, they are
> merely offering to those who may disagree with some of the Social
> Republic's economic proposals a pretext to reject or postpone the
> decision to take up arms for the salvation of our very lives and
> existence.[39]

Here the 'Ras of Cremona' was also voicing the feelings of the
Germans, who were worried by Mussolini's manœuvre, which had
reawakened the wild hopes of the Italian National Socialists and
might lead to something that he himself could not control. But in
this respect Mussolini was a better judge than the Nazis. He was
well aware of the disrepute, of the moral and political isolation

of men like Cione or ex-maximalists like Nicola Bombacci, in short of all the Fascist and anarchoid waifs and strays who supported the Italian Social Republic in this paradoxical comedy of the 're-turn to the origins'. He knew that it was mere propaganda, a verbal subterfuge, an expedient to make a struggle for survival seem more noble. Moreover, the Republic was wasting its time in futile internal discussions, in which old antipathies and differ-ences of opinion in the past were the real reasons for the squabbles among the leaders. The villas on Lake Garda, watched over by the SS and the Gestapo, were peopled by ghosts, and outside gov-ernment circles, which in themselves counted for nothing, the in-credible monologue of the 'left-wing' Fascists went on and on. The *Italia del Popolo* appealed to all the adversaries of Fascism to form a national *rassemblement*, which would—or so it main-tained—smooth out all differences and put an end to all the long-standing quarrels. 'Our old comrades of the same faith, the Socialists and Communists and the young men who support them, they, too, must overcome their preconceived hostility,' wrote Pulvio Zocchi. 'The Christian Democrats can and must come over to our side, and we can and must accept their help with cordial sincerity . . . Then there are the Liberals and the so-called Democrats . . . Only one course is open to the Liberals today—to await the coming of the liberators . . . The Democrats are bound to adhere to our cause.'[40] 'We who are real revolutionaries', declared Cione in the same paper, 'and who for twenty years have borne the burden, shall not lack the courage to guide. That being so, let us go even further . . . A bold social programme might well turn out to be a bridge which will unite Italians of both sides, a bridge on which we can meet and join forces in order to save Italy. Today the social question is far more important than any purely political problem, and that is why we brand as the real enemies of Italy the plutocrats, the conservatives and the reactionaries.'[41] Internal peace and the 'social revolution' became the slogans of this Fascism which pretended that it wanted to commit political suicide by merging into a formless mass, in order to 'save Italy'. Such attitudes were a mere camouflage for the desire to create a moral and poli-tical alibi, which would be all the more convenient because it would put Fascism on the same footing as any other political movement, would justify the plea that the past should be forgiven and present the Fascists in the guise of redeemers of the mistakes for which they themselves were responsible.

The Fascists were thus ready to enter into a discussion which they had terminated by violence twenty years before, and even to give due consideration to the hypothesis that the 'new order' could not be brought into being with the aid of Adolf Hitler's secret weapons or reprisals carried out by the 'black brigades' of Salò. They were willing to accept the re-entry of their adversaries into normal political life, provided these adversaries would renounce the privilege of calling themselves anti-Fascists and refrain from criticizing what had been done or the men in the régime. In the light of the new theories which matured as the Social Republic drew towards its end, political democracy, class interests, violations of the constitution and the catastrophe brought about by the war were reduced to the level of unimportant concepts or negligible factors, which had occurred in the course of a process that Fate had brought upon the Italian nation.

The arguments which this moribund Fascism propounded did not die with the Social Republic. On the contrary, they became a heritage of doctrines which were dusted off as soon as the atmosphere of popular insurrections and Italian and European resistance movements had been dissolved by the powerful blast of conservative reaction. The Fascists who took advantage of this situation reappeared one by one, taking their cues from the line of argument which marked the last days of Salò. Fascism rose again thanks to the appeal for reconciliation, for the abolition of the distinction between the 'vanquished' and the 'victors' in the civil war, for the granting of equal status to the 'moral and ideal motives' of the former and to the values for which the latter fought. Starting in the key of an ambiguous, sentimental and Christian appeal which was then transposed into a banal form reminiscent of a popular song—'what's done cannot be undone, he who has given has given, let's all forget about the past'—the message of Fascism was adapted to the situation just sufficiently to enable it to claim that it was the first-born child of European anti-Communism and a 'social' factor forming part of the schemes for 'ordered progress', 'equal sacrifices by both employers and employed', etc., etc. Within this framework the Fascism of the post-war years found an opportunity not only to take its place and clear its name, but also to enter into a vaster alliance which, while repudiating its principles, gave it both a chance to prosper and ample room for political manœuvring. Thus in a different context and in different circumstances, the objectives of the wave of reaction controlled by international capitalism favoured the resurgence of dangerous authoritarian trends closely interwoven with the formulas and attitudes of the subversive extreme right wing. The curtain rose on a stage full of actors reciting the script of the 'new order', and their activities are undoubtedly of great topical interest at the present day.

4 The 'Internationals'

The Nazis think of the future

On 10 August 1944, while Montgomery's armies were sweeping into France and the Red Army was rapidly approaching the frontiers of Germany, a top-secret meeting was held at the Hôtel Maison Rouge in Strasbourg, between representatives of German industry and functionaries of the German Foreign Office and Ministry of Munitions. It had been called to consider how Nazism and many of the men who had served its cause could carry on after the defeat. After careful discussion of the various suggestions a plan was adopted which provided for the concealment and subsequent transfer abroad of a large part of the Third Reich's funds, while the Nazi Party itself was to go underground immediately after the collapse and wait for the day when, with the help of the hidden funds, it would be able to reconstitute itself, or at all events make its influence felt in various ways. This plan was put into execution at once. A sum equivalent to about 500 million dollars was transferred to banks in Switzerland, Liechtenstein, Austria, Portugal, Spain, Argentina and other South American countries which were not at war with Germany. In the years immediately following the war, according to American experts, some of this money was used to acquire a controlling interest in several hundred companies spread over the various countries as follows: 214 in Switzerland, 158 in Portugal, 112 in Spain, 98 in Argentina, 35 in Turkey. The purpose of this operation was twofold: it would help to develop the economies of friendly neutral countries which had accepted deposits from the Third Reich, and it would enable those Nazis who took refuge in these countries to find employment and assistance. Doubts have quite understandably been expressed as to the truth of this somewhat sensational story, but after the fall of Perón in 1956 and the government inquiry into his activities, it came to light that the asylum granted in Argentina to thousands of German and Austrian Nazis and Italian, Croat and Slovak Fascists was not merely a gesture of comradely solidarity, but one of the most lucrative business deals that Perón ever made. It has been calculated that the Argentine authorities issued, against payment, no fewer than 7,000 false identity-cards for the use of Nazi and Fascist fugitives from Europe.

The rebirth of Nazism which we have witnessed during the past few years was thus not the result of improvisation or of a spontaneous reaction, but of an operation decided upon and planned at least a year before the German collapse. The hidden funds were to be used for the following main purposes: 1) the evacuation from Germany and Austria of Nazis liable to prosecution as war criminals; 2) settling these Nazis in countries which it was known would be ready to receive them; 3) providing legal assistance for Nazis brought before the courts (finding bail, appointing defence counsel, etc.); 4) the formation of associations of ex-prisoners-of-war; 5) launching a campaign to rehabilitate the German soldier, and in particular the Waffen-SS; 6) launching a similar campaign to secure the release of war criminals and refute the theory of German war-guilt; 7) the financing of neo-Nazi groups in countries which had previously been the targets of the propaganda carried out by Rosenberg's APA. Twenty years after the preparation of this plan it can be said that practically all its aims have been achieved. Tens of thousands of war criminals have been able to escape being tried; the honour of the German soldier has been vindicated, despite the accusations to be found in the forty-two volumes of records of the Nuremberg trial; the Waffen-SS have been rehabilitated, and posterity is now being told that they were the only real 'defenders of Western civilization'.

The ODESSA organization

Let us now examine in detail the operation which made it possible to save those Nazis who were in the greatest danger. Among the 'mutual aid societies' the most efficient was undoubtedly that known as ODESSA (*Organisation der ehemaligen SS-Angehörigen*), created by a man who had a genius for organization, ex-SS Colonel Otto Skorzeny, and by a distinguished *Luftwaffe* pilot, Colonel Hans Ulrich Rudel. In evacuating Nazis from Germany ODESSA normally made use of the Italian route. 'Between 1949 and 1952,' Simon Wiesenthal told us, 'I paid particular attention to this "Italian route". They called it the B-B line, i.e. Bremen-Bari. Every fifty kilometres along this imaginary line the organization established posts of five men each; these kept in close contact and thus enabled the fleeing Nazis to move about with the utmost secrecy and afforded them protection. One of those who used the B-B line to reach Argentina was Adolf Eichmann.' Along the 2500 kilometres separating Bremen from Bari Skorzeny thus had 250 agents who worked for years on end, and this gives us some idea of the cost of this rescue operation. Bari, however, was only the first stage of the journey. Other agents were stationed all over Argentina and Spain, and in many cities of the Middle East, to receive the fugitives, provide them with false documents and attend to their economic needs. Even after it had fulfilled its original mission, ODESSA was not disbanded, and in 1958 it was able to ensure the safety of the anti-Semite Ludwig Zind and the Buchenwald torturer Dr Hans Eisele.[1]

While Skorzeny and Rudel were thus carrying out their task efficiently, a number of former SS generals—among them Kurt 'Panzer' Meyer and Sepp Dietrich, who had been released from prison despite the fact that they had been sentenced to death by the tribunal which first tried them—reorganized, at first on a national and later on a European scale, the hundreds and thousands of SS-men whom the Nuremberg international court had branded as members of a 'criminal organization'. Soon after its formation the HIAG (*Hilfsorganisation auf Gegenseitigkeit der Waffen-SS =* Waffen-SS Mutual Aid Association) was given the official status of an association engaged in tracing missing members of the SS and assisting the families of the fallen, and in view of these aims the government of the German Federal Republic recognized it as a public utility undertaking. But behind the screen of these charitable activities the SS began from 1950 on to clamour for their moral 'rehabilitation' and economic welfare by launching a propaganda campaign in publications like the *Wiking-Ruf, Der Freiwillige* and the *Deutsche Soldaten-Zeitung*, the aim being to make the German public believe that the real war criminals were the Allies and that the Nuremberg trial had been a farce, and also, by arranging frequent meetings, to keep alive the *esprit de corps* of Hitler's crack troops, who from Paris to Smolensk and from Narvik to Tripoli had sung '*Heute gehört uns Deutschland, morgen die ganze Welt*' ('Today we are masters of Germany, tomorrow of all the world'). Thanks to the good offices of that respectable 'mutual aid society' called the HIAG, thousands of former SS-men were able to re-enter the ranks of the public administration as police functionaries, magistrates, mayors, and teachers, and over the years they succeeded in establishing a well-organized *mafia* which hampered the search for war criminals and saved them from punishment.[2]

But the ambitions of the SS extended outside the frontiers of Germany. An 'external organization' was set up, again under the leadership of Otto Skorzeny and Hans Ulrich Rudel, subordinate roles being entrusted to Himmler's principal agent in Italy, SS-Colonel Eugen Dollmann, the former commander of the *Légion Wallonie* Léon Degrelle, and the Jew-baiter SS-Colonel Johann von Leers. These men were responsible for the first attempt to group together in an 'International' the neo-Nazi movements that had sprung up immediately after the war in Europe and Latin America. From about 1951 on, the 'external organization' had its headquarters in Madrid, within easy reach of one of the largest secret hoards of money. From that time on the presence of Skorzeny was reported in Cairo, Malmö, Tangier, Buenos Aires and Rome, as well as in many German and Austrian towns. In 1956 the Bonn correspondent of a Washington daily wrote: 'Observers in Bonn have traced the increasing activity of former Nazis who travel between Germany and the main centers of the International —Spain, Sweden, Switzerland, Egypt and Argentina. They often work for import-export firms and agencies and for German motor-manufacturers. They are able to tap "buried" Nazi assets abroad, which may be providing the main financial backing for Nationalist activities inside Germany.'[3]

Skorzeny was, in fact, a commercial traveller and passed himself off as a businessman with a somewhat eventful past who was now more interested in money than in an adventurous life. In reality, however, it would seem that from 1945 down to the present day he has had a finger in every single delicate operation undertaken by the neo-Nazis, or has at least acted as expert adviser on subversive matters. This was not only because during the war he had been entrusted by Hitler with several dangerous tasks (rescuing Mussolini from the Gran Sasso, sabotage behind the Allied lines in the Ardennes), but also because through his wife, who was a niece of Hitler's Finance Minister, Hjalmar Schacht, he had valuable contacts, not only in Germany, with the leading figures in industrial and high financial circles. From the 'centre' in Madrid, where for more than ten years he enjoyed the protection of General Franco and from 1956 the support of the ex-dictator

Perón, Skorzeny completed the task of ODESSA, sold at a profit the supplies of weapons hidden by the SS in France, Austria and Italy, played an important role, through Karl-Heinz Priester, in the formation of the Malmö International, and had a finger in the anti-British conspiracy which led to Nasser's accession to power. After 1956 he had something to do with the founding of an SS colony in Eire, which appears to have considerable funds at its disposal and ostensibly is interested only in investing money in hotels and land, though it is said that in reality it is a cover for the transfer *en bloc* of the 'external organization's' headquarters from Madrid to Ireland. Skorzeny is in a better position than most people to estimate the precariousness of the Franco régime and would obviously prefer not to be in Madrid when the collapse comes.

The 'Malmö International'

The first post-war 'neo-Nazi International' about which we have reliable information was thus created by survivors of Hitler's *garde d'élite*, which during the war had numbered at least a million men, one-third of whom came from a score of European and Middle Eastern countries.[4] For the HIAG it was an easy matter to re-establish contact with SS-men who had returned to their respective countries of origin. A proof of this is that at Hameln, in 1959, a meeting presided over by Generals Kurt Meyer, Gille, Steiner, Simon, Harmel, Lammerding, Ullrich, Schreiber and Sepp Dietrich was attended by as many as 16,000 men from Austria, France, Italy, Belgium, Holland and the Scandinavian countries.[5]

Thanks to the alleged humanitarian aims we have mentioned above, ex-members of the Waffen-SS had no difficulty in re-establishing contacts with one another, but this was a far more difficult matter for the survivors of the various Fascist parties, who as early as 1946 were endeavouring to re-form their shattered movements. As Maurice Bardèche, one of the leaders of French neo-Fascism, reminds us:

> The neo-Fascist sects were very quickly reconstituted, much more quickly than is generally believed. Amidst the whirlwinds of defeat and persecution they formed themselves into bands . . . Their leaders were unknown men, who had held no offices and whose very obscurity enabled them to slip through the meshes of the net spread from Königsberg to Hendaye.[6]

What did they want, what hopes did they cherish, these little groups which sprang up in ever-increasing numbers in Germany, Italy, France and Japan, despite the presence of the forces of occupation and the denazification tribunals? As regards those in Europe, we can again quote Bardèche:

> In the early days, in all these men without exception—there was a nostalgia for what Fascism had failed to achieve—Socialism and European unity . . . But Socialism and Europe as conceived by Fascism had nothing in common with the ordinary man's Socialism and Europe. Fascist Socialism is authoritarian and at times deliberately brutal . . . The Europe of Fascism has nothing in common with the Europe of our cabinets and politicians. Its ambition is to be a 'third force' between the American and Soviet *blocs* . . . This imaginary island lying between two hostile continents was conceived by doctrinaire Fascists between 1946 and 1948.[7]

This dream of reconstructing the European empire which Hitler during the war years had merely hewn in the rough was not, however, approved by all the neo-Fascist groups. The more powerful organizations such as the *Movimento Sociale Italiano* (MSI) and the *Deutsche Reichspartei* (DRP) were in fact busy making a fresh start, in the hope of winning over at least part of the electorate, and, at all events officially, had resigned themselves to playing the democratic game. The notions of a 'brutal Socialism' and 'Europe as a third force' were thus cultivated by the smaller groups consisting of 'nostalgics' and extremists. And in the course of the last twenty years it is these radical groups who have created the dozen or so 'Internationals' of whose existence we know. Naturally, the MSI and the DRP also sent their delegates to the European congresses, but without showing much enthusiasm and without compromising themselves too deeply, thus justifying Bardèche's claim that 'for the majority of Fascists, nationalism is still the mainspring of their doctrine and feelings'.[8]

A first meeting of exponents of the various neo-Fascist and neo-Nazi parties and movements took place in Rome in March 1950, but at this conference, which was organized by the MSI and some representatives of Swedish Fascism, no important decisions were made, except that another meeting should be held, if possible in a climate less hostile to demonstrations of this sort than Rome. In fact, the choice fell upon Malmö, a quiet little town in the extreme south of Sweden, where for many years a great admirer of Mussolini, Per Engdahl, had been running the *Nysvenska Rörel-*

sen Fascist party and publishing a periodical called *Vaegen Framat* without being molested.[9] At the end of May 1951, about a hundred delegates from the principal German, Italian, Austrian, French, Spanish, Hungarian and Swedish parties and groups assembled at Malmö. Among those present Sir Oswald Mosley was the only man who had held an important post in the defunct Nazi and Fascist parties. We must, however, note the presence of Maurice Bardèche, who had placed his pen at the disposal of the neo-Fascists after his brother-in-law, Robert Brasillach, had been shot. At Malmö Bardèche represented the *Comité National Français*. In addition to this professor of literature, author of a learned degree thesis on Balzac, others present included a former leader of the *Hitler-Jugend*, Karl-Heinz Priester, who had some connexion with the SS International, Professor Ernesto Massi, who shortly afterwards broke away from the MSI, and the German Fritz Rössler, who after the banning of the *Sozialistische Reichspartei* took refuge in Egypt. These men, whose backgrounds and pasts had been so different, founded the 'European Social Movement', which later became more widely known as the 'Malmö International'. This 'European Social Movement' advocated a 'third force' Europe and claimed to be anti-Communist, but it was nevertheless an abstract creation of moderates like Mosley and literary men like Bardèche rather than an answer to the dreams of the younger generations, who demanded action and were steeped in racialist ideas which were far too openly professed and compromising. This archetype of neo-Fascist Internationals, however, soon found itself in difficulties and lost the support of its right wing, which in September 1951 founded, at Zürich, the *Nouvel Ordre Européen* (NOE), an international organization characterized by its extreme and virulent anti-Semitism. As for the 'European Social Movement', which is still under the leadership of Per Engdahl, it still keeps in touch with about forty neo-Fascist groups in a dozen or more countries, but in the course of fifteen years it has never succeeded in consolidating its structure or exerting influence on a European scale.[10]

The 'NOE'

The new International's first declaration after its inauguration on 28 September 1951 under the presidency of the Frenchman René Binet and the Swiss Guy Amaudruz, was decidedly racialistic in tone. 'We maintain the necessity', runs the resolution passed at the

first NOE congress, 'of a European racial policy with the following aims: 1) marriages between Europeans and non-Europeans
must be subject to controls; 2) the hereditary qualities of our
peoples must be improved by medical and scientific measures.'
Ten years later, at the seventh congress held in Lausanne, the
problem to which the NOE delegates devoted their closest attention was still the 'decline of Europe', the symptoms of which
were alleged to be the following: '1) the falling birth-rate; 2) the
weakening of racial characteristics; 3) the deterioration in the
physique of the whole population.'[11] From the advocacy of a programme for the defence of the race to a return to the old themes
of anti-Semitism was but a short step, and in fact, in another
paragraph of the 1962 resolution we read: 'Our policy is hostile
to the power of international finance. To further this end, laws
must be promulgated to check the activities of parasites, whether
they be Jews or non-Jews. Like all other citizens, Jews must either
obey the laws of the country or leave it.'[12] Such was the tone of
the official announcements. When, on the other hand, we turn to
NOE publications, we find anti-Semitism in its most virulent and
objectionable form: 'Those who shed tears over the fate of Anne
Frank are as despicable as the stupid herds of young Europeans,
and especially Germans, who weep while they scatter flowers in
the heroine's garret,' wrote Roland Cavallier, and the same author
dismisses the Nazi massacres in the concentration camps in these
words: 'a few thousand Jews and degenerates who died of typhus
in the labour camps'. The supporters of the NOE were also in
favour of a 'third force' Europe which would resist the pressure of
both Americans and Bolsheviks, these being 'expressions of the
coarsest materialism'.[13] This Europe was to rely for its strength on
'national armies', would refuse to accept as permanent the frontiers
of 1945, proclaim its intention to rescue the satellite states from their
subjection to the Communist world, and condemn the defeatist
policy of the European great powers which had led to their giving
up their possessions beyond the seas. According to the Italian NOE
theorists this new Europe would have to be built up round the
Berlin-Rome axis, which the 'historians drawing their inspiration
from Freemasonry and Marxist socialism' had attempted to undermine by talking about the 'German invader'. And with a melancholy nostalgia Pietro Biocotino affirmed in *Ordine Nuovo*:

> During the closing weeks of the war Goffredo Coppola was still
> able to declare with pride that 'to restrain the savage materialism

D

of the barbarians amidst the fires of the burning cities of Europe, to stop the blind and arrogant progress of the descendants of Genghis Khan, I maintain—because I know it to be true—that the sword of the Nibelung and the lictor's axe will suffice'. And in fact the Nibelung in Aryan-Germanic guise and the Aryan-Roman lictor fought side by side to the last, and by their reciprocal fidelity and the tragic fate of their alliance put the seal on that friendship and that kinship which are the most precious heritage of the real German and Italian peoples.[14]

By exalting not only Hitler's Europe, but also the blood myths, Nietzsche's superman and Bachofen's theory of the struggle between 'telluric' and 'Olympic' civilizations, the NOE achieved a certain amount of success between 1955 and 1961, especially among those youthful neo-Nazis who were still dreaming of Orders, initiation ceremonies, aristocracies and solar civilizations. In Italy they took down from the dusty shelves the works of Julius Evola, who during the twenty years of Fascist rule had preached racialism together with Preziosi and Telesio Interlandi. Once the NOE had succeeded in planting its roots in a score of countries, from Scandinavia to the Middle East and from South Africa to the United States of America, the executive decided at the Milan congress[15] held in 1958 to turn its attention in particular to the younger generation, entrusting this task to the former German member of the SS Jean Baumann, the Italian Nino Capotondi, the Belgian Jean-Robert Debbaudt and the Portuguese Zarco Ferreira—the task, that is to say, of grouping the various neo-Fascist youth movements into one organism, the 'Young European Legion'. This, however, was a failure and the NOE itself soon ran into trouble, owing to the rivalries, dissensions and inevitable schisms among its members.

In fact, the years between 1960 and 1963 witnessed the birth in Europe of other Internationals, all of which made use of the same men, who shifted from one to the other with the utmost nonchalance or even belonged to two or more Internationals at one and the same time. On the other hand, except for the varying doses of racial and anti-Semitic ingredients and a more or less sincere devotion to the idea of Europe as a third force, no great differences are discernible between the ideologies of these neo-Fascist Internationals. Any quarrels were due, not to disagreements regarding doctrine, but to rivalry among the leaders who were squabbling over the subsidies or trying to enlist the support of the extremists, who in any case were far from numerous. To follow their gyrations during the last fifteen years thus becomes an almost impossible task (and in reality hardly necessary). We would therefore ask our readers to pardon us if, in the course of our study, we are guilty of one or two errors of classification. To quote only one example, according to neo-Fascist publications the Belgian Debbaudt would appear at the beginning of 1964 to have had contacts with at least five Internationals, and it is far from easy—and even he himself might find it so—to discover any method in his complicated political relationships.

'Jeune Europe' and the OAS

We must not, however, let ourselves be misled by the word 'International'. Even in its heyday the NOE never comprised more than fifty movements, which means no more than a few thousand 'nostalgics' scattered over four continents. The activities of these Internationals were limited to exchanges of information, a few 'teach-ins', occasional camping holidays for the younger members, the printing and distribution of periodicals and leaflets (most of them anti-Jewish) and taking part in anti-Communist demonstrations. The outbreaks of anti-Semitism in 1959–60 were undoubtedly due to MSI and NOE propaganda and instructions issued by them, but these were reactions that could be easily checked by normal police measures. The groups with branches abroad became more dangerous, however, when they found a leader with a gift for organization who knew how to take advantage of a favourable political situation. The case of the Belgian Jean Thiriart is the most significant example.

Thiriart, undoubtedly one of the few men of action in international neo-Fascism today, saw in 1960 that he could exploit the discontent caused in Belgium by the loss of the Congo and at the same time enter into an alliance with the French extremists who were trying to delay any settlement of the Algerian question. He therefore agreed to become the principal agent of the OAS in Belgium, printed the communiqués of the Salan organization in his weekly, *Nation-Europe*, found shelter for terrorists who were being hounded by the French police, and used the international organization of which he was the head—*Jeune Europe*—to mobilize large numbers of activists in support of the OAS and its campaign.[16] In the last paragraph of his *Manifesto to the European Nation*, which summarizes the movement's demands and is one of the few neo-Fascist political documents to show a certain originality, Thiriart makes himself quite clear:

> Europe must be defended at Algiers as well as in Britain. It is the same campaign. We are partisans of a European Algeria. We cannot tolerate a control of the Mediterranean by the enemies of Europe. We shall remain in Algeria and help our European compatriots, who are fighting FOR US.[17]

Thiriart's calculations were not altogether wrong. For the first time since the Second World War the puny forces of neo-Fascism were given a chance to take part in an operation on the grand scale, which offered them a more or less respectable excuse and brought in subsidies needed to give new strength to the sclerotic militias of subversion. Between 1960 and 1962 Europe witnessed a revival in the activities of the neo-Fascist groups, galvanized by the hope that Algeria would prove to be a repetition of Spain in 1936. But as Bardèche says, neo-Fascism was not equal to the occasion: 'Whereas the Communists immediately transposed the Algerian problem into terms of international Communism, the Fascists never thought for a moment of expressing it in terms of a Fascist International.'[18] Notwithstanding Thiriart's appeals, not a single Belgian or French neo-Fascist (except those who were already serving in the Foreign Legion) tore himself away from the ordinary round of drawing-room intrigues in order to rush to Algiers and fight on the barricades to 'defend the West and Christian civilization'. The neo-Fascist International was quite efficient in providing safe hideouts for OAS leaders and, after the liquidation of the OAS, in using some of its elements to train South Tyrolese dynamitards, but that was all it did; it never managed to co-ordinate the various subversive activities, and after the signing of the Évian agreement it began to decline, since it was no longer receiving subsidies or material suitable for propaganda.

In the summer of 1963 *Jeune Europe*, too, had a schism within its own ranks, which we shall discuss here because it offers a curious illustration of the struggles within an International and of the not always edifying motives that inspired them. The clash between the opposing forces and the subsequent schism were brought to a head by Thiriart's decision to stand as a candidate in the Belgian municipal elections in 1964 and in the general election of the following year, a decision which was regarded by the secessionists as a renunciation of revolutionary methods. Another grave bone of contention was the Alto Adige question. The German-speaking delegates were in favour of supporting guerrilla warfare with the aim of creating an independent Tyrolese State, but Thiriart and the Italian delegates thought that any form of irredentism would harm the cause of European unity, and consequently they favoured a settlement of the controversy between Austria and Italy by means of negotiations.[19] These dissensions induced a number of groups to abandon *Jeune Europe* and create a new International, which they called the *Europafront*, under the leadership of Fred Borth, who was an Austrian. The only consolation for Thiriart was to wreak a partial revenge by accusing his adversaries of neo-Nazism (!) and expelling them.[20]

The 'National European Party' and the WUNS

At the beginning of 1962 the larger neo-Fascist parties in Europe decided to forge closer links between them by founding a 'National European Party', and in Venice they solemnly signed a *Protocol*, the preamble to which runs as follows:

> The date of 4 March 1962 is one to be remembered. It marks the creation of a 'National European Party' based on the idea of European unity. Unlike all other so-called European movements, this new party: 1) refuses to admit that Europe is a satellite of the United States; 2) still cherishes hopes of a reunification of Europe including the recovery of our eastern territories from Poland to Hungary and Bulgaria.[21]

This *Protocol* was signed by Adolf von Thadden for the *Deutsche Reichs Partei*; Sir Oswald Mosley for the *Union Movement*; Jean Thiriart for *Jeune Europe* and the *Mouvement d'Action Civique*; Giovanni Lanfré, A. Mellini Ponce de Leon and Count Alvise Loredan for the *Movimento Sociale Italiano*.

The *Protocol*, which reiterated in still clearer terms and in a more intelligent way the concepts to be found in previous pan-European manifestos issued by neo-Fascists, advocated the creation of a central European government, to be re-elected every four years; demanded the 'immediate withdrawal of Russian and American forces from the territories and military bases now occupied by them', and 'the end of political and military intervention on the part of the United Nations'; it assigned two-thirds of their continent to the Africans, leaving the remaining third to the Whites; and finally it maintained that it was necessary to create a 'third system, a State of producers, based on a free society which would be superior to those dominated by American-controlled capitalism and by a tyrannical Communist bureaucracy'. This attempt by the neo-Fascist parties to make themselves paladins of a reunification of the 'real' Europe stretching 'from Brest to Bucharest' never got further than the signing of this *Protocol*. The signatories took good care not to change the names of their parties, as had been suggested at the Venice conference, and only Mosley's Union Movement, which had sponsored the conference, adopted lightning as its new symbol. Since then no one has heard anything more of this International, and in any case, politically speaking, it was merely a supreme effort on the part of neo-Fascism to discard its 'nostalgic' attitude and, in its own way, face up to the political and social realities of the 1960s.

Although professing very extreme ideas, the men who created the Internationals we have hitherto mentioned never dared to give their organizations names which might remind anyone too vividly of the past. This circumspect attitude was abandoned for the first time on 15 August 1962 by the English neo-Nazi Colin Jordan, when at the end of a reunion attended by delegates from Belgium, Holland, Germany, Austria, Italy, Spain, France and the United States he announced the birth of a 'World Union of National Socialists' (WUNS), an international body which made no claim to being respectable, but defiantly adopted Hitler's swastika as its symbol, took the SS man as the model for its behaviour, and announced that it would openly wage an anti-Semitic and anti-democratic campaign.[22] With its radical programme the WUNS soon lured many adherents away from the NOE, and at the beginning of 1964 it was able to announce that it had founded sections in France, Belgium, Switzerland, Chile, Argentina, the United States, Australia, Germany and Denmark.[23] After the arrest of Colin Jordan in 1963 the leadership of the WUNS passed to Lincoln Rockwell, leader of the 'American Nazi Party', who was a United States citizen.

At the conclusion of this voyage of exploration among the neo-Fascist Internationals we must mention the 'Northern European League' (NEL), which was founded at the beginning of 1960 by the 'British National Party' and has branches in Scotland, Sweden, Norway and Iceland. The NEL has adopted the Celtic cross as its emblem and it passes itself off as an association interested only in promoting friendly relations between the Nordic countries.

Lastly, we must not forget the groups of Hungarian, Croat, Rumanian, Slovak and Ukrainian Fascists who in 1945 (and also after 1956 in the case of the Hungarians) managed to escape from their countries of origin and find refuge in certain obliging European countries, in the two Americas and in Australia. According to the West German Ministry of the Interior, in Germany alone they number 200,000, grouped in 200 organizations.[24] These refugees have established close contacts with one another, exchange their *revanchiste* publications and have formed an International of their own, which has shown a greater liking for terrorist activities than for doctrinaire dissertations.

The groups which have hitherto given the police forces of Europe most trouble are the *Ustaše* of the ex-*Poglavnik* of Croatia, Ante Pavelich, who until his death in 1959 never despaired of enticing Croatia away from the government of Tito. The 'Croat Liberation Movement' has its headquarters in Argentina, where it is run by the ex-*Ustaše* Minister, Stjepan Hefer. Other 'centres' are in West Germany, Spain and Britain. Some of the groups operating in Germany carried their audacity so far as to make an attack in force, on 29 November 1963, on the premises of the Yugoslav Economic Commission at Bad Godesberg, during which they killed the custodian and set fire to the buildings.[25] Other *Ustaše* groups who were trained in guerrilla warfare and sabotage penetrated secretly into Slovenia in July 1963, but were arrested before they had had time to start their subversive activities. In West Germany the *Ustaše* organizations are allowed to publish dozens of periodicals—for example, *Free Croatia*, the *Croat People*, *Drina*, *Ustascia*—in which terrorism is glorified and the massacres of Serbs during the last war are hailed as laudable achievements of Ante Pavelich's régime.

Classical Fascism and the reactionary right wing

The theme of this second part of our volume will be the Internationals, parties, movements and microgroups of Fascists and their activities from 1945 down to the present day. According to the *Frankfurter Rundschau* these fifth columns of subversion exist in sixty-four countries,[26] a number which coincides with that which we ourselves were able to establish during the investigations we made between the end of 1961 and the winter of 1964. We visited most of the countries we are about to discuss and obtained information often directly from neo-Fascist sources, in order to fill the gaps left by their propaganda, which, as is well known, is full of rhetorical statements and inconclusive polemics, but very reticent when it comes to supplying data on the real composition of the neo-Fascist groups, their sources of money and even their programmes (this being sometimes due to the fact that the latter are confused and almost non-existent).

In this second part of the volume we cannot afford to ignore those Fascist parties which are still in power and have already been mentioned above, partly because of the hospitality they have offered to the leaders of international neo-Fascism during the post-war years and also because of the radio transmitters they have placed at their disposal (for example, the transmission by Radio Lisbon of the 'Voice of the West' programme, run by Jacques Ploncard d'Assac, a disciple of Maurras), the use of neo-Fascist Internationals for propaganda and even for police purposes, and lastly the economic, diplomatic and military assistance given to certain terrorist organizations (e.g. the full support given by Madrid to General Raoul Salan and other OAS leaders).

Lastly, we shall deal with those authoritarian régimes which, although they do not openly claim to be Fascist, are nevertheless inspired by Fascist ideology or apply and imitate certain methods and principles. Naturally, in our examination of these neo-Fascist groups we shall often have to include a number of militaristic organizations, *revanchiste* associations, racialist groups and reactionary right wings, which are often the allies of the organisms forming the main theme of our book. Having, in this chapter, outlined the process of formation and the topography of the subversive Internationals, we shall in the following pages consider the neo-Fascist phenomenon on a reduced scale, as seen in each individual country, and this will enable us to make a deeper study of our subject.

5 Germany

The Wise and the Foolish Nazis

Every year, usually in March, the government of the German Federal Republic issues a report on neo-Nazism compiled by the Ministry of the Interior. To all appearances it is very carefully compiled, for it gives an overall picture of right-wing extremism, analyses its programmes and slogans, shows what contacts it maintains with international Fascism, lists all the anti-Semitic incidents, and finally gives an account of the measures taken against the neo-Nazis.

If we are to believe the figures given by this official publication, the membership of extremist organizations fell from 78,000 in 1954 to 24,600 at the end of 1963; Nazi or anti-Semitic incidents numbered only 177 in 1963, as against 205 in 1962, 389 in 1961 and 1,205 in 1960; the tendency to split up into smaller bodies seems to have continued, since the number of extremist groups rose from 85 in 1959 to 123 in 1963; while the total circulation of the fifty-two publications sponsored by subversive organizations rose from 129,500 copies in 1959 to 233,000 in 1963. In view of these extremely modest figures, it is hardly surprising that one of these reports should end on a somewhat optimistic note. 'Right-wing extremism in the Federal Republic,' we are told,

> is feeble and has no unified organization. On the plane of political ideology it is confused and contradictory, and offers few attractions. The reason is that it has never managed to play any part in the political development of our country or to attract any considerable portion of the population into its ranks. Every time the parties of the extreme Right have taken part in electoral campaigns during the last ten years, the result has been a failure.[1]

These 'reports' are certainly accurate, but at the same time they are one of the most incredible examples of misleading information that public opinion has ever been expected to swallow. They are accurate because they deliberately confine themselves to studying what the Americans call the 'lunatic fringe' and present a balance-sheet of figures against which we can find nothing to say. But on the other hand they represent a serious distortion of the facts, because they tend to show that right-wing extremism in Germany is limited to the 123 neo-Nazi movements examined, whereas it is common knowledge that more than half of the members of ex-Servicemen's associations (HIAG, *Stahlhelm, Deutscher Soldatenbund, Kyffhäuserbund*), of the East German refugee organizations *(Landsmannschaften)* and leagues of 'victims of denazification' are Third Reich 'nostalgics', who have also infiltrated in large numbers into the administration of the State, thanks to the complicity of government circles. It would consequently be a grave error to imagine that neo-Nazism is a factor completely extraneous to the State, when we know for a fact that it was born and has been nurtured within the State. Moreover, how could the functionaries of the *Bundesamt für Verfassungsschutz* (Federal Office for the Defence of the Constitution), which submits these reports to the Ministry of the Interior, be expected to be objective if, as a weekly review—*Der Stern*—revealed in 1963 (and Minister Höcherl could only confirm the allegation), one-third of them are former Nazi functionaries and some of them even served in the SS? When the defence of democracy is entrusted to the SS, it would be more than naïve to expect reports on neo-Nazism to give a complete picture of the phenomenon.

When, in the autumn of 1962, we visited Germany for the first time and told German friends that we would like to start our investigations by collecting information on neo-Nazi movements, one of them felt it incumbent upon him to warn us that 'the most dangerous Nazis are not to be found in the ranks of the *Deutsche Reichspartei*, but in the government and Ministries, in the police and the judiciary, and in the army'. And he went on:

That is where you ought to begin. In the extremist parties and movements you will find only fools and fanatics. Old fogies like Otto Strasser. Diehard generals like Erich Kernmayr and Ernst Remer. Fanatical agitators like Karl-Heinz Priester, Paul Hoffmann and Raoul Nahrath. And then people who are still pining for the days of Kaiser Wilhelm, desecrators of Jewish cemeteries, impatient *revanchistes* and young racialists. By and large a few tens of thousands of restless men who are still dreaming of a Fourth Reich which will resume the interrupted march on Stalingrad and settle accounts with Masonic Jewry.

The wise ones have taken care not to get involved with the 'nostalgics', who are alternately bitter and tearful, angry and exhibitionist.

Exploiting the failure of denazification and the opportunities offered by the Cold War, they have joined the big political parties with democratic labels and have managed to get back the same jobs they had under Hitler. Old Adenauer makes people laugh when he tries to make out that by inserting a special clause in the electoral law he has managed to keep the Nazis out of the *Bundestag* and the *Bundesrat*. It may be true that he has prevented the parties which made no bones about their neo-Nazi ideas from sending Deputies to the Federal parliament, but it is equally true that at least a quarter of the Deputies have had Nazi pasts, but nevertheless entered parliament by the front door, using the democratic parties as Trojan horses.[2] The same mass infiltration of ex-Nazis can be seen in all the other State organizations. Just to take an example, presiding over our courts of justice there are now 1,155 former *NS-Reichswahrer*, who for years, as everyone knows, administered National Socialist justice all over Europe, sentencing patriots to death and keeping the concentration camps full. In one way or another the 9 million members of the National Socialist Party are still serving the Eternal Germany, pretending to be democrats, but without repudiating the political aims of the defunct régime. 'Collective simulation?' the students of German affairs ask themselves. 'Collective amnesia?' No, it's sheer opportunism. The Nazis who really count, those who during the last few years have contributed to the restoration of the German State and its old ruling class, know that there is no point in digging up the past and that it is far better to change their methods and prepare for revenge by practising a subtle and patient diplomacy. Obviously they only laugh at the fanatics who immolate themselves on the altar of memories and have so little imagination that they can't see that Hitler was not a unique phenomenon, but a product of the irrepressible German arrogance, the same arrogance that produced Frederick II, Bismarck and Nietzsche, and will continue to produce leaders. Why shed tears over the fate of Hitler, they ask with a realism that cannot be denied, when every single German is as arrogant as he was?

The distinction which our German friend drew between 'wise' and 'foolish' Nazis has no real scientific foundation, but we shall nevertheless adopt it, since it provides a reasonably accurate definition of the two categories; and we shall first deal with the activities of the latter. Whereas Italian neo-Fascism was born during the retreat to the Valtellina, its German equivalent saw the light of day in the streets of a Berlin beleaguered by the Russians, amidst the ruins of the Chancellery and the legends surrounding the demoniacal end of Hitler. The SS man, who for five years had been absolute master of Europe and had left his infamous mark everywhere, did not, after the defeat, become a *Werwolf* and continue the fight in the mountains of Styria. Nevertheless, he could not forget in an instant that he was the proud possessor of four Aryan grandparents, he could not forget the oath he had sworn at midnight in the cathedral of Brunswick before the tomb of Henry the Fowler, or that he had carried his own symbols of death to the gates of Moscow, along the road to Cairo and as far as the Barents Sea. Even before the war was over Benedetto Croce realized that the Hitlerian epic was destined to become part of the *Nibelungenlied*, when he wrote in an article for *Critica*:

> Will not the Germans be able to boast, as they did at the time of the barbarian invasions and dominations, that they turned Europe upside-down and devastated it, that they shed the blood of millions of men and showed the meaning of those words *titanisch* and *kolossal* which are always on their lips and captivate their imagination? Will Germany's fight against the rest of Europe continue?[3]

Hitler's successors fall out

The exalted state of mind foreseen by Croce did in fact return, but not immediately. The first thing the Nazis had to think about was how to save those of them who were exposed to the gravest danger. Even in the prison camps associations were formed, like the *Bruderschaft* and the *Kameraden-Hilfswerk*, to provide legal assistance and shelter for war criminals, while groups such as *Die Spinnen* and ODESSA helped members of Hitler's 'Black Guard' to flee to safety abroad. The result of this was that when the ponderous machinery of justice got moving it was already too late, and during the whole post-war period only a few thousand Nazis were brought to trial, not all of whom were among the worst culprits.[4] The blame for this cannot be laid entirely on the Germans, and part of it must be borne by the Allies who, as soon as the Cold War started, abandoned their 'punitive' attitude towards Germany (just as they did in the case of Japan) in the hope of winning her over to their side in the struggle against the Soviet Union. The first man to realize this abrupt change in policy was the mayor of the little town of Stadtoldendorf, who together with all the members of the town council marched to the furnaces of the local gasworks and burned all the denazification certificates required by the occupying powers. The punishment of a nation which had been second to none in devastating and robbing Europe was thus brought to a grotesque termination in front of a little gasometer.

When denazification turned out to be nothing but a farce, new parties began to spring up which drew their inspiration from National Socialism, among them the *Deutsche Reichspartei* (DRP), the *Deutscher Block*, the *Konservative Partei* and the *Sozialistische Reichspartei* (SRP), the last-named under the leadership of Otto Ernst Remer, who had earned his promotion to the rank of general by the zeal he had displayed in foiling the plot of 20 July 1944 against Hitler. In the 1951 elections the SRP polled 11 per cent of the votes cast and obtained sixteen seats in the Lower Saxony parliament. But Remer was in too much of a hurry; he accentuated the polemical tone of his anti-American policy, accused the Allies of having built the gas-chambers at Dachau in order to throw discredit on the Germans, and attacked the government of Adenauer and the 'criminals of 20 July'. As a result of all this he was sentenced to three months' imprisonment and his party was banned.[5]

The heritage of the SRP passed to the DRP, which from 1952 on became the most influential extremist movement, despite the fact that it never had more than 16,000 members, and only a few seats in the little parliaments of the *Länder*, and normally did not poll more than half a million votes at general elections (in 1961 it received only 264,000). Among the leading lights in this party, which was under the leadership of Adolf von Thadden, we find the ex-Secretary of State Werner Naumann,[6] the honorary general of the SS and Reichstag Deputy Wilhelm Meinberg, the *Luftwaffe* ace Heinz Ulrich Rudel, ex-Generals Waldemar Magunia and Alexander Andrae, the former *SA-Standartenführer* Heinrich Kunstmann (who left the party in 1961 to found the *Deutsche Freiheitspartei*) and Otto Hess. Warned by the fate of Remer's party, the DRP took good care not to attack Adenauer's government and concentrated mainly on the task of cultivating the most chauvinist trends in the country and fostering the wildest hopes. 'When the last foreign soldier has left German soil,' declared one of the regional chairmen, Hans Schikora, 'we shall once again become a powerful nation, united under the swastika.'[7] And Rudel expressed his sympathy for war criminals by saying: 'I trust that General Kappler and Major Reder will not be discouraged by calumny. They should know that the vast majority of German soldiers support them and understand that the right of the conqueror has made it possible to distort the truth.'[8] Ivan Jungbluth, leader of the DRP in Berlin, maintained that 'in many ways Hitler was a genius, and the party to which I belong will restore Germany to its one-time greatness', and deplored the

accusation that the DRP was monopolizing neo-Nazism, remarking
that: 'There are Nazis everywhere, and I fail to understand why
anyone should try to show that all the bad Nazis are with us and
all the good ones somewhere else.' And when two DRP members,
Paul Schoenen and Arnold Strunk, were charged with painting
swastikas on the walls of the synagogue in Cologne on Christmas
Eve 1959, a former chairman of the party, Wilhelm Meinberg, said:
'My party is being accused, but we have nothing to fear. I have
not, like Herr Globke, the Secretary of State to the Chancellery,
written articles criticizing the racial laws. I have never, like Oberländer, the present Minister for Refugees, asked to be decorated
with the Order of the Blood.'[9]

On 21 June 1964, having escaped being banned several times
and suffered a heavy defeat at the 1961 election, the DRP decided
at its thirteenth conference to change its name and assume the more
respectable (though still ambiguous) denomination of 'National
Democratic Union'. But even this subterfuge could not save Adolf
von Thadden's party and on 4 December 1965, when its membership had fallen to 4,000, this oldest of German neo-Nazi parties
was formally dissolved in Göttingen. After its disappearance 3,000
of its former members found refuge in the *Nationaldemokratische
Partei* (NPD).

In the post-war period, as soon as the authorities in Bonn had
decided to rearm, besides the DRP at least a hundred parties,
associations, leagues or movements sprang up, all of them claiming
more or less officially to be the legitimate heirs of Hitlerism. Once
the veneer of a generic anti-Communism had worn off, they
appeared in their true colours as a mixture of violent resentment
provoked by the German defeat and the presence of foreign troops,
the conviction that they represented an *élite*, wild hopes of being
able to create a Fourth Reich which would take its place as a
'third force' between the two great *blocs,* a great longing for the
wide open spaces to the East, and lastly a more or less virulent
anti-Semitism. Generally speaking, none of them had more than
three or four hundred members, their activities were on a purely
regional scale, they were more like clubs than parties, led an
ephemeral existence and never became integral parts of the parliamentary opposition, however much they might claim that they
belonged to it.

Among the more active groups we will mention the *Deutsche
Gemeinschaft*, with its rather vague policy of 'universal national-

ism', the meaning of which becomes clearer when we find one of its leaders maintaining that the 'Nazi concentration camps were not strict enough'; the *Deutscher Block*, which after its poor show-ing at the polls decided to wait for better times and then seize power by force; the *Nationale Partei Deutschlands*, led by a retired general, Horiz von Faber Du Faur and consisting of some 300 Hessian officers and intellectuals who toy with fantastic ideas for reunifying Germany with the support of the Soviet Union; the *Deutscher Mittelstand*, headed by a former civil servant named Freybe, which appeals to the middle class and shows a marked preference for 'common man' ideas; the *Gesamtdeutsche Union*, advocating *revanchiste* pan-German ideas and led by Paul Hoff-mann; the *Gesamtdeutsche Partei*, offspring of a merger in 1961 between the *Deutsche Partei* and the BHE (*Bund der Heimatlosen und Entrechteten*=Union of Refugees and Victims of Injustice); the *Deutsche Soziale Union*; the *Nation Europa*, headed by a former Waffen-SS officer, Arthur Ehrhard. The list could be con-tinued to cover many pages. As John Dornberg reminds us in his *Schizophrenic Germany*:

> There are or have been a German National Party, National Demo-cratic Party, German Workers' Party, National German Workers' Party, Radical Socialist Freedom Party, Party of Good Germans, Bavarian Homeland and Royalist Party, German Conservative Party, and a European Party. The list has included such innocent-sounding right-radical front organizations as the Reich Movement, League of Reich Royalists, The Never-Forgotten-Homeland Associa-tion, League of Prussians, The German Circle, Historical Association, and Union of Independent Democrats. Some have mysterious titles such as Circle of Friends for the Preservation of Nordic Culture, Federation for the Determination of Historic Truths, and Spear-head Squad against Bolshevik Subversion. Others are more blunt, calling themselves Reich Front, Black Legion and Black Corps.[10]

In the post-war period only Japan can offer a greater number of Fascist or near-Fascist organizations with titles revealing such a wealth of imagination.

At the moment of writing many of the parties and groups listed above have already disappeared, while others are destined shortly to do so and others again have been suppressed by the German authorities. Among the latter we must mention the Ludendorff movement, which existed before Hitler came to power and was notorious for its rabid anti-Semitism; the *Freikorps Grossdeutsch-*

land, which tried to raise 'assault battalions' under the command
of Günther Sonnemann to ensure the physical removal of anti-Nazi
members of the government; the *Bund Nationaler Studenten*, some
of whose members, on the night of 2/3 January 1960, celebrated
the Teutonic solstice in Glienicke Park in Berlin by chanting Nazi
songs and waving swastika flags. When one of these parties dies, we
can expect that at least two new ones will spring up. One of the
latest is the *Deutsche Nationale Volkspartei* (DNVP), a new version
of the old party led by Franz von Papen, the ex-Chancellor of
the Reich who in his day helped Hitler to overthrow the Weimar
Republic. This party was secretly re-formed on 29 July 1962 by a
conservative, Heinrich Fassbender, together with Baron von
Koenig, the landowner Heinrich Thie and the former Nazi Deputy
Albert Abich. On the following 22 September the DNVP made its
bow to the public at a press-conference during which Fassbender
claimed to be speaking 'in the Kaiser's name'; he explained that
the party motto—'Thou shalt believe in the future of Germany'—
was a line from a poem by Ernst Moritz Arndt, expressed the hope
that the army would be reconstituted on Prussian lines, and finally
announced that the aim of the DNVP was the rebuilding of a
Greater Germany. 'Regarding this,' he said, 'and the partition of
Europe, Asia and Africa, we shall reach an agreement with
Moscow.'

At the beginning of 1960, having perceived the futility of all these
groups, which were far too small and often in competition with one
another, Karl-Heinz Priester, an ex-functionary of the *Hitler-Jugend*,
SS officer, chairman of the *Deutsche Soziale Bewegung* and one
of the five founders of the Malmö neo-Nazi International, appealed
to all 'associations faithful to the Reich' to send delegates to an
extraordinary meeting in Wiesbaden, at which the constitution of a
single right-wing organization was to be proposed. But Priester's
death on 16 April of the same year nipped this 'great plan' in the
bud.[11] The idea of uniting all the right-wing organizations was,
however, taken up again in 1964, in view of the 1965 *Bundestag*
elections. For example, at Kiel on 7 and 8 March, a 'working party
for a national policy' met under the patronage of the *Gesamtdeutsche Partei*, the *Deutscher Block*, the *Deutsche Freiheitspartei*
and the *Notgemeinschaft Deutscher Bauern*. The aim of these
parties was the formation of a middle-class nationalist front to
fight the elections on the right flank of the Christian Democrats,
in the hope of obtaining the votes, not only of the Reich 'nostalgics',

but also of the neutralists, who wanted a completely independent Germany no longer under the influence of NATO. Among the newspapers the chief supporter of this reunification was the Munich *Deutsche National-Zeitung und Soldaten-Zeitung*, whose circulation was rising steadily and was larger than that of any other right-wing publication.[12] Its efforts led to the formation, on 28 November 1964, at Hanover, of the *Nationaldemokratische Partei Deutschlands* (NPD); the chairman of this new party was Friedrich Thielen, a 'German Party' member of the Bremen parliament; co-chairman was Adolf von Thadden, leader of the DRP, while its vice-chairmen were Heinrich Fassbender, of the *Deutsche Nationale Volkspartei*, and Wilhelm Guttman, of the *Gesamtdeutsche Partei*. Seven hundred delegates hailed the birth of the new party by shouting: 'Long live our down-trodden and humiliated people, long live our divided Fatherland, we want one Germany, long live Germany!'

From the very beginning it was clear that the members of the NPD were men who regretted the passing of the Nazi régime and that they were conservatives and fanatics rather than traditionalists. The composition of the party's Federal Committee affords ample proof of this. Out of eighteen members, twelve had previously served in the SS or had joined the Nazi party before 1932. The party's Press and propaganda were run by men who were all too well known, for example Otto Hess, a former colonel in the SS; Heinrich Härtle, one-time secretary to Alfred Rosenberg, the Nazi party's ideologist who was hanged at Nuremberg; the former *SS-Hauptsturmführer* Waldemar Schütz; Erich Kern, who had served as an officer in the Adolf Hitler Division of the SS, and the former *SS-Obersturmbannführer* Peter Kleist.

As regards the party's programme, although it is sufficiently racialist and aggressive to attract those who are still mourning the collapse of the 'great thousand-year Reich', it cannot be said that it has made a very promising start. At the general election in September 1965 the NPD polled only 664,000 votes (2·1 per cent of the total votes cast) and since this was less than the minimum 5 per cent required, it did not obtain a single seat in the Federal Parliament. In the local elections held in three of the *Länder* six months later, however, the NPD fared rather better, obtaining 10 per cent of the votes cast in Schleswig-Holstein and 3·9 per cent in Hamburg. In Bavaria as a whole it polled only 2·1 per cent of the total, but in certain cities, e.g. Nuremberg, Ansbach and Bayreuth, it obtained more than 8 per cent. The chairman of the party,

Fritz Thielen, felt that this justified his telling the second NPD congress held on 18 June 1966 in the Schwarzwaldhalle at Karlsruhe that 'the time to speak the truth has come' and that the NPD was 'the reserve army of all German nationalists' and would provide 'the framework of the new German nation'.[13]

Eight months later, in November 1966, the NPD achieved another, even more spectacular success. In Hesse it obtained 7·9 per cent of the votes and eight seats, in Bavaria 7·4 per cent of the votes and fifteen seats. The neo-Nazis were naturally jubilant, and their vice-chairman, Adolf von Thadden, announced that by 1969 they would be in a position to choose who was to be Chancellor, while Otto Hess told a *Spiegel* reporter that in the 1969 general election the NPD would be certain to obtain not less than 3 million votes and between sixty and ninety seats in the *Bundestag*. This euphoria, however, was somewhat damped by the results of the local elections held on 23 April 1967 in the Rhenish Palatinate and in Schleswig-Holstein. Although the NPD had triumphantly proclaimed that it would poll 10 or perhaps even 15 per cent of the votes, it actually polled only 5·8 per cent, equivalent to four seats, in Schleswig-Holstein, and 6·9 per cent (four seats) in the Rhenish Palatinate. The chief reason for these modest results was undoubtedly the serious difference of opinion between Fritz Thielen and Adolf von Thadden, which at the beginning of May 1967 led to a split in the ranks of the NPD, followed by the resignation of Fritz Thielen and several thousand 'moderates'. Since this breakaway of the conservative wing headed by Thielen the NPD has become to an even greater extent an extremist party, consisting solely of old and new Nazis.

The successes achieved by the NPD caused alarm in certain government circles, who normally tend to minimize the danger of a right-wing revival. On 31 January 1967 the Federal Minister of the Interior, Paul Lücke, told delegates from the UIRD (*Union Internationale de la Résistance et de la Déportation*) that the NPD is undoubtedly 'the most formidable extremist party that has emerged in Germany since 1945'.[14]

The militarist associations

While the 'foolish' Nazis were squabbling over the heritage of Hitler, the political atmosphere created after 1950 by the Bonn government's decision to rearm Germany led to the formation of numerous ex-Servicemen's associations which served to strengthen the ranks of the nationalistic right wing and exerted a species of blackmail on the government. 'One of the HIAG's primary functions,' John Dornberg remarks when discussing this association of ex-SS-men, 'is political lobbying.'

> Unfortunately the former SS members are considered an important 'vote potential' by even liberal politicians and members of the parliament. While the HIAG is a veterans' organization fighting for legitimacy of its members, other more conservative, often traditional, organizations have become increasingly active and powerful. They are all closely associated with rightist and nationalist political movements and parties.[15]

Today there are over 1,200 military associations, and a mere list of them fills no fewer than thirty pages in the *Deutscher Soldatenkalender*.[16] Among them we find large bodies like the *Stahlhelm*, the *Kyffhäuserbund*, the *Deutscher Soldatenbund* and the *HIAG der Waffen-SS*, to which must be added several hundred *Traditionsverbände*, each of them representing a unit of the defunct *Wehrmacht*. The *Kalender*, which every year provides valuable information on the Bundesrepublik's militarist forces, openly defends Hitler's war of aggression (see, for example, the 1961 edition), inveighs against the Nuremberg verdict, harps on the myth that 'the German soldier was never beaten in the field', and pays homage to General Jodl (hanged at Nuremberg) and to the war criminal Field-Marshal Kesselring, who for the occasion is hailed as 'protector of the Italian people'.

The HIAG will serve as an example of the extent to which the Federal government has encouraged the revival of militarism. Although the Nuremberg tribunal declared the SS to be a 'criminal association' and any attempt to revive it was specifically forbidden under the Potsdam agreement,[17] this did not prevent Chancellor Adenauer from declaring in 1953 that 'the men of the SS were soldiers like the rest', an opinion which was later confirmed by the Minister for Defence, Strauss, when he said: 'Naturally I include them in the respect I feel for the German soldier of the Second World War.'

One result of these statements was that on 6 October 1959 the HIAG was classified in a decree as a 'public utility', and the SS men of the notorious *Wiking, Das Reich, Italien, Horst Wessel* and *Totenkopf* divisions, who had left grim memorials of their exploits at Marzabotto and Oradour-sur-Glane, were granted the right to draw pensions.[18] From 1 September 1956 they have also been allowed to enlist in the *Bundeswehr*, provided they had not held the rank of lieutenant-colonel and upwards under the Hitler régime, and since 28 June 1957 they have been allowed to wear all their Nazi decorations, including the award personally instituted by the Führer for those who participated in the struggle against the partisans. There are today 97,000 German citizens who are entitled to wear this *Bandenkampfabzeichen* (a dagger piercing a nest of vipers, surmounted by a swastika and a skull).

Since these militarist groups knew that they had the unconditional support of the government, it is hardly surprising that the meetings of the HIAG and other associations became blatant and noisy apologies for the Nazi régime. The country towns in Germany were, according to an American observer, literally *vom Feinde besetzt*—occupied by the Fascist enemy. And in fact the 'nostalgics' preferred to steer clear of the large cities, most of which had Social Democrat councils, and to pour into the little provincial towns. Among the thousands of such gatherings two were particularly memorable—those held at Hameln and at Windsheim. At the former, which was attended by 16,000 ex-members of the SS, the one-time commander of the SS *Das Reich* division—General Lammerding, the man responsible for the massacre of the population of Oradour, whom Bonn has consistently refused to hand over to the French authorities—and Sepp Dietrich, who had once commanded the *Adolf Hitler* SS division, were the guests of honour. During the meeting another equally notorious general, Kurt Meyer, said:

> We intend to enter this State not by the tradesmen's entrance, but by the front door . . . A few years ago a demonstration like this meeting at Hameln would have been quite impossible, and I must tell you that it would not have been possible now had it not been for the intelligent comprehension shown by influential men in the government as well as in the opposition parties. Yes, my comrades, this Federal Republic is really our State.[19]

And a year later, at Windsheim on 6 June, in the presence of the inevitable Sepp Dietrich and 1,500 SS men who had come from every part of Europe. Colonel Schreiber had the impudence to say: 'We intend to restore to the terms liberty, honour and Fatherland the meanings they used to have.'[20] After the speeches the SS men marched through the streets of the town, singing songs like 'We are the Black Guard whom Hitler loved' and 'Even if all are unfaithful we shall remain true'. When the townspeople protested, the chief of police declared that these songs were not on the list of Nazi songs prohibited in Bavaria.

Moreover, the Windsheim meeting, though spectacular, was not an exceptional occurrence. At every such gathering the law was flagrantly violated without any interference from the authorities. At Verden, in October 1952, the ex-general of a parachute division, Bernhard Ramcke, could say: 'The real war criminals are the Allies. The black list of criminal organizations in which the name of the SS figures will soon be a roll of honour.'[21] At Hamburg the former *Luftwaffe* general Röder demanded the reintroduction of the death penalty for anti-Fascists who had taken part in the resistance movement, and the suppression of the workers' parties and all democratic organizations. At Goslar the police charged a crowd of workmen who were trying to stop a meeting at which Kesselring, the 'protector of the Italians', was to speak. And in October 1960 the HIAG's periodical *Der Freiwillige* was able to note with satisfaction that 'the ban which has lasted fifteen years has now been lifted. The Waffen-SS has emerged from the "defamation zone".' In defiant tones the former SS general Erich Kernmayr, head of the HIAG press bureau, rubbed it in by declaring that 'the Federal Ministry of Defence takes no decision, however secret, without its being known to the HIAG within twenty-four hours. Our friends in the army keep their eyes open.'[22]

Revanchisme and anti-Semitism

Next to the militarists, the other body which supported—and not only as regards ideas—the nationalist *bourgeois* groups of avowed neo-Nazis was that of the refugees from East Germany, who represented 15 per cent of the entire population of West Germany and, since they were the most influential single group in the country, were a valuable card in the hands of those who were running German politics. The value of these millions of refugees was appreciated—perhaps even more than it was by Adenauer—by the older Nazis, who in a confidential circular issued in 1950 by their 'centre' in Madrid were already making plans to exploit this great exodus:

> The millions of expellees must be regarded as a valuable trump card in our policy toward the restoration of German power . . . The expulsion of ten million German racial comrades was a blessing for the Reich. The expellees strengthened the biological substance

of our race, and from the beginning they became a valuable asset
to our propaganda. The expellees, discontented with their fate,
infused a strong political dynamism in our demands. Very soon we
were able to drown out the noisy propaganda about German 'crimes'
without counter-accusation about the heinous misdeeds committed
against ten million German racial comrades . . . The distress of
the refugees has created a common political ground among all
Germans, regardless of political affiliation. The demand for the
restitution of the stolen German territories keeps our political
agitation alive. The militant elements among the refugees are working according to the best traditions of National Socialism, whereas
the broad masses among the expellees are kept close together in
well disciplined homeland organizations . . . The expulsion of
millions of our racial comrades provides us with a heaven-sent
opportunity to exacerbate the problem of the bleeding border and to
hammer constantly for its revision.[23]

In obedience to orders received from Madrid and with the
consent of the West German government, a start was made
in 1950 with the founding of *Landsmannschaften*, which today
have already reached the conspicuous number of twenty-eight with
a total membership of $2\frac{1}{2}$ millions.[24] Together they make up the
Bund der Vertriebenen, and they have a score of youth organizations[25] and publish 350 periodicals with a total circulation of
2 million copies.[26] From the government they receive an annual
subsidy which in 1963 amounted to 244 million marks, and
these *revanchiste* bodies can thus bring considerable pressure
to bear on the decisions taken by the Bonn government, since with
their ever more sweeping claims and their crude anti-Bolshevism
they make it difficult to follow a more elastic and realistic policy.
While the government parties—and the opposition as well—take
good care not to underestimate the political importance of the ex-
Servicemen's associations, they are to an even greater degree obliged
to pay court to the wild crowds of refugees from the East, even if
their leaders are well-known Nazis[27] and what they claim is virtually the unleashing of a Third World War which will enable them
to resume their interrupted march towards the East *(der Drang
nach Osten)*.

Although the Western democracies and the countries behind the
Iron Curtain are not impressed by pagan celebrations of the Teutonic solstice or by mythical fires lighted on the Bavarian mountains, they cannot ignore the inflammatory meetings which the
Landsmannschaften hold every year. At these gatherings Ministers
of the central and *Land* governments vie with the extremists in

demanding ever greater extensions of the present German frontiers, using language so aggressive that from time to time they cause alarm in the Chancelleries of Europe. From the now monumental list of their claims we will quote a few passages showing the dimensions of the threat to peace constituted by this mass of refugees and these agitators who for the last fifteen years have kept them in a state of restlessness and longing for a speedy revenge. 'The European task of the younger generation lies to the East,' declared the former *Bundesminister* Theodor Oberländer. 'Absolute unity among the young is essential if we are to be the advance-guard of the West.'[28] And on another occasion: 'We are determined to recover East Germany. Neither wars, nor millions of dead, nor famine, have ever been able to stop the German people.'[29] At subsequent meetings Oberländer was more explicit as to what he meant by East Germany: 'There, in Russia, the land is waiting for us. There we shall plant our roots.'[30] While Oberländer is thus looking East, the ex-minister Jakob Kaiser brings the western frontiers into the discussion. 'A real Europe,' he said in Salzburg, 'will never exist until the unity of Germany has been achieved. And this, I would remind you, includes not only Germany and Austria, but also part of Switzerland, the Saar and Alsace-Lorraine.'[31] In order to go one better than his Christian Democrat colleagues, the Social Democrat Wenzel Jaksch, the late chairman of the *Landsmannschaften*, wrote in the *Ost-West Kurier* in 1960 that 'the time has come to mobilize the political, moral and spiritual potential of the German refugees, so that at the right moment they can be thrown with decisive effect into the balance of destiny'.

The man whose outbursts have caused the biggest sensation and aroused most indignation is, however, undoubtedly the present Federal Transport Minister, Hans-Christoph Seebohm.[32] In Munich, at the annual conference of Sudeten refugees held on 4 June 1960, Seebohm asserted the right of all Sudeten Germans to return to their homeland, and to a crowd of 350,000 assembled in the Königsplatz he said: 'Our consciences and our hearts remain in our lost Fatherland.' Two years later, at a similar demonstration in Frankfurt, Seebohm prophesied that the boundaries of Germany would once again stretch from the Moselle to the Memel, from the Upper Adige to the Belt, and he made it quite clear that by East Germany he did not mean the area between the Elbe and the Oder, but included Bohemia, Moravia and all other territories formerly inhabited by Germans. On 17 May 1964 he told 400,000 refugees assembled in Nuremberg that the Munich agreement was still valid, and ended his speech with the following passionate appeal:

> There must be no renunciation! Justice must be done! In plain words that means the return of the Sudeten lands stolen from the Germans . . . We Sudeten Germans have never renounced our claim and we will never do so . . . There are no grounds whatsoever for maintaining, for example, that the Munich agreement is no longer valid. It was a convention drawn up in full conformity with international law.[33]

Although he was rebuked by Chancellor Erhard and asked to behave in future with a greater sense of responsibility, only a fortnight later Seebohm defiantly reiterated his claims. For that matter, Ludwig Erhard himself is not altogether blameless in this respect. On 22 March 1964 he told a meeting of *Landsmannschaften* in Bonn that 'We shall never renounce our claim—in view of our responsibilities to the German people, to justice and history, we cannot give up territories which are the natural home of so many of our German brothers and sisters'.[34]

The ambiguity of the Federal government's attitude towards the neo-Nazi, militarist and *revanchiste* organizations we have mentioned above undoubtedly tends to encourage certain dangerous trends among the German people, and above all anti-Semitism. According to the findings of a commission set up by the *Bundeskriminalamt*, out of 1,700 Jewish cemeteries existing in West Germany, 176 were desecrated between 1948 and 1957. The wave of outrages reached its highest point in the winter of 1959, when 850 cases of anti-Semitic vandalism were reported in the course of six weeks, which made many people think that a repetition of the *Kristallnacht* was imminent. 'There is no future for Jews in Germany,' said the Chief Rabbi of Cologne. 'So long as the Germans are busy getting rich, they won't do us any harm. But the moment difficulties arise, anti-Semitism will return with all its violence. That is why almost all the Jewish babies born in Germany are being sent to Israel.' At the time of writing there are only 25,694 Jews in West Germany (under the Weimar Republic there were 564,379), but according to an opinion poll taken in January 1966, one in every five German adults thinks this is too many and that they already have too much influence in the country. Another opinion poll showed that 7 per cent of Germans openly declared that they hated the Jews, while 70 per cent would have refused to marry an Israelite. In March 1963, in an interview granted to the Frankfurt daily *Abendpost*, Heinz Galinski, head of the Jewish community in Berlin, said that in his opinion the persistence of anti-Semitism was, practically speaking, encouraged 'from above'. 'If the West German authorities themselves set a bad example by appointing men of the Third Reich to responsible posts,' Galinski asked, 'what will be the repercussions in a society which sees that at the top nothing has changed?' The appointments—of 'wise' Nazis —mentioned by Galinski were made during the long years of the reign of Konrad Adenauer, and even now it is hard to understand why this old middle-class statesman, who had never been a Nazi and had never had any sympathy with Nazism, should have surrounded himself with so many men who had gravely compromised themselves during the Hitler régime.

The reign of Adenauer

The Old Gentleman of Rhöndorf's 'masterpiece' was not just the fact that he managed to stay in office for fourteen years. Or that as a politician he survived the death of John Foster Dulles and the end of his era. Nor was it that he patiently and cunningly exploited pan-European ideals with the sole purpose of accelerating the economic and military development of Germany. Konrad Adenauer's 'masterpiece' is the claim that he succeeded in bringing Germany back to the path of democracy with the help—paradoxically enough—of Nazi collaborators. What can have induced him to play this dangerous game? Mere opportunism, or that contempt for all other men and their ideas which everyone attributes to him? Was it the hope of redeeming these 'creatures of Hitler', or confidence in those supreme qualities of dutifulness and obedience which—as Madame de Staël observed more than a century ago—make every German a faithful servant of the State?

If we want to explain Adenauer's actions, we must first of all remember his primitive conception of Good and Evil as applied to politics. For a whole-hearted Catholic like Adenauer Good always means order and the Church, whereas Bolshevism is the incarnation of Evil, just as it was for the Nazis. Having, throughout his reign, based his policy on the psychosis of the 'mortal foe' in the East, he does not seem after all to have been so very inconsistent when he made use of men who had distinguished themselves in the service of Hitler by combating Communism and could therefore be 'saved' precisely because they were experts in that sphere. After all, Adenauer never attempted to deny that the Nazis had returned in force to all the leading positions in the State, and everyone knows with what loving care he always defended his 'circle' of experts and advisers (from Globke to Gehlen), how he was distressed by the forced retirement of Oberländer and did his best to rehabilitate him. On 22 October 1952, replying to the Deputy Erler, who had been instructed by the *Bundestag* to report on the infiltration of ex-Nazis into the Ministry for Foreign Affairs, Adenauer admitted:

> Erler has declared, in the most convincing way, that the higher one goes, the more Nazis one finds in State appointments, I assume that he meant from heads of departments upwards. That is true. It is true that 66 per cent of the functionaries mentioned by Erler were members of the Nazi party. But I believe that if you will view the matter calmly, you must admit that we could not have acted differently. You cannot form a Ministry for Foreign Affairs unless you have men who know their jobs in the key posts. In my opinion, we ought to stop this hunting for Nazis, because you may be certain that if we once start doing that, nobody can tell where we shall end up.

In obedience to this criterion, Adenauer introduced into the circle of his more intimate collaborators the old Cologne banker Robert Pferdmenges, who had been a banker in the Third Reich; he promoted to the rank of *Staatssekretär* a much discussed personage like Hans Globke, who was known to have rendered service to Hitler by devising the anti-Jewish laws which had led to his inclusion in the list of war criminals, but who at the same time was a first-rate civil servant and particularly competent when it came to Eastern problems;[35] and the same could be said of Theodor Oberländer, whom Adenauer made Minister for Refugees and his personal adviser on East German problems, despite the fact that he knew he had been political instructor to the *SS-Nachtigall* battalion, which was responsible for the killing of thousands of Polish Jews.[36] As Ernesto Ragionieri has pointed out in his article entitled '*Considerazioni sulla continuità dell'apparato statale dell'imperialismo tedesco*' (published in *Nuovi Argomenti*, November 1960/February 1961), out of nineteen Ministers and Secretaries of State who in 1960 made up the government of the *Bundesrepublik*, as many as twelve had compromised themselves by acting as advisers, ideologists or supporters of Nazism.

The system used in choosing top civil servants was also applied to army generals. After all, who could provide Germany with better safeguards against the Eastern menace than Hitler's strategists, who had had such valuable experience on the Eastern front? Franz-Josef Strauss—who as recently as 1948 had declared that any man who still wanted to handle a weapon ought to have his hands amputated, and in order to cover up his (admittedly modest) Nazi past, tried to make people believe the story that he had once committed a gallant act of resistance (he claimed to have scrawled the word 'swine' on Himmler's car)—when he was given the task of reorganizing the army had not the slightest hesitation in choosing men who had served Hitler, e.g. Heusinger, Speidel, Foertsch, Trettner, Ruge, Kammhuber, Kusserov, Zenker, von Zawadzki, Plocher, Johanneson, Trautloft. The American magazine *Time* called the Bavarian Strauss 'the man to watch', while the British Press described him as 'the most dangerous man in Europe'. And this man now became the associate of Adolf Heusinger, who as chief of general staff at Hitler's headquarters had been responsible for the 'Sea-lion' plan for the invasion of Britain, the 'Attila' plan for the overrunning of France, the 'Fir-tree' plan for the occupation of Switzerland, the 'Maritza' plan for the attack against Yugoslavia and the 'Barbarossa' plan for the invasion of Soviet Russia.[37] This close alliance gave birth to the *Bundeswehr*, which with its 500,000 men, its tactical bases in France, Spain, Portugal, Italy and South Africa, its 1,000 jet aircraft, its remote-controlled missiles and its brand-new fleet, is today the most modern instrument of war in Europe, lacking only atomic weapons (which Strauss and his successor von Hassel have so insistently asked for) in order to become even more formidable.

In the Koblenzerstrasse the return of the Nazis was on an even larger scale, as Adenauer himself had to admit. In 1958, according to the annual report of the German Ministry of the Interior, it was calculated that 84 per cent of the ambassadors and heads of departments employed by the Foreign Ministry had held office in the days of Ribbentrop. In that same year key posts were occupied by ex-Nazis in seventy-two out of eighty-three missions abroad, while Nazis were in charge of fourteen out of sixteen embassies or legations in South America and of fifteen in the Near and Middle East.

Diplomats involved in the deportation of Jews, in the elaboration of plans of aggression or in other operations implying obvious fidelity to the Nazi régime—Werner von Bergen, Wilhelm Grewe, Heinz Trützschler von Falkenstein, Ernst Günther Mohr, Otto Fürst von Bismarck, Manfred Klaiber, Kurt Munzel, Walther Hess, Hans Bidder, Andreas Nüsslein—were representing Bonn in the most important capitals and in the most delicate situations. 'Every one of these men,' writes Wolfgang Hans Edler Putlitz, the only diplomat who broke with Ribbentrop and resigned in 1939, 'was perfectly well aware of what was going on and of the state of barbarism existing under the Nazi régime.' T. H. Tetens, who from 1946 to 1948 worked for the American War Crimes Commission and has personal knowledge of the archives of Hitler's Foreign Ministry, is even more severe in his treatment of the ex-Nazis in the *Auswärtige Amt*:

> Most of these men had been actively involved in preparing Hitler's aggressive moves by spreading propaganda and lies among the future victims and by financing and directing 'fifth column' and espionage networks abroad. In some countries these diplomats gave all-out support to groups which organized rebellions against lawfully elected governments, as, for example, in Austria, Spain, Czechoslovakia, and Iraq. They were implicated in kidnappings, the plotting of murder, mass deportation and gassing of Jews, the killing of hostages, and looting of whole countries.[38]

Obviously, the police and the judiciary were not exempt from this invasion by 'wise' Nazis whose 'competence' was their salvation. An inquiry instituted by the Civil Servants' Association in 1959 showed that in that year almost all the criminal police services in Dortmund, Cologne, Essen, Bonn, Düsseldorf, Gelsenkirchen, Krefeld, Mülheim/Ruhr, were in the hands of senior SS officers, almost all of whom had served in Himmler's Security Police.[39] Before he was tried in 1962 and convicted of massacring 30,000 Jews, the SS colonel Georg Heuser had managed to become chief of police for the whole of the Rhenish Palatinate. An equally rapid career was that of the ex-SS captain Theo Saewecke who, before he was dismissed in 1963 because he was accused of having committed a number of crimes in Germany and Italy, had held a high post in the Security Police of the German capital. In a biting comment on the 'Saewecke case', a Frankfurt newspaper expressed itself as follows:

When Theo Saewecke's superiors are asked why this man—a former officer in the SS—was holding an important post in the Bonn Security Police, they reply that he had all the qualifications for the job. At that rate, if Goebbels were still alive, he ought to be head of the Federal Press Bureau.[40]

At question time in the House of Commons on 19 November 1959 Mr Zilliacus asked the Prime Minister whether he intended to request Adenauer to take measures against the 1,155 judges 'responsible for crimes against humanity' who were still administering justice in the *Bundesrepublik*, in violation of the Potsdam agreement (III, A, 8). These judges and prosecutors had been members either of the notorious Berlin *Volksgerichtshof* (People's Court) or of the 'special tribunals' which together, between 1933 and 1945, had passed sentence of death on 45,000 Germans and citizens of the occupied countries guilty of having infringed Hitler's laws, and had later re-entered the judiciary of the Federal Republic in time to save the few Nazis who appeared in the dock. In fact Brian Connell attributes the frequent acquittals of Nazi war criminals (especially between 1950 and 1958) to the fact that there was 'little ideological difference between a judiciary partly staffed by ex-Nazis and the accused'.[41] On 14 June 1961, as a result of the indignation caused by these revelations, the *Bundestag* passed a law authorizing the optional retirement before reaching the age-limit of judges who had inflicted capital sentences under the Hitler régime. According to a communiqué of the German press agency, 153 judges did in fact retire before the prescribed date of 30 June 1962, but others with Nazi pasts remained in office and are still there. 'If we take into account those who retired on reaching the age-limit,' says Wolfgang Zwielicht, 'the number of functionaries with "murky pasts" who are still in office must be somewhere around seven hundred.' On the other hand it seems to us that Albert Norden, a member of the *Politbüro* of the SED (United Socialist Party of East Germany) was exaggerating when he told a Press conference in East Berlin that 'three-quarters of the 11,600 West German judges were in office under Hitler and belonged to the Nazi Party'.[42]

The omnipotent *Wehrwirtschaftsführer*, the men who ran Germany's war economy, found new jobs managing the big trusts which according to the Potsdam agreement were to be broken up, but today are more powerful than ever, and have brought increased prosperity to the various Krupps, Thyssens, Flicks, Quandts,

Haniels and Kloeckners. Yet the decentralization of economic power had not only been stipulated by the Allies at Potsdam, but had also been recognized as necessary by the CDU (*Christlich-Demokratische Union*). In the 'Ahlen programme', approved by the future rulers of West Germany on 3 February 1947, we read in fact that:

> The capitalistic economic system has shown that it is unable to meet the demands of the German people's economic life . . . The concentration of power in the hands of particular groups must be prevented . . . Coal is the product that dominates the whole of the German economy. We demand the socialization of the mines . . . Socialization is also necessary in the steel industry . . .

But here again, as in 1918, the Germans missed the chance to effect those reforms in their economic structure which would have brought about a radical transformation in the most dangerous country in Europe. Very soon, in fact, conservatives like Adenauer and Erhard managed to put the CDU reformers in a minority and, after a brief interval due to forced decentralization, they fostered the resurgence of the traditional monopolies, with the approval of the Americans who wanted to use Germany as a pawn in their battle with the Soviet Union, as they had already used Japan.

The Korean war, which marked the rebirth of the big Japanese trusts, also put the owners of the huge German combines on their feet again. Flick and Krupp, whom the Nuremberg tribunal had sentenced as war criminals, returned to the helms of their economic empires and made them even more powerful thanks to the financial aid received under the Marshall Plan. Abs and Pferdmenges, once more became the symbols of the concentration of economic power. Indispensable figures in the I.G. Farben group and in other key industries were once again the Ter Meers, the Mennes, the Haberland-Winneckers, the Ambros and the Fausts who had been accused of complicity in the deportation and extermination of the Auschwitz 'slaves'. Even Dr Petersen, the man who is said to have supplied the extermination camps with the deadly *Zyklon D* gas, returned to his post as manager of the *Degussa* in Frankfurt. The reconstitution of the big *Konzerne* began on the quiet in 1952 and may be said to have been completed in 1963 when the *August Thyssen Hütte* was merged with the *Phoenix Rheinrohr*, a merger which allows one German company to produce 7 million tons of steel every year. Commenting on the restoration of the German economic oligarchy, Robert Jungk pointed out that 'the government party has strengthened German capitalism to such a degree that, despite the "decartelization measures" taken by the conquerors, economic power is today concentrated in even fewer hands than before the war'.[43] And Meyers, the Minister-President of North Rhine-Westphalia, remembering how the giants of the Rhineland and the Ruhr wrecked the Weimar Republic, suggested that a stricter control over them is needed, because 'one industrial giant could support another Hitler, and then all measures to ensure the maintenance of democratic order would prove to be inadequate'.[44]

A detailed analysis of this reabsorption of Nazis into the Federal Republic's civil service would occupy many pages, and we will therefore limit ourselves to citing only two more examples— the case of General Reinhard Gehlen and the choice of Ministers for Refugees. The story of Gehlen is fairly well known, but it is very significant. The right-hand man of Walter Schellenberg (head of SS Intelligence), he was reputed to know more about the Soviet Union than anyone else. In 1945 Gehlen was picked up by the Americans together with his small army of spies and experts (most of them ex-SS officers or ex-agents of the Security Service) and utilized as 'America's Number One Spy abroad'.[45] In 1955, when Germany regained her full sovereignty, Gehlen's espionage network was immediately transformed into a government department under the direct control of another ex-Nazi, Hans Globke. The second episode seems almost incredible. Three well-known former Nazis—Theodor Oberländer, Hans Krüger and Ernst Lemmer—have held the post of Minister for Refugees between 1953 and the present day. The first of these was dismissed because of his past record as an SS officer. The second resigned when it was discovered that he had been a judge in one of the 'special tribunals'. The third, still in office, was in Nazi days a journalist under Goebbels. There would seem to be a moral in all this. Either the Federal Republic thinks that it has no other men better fitted than these ex-Nazis to take charge of the Ministry for Refugees, or else this Ministry, in view of its special functions, must inevitably be run by an ex-Nazi.

A State within the State

What we have just described is the State which Konrad Adenauer, at the age of eighty-seven, handed over to his successor, Professor Ludwig Erhard, in 1963. A State whose essential problems were concealed from the eyes of superficial observers by the veil of the 'economic miracle'. A State which had undergone no fundamental transformation and was wavering between a return to pre-Nazi democracy with its poverty of ideas, its adherence to rules of procedure and its opportunism, and a return to a nationalism inspired by the desire for revenge, advocated more and more openly by the Nazi elements who had re-entered the government services. In an article on Adenauer's Germany which appeared in the *Tribune des Nations* in November 1963, Bernard Lavergne reached the following conclusions:

> A warm supporter of the Cold War, if not of war *tout court*, of intensive rearmament and of the renazification of Germany, that is what Chancellor Adenauer has been. During the fourteen years of his reign no one in the West, not a single Minister or politician who was not a Communist, has had the courage to tell the truth about West Germany . . . When the history of our sorrowful epoch is written, what will be the verdict on these West European politicians, who all of them, from the first to the last, in their efforts to flatter the Federal Republic have encouraged its worst errors?

The alliance between this old exponent of the Catholic *Zentrum* and the 'respectable' wing of Nazism has led to the reconstitution of a Germany which even lays claim to the imperial frontiers of 1914, substituting Christian pan-European slogans for the worn-out ideas of pan-Germanism, and also of an army which seizes every opportunity to proclaim that it does not intend 'to take part only in parades'. This, incidentally, had already been predicted by a Liberal, Reinhold Maier, when he said: 'Remember that the German army never keeps its place; it always takes the first place in the State.' While a Social Democrat, the editor of *Vorwärts*, Jesso von Puttkamer, wrote that 'the General Staff which has reconstituted the *Bundeswehr* is the same General Staff that folded up its maps at Zossen. And as regards the prevailing atmosphere, there is little to choose between Zossen and Bonn',[46]

Army interference in government matters made itself felt sooner than anyone had anticipated. On 20 August 1960 the German

military chiefs made their demands public in a memorandum entitled 'Conditions for an adequate defence', which sponsored the
cause of atomic weapons and revealed the traditional intolerance
of the army *vis-à-vis* the civil power. What they expressed in this
memorandum was not merely their professional opinion, but a
clearly political judgement. Not only did they think that atomic
weapons were the only adequate defence against the Bolshevik
'mortal foe', but they maintained that the Soviet Union was Germany's 'only possible enemy', and this was equivalent to a definite
intervention in foreign policy. 'In this way,' wrote a Frankfurt
daily, commenting on the episode, 'Inspectors Heusinger, Ruge,
Kammhuber and Zenker, who during the Second World War all
held responsible posts in Adolf Hitler's armed forces, are leading
the *Bundeswehr* into a position which ignores the teachings of two
great political and military catastrophes.'[47] A few months later,
when the Defence Minister, Franz-Josef Strauss, was involved in
the 'Fibag scandal', the heads of the three Services made it known
through Inspector-General Foertsch that the *Bundeswehr* was
solidly behind Strauss because of its personal ties of loyalty to
him, and demanded that he should remain in his high office. After
interfering in politics, the generals thus resorted to intimidation
and blackmail.

In any case, how could such a typical product of the Cold War
as the *Bundeswehr* remain the democratic instrument that Colonel
Baudissin had hoped to create? Eight years after it had been
formed, certain democratic measures like the *Soldatengesetz* (the
law defining the duties and rights of soldiers) and the appointment
of *Vertrauensmänner* (confidential advisers of Servicemen) were
undoubtedly still functioning, but they went into a rapid decline
as soon as the old militarist tradition had been re-established.
Similarly, the post of 'parliamentary commissar for military matters'
still exists, but we need only remember what happened to the
'commissars' Helmuth von Grolman and Hellmuth Heye in order
to convince ourselves that the *Bundeswehr* will never tolerate in-
trusions by civilian controllers into its own sphere. Von Grolman
took up his duties in April 1959, and a year later, in his 'report'
to the *Bundestag*, he maintained, among other accusations, that the
principle of 'citizens in uniform' had clearly been misunderstood
by many officers and N.C.O's, who were far from being convinced of the usefulness of a democratic army. This report and
the following ones provoked violent reactions from Strauss and

E

certain conservative elements in the parliament and government. Grolman was obliged to resign, and later even attempted to take his own life, while the Minister of Justice for the Rhineland and Westphalia instituted an inquiry into his private life, hinting that he was a homosexual. Using the same pretext, later proved to be false, Hitler had succeeded in 1938 in removing the commander-in-chief of the *Wehrmacht*, General Werner von Fritsch. Memories of this episode convinced many Germans that Grolman, too, must have been the victim of a plot.

His successor was a retired vice-admiral, Hellmuth Heye, who until 1961 had been a CDU Deputy in the *Bundestag*. Heye soon ran into the same trouble that had led Grolman to try to kill himself, but profiting by his predecessor's experience he was more wary, and in June 1964, realizing that he would never be allowed to say in Parliament what he really thought of the *Bundeswehr*, he decided to vent his opinons through the columns of *Quick*, the Munich weekly. 'In writing these lines,' the former CDU Deputy began:

> I am asserting my right and my duty to take a stand on a number of matters which to my mind are dangerous . . . If something is not done soon, the *Bundeswehr* will become an institution of a kind that none of us can certainly want to see. It is clear that it is tending to become a State within the State . . . When I took office, I was convinced that I would be able to exert a positive influence on the *Bundeswehr*. Today I must confess that this was an illusion. I now have to ask myself whether most of the new German officers are willing to admit that democratic parliamentary control must be supreme. I have serious doubts whether they are. The training of our troops is based on ideas which are not in accordance with the times, which are in fact reprehensible and shatter the confidence of those members of the younger generation who are serving in the *Bundeswehr* . . . In our army the system of training is antiquated and based on the principles of rigid discipline. Such methods may be suitable for training animals, but certainly not for training men. These methods date from the days of mercenaries and are unhappily so common that I feel it to be my duty to warn the public against any attempt to minimize them.

In a second article Heye amplified what he said about the *Bundeswehr*:

> Notwithstanding the Federal Government's efforts to instil a new spirit into the *Bundeswehr*, the old traditional ideas are still prevalent in our army. Even the unsuccessful military plot against Hitler on 20 July 1944 is still a subject of controversy among our army

officers. We need only remember what General Hans Roettinger, a former Inspector-General of the *Bundeswehr*, told the cadets at a training school for tank units. 'No matter who tries to stop us,' said Roettinger, 'we shall reconstitute the Tank Corps with all its old spirit.'

Hitherto accusations of this kind had come only from the ranks of the extreme left wing, and it was unprecedented that they should now be made by a Christian Democrat. Hellmuth Heye, too, was severely rebuked; Chancellor Erhard defended the *Bundeswehr* and everything was done to ensure that the incident would be speedily forgotten. On 3 November 1964, in fact, Vice-Admiral Heye was compelled, as Grolman had been, to hand in his resignation.

Actually there is no other body in West Germany—as we shall see when we come to the '*Spiegel* affair'—so shrouded in secrecy as the army, that colossus which costs the Federal Treasury millions of marks every year and 'according to the experts is today far more powerful than the Hitlerian army which occupied Czechoslovakia in 1938 after imposing the *Anschluss* on Austria. But whereas Hitler's Germany strove to exaggerate its military power, the watchword today is to minimize it, and (with a pious lowering of the eyelids) what is really deliberate camouflage is described as "modesty".[48] Despite the strategic advantages which the West hopes to achieve thanks to the *Bundeswehr*, it is more and more widely felt that the rearmament of Germany, in the light of the incidents we have just mentioned, might well be turned against those very nations which have sponsored it. On 11th April 1963, Senator Claiborne Pell made himself the mouthpiece of these fears when he said in the American Senate:

> . . . the recollection that Germany has engaged in three aggressive wars in the last 100 years . . . is a fact very much in the European mind. It is one of the reasons . . . for the general acceptance of the fact that Germany should not have nuclear weapons . . . This is perhaps the most important single policy that we and the Soviets share. Accordingly, I think we should give our present policy toward Germany a critical re-examination with a view toward acceptance of the fact that Germany is divided as long as we have not reached the millenium of a world and a time when we can achieve a unified, unarmed Germany . . .[49]

The '*Spiegel Affair*'

An ordinary article in a weekly magazine, which in other circumstances and with a different 'team' in power might have passed unnoticed, showed that democracy in the Federal Republic was but a fragile plant and that the men entrusted with the task of modelling their country on democratic lines were not up to their jobs. On 10 October 1962, under the title 'Fit for defence in limited circumstances', the Hamburg weekly *Der Spiegel* published a long article on the NATO military manœuvres (*Fallex 62*), containing caustic criticisms of the *Bundeswehr's* equipment and (not for the first time) allegations against the Defence Minister, Franz-Josef Strauss. Three weeks after the publication of this article agents of the Federal Police made a 'Gestapo-like swoop'[50] on the *Spiegel* offices and arrested the leading members of the editorial staff on charges of high treason, betrayal of military secrets, making false statements damaging to the State and wholesale bribery. In making these arrests and perquisitions the police used methods which the *Christian Science Monitor* described as being 'in a manner reminiscent of Nazi days'.[51]

Chancellor Adenauer reacted by telling parliament that 'he did not think much of people who advertised in a magazine that periodically committed treason'.[52] In reality there had been no treason. *Der Spiegel's* editor had merely criticized the government's official line. But that was enough for Adenauer, and accordingly Augstein had to be punished.

Quite apart from the specific criticisms contained in the incriminated article, the '*Spiegel* affair' revealed a series of most disconcerting violations of law and normal procedure, of episodes showing a complete disregard for democratic practice. Let us list the principal features. 1) The agents raided the *Spiegel* offices by night, which was a breach of paragraph 104 of the police regulations; 2) deliberately by-passing the normal channels of diplomacy and the Interpol, the Defence Minister, Strauss, personally asked the Military Attaché to the German Embassy in Madrid to persuade the Spanish police to arrest the journalist Conrad Ahlers, who was on holiday near Malaga; 3) on the night of the raid the police asked to see the proofs of the issue that was just going to press, thereby violating the freedom of the Press and article 1, paragraph 5, subparagraph 3 of the Constitution; 4) as legal justification for the arrest of the editors of the magazine the German Government quoted paragraphs 100 A and 100 C of a law against treason which Hitler had caused to be passed in 1934, which had been abrogated by the Allies in 1946 and later restored by the Federal Government in 1951; 5) the arrests had been made without the knowledge of the

Minister of Justice, Wolfgang Stammberger, who in accordance with normal procedure should have been the first person to be informed; 6) disregarding the distinctions between the jurisdiction of the Federal Government and that of the regional administration, the agents of the Federal Police had raided the *Spiegel* offices in Bonn, which is in North Rhine-Westphalia, without first consulting the Minister of the Interior for that *Land*; 7) contrary to German law, the telephone exchange of the *Spiegel* and the private telephones of its sub-editors had been tapped for several weeks before the raid took place; 8) two minor details should not be overlooked: the man who denounced *Der Spiegel*, Baron Friedrich August von der Heydte, was a close friend of Strauss and had served in the SA during the Hitler régime, while the man who directed the police operations, Theo Saewecke, had in Hitler's time been an SS officer.

The ensuing scandal brought about the fall of Adenauer's fourth government and the exclusion of Strauss from the new cabinet.[53] The flagrant violation of the law and the employment of Nazis and Nazi regulations to silence the few opposition periodicals in West Germany aroused the anger of a large part of the Press and the more progressive elements in the Federal Republic. Thousands of students demonstrated in Berlin, Hamburg and Frankfurt, carrying posters bearing the words 'My God, what will happen to Germany?' 'Carl von Ossietzky 1931—Augstein 1962?' Protests also came from the universities of Cologne and Göttingen, and from the intellectuals of the 'Group 47'; but once the storm had blown over, the voices which had dared to protest were themselves accused of treason and complicity in the eternal conspiracy against Germany, while public opinion, which had not entirely grasped the dimensions of the scandal, was placated, anaesthetized as usual by its economic well-being and by the reassuring words of Adenauer, that elder statesman who had made people believe that he would think of everything *(Der Alte denkt an alles).*

In a communiqué on the *'Spiegel* affair' the German trade unions pointed out that the episode had revealed 'notable flaws in the immature German democracy', while one of the most ardent champions of German unity, Lord Boothby, in a letter to *The Times* even demanded that the negotiations in Brussels concerning the entry of Britain into the Common Market should be broken off because 'the recent actions of President De Gaulle, which are entirely unconstitutional, and of Dr Adenauer's Government in the

Der Spiegel affair, prove conclusively that neither France nor Germany are any longer democracies in the sense that we understand the term.'[54] It should, however, be added that the responsibility for the present political tendency in West Germany must not be attributed to the larger parties alone, but to the smaller groups as well, since they no longer constitute an effective opposition, this being due either to the subjection in which they were held for fourteen years by the paternalistic dictatorship of Adenauer, or else to the decay of democratic institutions and the acceptance of nationalism as the programme for all. We are far from the days when the Social Democrats opposed rearmament, and the Protestant middle class, concentrated in the Liberal Party, strove to achieve a neutralist solution. Today opposition is confined to ever more restricted circles, courageous and pugnacious though they may be.

The other Germany

Let us once more allow figures and documents to speak for themselves. In March 1963, in an analysis of the results of various opinion polls in West Germany, the Munich magazine *Quick* gave the following disconcerting details. Seven per cent of the population of the Federal Republic would welcome a return of Nazism; 12 per cent replied that they 'had not the slightest idea how they would react', 29 per cent said they did not mind whether there was another dictatorship or not; and only 34 per cent of Germans declared that they would defend democracy even if they had to take up arms. 'A sorry balance!', was the comment of *Quick*, which can hardly be called a progressive publication. Most foreign writers and those German anti-conformists who have made a close study of the Federal Republic over the last few years agree that, although she now possesses all the necessary democratic institutions, Germany has not yet learned the lesson of democracy. 'The Germans,' says Dornberg, 'are going through the motions of living in a democratic society without really knowing what it is supposed to be.'[55] And T. H. Tetens quotes the astonishing admission of Friedrich von der Heydte, one of the founders of Adenauer's party: 'Today it is fashionable in Germany to be a democrat. Every German is a good democrat as a matter of course—if you want to "belong" you have to be. But basically the Germans do not cherish democracy.

They submit to it as perhaps people submit to a fashion although deep inside they resent their uncomfortable plight.'[56] One of the most courageous German journalists, Heinz Abosch, after stressing the fact that Germany's economic miracle is merely a proof of the German people's capacity for hard work and of their flair for organization, adds that 'a real miracle would have been an authentic democratization, the elimination of the old *élites*, and a break with reactionary tradition. Unfortunately nothing of the kind has happened.'[57]

Has Germany, then, once again become a danger to herself and to others? Sad to relate, Heinz Abosch is convinced that she has. In fact his whole study tends to confirm the re-emergence in Germany of a highly dangerous nationalistic egocentrism coupled with a frenzied desire for power, 'a voluptuous delight in catastrophe', a tendency to relegate to the recesses of the mind all disagreeable thoughts *(unbewältigte Vergangenheit)* and the conviction that the hour of destiny is about to strike for their country. Interpreting the fears of the more progressive elements, Pastor Grüber made this stirring appeal:

> The concentration camps no longer exist, but all the other elements of the past are still with us. Not only attempts to spy on the people and X-ray them, but also attempts to push men in a specific direction, to draw them into mass movements guided by the authorities. During the Nazi era we often used to ask ourselves: 'Is it possible that the politicians of other lands do not realize what is going on in our country?' Today my friends and I myself ask the same question: 'Can't people abroad understand what is going on here?[58]

Although a study of the forces opposed to any renazification of Germany is partly outside the scope of our study, we shall nevertheless make a brief mention of them here, in order to conclude our remarks and show that 'another Germany' does actually exist, as it has always existed, even in the darkest days of Nazism. It is a minority Germany which has its strongholds, not among the workers, who are unfortunately blinded by economic prosperity, but in the religious and intellectual spheres. It is the Germany of Pastors Niemöller and Grüber. The Germany of writers like Erich Kuby, Eugen Kogon, Heinrich Böll, Arno Schmidt, Alfred Andersch, and the editors of *Merkur*, of the *Frankfurter Hefte* and of *Konkret*. The Germany of the Catholic Bishop of Limburg, Walther Kampe, who warns us that 'our German

people has not yet overcome National Socialism spiritually' and
that 'to let grass grow over the past simply won't do'.[59] The Germany of the Protestant bishops, who in 1963 exhorted their fellow-
countrymen not to take the trials of Nazi war criminals too lightly,
because 'even those citizens who have committed no crimes, and
those who never knew that any were being committed, are co-
responsible because they remained indifferent to the violation of all
the precepts of morals and the law'.[60] The Germany of those who
have fought to prevent the resurgence of German Nazism, like
Klara-Marie Fassbinder, Gustav Schmidt-Küster and Gustav Heinemann. The Germany of the historians Golo Mann and Michael
Freund, who do not hesitate to describe as 'arrogant' and 'suicidal'
the claims of the nationalists. The Germany of those who escaped the
gas-chambers and now belong to the persecuted *Vereinigung der
Verfolgten des Naziregimes* (VVN=Association of Victims of the
Nazi Régime), which has adopted the motto of the inmates of
Buchenwald—'Prevent Europe from becoming an SS Europe'.[61]
The Germany of all those who have meditated on Bertolt Brecht's
warning in the last scene of *Arturo Ui*: 'The womb that brought
forth this unclean thing is still fruitful.'

But who listens to this minority Germany? How are its counsels
received? If we take as an example the reception given to a volume
of political essays by the philosopher Karl Jaspers, *Freiheit und
Wiedervereinigung*, we are bound to admit that the majority of
Germans refuse to listen to advice and react angrily to every appeal
for moderation and common sense. Observing that the Germany
predicted by Adenauer was the same as that of which the neo-
Fascist International dreamed, the German philosopher asked in his
book whether, instead of pursuing the 'chimeras' of reunification
and redemption of lost territories, Germany would not have done
better to try, for the first time in her history, to 'realize the democratic idea'. Jaspers also suggested that it was wrong to foster
'false hopes' among the refugees from the East and warned that,
'if the Federal Army were once more to become a national army,
fresh disasters were only to be expected', while the rapid economic
and military expansion of the Federal Republic might lead people
to believe—once again—that 'the economy and the army determine
the truths of history'. And in conclusion:

> There is raving in those very circles which disown Hitler and
> National Socialism in the most categorical manner, but in which
> at the same time a similar—or rather, identical—way of thinking

is reborn. And in actual fact it is not National Socialism that is reborn. The same calamity merely assumes different aspects.[62]

This was a keen and pitiless diagnosis of the temptations and inclinations of present-day Germany, and, as the Bonn correspondent of the *Basler National-Zeitung* pointed out, it brought forth 'indignant reaction from the parties, political organizations and newspapers of the Federal Republic. Khrushchev himself had never succeeded in evoking such a demonstration of unanimity.'[63]

6 Italy

'The Great Mother'

In November 1945 the Italian Liberal Party (PLI) instructed its secretary Leone Cattani to accompany the Minister for the National Assembly, Manlio Brosio, to Palazzo Chigi in order to discuss with the then Foreign Minister, Alcide De Gasperi, 'the probable date and form' of a crisis in the coalition government of which Ferruccio Parri was the Premier. The two PLI envoys had been entrusted by their party with the task of working out the procedure to be followed during the coming crisis and the conditions for the entry of the PLI into a new government of which De Gasperi was to be the head.[1]

On the evening of 23 November the Premier suddenly called the representatives of the Italian and foreign Press to a conference, at which, in his usual deprecatory but firm manner, he announced that the Liberals and Christian Democrats were planning a *coup d'état* behind the backs of the government in which they held some of the most important posts. Parri was obviously worried. He spoke of manœuvres which were subtly and effectively undermining the government from within, with ramifications outside the coalition. These manœuvres were reflections, hopes and intrigues of right-wing elements, who were preparing to launch an attack against the democratic régime set up by the Resistance Movement in the hope of preventing a renewal of the system which its programme envisaged. On the surface Parri remained calm, but the gist of his words was serious. When he had finished speaking, De Gasperi rose in order 'to implore the foreign journalists, as Foreign Minister, not to take Parri's reference to a *coup d'état* too literally, and to defend the Christian Democratic Party (DC) against any accusation of disloyalty'. De Gasperi maintained that his party had been actuated solely by the desire to 'defend the democratic system and methods'.[2]

The Parri cabinet had been formed five months earlier, on 21 June 1945. During these months it had become clear beyond all possibility of misunderstanding that the PLI and the DC were trying to deprive the National Liberation Committee (CLN) of its authority and destroy the coalition, their ultimate aim being to lay the foundations of a broader policy of restoration. It became known that they had received offers of support from the monarchical right wing and from Umberto di Savoia, then Lieutenant of the Realm, who hoped that the fall of the Parri government would strengthen the tottering monarchy.[3] When the man who had led the Italian Resistance resigned, the choice of a successor fell upon De Gasperi. On 4 December the PLI explained the conditions on which they were willing to collaborate with the new government, set out in a memorandum in which the secretariat of the Action Party immediately detected the presence of 'claims which, taken in their entirety, aim at suppressing the democratic and anti-Fascist character of the government'. 'It will suffice,' the Action Party's communiqué continued, 'if we note the demands for the cessation of all the CLN's functions, for the abolition of the tribunals recently approved by the Assembly for the trial of Fascists, and for the dismissal of politically-minded prefects and chiefs of police, even of those who had shown that they provided the best and most impartial line of defence against a return of Fascists to the more important offices; and added to all this we have the insidious reservations regarding the powers of the Assembly.'[4] The PLI memorandum was in fact neither more nor less than a list, couched in bureaucratic terms, of the measures which it was thought the new government ought to introduce in order to get rid of the men and institutions that had emerged from the struggle against Fascism, to bring back the political and administrative system of pre-Fascist days, and to entrust the execution of these measures to men outside the democratic movement. The Liberals were to act as a kind of militant advance-guard during these manœuvres; when the crisis was over, they would appear to have suffered a defeat, since they would not form part of the new coalition cabinet under De Gasperi, but in reality the new Premier hoped to bring them into the cabinet at the first opportunity, and in fact he hastened to tell the press that their return was 'an objective which must be achieved as soon as possible'.[5] In a personal letter addressed to the secretariat of the PLI he mentioned the conditions laid down by the Liberals and assured them that he was prepared to accept 90 per cent of them. Consequently, the PLI felt reassured as to the temporary nature of the pact concluded by De Gasperi with the left-wing parties when he launched his new government. It was merely a question of time and tactics, but the Liberals, like the Christian Democrats, knew that a policy of restoration was one which would not be reversed.

It was not by mere chance that, during the controversy within the coalition and the attack on the Parri government, the PLI had chosen to make the question of the 'purge' the main plank in its platform. To further their aim, they launched a vigorous campaign, in the course of which alarmist rumours were coupled with allegations that the Premier and the left-wing parties were using the tribunals set up to ascertain the guilt of Fascists as a pretext for the persecution of thousands of innocent people or of individuals who had received only trivial benefits from the defunct régime. The purge was of course the exact opposite of the picture which the PLI chose to paint of it. Quite apart from the fact that it had punished only an absurdly small percentage of those responsible for the past, it had allowed the chief culprits to escape through the meshes of its net, these being the men belonging to that category of industrialists and financiers who had made the biggest profits out of their collaboration with Fascism. In demanding the cessation of this alleged discrimination, the PLI was really acting on behalf of these men, who, once they had got over their fear that a democratic régime might make a thorough investigation of their activities, were indignant at being charged as accomplices. Moreover, the PLI raised the banner of a 'return to normal', knowing perfectly well that this would win them the sympathies and approval of the conservative and reactionary front, which the PLI ambitiously aspired to lead.

Thus the bracing 'north wind' died away and was followed by a sandstorm which buried all the hopes and achievements of the Resistance. A few months after the liberation, the right-wing parties carefully garnered all the seeds of weariness and discontent, of the moral and political bewilderment which had followed the end of the war, bound them together with the threads of a professed 'legalitarianism' and the bogies of 'revolution', and turned them against the State.

The unnerving experience of the war and the two years of the sanguinary battle against the Republic of Salò, the destruction and the misery, together with the moral and spiritual decline resulting from that long affliction, had brought about a natural desire for more peaceful times. In the minds of millions of Italians a feeling of scepticism and boredom regarding so many of the values and arguments over which the opposing parties were squabbling got the better of any desire they might have had to discover the mistakes which had led to the catastrophe and the methods which alone could lead them back to a more civilized way of life free from any risk of regression. Half the country had known nothing of the uprising of the people; the other half had been occupied territory in which the population had been desperately trying not to die of starvation. The fortunes amassed in the past had grown still larger, the poverty of earlier days had reached an abysmal level. Mountains of disillusionment, fallen idols, bitterness and rancour had risen to the surface of a country still subject to Allied control, threatened at the top by an aggressive conservative faction, and in its foundations by the absence of any solid, age-old traditions. At Salerno the compromise between Togliatti and Badoglio—quite apart from any opinion as to its merits—had brought back to the corridors of power the ghosts and theoreticians of a deliberate wait-and-see policy. Such people had never imagined that a post-liberation Italy could be anything but a return to pre-Fascist times. In these troubled waters the anti-democratic counter-offensive could fling its bait in the hope of catching men whose state of mind was such that they were ready to swallow anything which would dispel the prevailing discontent and malaise and excite their critical faculties, since they were only too anxious to find moralistic and popular solutions.

It was at this moment that there rose above the horizon the star of Guglielmo Giannini, a mediocre and pretentious playwright, who, however, had a certain instinctive feeling for those lukewarm desires which were emerging from the recesses of the mass psyche. On 27 December 1944 he founded a paper called *L'Uomo Qualunque* ('The Common Man'), whose circulation rose in a very short time to hundreds of thousands of copies. When he began putting out feelers towards the PLI, he was repulsed, because it was feared that he might soon come to represent a majority within its ranks, since he lacked neither the means nor the histrionic qualities necessary to win his readers over to Liberalism.[6] Later, he asked Croce, Nitti, Orlando and Bonomi to take over the leadership of the party he intended to create, but 'only the last-named', Catalano tells us, 'did not refuse on the spot'.[7] Finally, on 8 August 1945, the playwright himself assumed the leadership of his political enterprise. The programme of the *Uomo Qualunque* had already been published in the paper and consisted of a few demagogic formulas—abolition of all parties, a business government, absolute freedom from 'party rule', 'safeguards for the taxpayer', etc., etc. The movement's emblem showed a little man crushed beneath the press of political vexations and the burdens everyone was placing upon his shoulders—the forces of occupation, the left and right wings, the centre parties, the bureaucracy, and so on.

Giannini's political tactics were based solely on protestations, and the fate of the movement was sealed when its founder carried to the point of exaggeration his scornful and devastating attitude towards everything that might form the object of discussion—ideas, the strengthening of democracy or an appeal for a social renewal. Giannini had conceived his paper—which was the real instrument of his political success—as a chronicle of vulgar scandals, of street-corner gossip to which he added a few flashes of wit and stale relics of former controversies. In this Neapolitan playwright's prose a few sallies were to be found which were typical products of drawing-room snobbery, but above all it contained an astonishing profusion of abuse, slander and vulgar double meanings. Italy resounded with Giannini-esque orations, which introduced into the dialogue with the public the quips of journalists mingled with invocations to the 'Great Mother of us all' who must at all costs be saved; but whenever Giannini stopped cracking jokes and plunged into moralistic tirades, he displayed a typically Fascist style. *'Qualunquismo'* managed in this way to hover on the fringes of the big parties, and its leader, eager to make capital by advertising his success, endowed the movement with ambitions on a Continental scale by founding another paper, *Europa qualunque*, the organ of an outlandish European federalism of malcontents and 'plain men' who did not want to hear of any parties and demanded only that they should not be 'messed about'.

The campaign of slander and abuse which *'Qualunquismo'* hurled at democracy made a considerable impression on millions of citizens and showed how 'the Italians still carried deeply impressed on their hearts the memories of a dictatorship which had accustomed them not to take any interest in public affairs', and how 'the activities of political parties' were held to be 'intolerable forms of compulsion'.[8] Those who mourned the passing of Fascism or who had fought for the Republic of Salò recognized in these things another decisive factor—the impunity which would shield them if they indulged in attacks on democratic institutions, on the adversaries

of Fascism and on the Resistance. This emboldened them sufficiently to persuade them to emerge from hiding and make their
reappearance on the political stage, in an atmosphere which intensified the malaise prevailing in the country, since the forces of
democracy showed that they were paralysed when it came to dealing
with urgent problems and were squandering their time in internecine
quarrels of which only the 'initiates' could understand the terms.
After the liberation, the Fascist camp had maintained a discreet
silence, which was a mixture of fear and discouragement. Gradually,
little groups of 'nostalgics' created organizations most of which
were very small and had a purely local character, and surrounded
themselves with a veil of profound secrecy. Such movements were
the FAR *(Fasci di Azione Rivoluzionaria)*, the ECA *(Esercito
Clandestino Anticomunista)*, the AIL *(Armata Italiana di Libera-
zione)*, the FAI *(Fronte Antibolscevico Italiano)*, the PNL *(Partito
Nazionale del Lavoro)*, the SAM *(Squadre di Azione Mussolini)*,
the RAAM *(Reparti di Azione Anticomunista Monarchici)*, the
ABIRAC *(Arditi Bianchi Italiani Reparti Anticomunisti)*, and so
on. None of these formations had the attributes which would justify
their being called conspiracies; more often they were just bands,
little units hoping to be used in the struggle against Communism,
or else tiny groups waiting for the creation of a new great party,
a 'national front' against the 'red peril'. Meanwhile they were split
by personal rivalries or by differences of opinion which often
brought them into conflict with one another. The activities of these
clandestine armed bands were sporadic and of modest proportions—
attacks on the premises of the democratic parties, and in particular
on those of the Communist Party, the distribution of leaflets and
'souvenirs' of the defunct Duce, the laying of black banners near
plaques commemorating partisans, and so on.

These extremists gave their exploits names reminiscent of adventure stories, such as 'Black Bear', 'Camel', or 'Scorpion', thereby
showing that most of their members were mere schoolboys or
readers of comic strips. On 22 April 1946 Domenico Leccisi, who
later became an MSI deputy, stole Mussolini's body from the
Musocco cemetery in Milan. After his arrest a letter was found in
his pocket addressed to the President of the Republic, which said:
'You think that you have suppressed the Fascist movement because
Mussolini's body has been recovered. It isn't true; the idea will
live on.' And Leccisi had left a tragi-comic message in the grave
at Musocco: 'At last, O Duce, we have you with us. We will

surround you with roses, but the odour of your virtues will be stronger than that of the roses.'⁹

In the summer of 1946, after the arrest of Captain Faccini, the public was informed of the existence in Lombardy of a clandestine army of 25,000 Fascists, 'armed to the teeth' and 'mobilizable within four hours'.¹⁰ But these were the ravings of fanatics, the braggings of a melodramatic 'terrorism'. In reality the neo-Fascist revival had safer refuges; the *Uomo Qualunque* provided a rallying-point for the less courageous 'nostalgics', who were undoubtedly in the majority; the others met a few at a time; they had neither the ability nor the courage to organize themselves and were content to be merely supporters of *'Qualunquismo'*. In any case, Giannini's party could not satisfy the expectations of the Fascists. 'Qualun-quismo' rejected all accusations of nostalgia, fostered tendencies which Mussolini's disciples described as 'belly-filling' and sought to ally itself with the conservative right wing. Moreover, the play-wright who was its leader did not seem inclined to associate with personages of the defunct régime, and when he did throw out feelers in the political sphere, they were towards the Liberals and Christian Democrats rather than the other parties. In fact, when Francesco Saverio Nitti was about to form his 'National Reconstruction Front' with its semi-qualunquista programme, Giannini approached him, and negotiations were started with a view to amalgamating the two movements; this caused anxiety among the Liberals, since the constitution of such a *bloc* might have left them behind in the race to capture the votes of conservative elements.

This backsliding of the *Uomo Qualunque* into democratic alliances and the by this time obvious passive attitude of the State towards 'nostalgic' outbursts, convinced a number of former Fascist leaders that the time was now ripe for an official reappear-ance of Fascism. On 26 December 1946, at a house in Via Regina Elena, Rome, there was a meeting between a certified public accountant named Arturo Michelini, former vice-secretary of the party in Rome, the journalist Giorgio Pini, the archaeologist Biagio Pace, Pino Romualdi, who claimed to be an illegitimate son of Mussolini, and the trade unionist Francesco Galanti. They decided to form the *Movimento Sociale Italiano* (MSI), based on the political ideas which had inspired the 'revolutionary' Fascism of 1919 and the 'eighteen points' of the Verona manifesto. A party statute was drawn up, article one reading as follows: 'The MSI is a political organization, inspired by an ethical conception of life, its aim being to defend the dignity and the interests of the Italian people and realize a social ideal in the uninterrupted progress of history . . .'; while in article four we read: 'The following are unworthy to belong to the MSI: a) those who are proved to have shown grave incoherence in their political ideas; b) those who have betrayed their country and failed in their duties as citizens and soldiers.'[11]

The birth of this party, which adopted the symbol of a funeral bier with an Italian tricolour protruding from it—the usual macabre Fascist allegory—denoting the perpetuity of an idea nourished by the body of the Duce, brought flocking into its ranks thousands of ex-supporters of the Republic of Salò and attracted such generous financial 'contributions' that within a few months the MSI was able to open branches all over Italy and to indulge in a costly publicity campaign. Approximate statistics show that between 1946 and 1950 twenty-five neo-Fascist publications were circulating in the country. One year after its foundation the MSI was able to enter the political arena reinforced by a large number of ex-followers of Giannini, who hastily abandoned the declining *Uomo Qualunque*. This was a promising beginning. Eulogies of Fascism filled the pages of the MSI periodicals or of others which supported it; abuse of the Resistance movement became the order of the day. The MSI promised to cleanse the 'stinking' atmosphere of Italy by throwing the revolutionary 'indefatigable younger generation' into the attack. The young men who eagerly clamoured for the formation of armed squads were employed in operations for which the MSI naturally accepted no responsibility, but with which it sympathized in a pretty obvious way. In February 1946, for example, a group of these *arditi* managed to occupy the radio station on Monte Mario near Rome and broadcast propaganda slogans accompanied by the cadences of *Giovinezza*. The party denied having organized this exploit, but left no one in doubt that it approved the idea.

In view of the increasing audacity shown by the 'nostalgics', on 3 December 1947 the government and parliament passed the 'law for the repression of neo-Fascist activities'. This came into force during a phase in the political struggle which was unfavourable for its application by the organs of a State that was still to a great extent in the toils of the bureaucracy of the Fascist era. At that time the majority forming the government was appealing to all the 'healthy elements' to form a solid anti-Communist front in order to offer the necessary resistance to the subversive 'plans' of the

Left, which it was alleged would lead to a Bolshevist régime if the general election in the Spring of 1948 gave a victory to the 'Popular Front'.

The 'tame' Fascists and the 'hard core'

When Togliatti, the then Minister of Justice, proclaimed an amnesty in 1946, this was certainly not a positive contribution by the left wing to the efforts to prevent a Fascist revival. It was a good idea to introduce a measure which showed that democracy had no intention of persecuting thousands of citizens guilty of minor offences during the Salò régime, but it was speedily transformed into a legal instrument that could be interpreted in so many different ways that it afforded ample scope for over-indulgent judges—some of whom welcomed the opportunity—to apply it in a manner which favoured authentic criminals. The special assize courts dealt with a large number of cases in a remarkably speedy way, and by the end of 1947 most of the sentences covered by the amnesty had been reviewed and the majority of the accused had been acquitted, or at all events released from custody.[12]

This batch of ex-Fascists and ex-*Repubblichini* thought that they had been rehabilitated and restored to liberty by a State which had not sufficient energy to punish the crimes committed under Fascism, and that they could now exploit this easy-going and tolerant attitude which left them unpunished. Confidence in their immunity was thus added to a feeling that they had been victimized, and they rushed to join the ranks of the neo-Fascist activists. Moreover, the confusion of ideas and the making of false moral and political comparisons were heightened by the efforts made by the Communists to reconcile ex-partisans and 'bona fide' ex-*Repubblichini*. Striking examples were provided by the demonstrations at Perugia and in Rome, among those present being Ezio Maria Gray, General Operti, former commander of the Piedmontese partisans (who had for a few months commanded the regional corps of volunteers, but had quarrelled with the local liberation committee and been deprived of his command for contacting the Fascists with a view to putting an end to partisan warfare), and Cino Moscatelli, ex-commander of the 'Garibaldi' formations in the Ossola valley. These Communist initiatives met with little success; in fact they caused an indignant reaction among those who had fought as volunteers in the war of liberation, and even among Communist partisans.

Accordingly they were soon stopped, before they had achieved their aim, which was to attract those *Repubblichini* of good faith away from the 'nostalgics' (though nothing could have been more puerile than an 'equalization' of the two fronts as a preliminary to a real understanding). They had provided neo-Fascism with a fresh proof that the rulers of the democratic State were on the point of yielding, and fresh motives for vaunting their own role in the political arena. Then again, the atmosphere of an anti-Communist crusade, fanned by the Christian Democrat leaders, by the policy of the Vatican and the attitude of the conservative right wing, not only widened the scope of the MSI, but also gave it a role in the task which was being undertaken, that of reuniting the conservative and reactionary fronts. The Catholic Action movement and the 'civic committees' set up by Professor Luigi Gedda fomented a hysterical campaign based on fear of the Communists and a desire to 'appease' the Fascists. The Jesuit Father Lombardi, popularly known as 'God's microphone', travelled from one pulpit and one city square to another, preaching the most virulent anti-Communism, calling down curses on the 'Reds' and appealing to Heaven to smite all those who cherished left-wing ideas. There were feverish negotiations between the 'civic committees' and the nostalgic right-wingers, combined with exorcisms on the part of Professor Carlo Carretto, a Catholic Action delegate who, between writing essays on conjugal hygiene and dissertations on public morality, conducted a fanatical and grotesque campaign against any *rapprochement* between Catholics and 'subversives'. In November 1947 a 'committee for the defence of republican institutions' was set up, which had, as its chairman Randolfo Pacciardi, the vice-premier. The functions of this committee, Maurizio Ferrara tells us, 'were somewhat vague, but in reality it was a supra-Ministry for Internal Affairs, whose main concern was the electoral campaign. Its first resolutions were "measures designed to prevent disorder and subversive acts" and "precautions regarding problems arising from the known presence of foreign agitators".'[13]

Just before the general election in the spring of 1948 this clerico-conservative paroxysm reached its highest point. This was all to the advantage of neo-Fascism, so much so that the statistics of its organizations were enriched by the advent of new groups with an action-squad bias, such as the SFAI *(Schieramento Forze Anti-bolsceviche Italiane e Internazionali)*, the TN *(Truppe Nazionali)*, the MACI *(Movimento Anti Comunista Italiano)*, the **PARI**

(Partito Azione Rivoluzionaria Italiana), the CSI *(Circolo Solidarietà Internazionale)*, the MNS *(Missione Nazionale Sociale)*, the PFI *(Partito Fusionista Italiano)*, the PR *(Partito del Reduce*=Ex-soldiers' Party), the MIF *(Movimento Italiano Femminile)*, and so on. At the general election on 18 April 1948 the MSI polled 525,408 votes, obtaining six seats in the Lower House and one in the Senate. Amidst the exultation of the conservative and right-wing elements caused by the defeat of the Popular Front, this achievement of the MSI, by no means sensational but nevertheless noteworthy, was held to be what it actually was—half a million 'nostalgics' ready to join forces with the anti-Communist and anti-Socialist elements and eventually to form part of a united right-wing front. Meanwhile, among the neo-Fascists those elements began to gain ground who favoured a solution of this sort, especially when it came to the question of an alliance with the monarchists. The columns of the neo-Fascist papers were filled with articles calling for a change in the MSI's emblem, by adding beneath the bier the heraldic figure-of-eight knot of the Savoy family and thus proclaiming the renewed loyalty of the Fascists to the monarchy.[14] Attilio Crepas, a journalist of the Fascist régime, was offered the weekly *Brancaleone* so that he might conduct a campaign in favour of a *rapprochement* with the Catholics and show that the Fascists were the only true defenders of the Church. Signs of a reunion with the 'national forces' also came from the resurrected 'D'Annunzio groups', who devoted themselves to glorifying the poet of Gardone and welcomed into their ranks ex-Fiume legionaries, nationalists of the old school and retired generals.

The new leader of the MSI was Giorgio Almirante, ex-editor of the Fascist daily *Tevere*, former secretary to the editorial department of the racialist review *Difesa della Razza* and private secretary to the Minister for Popular Culture in the days of the Salò Republic. Nominally, the 'nostalgic' party was solidly behind Almirante and his committee, flourishing the eighteen points of the Verona manifesto, preaching the 'truths of revolutionary Fascism' and repudiating 'democratic pollution' and 'the vile practices of effete party politics'. But a process of erosion was already undermining the neo-Fascist front and preparing the way for differences of opinion which subsequently led to defections. A 'second wave' had entered the party—'hierarchs' of the Fascist régime and ex-inmates of the 'criminal Fascists' camps' like Roberto Mieville and Giovanni Roberti. Of those in the former category the most eminent were Marshal Rodolfo Graziani; Prince Junio Valerio Borghese, commander of the Tenth MTB Flotilla during the Salò period; Augusto De Marsanich, Assistant Postmaster-General during the Fascist era; Cesare Maria De Vecchi di Val Cismon, one of the 'quadrumvirs' at the time of the 'March on Rome'; Ezio Maria Gray, etc. These men brought to the MSI the opportunist and calculating realism of leaders who had learned from experience, who viewed with suspicion the 'socializers' of Salò and were determined to steer the party ship into the calmer waters of the traditional clericomonarchical right wing, seeking and, when it seemed advantageous, concluding very solid alliances by normal parliamentary means. In short, they thought that the 'subversivism' of the survivors of Salò was dangerous and liable to recoil upon itself; that the 'revolutionary' intransigence of such men lacked realism and might lead them into a blind alley of useless appeals to revolt or of clandestine activities which might eventually lead to the banning of all 'nostalgic' organizations, including the MSI. Since they favoured the formation of a large party to which even the 'traitors of 25 July' would be admitted, many of the leaders of this more moderate trend argued that the days of 'action squads' were over; for them the crucial problem was how to penetrate into the citadel of the democratic State through legitimate channels without missing any chance of forming part of the anti-Communist front, though they still thought it a good thing that the MSI should unofficially preserve its role of a party conducting a struggle outside the law. Their appearance and the first symptoms of the trend their policy was taking alarmed the left wing of the MSI headed by Pini, Concetto Pettinato, Ernesto Massi, Clavenzani and, more warily, by Almirante, as well as the scattered bands and groups of neo-Fascists with 'squadristic' or extreme views, prominent among them being the Milanese groups controlled by Domenico Leccisi.

These handfuls of 'pure' Fascists were scandalized by the offer made to the 'traitors of 25 July' to join the ranks of the MSI, and denounced in scathing terms the plans to repress the revolutionary spirit still prevalent among the 'hierarchs' who had just re-entered political life. The 'realist' wing led by Michelini, De Marsanich, Roberti and Caradonna, was bent on achieving its own aim, and at a committee meeting held in Lucca at the end of 1947 it seemed certain that the 'Saloists' would be decisively beaten. The reaction of the extremist faction was violent; they poured a torrent of abuse on the advocates of a swing towards the right and took their revenge by intensifying their campaign of sabotage and terrorism, throwing grenades and bombs at the offices of partisan associations, organizing punitive expeditions, scrawling slogans exalting the Republic of Salò on the walls of houses, etc., etc. The political atmosphere in the country after the fateful date of 18 April 1948 favoured a tolerant attitude towards these upsurgings of Fascism and in general towards anything that, originating on the right wing, gave indirect support to the government policy of a return to normal and to the counter-attack against the Left by organizing anti-Communist demonstrations in the streets or by political collaboration on the parliamentary level.

In 1950, the then Minister for the Interior, Scelba, acting on instructions received from the Christian Democrat leaders, put the finishing touches to the plan to raise a 'corps of civilian volunteers' to help the *carabinieri*, while on 23 August the cabinet, 'besides deciding to increase the strength of the police', created in the Ministry for the Interior a 'directorate-general of civil defence services' with power to enrol volunteers.[15] The government organs and the coalition 'centre' parties denied that the aim of this law authorizing the formation of a 'civil defence corps' was to create a party militia; but the text of the bill confirmed the most pessimistic fears, since it gave the government power to decide the nature of emergencies requiring the intervention of 'civilian volunteers' and foreshadowed the creation of a corps of recruits who would in reality be a kind of special 'guard' under the orders of the Minister for the Interior.[16] The law was passed in July 1951; in the same month Premier De Gasperi appeared at a congress of Catholic partisans and made a warm appeal to the delegates to hold themselves ready to play an active role in the defence of the country 'side by side with the forces of law and order, in the event of an emergency'.[17]

The congress discussed and approved the proposals put forward by the president of the association, the engineer Enrico Mattei, chairman of the *Azienda Generale Italiana Petroli* (AGIP). These included the appointment of members of the association as 'white guards' with the following duties:

1) In factories and offices, to keep under observation any groups advocating disobedience, which is an embryonic form of sabotage, or any attempts to interfere with the freedom of association and the right to work, or any threats to the effective functioning and productivity of firms; 2) to prevent the execution of political plans

for passive resistance, whether open or camouflaged as trade-union activities; 3) to discover and forestall any attempt to create underground organizations, whether or not of a military character; 4) to watch out for and report on all the adversary's sources of funds and take the necessary measures regarding them; 5) to forestall and help to repress any clandestine attempts to obtain information concerning the country's nerve-centres, whether civil or military; 6) to co-operate with the forces of law and order in discovering caches of arms and ammunition, to find out where these came from and the methods and means used by subversives to obtain supplies, and all other matters connected therewith; 7) to combat the progressive poisoning of minds and prevent the weaker members of society from being influenced by hostile propaganda, especially when combined with forms of coercion; 8) to prevent the appointment of Communists to positions of authority and responsibility, having obtained which they become so many Pontecorvos; 9) to thwart the criminal solidarity whereby only Communist artists (painters, sculptors, musicians, authors, producers and so on) dominate exhibitions and competitions, obtain prizes awarded out of public funds, benefit undeservedly from publicity campaigns in the Press which bring them notoriety, and lastly poison the minds of all those who read, listen to and admire the works for which prizes are awarded; 10) to accustom themselves and to accustom others to think that the whole world, the concept of good and evil, the sense of honour and respect for the human individual, have different meanings for Communists than they have for other people.[18]

This decalogue, which might have been drawn up by the *Opus Dei*, the Spanish clerical-Fascist organization, remained a dead letter for most partisans, and the same might be said of the 'civil defence' law (approved in parliament by a tiny majority), but both of them bear witness to the prevailing atmosphere of entreaties, appeals and exhortations to which the neo-Fascists complacently responded, asserting that for them, too, the problem was more or less the same and that as for keeping an eye on Communism (by this time 'anti-Communism' had come to mean repressive action against the workers' trade unions and the sabotaging of political movements which did not see eye to eye with the government), they had undoubtedly been first in the field.

The trend towards the right introduced into Italian politics by the Christian Democrat leaders culminated in April 1952 in the proposal put forward by Don Sturzo, just before the municipal elections in Rome, that a 'civic' list of candidates should be prepared by the four parties in power and that it should include candidates from the National Monarchical Party and the MSI. Don Sturzo's initiative, the aim of which was to 'prevent Rome, the capital of Christendom, from becoming a branch-office of Moscow and an obedient servant of the Kremlin',[19] was supported by Professor Gedda and the right-wing Christian Democrats. It failed because it put the De Gasperi government in an awkward position and was opposed by the other parties to the coalition, but it was taken up again in other quarters and marked the beginning of attempts to conclude alliances between the Christian Democrats and the parties of the extreme right wing. This introduced the MSI into local government affairs and made it a kind of sub-government, no longer isolated as it had been hitherto.

The 'nostalgics' were busily expanding their organizations and approved the legal proceedings against partisans which the courts had started in the meantime, while at the same time there were sensational acquittals of men who had fought for the Republic of Salò, of Fascist leaders and of those who had made money out of the Fascist régime. In June 1952 the Scelba law came into force, which provided for the disbanding of all parties obviously drawing their inspiration from Fascist programmes and methods. This law, as the Minister who introduced it was at pains to make clear, was aimed at the MSI and the neo-Fascist groups, but Concetto Pettinato, whose break with the party of Michelini was by now a foregone conclusion, gave an interpretation of it which was not very far from the truth when he wrote in the *Meridiano d'Italia*:

> The aim is to make the MSI a more or less moderate, clerical and pro-NATO party which will not only cease to be a nuisance to the government, but will also be useful because it will provide the government with an organization which may at last bridge the gap between the old and the new ruling class, between the clericals of today and the Fascists of yesterday.[20]

In other words, Pettinato maintained that the Scelba law was a species of blackmail rather than a threat to use the police; and in fact it was never applied. At the party conference held in L'Aquila exactly a month after the passing of the Scelba law, the general staff of the 'old guard' won the day. Prince Valerio Borghese indignantly repudiated the accusations of totalitarianism brought against the party; De Marsanich stressed the need for 'national appeasement' and deplored all violence and thirst for vengeance; Caradonna offered the Church the support of the neo-Fascists, which he claimed would be more valuable and sincere than that of the Christian Democrat Party. The MSI's original slogan: 'There are three solutions—Russia, United States, or MSI', disappeared from its propaganda. The neo-Fascists of Michelini—who was steadily outdistancing his colleagues in the race for the leadership—became supporters of the Atlantic Treaty and left all the theorizing about a 'third force' to Edmondo Cione, who had resumed his efforts to propound the ideas which had been the main reason for Mussolini's somewhat uncomplimentary remarks.

The three opposing trends within the MSI could now be roughly defined as follows. The 'old hands' and the 'realists' strove to obtain a firm foothold in the right-wing front, abandoning all ideological formulas and accepting the help of any allies they could find. In February 1950, in the course of a speech he made in the Adriano theatre in Rome, De Marsanich suggested an alliance with the Monarchists and the Liberals, and it was in this direction that his faction tended. Then there was a 'left wing' of 'corporative socializers' who took as their basis the Verona manifesto and criticized the old Fascist régime. And lastly there was a trend, destined soon to disappear, which attracted all those who called themselves 'spiritualists' and, practically speaking, were racialist disciples of Julius Evola or the neo-Nazis, open to the ideas of Priester and Engdahl. European unity again occupied a prominent place in neo-Fascist appeals, and since there was much talk of European federalism, to which the Western powers gave a marked anti-Communist bias, the MSI asserted that Fascists had always believed in European unity as 'a bulwark of Western ideas against Bolshevism' and had done their best to achieve it.

The reaction of the 'extreme left wing' towards this sudden swing towards the right on the part of the MSI leaders was, as we have already said, violent. In reply to an article in *Lotta d'Italia*, the organ of the pro-NATO faction, which said: 'We choose the West, without mincing words, without any false regrets and without hesitation; and unarmed neutralism will certainly not be able to stop the Bolshevik armies,'[21] Concetto Pettinato published in the *Meridiano d'Italia* a 'warning to industrialists', hinting that support of the Atlantic Treaty was contrary to their own interests. 'Beware of putting a cord round your necks with your own hands!' the Fascist journalist wrote:

> Send to Palazzo Chigi a man who's got a head on his shoulders and will return to the policy of the years 1933–34, the policy which led no less a man than Mussolini to sign a pact of friendship with Russia and made Russia the most faithful supporter of internal

order in our country. Help to free Europe from the mad idea that it is impossible to co-exist with a régime with which we—yes, we—lived on amicable terms from 1920 to 1941, until we made our greatest mistake, the consequences of which have been tragic—the error of not continuing to live in peace with Russia, instead of waging war against her.[22]

Another journalist, Stanis Ruinas, editor of *Il Pensiero Nazionale*, who had been a student during the Fascist years, took up an extreme left-wing position, firing over open sights at Atlantic Treaty capitalism and professing such pro-Soviet ideas that he attracted the attention of the Communist Party. In the lower strata of the extremist opposition, the controversy with the Fascist leaders was carried on by means of broadsides of a typically Fascist kind. 'So we are back on the dunghill of compromises!' we read in *Avanti Ardito!*, '. . . those poltroons who, the moment they come up against opposition, are ready to let their pants down, they and their wives as well.'[23] *Asso di Bastoni*, the Fascist weekly with the largest circulation (perhaps 100,000 copies between 1950 and 1952), edited by Caporilli, a former editor of the *Domenica del Corriere* in the days of the Salò Republic, was anticlerical and 'Farinaccian', and proclaimed that 'we will spit in the faces of those who have sold themselves to Russia, to America and to the Vatican'.[24] In *Lotta d'Italia* Arturo Giuliano remarked that in the party there was still 'babelic confusion and uncertainty at the bottom, and at the top a frantic chaos of little men running after one another as if they were on a roundabout in their efforts to win the prize, while Italy—the real Italy—is the Great Absentee.'[25]

The dissident Milanese and Roman Fascists were the most violent of all in their accusations against the MSI and in searching for opportunities to proclaim their loyalty to the past. On 4 October 1952, the anniversary of the formation of the Salò army and of the speech made by Marshal Graziani at the Adriano theatre urging Italians to support the Social Republic, two coachloads of former 'hierarchs', 'seniors' and 'centurions' of the Fascist militia left Milan and travelled the length of Italy to reach the Arcinazzo estate in the Pontine Marshes where the ex-Marshal of Italy had established his residence. They were under the command of two men 'all too well known in Milan', Asvero Gravelli, former chief of staff of the Republican National Guard, and Ampelio Spadoni, a former colonel on the staff of the 'Ettore Muti' Black Brigade. The 'nostalgics' pitched their tents in the grounds of the 'Lion of Neghelli's' house, changed from civilian clothes into Fascist uniforms (black shirts, daggers, fezes and leggings) and paraded in front of Graziani, who, with his shoulders covered by a threadbare greatcoat, inspected them and gave the Fascist salute. After this ceremony, a 'comradely meal' was consumed by those present.[26] Immediately afterwards, all over the country there were attacks on the premises of partisan clubs and left-wing organizations and assaults on anti-Fascists, while 'nostalgic' slogans and emblems were scrawled on the walls of houses. Giorgio Pini resigned from the MSI, and his parting words were: 'The MSI is now a reactionary party without a future.'

The Roman 'Ducetto'

'Why should I make a secret of it? Between 1949 and 1955 I took part in all the punitive expeditions. I began when I was fifteen and stopped when I was twenty-one. I was in the punch-ups in Via Margutta and outside Montecitorio. I took part in the raid on the *Rinascita* bookshop in Via delle Botteghe Oscure. I learnt to make bombs out of stuff left in military dumps; I've thrown "crackers"; I've used knuckledusters and truncheons, crowbars and bicycle-chains in scraps with the police and the Reds. I'd be a rich man now if I had as many thousand-lira notes as I've given punches. At eighteen I was an MSI section-leader and my pals used to call me the *"ducetto"*.'[27]

The *'ducetto'* paused for a moment and looked at us as if to gauge our reaction to his opening words. He was a young man not over thirty, prematurely bald and corpulent. If we had not been aware of the real reasons behind his 'conversion', we might have thought that the taverns of Trastevere, which cropped up so often during our conversation, had been responsible for undermining his ability to use a knuckleduster.

'If you're interested,' he went on, 'I can tell you all about the Via Margutta expedition against the supporters of Renzi and Aristarco. You remember what happened? I think it was in 1953, in the autumn; anyway, it was in the afternoon. They told us to assemble at the Prati district office, and we knew why. There must have been about fifty of us, and we were all excited and itching to use our fists. As for me, I hated those two, Renzi and Aristarco, because they said things about the military virtues of the Italian soldier.[28] I remember I started singing: "To arms! We're Fascists," and that I sang it at the top of my voice, getting more and more excited. Then we sang *Giovinezza* and after that *Battaglioni M*, and we didn't stop until the "chief" told us to, and then he started talking about race. He said we were an élite, defenders of the most precious things in Italy and a bulwark against Red barbarism. He said we were "children of the sun" and that pure blood can never lie, and he told us to hit hard. Before we left, someone brought out four bottles of vermouth, which we polished off at a gulp. Then in little groups, so as not to attract attention, we went to the Villa Borghese, where we found a truck with the truncheons. They were wrapped up in newspapers, and carrying them under our arms we went to Via Margutta. Well, I guess you know the rest. It was a scrap to be remembered. I lost a tooth and a tuft of my hair. Nowadays I feel like a criminal when I think of what I did. But you wanted me to tell you everything just as it happened, as if I was speaking just after the fight.'

The story of the man who was speaking to us had begun in the days when the 'vanquished of Salò' were handing on the torch to the young recruits. 'In 1949,' the *'ducetto'* went on, 'I came back to Italy with my family from Asmara. In the Roman suburb where we went to live, we found a whole lot of refugees and ex-soldiers, fed up because of all the unemployment and the overcrowding. The feeling of poverty and discontent couldn't have been more depressing. Was this the Italy, I asked myself, that I used to dream of among the hills of Asmara? Was this collection of hovels, this band of down-and-outs, the imperial Italy my father was always talking about? At the local offices of the MSI, which had just been opened, I found plenty of people ready to answer my questions. There for the first time I heard of the "eighteen points of the Verona manifesto" and of the "Republic of Salò", which had socialized factories, confiscated land and appointed factory committees; of course, nobody told me that this revolution had only been on paper, and I began to dream of a perfect and just world, which only the bloody-mindedness of Communist partisans had succeeded in destroying. After school I always used to go to the local party office. There I always found someone who had served in the army of the Salò Republic and was ready to talk about it. There was one man who had been in the "Barbarigo" battalion, and another who had been with an anti-tank unit in the Gothic Line. The "old 'uns" didn't need to tell us anything about Fascist mysticism to get us all het-up; their stories were quite enough. Soon we found ourselves ready to take their places on expeditions, especially if they were too well known to the police. I got on quickly, because I used to train by boxing in the gym and I was the most determined. My motto was: "We'll put the eighteen points of Verona across with tommy-guns." Today I must confess that neither I nor any of the others knew exactly what the eighteen points were. That didn't matter. We couldn't have cared less about ideology. All we wanted was to feel angry. Personally it tickled me to death when they called me *"ducetto".*' The young man paused for a moment and then made a gesture of boredom. 'You can count by thousands the "actions" that we of the MSI and the other groups carried out in those days,' he said; 'raiding party offices, smashing tablets commemorating partisans, desecrating Jewish cemeteries, setting fire to trade-union offices, anti-Semitic demonstrations, blowing things up, beating people up and throwing paper bombs. What's surprising about that? And then, it wasn't all that dangerous. They nicked us more than once, but they never managed to get us as far as Regina Coeli. Before the seven days were up,[29] we always managed to get away with it. Now, with this centre-left government, things have changed a bit. The fellows who interrupted the celebrations of the seventieth anniversary of the foundation of the Italian Socialist Party ended up in the clink and had to pay the bill for the rest. But in the old days it was grand!'

The Cold War, the pressure exerted by the industrialists in the hope of curbing the claims of the working classes with the help of the authorities and thus completing the process of reorganizing production on monopolistic lines at the expense of the community, the veritable crusade launched by certain ecclesiastical hierarchies and Catholic integralist circles against the left wing—between 1950 and 1952 all these factors provided excellent opportunities for an expansion of the MSI brand of 'legalitarian' neo-Fascism, and at the same time encouraged the subversive and dissident groups within the party. The twenty years of the Mussolini era were glorified even by the Jesuits. On 18 March 1950, the magazine *Civiltà Cattolica* wrote that 'to consider as completely negative the twenty years of Fascist rule has been the not exactly noble achievement of a few Italians, who to the humiliation of the defeat have added the still greater humiliation of a slander on their own country.'[30] At the municipal elections in the spring of 1952 the MSI polled as many as 1,699,859 votes, while at the parliamentary elections on 7 June 1953 they were almost equally successful—1,579,880 votes, equivalent to 5·9 per cent of the total electorate, which gave them twenty-nine seats in the Lower Chamber and eighteen in the Senate. When, after the election, the De Gasperi cabinet fell, the new government under Pella tackled the problem of Trieste and the Free Territory, which had been hanging fire since 1944, thus providing the 'nostalgics' with a chance to transform into violent anti-Yugoslav demonstrations the terms of a delicate problem which had placed democratic Italy in the position of having to pay for all the crimes committed by the Fascist régime against the Slavs.

The swing to the right in government policy received a fresh impulse from the Scelba cabinet, which was a blend of Christian and Social Democrats and took office on 10 March 1954. The new government carried the policy of repression even further than the preceding cabinets, especially in the field of cultural activities and discrimination against the workers (it was the Prime Minister himself who coined the contemptuous term *culturame* to denote left-wing culture). Neo-Fascists swarmed into the streets, celebrating their rites and committing assaults, dressed in the uniforms of the Salò Republic or of the Nazis, and openly glorifying the Fascist régime. The year 1949 saw the formation of the 'National Association of Republican ex-Servicemen' under the chairmanship of Marshal Rodolfo Graziani, which attracted the men who had served in the armed forces or militia of the Salò Republic. On 14 January 1955 the *Associazione Nazionale Arma Milizia* (ANAM) was formed, after which all sorts of groups of ex-*Repubblichini* sprang up, for example those of ex-members of the 'Black Brigades', of the 'Ettore Muti Black Brigade Legion', of the 'Tenth MTB Flotilla', of 'Disabled and Wounded Soldiers of the Social Republic', and so on. The MSI daily, *Il Secolo*, heaped insults on the Resistance and the demonstrations held to commemorate the tenth anniversary of the partisan war, dedicating whole pages to the 'atrocities' committed by partisan bands and glorifying the leading figures of the old régime.[31] In parliament, the government accepted the support of the right-wing parties and the MSI on the question of the Western European Union, in other words the rearming of the German army. In a comment on the looting of the *Rinascita* bookshop in Rome, which appeared in its number for March 1955, *Il Ponte*, the radical magazine, wrote:

> To us it seems that the government is wholly responsible, because—
> even on the parliamentary level and not only outside parliament
> as was the case with the preceding governments—it has finally

accepted the more or less fortuitous alliances and compromises with the forces of the extreme Right. Once again, in the brief history of a united Italy, the decisive factor in the internal democratic development of the country seems to have been foreign policy, in which all 'right-minded' people believe with such a religious fervour that anyone who objects to the rearmament of Germany—whether his reasons be good or bad—is looked upon as a Communist, while those who are in favour of it do not dare to reject the captious interpretation which the Fascists give of this rearmament.[32]

At the MSI's fourth party conference, held at Viareggio in January 1954, the 'swing to the right' suffered a setback. Despite its successes at the elections, the party's 'realist' wing found itself in difficulties, mainly because the implications of the votes it had received and the fact that it had consolidated its position within the right wing, induced the Christian Democrats to try and absorb this faction and thus 'nibble away' the ground beneath the feet of the neo-Fascists. The government's policy, in fact, tended to hamper the MSI's scope for manœuvre, even though it gave the activists among the neo-Fascists a better chance to make themselves heard, and tolerated to a degree it had never done before the attacks on the Resistance launched by 'nostalgic' periodicals and propaganda. At the MSI conference the Christian Democrat Party was consequently described as 'Public Enemy Number One', amidst shouts of 'Down with Churchill' and 'God strafe England' (slogans coined by Mario Appelius in his broadcasts during the closing months of the war), while Giorgio Almirante announced that 'the MSI is the only proletarian party and the only one that has no masters', and Pino Rauti asserted that 'democracy is a disease of the mind'. In 1952 Scelba had asked the '*Missini*' the following question:

> How can anyone maintain that there is any difference between the MSI and Fascism, when everything the Fascists ever did is glorified—and not only in programmes and gestures? If in its songs and its gestures, in its tone and its methods, in its language and its liturgy, the MSI borrows everything from Fascism?[33]

The 'nostalgics' did not even take the trouble to refute these accusations in public. At the funeral of Rodolfo Graziani, who died in January 1955, tens of thousands of neo-Fascists paraded shouting '*Duce! Duce!*' and singing Fascist songs. And the police did not intervene.

By now the MSI had become a full-size party, with a very active youth organization, the *Giovane Italia*; it also had a *Fronte Univer-*

sitario di Azione Nazionale (FUAN) for university students, which (sometimes in alliance with the Monarchists) nominated Fascist or quasi-Fascist candidates at the Students' Union elections, and a trade union called the *Confederazione Italiana Sindacati Nazionali Liberi* (CISNAL), which had few members but ample funds. Under Pella's one-party Christian Democrat government representatives of this Fascist trade union were received for the first time by the Premier, together with those of the other trade unions (CGIL, CISL and UIL), this implying official recognition of its existence as a national organization. The twofold expansion of 'legalitarian' and subversive Fascism proceeded on almost parallel lines. The moral scandals which marked the term in office of the 'centrist' government of Scelba and the Social Democrats helped the Fascist onslaught on the democratic system and created a fresh wave of *'Qualunquismo'*, but this time it was not led by Guglielmo Giannini, but by the faction of Michelini and De Marsanich, with the support of the extremist associations and movements that had sprung up in the meantime. In Turin (where the MSI led a hard life and the other groups numbered only a few adherents) Colonel Massimo Invrea, a dissident member of the MSI, founded a group called *Socialismo Nazionale*, which ran a small periodical of its own, *La prima fiamma*, and demanded the overthrow of the democratic régime and a return to the principles of the Salò Republic. In the same city a judge named Giovanni Durando, editor of *La Voce della Giustizia*, tried to rally proselytes to his dreams of a right-wing clerico-Fascist *rassemblement*, which toyed with the idea of installing a Franco-type authoritarian régime in Italy, with the papacy restored to its role of supreme head of the political system.

Little groups like these were not strong enough to rank as parties or even to extend their activities outside the borders of journalistic controversy. Nevertheless, the very fact that they could voice their opinions in a city with such fervid anti-Fascist and partisan traditions showed how easy-going the authorities were when it came to dealing with the extreme right wing and the spread of 'nostalgic' ideas. Some of these neo-Fascist groups were almost entirely the outcome of the bitter personal quarrels and clan rivalries raging in the 'nostalgic' camp. To take an example, it is quite impossible to grasp what ideological and political differences of opinion distinguished *Socialismo Nazionale* from another group called *Raggruppamento Sociale Repubblicano*, which was founded in Milan and was likewise a haven for ex-*Repubblichini* who had broken away from the MSI. Parties and movements sporting neo-Fascist symbols were born and died within the space of a few months, often without ever getting any further than publishing a manifesto announcing their formation. Normally, all such groups claimed to be the sole owners of the social 'truths' and 'coherence of ideas' of Fascism, pouring accusations and abuse on the other Fascist groups as well as on their anti-Fascist adversaries. Inside the MSI more or less the same thing went on; the major and minor trends exchanged abuse and sanguinary insinuations and were torn by irremedial dissensions. In October 1953, Bruno Spampanato wrote in his weekly magazine, *Noi*:

> Let us try to calculate how many parties we should have to found if we wanted to represent all the trends in the MSI or the fringe parties; there would have to be a 'Corporative State' party, a 'socialization' party, a pro-NATO and Western party, an anti-NATO and mildly pro-East party, one which was both anti-West and anti-East . . . Just count . . . one, two, three, four . . . and we shall get to about twenty.[34]

The depressing interlude of Scelba's 'centrist' government came to an end and the first signs appeared of a revival of the democratic and anti-Fascist elements within the Christian Democrat Party as well as in the left-wing parties as a whole. But it was in these very years and during the leadership crisis in the Christian Democrat Party after the death of De Gasperi that neo-Fascism displayed an unprecedented vitality. The cabinets of Pella and Segni, and more especially the one-party government headed by Zoli, adopted the same easy-going attitude towards the neo-Fascists as their predecessors, condemning them by word of mouth, but including them in their coalitions when it came to municipal elections, and allowing them to carry on their work all over the country without any serious interference. Michelini, who soon showed himself to be a skilful organizer and a clever mediator in the roaring jungle of the MSI, took advantage of the opportunity to get rid of the 'left-wing' elements in his party one by one. His policy, based on an alliance with the Monarchists and offering the Christian Democrats the support of the neo-Fascists whenever they needed it, really brought the party out of its isolation and made it a component part of the Right, which the more important elements among the Christian Democrats treated with due respect.

Worried by the outbursts of internal dissension, Michelini decided to try appeasement; his efforts to reach a compromise with the chaotic but virulent ensemble of Milanese opposition groups were conducted sometimes in pleading and sometimes in imperious tones, but they all proved abortive. Consequently, this ex-Federal Secretary of the Fascist Party in Rome decided that there would have to be a showdown at the next party conference. At the fifth such conference, held at the Dal Verme theatre in Milan in November 1956, the seven hundred MSI delegates, amidst scuffles, shouting and general uproar, heard their leader declare that the party must concentrate on two immediate and concrete objectives—the banning of the Communist Party and the immediate holding of a general election, in order to mobilize public opinion, which had been aroused by the events in Hungary, and take advantage of the situation. 'The MSI', said Michelini, 'is alive and here today; it scorns the idea of remaining stuck in the past.' The extremists hastily circulated their latest slogan—'fewer double-breasted jackets and more knuckledusters'—but they failed to win the day. Giorgio Almirante, who had become the exponent of the adversaries of a 'soft' policy, had had sixteen out of thirty members of the executive committee solidly behind him on the eve of the conference, and they had tendered their resignations in order to show their disapproval of Michelini; but by the end of the session the alliance between centre and right had enabled Michelini to get his resolutions passed and preserve his majority.

This was a setback for Milanese Fascism, and soon afterwards Michelini decided to storm the last outposts in his own baliwicks by making use of faithful followers like Senator Gastone Nencione and the journalist Franco Maria Servello, nephew of D'Agazio, the founder of the *Meridiano d'Italia*, from whom he had inherited that daily.[35]

The 'legalitarian' palingenesis of the MSI for which the 'realists' longed did not definitely exclude subversive activities or glorifications of the old Fascist régime. It wanted both of these to continue without, however, involving the responsibility of the party, in fact in apparent opposition to its methods and precepts. There can be no doubt that the 'realist' controlling faction in the MSI had not the slightest intention of getting involved with the 'commando-type' enterprises of the dozens of subversive groups which flourished in the shadow of the party, nor did they wish to see their own organizations involved in a systematic campaign of sabotage and acts of terrorism. Nevertheless, they could not rid themselves of the action-squad armoury which provided them with the weapons required to attract the younger generation and with the watch-words they needed to keep up their enthusiasm, despite the competition of the heresies fomented by the 'left wing'.

Michelini wanted the MSI to acquire a middle-class respectability, but he could not ignore the fact that his position in parliament and his opportunism needed to be counterbalanced by at least a minimum of 'fidelity' to the formulas of the Blackshirt *avant-garde*; otherwise, the younger generation, on which the party's foundations rested and which was attracted only by exaltations of the past and by revolutionary activist myths, would have drifted away. It was for this reason that the MSI's youth organization, *Giovane Italia*, consisting mainly of secondary school students and led by Massimo Anderson and Giulio Caradonna, maintained its own character of an organization which engaged in provocative demonstrations against anti-Fascists, the looting of left-wing bookshops, the beating-up of individuals and punitive expeditions. In the long list of neo-Fascist exploits, the mark of the *Giovane Italia* could be seen time after time, and the names of some of its members also appeared. This proves that the MSI, although it claimed to know nothing about such episodes, was in reality pursuing a policy of subversive activities, to which it resorted whenever they seemed to serve its own ends.[36]

Fernando Tambroni, a would-be dictator

The heretical groups within the MSI deliberately kept aloof from normal political activities and devoted themselves to studying the theorists of racialism and the National Socialist rehashes produced by men like Karl-Heinz Priester, Einar Aberg, Per Engdahl, Gunnar Cedeberg, Julius Evola, and so on. In Rome a section of *Ordine Nuovo* was founded, a movement drawing its inspiration from the themes of the *Nouvel Ordre Européen* on the one hand and the racialist theories of Evola on the other. Pino Rauti, an exponent of the MSI 'left wing', took command of this group and 'cells' were soon set up in several Italian cities. With *Ordine Nuovo* there reappeared in Italy in an integral form those vitalistic myths and pan-European visions with which we dealt when discussing the years of the Second World War. Naturally, squabbles and rivalries soon broke out in this new movement, which, as a result of a whole series of schisms, gave birth to the 'aristocratic' sect of the 'Children of the Sun', the 'National Youth Front', and the '*Avant-garde*

of National Youth', microcosms which soon exhausted the
supply of recruits from certain middle-class circles and the
Roman *jeunesse dorée*, and abandoned themselves to the pleasures
of celebrating esoteric rites (for example, the '*Avant-garde* of National Youth', despite its dynamic name, would appear to have
consisted of Stefano Dalle Chiaie and four of his friends, who
achieved notoriety in 1961 thanks to a 'courageous' exploit—the
removal of the flag of the Resistance, decorated with the gold medal
for valour, from the Tomb of the Unknown Soldier in Rome).
Most of these groups maintained (and still maintain) their links
with the MSI, if for no other reason because Michelini's party
used to summon them, together with *Giovane Italia*, whenever it
was in its own interest to use them for the customary *coups de
main*. Other sects, for example *Giovane Nazione* (which had its
headquarters in Milan), adopted polemical attitudes towards the
MSI and sometimes caused embarrassment as regards relations with
neo-Fascist and neo-Nazi organizations in other countries.[37]

The beginning of a 'thaw' in international politics and the consequent slowing-down of right-wing activities took some of the
bite out of neo-Fascist policy after 1956. The little groups and
extremist factions continued to let off steam by committing the customary acts of sabotage, but on occasions they encountered a more
prompt and drastic reaction from the police. Having broken with
the Monarchists and finding itself hampered by the quenching of
the fires which had encouraged the more extreme aspects of the
'crusade' against Communism, the MSI relapsed into its former
isolation, notwithstanding all its efforts not to lose touch with the
right-wing Christian Democrats and their claims, which still had a
preponderating influence on government policy. For the 'nostalgics',
however, the outlook seemed gloomy. The 'thaw' had stolen much
of their thunder and made it embarrassing and inopportune for the
Christian Democrats and Liberals to maintain the alliance with the
MSI which they had concluded a few years before. The remarkable
economic boom in the country and the new dimensions assumed
by the problem of marketing products made it essential for the
more progressive monopolistic groups to change their attitude towards the workers, since the new planned economy was guided
by directives more consonant with the new turn events were taking.
A strategy based on the idea of 'one wall against another', on a
frontal attack on the workers, on 'witch-hunting' and McCarthyism,
proved to be inadequate and was abandoned by these dynamic

sectors of capitalism in favour of methods for which activist neo-Fascism was neither suitable nor opportune. The neo-capitalist choice of a policy of reform (made possible by the very high level of profits), and the consequent preference for political alliances which would help to realize that policy, relegated the extremist forces of the old-fashioned right wing to the background, those very forces that had been the protagonists of the reconstruction period.

This new turn in events paved the way for the political trend generally known as the 'centre-left'. But its emergence in the first few months of 1960 caused immediate alarm among all the more reactionary elements of the conservative front. In the Christian Democrat Party, the right wing and the 'Scelbian' centre at once tried to avert this danger. The right-wing Vatican hierarchies, led by prelates like the Cardinal-Archbishop of Genoa, Monsignor Siri, aided and abetted this alarmist campaign and openly sided with the adversaries of the 'centre-left' trend; the *Confederazione Generale dell'Industria Italiana*, mainly through the *Assolombarda* (association of Lombard industrialists), manœuvred to intimidate the majority party by using men like Pella and Togni, who were the mouthpieces of the most retrograde sectors of Italian finance. After the failure in March of the negotiations to form a centre-left government—negotiations which were thought to have already been concluded—a cabinet was formed under the premiership of Fernando Tambroni. If we are to believe official sources, the Tambroni government was intended to be a 'caretaker' or 'business' government pending a resumption of negotiations as soon as the horizon had cleared, with the ultimate aim of finding a 'centre-left' solution. On the other hand it was observed that the new Prime Minister belonged to that 'left-wing' sector of the Christian Democrat Party which was favourable to the new trend in policy; for which reason —it was explained—the centre-left programme would find in him a man who in a certain sense was its forerunner. And lastly—still according to official sources—Tambroni enjoyed the confidence of the President of the Republic, Giovanni Gronchi, whose ideas tallied with those of the Deputy from the Marches. Nevertheless, in the brief space of a few months it became clear that Tambroni intended to tackle the problems of pressure from the workers (which had become more urgent owing to the disparity between profits and wages, between the cost of living and the purchasing power of money) by resorting to methods dating from the days of the Scelba government. The police and *carabinieri* proceeded to deal with strikes in a brutal way undoubtedly inspired by instructions from above; the government's economic measures seemed to be merely safeguarding the speculation which was rife throughout the country; an atmosphere of blackmail and sinister intrigue pervaded the top levels of political life, and rumours were current that the Premier himself had ordered the police to check up on all members of parliament and on his own colleagues in the government.

From the very beginning the cabinet was torn by dissensions in the ranks of the DC and these brought about its fall on the eve of 25 April. Negotiations were then resumed with a view to forming a centre-left government with Fanfani as Prime Minister, but a week later there was another dispute and Tambroni's name was again put forward. At the beginning of May his second cabinet was launched, thanks to the support of the MSI. Two months later the situation, which had already been tense, became explosive. The Prime Minister, hailed in certain Vatican circles as 'the wise and strong man', showed arrogant authoritarian tendencies, while the 'nostalgics', emboldened by their unaccustomed success, which had brought them to power, demanded that the government should adopt a 'policy of force' in dealing with the agitation among workers and 'restore order'. The MSI leaders thought that the time had come to convene a party conference and announced that, with the consent of the government, it would be held in Genoa, under the chairmanship of Carlo Emanuele Basile, a former Fascist prefect of the city, whose name had figured in the list of war criminals. The provocative nature of this announcement was obvious.

Genoa, which had been awarded the gold medal of the Resistance, reacted by appealing to all the anti-Fascist elements in Italy. An anti-Fascist demonstration was organized in the Ligurian capital on 30 June; the police turned out armed to the teeth and charged the crowd. This was the signal for a veritable revolt of the population. For almost forty-eight hours, after the police had been reduced to impotence, the city remained practically in the hands of the insurgent anti-Fascists and workers. The 'Federal Council of the Resistance', which had established itself in the city, asked the Prime Minister to cancel the permit given to the MSI to hold its conference in Genoa. The 'nostalgics', besieged in their hotels, had to depart a few at a time in police jeeps. The government was obliged to capitulate, but a few days later, at Reggio Emilia, the police reacted even more violently against the demonstrators, killing five of them. The anti-Fascists at once mobilized their forces to counter this resurgence of authoritarianism. Tambroni then made preparations to use troops and went to the President of the Republic to obtain emergency powers. Giovanni Gronchi, whose attitude during the whole matter had not been too clear, was compelled to ask Tambroni to resign. The country was a powder-magazine. The right-wing parties were cowed by the reaction of the masses in Genoa and Reggio Emilia.[38]

That was the end of the Tambroni government, but its term of office had shown only too clearly that the resurgence of Fascism was due to the prevalence among the DC and its ramifications of subversive reactionary ideas which linked the 'Dorothean' (or right-wing) and 'Scelbian' tendencies with certain Vatican circles and with important elements in the worlds of industry and finance, with probable ramifications in the army and among the *carabinieri*. The MSI had played the part of shock-troops, had provided parliamentary support for the manœuvre and its action squads for the first clash in the streets, which was necessary in order to give the State an excuse to intervene against the Left and anti-Fascism in general.

Michelini's 'nostalgics' felt that they had never before been so close to realizing their most fervid aspirations. 'We went to Genoa animated by the best intentions,' Filippo Anfuso said later:

> If they had only let us hold our conference there, we would have explained our programme, outlined our democratic convictions and given guarantees. I will even say more. If the DC had made an effort to understand our intentions and had welcomed us into the government, we should have disappeared as a party. Instead of which they threw us overboard, in the way everyone knows. But we shall continue to refute all accusations of totalitarianism, because the electorate has conferred upon us the blessings of legality. It was the electors with their votes who sent us to Montecitorio and have furnished the best proof that we are democrats.[39]

It may well be true that the Genoa party conference was intended to emphasize the complete adherence of the MSI to the type of 'legality' and 'democratic spirit' installed in Italy by the Tambroni government. It is, however, less likely that the 'nostalgics' were ready to commit political suicide by disappearing as a separate party, unless we are to believe that the DC's *volte-face* had been so rapid and on such a scale that the Catholic elements in the party were willing to act as guardians of a Salazar-type régime or something similar. This, however, is a matter for pure conjecture. What was a reality was that, fifteen years after the collapse of the

Fascist régime, the neo-Fascists had come very close to getting back to power, not by their own efforts, but by acting as shock-troops for the Right, always on the lookout for a *casus belli* that would enable it to crush Italian democracy.

The striking feature about the events of July 1960 was that they showed that the danger of a return to an authoritarian régime of the Mussolini type came from the very party which was then in power; that Fascist aspirations lay hidden in those very institutions whose duty it was to safeguard republican democracy, and that Tambroni's experiment had had the tacit consent or connivance of Catholic leaders who were believed to be staunch supporters of the democratic spirit and of progressive ideas. All these things were far more important than any criticism of the part played by the MSI and the other 'nostalgic' organizations in the attempted *coup d'état*. As usual, they had preferred to play a subordinate role, in the hope of reaping rewards for their services.

The disciples of Rosenberg

In November 1957, Count Vanni Teodorani, a nephew of Mussolini and a leading figure in Italian neo-Fascism, was sent to trial for stating: 'We used to burn Jews in the furnaces.'[40] In May 1958 members of the MSI marched through the streets of Rome cheering Mussolini and shouting 'Death to the Jews', and tablets commemorating Jews who had died in the concentration camps were defaced by 'nostalgics'. This racial hatred on the part of the neo-Fascists vented itself in July 1960 on the Jewish quarter of the capital; bands of youths, armed with sticks and chains and shouting Fascist slogans, looted shops and beat up passers-by. The Jews reacted and the leader of the expedition, Franco Cecchetti, was injured and admitted to hospital.

The capture and subsequent trial of Adolf Eichmann in 1961 caused the anti-Jewish agitation to flare up again. Giovanni Durando, the editor of *La Voce della Giustizia*, who in the meantime had become adviser to the 'Civil Order Centre' in Turin, appeared before a court in Genoa charged with having written a newspaper article in which, among other monstrous statements, he attempted to clear the names of the Nazi murderers by saying that 'the Jews, because they refused to recognize, officially and juridically, the divine innocence of Christ, must be considered deicides in the legal sense of the term, deliberate and perpetual authors of the crucifixion of Jesus, who for that reason must be deprived of the authority to judge anyone not of their persuasion'; and in another passage: 'The Jews have no moral sense that can be considered to have any weight whatsoever.'[41] The judges found that their colleague had not committed an indictable offence and the neo-Fascists greeted the news of his acquittal with jubilation.

Swastikas and anti-Jewish slogans were painted on the houses and pavements of many Italian cities to honour the memory of Eichmann, when he was hanged in Israel after a trial which had revealed the most revolting aspects of the Nazi criminal machine down to the minutest detail to public opinion throughout the world. Benito De Domenico, secretary of *Giovane Italia*, distributed leaflets printed by his organization, saying:

> International Jewry, with the tacit consent of the Western democracies, has made a new victim in the person of Eichmann, the noble survivor of a heroic phalanx most of whose members gave their lives at Nuremberg, in the name of the sublime principles which were to have created a New European Order. Eichmann, we swear never to forget you, and to avenge you when the moment shall come![42]

De Domenico was arrested and the same fate usually befell those of his imitators whom the police could identify. After the Tambroni interlude, in fact, the organs of the State showed less tolerance in their attitude towards neo-Fascist demonstrations, this being in harmony with the trend of the political situation, which had brought a centre-left government to power. But the suppression of the more brazen outbreaks of nostalgia, of the anti-Jewish campaign and of the more impudent glorifications of Fascism, did not alter the fact that agents and leaders of the French and Belgian OAS found hospitality and freedom of movement in Italy, or that neo-Fascist organizations like *Giovane Italia* could make them known by taking them all round Italy, or, like the *Fronte Nazionale Giovanile*, borrow emblems and operational schemes from them. Rekindled by the trials of Nazi war criminals, anti-Semitism and racialism were mingled with colonialist propaganda against the liberation movements of the Afro-Asian peoples, and became part of the noisy campaign in which all the most important sectors of the European Right indulged. The exploits of the OAS and of the notorious 'Red Hand', a French extreme right-wing organization which according to the press had contacts in the *Deuxième Bureau*, raised the enthusiasm of Italian neo-Fascists to the highest pitch.

F*

Following investigations made by their correspondents, several
Italian and French newspapers reported the existence of a very
close collaboration between the internal and external organs of
the MSI and the French, Belgian and Spanish extremists whose
movements had sprung up during the war in Algeria and the
rebellion in the Congo.[43]

While the MSI was fighting a pitched battle against the 'centre-
left', describing Fanfani as a 'stakhanovite under the orders of
Nenni', and revealing the 'Marxist vocation' of Moro, the pro-OAS
and pro-Nazi groups multiplied to such an extent that it became
difficult to distinguish them. Racialism, anti-Communism, colonialism and opposition to the 'centre-left' formula became one and the
same thing. A leaflet issued by the 'Italian section' of the 'Circle' (the
emblem of *Giovane Europa*) contained the following appeal: [44]

ITALIANS
After twenty years of 'pornocracy' we appeal to you to restore the
right and obligation to defend our Race.
ITALIANS
Join us beneath the symbol of THE CIRCLE, which denotes that
NAZI-FASCISM has risen again in Italy too.
ITALIANS
Fight with us against the Communists, Jews and perverts, in order
to cleanse our homeland from the subversive plague that is seeking
to destroy it.
ITALIANS
Let us boycott our enemies, using every means to stop them, let us
daub the infamous star of David on the shops of the Jews and
write P. P. P. (the initials of Piss-Pot Pasolini) on the houses of
Communists and perverts.
EUROPE—UNITED, GREAT, FREE
beneath 'THE CIRCLE' of European Nazi-Fascism.
                    WE SHALL CONQUER

Viva Mussolini.   Heil Hitler.

The epithets used to describe the leading figures of the centre-
left coalition included calling Saragat an 'Italiot gargoyle' and
'spiritual head' of all Italian 'pimps', that 'physically indistinguish-
able, despicable and cowardly rabble' who—according to *Aristocrazia*, the 'political action organ' of the Novara branch of the
MSI—had made money out of the Fascist régime and then deserted
it.[45]

Thanks to their definitely Nazi leanings, the contacts they maintained with kindred organizations abroad and the fact that they
sent their acolytes to special training camps in Belgium, where they

learned the techniques of OAS and Nazi propaganda, the *Ordine Nuovo* and *Giovane Nazione* movements virtually dominated the other 'nostalgic' groups and acquired a kind of pre-eminence in the fields of Italian colonialism, racialism and—needless to say—'Europeanism'. In an article written for *Europa Combattente*, a magazine which appeared at irregular intervals under the auspices of *Giovane Nazione*, Antonio De Bono described the struggle the Angolans were waging against 'Soviet penetration' into Africa, maintaining that the first seeds of 'rebelliousness' had been sown among the black races by the British and the French, since the former had made use of Ethiopian guerrillas to drive out the Italian troops, while the latter had recruited the coloured races into their army. At the end of the Second World War the African nationalists had 'perhaps unconsciously' become tools of Moscow and had accordingly been given a free hand to stir up trouble in the Dark Continent. 'Angola,' De Bono tells us:

> is perhaps the only African country that for years past has never experienced racialism, oppression or exploitation. The Negroes are treated as Portuguese citizens; they can rise to the highest positions in the State (the last governor of Angola but one was a Negro) and the percentage of half-breeds is also very high. And yet we see what is happening there. The truth is that the Negroes were quite happy under white rule (the Italians are still mourned by vast sectors of the native population in our ex-colonies, especially in Eritrea), and all the rest is just propaganda. It is Moscow's aim to conquer all the African countries one by one; after that, Europe will have been definitely encircled and then it will be our turn. That is why we must realize that the Portuguese campaign in Angola is our own, a fight to defend our civilization, a fight for Europe.[46]

Anti-Communism and anti-Russian feeling found their counterparts in anti-capitalism and hatred of the Americans, who had been the 'ruin of Europe' because they were determined to conquer and dominate her markets.[47] The above-quoted De Bono supported the thesis that American goods ought to be boycotted because they were vehicles of cancer.[48] Dollar capitalism was 'disintegrating' the national economies of European countries to its own advantage, pretending to help the 'cause of Niggerdom' in order to drive European products out of the African markets.[49] Europe must therefore unite and form an autonomous block to resist the 'aggressiveness' both of the Soviet Union and of the United States.

But what kind of place was this 'United Europe' to be? When

called upon to elucidate this point, the neo-Nazis of *Europa Combattente* immediately sought refuge in vagueness. 'Europe must be spiritually and materially united,' we are told by Gianni Albertini, 'because a united Europe would be a State the like of which has never been seen before. The old Europe with its numerous States fighting among themselves first on the battlefields and then in politics, was just a skeleton,' Albertini continues,

> but a skeleton which at one wave of the magic wand of faith in a united Europe could be transformed into a magnificently powerful wild animal. 350 million European souls, 208 million behind the Russian steam-roller, 151 million in the United States. 350 million souls manning the bulwark between the Red Army and the material and moral invasion from the United States. Europe must tomorrow become a reality; it might have been one today, had not our consciences been lulled by vain dreams . . . That is why we want Europe to be one united nation, just as the Americans are of their own free will, and the USSR rather less voluntarily. It is on this basis that we intend to fight for a YOUNG NATION—EUROPE.[50]

Certain passages in *A European's Prayer* by Carlo De Agostinis are more explicit about the kind of Europe for which the neo-Fascists were longing:

> I love, O Lord, the Europe of today which suffers and dares, relying on pistols and poetry and laughing at Bolshevism. The Europe of Berlin, Poznan and Budapest, which does not believe the anti-Communist broadcasts from Munich and beyond the ocean. I love her because she destroyed the tanks and conquered the streets, only to be abandoned to her fate and crushed by a new and greater horde of invaders. I love, O Lord, the Europe of those who know the weight of a plastic bomb and fall in the streets, slain by the bullets of the police. The Europe that is being defended in Africa, in the lands cultivated by the determination and courage of generations of Europeans . . . I leave to others, O Lord, the Europe of soft carpets, of applause, of medals and victory parades. My carpets have been burned by phosphorus, my applause has fallen on empty ears, my medals have been worn again but, shorn of their ancient symbols, they can but contemplate the rows of Crosses on the Tombs of my defeated soldiers. In the shadows, in the dwelling-places of the wicked, in my hiding-place, I await the moment when at last our red and black banners will be raised skywards and the bullets of the execution squads will pierce new bodies. Till then, O Lord, O Awful God of Vengeance and Victory, give me the strength to continue fighting for this resentful Europe.[51]

The decadent and illiterate aestheticism of the neo-D'Annunzians declared that it abhorred an 'abstract Nazism, stereotyped and made to measure in order to include under the term "Nazism" all those who fight against Bolshevism and international capitalism'. According to *Europa Combattente* Nazism was now more than ever before the 'morning star' and ought not to be judged in terms of concentration camps and gas-chambers.[52]

Spartaco Paganini was at pains to stress the notion of 'revolution' prevalent among the 'Europeanists' in the movement:

> Ours is and always will be a revolution of ideas; if necessary, it will become a revolution of the people. Ours is a continual warfare against all the haggling, middle-class institutions, against the servility of Europe towards America and Russia . . . The moment has come when we must choose between spiritual death for the sake of democracy and a revolutionary anti-conformism which will strive to create a new, united commonwealth State—Europe. Think it over and make your choice. If you follow us, life will have a sense and purpose. If you follow the others, you will have to rest content with work and the family (sacred institutions, but which do not make the complete man), and at the very most with cultural clubs. So long live the revolution! May the streets be plastered with posters! May our challenge to Communism prosper! Long live the Celtic cross on its red background! Either live with us or die a spiritual death![53]

Pending the moment when they would be able to unify Europe, the 'nostalgics' encountered serious difficulties in unifying themselves. On 30 June 1963, a meeting of representatives of the 'various traditionalist and national-revolutionary groups in Italy' was held in Milan under the auspices of the FNCRSI *(Federazione Nazionale Combattenti della Repubblica Sociale Italiana)*. One of the items on the agenda, according to *Europa Combattente,* was the 'need to unify, or at all events co-ordinate, the operations of the numerous youth associations in the country, which hitherto have for the most part been in a state of anarchy and chaos that has compelled them to lead a hard life and follow an incoherent policy too often overshadowed by that of a political party'.[54] One result of this meeting was the formation of the 'National Revolutionary Alliance', a 'federative organ' the task of which was to be the co-ordination of the organizations composing it. This pact was signed by Pierfranco Bruschi for *Giovane Nazione,* by Paolo Molin for the national committee of *Ordine Nuovo* and by Egidio Muraglia for the *Forze Nazionali Giovanili della Sardegna,* as well as by representatives of various local groups.

'Will the chaos reigning in our associations now end?' the neo-
Nazi periodical asked. 'We are not in the habit of making prophecies,
but what we can say is that, in order to restore some sort of order,
it is essential that all the youth organizations in Italy should unite,
and that the men at the top should agree on a common policy, on
one method of conducting our campaign, under one symbol and
under one leader.'[55]

The chaos in 'nostalgic' circles went on. Dozens of 'research
centres' for the 'formation of cadres', each independent of and
unknown to the others, sprang up on every side, usually consisting
of not more than five to ten people with ill-defined programmes of
'research' and 'ideological preparation'.[56] Rauti's *Ordine Nuovo*
and Bruschi's *Giovane Nazione*, however, remained the most
prominent among these organizations. It was presumably at their
instigation that a 'violently racialist and anti-Semitic' volume of
617 pages entitled *Cospirazione contro la Chiesa* ('Plot against the
Church') was published and distributed to all the prelates attending
the January 1963 session of the Oecumenical Council convened by
Pope John XXIII.[57] This work, written in Italian by a certain
Maurice Pinay, contained, for example, chapters on 'The secret
wheels within wheels of Communism', 'The occult power of
Freemasonry' and 'The Jewish fifth column among the Clergy'.
This was the most carefully organized gesture of European neo-
Nazism (the money to cover publication costs was probably found
by Nazis who had taken refuge in Egypt) against the tendency which
had been imparted to the Church by the exceptional missionary
zeal and profound sensibility of the late Pope.

The task of conducting a more indirect campaign against the
Pope's 'saintly folly' was left to the MSI, who, for example, published in *Il Secolo* a report on the religious massacres in Spain
during the civil war, as a warning against the dangers of the
political and social 'overtures' sponsored by the Vatican, while at
the same time the neo-Nazis tried to find out what Julius Evola
thought about solving the 'racial problem' in a united Europe. After
first drawing attention to the existence of 'a first racial category,
dependent on physical and biological factors; a second category
forming part of the domain of the soul, which can be identified by
its style, etc. . . . and a third category, that of the spirit . . .' the
author of *Il Mito del Sangue* asserted that it was difficult to accept
'the facile racialism so widespread in Germany' and that 'bearing
in mind the above three categories . . . a Germanic race has its

counterpart in a joint Spartan-Roman race'. Evola, however, was sceptical as to the possibility of solving the racial problem in Europe. 'That would be impossible in a traditional Europe,' he declared. 'It might be feasible in a political Europe, but that does not interest us here. It is nevertheless true that decadence began earlier in Europe than elsewhere, and for that very reason it may end sooner. For the moment no signs of this can be seen. Our only hope,' the racialist thinker concluded, 'lies in an existential anarchy, extraneous to politics.'[58]

Side by side with unadulterated pro-Nazism and glorifications of OAS methods, which were unfavourably compared with the MSI's 'gradual trend towards *bourgeois* ways and outlook', themes of this kind filled the pages of a new review published in Turin by the local branch of *Giovane Nazione* and edited by Salvatore Francia, a television cameraman. The *Quaderni Neri*—such was the title of this new periodical—aspired to become an international review of 'revolutionary' neo-Fascism and neo-Nazism, drawing its readers' attention in particular to the problems of 'power', of a regeneration of Europe by means of a revolutionary upsurge which would break her chains and follow the 'path of Nietzsche's super-man' and 'European Nationalism'. Among its contributors were Mosley, Jean Thiriart, Angel Ruiz Ayucar and other well-known exponents of Continental neo-Fascism, and it maintained contacts with the headquarters of 'nostalgic' groups in Belgium, France, Portugal and Canada.

The second number of the review was confiscated when a charge of 'apology for Fascism' and a libel action were brought against it by certain partisan leaders, and its editor was duly tried and found guilty.[59]

On 27 October 1963, the efforts made by the *Giovane Nazione* extremists to bring about some sort of unification achieved a partial and mediocre success at a conference held for this purpose in Bologna. In a number bearing the sub-title *Organo di Giovane Europa, Europa Combattente* announced that this conference had been attended by 'the leaders of the most important and most active pan-European organizations'.[60] But when we glance through the list of delegates as given by the journal, we can but feel that this claim was somewhat exaggerated and that 'the most important and most active' Italian National Socialist organizations must have been very few in number. The delegates mentioned by the journal as being present were Bruschi, De Bono and Cinquemani of

Giovane Nazione, Cesarini, Smantelli and Gigliarelli from the Perugia branch of *Ordine Nuovo,* Pintus of the La Spezia branch of the FNG *(Federazione Nazionale Giovanile),* Paganini of the *Gruppo Valerio Catullo* in Verona, Andrioni of the Neapolitan branch of the FISN, together with 'other friends from Grosseto, Catania, Reggio Calabria and Messina'. In any case the delegates—still according to *Europa Combattente*—discussed 'in an atmosphere of cordial comradeship' new plans for reorganization, new tactics and new methods of carrying on 'the struggle'; none of the delegates present brought forward any pretexts, 'as is usually the case', for remaining independent of the others. The upshot of the meeting was that *Giovane Nazione,* the Perugia branch of *Ordine Nuovo,* the FNG of La Spezia and the Valerio Catullo Group from Verona were merged into a new organization called *Giovane Europa.* 'The other delegates,' *Europa Combattente* reported, 'regretted that circumstances of a temporary nature or the absence of definite instructions to that effect prevented them from joining this coalition, but at the same time said that the aims of *Giovane Europa* had their unconditional support and that their groups would join it in a not too distant future'. The average age of the supporters of these movements ranged from twenty to twenty-five; most of them were students and almost without exception they came from the lower middle class. Among the exceptions were some of the leaders, for example Bruschi, who belonged to the war generation, and Pino Rauti, who had matured in the ranks of the MSI during the 'heroic years'. Emilio Gay, a thirty-year-old student who during the March 1963 election campaign had thrown a bundle of income-tax declaration forms and blank bills of exchange at Fanfani during a meeting in Novara, was considered a veteran in the organizing of 'nostalgic' groups and exploits.[61] Inveterate adversaries of the MSI or men who had quarrelled with Michelini's party over methods, these men nevertheless agreed with the principles of the *'Giovane Italia* charter', which had defined the supreme laws of Fascist 'idealism' as follows:

> For us the younger generation is not a matter for statistics or biological studies, but is essentially a spiritual attitude, as regards both its tone and its way of life. It is characterized by the enthusiasm and generosity of those who follow an ideal merely because they love that ideal, by their determination to give their unconditional support, quite apart from any idealism; by the joy of action; by a desire for renewal and progress; by contempt for a comfortable life . . .'[62]

The 'Last Shot'

'Look at my jaw, note the magnetism of my eyes. Could I be a Liberal with a jaw like this? To that there is only one plain answer —No . . . I'm the "Last Shot"; that's my nickname. Why? Because on 27 April [1945] I got hold of a motor-ambulance, went to the Motta factory, threw four hand-grenades and fired a burst from a tommy-gun, the very last shots of the war. Then I hopped it. They arrested me at Nervi and they tortured me—here, here and here . . . I was in the San Vittore prison in Milan for two years, until I was released in 1947 and went overseas. Brazil, Argentina, Peru, Uruguay, Haiti, Jamaica, Mexico. I went into business, but still found time to take part in a revolution in Bolivia, and in 1952 I went to Cuba. Then Batista came along, and I saw which way the wind was blowing and backed him. In short, I became Batista's right-hand man and made pots of money . . .'[63]

That is what Ernesto Brivio, alias the 'Last Shot', said to a reporter from a Milanese daily, only a few months after his victory at the Roman municipal elections in June 1962. Together with De Marsanich and other well-known 'nostalgics' Brivio had stood as an MSI candidate, and his election campaign had attracted attention owing to the enormous amount of propaganda this clever business-man had employed. His election expenses ran into hundreds of millions of lire, and he had polled more votes than any other of his 'comrades' from the same party, not excluding De Marsanich, since he had obtained no fewer than 35,599 preferential votes. Chairman of the 'Lazio' football club, film-producer, racehorse-breeder, owner of the 'Italian Press Agency' and of a transport undertaking in Paraguay, this singular personage had contributed not a little to the success of the MSI at these municipal elections. In Rome Michelini's party had polled four-fifths of the total number of votes cast for the MSI in the whole country, the party's percentage rising from 9.7 to exactly 10 per cent of the whole electorate. This swash-buckling braggart soon became the star performer of Roman neo-Fascism, but not long afterwards he became involved in a bank-ruptcy no less sensational than his luxurious way of life and the systems he had excogitated to attract the astonished attention of his fellow-citizens. Hounded by his creditors, Brivio disappeared from the Italian scene just in time to avoid being arrested, after a whole series of phoney business deals which resulted in huge overdrafts.[64]

For the political secretariat of the MSI controlled by Arturo Michelini, however, Brivio's brief venture into politics had been only one out of many worries. The former 'Federal Secretary' of the Roman Fascist Party had to engage in yet another battle against adversaries inside his own party. The faction headed by Almirante, Romualdi, Ezio Maria Gray and Massimo Anderson—in other words the so-called 'left wing' of the 'spirituals'—had become somewhat bolder and acquired a certain importance within the party, after having been virtually relegated to the fringe areas ever since Michelini took over the secretariat in 1956. Now they accused the party secretary of making a too personal use of the funds allotted to the MSI's daily newspaper, *Il Secolo d'Italia*, and above all of not employing a 'truly Fascist style'. His adversaries resented the fact that Michelini had protested to the President of the Chamber of Deputies because his fellow-deputies had referred to the MSI as a neo-Fascist party, and also because just before the parliamentary election campaign he had circulated a letter to all party branches advising speakers to refrain from raking up the twenty years of the Fascist régime. Michelini had likewise been criticized for using the pronoun *lei* when speaking to 'comrades' and for a whole series of measures taken—according to his critics—with a view to winding up the semi-military formations of the 'nostalgics'.[65] The squabble became more bitter when the results of the general election became known, since the MSI polled only 1,570,282 votes (5.1 per cent of the electorate), thus confirming what had already been clear at the time of the 1958 election, namely that the party was not progressing, but was obtaining a smaller percentage of votes. The 'left wing' attributed this stagnation to a falling-off in 'revolutionary' spirit resulting from the tactics employed by Michelini, to which he retorted by maintaining that his opponents were to blame, since the lack of progress was due to their stubbornness in assuming subversive attitudes which were not justified by any possibility of expansion towards the right.

The atmosphere within the party soon became heated. Even the MSI's daily newspaper reflected this situation when it was subjected to censorship by no fewer than five editors—Franz Turchi, Filippo Anfuso, Giorgio Almirante, Nino Tripodi and Dante Maria Tuninetti, three of these being supporters of Michelini (Anfuso, Tripodi and Tuninetti) and the other two 'left-wingers'. Almirante, who was now leading a new trend calling itself *Rinnovamento*, was plotting to transform the party conference due to be held in

Rome in August 1963 into an arena for his attack on Michelini's secretaryship. For months the opposing trends clashed both at the centre and on the outskirts, conducting a struggle in the course of which no holds were barred. On 2 August, at the opening session of the seventh party conference, held at the exhibition buildings in Rome, the opposing factions faced each other with apparently unshakable resolution. Michelini made a conciliatory opening address, but he spoke of a 'party of those who believe in serving their country' and claimed that the 'realistic' policy which had enabled the MSI to become one of the big political parties in the country was the right one.[66] The reactions to this speech of his were so violent that the conference was transformed into a cockpit of scuffles, accompanied by insults and reciprocal accusations of the utmost gravity. Almirante, in his speech, demanded the reconstitution of a 'more Fascist' party, while most of the 'left-wing' orators stressed the fact that the points of the Verona manifesto must become integral parts of the MSI's policy. In the midst of continual brawling, at a given signal the 'left-wingers' walked out of the hall and held a meeting of their own, in the course of which they threatened to form a new party. Almirante, Gray, Angioy, Servello, Delfino and Leccisi demanded an extraordinary meeting, failing which they threatened to secede from the party. Michelini appeared to be shattered by the number of his followers who supported his adversaries and resorted to negotiations with a view to composing the differences of opinion. The talks, exchanges of messages, suspensions and resumptions of sittings went on for months. In the end Almirante and the dissidents sheathed their swords and expressed their willingness to rejoin the committee of the MSI—a compromise which the *Giovane Europa* extremists considered dangerous and due to nothing less than a desire to surrender.[67] Almirante was also accused of being an 'opportunist' and a 'rabbit', while Michelini was branded as an anti-Fascist, this being the most deadly insult that a 'nostalgic' could hurl at a colleague.

The reabsorption of Almirante's 'left wing' into the official 'centre-left' faction was the result of negotiations which ended in the appointment of dissidents to leading posts within the party and provided yet another proof of Michelini's skill in reconciling warring elements. But it is quite possible that Almirante, who was an intelligent man with a keen understanding of politics, was well aware that if he withdrew altogether from the MSI, he might find himself in the arms of sectarians who had no real influence in political matters and be reduced to the rank of leader of a tiny faction without a future. And indeed, at the eighth party conference held at Pescara on 12-14 June 1965, Michelini found himself in a minority facing a crowd of vociferous delegates who greeted the words of the 'left-wing' leader with enthusiastic applause, but despite this he managed to persuade Almirante to accept a compromise which in reality was a victory for his own policy, since this was eventually approved after a sitting continually interrupted by scuffles, loud threats to secede from the party and the singing of Fascist songs. Romualdi obtained about 20 per cent of the votes and became leader of the dissident minority, but the pact between the party's two most prominent leaders reduced the dissidents to impotence. The outcome was that Almirante, the 'pure left-winger', had allowed himself to be corrupted by the 'lukewarm' Michelini, and for this the more rabid extremists never forgave him.

Moreover, this 'act of treason' on the part of Telesio Interlandi's ex-disciple was committed at the very moment when the entry of 'Marxists' into the government seemed to stress the necessity of some 'revolutionary' gesture, and consequently the intransigent 'nostalgics' tried to console themselves by organizing the usual 'punitive expeditions' and devoting themselves to rites commemorating the past. It was at this point that the already existing formations were reinforced by the emergence of the groups known as 'Greenshirts'. In January 1965, while investigating an attack on the headquarters of the Christian Democrat Party, the police arrested Romano Fassio, the 'commissar' of the MSI's Savona branch, who was charged with having recruited and given military training to neo-Fascist 'Greenshirt' groups which had already been in existence for several years and favoured 'violent action'.

During 1962 and 1963, determined efforts had been made to stop the proliferation of 'nostalgic' groups, perhaps because of pressure from foreign organizations and as a result of the international political situation, and there was a growing tendency to regard Gaullist 'Caesarism' as a touchstone for that future authoritarianism which was the cherished dream of all right-wing extremists. But internal discord undermined every attempt at unification and split the party even more. The personal ambitions of the leaders and local bosses were irreconcilable and in most cases, quite apart from any disagreement as to tactics and strategy, merely led to a further splitting-up into groups. The same might be said of the associations formed by ex-Servicemen of the Salò Republic, whose federation, first under the chairmanship of Graziani and then under that of Prince Borghese, was deserted in 1955 by a number of local organizations who formed the *Unione Combattenti della Repubblica Sociale Italiana* and appointed as their chairman Colonel Languasco, former commander of the corps of 'Apennine *chasseurs*'. This defection annoyed Borghese, who resigned, whereupon the leadership of the federation passed to General Farina (according to some MSI sources, Borghese, the ex-commander of the Tenth MTB Flotilla, approved of the *Unione Combattenti*, though he never actually joined it). Some of the branches, however, took advantage of the opportunity to achieve independence (e.g. Turin, under the leadership of Colonel Botto). Officially, the split was due to clashes between supporters of 'politically-minded' associations and those who wanted them to be merely ex-Servicemen's organizations, free from any control by the MSI or by 'nostalgic' elements, but the neo-Fascists themselves admitted that the real reason was to be found in disagreements among the leading figures and the desire of each one of them to become arbiter and trustee of the organization's aims.[68]

The slump, which in Italy followed immediately in the wake of the 'economic miracle', revealed all those defects which the period of maximum productive development had not only failed to remedy, but had actually accentuated by introducing new factors, and showed how precarious was the 'prosperity' that had been achieved without rectifying the anomalies of the system. At the first signs of an approaching slump the economic right wing adopted a demagogic attitude and hastened to lay the whole blame for the crisis on the workers, clamouring at the same time for a unilateral 'austerity'. Contemporaneously the conservative front opposed every attempt made by the centre-left government to introduce reforms which might obstruct the increasing tendency towards monopolistic concentration or lower the level of profits in the interests of the nation as a whole. In the course of their offensive the right-wing parties resorted to the methods usually adopted by reactionaries in order to win over the middle class, who had been adversely affected by the crisis, and to set them against the State, against democracy and against the reforms (which had not yet become operative).

One result of this campaign was that the neo-Fascists found themselves obliged to support those appeals to unite 'the forces of the nation' which are inevitably made whenever an economic recession occurs. Anti-Communism and anti-Socialism likewise received a fresh boost, and the ensemble of these forms of pressure exerted by the right wing favoured the advent in Italy of 'Gaullism'. General De Gaulle's régime became a model for 'nostalgics' of every hue, as well as for those conservative elements who were ready to embark on any totalitarian experiment that seemed able to guarantee their survival. In 'Gaullism' the neo-Fascists claimed to see that authentic 'Pan-European wisdom' which advocated a *'Europe des Patries'*, anti-British and chauvinistic, and at the same time very similar to the one they themselves were striving to achieve. In February 1963 *Il Secolo d'Italia* wrote that 'these two men, De Gaulle and Adenauer (and also the aged Chancellor's future successor, who is just as intransigent as he is when it comes to anti-Communism) represent an effective and substantial guarantee for the defence of Europe'.[69]

The attractions of 'Gaullism', invariably starting with the theme of 'national unity', thus led to an exhumation of appeals couched in this vein, for which the MSI possessed plenty of material, while the right-wing parties in general let their imagination run riot and were not averse to spending money in order to propagate such ideas. The phenomenon assumed the twofold form—common to all reactionary movements of this sort—of attacks on the democratic system and the spreading of alarming rumours of an impending seizure of power by the Communists, the starting-point of this campaign being the inclusion of PSI Socialists in the cabinet. This explains why certain Catholic sectors were now accused of becoming the tools of 'Marxism' and of the expansionist aims of Bolshevism, which it was claimed would be filtered down through the Socialists. According to the neo-Fascists, conservatives and 'Gaullists' from various parties, it was essential to act quickly and create a new movement on a very wide basis which would rally all right-minded Italians round the forces capable of defeating this conspiracy.

Towards the end of 1963 and the beginning of 1964, these 'patriotic' sentiments, manipulated or influenced by the economic right wing, hoodwinked one of the leading exponents of militant anti-Fascism, Randolfo Pacciardi, former commander of a 'Garibaldi' battalion of Italian exiles who had gone to Spain to defend the Republic. Pacciardi was a strenuous opponent of the centre-left government, and when the Republican Party (PRI), to which he belonged, voted to support the new régime, he did not confine himself merely to voicing his disapproval, but voted in parliament against the cabinet of which some of his PRI colleagues were members. When he was summoned before the party committee to explain this act of insubordination, he refused to appear and sent the committee a telegram reminiscent in its style of Fascism and including the five-letter word made famous by Cambronne. For this he was expelled from the PRI, but he found no difficulty in obtaining the funds necessary to start a periodical called *Folla,* which soon achieved a large circulation and, besides attacking democracy and the party system, published patent eulogies of the *Confindustria* [Federation of Industrialists] and appeals to re-establish the 'authority' of the State and to wage a struggle without quarter against Communism.

From the editing of a review to the formation of a political movement the step was only a short one. In the early months of 1964 this ex-PRI deputy announced the formation of a 'Second Republic' movement, which later adopted the name of 'Popular and Democratic Union for a New Republic'. Pacciardi toured Italy to explain his new creation's aims and at the same time establish contacts with the leaders of industry and high finance. The 'Union' had a generically right-wing and pro-De Gaulle programme, and it was ferociously anti-Communist and fond of making appeals reminiscent of Guglielmo Giannini's *'Qualunquismo'.* Pacciardi's followers placed him on a pedestal similar to that of De Gaulle and his supporters believed that he was the long-awaited leader of a 'national front' which would oppose the 'red subversives'. In June 1964, at a conference held in Bari by the 'agrarian action centres', an extremist movement sponsored by right-wing landowners, the secretary of the organization, Oronzo Melpignano, welcomed the presence of the Union's founder at a meeting held in the Piccinni theatre. 'You, who have always been an anti-Fascist,' Melpignano exclaimed, 'have embraced the soldiers of the Social Republic in the name of the new Italy.' And in fact Pacciardi concluded a fraternal alliance with the *'Repubblichini'* present on that occasion and proclaimed the need for a general 'reconciliation'. When the conference was over, a crowd of neo-Fascists and landowners carried Pacciardi shoulder-high out of the theatre. About the same time a former parachutist officer of the Salò army named Giorgio Pisanò, who was one of the founders of the FUAN and editor of the *Secolo Ventesimo,* a review published in Milan by adversaries of the MSI, started a similar movement. Pisanò wanted to create a 'Second Republic' party consisting of ex-*Repubblichini* and ex-partisans who were willing to bury the hatchet in order to 'save the country', and he found a certain amount of support among ex-members of the Social Republic's armed forces and minor figures in the Resistance movement. He had previously written a book on the 'terrifying truths' of partisan warfare and the German occupation, and now he hoped to 'bridge the ditch of blood' separating the Fascists and anti-Fascists who had fought on opposite sides in the civil war and to unite them in the battle against Communism. Salvatore Francia and Emilio Gay, together with other 'nostalgics' whom we have encountered in the course of our narrative, created branches of the movement in a number of cities and claimed to have received 'avalanches of approval'. A national committee was set up in Turin, consisting of Pisanò himself, Francia, Persano, Pastore, Bandioli and Bussano. Contact was established with Pacciardi, with a view to joining forces, but the ex-commander of the 'Garibaldi' battalion did not wish to compromise himself by collaborating with neo-Fascists.[70]

Shortly afterwards, at a meeting held in Turin to establish a programme for the new movement, differences of opinion arose between Pisanò and those who, like him, were content with a vague unification programme on the one side, and on the other the trend headed by Francia and Gay, who insisted that the 'Second Republic' ought to have clearly defined political aims, or in other words ought to align itself more or less with the 'nostalgic' groups of the 'left wing'. This resulted in a quarrel, which eventually led to the break-up of the movement and the paralysing of its activities.

Meanwhile Pacciardi went his own way. The MSI watched him apprehensively, because it realized that he and his movement might become competitors who were not to be despised. The 'Union' repudiated all accusations of neo-Fascism, and the former exile may well have been convinced that he was not betraying his own past. But, as Pietro Nenni said, 'the fact of having been anti-Fascists and members of the Resistance does not mean that one can resist the allurements held out by [right-wing economic] groups which are able to exert pressure'.[71] The 'Pacciardi case' was only an episode, but a very significant and ominous one, in a more complex manœuvre of the right wing, comprising all those forces which might eventually be utilized to give the Italian political situation a swing towards a solution of the De Gaulle type. Each one of these formations and groups, from the MSI to the 'Union for a New Republic' and the *Giovane Europa* bands, had no chance of achieving success on its own. Pacciardi was a caricature of De Gaulle, while Fassio's 'Greenshirt *arditi*' and Julius Evola's racialists were merely extrovert small fry torn by innumerable internal squabbles and incapable of even perceiving their own shortcomings. Nevertheless, should a Gaullist or neo-Fascist solution ever prevail in the economic right wing and among the political trends representing its vested interests in the sphere of the Catholic and Liberal-Monarchical parties, some or most of these scattered outposts of extremism might play the role that the Tambroni government in July 1960 allowed the action-squads to play in Genoa and Reggio Emilia. And their spirit and aims would in any case serve to strengthen any régime that might receive their support.

7 France

The great opportunity

After the Second World War, during the anxious years characterized by the Manichaean controversy between East and West, the
extreme right-wing parties and movements were certainly offered
plenty of opportunities to get going again and furbish up their
ancient myths. We need only mention the Hungarian insurrection,
the recent colonial war in North Africa, the guerrilla warfare in the
Alto Adige and the Berlin Wall. Although they never managed to
co-ordinate their operations properly or achieve decisive results,
the neo-Fascists were quick to take advantage of favourable circumstances, and if they did nothing else, they at least confirmed the
prophetic words spoken by the leading theoretician of Nazism,
Alfred Rosenberg, as he was being led to the gallows in Nuremberg:
'In fifteen years' time people will start talking about us again, and
in twenty Nazism will once more be a force to be reckoned with.'

There is no denying that towards the end of the 1950s, the neo-
Fascists were getting themselves talked about, and in Algeria, before
the date predicted by Rosenberg, they very nearly achieved their
first victory. Though they failed to carry through their plan to install
a new régime in France, they were nevertheless in a position to
exercise almost absolute control over a large country like Algeria,
they introduced subversion into the mother country and were
instrumental in reviving certain hateful practices which it was
thought had disappeared for ever with the end of the Third Reich.

For six years, from 1956 to 1962, Algeria was, in fact, the testing
bench for all the forces of French subversion, from the ultra-
nationalists to those who drew their inspiration from Catholic
integralism, from the definitely Fascist trends to those deriving from
Maurras, and all of them found common ground in their attacks
on parliamentary democracy and their liking for authoritarian
solutions. In a short article on French Fascism, written in the early
days of this period, Paul Sérant, a man who has never attempted
to conceal his admiration for the intellectuals of the extreme right

174

wing, felt obliged to admit that 'if by "Fascism" we mean a predilection for authoritarian rule, then there exists in France today a
"pre-Fascist" situation far more tense than before the war. In 1936
the "Leagues" had considerable success, but most of their adherents
were merely voicing their own discontent; they did not really want
an authoritarian régime.'[1] After the war and the ensuing purge,
faithful followers of Pétain like Darnand, and ardent disciples of
Maurras like the worshippers of the Celtic cross could think of
nothing but revenge, counter-revolution, *coups d'état* and 'the edifi-
cation of a new State, authoritarian and at the same time popular,
national and social',[2] within the framework of a Europe sufficiently
strong to be able to defend herself against the joint 'aggression' of
Jews, Arabs, Negroes and Asiatics. 'Down with the Europe of
Strasbourg!, down with the Europe of the Federalists!, down with
the Europe of the slaves of Russian or American imperialism!'
shouted René Binet, an anti-Semite and ex-member of the SS. 'Each
one of us must strive to forge links between the nationalists of
every country in Europe—links which will enable us to form an
alliance of national workers' States in Europe, the rights and independence of each nation being respected.'[3]

These groups of such hybrid origins found common ground in
their anti-Communism, while at the same time they described the
African and Asian independence movements as auxiliaries of Communism which must be combated by the use of violence. In the
eyes of these right-wing extremists the defence of Algeria to the
last gasp became a campaign in defence of the values of 'Western
Christian civilization', and in one of his proclamations General
Raoul Salan declared that 'even if tomorrow Algiers should become
a second Budapest, that would not matter. With our eyes fixed on
the shining example of Joan of Arc, we shall embark on this last
crusade, on which the fate of Humanity depends.' Without perceiving that he was making himself ridiculous, Robert Martel resorted
to rhetoric while haranguing, the Mitidja settlers: 'Brandish aloft
the symbol of the Heart surmounted by the Cross, and like Father
de Foucauld, like Saint Joan of Arc, concentrate your energies in
order that the Sacred Heart of Jesus may rule the world.'[4] And
Joseph Ortiz, a 'Mediterranean by race and blood', appealed to
his fellow-countrymen in Spain, Italy, Greece and Turkey to 'unite
all the forces of the Mediterranean against the Soviet policy of
enslavement'.[5]

In the years immediately following the war, as Pierre Fougeyrollas has pointed out, 'monarchists, neo-Fascists and ultra-nationalists were only small groups and impotent minorities':

> The same could be said of the integralists in French Catholicism. But the wars in Indo-China and Algeria and, in a more general sense, the circumstances accompanying the end of the French colonial empire, made it possible for these minorities to exert pressure on people in high places and thus to play a far from negligible rôle in French politics between 1956 and 1962. The European population in Algeria, a number of officers in the army and some of the more moderate electors were for a certain time converted to ultra-nationalism and the tactical principles of the extreme Right.[6]

During six long years Algeria was the theatre for every kind of experiment in psychological warfare and counter-revolution. The men of the SS reappeared, this time camouflaged in the uniforms of paratroopers. Old tattered remnants of the *Cagoule* fought side by side with raw neo-Fascist recruits. Every kind of symbol was brandished—from the Celtic cross to the swastika, from the Cross of Jesus Christ to that of Lorraine. No matter whether they were atheists or Catholics, Nazis or National Communists, conservatives or revolutionaries, integralists or advocates of a Corporative State, the men who reached the zenith of their careers under the banner of the OAS showed once again that Fascism can assume a new form, that it seeks to renew itself in the hope of widening the basis of its appeal, and that it is prepared to enter into any alliance provided it is able to assert itself. 'We are dangerous,' André Rossfelder wrote in *L'Esprit Public*, 'because we are impatient. We must start a revolution in every European country.' They did not succeed in starting one, not even in France, because, as René Rémond has pointed out:

> Such forms of nationalism never remain united for long; either success or the lack of it causes them to split and the squabbles among the remnants of the OAS, between Château-Jobert's counter-revolutionary faction and the pro-Fascist supporters of Argoud, reveal the impotence of nationalism when it comes to devising a positive plan of action around which all the centrifugal trends can rally.[7]

But it is, to say the least, certain that for a few months in 1961 the forces of the French extreme Right came very near to winning, and on 13 May 1958 they contributed to the overthrow of the Fourth Republic and at the same time helped a party which to a certain extent was their rival—that of De Gaulle—to install the authoritarian régime they wanted, which in the end will disarm and absorb them. As it has already done to a certain extent.

The revival of the extreme Right

Seventeen years elapsed between the purge following the fall of the Vichy government and the battle for Algiers. Let us see how during these years the French extreme Right managed to rise again, patiently weaving its plots while awaiting the day when it would be able to look upon the Élysée as a not unachievable goal. Elsewhere in this volume, when dealing with the authoritarian movements of the 1930s, we said that the French extreme Right cannot be dubbed Fascist *tout court*; the term might prove to be too restrictive, too generic, or even wrong. After the Second World War, however, together with groups clearly recognizable as neo-Fascist or neo-Nazi, we find a whole range of authoritarian, anti-democratic or racialist movements which cannot be bundled together under the single label of 'Fascism', but which, like the Fascists, dreamed of revenge, and did not disdain to collaborate with them.

The first to raise their heads again were the disciples of Maurras and the *Action Française*. Hardly had General Leclerc's motorized columns occupied Paris when these supporters of a monarchical restoration secretly launched a periodical called *Documents Nationaux*, in which they defended Charles Maurras's wholehearted support of Pétain and his *révolution nationale*.[8] The next to emerge, clad in Nazi uniforms, were the militants of the LVF *(Légion des Volontaires Français)*, who in the columns of their *Combattant Français* announced that they intended to form a 'National Socialist Revolution Party', which was to purge the French race of the Jews, Negroes and Asiatics who were contaminating it. They also wallowed in their recollections of the great battles in the East, whither Pétain had dispatched them in order that they might share with the Germans the honours and the burdens of the 'anti-Bolshevik crusade'. Years later—in 1963—one of them, Marc Augier, under the pseudonym of Saint-Loup, wrote a history of their epic struggle in Russia and, commenting on the *rapprochement* between France and Germany sponsored by De Gaulle, went so far as to say:

> There can be no doubt that we inaugurated the policy of collaboration with the Germans too soon and at the wrong moment. It would be pointless . . . to ask whether these men were the 'lost

generation' of an epoch that dared to condemn them, or the 'heroic precursors of a united Europe', of 'Franco-German collaboration', of a 'Franco-German brotherhood in arms'.[9]

Between 1947 and 1951, as *le système* showed itself to be more and more fragile and one cabinet after another fell, even the more important 'purgees', hitherto regarded as the scum of the nation, began to pluck up courage. At the general election held on 17 June 1951 the faithful adherents of Vichy were grouped under the somewhat vague denomination of *Unité des Indépendants Républicains*, their candidates being the lawyer Isorni, Admiral Decoux, Loustanau-Lacau, Trochu and Leroy-Ladurie. In that same year there re-entered the political fray the extremist author Maurice Bardèche, who in 1947 had already drawn attention to himself by libelling the Resistance movement (in *Lettre à François Mauriac*) and a year later by publishing a controversial book in defence of the war criminals sentenced at Nuremberg, in which, *inter alia*, he wrote: 'In the pious hope of appearing more plausible, they [i.e. the Allies] built extra crematoria at Auschwitz and Dachau, in order to allay any scruples that might have arisen in the minds of mathematicians. That is the way history is written.'[10] In 1951 Bardèche founded the *Mouvement Social Européen* and a few months later we find him as one of the founders of the neo-Fascist Malmö 'International'. A brother-in-law of the 'martyr' Robert Brasillach (shot as a collaborationist on 6 February 1945), a skilful controversialist and a man of undoubted intelligence, Bardèche seemed at first sight to have all the necessary qualifications for leadership of the French Fascists, but later he proved to be an incompetent leader and organizer, and in any case could not be compared with the 'providential men' of the 1930s, for example, Georges Valois, Marcel Bouchard, Jacques Doriot. In 1954, together with the ex-Minister of the Vichy régime Jean Louis Tixier-Vignancour, he founded the *Rassemblement National Français*, from which he resigned shortly afterwards as the result of a quarrel with the anti-Semite René Binet. After this he started the *Comité de coordination des forces nationales françaises*, now defunct. Bardèche was an intellectual rather than a man of action, and moreover he was obsessed by the idea of restoring Fascist ideology to its original purity, which, according to him, had been contaminated by the events of the last decades. For this reason he did not hesitate, in 1961, to indulge in self-criticism, when he stated, in what is perhaps the most original book on neo-Fascism yet written, that 'together with one or two others I have defended the Vichy régime. Nevertheless, in the depths of my heart, I repudiate three-quarters of what Vichy did. I have defended those who were accused at Nuremberg; some of them, if I had obeyed the promptings of my heart, I would perhaps have condemned. But that was not the moment to make distinctions. The injustice was indivisible, and the response had to be the same. Today, however, we can speak the truth without fear of being called cowards. We must be sincere; there were certain aspects of the Fascism that was which the Fascism of today must refuse to accept.'[11]

By thus stripping Fascism of its dead wood, Bardèche showed his approval of the programme launched by Mussolini in 1944, when events compelled the Duce to give republican Fascism (at all events on paper) the appearance of tending towards social reform. Bardèche, however, reproached both the Fascism of Mussolini and National Socialism with having failed in 'their essential mission, which was the realization of true National Socialism. As for Fascist doctrine, if it has not remained a perennial fountainhead, the chief reason is that, practically speaking, Fascism never had a doctrine. We seek in vain the *book* of Fascism; no such bible exists.'[12] But the lack of such a bible did not worry Professor Bardèche, since he was convinced that 'Fascism is not a doctrine' but 'an obscure and remote longing written in our blood and in our souls', and that those who 'carry on the Fascist idea are men who feel, more deeply and more desperately than other men, that it is a means of salvation, the secret of life and well-being which every zoological species preserves like an instinct in the depths of its conscience. And that can also be said of German racialism'.[13] Concerning the future of Fascism Bardèche was very optimistic. He did not believe in the 'third force' Europe of which the neo-Fascists dreamed, simply because he could not see that it had yet been realized in any way. He has rather harsh things to say of the *Movimento Sociale Italiano*, which 'takes refuge in memories', and of the *Deutsche Reichspartei*, which 'can't even do that'. He attacks the 'myth of a heaven-sent leader' and advises the neo-Fascists to think twice about the utility of party directives. And in conclusion he dismisses half a century of Fascism with these words: 'I do not say, "this is what there was"; I say, "this is what might have been and occasionally was". This was Fascism's dream, but it was nothing more than a dream and the inspiration of a few men.'[14]

According to Bardèche, only one thing could bring about a revival of Fascism, and that was if the West were to make it a bulwark against Communism.

> It was Lenin who prophesied that Fascism would be the ultimate form of government every country would have to adopt if it wanted to survive and not surrender without a struggle to the dictatorship of Communism. If the West were to become powerless, if it were to disappear like a drowning old man, we could do nothing to save it. But if it made up its mind to resist, Lenin's prophecy might well be realized under another name, with a different aspect, and certainly without the slightest reminder of the past; it would have the face of an innocent child whom we would not recognize, the head of a youthful Medusa, and the Spartan order would be born again; and paradoxically enough, it would then become the last bulwark of Liberty and of the sweetness of living.[15]

These are the closing words of this *Mein Kampf* of the 1960s, too pessimistic to serve as a textbook of Fascism, but sufficiently rich in muddled Utopias and wonderful expectations to earn it a worthy place in the ideological literature of the movement.

In 1951, the year of Bardèche's début, the four Sidos brothers, sons of one of Darnand's henchmen who had been shot in 1945 near La Rochelle, founded *Jeune Nation*, an ultra-nationalistic movement which took as its emblem the Celtic cross. This symbol was intended to be a reminder of the legendary past of France, and the Sidos brothers described it as 'the most suitable emblematic representation of our determination to combine memories of our nation's distant past with our hopes of an even greater future'.[16] During the ensuing years, in fact, this late edition of the swastika was to appear everywhere in the crumbling French empire—scrawled on the walls of Saigon, daubed on the barricades in Algiers, branded on the flesh of Tunisian volunteers during the battle for Bizerta. The Sidos brothers—Pierre and Charles in particular—had a hand in all the plots and revolts organized in Algeria and fought side by side with the OAS. They appeared several times before the courts, and when, in 1964, they at last realized that 'the nationalists of this country, when they wish to draw attention to the problem of national defence, can no longer avail themselves of that formidable weapon which the preservation of a French province used to provide', they could think of nothing better than to advise their friends to support 'the magnificent fight which is being waged by Portugal and South Africa' and to clamour for an amnesty for the activists of the OAS and other extremist movements.[17]

Another movement in the tradition of neo-Nazism, anti-Semitism and anti-Communism was the *Phalange Française*, founded by Charles Luca, alias Charles Gastaut, a former agent of Marcel Déat. It was particularly active in Algeria and was suppressed after 13 May 1958. Very soon, however, it cropped up once more under another name, *Mouvement Populaire Français*, and with a very bellicose slogan—'One doctrine, one cause—National Socialism! De Gaulle has destroyed the Empire; the National Socialists swear to reconquer it!' The year 1954, in the course of which the Algerian revolution broke out, also saw the birth of most of the forty-seven extreme right-wing organizations which remained more or less active until 1962.

The situation in Algeria—where the civil authorities were becoming more and more obsequious to the military and hopes of saving the African 'provinces' were slowly fading—could hardly have been more propitious for the budding of ultra-patriotic and racialist groups. The most aggressive of these movements was headed by a Corsican lawyer named Jean-Baptiste Biaggi and provided a haven of refuge for disgruntled paratroopers just back from Indo-China and for National Socialist students. Under Biaggi's leadership this *Parti Patriotique Révolutionnaire* was soon transformed into a semi-military organization, and the turbulent Corsican's 'commandos' soon made themselves famous. Biaggi had himself photographed holding a tommy-gun and leaping over the obstacles of an 'assault course'. After providing the illustrated papers with much sensational material, the commandos turned their attention to more serious matters. In February 1956 they staged a *putsch* in Algiers, and in November of the same year they set fire to the premises of the Communist newspaper *Humanité* in Paris. The activists of the PPR did not bother about ideas—they were men of action, not politicians. This was noticed by the journalist Henri-François Rey when he interviewed four of them:

I tried to get them to talk. Had they a theory, had they leaders? The oldest of the four did his best, but he was inarticulate. What about Hitler? He's a washout. And Mussolini? A clown. Franco? He's a rotter, and besides, he's a Freemason. Pétain? Loud laughter. It was like a game of ninepins. What about Poujade? More laughter, accompanied by a gesture of flicking away dust. I tried to think of other names, because, like Pavlov's dogs, they reacted only to words. Juin? He's like the rest, he belongs to the *système*. The word *système* reminds me of De Gaulle, but for them De Gaulle is a thing of the past. The names of Doriot and Déat were equally

G

unsuccessful. They didn't quite know what they stood for. We went on to the theoreticians. Another list of names. Maurras? Only one of them had ever read anything he wrote. 'He's an old bore.' Sorel? Never heard of him. The only name that seemed to strike a chord was Soustelle's, curiously enough. 'And as for theories,' said one of them, 'we don't need any. The intellectuals bore us stiff . . . *De l'action directe . . .*'[18]

Direct action was what they wanted; they wanted to shoot, to exhume the plastic bombs of the *Cagoule* once again. And soon afterwards they did, as soon as the military men had been converted to their ideas and dared to defy Paris.

Early Gaullism

Let us now leave these groups of ultra-nationalists while they are getting ready for the *putsch* on 13 May 1958 (which for them was the beginning of the end) and retrace our steps in order to examine Gaullism and Poujadism—two movements more typical than any of the others of post-war France, and which likewise turned up punctually at the great Algerian showdown on 13 May.

Even before Gaullism became a mass movement and gave vent to its anti-parliamentary and anti-republican sentiments through the pseudo-parties known as the *Union Gaulliste* and the *Rassemblement du Peuple Français*, Charles de Gaulle was the man whom many French democrats distrusted more than any other. It is true that during the Resistance all the anti-Fascist forces—Communists included—accepted his leadership, but they thought that they had a safeguard against any 'exploiter of the victory' in the 'Programme of the National Resistance Committee', which stated explicitly that 'united as regards the goals to be achieved and the methods to be employed in liberating the country, the representatives of the movements, groups, parties or political trends on the National Resistance Committee proclaim that they are determined to remain united after the liberation'. This was a magnificent Utopia, and as soon as the shooting was over De Gaulle hastened to prove it. De Gaulle, in fact, could not possibly become the leader of a new Popular Front. In any case, he would not have been willing to give practical application to Point Five in the Committee's programme, which demanded the elimination of 'economic and financial feudalism'. By origin and cultural formation he was a man of the Right, a right-wing nationalist. His old-fashioned conception of politics and society, his monarchical and theocratic notions, undoubtedly owed much to the influence of Maurras's *Action Française*, while his authoritarianism seemed to make him a direct disciple of Pétain. 'When I want to know what France is thinking,' he said in London in 1941, 'I just ask myself.'

The role of undisputed leader was undoubtedly one that had always attracted him. As early as 1932, in that revealing little volume entitled *Le fil de l'épée*, he showed his desire for power, for the right to take decisions, and his conception of the ideal leader (i.e. himself): 'Emerging from obscurity, the military leader is suddenly invested with a frightening authority. In a moment his rights, as well as his duties, become limitless. He can dispose of the lives of others. The future of the country depends directly on his decisions. An entire nation turns to him in anguish.'[19] And when, in 1940, events had actually made him the leader and symbol of 'Free France', he believed that he owed his appointment to Divine Providence, and wrote: 'Standing on the brink of a general renunciation, my mission was suddenly revealed to me, clear and terrible. At that moment, the worst in her history, *c'était à moi d'assumer la France*.'[20] But a man who believed that he was the incarnation of France at the moment of her most appalling disaster and who preferred authoritarian solutions and plebiscitary approval of his actions, could not be expected to tolerate for long the *jeux stériles* of French party politics. On 20 January 1946, after sixteen months of stormy rule, without waiting for a vote or troubling about parliamentary procedure, De Gaulle resigned, but not before he had expressed an opinion which was in itself a threat and a harbinger of his future line of action. 'The exclusive party system has returned. I do not approve of it. But unless I establish a dictatorship by force, which I do not want to do because it would undoubtedly lead to disaster, I have no means of forestalling this experiment. It is therefore essential that I should retire.'[21]

De Gaulle withdrew to the solitude of Colombey-les-Deux-Églises and remained silent until March 1947, while one of his followers, René Capitant, founded the *Union Gaulliste*, which twenty-two members of the Chamber of Deputies joined. But it was still too early to talk of a Gaullist party. The General's return to the political arena took place later and coincided with the beginnings of the Cold War, when it became customary to describe the Communist parties of Western Europe as 'subversive' and 'separatist' organizations. In his speeches at Bruneval and Strasbourg De Gaulle outlined the character and aims of his movement, which of course was not a party, but a *rassemblement*, the aim of which was 'to promote and achieve, despite all our differences, the union of our people, the removal and reform of the State'. The ideology of early Gaullism is contained in these few words. In them we have, in fact, the theme of national grandeur, which must be preserved at all costs, and that of public welfare, which at home must be given priority, despite the party system and Communist action. At first the *Rassemblement du Peuple Français* (RPF) was a huge success. In a fortnight it enrolled 800,000 adherents, most of them nationalists and anti-Communists, men who were opposed to any form of Socialism or State planning and viewed social and colonial upheavals with distaste. At the 1947 general election the RPF achieved another success, polling 17·2 per cent of the votes cast and becoming at one blow the second largest party in France after the Communists. As Carlo Casalegno says,

> Some of the reasons for this triumph are evident. The first was the fear of Communism, at a time when disturbances were becoming particularly serious and frequent and the nightmare of Russia still haunted the disarmed West; the RPF received an avalanche of anti-Communist votes, just as the Christian Democrats did in Italy on 18 April of the following year. Another important reason was the defection of many electors from the MRP *(Mouvement Républicain Populaire)*, whose percentage of votes fell from 25 to little more than 10 per cent. While the French Christian Democrats, who had at one time been the General's most faithful supporters, were hesitating whether to break away from the Left and openly support nationalism, De Gaulle did both these things in a most decisive fashion.[22]

The success of the *Rassemblement* at the polls, its organization, which made it seem more like a militia than a political party, and its definitely anti-parliamentary bias increased the distrust which the left-wing parties had always felt for De Gaulle. In 1948 the leader of the French Resistance was for the first time called a 'Fascist'. The accusation was first made by the *Rassemblement Démocratique Révolutionnaire*, which drew its inspiration from the philosopher Jean-Paul Sartre and from David Rousset. Later the cry was taken up by the Communists, who until then had limited themselves to describing the RPF as a 'factious party'. In February 1950 Étienne Fajon wrote as follows:

> That De Gaulle's speech at the Vélodrome d'Hiver on Saturday was the speech of a Fascist is beyond all question. The attacks on the constitution of the Republic, the exaltation of a 'strong government', the Mussolinian slogan of an alliance between capital and labour, the suggestion that working-class agitation ought to be forcibly suppressed, the appeal to unite around his own person—this apprentice-dictator omitted nothing in his harangue.[23]

The Fascist trend in the *Rassemblement* was also stressed—but this time with lively satisfaction—by the Right, in particular by the *Movimento Sociale Italiano*, and although Maurice Bardèche tried to throw cold water on the enthusiasm of his comrades beyond the Alps by pointing out, in his *Défense de l'Occident*, that De Gaulle, a member of the Resistance and a 'purger', could never become the leader of a Fascist party, the MSI still persisted in admiring De Gaulle and even envied France for having such a man.

Nowadays we can judge these things with more detachment, and in the light of the second and more complex Gaullist experiment we can safely say that the RPF certainly did have '*Qualunquista*' and Fascist tendencies, but that was not all. Like Giannini's 'Common Man' movement, Gaullism showed a liking for authoritarian forms of government and a great contempt for the party system and the intrigues of professional politicians, but its aims were not purely negative, as those of Giannini's party were. As for the RPF's anti-Communist 'commandos', they undoubtedly remind us of the Fascist 'action squads' of the 1920s, but it cannot be said that De Gaulle, whose constant ambition it was to act as mediator between the State and its citizens, ever thought of using them to seize power. Made up as it was of heterogeneous elements, the RPF could not be dominated even by De Gaulle himself, and on 6 May 1953, after the failure of his attempt to overthrow the party system and reform the State, he himself disbanded it. Stalin had died barely two months before, and soon the thaw set in and a new era of relaxation dawned. But Gaullism survived the Cold War and its own first defeat, only to reappear with its two aspects still more clearly distinguishable—the aspect inspired by Spengler and the ethnologist Jacques Soustelle, and the authoritarian and conservative views of General De Gaulle.

Poujadolf

When a disappointed and angry De Gaulle withdrew for the second
time to Colombey-les-Deux-Églises and devoted himself to writing
his memoirs, his role in the political drama was taken over by a
bookseller from Saint-Céré, the youthful and energetic Pierre Poujade. On 23 July 1953, two months after the demise of the *Rassemblement*, Poujade organized in his own little town the first demonstration against the Inland Revenue. The success of this enterprise
induced him to propagate his ideas elsewhere and to transform his
campaign into 'a crusade' against the system of taxation, monopolies and the neo-feudalism of high finance, which according to
him were in league with one another to exploit the small fry of
shopkeepers, artisans and peasants, the 'little men' and the 'no-
bodies'. At first, this amounted to little more than protesting against
the interference of the authorities in fiscal matters, but as it became
more comprehensive and political-minded, Poujadism appeared in
its true colours as an ultra-nationalistic, xenophobic, anti-Semitic
and anti-parliamentary movement. Poujade drew the attention of
the masses to the difference between himself, a 'son of the soil', a
Frenchman of solid peasant origin, and the wealthy Pierre Mendès-
France, who was a Jew and had 'not a drop of Gallic blood in his
veins'.[24] The Marxist parties he described as 'international trusts',
who had allied themselves with world capitalism in their anxiety
'to suppress our country'.[25] Everything foreign was viewed with
suspicion and resentment. 'We want to live as people live today on the
banks of the Seine and the Garonne. If anybody is curious to know
how people live on the banks of the Moskva or the Mississippi, let
him go there!'[26]

Both the Right and the Left were attacked, as well as big business, the Marxist parties, trade unions, the banks, the Jews, state-
planning and collectivism, the intellectuals and the rebels, and all
those who were seeking to undermine the French empire. Appealing to cheap popular sentiment, the bookseller from Saint-Céré
preached that the government ought to be in the hands of the citizens, and not of the parties, and demanded the convocation of the
States-General, to which, as in 1789, the representatives of all
categories of able-bodied citizens would be allowed to submit their
grievances and their claims. Poujade, who had all that was needed
to make him a popular hero, from his Rabelaisian appearance

down to his forceful and aggressive language, expounded his ideas in the market-places of French provincial towns, and in hysterical tones invited his partisans to hang him if he were one day to betray them. He posed as the defender of the people and willingly encouraged the cult of his own person. As a result the UDCA (*Union de Défense des Commerçants et Artisans*) increased its membership rapidly, and on 24 January 1955 150,000 of its adherents flocked to a rally in Paris from every Department in France. A year later, at the election held on 2 January, to the general surprise of foreign observers the UDCA polled 2,600,000 votes and obtained fifty-two seats in the Chamber of Deputies.

The unexpected and sensational success of the UDCA alarmed the French Left. The Communists, who in the early days had warmly supported Poujadism, drew in their horns, and their spokesman, Waldeck Rochet, expressed their disapproval of the attempts the bookseller from Saint-Céré was making to exploit the legitimate grievances of the small shopkeepers and artisans in order to further aims 'of a Fascist character'. The weekly *L'Express* started a violent campaign against Poujade and advocated the formation of a republican front to stem the impetus of his movement. Abroad, too, little tenderness was felt for the leader of the UDCA, and the British cartoonist Vicky immortalized him under the nickname of *Poujadolf*. The bookseller defended himself against these attacks: 'They accuse us of being Fascists. Is appealing to the people Fascism?' But his denials carried little weight, for the neo-Fascists hailed him as one of themselves and extolled him in their periodicals. Shortly after the election *Rivarol* wrote exultingly:

> There are grounds for hope and confidence. The 'system' has received a blow from which it will never recover. The triumph (the word is no exaggeration) of the Poujadist candidates at the polls can mean only one thing: the real France has shaken off its torpor and is preparing to kick out the criminals, traitors and nincompoops who have become scandalously rich by battening on the misfortunes of the country.[27]

The Maurras-monarchical *Aspects de la France* saw in Poujade the 'strong man' whom France needed, while the National Socialist *Fidélité*, the organ of the *Phalange Française*, made no attempt to hide its satisfaction: 'The Saint-Céré movement is the only one in the last ten years that has been greeted with enthusiasm by our members ... Pierre Poujade is of the same age as many members of the *Pha-*

lange . . . He speaks the same forceful language, intelligible to all, as we do—the language of a generation that has read the works of L. F. Céline.' And after pointing out that the Poujadist Deputies were 'rebels', but not yet revolutionaries, the journal added: 'The only unforgivable sin in politics is not carrying one's ideas to their logical conclusion. But sooner or later you will have to reach the stage that we reached years ago.'[28]

A section of the movement—which was faced with a serious crisis after the *putsch* on 13 May 1958—did in fact adopt the extremist attitude of the neo-Fascists and helped to swell the ranks of the *plastiqueurs*, but most of its members, even when Poujade opposed De Gaulle and indulged in a dangerous flirtation with Salan and the OAS, never gave any effective support to the partisans of a French Algeria, one of the reasons being that the influence of the UDCA in the country as a whole gradually declined and eventually became insignificant after its defeats at the polls and the settlement of the Algerian question. Lastly, although the psychology of Poujadism was closely akin to that of Fascism and although it was just as hostile to the working-class proletariat, to Jews, culture and intellectuals, the *Mouvement de Saint-Céré* never became sufficiently modern and industry-minded to justify its classification as a branch of Fascism, but was reduced to playing a subordinate role. We accordingly believe that Stanley Hoffmann was right when, in 1956, before Poujadism had had to tackle the Algerian problem, he expressed the opinion that the Poujadists were not ready for 'any political activity which frankly admitted that it was political, or for a "classic" type of Fascism according to which Fascism is a cult of the State and a philosophy of the absorption by the State of society as a whole':

> The France of the 'little men' was far too Girondist for that; the basis of the movement remained too rural, for it included too many people for whom mass action was a novelty, a thrilling adventure, but in the long run rather terrifying—a feeling which was unknown to the adepts of totalitarian movements. Fascism is above all the practice and mystic worship of violence; the Poujadists were certainly ready to commit occasional acts of violence of any sort, but they were unwilling to run serious risks and were too fond of order to 'approve such methods'.[29]

These methods were, however, approved by a minority whom we shall meet again during the clash on 13 May, under the leadership of Paul Chevallier, of the 'corporativist' Dr Lefebvre, and the café-proprietor Ortiz, all of them militant members of the UDCA, who played a prominent part in the Algerian drama.[30]

The 13 May Plots

The difficulties and contradictions resulting from the Algerian war hastened the decline of the Fourth Republic, and the forces of the French extreme Right saw that their moment had come. At first they tailed along behind Pierre Poujade's movement in the hope that it might shatter what Marshal Juin had once said was a 'board of directors' rather than a 'State'; but when Poujadism began to lose some of its vigour, they decided to play the Algerian card, that is to say, the card of exaggerated nationalism and subversion. The task of stirring up a population which already felt that it had been betrayed and sacrificed by the mother country and of finding allies among the military proved far easier than they had foreseen. Another reason was that in Algeria, in the course of the bitter fighting, a highly abnormal atmosphere had been created, in which anything was possible and permissible, even the most shameful things. In every district where fighting took place, in the Aurès or in Kabylia, the torture and killing of prisoners were everyday occurrences. The same thing happened in the camps and secret headquarters of the DOP *(Dispositif Opérationnel de Protection).* In a report dated 13 December 1955, the director-general of the *Sûreté Nationale,* who had himself investigated and denounced these criminal practices, states that 'the police have had a share in these atrocities, and so has the army. I cannot bear to think that by their behaviour the French police remind people of the methods of the Gestapo. And, as an officer of the Reserve, I cannot bear to hear French soldiers compared with the brutal German SS men.'[31] Notwithstanding these admissions and statements torture and murder continued throughout the war, because, as Pierre Vidal-Naquet points out, 'in Algeria, torture was for the most part the outcome of a defensive reaction on the part of a minority whose privileges were threatened, of an army entrusted with the protection of this minority which could think of no better way of carrying on the struggle, and of a government which for years, with the support of the bulk of the nation, had done everything it could to safeguard the privileges of that minority.'[32]

G*

The theoreticians of this merciless war were certain officers who had fought in the Tongking campaign and lost it and who blamed France for ceasing to take any interest in the Algerian war, just as she had done in Indo-China. In 1956 and 1957, while the battle for Algiers was raging, they perfected their theory of *action psychologique*, which was the product of an ill-digested assimilation of classic works on revolution—for example Marx, Lenin, Trotsky, and above all Mao Tse-tung—and in substance can be reduced to the concoction of a theory of torture as an instrument of warfare, and the practical transformation of Algeria into one huge concentration camp. But since, in order to justify in their own eyes this pitiless type of warfare, they felt an urge to create a new system of values, they proclaimed themselves defenders of the West and of Christian civilization against Evil, Islam and Marxism. The man who more than any other strove to bring about a symbiosis of integralistic Catholicism and extreme nationalism, was himself a renegade Communist, Georges Sauge, who took upon himself the mission of 'saving society from the Communism whirlwind'. The intolerance of this convert did not escape the notice of the army's psychological warfare department, who put him in touch with the *Cinquième Bureau* and sent him on frequent missions to Algeria, where he met the colonels of *Action Psychologique* and the Sidos brothers, leaders of *Jeune Europe*. To the Godards, Trinquiers, Lacheroys, Gardes and Argouds, and all the other theoreticians of revolutionary warfare,[33] Sauge thus brought the comforts of a religion which still had a medieval conception of evil and seemed to approve the methods of *Action Psychologique*.[34]

In this climate of violence and illegality, of exaggerated nationalism and a 'crusade against evil', the groups of the extreme right wing were able to operate undisturbed and to perfect their subversive plans, though they did not succeed in reaching a lasting agreement among themselves as to joint action and the choice of a candidate for the premiership.

On the eve of 13 May a hybrid assemblage of groups, some of them rivals of others, found themselves in the field. The best organized was the one led by Dr Félix Martin, ex-head of the *Cagoule*'s *Deuxième Bureau*, and by the mystic Robert Martel, who represented the Mitidja settlers. Their aim was to overthrow the régime, to keep Algeria French at all costs, and to install an authoritarian, nationalistic and corporative State. They relied on the army, and in particular on Generals Cherrière and Chassin. They maintained more or less close contact with Jean-Baptiste Biaggi's 'commandos', the activists of *Jeune Nation* and the Poujadists, who in Algeria were led by Joseph Ortiz and Dr Bernard Lefebvre; the latter was a theoretician of the Corporative State and the author of a book entitled *L'Occident en péril*, in which we read that 'the authorities must try to establish a terrestrial order which will be the image of the divine'. On the other hand plots were organized on their own account by groups of officers who were experts in the technique of 'revolutionary warfare', who dreamed of establishing an Algerian republic independent of France and evolved a theory of 'military Fascism'. Obviously the Gaullists were not absent from the arena, and since they knew all about the plots, they tried, through Léon Delbecque and Jacques Soustelle, to control them and bring them into line with their own plans. 'On 29 April,' one of De Gaulle's biographers tells us:

> Lucien Neuwirth, whom Delbecque had appointed as his chief collaborator in Algeria, insisted once again on knowing what De Gaulle would do if Algeria revolted and made an appeal to him. De Gaulle answered in these very words: 'I shall respond to it.' Thus on that day he knew—as many observers in Algiers did—that a crisis was coming on the further shores of the Mediterranean. He also knew that some of the Gaullists would try to sidetrack the revolt in such a way as to cause an appeal to him to be made.[35]

And that, in fact, is what actually happened. On 13 May Pierre Lagaillarde, a former president of the Algiers students' association, occupied the palace of the government and started the counter-revolution which Dr Martin had been preparing since 1954. But the activists of the extreme right wing soon showed that they had no combined strategy. Biaggi and the Deputies and ex-paratroopers Le Pen and Demarquet never even reached Algiers. General Chassin of the air force took to the woods in the neighbourhood of Lyons; but he waited in vain for the reinforcements of parachutist units which were supposed to arrive from Algeria. With undeniable skill the Gaullists managed to keep the revolt under control and exploit it for their own benefit. On 15 May Léon Delbecque persuaded General Salan to wind up his speech to the crowd assembled in the Forum by shouting 'Vive De Gaulle!' On the afternoon of that same day De Gaulle issued a communiqué in which he told the country that he was ready to take over the reins of government. And on 28 May he did. This day marks a break between Gaullism and the other counter-revolutionary movements. It is true that De Gaulle was raised to power by an illegal movement, but a *putsch*, but in order to reach the Élysée he had first to come to terms with the men of a régime which he detested and promise them that he would maintain the public liberties, the parliamentary régime and constitutional procedure. As De La Gorce points out, he also undertook to eliminate

> military domination, pre-war Fascism, right-wing extremism and economic traditionalism, whether corporative, nationalist or poujadist. It was on 28 May that there began, without anybody realizing it, the series of events which led De Gaulle to crush the military opposition, to go ahead with decolonization, to reduce the European community in Algeria to new dimensions, to destroy the OAS and to incur the risks of the attempts on his life at Pont-sur-Seine and Petit-Clamart.[36]

Life and death of the OAS

The activists of Algiers who had accepted the Gaullists' suggestion that they should use De Gaulle as their instrument soon found that they had been hoodwinked. Not only did De Gaulle hasten to launch a policy, both in Algeria and in France, which did not conform with their ideas, but he also recalled to France or removed from Algeria the military leaders who had been most closely involved in the 13 May *putsch*: Generals Salan and Vanuxem and Colonels Lacheroy, Trinquier, Ducasse, Faugas and Goussault. Even Gaullists like Jacques Soustelle were irritated by the steps taken by De Gaulle, for they had really hoped that the General would have followed the line of action suggested by the *ultras*. The idea of another *coup* thus began to circulate among the disappointed and angry activists, and from the summer of 1958 onwards efforts were made to reconstitute the extremist front that had failed to achieve its objectives on 13 May.

As in the past, this consisted of two categories of men—those who wanted to go on fighting, mainly in the hope of keeping Algeria as a preserve for the *pieds-noirs*, and those who saw in Algeria merely a springboard and were ready to sacrifice it if this would enable them to seize power in Paris. On 1st November 1958 Joseph Ortiz, Jean-Jacques Susini, who had become president of the Algiers students' association, and Dr Jean-Claude Perez founded the *Front*

National Français, (FNF) the first large organization of a definitely
Fascist type to be founded since the Algerian war. In accordance
with the best traditions it immediately began to organize armed
bands and borrowed from the Sidos brothers' *Jeune Nation* the
symbol of the Celtic cross, because this was 'the emblem of the
old Celtic tribes' and also of 'the conquest of Algeria, of which
we have no reason to feel ashamed and which reminds us of the
glory of France'.[37] About the same time Robert Martel founded
the *Mouvement Populaire du 13 Mai* (MP 13), in the hope of en-
rolling all the most violent reactionary elements among the settlers,
while Dr Bernard Lefebvre set up his *Mouvement pour l'instaura-
tion d'un ordre corporatif*, which cherished nostalgic memories of
Pétain's Vichy régime. The officers who had taken part in the
'revolutionary war' also remained on the *qui vive* and were quick
to seize any chance of sabotaging De Gaulle's orders, as Gérard
Périot tells us in his report on a speech made by Colonel Bigeard
to his officers:

> When General De Gaulle and Delouvrier came to Saida, they
> told me that torture must stop. So what I say to you, gentlemen,
> is 'Torture must stop!, but of course . . . that means that you'll
> carry on just the same,' and the colonel added that General De
> Gaulle's policy was to be followed only when it seemed to be
> 'reasonable'.[38]

On 16 September 1959, at eight o'clock in the evening, De Gaulle
announced the formula of self-determination, which was a decisive
step towards the final liquidation of French rule in Algeria. The
announcement caused dismay among the *pieds-noirs* and the activists realized that they would have to take time by the forelock.
In November, at a public meeting held in the Bab-el-Oued quarter
of Algiers, Dr Perez declared open war on the government and
appealed to 'fanatical patriots ready to give their lives' to take
action. On 18 December Robert Martel announced that his MP 13
group intended to overthrow the republican régime, and so, he
explained, 'we don't need slogans any more, we need armed organizations'.[39] The activists also established contact with Colonels
Gardes, Godard and Argoud, whose ideas coincided almost exactly
with those of the extremists, while territorial and reserve units of
the army were formed into one group and placed under the orders
of Marcel Ronda, who had secretly become a member of Ortiz's
Fascist FNF, which already counted 10,000 adherents. The plan for

another *putsch* was now ready, and it was a question of waiting for the right moment.

On 24 January 1960 the FNF thought the moment had come and it therefore appealed to the public to come out on the streets and demonstrate against De Gaulle's policy of 'renunciation'. In the course of the day the demonstration rapidly assumed the proportions of a veritable revolt; numerous barricades were erected and towards evening during an exchange of shots seventeen gendarmes and nine demonstrators were killed. From 24 January to 1st February several streets in the centre of Algiers remained in the hands of the insurgents, who were led by Lagaillarde and by Joseph Ortiz, while the army merely stood by, making no attempt to suppress the revolt, and some parachutist colonels even helped the rebels to strengthen the barricades. But this time there was a man at the Élysée who was not going to allow himself to be intimidated. On the evening of the 29th De Gaulle appeared on the television screens in his general's uniform and announced his intention to crush this insurrection which had been made possible by the 'complacent hesitation of certain military elements'. On the following day the barricades were abandoned. Lagaillarde was arrested and Ortiz managed to flee to Spain.

Once again the *putsch* had failed because the entente between the *ultras* and the army had shown itself to be a fragile thing, despite the fact that since 13 May there had been a systematic political penetration of the army, thanks to the underground activities of the experts in psychological warfare. After the surrender of Lagaillarde, De Gaulle lost no time. Colonels Argoud, Godard and Broizat were recalled to France; Colonel Gardes was placed under arrest pending trial, and it was also decided that the commander-in-chief, General Challe, should be relieved of his post; lastly, the territorial units were disbanded and the *Action Psychologique* centres suppressed, But by now the army had been contaminated. And by recalling these extremist officers De Gaulle committed the imprudence of reinforcing the bridgehead of the *ultras* in France. The OAS had not yet been born, but all its leading figures were now known by name, they had revealed what they were and what they wanted, and they began to forge links among themselves, determined this time that no obstacle should stop them from overthrowing Charles de Gaulle and his Fifth Republic.

The adventurous story of the OAS did not begin in Madrid in February 1961, as many writers have erroneously assumed, but at

Algiers on 10 and 11 December 1960, even though the initials OAS were as yet unknown and the walls for a long time to come were still covered with inscriptions exalting the FAF. This *Front de l'Algérie Française* was formed on 17 June 1960 from the remnants of the FNF and other activist groups. Having learned their lesson from the fiasco of 13 May and the 'week of the barricades', the *ultras* swore to forget their rivalries and their dissensions, and to form a united front of all the forces still prepared to fight for a French Algeria. They entrusted the leadership of this coalition to two men, Andros and Vignau, who had played only minor roles in the political life of Algeria. By eliminating from the top positions those leaders who had become too well known, they hoped to forestall any accusations of extremism and Fascism such as had been brought against the FNF and other groups of the extreme right wing. In a week the membership of the FAF reached 100,000 and the statute of its Parisian section was signed by the most illustrious names in right-wing radicalism: Tixier-Vignancour, Lacoste-Lareymondie, Le Pen, Jean Dides and Georges Sauge.

On 10 December, during De Gaulle's visit to Algeria, the FAF tried to persuade the European population to demonstrate, in the hope that the Muslims would react and that the army would thus be forced to intervene to protect the Whites. But times had changed and De Gaulle's new Algerian policy was already taking effect. The Muslims swarmed into the streets and faced the *pieds-noirs*, but this time the soldiers kept their heads and did not open fire, though the Europeans kept egging them on, shouting: 'Fire, make up your minds to fire! The Germans used to open fire for much less!'[40] The two communities faced each other in an atmosphere of tension and hatred that was a prelude to what the OAS was to install for a whole year, but nothing happened and the hopes of the *ultras* were frustrated. Salan, Lagaillarde and Susini, who were waiting for the signal to dash to Algiers, stayed in their hideout in Madrid, whither the headquarters of the conspiracy had moved a few months earlier. The great novelty, which was to result in the birth of the OAS, was that the army had shown that it was not prepared to support the insurgents. Generals Salan, Challe, Zeller and Jouhaud found this out to their cost when, on 22 April 1961, they seized Algiers after a *coup de main*, but owing to lack of support were compelled to give in four days later, some of them choosing to go to prison, while others went underground and carried on the struggle. For the *ultras* the only way out was to plunge into subversion, to apply the scorched earth policy to 'their' Algeria and to pin their hopes on the physical elimination of De Gaulle. As has been shrewdly pointed out, 'the death-wish took possession of this movement without a future. Thinking gave way to violence. Men became murderers. The OAS was the Fascism of negation.'[41]

From its very start the *Organisation de l'Armée Secrète* behaved very much like the Fascist *Cagoule* in 1936. They both had a predilection for conspiracy and violence. Though they were separated in time by thirty years, they spoke the same language; they used the same terms borrowed from science fiction, the same invectives, the same expressions of wild enthusiasm. They had no time to waste on drawing up political programmes. They had to confine themselves to damning their adversaries and clamouring for their destruction. Eugène Deloncle, the leader of the *Cagoule*, said in 1936: 'We intend to overthrow the State because it is impossible to live under a republic.'[42] Plastic bombs, used for the first time in history by the *Cagoule* in 1937, were adopted by the OAS as a means of convincing others, and during the aftermath of the Algerian war they caused the death of 415 persons and injured 1,145. The *commandos d'action ponctuelle* dogged the footsteps of De Gaulle, just as the commandos of the *Gagoule* had, more successfully, hounded down the Rosselli brothers.

For almost a year the OAS was quite successful, since it managed to mobilize and control all the groups of *ultras*, despite the eternal squabbling which had at one time threatened to disintegrate them. Under one and the same banner we find the theoreticians of psychological warfare, the armed bands of Ortiz's FNF, the settlers egged on by Robert Martel, the nationalistic students of *Jeune Nation* guided by Susini, a few scattered groups of Poujadists, the advocates of a Corporative State led by Dr Lefebvre, who like Jacques Soustelle was an ex-Gaullist, and even the Catholic Georges Bidault, who had been one of the leaders of the French Resistance during the war. With such a motley coalition—some of its members being revolutionaries and others extreme reactionaries—it was easy to wage guerrilla warfare, but not so easy to impose a doctrine. In fact the OAS never had a precise and definitive doctrine; it was obliged to be vague, in order to avoid offending one or other of its many factions. But even the rare pronouncements which were disseminated by means of clandestine publications tell us enough to enable us to classify the OAS doctrine as being typically Fascist.

In a muddle-headed programme of thirty-six points, published during the summer of 1961, the doctrinarians of the OAS started by announcing that a 'surgical operation is necessary' and that 'only the French nationalists are qualified to perform it'. After criticizing 'all the parties and all the men who have failed', they announce that when they come to power they will 'abolish all parties' and 'take over their offices, which will be considered as property of the nation', that they will 'immediately hand over to newly married couples and homeless French subjects the premises now occupied by parasitical organisms such as UNESCO, the League for the Rights of Man . . . adopt the Celtic cross as the official national emblem', etc., etc.[43]

In another publication the OAS stated that it wanted to bring about 'the fall of the Gaullist régime' and the establishment of a 'government of Public Safety' which would install 'a genuinely popular régime, opposing both the big capitalists and the Communist International; a régime which will safeguard our traditions, restore our links with Africa, rebuild Europe and restore to France her position in a West which will be proud of itself'.[44]

Tixier-Vignancour, the stubborn and skilful defender of Salan and other OAS leaders when they appeared before the courts, told us in an interview that 'the OAS has nothing to do with Fascism. The OAS is merely the reaction of a part of the French people, humiliated in their own patriotism and angry. If Fascism succeeds, the responsibility for that will be De Gaulle's.'[45] On the other hand, Maurice Bardèche admitted several things:

> The OAS is not Fascist; nevertheless there are among its supporters a number of people who are Fascists by temperament, who dream of a régime closely resembling Fascism. In a certain sense they are Fascists without knowing it . . . I believe that there will be a Fascist revival in France; under various aspects the trend can be seen everywhere. Fascism is in the air. It is an inevitable solution rather than a political force . . . And after all, De Gaulle has contributed a great deal to the spread of Fascism.[46]

In democratic circles opinions differed slightly as to whether the word 'Fascist' should be used or not. For Georges Montaron, editor of *Témoignage Chrétien*, the OAS was 'closer to the movements of Franco and Salazar than to the classical form of Fascism, because it seems to rely more on the support of the army and of Catholic integralism than on the National Socialist forces which are typical of Fascism'. For Jean-Marie Domenach, editor of *Esprit*:

> The OAS is unquestionably a Fascist movement, but only if we give a very broad meaning to the term 'Fascist'. Born of a feeling of rebelliousness, of the mental shock experienced by the whole nation after the loss of Algeria, it has transformed itself into a subversive movement and now resorts to the ideas and methods of Fascism, for example hysterical anti-Communism, hatred for any kind of discussion, and recourse to murder. Argoud, Bidault and Soustelle are three men united by their anger.

On the other hand, the Socialist Pierre Stibbe thought that the OAS was definitely a Fascist movement:

> The systematic recourse to attempts to kill those who are against the idea of a French Algeria, the clandestine organization of armed bands with a view to seizing power and installing a dictatorship, which are so characteristic of the OAS, reveal the close affinity between this movement and Fascism, and it is no mere chance that the survivors of Nazi formations have met once more in the ranks of the OAS and are fighting side by side with former members of the Resistance like Bidault and Soustelle, whose outdated colonialism and false conception of nationalism have prevailed over the Resistance's fidelity to the democratic spirit. But the essential basis of the OAS is the European community in Algeria, which stubbornly defended its privileges. And now that Algeria is independent, the OAS has lost all its *raison d'être*.

In July 1964, while the Curutchet trial was taking place, the OAS was virtually suppressed. Salan, Challe, Zeller, Jouhaud, Argoud and 4,000 other activists were imprisoned; Bidault, Soustelle, Gardes and Perez fled to Latin America; Gardy and Dufour went to Portugal; Lagaillarde and Château-Jobert to Spain; Susini to Denmark; Ortiz to the Balearics; Godard to Italy. The only man who remained active was Captain Philippe Sergent, who succeeded Gardy as leader of the OAS in May 1963. After the end of the Algerian war the various factions in the OAS ceased to be a united party and formed independent groups such as the MCR *(Mouvement de Combat Contre-révolutionnaire)* under Colonel Château-Jobert and the OASR *(Organisation Armée Secrète Révolutionnaire)*, whose leaders declared that they had previously belonged to the 'left wing', but had abandoned it because it 'supported Islamic fanaticism and that Fascism of the poor called

Gaullism'. Separated and hounded by the police the surviving members of the OAS (numbering some 5,000–6,000) wasted their energies on futile polemics. One group of them, adhering to the OAS-CNR, even found time in April 1964 to indulge in auto-criticism, which if it is nothing else, is at least drastic:

> The officers who had attended staff courses showed that they were very poor strategists. In France they did not find the same logistic support as in Algeria and they knew nothing about the French situation as a whole . . . The OAS has for too long underestimated the strength of the police in France. The best description of the OAS and of the police was given by De Gaulle himself after the attempt on his life at Petit-Clamart: 'I am surrounded by imbeciles who have to deal with nincompoops.'

Gaullism in power

In French left-wing circles the conviction is widespread that despite the revolt of the generals in Algiers and the attempts on De Gaulle's life there was never any real break between the OAS and Gaullism.[47] These two movements, both financed by that same *Patronat* which was still dreaming of the good old Vichy days, are said to have been competitors rather than enemies; they differed only in their methods and in reality represented two typical facets of Fascism—the violent and revolutionary aspect (OAS) and the paternalistic and corporative aspect (UNR). When he was court-martialled, Colonel Bastien-Thiry, leader of the 'commando' that tried to kill De Gaulle at Petit-Clamart, went so far as to accuse a Gaullist Minister, Giscard d'Estaing, of having been a member of the OAS under the cover-name of '12 B', adding:

> 'The Resistance movement established contacts with parliamentary circles and even with members of the UNR. I would like to add that we were financed by certain men—bankers and industrialists—who at the same time were financing the operations of the government with an eye to the future. These men were in contact with the UNR.'[48] Referring to Bastien-Thiry's allegations, his defending counsel, Tixier-Vignancour, said that for once he found himself in agreement with the Communists, who were fond of saying that the OAS and Gaullism were two branches of the same tree. 'I believe that they are perfectly right. The tree is the same, and if there are two branches, that is because of events which it was not their job to forestall. If Algeria had never existed, I would like to know what difference there would be between Colonel Bastien-Thiry and Lieutenant De la Tocnaye and you, gentlemen!'[49]

In a meeting held at the *Mutualité* in October 1962, during the election campaign, the Socialist Claude Bourdet said: 'The OAS is the UNR of yesterday. You have only got to strike out one name (De Gaulle) in order to see how ridiculous the whole system was.' Some time before this, in an attempt to prove the extreme duplicity of De Gaulle, the weekly *L'Express* went so far as to say (and so far as we know the statement has never been contradicted) that the Gaullist government financed the OAS indirectly, in order to keep up a certain tension in the country and heighten the fear of subversion, elements which Gaullism exploited in order to consolidate its own position. These accusations, made by both Fascists and democrats, would seem to be supported by the methods used to suppress the OAS, which never assumed the character of an operation in the interests of 'public safety'. In fact, immediately after it had created them, Gaullism hastened to dissolve all those organisms which were definitely anti-Fascist, for example the OCC (organization against clandestine movements) and the CDR (committees for the defence of the Republic), which had shown that they were taking the fight against the OAS very seriously. And though it is true that Déguelde and Bastien-Thiry were executed for their share in the attempt on De Gaulle's life, one cannot help feeling that a great measure of clemency was shown to high-ranking officers and thousands of other activists. Later on, most of those who received sentences were set free as a result of amnesties.

It may well be that no such pact of reconciliation was ever conceived or concluded, but it is undoubtedly true that Gaullism emerged victorious, but not pitiless, from the battle between the 'two branches of the same tree', and since then, thanks to its handling of foreign policy, it has managed to upset the equilibrium achieved at Yalta and has accelerated the trend towards corporativism, with the result that many men of the Right have once more joined its ranks. Is Gaullism, then, merely a modernized form of Fascism, as many maintain? Was Drieu La Rochelle (the theoretician of Fascism who committed suicide in 1945) perhaps right when he prophesied that De Gaulle would one day become the Duce of Fascism that Doriot had never contrived to be?

'It's absurd to say that the head of the Resistance couldn't possibly be a Fascist just because it seems impossible,' wrote a Socialist, Gilles Martinet. 'All the same, De Gaulle is not a Fascist. To compare him with Hitler and Mussolini is a grave error of judgement rather than an insult. But he is remarkably like Salazar, and like him he owes much of his political philosophy to Maurras.'[50] François Mitterand avoids using the word Fascist, but he is even more severe:

> Between De Gaulle and the Republicans there is, and there always will be, the question of his *coup d'état*. There's no getting over that. De Gaulle rose to power because he wanted to, because he worked patiently to that end, played his cards well and seized it boldly. Between 13 May and 3 June 1958 General De Gaulle brought off his first *coup*. After having encouraged a political plot and exploited sedition in the army, he overthrew the constituted but decadent order that called itself a Republic . . . What is Gaullism, now that it has achieved power after being born of an insurrection? Just a common or garden *coup d'état* . . . There are still Ministers in France. They even say that there is still a Prime Minister. But there is no longer a government. Only the President of the Republic can give orders and make decisions.[51]

According to Georges Montaron, 'De Gaulle is a nationalist puffed up with pride, but he is not a Fascist. Maybe he will humiliate parliament again by depriving it of still more of its powers, and he may even succeed in establishing a paternalistic dictatorship. But that won't be Fascism; it will be authoritarianism.' Jean-Marie Domenach is more or less of the same opinion:

> De Gaulle is a man of tradition and his mental make-up is miles away from Fascism. He dreams of establishing a kind of protectorate over democracy, and it is unfair to maintain that we are living under a dictatorship; it would be more correct to say that we have got as much democracy as the weakness of the parties in the France of today will allow. Nevertheless, there's no getting over the fact that by accustoming the country not to argue and not to think for itself, Gaullism is preparing the way for Fascism.

And according to Pierre Stibbe:

> I do not think that Gaullism is leading France towards Fascism. Of course, the circumstances under which De Gaulle returned to power in May 1958 after the Fascist rising in Algiers might well have generated a kind of Fascism, but they were closely bound up with the war in Algeria. To tell the truth, the régime installed by General De Gaulle could be described as a 'Liberal monocracy'; it is a personal régime, since all important decisions are taken by the President and are then subject to purely formal ratification by means of a nation-wide referendum. But it is not a one-party régime, and the opposition is still free to express its opinion and does not fail to do so. At one time there was a danger that the

ultras might kill De Gaulle and exploit the political void created by his death in order to seize power and bring in real Fascism, but that was an eventuality much more to be feared during the Algerian war than after peace had been restored.[52]

Replying to someone who asked whether De Gaulle had the soul of a dictator, the Socialist Guy Mollet said: 'I don't think he has it yet. Although grave wrong has been done to certain aspects of liberty—for example, the freedom of the Press—the fundamental liberties have been preserved.'[53] According to the former Radical Minister Pierre Cot, the Gaullist conception of personal power is more revolutionary and more dangerous than the concept of monarchy, and stressing the hidden dangers of plebiscites, of which the General is so fond, he adds: 'De Gaulle has benefited by the difficulties arising from the Algerian war, just as Hitler exploited the defeat of 1918 and Mussolini the disillusionment of the Italian people.'[54]

When we examine such statements, we note a certain reluctance to utter the word 'Fascist'. Everybody seems to prefer vaguer terms such as proud nationalist, authoritarian, or anti-Liberal, though all agree that De Gaulle moves in an atmosphere which, if it is not Fascist, is pre-Fascist, that practically speaking he is ruling France without anybody above him, that his power is greater than that of a Prince-President in a Bonapartist republic, and that he has had illustrious predecessors in MacMahon, Millerand, Charles X and Louis Napoleon. They avoid using the word 'Fascist', even though they all agree that De Gaulle is allergic to the idea of governing with the traditional powers and that he has therefore resorted to all the three precepts of dictatorship: 1) by creating a vacancy in the headship of the State; 2) by presenting himself as final arbiter above all parties; 3) by hastily launching the constitutional laws necessary to ratify a 'new order'. In fact, under the new constitution De Gaulle has reduced the powers of parliament (Article 37); under Article 38 he can promulgate decrees which for the time being will have the validity of laws; Article 16 authorizes him (without imposing any time-limit) to assume dictatorial powers if he thinks that the situation is 'grave'; under Article 11 he can, subject to a referendum, modify ordinary and organic laws which have already been approved by parliament; and under Article 12 he can dissolve the Assembly and order a general election. But that is not all; he has on occasion even violated his own constitution by reserving to himself the sole right to deal with the 'reserved sector', which comprises the most delicate instruments of a country's life such as diplomacy and national defence.

The reluctance displayed by De Gaulle's critics in using the word 'Fascist' is understandable, since it is not an accurate definition of the Gaullist régime. Although it contains a few elements of Fascism, Gaullism has to a certain extent gone beyond Fascism in order to conform with the demands and ways of a modern industrial society. As Richard Duflot has pointed out:

> The madness or the Fascism of De Gaulle must definitely be relegated to the limbo of outdated slogans, coined during periods of unrest (e.g. decolonization), which today have lost all their revolutionary truth; Gaullism is a *de facto* State, a modern and polyvalent reality which we must make up our minds to resist wherever it may appear, and not only with the weapons of satire, irony and iconoclastic nostalgia. This reality is called neo-capitalism— a capitalism brought up to date, intelligent, capable of planning, and productive.[55]

Although from time to time he has conferred upon himself the not exactly modest titles of 'symbol', 'guide' and 'trustee of democracy', De Gaulle nevertheless remains the representative of one class, the middle class of finance which supports him but imposes its own conditions, and strives to create, through his enlightened despotism, its own ideal State, which will provide for the effective, if not formal, abolition of the representative system and its replacement by a Corporative State. De Gaulle may claim to 'be France' and is convinced that he is filling the role of arbiter above all parties and classes, but in reality we have only to examine his birth-certificate, his social programme, the men he has chosen to be his collaborators, in order to see how untrue this legend is.

Charles André Joseph-Marie de Gaulle, in fact, belongs by birth to the landed gentry, which in northern France has become fused with the industrial middle class. He has chosen as his closest collaborators men like Pompidou, Couve de Murville, Giscard d'Estaing, Jacquinot, Berthoin, Mayer, Debré and Chalandon, representatives of big capital and of the largest French banks, such as the Banque de Paris et des Pays-Bas, the Banque Rothschild, the Banque de l'Union Parisienne, the Banque d'Indochine and the Banque Lazard. In all the key posts of the State administration he has placed trusted members of the financial oligarchy. And it was purely because of class solidarity that, when he was in power in 1945, he stopped the nationalization of the banks, and later, as leader of the RPF and then as President, he began to formulate a Socialist programme having all the characteristics and theoretical justifications of a Maurras-type corporativism—for example, the futility of the class struggle, the need for collaboration between capital and labour, the importance of creating a new type of trade-unionism 'purged to the bottom of politics' and of transforming the Senate into a kind of Corporative Council. In short, a programme the aim of which is to convince the French working classes that conditions can be improved without altering in any way the structure of a capitalistic society.[56] Even De Gaulle's foreign policy reflects the influence and pressure of the class to which the General belongs. The Carolingian empire of which De Gaulle dreams—excluding Britain because she is a dangerous competitor and spectator—is first of all a Europe of monopolies united against the trade unions. It is De Gaulle's ambition to use his *force de frappe* to enable France to play an important role in the Europe of the 'Six' and to make her a wedge between the two world *blocs*, and this coincides with the ideas of the technocrats and representatives of the great monopolies, who see in the agreements concluded with the German capitalists, in the Euro-African policy and in the recognition of China (for purely economic reasons), in the expansion of technical know-how and the huge increase in nuclear production (the works at Pierrelatte, Marcoule, La Hague, Mazzingarbe and Miramas), the realization of their hegemonic dream which had been interrupted by two world wars.

By this we do not mean to imply that De Gaulle is merely a tool in the hands of the financial oligarchy. Though he instinctively serves the interests of his own class, his personality is undoubtedly so individualistic that he feels it incumbent upon him to play a role that shall remain unique. In actual fact, the Gaullist 'system' has no precedents; it is not presidential rule on the American pattern, as some would like to make out, but in truth an absolute monarchy clad in republican robes, and it has resulted in a 'plebiscitarian democracy' not unlike the régimes installed by Franco and Salazar. With the new constitution and his demagogic appeal to the nation in order to obtain his investiture as President by a free and universal suffrage, De Gaulle has achieved practically all the aims he set himself. He has humiliated and reduced to impotence the parties opposed to him, he has made his own party (the UNR) a mere instrument for the production of Deputies ready to hand him a blank cheque, he has turned the Assembly into an empty hall where debates are tending more and more to become pure formalities. Lastly, he has urged the French to cease taking any interest in politics, in a speech which amounted approximately to saying 'Stop worrying about me and what I do, and I will look after you and your welfare.' The French are amused by Tisot's jokes about De Gaulle; they laugh when they listen to the gramophone-record *Autocirculation*, which is a parody of a speech by the General. But when it comes to voting, they vote *oui*, just as their President had foreseen. Because De Gaulle is a good psychologist, and he 'understands' them, he knows their weaknesses, which he exploits, and he manages to create a universal indifference. What are the underlying dangers of this bargain between De Gaulle and his France of yes-men? First of all, the depoliticization of the country (the 32 per cent of abstentions at the October 1962 election was the first grave symptom of this). Next, the perilous strengthening of the powers of the executive. About forty years ago Mussolini wrote that 'one of the reasons for the decline of the democratic and Liberal State has been the disproportionate increase in the powers of the elected chamber to the detriment of the executive power'. De Gaulle would agree with this diagnosis and has provided a remedy: 'The executive power must lie with the head of the State, who is above all parties.' These words were spoken at Bayeux in 1946. Today, after various revisions of the constitution, he has almost achieved this final aim. But De Gaulle, as the editor of *Le Monde*, Hubert Beuve-Méry, remarks, is not the sort of man to rest content with being the holder of power; he also wants to be its 'fountainhead':

> Rarely has the theory of absolute power been expounded with such complacency, clarity and vigour . . . But if we admit that everything in the country must be in the hands of one man and that liberties are founded on a concession and tolerance that can always be revoked, rather than on a State in its own right, then we already have the germs of a more or less totalitarian dictatorship.[57]

But the worst service that the *Homme de la Nation* has rendered to the French and, in the last analysis, to all Europeans, is that he has officially revived the cult of nationalism and has restored to France the notion of her *grandeur*. If we glance through the French newspapers, we find that nowadays they are as often as not full of chauvinistic appeals for recognition of the fact that France is the hub of Europe. At the same time writers like Charles Becquet—

who has won particular favour with the régime—urge the French 'not to immure themselves in the hexagon of the Maginot Line', but to think of the fate of the French-speaking peoples living in Belgium, Switzerland, Val d'Aosta and Canada.[58] Nevertheless, a France with 45 million inhabitants cannot hope to compete with the Russian and American colossi, and so De Gaulle asks the French to forget the teachings of Malthus and the theory of the only child, and launches a campaign to increase the birth-rate: 'A modern France could have 100 million inhabitants. How welcome will be the babies who are born in 1963!'[59] Still inspired by the romantic nationalism of Barrès and Maurras, De Gaulle is thus doing his best to convince the French that the days of Napoleon and Louis XIV are here again and that the moment will soon come for France to take over the leadership of Europe. There is, however, a risk that, as the English historian Arnold Toynbee has pointed out, this policy of his will lead to results which are the exact opposite of what he hopes:

> Charles de Gaulle is not the first patriotic and intelligent states-man who has 'worked for the King of Prussia' without knowing it. If he succeeds in turning the Common Market into a French empire, who knows whether this empire will still be French when it eventually breaks up? And that sad day would certainly see Germany, not France, in command.[60]

And lastly, by substituting a *Europe des patries* for an integrated Europe, De Gaulle has deprived the Germans of their hope for a rapid unification of Europe, which for them is the only alternative to nationalism. 'In many ways,' says Maurice Duverger,

> De Gaulle seems to have been one of the men responsible for the reawakening of German nationalism. On the further bank of the Rhine the name 'Gaullist' is applied to those who favour such a revival and maintain that the unification of Europe is a Utopia, and the name is a very apt one. And that in his heart the President of the Republic is aware of the danger of a German revival does not in any way alter the results of his policy or calm the fears that it evokes.[61]

Addressing the young Socialists of the SFIO *(Section Française de l'Internationale Ouvrière)* and submitting to their attention a plan for opposing De Gaulle, Guy Mollet did not forget to mention this poisoned gift which De Gaulle has made to France, and he ended his speech with this dramatic appeal: 'Your chief aim must be to kill that French nationalism which is being reborn.'[62]

The presidential election in November 1965 was a first important indication of the failure of the Gaullist programme. De Gaulle was confident that he would receive a plebiscitarian approval of his policy, which at the same time would be a confirmation of his personal popularity, and the fact that he failed to do so reveals on the one hand the fears and opposition aroused by the prospect of a dictatorial régime, and on the other a gradual falling-away of certain sectors of French Gaullism from the Gaullist policy of hostility to the Common Market and, more generally speaking, to the integrated economic area envisaged by the Atlantic system.

8 Austria

The Horsemen of the Apocalypse

'A European civil war will probably start about 1967, when the Europe of monopolies and nationalist states, by its failure to solve its fundamental problems, will have strengthened the position of the Communists to a dangerous degree and, conversely, that of right-wing extremism as well. The flames of civil war, fanned by the countries of the Eastern *bloc*, will flare up in France, after an unsuccessful attempt to bring a "popular front" to power, and in Belgium, as the result of a violent clash between the Walloons and the Flemings. As soon as the news of the first clashes spreads, the Germans, tired of twenty years of humiliation and compromise, will take up arms, and there will be war between the two Germanys. In Spain the syndicalists will turn Franco out, in order to be in a better position to resist the *coup d'état* planned by the Communists. And as for Northern Italy . . .'[1]

The man who told us all this was called Fred Borth and he was born in 1928 in a Lower Austrian village. He had a chubby, rubicund face and light-blue eyes—too blue, in fact, rather like those of a Dresden china angel. The story of his life showed that he belonged to a world of angry young men and avengers. At fifteen Fred Borth volunteered for service in the *Luftwaffe;* in early 1945 he asked to be transferred to the *Waffen-SS*, and when he was only seventeen he was promoted to the rank of second-lieutenant, commanded an assault group and was decorated with the Iron Cross. After the war he was sentenced to three years' imprisonment in Vienna, and when he came out he founded a paper called *Der Kamerad*, which was quickly suppressed by the Russian occupation authorities. Since then he has been connected with practically all the extreme right-wing groups. He ran the *Bund Heimattreuer Jugend* until it was banned in 1959, and after that the *Legion Europa*, the Austrian section of the Belgian Jean Thiriart's Fascist International. The police and the journalists reported Borth's presence in Munich, Nuremberg, Venice, Tivoli, Passau, Goslar and

Madrid. He made a point of attending all the rallies of 'nostalgics', where he could easily be recognized by his dirty and well-worn white raincoat. When South Africa's apartheid policy led to her leaving the Commonwealth, Borth wrote a letter to Premier Verwoerd, assuring him of the solidarity of the 'real' Europe. In reply, Verwoerd thanked him for this gesture, but President Gronchi did not reply when Borth wrote that 'thousands of young Europeans are willing to come to Italy and work there without pay on development schemes, providing you will grant South Tyrol the right of self-determination'.[2]

Jean Thiriart's definition of himself, Fred Borth and his companions gives us a pretty clear idea of the mad world they lived in. 'The men of *Jeune Europe*', he said, 'might be called the Horsemen of the Apocalypse, the ideal men for a desperate situation. As soon as something serious happens and the feeble governments of today fall, history will need us.'[3] Sipping a glass of beer as he sat at our table in a café full of mirrors and plush-covered settees, Fred Borth talked about this historical moment:

> As soon as the Communists try to seize power, we shall organize risings in every country of Europe, and the United States, whether they like it or not, will have to support us, because we have a twofold aim—to settle things once and for all in Europe and to build a wall against Communism which won't run along the banks of the Elbe, but will be to the east of Bucharest. The Europe that will emerge from this total revolution will not be a *'Europe des patries'*, but the Europe of one nation, in which all the squabbles between Walloons and Flemings, Italians and Austrians, Slovaks and Czechs, will cease to have any significance.

And Thiriart tells us that this Europe 'will need men who know how to use their fists; it will need soldiers a hundred times more than it needs lawyers; steel, not literature; leaders, not do-gooders.'[4]

Among the leaders, however, there are differences of opinion, the chief bone of contention being the 'South Tyrol' question. Some of the leaders of *Jeune Europe* would like to support the terrorists (and in fact have already done so); others (and the Italians among them) are in favour of settling the question by means of negotiations. This squabble brought about the downfall of Jean Thiriart's International, from the ashes of which arose, in the summer of 1963, a new party calling itself the *Europafront*, under the leadership of Fred Borth, who found adherents among those who were in favour of carrying on guerrilla warfare in the Alto Adige until this region is reunited to the German-speaking world.[5] Incidentally, Borth had made his attitude to the Alto Adige problem quite clear in 1961 when, among other 'solutions', he suggested 'supporting the South Tyrolese partisans in every possible way. Although we deplore this conflict with Italian national elements [in other words the neo-Fascists], the fact remains that a continuation of partisan warfare in South Tyrol will attract the attention of the whole world.'[6] But even after he had become supreme head of the *Europafront*, Borth was not satisfied. His restless spirit even led him to suggest to Verwoerd that a line of *Kibbutzim*, manned by young Aryans, should be set up along the frontiers of the South African Union, to halt the advance of the native Africans and save the last outpost of white civilization in Africa.

The neo-Nazi front

An investigation made in 1960 by the magazine *Forum* showed that in Austria there were at least forty neo-Nazi movements, either officially recognized, semi-clandestine or secret. To these, as in West Germany, must be added the ex-Servicemen's associations like the *Österreichische Kameradschaftsbund* (180,000 members) and the *Österreichische Soldatenbund* (120,000), which openly criticize Austria's policy of neutrality and demand that their country be re-annexed to Germany;[7] then there are youth associations like the *Bund Heimattreuer Jugend* (reconstituted under another name after being banned)[8] and the student associations with all too significant names like *Olympia, Alemannia, Nibelungia, Teutonia, Vandalia, Sudetia, Gothia*, which in their statutes openly extol the ideals of pan-Germanism.[9] And there are the athletic clubs like the *Turnerbund*, the eight associations of refugees (*Sudetendeutsche, Karpatendeutsche*, etc.),[10] and the *Freiheitliche Partei Österreichs*, (FPÖ) which is the third biggest party in Austria and has seven seats in parliament.[11]

The neo-Nazi front in Austria thus ranges from the Austrian section of Fred Borth's *Europafront* to Willfried Gredler's FPÖ. On the one hand there are professional agitators like Fred Borth, the printer Konrad Windisch, the three leaders of the *Österreichische Soziale Bewegung* (Karl Zimmermann, Hans Wagner and Wilhelm Landing),[12] the president of the *Ring Volkstreuer Verbände* (Roland Timmel), the leader of the *Sozialorganische Ordnungsbewegung Europas* (Theodor Soucek),[13] the university professor Norbert Burger, and Graf Albrecht Alberti. On the other hand we have intellectuals like Hitler's poet laureate Mirko Jelusich, Professor Taras von Borodajkewicz, and some of the leading lights of the FPÖ, while there are also 'respectable' and 'drawing-room' Nazis like Deputy Claus Mahnert, the former deputy-Gauleiter of the Tyrol, and the chairman of the FPÖ Gredler, who still remembers with pride his Nazi past though he denies ever having been in contact with neo-Nazi organizations. 'In 1936,' Gredler told us,

> there were not many alternatives for us Austrians; with 600,000 unemployed the only alternative to Nazism was Communism. The younger generation accordingly greeted Hitler as a liberator; they believed that his empire would last a thousand years and they followed him to the last catastrophic conclusion, serving in those armies of his which were conquering the world. I should be distorting the truth if I concealed the fact that I felt a real exultation when we entered Paris and marched under the *Arc de Triomphe*.[14]

Gredler's exultation is a confirmation of the irrepressible imperial ambitions of certain Austrian circles and helps to explain why Nazism was so successful in Austria. Reduced to the rank of a third-rate power after the defeat in 1918, Austria was unable to resist the blandishments of Hitler, who promised to let her share in the conquest of an empire such as the world had never seen. But once the alliance had been concluded over the dead body of Dollfuss, Nazism made haste to reduce Austria to the status of a mere province of the Reich. Despite this negative experience, Austria was still open to the appeal of pan-Germanism, and even though they abhorred the excesses of the Nazi régime, all but the shrewdest Austrians failed to repudiate its ideology *en bloc*. This is not surprising when we remember that in proportion to her population Austria provided more members of the National Socialist Party than did Germany herself, and that men like Hitler, Kaltenbrunner, Seyss-Inquart, Eichmann, Rajakovic, Rintelen and Skorzeny were all Austrians, and not Germans.

The rebirth of Nazism after the Second World War was thus helped not only by the age-old and frustrated imperial ambitions, but also by memories of defeat, the humiliation of the long occupation by the Russians, the anti-Italian campaign in the Alto Adige, and the economic difficulties caused by a state of uneasy neutrality. For these reasons the *Dietwarte* found that it was not very difficult to persuade the younger generation to respond to the ideal of a 'Greater Germany'. At a congress in Florence in February 1959, the theme of which was 'The Resistance and the younger generation', one of the Austrian speakers, Leopold Voller, told a little story which is typical of the methods employed:

> It was in 1950, six thousand feet up in the mountains on the border between Austria and West Germany. A score of boys and girls, from fifteen to twenty-two years old, were standing in a circle right on the frontier between the two countries, so that half of them were on German soil and half on Austrian. When a young man of about twenty-eight gave the order, they sang 'Were all to be unfaithful, we should still be true'. It was this song that first attracted my attention, because I knew that diehard Nazis always sing it when they want to show their fidelity to Nazism. After the song, the 'Führer' of the group started a kind of 'lesson'. First he asked those who were standing on German soil: 'In what country are you?', to which the young people replied: 'On German soil.' The leader then addressed the whole group. 'Can you see any difference between the soil on the right of the frontier and the soil on the left?' The answer was unanimous: 'No, it's the same soil.' Then the leader said: 'So it's the same soil, and this frontier has been artificially created by the enemies of Germany and he who recognizes it is a traitor.' Then he went on: 'Are the people on this side of the frontier different from the people on the other side? Don't they all speak the same language? What are we to conclude from that? That we have one country, that we are one nation, and we are therefore entitled to have one Reich and what we need is a Führer.'[15]

Since then, pilgrimages to the mountains near Salzburg, Kufstein and Innsbruck have become more and more frequent. And from naïve talk about 'artificial frontiers' the *Dietwarte* have gone on to discuss more complex and more promising topics. With the result that after the harmless lighting of mythical bonfires along the frontier came the 'night of the fires' in the Alto Adige. And the song 'Were all to be unfaithful' has been replaced by a more aggressive and provocative ballad which runs:

> The gas-chambers were not big enough;
> We must build bigger ones.
> There will be room in them for all of you,
> You can rely on that.[16]

A government that is far too tolerant

Nevertheless, we should be failing in our duty to be impartial if we did not contrast this nostalgic and exalted Austria with the other Austria which was not an accomplice, but a victim, of the Nazis. The Austria of the 185,000 patriots who were killed or persecuted by Hitler, the Austria which in 1945 rose in revolt under the leadership of Major Szokoll in Vienna, the Austria which today is trying to stop any resurgence of Nazism and is ready to pour into the streets, as it did on 19 October 1959 in Vienna, and drive the 'nostalgics' out of the square in front of the City Hall, shouting *Weg mit dem Nazispuk, wir haben von Hitler genug*! (Out with the spectres of Nazism! we've had enough of Hitler!). And which, at Berndorf in Lower Austria on 7 October 1962, broke up a meeting of Nazi ex-Servicemen, organized by the *Kameradschaftsbund*, and tore the Iron Crosses and other Nazi decorations from their breasts.[17]

But the Austrians who protest and give vent to their indignation are only a despairing minority—former members of the Resistance movement, ex-inmates of the concentration camps, Socialist students and progressive Catholics. The official Austria maintains a vague and sometimes ambiguous attitude towards Nazism. 'Recently,' we read in the Catholic weekly *Die Furche* after the wave of anti-Semitism in 1960, 'when it has been a question of doing something to help the Austrian Resistance, our statesmen and government have always drawn in their horns and avoided showing themselves, except on a few rare occasions. But whenever there have been festivals or commemorations organized by bodies whose loyalty to Austrian liberty and democracy is somewhat doubtful . . .' The presence of the authorities was, in fact, conspicuous at Klagenfurt when the anniversary of the Nazi attack on Narvik was being celebrated; at a meeting in Zwetter organized by the *Kameradschaftsbund*; at the 'gymnastic rally' held in Graz on 15 July 1960; at the commemoration of the 150th anniversary of Andreas Hofer's death. Commenting on the attitude of the authorities on the occasion of the rally in Graz, *Die Furche* said: 'If we want to describe tolerance of this kind, the word "cowardly" is perhaps too mild.' At Graz the *Turnerbund* exploited an athletics meeting as a pretext for assembling 20,000 young neo-Fascists from every country in Europe, who between one event and another demanded the reunion of the

'South Tyrolese ethnical group to the other German peoples', and sang with provocative intent the (officially prohibited) hymn of German unity:

Carinthians and South Tyrolese,
Germans from the North and South,
From Westphalia and Salzkammergut,
From Berlin and Lower Austria,
Saxons and Prussians,
Dwellers on the Danube and the Rhine,
We have but one conviction,
One only and unshakable:
We are an inseparable whole.

On the anniversary of Andreas Hofer's death the deputy-burgomaster of Innsbruck, Otto Gamper, announced that 'peaceful coexistence in Europe will not be possible until the unification of Tyrol and the German Reich has been achieved'. On that same occasion, as if Gamper had not made his meaning clear enough, Dr Friedrich Mang added:

The preservation of *Deutschtum* in the southern portion of our *Land* must inevitably be the ardent desire of every German heart. But unfortunately the claims of the Tyrol have now almost vanished from the consciences and national feelings of Germans. We must make it our first task to be present everywhere in the name of German national pride [*deutscher Nationalstolz*]. He who disowns his own people is unworthy of his ancestors. Frontiers may change, but no one can change his race [*Volkstum*] without becoming a renegade. That is why we will not hear of any *Verschweizerung* [Swissification] or of becoming part of an Austrian nation. We want to be what our fathers and forefathers were—German men in a German land.[18]

For years the Catholic-Socialist coalition government allowed emotional speeches of this kind to be made; it pretended not to know that thousands of Nazi criminals had taken refuge in Austria; it even granted Austrian citizenship to the Belgian SS-General Jan Verbelen (who was not arrested until 1962);[19] it conferred a high honour on the German racialist Globke, who had already been decorated by Hitler for 'valuable services in connexion with the integration of Austria into the German Reich'; and only in 1962, when the Eichmann trial had resulted in too many compromising documents from the Jerusalem archives becoming known to the public, did it allow proceedings to be taken against the *SS-Obersturmbannführer* Hermann Höfle, responsible for the genocide of over a million people, and against Otto Skorzeny, accused of setting fire to several synagogues in Vienna and of massacres in Czechoslovakia; while dozens of other Nazis have been acquitted and carried shoulder-high by the crowds, despite the fact that their guilt had been clearly proved during their trials.[20] The ambiguous policy followed by the Austrian government has undoubtedly contributed to the spread of neo-Nazism in Austria, and a proof of this is the striking success achieved in the 1962 university elections by the *Ring Freiheitlicher Studenten*. After trebling in one year the number of votes it received, this neo-Nazi association polled 5,900 votes in 1962 as against 2,900 received by the Socialist students' association.

The testing-bench of the Alto Adige

Where, however, the Austrian government's wavering attitude to neo-Nazism has been fraught with most serious consequences is in its handling of the Alto Adige question. Because they were afraid of losing votes in Tyrol, Styria and Carinthia, both the Catholic *Volkspartei* and the Socialists have for years past been supporting the extremist policy of the *Berg Isel Bund* (which today is still clamouring for the annexation of South Tyrol to Austria), and have light-heartedly accepted the collaboration of well-known terrorists, pan-Germanists and neo-Nazis, as well as that of sincere and respectable patriots. It was only as the result of worldwide reaction to the outrages in the Alto Adige that Vienna went through the motions of abandoning this extremist association to its fate; but on reflection, and thinking the *Bund* might prove useful on some future occasion, the authorities pigeon-holed the order banning it which had already been drawn up. All this despite the fact that in February 1962 the Viennese *Kurier* had revealed that the *Berg Isel Bund* was not just an association of irredentists, but a hive of Nazis, and that its president, the former Foreign Secretary Gschnitzer, had been forced to resign because a resolution he had proposed had been rejected by the majority of its members. The resolution was to the effect that any kind of neo-Nazi activity would be incompatible with the aims and tasks of the *Berg Isel Bund*, and consequently, only those who repudiated National Socialism and declared that they are loyal Austrian subjects should be eligible for membership of the association or able to hold any office therein. 'The *Berg Isel Bund* is an organization which will employ only legal methods in its campaign to protect the South Tyrolese.'[21]

In order to understand the risky game Vienna was playing, we must go back to the beginnings of the Alto Adige dispute, which started some fifty years ago and, like all questions which are never solved and remain smouldering, has become far more complicated with the passage of the years and is today a problem and a thorn in the flesh for the whole of Europe. Immediately after the First World War, successive conservative governments of Italy had other more pressing matters to deal with, and in any case they had no time to spare for a detailed study of the whole problem. The Fascists, always inclined to be slapdash, thought they would be able to settle the question if they first adopted a vigorous policy of denationalization of the German-speaking ethnical group and encouraged an artificial emigration of Italians to the area north of Salorno (the southernmost German-speaking locality in the Alto Adige); subsequently, they reached an agreement with Hitler whereby those inhabitants of the Alto Adige who were of Germanic origin should be transferred to the Reich. But after the Cassibile armistice in 1943, Hitler sent *Gauleiter* into the Alto Adige, thus showing that he not only wanted to penalize Germany's ex-ally, but also intended to incorporate 'South Tyrol' permanently into a Greater Germany. When the war ended and the Allies were engaged in trying to restore order in Europe, the Austrian government, quoting the principles laid down in the Atlantic Charter, asked that the 300,000 German-speaking inhabitants of the Alto Adige should be given the right of self-determination. But the Allies, to avoid offending the Italians, who were already worried about the fate of Trieste, rejected the Austrian demand and ruled that the Alto Adige should remain Italian in accordance with the provisions of the treaty of St-Germain-en-Laye. De Gasperi, who had doubts as to the legal validity of this 1919 treaty, hastened to allay the suspicion felt by the Austrians that a democratic Italian government might follow the same policy of oppression as the Fascists had done, and in Paris he signed an agreement with the Austrian envoy, Grüber, the aim of which was to guarantee that the Germans in the Alto Adige would enjoy the same rights as Italians, thus creating 'a bridge, not a barrier, between the two civilizations'.

The terms of this agreement were, however, vague, and the Italians soon took advantage of this fact and began to restrict the autonomy of the Alto Adige, whereas Austria made every effort to have it extended, first by demanding that the stipulations of the Paris agreement should be put into force immediately, and later by suggesting that a 'special zone' should be created consisting only of the province of Bolzano. Finally, Austria demanded a plebiscite, which would virtually have meant the annexation of the Alto Adige to Austria. Eighteen years of shilly-shallying, niggling and contradictions on the Italian side, and of exorbitant demands and encouragement of terrorist activities on the Austrian, made the Alto Adige one of Europe's 'hot spots', the scene of plots, outrages and clashes, and, what is even worse, turned it into a testing-bench for German *revanchisme*.

Although Italy deserves to be blamed for not taking the question seriously, the fact remains that ever since Austria has taken on the role of defender of the Alto Adige, her attitude in this controversy has always been ambiguous, even if we admit that it was due to a justifiable feeling of resentment. In the first place she has never (or only rarely and reluctantly) attempted to carry out the provisions of the 1955 treaty, whereby she undertook 'to dissolve all Fascist, politico-military and semi-military organizations', which have inevitably been the nurseries of terrorism in the Alto Adige. To this we must add her failure to collaborate with the Italian authorities in forestalling and suppressing terrorist activities, which have their ideological nerve-centres, their supply-bases and their safe hideouts in Austria. This attitude has enabled the *Berg Isel Bund* to conduct an increasingly violent campaign, to establish links with kindred irredentist associations in West Germany, and lastly to set up a militaristic organization called the *Befreiungsaktion für Südtirol* (BAS), which since 1955 has welcomed to its ranks many violent, though sincere, irredentists, together with ex-Nazis pining for revenge, Austrian and German neo-Fascists, former OAS *plastiqueurs* and other disreputable characters from the Nazi-Fascist Internationals, all firmly convinced that in the Alto Adige they had found a providential headquarters, from which, when the moment came, they would be able to sow discord among the European family of nations.[22]

On the rare occasions when the Austrian police have made any arrests, the judiciary or the government have intervened to mitigate or revoke such measures. Let us quote a few examples. On 5 April 1962, the Austrian Minister of Justice, Christian Broda, announced that there would be 'a whole series of trials for offences connected

with the Alto Adige question'. And in fact a number of men known
to be responsible for acts of terrorism were duly charged—Professor
Norbert Burger, an ex-major of the *Schützen* named Georg Klotz,
the dynamitard Kurt Welser, Oberhammer, who was one of the
leaders of the *Berg Isel Bund*, and half-a-dozen other activists—
but two months later the cabinet decided to pigeon-hole the proceedings. Later, in April 1964, the police arrested two South Tyrolese,
Alois Amplatz and Georg Klotz, who had informed representatives of the German Press that they had been responsible for almost
all the terrorist outrages in Italy, that they had smuggled explosives
into the Alto Adige, and that at Absam near Innsbruck they had
even started a 'school for terrorists'. It certainly cannot be said
that there was any lack of evidence, but after being detained for two
months both these men were released and granted political asylum,
which was likewise granted to twenty other men from the Alto
Adige. Thanks to this act of clemency, Klotz and Amplatz were able
to reorganize the BAS, and on 29 August 1964 they recrossed the
frontier and resumed their guerrilla warfare, as a result of which
the Italian anti-sabotage units had three men killed and seventeen
wounded. In the early days of what the BAS calls the 'summer of
blood', Amplatz was killed in an Alpine hut on the slopes of Monte
La Clava, in circumstances which are still not clear. The funeral of
this BAS leader took place in Bolzano, and after the religious
ceremony it was transformed into a Nazi rite, among those participating being two representatives of the neo-Nazi *Deutsche Freiheitspartei*. As they were laying a wreath on the coffin, one of them
exclaimed: 'Alois Amplatz, your cause is ours!' If anyone still
had any doubts as to the links between the neo-Nazi headquarters
in Munich and the BAS, they were eliminated by the presence of
the two men and these words.

Often the whole matter was hushed up; in a few cases trials took
place in Graz or Innsbruck, where within living memory no Nazi
criminal, exterminator of Jews or South Tyrolese terrorist has ever
been convicted by a jury. And in fact, among the many acquittals
in Graz are those of Wolfgang Pfaundler, who organized the 'night
of fires' in the summer of 1961, of Ottokar Destaller and Ludwig
Messerklinger. In other cases the terrorists would be warned that
the police were about to issue warrants for their arrest and advised to move to neighbouring Bavaria. This was the case with
Norbert Burger, who, after his escape to Munich, boasted that he
had been back to Austria several times and had always been allowed

to move about freely, because he knew too much and his arrest would certainly have had unpleasant consequences for 'the men in the two parties forming the coalition government who from the beginning had benevolently encouraged the dynamite outrages'.[23] This was an impudent challenge which the Austrian police at last felt they must take up, and Burger was arrested on 21 June 1964 a few hours after arriving in Klagenfurt.[24] But when he was tried sixteen months later, in October 1965, the jury at the Graz assizes acquitted him together with twenty-six other terrorists. This leniency on the part of the Austrian courts prompted an immediate resumption of neo-Nazi activities, and at the beginning of 1966 they started making clandestine broadcasts from 'Radio Free Tyrol'.

Obviously the *Berg Isel Bund* and the student associations were not the only people who wanted the state of unrest in the Alto Adige to continue. The German extremists—who were particularly active in Bavaria—did their best to keep the question alive, in order that it might remain a permanent hotbed of nationalistic agitation. Since, at all events for the time being, they had been obliged to drop their agitation against Gaullist France and their bitter resentment at the loss of Germany's eastern territories had to be confined to words, the German *revanchistes* felt that the Brenner frontier was the weakest link in the chain and that the Alto Adige would serve as a providential testing-bench for their irredentist ideas. By encouraging and financing terrorism, they hoped to force Italy to take more severe repressive measures, which in turn would compel the nationalistic elements in Austria and Germany to give more open support to the cause of the BAS, whose members, at the beginning of 1964, were even toying with the idea of calling themselves a 'provisional government' and establishing their headquarters at Vaduz in Liechtenstein.

The collusion between German extremists and South Tyrolese terrorists was repeatedly admitted by the accused during the Milan trial in 1963–64. Below we give an extract from the examination of Josef Kerschbaumer, one of the militant leaders of the BAS:

PRESIDING JUDGE: Did Pfaundler send men from Austria and Germany?

KERSCHBAUMER: Yes, I personally asked him to do so.

JUDGE: Why from Germany as well?

KERSCHBAUMER: Because the Bavarians are very partial to us Tyrolese.

JUDGE: Who was the German you met at Scena, just after the 'night of the fires'?

KERSCHBAUMER: I don't know his name. Before that I had only seen him once, when he brought us the explosives which were to be used on the 'night of the fires'.

JUDGE: And what did he say when you saw him at Scena?

KERSCHBAUMER: The German told me that very soon he would be coming back to the 'old provinces' in Italy to carry out other operations.

JUDGE: And in fact, a few days later there were other outrages in the provinces of Verona, Novara and Varese.[25]

The address of the Bavarian extremists' headquarters—as Mario Martin, the investigating magistrate who spent three years trying to find out where the South Tyrolese terrorists got their supplies from, was able to ascertain—was Karlsplatz II/320, Munich (according to the Viennese daily *Volksstimme* it was moved shortly afterwards to Neuhäuserstrasse 34) and it camouflaged itself under the innocuous denomination of *Kulturwerk für Südtirol*.[26] It was this 'cultural organization' that remitted to the *Berg Isel Bund* (for transmission to the BAS) a large proportion of the funds that served to keep terrorism going. The *Kulturwerk* is in its turn a subsidiary of the *Sudetendeutsche Landsmannschaft*, of which 1½ million Sudeten refugees are members.

In the dispute between Italy and Austria over the Alto Adige, the West German government has hitherto preferred to adopt a neutral attitude, but some of its Ministers (Seebohm, Bücher, Krüger) and certain supporting elements (Mende's Liberals and the Christian Democrats headed by Strauss) have more or less openly approved the claims made by the *Berg Isel Bund*.[27] To quote only one instance of the support the extremists receive even from 'respectable' quarters, on 4 January 1964 the journal of the Liberal Vice-Chancellor Mende, *Das Freie Wort*, deplored the indifference shown by German public opinion to developments in the Alto Adige and the Milan trial, and suspected that people thought it was 'more convenient to get excited about a few Negroes than about a German ethnical group'; which prompted the journal to ask whether 'the national feelings of the Germans have fallen into a state of coma'. It is thus clear that the tension in the Alto Adige is not entirely due to the plottings of a few groups of 'nostalgics', but that it is also the result of concerted action by neo-Nazis and 'respectable' elements in the two German-speaking countries, which have discovered that when it comes to a flat refusal of the 1945 European settlement, this is a point on which they are both agreed.

An unenviable record

In 1962 some of the experts of the UIRD (*Union Internationale de la Résistance et de la Déportation*) expressed the opinion, which to our mind still holds good, that the European country in which neo-Nazism has made most progress is Austria. When we raised this point in the course of an interview, the Secretary of State for the Interior, Otto Kranzlmayr of the *Volkspartei*, replied that 'in Austria no danger of Fascism exists', and that to stop any such movement 'all that one need do is to keep an eye on a group of "incorrigibles" and prevent them from contaminating the younger generation'. Kranzlmayr also denied that the 'purge' had been only a farce and that the competent authorities had failed to investigate the Nazi pasts of Austrians. 'I reject, in any case, any kind of accusation that is not supported by concrete proofs. In order to obtain sure proofs of the guilt or innocence of a few Austrian citizens, we sent two observers to the Eichmann trial.'[28]

The Minister for the Interior, Josef Afritsch, was less optimistic. When he was seeking to reassure Austrian public opinion, which had been badly shaken by some grave episodes that occurred just after the Eichmann trial had opened in Jerusalem, the Minister admitted that there was a disgraceful resurgence of Nazism in the country and said that, in an effort to stem this tide, the courts had sentenced 120 young men who were found guilty of distributing anti-Semitic literature and daubing swastikas on walls. A similar opinion was expressed by the Minister of Justice, Christian Broda. In 1962, speaking of the risks Austria was running as a result of the long irredentist and pan-Germanic campaign, the Socialist Minister tried to find a way out by warmly supporting a law 'to restore internal peace' which provides for severe penalties against those who revile the 'Republic and its federal *Länder*', insult 'the Austrian emblems, colours, flag or national anthem', or persecute groups of persons 'on account of their racial origin or religion'. But it was left to the successor of Afritsch, the Socialist Franz Olah, to discover that far more serious things were going on in this neutral and democratic Austria than the daubing of swastikas on walls. On the evening of 28 January 1964, in the course of a dramatic appearance on the television screens, the Minister accused the State police of being a band of spies, of checking up on thousands of citizens as if Austria were under a dictatorship, and of compiling

H*

thousands of secret files, many of which contained false and slanderous accusations.

Feeling that she is threatened by both the old and the new Nazis, Austria has taken steps to defend herself. But can the passions which the Republic, with its miscalculations and frivolous attitudes, has helped to unleash, now be held in check? The desecration of Jewish cemeteries, the shots fired at the parliament buildings, the burning of Austrian flags—these are all episodes bearing the signature of the extremists who supported the *Anschluss* in 1938, or of their disciples. As for their final objective, it was indicated nearly a hundred years ago in a song written by Ernst Moritz Arndt, which the Gorbachs, Kreiskys and Gschnitzers have for too long allowed to be sung with impunity:

> There is only one ideal,
> In Bavaria or the Banat,
> In Berlin or South Tyrol,
> In Burgenland or in Prussia,
> In Salzkammergut or Westphalia:
> THE GERMAN PEOPLE.

9 Belgium

The Vikings of the twentieth century

Léon Degrelle, the founder and leader of 'Rexism', now lives in Spain, whither he fled at the end of the Second World War, before his fellow-countrymen could call him to account for the services he had rendered to Nazism. Officially he is under police supervision, but in recent photographs he looks flourishing and arrogant, faultlessly dressed in the white uniform of a functionary of the Falange, with the decorations he received from Hitler very much in evidence. From time to time this former commander of the *Légion SS-Wallonie* writes 'open letters' to the Belgian papers, which duly appear in the monthly *L'Europe Réelle,* a 'periodical which is fighting for a new order in Europe', published by the *Mouvement Social Belge* (MSB). The MSB is the Belgian section of the Malmö International, and it welcomes to its ranks all surviving members of the Walloon and Flemish collaborationist organizations. The chief planks in its programme are the Corporative State, the fight against monopolies and 'hypercapitalism', and opposition to Communism and 'all those political, economic and philosophical groups which are playing the Communist game by dividing the nation'.[1] It is the only group with a neo-Fascist intonation that recognizes the claims of the Arab countries to independence, this being perhaps meant as a tribute to Nasser's Nazi sympathies or as an attempt to give it a veneer of originality in comparison with other 'nostalgic' groups. From the start its influence was only slight, and it declined even more during the postwar years. At the 1954 election the MSB polled less than 500 votes, and since then it has never re-entered the political arena at election times.

The anti-Semitic and neo-Nazi friends of the founder of Rexism eke out their political existence as members of a *Mouvement pour le retour de Degrelle*, organizing meetings to recall the military 'glories' of the Belgian SS and singing Nazi songs in a café in the Rue de Brabant in Brussels The MSB is only a little group of 'nostalgics' forming the rearguard of the pro-Nazi or tradition-alistic Belgian right wing, whose organizations enjoyed a brief moment of celebrity during the more heated phases of the controversy over the behaviour of King Leopold III, accused by the democrats of having placed himself under German protection at the time of the armistice and criticized for his marriage to Liliane de Rethy. In defence of the monarchy, which had suffered as a result of the criticisms levelled at the sovereign, other movements were formed, e.g. the *Mouvement National Royaliste*, consisting of ex-members of the Resistance who sympathized with Leopold and which has now practically ceased to exist, and the *Mouvement pour l'Ordre et la Liberté*, which gave birth to the *Organisation du Salut Public*, consisting of a few dozen avowed ultra-nationalists, royalists, opponents of a united Europe and reactionaries. The influence of both these organizations is rapidly declining.

It was, however, the 'Congo affair' that gave the greatest impetus to the development of extreme right-wing organizations. The loss of this rich African colony induced all the radical and colonialist groups of the conservative front to unite and demand with one voice a fight to the finish, and in this they were backed up by the industrial and commercial monopolies, which looked on the Congo as their most fertile territory for exploitation. This led to the rise of a dozen or more parties which made the 'presence of Belgium' in the Congo the main plank in their platforms, though they took care to include in their programmes the usual attacks on Communism and democracy. Among these parties were the *Parti National Belge*, founded in 1961 and drawing its inspiration from Maurras; the *Comité de défense des Belges au Congo*, dating from July 1960, which subsequently changed its name to *Rassemblement pour la défense de l'œuvre belge au Congo*; *Les Amitiés Belgo-Katangaises*, an association created to help Tshombe's separatist government; and the *Parti Social Indépendant*, founded by Albert L'Allemand, a businessman who had formerly lived in the Congo. To complete the picture of the agitation resulting from the 'Congo affair' we must add the *Parti Indépendant* (PI), founded in February 1961 and inspired by Poujadist ideas; the *Union Nationale des Indépendants* (UNI), with a policy practically the same as that of the PI; and the *Manifeste de Rénovation Nationale*, an extreme right-wing faction consisting mainly of aristocratic Catholics who had quarrelled with the Christian Social Party.[2] The founders of all these groups, however, had no wish to take over the legacy of

Nazism and Fascism (on the contrary, some of them indignantly repudiated it) or to adhere to the principles of neo-Fascism, whose methods the OAS had made famous. This task was left to Jean-François Thiriart, owner of a chain of shops selling optical instruments, who had been imprisoned as a collaborationist and was a member of the AGRA *(Amis du Grand Reich Allemand)*. 'The plastic bomb will be the loudspeaker of anti-Communism in the latter half of the twentieth century'—such was the slogan coined by Thiriart, to make his intentions quite clear.

The 'Congo affair' was exploited by this dealer in optical instruments with a cleverness that could hardly have been bettered. On 8 July 1960, at the Café Tanganyika in Etterbeek, a group of nationalists founded a *Comité d'Action et de Défense des Belges d'Afrique* (CADBA), hoping to unite all the ex-settlers in one movement and to bring pressure to bear on the government regarding armed intervention in the Congo. Although the CADBA's programme was definitely anti-parliamentary and Poujadist, its leaders had blameless pasts—Auguste Minet, severely wounded in the 1914–18 war, had been sentenced to death by the Nazis and imprisoned for four years for helping British Intelligence; Raphael Mathyn was an ex-member of the Resistance movement and an ex-inmate of Dachau; Verlinden was a retired colonel of the Reserve, who had achieved fame by escaping from Belgium to London in 1942. But the CADBA was also joined by two men who later made radical changes in its policy, though they continued to exploit the prevailing discontent and to make use of the association's funds. These two men who emerged from the Trojan horse that had penetrated into the CADBA were Jean-François Thiriart and Dr Paul Teichmann, the latter being a Belgian supporter of Poujade and subsequently of the OAS. Although they remained behind the scenes and continued to exploit the names and pasts of the nominal leaders, Thiriart and Teichmann became the masters of the *Comité*, which in the meantime had changed its name to MAC *(Mouvement d'Action Civique)*.

From that time on the neo-Fascist campaign progressed by regular stages. The MAC adopted as its emblem the Celtic cross, which had previously been used in France by the extremists of *Jeune Nation*. It tried to unite all the extremist groups of the right wing; it began daubing the walls of Brussels with inscriptions attacking the UN and the Communists; it espoused the cause of Katangan independence, and maintained that the men who deserved to be

helped were Tshombe, Welensky, Verwoerd and Salazar; it became
the chief agency in Belgium of the OAS, publishing the latter's communiqués in its own periodicals, delivering messages to activists,
and even inserting absurd advertisements for women willing to act
as 'godmothers' to members of the organization who had ended
up in gaol; it clashed with the 'Young Socialist Guards', became the
Belgian section of the neo-Nazi International *Jeune Europe* and
acted as its guide. In April 1962 Mathyn, the ex-member of the
Resistance, finally decided to resign, which gave Thiriart and Teichmann an excuse to liquidate the old nominal 'directorate' and get
themselves elected as official leaders of the movement. The operation had been successfully concluded.

Hyperfascism

The MAC's four years of life are a fascinating subject for students
of the neo-Fascist phenomenon. Since it had not been founded
until 1960, the MAC could not, like the Italian MSI, boast of its
'glorious past' or live on its memories. Since it was thus unable to
exploit the appeal of Fascism, the MAC tried to avoid the unpleasant consequences that might ensue if it called itself 'neo-
Fascist'. Accordingly Thiriart brusquely announced that Fascism
had perished in 1945 and that, as we read in the MAC's organ,
Nation Belgique, 'the members of the MAC are not Fascists, if for
no other reason because we have not the slightest desire to have
any contact with a corpse, however skilfully it may have been
embalmed'.[3]

But they were not neo-Fascists either, because the followers of
this creed—we are told by Thiriart—'waste their time in celebrating
moving but futile rites; they officiate before the altar of a dead
god'. This being the case, Thiriart cast around for a new name for
his movement. 'What do you think,' he asked the readers of *Nation
Belgique*, 'of hyperfascism or transcendent Fascism?' Then he
saw that a name of that sort would not do. He realized that some
striking new name was needed, that had something to do with
European unity or a community of nations—two pet themes of the
MAC. He turned again to his readers: 'I suggest that you play
the "christening game",' and he himself suggested syllables of words
like EUR, COM, UNI, which his readers could shake up in a hat
and then try to put together again.[4]

But a name is not everything. Some sort of ideology was also needed, and for this the quiz system seemed inappropriate. Here Thiriart found help in the person of the theoretician Henri Moreau, an ex-Socialist and notorious anti-Semite, who had lost both his hands while fighting in the ranks of the *Waffen-SS* in Russia. Like other anti-Semites, Moreau was convinced that high finance and trade based on the gold standard were inventions and prerogatives of the Jews, and he accordingly planned a 'communitarian society' free from subservience to gold and the influence of American 'plutocracy', a society controlled by a communitarian bank which would allow workmen to fix their own wages and retire at fifty as millionaires. 'In order to become part-owner of a factory, or just owner of a house,' the Belgian theoretician pointed out, 'the wage-earner or salaried employee must first of all have a bank-account. This, in my opinion, is an aim that every worker must achieve.'[5] 'Forward in the name of capitalistic Socialism,' Moreau cried, heedless of the meaning of words, and he proposed that having abolished 'the division of society into intellectuals and manual labourers', a 'trade-union Senate' should be set up, which was nothing more than the worn-out Fascist concept of a 'chamber of Fasces and corporations'.[6] This 'communitarianism' of the MAC (or, as Moreau called it, 'Communism without Marx'), was merely a shuffling of words and meanings, an exhumation of stock ideas based, in order to make them more palatable, on a shameless demagogy, but in reality still bound up with the old hatred of the working-classes and trade unions.[7] Later on the optician Thiriart quarrelled with the 'theoretician' Moreau, who founded on his own account a Belgian section of the *Mouvement Créditiste Canadien*, the mouthpiece of which was a journal called *Brisons la piège*. But the 'teachings' of Moreau remained the property of the MAC and became its 'ideological' foundation.

Thiriart was delighted. He now had all the ingredients he needed not only to provide the MAC with an ideology, but also to enable him to boost the neo-Nazi *Jeune Europe* International, of which he was now the undisputed 'Führer'. Pending the discovery of a better name, 'Fascism' would be called 'Communitarianism'. The revolution which was to free Europe from subservience to the Russians and Americans would be a 'social-European revolution'. The party behind this revolution would call itself the 'National European Party'. And armed with this paraphernalia of ideas and proposals Jean-François Thiriart set out for Venice to attend the conference organized by Mosley and the MSI, which three months later, on 4 March 1962, produced the 'Manifesto to the European Nation'.[8]

It is worth while pausing to consider what the Europe proposed by Thiriart really was. The 'Manifesto' begins with a slogan: 'Neither Moscow nor Washington.' Thiriart, in fact, wanted 'to build a great common homeland, a united, powerful and communitarian Europe', endowed with 'atomic strength' and determined to liberate 'millions of compatriots (East Germans, Poles, Czechs, Hungarians, Bulgarians, Rumanians and Yugoslavs) who for years have been the slaves of the Bolshevik dictatorship'. Not only did Thiriart intend to wipe out the memory of the 'betrayal at Yalta' and get Europe out of the 'UN circus', but he also repudiated 'the legal Europe, the Europe of Strasbourg and treachery'. Like Hitler's Europe, Thiriart's would at one and the same time 'carry on the struggle against both Communist and American materialism', replace 'chattering and corrupt parliamentarism' by a 'direct, hierarchical, stable and LIVE democracy', do away with the class struggle, and tolerate captitalism only if it were 'civic, disciplined and controlled by the nation'.[9]

In order to realize all this, Thiriart suggested that 'a European mysticism, a European nationalism must be created'. But if anyone thought that it would be difficult to create a mysticism of this kind, he had only to listen to the advice of Jean-Baptiste Biaggi, who had told the French Chamber of Deputies that 'if we want to build a new Europe, we shall, perhaps sooner than you think, have to appeal to the parachutist battalions. So far as I know, the only fraternization between the French and German armies was between the men of the parachutist battalions'. Thiriart was of the same opinion. His Europe, like Biaggi's was to be modelled on that of 1940, except that the paratroopers would take the place of the Waffen-SS.

We could afford to laugh at these revolutionary ideas, if it were not for the fact that they have since spread from Malmö to Cape Town, from São Paulo in Brazil to Tokyo, and have contaminated the minds of so many young men who, according to Henri Moreau, 'must not diverge either to the right or the left, but must go forward'. To these wild and 'categorical' imperatives we must add the enticements held out by Thiriart: 'The MAC is a staff college for the training of CADRES, a crucible of ÉLITES; the MAC has no use for shirkers, bystanders, spies, "nostalgics", restless souls or cranks.' Conversely, the enemies, the people who must be hated, are pointed out by Dr Teichmann. One of the favourite targets was Jean-Paul Sartre:

> The vicious thinking of this typical left-wing intellectual is written on his face. He is just like the country *curé* of Bernanos. He coughs and sweats; physically he is a poor devil. He has the same persecution complex as the Jews, the same grudge against society. He is physically deformed, and consequently mentally deformed as well.

And the neo-Nazis would certainly not tolerate weaknesses of this kind, since it is laid down in the 'Manifesto' that 'hyperfascism must first of all reintroduce the concept of virility into political relations'.[10]

As Michel Géoris-Reitshof has pointed out, the MAC is at present 'the only Fascist movement in Belgium that is serious and well organized',[11] though he also remarks that it is in the throes of a crisis regarding its policy and organization—a crisis due to the continual 'backsliding' of its adherents and its lack of success at the municipal elections held in October 1964, when its candidates in Brussels, Schaerbeek and Ganshoren (these last two being suburbs of Brussels) polled very few votes. Thanks to the *Jeune Europe* International, Thiriart and his colleagues have plenty of contacts in other countries, and to these they send instructions, printed matter and advice regarding organization.[12] Under the auspices of the Belgian neo-Nazis, 'seminars' are organized for the training of 'nostalgics' in the various countries, and these are probably run by ex-members of the OAS.[13] The agitation among Belgian doctors, which lasted throughout April and May 1964, had a Poujadist tinge, and *Jeune Europe* had a decisive influence on it.[14] The same might be said of the more violent demonstrations against the granting of independence to the Congo. The disciples of the various Fascist Internationals were told by *Jeune Europe* to paint Celtic crosses on walls, to practice judo, karate and savate, and to listen every evening, between 11 and 11.45, to the propaganda transmitted by Radio Portugal; all this while awaiting the coming of 'zero hour', which, as their leader is supposed to have said, will be struck by the 'clock of history'.

The split in the movement during the summer of 1963 and the emergence of Borth's *Europafront* impaired the prestige and influence of Thiriart, all the more so because he was accused of *embourgeoisement* when he announced that he intended to stand as a candidate at the municipal elections in 1964 and the parliamen-

tary elections in 1965. Moreover, Thiriart himself seemed to be
doing his best to make his party 'respectable', since he indignantly
repudiated all charges of 'anti-Semitism', 'Fascism' and 'Nazism',
as well as the mere suggestion that the use of violence was part of
Jeune Europe's system.[15] All this, however, had the flavour of
camouflage. *Jeune Europe* continued its attacks on the democratic
system, Communism and the Left in general, it predicted a series
of revolutionary outbreaks which would 'liberate' the 'brothers in
the East', and urged all free men to unite and fight the 'alliance
between Moscow and Washington'. It aimed its shafts at the traditional targets of every neo-Fascist and neo-Nazi movement; the
hatred the Fascists had always felt for Franklin Roosevelt was re-
exhumed by *Jeune Europe*; when Pandit Nehru died, it did not
even have the decency to stop its attacks on him, but instead published a most vulgar obituary notice; on the other hand it made
itself the paladin of the political attitude of Pope Pius XII and had
hard words for those who 'outraged' his memory.[16] The entry into
the political arena of Barry Goldwater as a candidate for the Presidency prompted the editors of its journals to express their sympathy with his ideas, though they took care to make all the necessary
reservations because he was an 'American' and therefore the representative of a continent with interests 'slightly different' from those
of Europe.[17] This exponent of extreme republicanism obtained their
support because he wanted to resume, and if necessary to carry
to its inevitable consequences, the policy of the Cold War and the
'crusade' against Communism and democracy.

'We shall be the Vikings of the twentieth century,' Thiriart wrote.
The metaphor is obscure, but Moreau hastened to explain it by
adding that 'Communitarianism' is 'a doctrine destined to become
universal'. According to this former theoretician of the MAC, 'If
we confine ourselves for the present to Europe, the reason is that
this part of the globe has been the humus which has fertilized all
the progress of the human race. This is our sincere conviction, and
I can see no reason why a Japanese, a Chilean, or even a Papuan,
should not accept Communitarianism.'[18]

In 1965 and 1966, after printing and distributing a bulky volume
in five languages entitled *An Empire of four hundred million men—
Europe*, in which he reiterated and amplified all the concepts contained in the 'Manifesto to the European Nation' and, as he himself
explained, 'eliminated every trace of romantic activism and pseudo-
military pomp' from the *Jeune Europe* movement, Jean-François

Thiriart devoted his attention to the consolidation of his party (in Brussels he purchased a five-storey building complete with all the plant for printing in offset), and to providing his followers with new organisms such as a 'staff college', a 'Communitarian trade union' and a 'European Communitarian party'. This latter—as Thiriart was at pains to stress—would take up its stand midway between the Right and the Left, and would thus form the 'hard core' and set up a 'revolutionary centre'. 'The persistence I show in developing the internal organization of the party', said Thiriart in 'Circular No 320 for members only', 'is based on one aim: to have at my disposal a revolutionary war-machine, powerful, well oiled and implacable. *Jeune Europe* is alternately a political church, a school of doctrine, a freemasonry and a *Mafia*.' Lastly, he wished to settle who his successor should be, and thus avoid any interruption of 'our long march on Bucharest'.

10 Spain

So dark a night . . .

In the corner of Europe lying between the Pyrenees and the Atlantic, we no longer need to follow the so often confused traces of neo-Fascism, because a clerico-military variant of real Fascism has been in power for twenty-six years in Spain and for thirty-three in Portugal. In the new Europe that has arisen from the ashes of what was to have been a thousand-year-old Reich, the Iberian peninsula has remained isolated down to the present day, almost as if it were separated by a kind of 'sanitary cordon'; as it actually was during the first years after the war. The reason for this isolation (now more symbolical than real) is that, although it is now only a fossil and an anachronism, the two-headed monster ruling over the Spanish and Portuguese peoples is still showing signs of life, and in the throes of its long agony can still paw the air, use its claws and even kill. Thirty-five million human beings, to whom we give the courtesy title of Europeans, but who in reality might be living in another continent, in an isolation which only now is being gradually mitigated, have in these last three decades lost all sense of reality, all the strength needed to put their faith in a change of régime. Those who are not in prison, in hiding or in exile, are living in a kind of vast limbo, where the only things they are allowed to do are to read sporting papers like the *Marca*, to believe in God (always provided that God does not become too progressive) and to beget children.

Those who have managed to escape from this limbo find that they cannot enjoy the liberty they have recovered, as if their senses had been numbed by the chill of the cells or by the vague outlines of their prison. One such man is Marcos Ana:

> It is nearly a year since I was released from the prison in Burgos, but my mind and my memories are still confined within those walls. I can see only the prison yard and the faces of my companions. I can hear only their voices—the rather hoarse voice of the miner Ismael Zapico, and the softer, more educated tones of the musician

Antonio Gil Bernat. I cannot get used to the light, or to seeing things far away. Remote horizons make my eyes water; to rest them, I have to look at a nearby wall, which reminds me of my prison.[1]

Marcos Ana spent twenty-two years in prison because as a boy he fought on the side of the Republicans, and he would not have been released until 1980, if there had not been a worldwide demand for an amnesty. Since his release in 1962 this peasant from Old Castile, who became a poet while in prison, has travelled all over a listless and indifferent Europe, telling people how the Franco régime, since it cannot rid itself of all its adversaries by killing them, seeks to break their spirit by means of years of imprisonment, torture and privations; how in the prisons of Burgos, Carabanchel and Puerto de Santa Maria there are still hundreds of people serving sentences passed on them under special laws promulgated during a war which ended more than twenty-five years ago. A war that was a victory for International Fascism and a dress-rehearsal for the Second World War.

Today, however, although Spain is still a Corporative State under a totalitarian régime, none of the government's supporters dare, at all events officially, to recall the old Fascist ideology, even if its symbols are still displayed and the instruments of dictatorship are still functioning. In order to adapt itself to the times, the 'totalitarian and national-syndicalist State' has become an 'organic democracy'; the Falange has discarded its 'revolutionary' impulses and has become an instrument of bureaucracy. And General Franco can even wax indignant when he hears that,

> abroad our régime is described as a dictatorship; as if the Spanish people would ever bow to a dictatorship! . . . In reality, our régime is something new, more progressive than many other régimes in other parts of the world. We do not need to worry when we find that our way of thinking is misunderstood; it is always a long time before revolutions are properly understood, and we are creating a living revolution.[2]

Nevertheless, although in Spain opportunism has become the State religion, facts count for more than words, and the 8,950 days Marcos Ana spent in prison are more important than Franco's 'living revolution'. The word 'Fascism' may have vanished from the official vocabulary of the régime, but its methods and style have remained. The successors of General Millan Astray no longer shout *Viva la muerte!* or *Abajo la inteligencia!*, but violence is still the dominant factor in the lives of Spaniards and intelligence is still trodden under foot. 'How sad it is,' Jesús López Pacheco remarks with some bitterness, 'that a land with so much sunshine should have so dark a night in the recesses of its heart!'[3]

The neo-Falangists

While Franco Spain was busy getting rid of the more conspicuous trappings of Fascism and doing its best to become respectable, a negligible minority with no official functions tried to revive the ideals of Fascism or, in the more extreme cases, to resume contact with the neo-Fascist International. The existence of neo-Falangist 'cells' was first reported in 1958, when the Falange, having lost more and more of its political significance, was active only in the field of literary rhetoric. The first nuclei appeared in the youth organizations of the *Movimiento Nacional*, among the *Guardias de Franco*. Disappointed with the Franco régime, which had first exploited the Falange in order to seize power and had then relegated it to a corner and neutralized it, the youthful neo-Falangists no longer looked to *el Grande Ausente*, José Antonio Primo de Rivera, but to Ramiro Ledesma Ramos, who in their opinion was the most outstanding and reliable theoretician of national syndicalism. Their revolt, however, came to an abrupt end soon afterwards, when a number of *Guardias de Franco* were arrested at the Atocha railway station in Madrid while they were distributing leaflets. Shortly after this, still dissatisfied with the régime, a whole 'century' of the Madrid *Guardias de Franco* started calling themselves *Hedillistas*, this being an act of homage to an old *camisa vieja* [old shirt— veteran Falangist], Manuel Hedilla, whom Franco had sent to prison for ten years in 1937 for opposing the amalgamation of the Falange and the other traditionalist militias.

These, however, were just acts of rebelliousness which were born and died amid the utmost confusion, and not the slightest trace of ideas or intentions can be discerned in them other than a myth-ical and generic desire to return to the origins. Another group formed about the same time and calling itself *Haz Ibérico* also exploited the name of Hedilla, who was the only leader of the Falangist old guard who had not compromised himself by sup-porting the Franco régime. But although this group was more num-erous and included among its members a large quota of civil war veterans, it never contrived to obtain nation-wide support for its campaign for a 'restoration' of authentic Falangism. *Haz Ibérico* is not, however, the only semi-clandestine neo-Fascist movement active in Spain at the present time. The various groups of dissidents are said to have a total membership of about 25,000.

To these must be added the groups directly connected with the Brussels neo-Fascist International, who have discarded the symbols of the arrows and yoke and adopted the Celtic cross as their emblem. In 1963 the Spanish section of *Jeune Europe* had committees in seventeen provinces, its secretary-general being the *camarada* Antonio Méndez García. More extremist than the other neo-Falangist groups, *Joven Europa*, like the other European sections concentrated on Jean Thiriart's pan-European notions, maintaining that what it feared most was a 'static mechanism, devoid of imagination, with no other resource than to be the expression of a bourgeois Europe of traders, the Europe of the big banks, of cowardice and fear, the Europe that hopes to open the gates of Moscow with the keys of Wall Street'.[4]

When, in January 1963, he prohibited the holding of a *Joven Europa* inaugural congress, General Franco thought that this would be an easy way of gaining credit among the European democracies, who were still undecided whether Spain ought to be admitted to the European Common Market or not. But the trick was too naïve and obvious, though it is true that *Joven Europa* had itself accused Franco on several occasions of having deserted Fascism and of becoming too liberal! *Joven Europa* also annoyed the *Falange*, which could not resign itself to sharing the monopoly of totalitarian ideology with any other group and, although it was the party behind the government, detected in the too daring activities of the neo-Fascists a negative element that might be harmful to Spain's tourist industry.

Decline of the Falange

Was it, then, the consciousness of the fact that they were responsible for governing the country that induced the authorities to apply the brake to the activities of what was still considered to be the third largest Fascist party in Europe? It was not so much a feeling of responsibility, but rather the corruption that was rife and Franco's ability in ridding himself of old allies whom he no longer needed and who were now merely a source of embarrassment. According to the poet Dionisio Ridruejo, who before his 'conversion' had achieved such high rank in the Falange that he was known as the 'Spanish Goebbels',[5] Falangism ceased to exist at the end of the Second World War and was replaced by Francoism, in other words by a military dictatorship of a rigidly conservative type. 'The liquidation of Falangism', says the author of *Cara al sol*,

> was more like a draining away; by the time it was over, there was nothing left. The party cadres consisted only of its own employees and the more or less large number of members who still had fixed and well-paid jobs in the rural centres. This makes it seem probable that Fascism will cease to play any part in Spanish life, for since it can never again become what it used to be, it will remain as a mere adjunct to the system.[6]

As an original movement Falangism had ceased to exist long before, in 1937, when Franco, to cool the revolutionary ardour of the Falange, weakened it by amalgamating it with the Carlist movement. Of this forced marriage Salvador de Madariaga says that it was 'very much as if the President of the United States organized the Republican-Democratic-Socialist-Communist-League-of-the-Daughters-of-the-American-Revolution in the hope of unifying American politics'.[7] The liquidation of Falangism continued rapidly after 1945, when Franco, alarmed by Spain's isolation, was trying to make everyone forget the Fascist origins of his régime, and on 7 June 1947 he transformed the totalitarian national-syndicalist State—at all events on paper—into a traditionalist and Catholic monarchy, thus eliminating Point 6 in the Falangist programme, which advocated the separation of the State from the Church. The Fascist salute was forbidden, the militia was disbanded and the portraits of José Antonio disappeared from office walls, while even the name *Falange Española Tradicionalista y de las Juntas de Ofensiva Nacional-Sindicalista* was changed to the more generic denomination of *Movimiento Nacional*. Ramón Serrano Suñer, who at the time when the Axis was winning sensational victories had perhaps toyed with the idea that he might one day, with the help of the Falange, supplant Franco, definitely buried it in 1947 when he said: 'In reality the Falange was just a political movement that never grew to maturity.'[8]

For three years, until 1948, the Falange, which had been deprived of its control of the press, was left without a Minister and secretary-general, and the only sector in which it was still allowed to operate was that of the trade unions. But by now it was too late for it to organize political influence among the workers. Demagogic promises could not cancel the resentment at the treatment of the workers, which became harsher every year. Following the technique used by all Fascist parties, the Falange maintained that it was anti-capitalist and anti-bourgeois, and even asserted that it was more Socialist than the Socialist parties themselves, but it never kept even one of its promises. Its last attempt to introduce agrarian reforms was made in 1951, but like all reforms which affect the banks and industry they remained a dead letter. Its protests became more and more sporadic as its members found posts in the administration. The leaders of what Ridruejo calls the 'hypothetical Falange' ('something that never existed historically speaking, but which is a more or less faithful reflection of the interesting, complicated and often contradictory theories of its founder'[9]) continued to grumble and stress the necessity of presenting Franco with an ultimatum, but with the passing of the years such intrigues never got beyond the drawing-room stage, while the protests and lamentations assumed an almost comical tone.

The same can be said of the lachrymose and insincere commemoration of the twentieth anniversary of the death of José Antonio Primo de Rivera in a speech broadcast over the Spanish radio by José Luis Arrese. 'José Antonio,' the Minister and secretary-general of the Falange asked, 'are you pleased with us? I think not.'

> And I think this because you fought against materialism and selfishness, whereas today men have forgotten the greatness of your words and follow the path of materialism and selfishness, behaving like madmen. You dreamed of a country of poets and visionaries striving to achieve a hard-won glory, whereas the men of today want only a country that will provide for them and feed them well. No, you cannot approve of this mediocre and sensual existence.[10]

More sincere (and more significant) were the words 'Franco, you're a traitor!', which a young soldier named José Urdiales shouted at the *Caudillo* on 22 November 1960 in the subterranean church of Santa Cruz de los Caídos, at the very moment of the elevation of the Host. This was not the cry of an adversary, but that of a young Falangist accusing Franco of betraying the party that had raised him to power. This gesture, which cost Urdiales a sentence of twelve years' imprisonment, was not the only episode of its kind. In November 1957, when Franco arrived at the Escorial to attend a mass for the soul of the Founder of the Falange, wear-

ing the uniform of an army general instead of that of the party, he
was greeted with shouts of 'Falange! Falange!' In retaliation,
Franco dismissed the leader of the Falangist youth movement and
the president of the university students' association. In a subsequent
speech he defined his attitude to Falangism by pointing out that
'when a movement becomes national, it has to rid itself of its old
prejudices; it has a right to be proud of the days when it served in
the front line, but since the war is over, it is our duty not to conquer,
but to convince'. This was an invitation that the *camisas viejas*
could hardly be expected to accept, and they regularly forget it
when the anniversary of José Antonio's death comes round. On 19
November 1963 about a thousand Falangists marched through the
streets of Madrid shouting *'Falange sí, Opus Dei no!'* and singing
an old Falangist song which had long ago been prohibited, its title
being 'Death to capital!' There were, however, sporadic outbursts
which the authorities tolerated or pretended to ignore, because
they were too busy suppressing another kind of opposition—the
real democratic opposition which also had the support of public
opinion all over the world.

The growth of this opposition to Franco, however, had a curious
sequel inside the Falange. From 1956 on, the left wing of the
movement, consisting of the old guard still firmly attached to
orthodox Falangist ideas, assumed a more and more independent
attitude, indulged in systematic criticism of the régime and, very
discreetly, began to establish contacts with the more moderate
elements among Franco's opponents. Thus, thirty years after José
Antonio Primo de Rivera's attempt to come to an agreement with
the Socialist Indalecio Prieto,[11] we find the more radical elements
in the Falange trying to escape from their isolation and join up with
the opposition forces, in the hope that their 'populist' and anticlerical views would enable them to survive the fall of the Franco
régime.

The 'José Antonio Club'

This change of attitude among the Falangist left-wingers began after
the great disappointment of 1956. In that year, still following his
policy of turning first to one and then to another of the forces
supporting his régime, Franco decided to strengthen the by now
weak position of the Falange by authorizing it to appoint a committee to revise the movement's statutes and draw up plans for

reforming the 'fundamental laws', thus broadening the bases on which the régime rested. This new approach to the Falange on the *Caudillo*'s part resulted, for the first time since the war, in an increased membership (35,000 new subscribers).[12] But what the *camisas viejas* thought was their last chance turned out to be a complete fiasco, for when the committee laid its recommendations before the National Council of the Falange (on which the real Falangists were in a minority) the representatives of the army, the Church and high finance opposed the reforms, and that was the end of it.

In a letter addressed to Arrese, the party's secretary-general[13] Luis González Vicén, who subsequently became the recognized leader of the Falangist 'left wing', revealed the misgivings felt by the old guard, attacking with unaccustomed violence the persistence of the dictatorship and making bitter and detailed criticisms of the régime. In order to fill the void surrounding the régime and save the country from disaster, he suggested that the party should be transformed into a 'system' and that the National Council should become the highest organ in the State, with the right to nominate candidates for ministerial posts and to veto any decision taken by the government. This, according to Vicén, would put an end to the *Caudillo*'s arbitrary and personal powers, reduce the influence of the army and the clergy, settle all outstanding matters left over from the civil war and create a more representative government. It was the old guard's last attempt to 'refalangize' Spain. In his letter to Arrese Vicén made no attempt to conceal the fact that the very existence of the Falange would be endangered if it did not regain its authority before Franco disappeared. 'It is more probable that we would be cast out by the monarchists and the king himself, who very logically would wish to remove the presence of a Falange in part imposed, but not loved.'[14]

After the failure of this attempt in 1956, the Falange once more became a mere instrument of Franco's dictatorship. But soon its 'left wing', the basis of which was the 'José Antonio Study Club', gradually began to adopt a more critical attitude towards the régime. In January 1961 a group of left-wing Falangists, after a 'national congress of the council of the old guard', sent a long report to Franco in which they analysed the situation and made certain recommendations, among them the constitution of an Upper Chamber and the resumption of diplomatic relations with the Soviet Union for purely economic purposes. Having thus warned Franco, this group, led by the former commander of Franco's guard, Vicén, by José Antonio's brother Miguel and his sister Pilar, and by a former secretary-general of the party, Raimundo Fernández Cuesta, began making systematic attacks on their rivals on the government side, these being the *Opus Dei*, which held a kind of monopoly over the finance ministries; the monarchists, who demanded the return of the Bourbons; and high finance, to which various labels were applied, e.g. 'the banks', 'international capitalism', 'pressure groups'.

This offensive became more organized in early January 1963, when the Falangist 'left wing' was given permission to publish a quarterly review dealing with current affairs, called *Es Así* ('It is so'). In the four numbers which appeared in 1963 (the third was withdrawn from circulation by order of the minister-secretary of the *Movimiento*, Solis Ruiz, then allowed to circulate again; the review was definitely suppressed in June 1964) the group gave a somewhat confused outline of its programme and indulged in increasingly violent attacks on rival groups.

For example, in the first issue, under the title 'Neither Fascism, nor a sect, nor an exclusive group', Luis González Vicén declared that 'the foundations on which the State rests are growing weaker every day' and that 'nobody would be surprised if there were to be a sensational collapse with tragic consequences'. After maintaining that 'syndicalism is the most suitable form of government', Vicén explained that what the Falange wanted was

> a government chosen by the people and a two-chamber system. We shall fight against any form of capricious and personal government. The spectacle of a régime that governs by decree is contrary to the very conception of the *Cortes*, and any government violating the constitution which it has itself proclaimed must for this very reason be held to be outside the law and exercising illicit power.

Criticizing the economic planning of the *Opus Dei,* he added: 'We shall oppose any government that, using the excuse that it is reinforcing the country's economy, does this at the expense of the poorest classes. The Spanish workers have had to bear most of the burden of the stabilization plan.' After insisting that the resumption of diplomatic relations with the Soviet Union was a prime necessity, Vicén ended by declaring that the European Common Market 'must become a reality, but without our having to make any dishonourable concessions, since we shall be admitted anyway, provided we make a firm stand'.[15]

The second number of *Es Así*, in an article signed by Miguel Primo de Rivera, returned to the attack on 'the pressure groups rooted in the *Opus Dei*, which have driven the country into a policy of economic stabilization the results of which have been completely negative for the country as a whole, and have often carried out a veritable seizure of the State and of its sovereignty'. In yet another article, which was an obvious attempt to win over certain elements among the working classes, Vicén criticized the prevailing conception of trade unions, maintaining, 'it is no use trying to bring together, in one national trade union, technicians and executives, when they are separated in their daily work', and suggesting that each undertaking ought to have its own trade union, and at the same time defending the right to strike.[16] In the third number Villonia asserted that 'the dictatorial and totalitarian way of thinking leaves no room for hope. We want a presidential and representative State under a revolutionary trade-union régime'. Referring to the twenty-seventh anniversary of the Franco revolt on 18 July, *Es Así* said: 'An historical date is not enough for the younger generation; they need some more attractive symbol offering them the prospect of new solutions.'[17]

Perhaps because he was alarmed by the agitation and discontent prevailing in the Falange, Francisco Franco allowed the National Council of the *Movimiento*, which had not met for eleven years, to assemble in Madrid on 5 March 1963. At the final session, the *Caudillo* instructed the Council to formulate a basic law defining the organization of the *Movimiento* (hitherto based only on a decree), because, as he explained, 'the political and administrative organization of the *Movimiento* is still a reality subject to the erosion of time and to the characteristics and demands of problems'; consequently, what was needed was 'a stable organization which will see that its various structures are perfected, its cadres renewed and its foundations strengthened; that is what it needs to enable it to accomplish its task'.[18]

But this purely tactical and instrumental, umpteenth attempt to instil new life into the National Council of the Falange, which was by now generally regarded as a purely ornamental body, did not deceive the Falangist 'left wing' which, on the contrary, accentuated its 'revolutionary and anti-capitalist' attitude to the point of approving, in October 1963, the protests of the '102 intellectuals' against the tortures inflicted on the Asturian miners. In a letter to Solis Ruiz, Luis González Vicén and fifty-one Falangists of the old guard, after demanding an inquiry into the grave episodes in the Asturias, attacked the régime's policy as being based on 'the most retrograde capitalistic notions' and warned that if the workers were not given a new deal, they would have no other alternative than that of revolt, so that Spain and the world might know that they disapproved of the régime's policy. The letter ends with this significant warning: 'It would not be surprising if one day the workers were to respond with violence to the violence to which they have been subjected.'[19]

This attitude on the part of the Falangist 'left wing', which incidentally only represented a minority within the *Movimiento Nacional*, must not lead us to draw wrong conclusions. Notwithstanding Franco's poignant appeals, the criticisms levelled at the régime, the protest marches, it would be wrong to judge it by the same standards that we use when judging other democratic parties. Ever since 1945, Arrese, the former secretary of the Falange, had been trying to prove that the Falange had never been Fascist,[20] but in the editorials he wrote for *Es Así* we find no trace of his ever having renounced his totalitarian principles or his aversion to the multi-party system. The generic 'populism' that he professed, together with his hostility to the capitalist pressure groups and the republican creed, are proofs, not of an evolution towards more Liberal forms, but of a nostalgic return to the 'national-syndicalist and revolutionary' origins of the Falange and to its original programme, which Franco utilized so long as it suited his purpose and then consigned to the lumber-room.

It remains to be seen how the Falange will behave on the day Franco falls. According to Dionisio Ridruejo, the Falangists will then be faced with the following alternatives: 1) they could die a 'beautiful death' defending the régime and their revolution that has failed (though in view of all the accumulated delusions it is most unlikely that they would choose to do this); 2) they could, as they did in 1936, join forces with the reactionary and conservative fronts (the right wing of the *Movimiento* headed by Admiral Carrero Blanco might well do this); or 3) they might swing to the left, thanks to the efforts of the more dynamic elements and in view of the social reforms that they have never succeeded in realizing.[21]

Entrenched within its last syndicalist stronghold, the old Falange is at the moment trying to win the workers over by promising new collective labour agreements and by allowing elections to be held, as they were between March and November 1963, in conditions of relative liberty. But the 'vertical' trade unions are still a totalitarian and hierarchical organization, and the accusations made by 339 Basque priests still hold good: 'The Spanish trade union is not a trade union, and it is not even Christian. It is a State organism which defends the interests of the State.'[22] In other words, the Falange is still serving the Franco régime, and it is still thriving on, and must therefore share the responsibility for, all the crimes that have been committed. It is still fulfilling that function which Payne has so lucidly defined: 'The Falange, far from controlling the State, was no more than an instrument for holding the State together.'[23]

The Spain of hope and the garrotte

'In 1937, by raising the programme of the Fascist Falange to the level of an ideology of the State, General Franco, as he himself has said, intended to make Spain a totalitarian State.' That is the conclusion reached by the 'white book' published by the International Commission of Jurists:

> Later, and especially after the Second World War, he made certain statements in which he adopted a more aloof attitude towards totalitarianism, without ever abandoning that intolerance which is so characteristic of totalitarian régimes and without ceasing in his attempts to crush all opposition.[24]

But even if a world war and the collapse of the Axis powers had not induced Franco to relegate Falangism to the background, it is highly probable that, like Hitler and Mussolini after they had consolidated their own personal power, he would have got rid of the more noisy and plebeian elements among his Greenshirts and would, as he actually did later, have transformed his 'national-syndicalist revolution into a military and police dictatorship, for the benefit of the big landowners, industrialists and capitalists'.[25]

Having reduced the 'Falangist revolution' to its proper dimensions, Franco allowed the doctrine of *Caudillaje* (very similar to that of the German National Socialist *Führerstaat*) to be evolved around his own person, thus making the *Caudillo* the key man in the régime.[26] The status of the *Caudillo* is defined as follows in Article 12 of the Falange's statutes: 'As initiator of an historical epoch, during which Spain acquired the ability to fulfil her historical destiny and at the same time achieve the aims of the *Movimiento*, the *Caudillo* is invested with absolute power in the fullest sense

of the term. The *Caudillo* is responsible to God and to posterity.'
Article 40 of the statutes also lays down that 'the *Caudillo* will
also nominate his successor, who will be proclaimed by the Council after the *Caudillo*'s death'. This is a regulation which in theory
should ensure the continuity of the Franco régime.

Caudillaje is essentially an attempt to legitimize a régime which
was the product of a military insurrection, and we look in vain for
any ideology underlying the Franco régime.[27] 'Supported by high
finance, guarded by the army, robed in the symbols of a moribund
Fascism, bearing the stamp of absolute power, Francoism breathes
the air of the Cold War, survives thanks to the tension prevailing
in international affairs, and lastly, tries to perpetuate the myth of a
régime waging a holy war and to claim that it is in the forefront
of the battle against Communism.'[28] With his profound understanding of his own country Francisco Franco-Bahamonde knows how
to keep it divided, exploiting his greatest gift, which is his ability
to arbitrate and cajole first the Falange and then the Church,[29]
one day humiliating the Falange by turning to the *Opus Dei*,[30] and
the next day making the monarchists believe that restoration is
imminent,[31] but always nipping all opposition in the bud without
ever changing his attitude towards the army[32] and high finance,
the two forces on which he relies and which derive the greatest
benefits from his régime. Displaying his skill in manœuvring and
carrying repression to the point of perfection, Franco has been able
to preserve his régime for twenty-six years—a régime described
by Herbert Rutledge Southworth as 'a living monument to all the
work of Hitler and Mussolini'.[33]

But however anachronistic this régime may be, it manages to
survive, and a close examination of Spanish history over the last
few years invariably leads to one conclusion. The régime always
seems to be on its last legs, but it never falls. From time to time
the squabbles between the various factions become more violent,
but the only result is to give the *Caudillo* a chance to show his
skill in arbitration. The Church holds itself aloof from the régime,
but the *Opus Dei* is in reality its brain. The opposition is active,
but atones with thousands of years of imprisonment for its inability
to find a basis for collaboration. And the upshot is that we do not
know how much faith we can have in the atmosphere of expectancy which has lasted ever since the big Asturian strikes in 1957
without producing any concrete results. With bitterness, not un-
mixed with a certain dose of realism, Juan Goytisolo has tried to

find an explanation for these vain hopes, and he maintains that the heroic behaviour of a people at a particular moment in its history does not authorize us to think that it will remain a heroic nation for all time to come and to treat it accordingly.[34]

As regards this atmosphere of expectancy, 1963 did not differ from the preceding years. On New Year's Day, for the first time for twenty-five years, the Spanish radio omitted from its news-bulletins the ritual playing of the Falangist hymn and the cry of *Viva Franco!, Arriba España!* On 1st March the Generalissimo himself, replying to criticism from the Falangist 'left wing', admitted that the Spanish State ought to become more democratic and promised to grant the trade unions a larger measure of independence. but the change in the ritual of the news-bulletins, the desire of the Falange for a 'defascisticization' of the régime and Franco's democratic proposals would seem to be nothing more than expedients to avoid raising internal tension to combustion point and to ingratiate Europe by adopting a more serene and more acceptable attitude. This, however, does not mean that the Franco régime has changed its nature, or has the slightest intention of changing it, since it is still a totalitarian police State, just as it was in the 1940s.

Now that the world situation as a whole has become less strained and Spain has concluded a military pact with the United States, summary executions of adversaries are, of course, no longer possible. Between April 1939 and June 1944 there was wholesale slaughter,[35] but since then executions have become increasingly rare, and have invariably been preceded by the pretence of a trial. But if we study the activities of the régime's repressive organs, even in the year 1963 alone, we cannot help being struck by their ruthlessness, this in itself being a confirmation of the aggressive and typically Fascist nature of this régime, which, twenty-five years after the ending of the civil war and despite the lip-service it pays to reconciliation, cannot rid itself of the idea of revenge; thus perpetuating 'the invisible demarcation-line of the blood that has been shed'[36] and remaining faithful to the concept expressed in 1951 by the then minister-secretary of the Falange, Fernández Cuesta: 'Between their Spain and ours lies a gap that can never be filled, unless they repent and accept our doctrine. Otherwise, they will remain on the other side of the gap, and if they attempt to cross it secretly, they will perish.'[37]

Between 25 January and 18 April 1963 alone, the investigating

I

magistrate, Colonel Enrique Eymar Fernández, sent about 200 men charged with armed rebellion for trial before the *Sumarísimo* War Council. Of these, 128 were sentenced to terms of imprisonment ranging from one to thirty years. On 20 April Julian Grimau García was shot for 'war crimes' which could not be proved and had in any case been committed twenty-five years before. 'I shall be the last victim of Francoism,' Grimau told his fellow-prisoners on the eve of his execution. But on 17 August two anarchists, Joaquín Delgado Martínez and Francisco Franados Gata, were executed for having allegedly committed acts of terrorism in Madrid. To make the sentence more exemplary, the medieval method of garrotting was chosen. And lastly, to stop the continual strikes during that year in the Basque lands and the Asturias, the police arrested thousands of people and subjected many of them to beatings and torture.[38]

For several weeks, and more especially after the execution of Grimau, public opinon all over the world realized that Franco had not changed and that 'people are still dying in Madrid'. To quote François Mauriac: 'My opinion of Franco is today the same as it was at the time of Guernica.'[39] In an article entitled '*Rompre avec l'Espagne?*', Maurice Duverger says that although it is still possible to maintain relations with a dictatorship, 'its dictatorial nature cannot be denied, and we cannot officially recognize it as a democracy. Doubts as to its democratic principles will consequently arise in the minds of its own citizens as well as in those of citizens of the free countries'.[40] Discussing the reasons behind the *Caudillo*'s refusal to reprieve Grimau, Jean Daniel observes that 'Franco thinks this is the moment to show that he is still there, still holding the reins of government firmly and still implacable. So everyone is against the execution? Very well, the execution will take place'.[41] And Dionisio Ridruejo, who knows Franco and Spain even better, adds:

> The execution of Grimau was, in a certain sense, an act of reprisal, the blow that toppled the house of cards erected by progressive collaborators, by pan-Europeans and by the 'liberal-minded' supporters of the régime, the *fait accompli* that will compel them to acknowledge that they are nothing less than accomplices of a system based on violence and brutal authority. Franco remains true to form. For him there is no room for pity when it is a question of staying in power; the real interests of the country are subordinated to the preservation of his power; and lastly, the internal problem outweighs all considerations of prestige which might affect Spain's

relations with the outside world. Once again he has defied the moral conscience of the world in order to avoid any danger of his system being undermined.[42]

Public indignation rose to such a pitch that on 4 May 1963 a 'special Western European conference to discuss Spain' was convened in Paris, at the end of which a resolution was passed 'denouncing this régime as the most typical survival of Fascism in Europe and as one which is sheltering many war criminals,[43] . . . It continued:

> This meeting appeals to the U.N. to include in the agenda of its next general assembly an examination of the Spanish question and of the possibility of taking measures to ensure that Spain should have a government based on the elementary principles of law . . . The meeting also considers that all military, economic and financial aid to Franco Spain on the basis of bilateral pacts should cease, since the effect of such aid would be to prolong the existence of the Franco régime.

But these appeals fell upon deaf ears. On 27 September the United States renewed its military and economic agreements of 1953 for a further five years and Western Germany made huge loans to the Madrid government. Instead of finding himself isolated, Franco received help in overcoming his economic difficulties, and time placated the indignation of the democrats as their posters faded on the walls.

Once again silence clamped down upon Spain, betrayed in 1936 as she was in 1945 and always is. Silence fell on the Spain of the Asturian women whose heads had been shaved in mockery and on the Spain of the Madonnas decorated with Nazi Iron Crosses. On the Spain of tortured prisoners and on the Spain of judges who swear 'by God and the Holy Gospels to obey without question the orders of the *Caudillo* of Spain'.[44] On the Spain of protests and censorship, on the Spain of hope and the garrotte.

11 Portugal

Happy countries have no history

Unaffected by European progress and knowing nothing whatsoever of modern ideas, Portugal, to an even greater extent than Spain, has tried to turn her isolation to advantage by using every possible subterfuge in order to camouflage the real nature of her government. But the respectable façade of the *Estado Novo* ('Happy countries have no history,' was Salazar's reply to someone who asked him why it was that 'apparently' nothing ever happened in Portugal) was rudely shattered by the seizure of the liner *Santa Maria* and by the insurrection in Angola, and public opinion all over the world suddenly realized that the oldest Fascist régime in Europe was still intact and, in the course of the long and secret struggle against democracy, had even perfected its use of violence and its skill in suppressing all opposition.

'On the day after Hitler's suicide in the bunker of the Chancellery,' we were told by the Angolan poet Costa Andrade in 1962, shortly after he had escaped from Salazar's prisons,

Portugal was the only country in the world where flags were flown at half-mast. And yet she has managed to become a member of NATO and to make people believe, down to 1959, that the 'Salazarian order' is something just, respectable and efficient, whereas in reality it is only a police régime trying to cover up the complete failure of the Corporative State. Take a glance at the official statistics issued by the Bank of Portugal and you will see that a skilled workman earns £20 ($56) a month, a labourer £15 ($42) and a peasant from £5 to £10 ($14 to $28), while four big landowners between them own over 250,000 acres of land.[1] Look at other statistics, and you will find that 40 per cent of the inhabitants are illiterates, that the annual income per head—about £75—is the lowest in Europe, that a million people live in villages that have no roads, that 48 per cent of the communes have no electric light, and that the infant mortality is the highest in Europe.[2] That is the result of being governed for thirty-four years by Professor Antonio de Oliveira Salazar, who hides behind the legend of the solitary man who doesn't like crowds or making demagogic speeches—frugal, ascetic and always communing with God; a dictator like all the others, who keeps himself in power with the help of the secret police, the Fascists of the 'Republican National Guard' and the 'Portuguese Legion'.[3]

We need say nothing more of the Corporative State, since we have already dealt with it in the first part of this volume, but it would seem appropriate to mention here the Archbishop of Oporto's definition of it: 'In practice the Corporative State has shown that it is a way of exploiting the workers.' This opinion, expressed by the prelate in a letter he wrote to Salazar in 1958—and for writing it, he was exiled—marks an important date, since it coincided with the abandonment of the régime by the more enlightened clergy and the Catholic masses. In the beginning the Salazar régime received the unconditional support of the Church, the army, the big landowners, a dozen or so large monopolistic enterprises and the middle classes, but on this occasion it lost one of its most precious allies. The breach became even wider a few years later, when a score or more priests were arrested, deported or killed in Angola.

The crisis in Portuguese Fascism became evident at the time of the 1958 presidential election. For the first time,[4] the democratic opposition put forward a candidate, General Humberto Delgado, who, despite all difficulties, polled 236,528 votes as against the 758,998 cast for the government candidate, Américo Tomás. This was a great achievement, and all the more so when we remember that the electoral laws deprived more than half the population of the right to vote. As Peter Fryer and Patricia McGowan Pinheiro aptly point out,[5] Salazar has at least seven different ways of preventing elections from being really free: 1) opposition candidates have to be approved by the government; 2) paupers and illiterates cannot vote; 3) each citizen has to apply to be put on the electoral register; 4) any elector can be struck off the register at the discretion of the government; 5) no representatives of the opposition candidates are allowed to be present at the counting of the votes; 6) ballot-papers containing votes for the opposition can be confiscated by the police; 7) members of the opposition are liable to be arrested. But despite all these precautions on the part of the régime, Delgado received a quarter of a million votes, with a programme which openly demanded the abolition of the Fascist régime and the restoration of democratic liberties. His success was of fundamental importance, since it was achieved thanks to a pact between all the opposition parties, ranging from *os velhos republicanos* to the Communists, from the Socialists to the Catholics and all the other democratic groups that have sprung up since 1956, the year of the *détente* in the international situation. On polling day, repeating the bold exploit of the Italian poet De Bosis, who flew over Milan during the Fascist régime, an airman of the opposition flew his plane over Lisbon and dropped anti-Fascist leaflets on the city.

The government reacted promptly. Humberto Delgado was relieved of his post as director-general of civil aviation and threatened with arrest. (Subsequently he took refuge in the Brazilian embassy in Lisbon, where he stayed until he was granted a safe-conduct which enabled him to reach Latin America; after that he went to live in Algeria, where he continued his campaign against the Salazar régime; on 13 February 1965 he was murdered near the frontier between Spain and Portugal, in circumstances which are still far from clear.) Another grave retaliatory measure was a change in the constitution, the effect of which was to carry Portugal still further along the road towards totalitarianism, instead of granting her greater freedom. After suppressing the last pitiable remnants of liberal ideas, Salazar abolished presidential elections on a universal suffrage basis; future presidents were to be elected by the five hundred members of the National Assembly and Chambers of the Corporations, in accordance with the best traditions of Fascism. As a result of this manœuvre, which throws into even clearer relief the Coimbra professor's contempt for democratic institutions and his ideal of *catedratocia* (government by university professors, by an enlightened élite), the régime lost the support of the middle classes, who had been hoping for a gradual liberalization of the country and its inclusion in the 'Europe of the Six'.

But this was not the last defection. In April 1961 it was the turn of the army, which in 1926 had made the Fascist *coup d'état* possible, but now attempted to overthrow the Salazar régime. A few high-ranking officers, led by the Minister of War, Botelho Monis, tried to organize a revolt in Portuguese Africa. This attempt failed and General Monis, who had written letters to Salazar and President Tomás demanding a return to the republican constitution of 1910, was dismissed. In many respects this '13 April' of the Portuguese generals resembled the '13 May' of the French *ultras* and also the '25 July' of the Italian Fascist Grand Council. Monis belonged, in fact, to a conservative group consisting mainly of former collaborators of Salazar who wished to retain the Fascist régime, which was useful to the big capitalists, but to get rid of the old dictator, who had now incurred the hostility of public opinion all over the world and was far too rigid in his decisions. Behind this conservative group (of which the former head of the President's cabinet, Marcelo Caetano, and a former Minister of the Interior, Trigo de Negreiros, were also members) stood the CUF *(Companhia União Fabril)*, the biggest Portuguese monopoly, and other trusts linked with international capitalism, which would have favoured the advent of a régime of the Gaullist type and the removal of the Coimbra professor, who had compromised himself far too deeply.[6]

Discontent in army circles became even more widespread after the loss of Goa and the other Portuguese possessions in India, and especially after the insurrection in Angola. This time, however, it was not only the senior officers who rebelled, but the rank and file and the junior Reserve officers. Some soldiers refused to embark for Angola, went on hunger-strike and organized demonstrations on the quays, joining civilians in shouting 'Peace in Angola', 'Amnesty!' and 'Free Elections!', and finally hundreds of them deserted. The opposition exploited this discontent, distributing a clandestine publication called *Tribuna Militar* among the soldiers and forming increasingly solid contacts with the army. The upshot of this campaign was the attack on the Beja barracks on New Year's Day, 1962. True to the traditions of Iberian insurrections, the attack was led by an officer, Captain Varela Gomes, and by a Catholic, Manuel Serra, and it ended in a dismal fiasco after seven hours of fighting. Nevertheless, it was significant because, like the 'act of piracy' committed a year before by Captain Galvão when he seized the liner *Santa Maria*, it drew the attention of Portugal and the whole world to the necessity of overthrowing the Fascist régime.

From the beginning of 1962 onwards Salazar could rely with certainty only on the support of the police and the Fascist military or semi-military organizations. The dictator now began to adopt a more cautious policy and, after a thorough reshuffle, he surrounded himself with the most extreme elements in Portuguese Fascism—men like General Calouzo de Arriaga, Admiral Henriques and the Nazi Santos Costa. Since he no longer trusted the army, he placed the arsenals, the motor-transport depots and the tank-workshops under the protection of the 'Republican National Guard' (one of the régime's three police forces). Such precautions could not be called excessive, for the democratic opposition was becoming more and more aggressive and had at last managed to create a united and effective organization, the *Junta de Ação Patriótica*, and even to set up a 'Portuguese National Liberation Front' (21 December 1962). The solidarity of these anti-Fascist forces was proved by the success of the demonstrations against the régime, which began on 1 May 1962 and continued throughout the summer—that summer which was described as the 'hottest' Portugal had ever experienced. Against the thousands of citizens who thronged the streets protesting against the régime and the war in Angola, Salazar's police force used all its weapons and all its ferocity. In the second part of this chapter we shall examine this instrument of Salazarian oppression.[7]

The PIDE versus the opposition

In a country where parliament is in session for only three months in the year, while for the rest of the time Salazar governs by means of decrees, where strikes and trade unions are illegal, where the only authorized party is the *União Nacional*, where boys between eight and seventeen are conscripted into the *Mocidade Portuguesa* and made to wear green shirts and a belt with the dictator's monogram engraved on the buckles, the size and functions of the security forces are bound to play a preponderating role, as they do under all authoritarian régimes. In Portugal there are, in fact, five armed security police forces: the secret police (PIDE = *Policia Internacional e de Defensa do Estado*); the municipal police (PSP); the Republican National Guard (GNR); the *Legião Portuguesa*, consisting of Greenshirt volunteers; and the *Guardia Fiscal*, which is also armed.

The most notorious of these, on account of the brutal methods it employs, is the PIDE, formed in 1940 on the initiative of the then Minister of Defence, the pro-German and racialist Santos Costa. Its first functionaries were, in fact, trained by Gestapo agents and one of its first chiefs, Neves Graça, was a pupil of *Obersturmbannführer* Kramer, who in 1942 was appointed commandant of the Belsen concentration camp.[8] The PIDE employs thousands of informers (it is calculated that Salazar has engaged at least 100,000 of these wretches to spy on the rest of the population), controls the whole country in the most meticulous manner and manages to create an atmosphere of suspicion and terror.

Working in close collaboration with the PIDE we have the *Legião*

Portuguesa, founded in 1936 on the model of the German SA and the Italian Fascist militia (MVSN). According to Salazar himself this is 'an organization of volunteers for the preservation of order, with special reference to the struggle against Communism; its military training undoubtedly makes it most suitable for this purpose and it is therefore intended that it should collaborate with the police, the territorial army and the navy'. For the régime this army of volunteers, 87,000 strong, represents an important military and political reserve.[9] For suppressing riots and strikes the authorities prefer to make use of the ordinary police (PSP), which has an establishment of 10,000 men, or of the Republican National Guard, which is heavily armed and equipped with armoured cars and tear-gas, and has a strength of about 20,000 men.

'The powers of the PIDE are unlimited,' we were told by the Angolan poet Costa Andrade, who bears on his chest the marks of the lighted cigarettes which PIDE agents pressed against it to make him talk. 'Perhaps even greater than those of the Gestapo or the Hungarian AVH.' Costa Andrade is one of the 52,970 people who, between 1926 and 1961 have been imprisoned in Portugal simply on account of their opinions. He is one of the few who have managed to escape and can therefore give an accurate account of the 'reign of terror' established by the *Estado Novo*, on the hurried trials before the *Tribunalis Plenários*, of the sufferings of thousands of political prisoners in the jails of Caxias, Alijbe, Peniche, Santa Cruz do Bispo and Poços de Ferreira, of the tortures and faked suicides, and of the reopening of the concentration camps at Tarrafal and São Tomé.

The powers of the PIDE were legally established by decree No 35042 of 20 October 1945, six months after Nazism and Fascism had vanished from the rest of Europe. The decree authorizes the PIDE to arrest anybody without preferring any specific charge, and to keep them in detention for a period of three months, which can be extended to six by order of the Ministry for the Interior. A subsequent decree (No 40550 of 12 March 1956) authorizes the secret police to prolong the period of detention for a further three years and, by means of successive prolongations to transform it, practically speaking, into a life sentence. 'The indefinite duration of the period of confinement,' we read in this notorious decree, 'will enable the detainee to convince himself that his release depends upon himself, and this will be a most efficacious method of inducing the proper reactions in his mind.' Although the decree specifies that

1*

trials must take place before the expiration of the maximum limit of one year from the date of arrest, this is never the case, because the PIDE invariably raises objections. This explains why the Communist leader Manuel Rodrigues da Silva spent ten years in Tarrafal concentration camp without ever being brought before a court, Rolando Verdial six years, Carlos Costa four, Maria Angela Vidal four and Ivonne Dias Lourenço three.[10]

The PIDE also makes sure that the accused cannot be properly defended during his trial, so that the proceedings of the *Tribunalis Plenários* are transformed into tragic farces, during which the judges show that they are obsequious servants of the régime, while defending lawyers are often threatened, witnesses are frequently arrested immediately after giving evidence, and the accused—as happened recently to Antonio Gervasio—is beaten up by PIDE agents during the actual hearing. In order to break the spirit of political detainees the secret police have even invented a new and incredible offence— 'subversive activities while in prison'—which allows it to prolong any sentence for as long as it likes. But the most shameful aspects of the activities of Salazar's police are the ill-treatment of prisoners in the insalubrious penal establishments and the use of torture in order to extract confessions.

The things that happen at the Lisbon headquarters of the PIDE— in Via Cardoso, in the very heart of the city—as well as in Oporto and in the above-mentioned prisons, are obviously derived from the teachings of the Gestapo torturers, as regards both methods of psychological intimidation, the technique used to prolong suffering and the scientific methods of concealing the marks of torture. Beatings-up, solitary confinement for months on end and brainwashing are the systems normally employed in order to break down the will-power of political adversaries. But the PIDE's favourite method is that known as 'the statue', which the report mentioned in Note 10 describes as follows:

> The method of torture known as 'the statue' consists of making the prisoner stand still with his face to a wall on which the questions asked by the police, and which they want him to answer, are posted up on a level with his eyes. The detainee remains in this position for days and nights on end, without being able to sleep, eating a few mouthfuls while standing up, and liable to be beaten the moment he shows any signs of weakness due to fatigue or sleepiness. After a few hours of this his legs begin to swell and cause him pain; his feet, in particular, become enormously swollen and the prisoner cannot put on his socks or shoes. At the same time the

lack of sleep causes hallucinations, impairs the faculty of vision and causes intolerable distress.[11]

Francisco Miguel, who was detained in the fortress of Caixas, is probably the man who has had most experience of this treatment. Three times in succession he was subjected to the 'statue' torture for 732 hours (thirty days); Hernani Silva, a student, underwent it for seven consecutive days and nights; Joaquim Dias for sixteen days with two breaks; Domingo Abrantes for twenty days with one or two breaks; Ilidio Esteves for thirteen days with two breaks. It seldom happens that a detainee escapes being subjected to this or some other form of torture. Salazar himself admits all this and even tries to justify it, as his official biographer, Antonio Ferro, tells us:

> We came to the conclusion that the prisoners who had been ill-treated were, almost without exception, terrorists of the worst type—men who manufactured bombs or who, despite lengthy interrogation by the police, refused to reveal where they had hidden their nefarious and murderous weapons. It was only after violent methods had been used that they decided to tell the truth. I ask myself whether, if we were to prevent such action by the police, the lives of defenceless people, the lives of children would not be sufficient justification for giving these wretched creatures a good half-dozen beatings.[12]

In 1957 General Massu claimed the same right to obtain information by using torture. And it is curious that Massu, like Salazar, hypocritically pretends that the violence used against prisoners was limited to 'a dozen lashes' and 'a few clips on the ear'.

Such hypocrisy becomes even graver when we remember that the tortures inflicted by PIDE agents are known to have caused the deaths of scores of anti-Fascists. Since the death penalty was abolished in Portugal in the course of the last century, the Salazar régime can get rid of its opponents only by resorting to torture, by treating them brutally in the concentration camps, by refusing them medical aid, and by means of traps and bursts of machine-gun fire. What were really murders are frequently camouflaged as suicides, as in the case of those of the trade-union leader Manuel Vieira Tomé, of the office-worker Francisco Ferreira Marques, of José Moreira, Raul Alves and, more recently, of the sculptor José Dias Coelho and Colonel Lucio Lunha Serra.

As the régime gradually becomes more and more insecure, the work of the PIDE increases. On an average it carries out three assassinations every day. In 1962 alone it made 5,000 arrests, an average of sixteen a day. Incidentally, the orders it receives leave no room for misunderstanding. 'From now on,' José Rosa Carval-hal, the head of the PIDE, told his colleagues in 1963, 'we shall make ourselves understood even by those who can't understand us. We shall fight the Demon without any scruples.' To destroy the demon of the opposition, the PIDE has recently thought of a new system, which is a prelude to the installation of gas-chambers. News has leaked out that the secret police are using prisoners to test the effect of pumping poison-gas slowly into overheated rooms. This is a grim story, but it is constantly being repeated. When a régime is at its last gasp, it resorts to extreme measures, almost as if it were afraid of not being taken for what it really is.

The insurrection in Angola

While the Salazar régime was in the middle of a crisis, Angola rose in rebellion.[13] On 4 February 1961 African nationalists stormed the prison of São Paulo in Luanda and on 16 March of the same year the rebellion spread from the 'Primavera' *fazenda* at São Salvador do Congo to the whole of the northern part of the colony. The only people to be surprised were the Portuguese authorities, and Salazar hastened to deny that it was due to the 'fatality of a historical movement' and to throw all the blame on 'inflammatory ideas imported from outside'.

The official line, which was reiterated in 1961 by the then Minister for the Overseas Provinces, Adreano Moreira, was that Portuguese colonialism was quite different from that of the capitalistic nations. In the case of the latter, human relationships in their colonies were based on racial segregation, whereas the Portuguese system was a 'missionary colonialism' which was doing its best to bring the races into contact and redeem 'our black brethren' (as one of the leaders of Portuguese Fascism, Castro Fernandes, called them) from moral chaos. 'Colonization', said another eminent representative of the Salazar régime, 'means teaching and training.' These noble professions of faith were contradicted, not only by the facts, but also by certain frank admissions made by, among others, Marcelo Caetano: 'Africa is something more than a country ripe for exploitation . . . For us Africa is a moral justification and the *raison d'être* of our existence as a power. Without Africa we would be a tiny nation; with it we are a great country.' And Portugal certainly was the third biggest colonial power in the world.

Per Wästberg points out that Salazar's colonial philosophy is founded on a mystical dream of a pan-Lusitanian commonwealth, held together by the spiritual qualities characteristic of Portuguese culture.[14] Ever since the early days of his dictatorship the Coimbra professor has been doing his best to spread this mystical nationalism in his country, this 'missionary Lusitanianism', not unlike Nazi pan-Germanism in its irrationality, the vagueness of its doctrines and the brutal methods it employs. Despite official statements to the contrary, there was no *pax lusitana in* Angola, Mozambique or Guinea, in the Cape Verde Islands or at São Tomé, unless we apply the term to a régime based on the PIDE, on slave labour, deportations and lessons instilled with the aid of that medieval instrument of torture known as the *palmatória*.[15] Salazar's only exports to the colonies (in deference to the UN they were called 'overseas provinces' after 1951) were Fascist methods, rendered even more brutal by the prevalence of racial hatred. Salazar's record in Africa was even worse than it was in Portugal. Taking as an example Angola, which is the richest Portuguese colony and the one to which they have devoted most 'care', we find that illiteracy reaches the record figure of 99.3 per cent, while infant mortality stands at 55 per cent; that the average annual income per head is about £7 ($20) and that there is only one doctor for every 21,000 inhabitants; and that the Whites own most of the land and all the industrial and commercial undertakings, banks and financial capital.

Salazar's colonial mysticism also boasts that it systematically rejects and condemns every form of racialism, but the facts give the lie to this claim. The much vaunted fraternal feeling between the two races is typified by the notorious *caderneta indígena*, which is the equivalent of the famous 'pass' that the racialist authorities in Pretoria make all Negroes—and only the Negroes—carry. It is true that in Luanda segregation has not been made a law as it has been in Johannesburg, but all the same the Africans live in separate quarters of the town, special wards are reserved for them in hospitals and the education received by the few who qualify for it (the *ensino primario de adaptaçao*) is definitely inferior to the *ensino oficial*. Despite the fact that recently, as a result of UN pressure, the *Estatuto dos indígenos* dividing Africans into *assimilados* and *indígenos* has been abolished, the social condition of the Angolans has not changed and they still have no political rights whatsoever. According to the Portuguese, being kept in a species of limbo is in the Africans' own interests. As for the confusion existing in the rest of Africa, the above-mentioned Castro Fernandes gave his own explanation of it when he said: 'The introduction of the parliamentary system has added new causes of dissension and quarrels to the already existing ancestral hatreds and vendettas.' In reality, the only thing the Africans are taught is the love of work. As the then Minister for the Colonies, Vieira Machado, said in 1943: 'We must get the idea of work into the Negroes' heads and convince them that they must stop being idle and discontented; otherwise it will not be possible to defend them by colonizing them.'

What discouraged the natives in the Portuguese colonies and induced them to revolt in 1961 was precisely the meaning Salazar gave to 'work', i.e. forced labour. In Angola the *shibalos* represent over a third of the total labour force; in Mozambique over 400,000 Africans have been sent under official auspices to work in the copper-mines of Zambia or in the South African gold-mines. Before Henrique Galvão, the hero of the *Santa Maria* exploit, became an opponent of Salazar, he was an inspector in the colonial service and one of his reports put the Lisbon government in a very embarrassing position. 'In many respects,' Galvão wrote,

> the natives employed on forced labour are worse off than they were as slaves. Under slavery, the owner who had bought a slave had an interest in keeping him fit. Today it does not matter to the entrepreneur at all if his natives fall sick or die; what matters is that they should work while they are alive. When they are dead, one need only send in a new indent in order to receive a fresh supply of slaves.[16]

Angolan nationalists are treated almost as badly as Portuguese democrats are in the home country. As Henrique Galvão points out:

> In the Portuguese provinces in Africa Salazar uses the same methods as he does in the mother country in order to rule and enforce the Salazar peace, that Salazarian order which his propaganda is always proclaiming so loudly. Only those who are at rest in the cemeteries know what this peace and this order are.[17]

Like Verwoerd, the Portuguese dictator laughs at the manœuvres of the Afro-Asiatics in that big glass palace in Manhattan, and speaking in parliament on 30 June 1961 he described the UN appeal to stop repression in Angola as a 'theatrical gesture'. In adopting this contemptuous attitude he relies on the support of Great Britain and the United States who, in defiance of the principles they normally proclaim, support his régime because they are afraid of losing the big profits they receive from their investments in Portugal and her overseas provinces.[18] Another weapon frequently used by Salazar is blackmail. After the loss of Goa he never stopped predicting that the end of the world was at hand, and every time he needs arms to intensify his operations in Angola or Guinea, he threatens to leave NATO, warning public opinion all over the world, in the tones of the only man still capable of reasoning, that 'many nations are beginning to doubt the validity of their previous policies' and that today only Portugal is 'defending Europe on the only fronts where she can still be defended'.

After the first risings in Angola, Salazar reinforced the PIDE by dispatching an expeditionary force of 50,000 men, made up of paratroopers, 'special units' and detachments of the Fascist *Legião Portuguesa*. Portugal's 'civilizing mission' was promptly forgotten. Speaking on 5 May 1961 to 3,000 young men who were about to embark for Angola, Mario Silva, the Defence Minister, uttered this warning: 'We are fighting against savages. We are fighting against wild beasts . . . who are not Portuguese because they are taking their orders from the Communist International. We have to deal with terrorists, who must be shot down just as we shoot down wild beasts.'[19] Since then repression and genocide as practised by the Nazis have become synonyms.

As a reprisal for the killing of seven policemen during rioting in Luanda on 4 February 1961 3,000 Angolans were massacred. And the deaths of 200 white settlers in the region bordering on the Congo were avenged by exterminating 30,000 Angolans. Even the massacre of the Hereros by the Germans at the beginning of this century can hardly be compared with this. On 3 May 1961 a Portuguese told the Luanda correspondent of the *Daily Mirror* that there were probably 100,000 more rebels still operating in the bush and that they would be killed as soon as the dry season set in, while the correspondent of *The Observer* reported that a car with a loudspeaker drove through the village of Tumbi announcing that the 'king' of the UPA (Holden Roberto, one of the leaders of the Angola revolt and since 1963 president of the 'revolutionary government of Angola in exile') was about to arrive by plane, and when a plane did arrive and a crowd gathered, the troops converged on the village and killed 300 of the inhabitants. Similar massacres took place in the villages of Libolo, Dembos, Golungo Alto, Ambaca, Dondo, Cacuso, Sanga, Tomboco, Mawuela, São Salvador and hundreds of other places. For the paratroopers and the settlers it became a form of sport to go hunting for natives in the woods, though they regretted that the Africans were such a poor kind of game (cf. report of the South African News Agency, 19 June 1961). The wives of extremist settlers handed in their jewels to help speed up the campaign of repression. Angolan patriots were shot as soon as they were captured, buried alive or dropped into the sea from aeroplanes. Heads of men were to be seen stuck on poles as in the darkest ages. Eight Methodist ministers accused of complicity with the partisans were shot, and the fate of seventy others is still unknown. The British Baptist Missionary Society reported the shooting of seventeen ministers and the arrest of 120 missionaries. Dozens of Catholic priests, including Joaquín Pinto de Andrade[20] and Monsignor Joaquín Mendes da Neves, vicar-general of the archbishopric of Luanda, were deported to Portugal. 150,000 Angolans fled to the Congo and 50,000 civilians were killed in the course of reprisals or as the result of air raids.

In the summer of 1962 a medical officer made the following statement to the Special Committee of the United Nations:

> My name is Marino Moutinho de Padoua; I am a doctor by profession and am twenty-six years old. I was an officer in the Portuguese army in Angola and I deserted in October 1961 after seeing with my own eyes the crimes committed against the Angolan people, crimes that nothing could justify. Our first sight of Luanda filled us with shame. The white settlers came to us and talked about the tortures they had inflicted on the Angolans, and they were proud of what they had done.

Then he went on to describe a round-up:

> After the first few miles, my men were horrified. In the courtyard of a farm lay the bodies of Angolans who had been shot, all of them with their ears cut off. Some veterans of the colonial war told us all about this gruesome joke—before being executed the condemned men were compelled to eat their own ears or those of one of their companions.

The doctor spoke for two hours and ended with these words:

> People who had been arrested were unloaded from trucks as if they were logs. If a soldier wanted to, he was allowed to select 'his victim' and kill him on the spot. The heads of the dead were cut off in order to spread terror among the living. The *machete* served as a guillotine.[21]

12   Great Britain

The importance of not being born in Predappio

'Am I a Fascist? Not on your life! Today my party is about as
far away from Fascism as British Liberalism was from the sanguinary fury of the French Revolution. By that I don't mean to
say that I disown my past. I don't take back a single word I said
in the past or a single gesture. I was a Fascist when I had to be
one, when there was no other alternative but action. But Fascism,
which in its essence is nationalism, has had its day. The nations
of Europe are too small to survive when they are caught between
two giants like the United States and Russia. That's why they
must unite, forget their old nationalist animosities and form a
united Europe as soon as they can. That's what I'm fighting for
now—for a new Europe.'[1]

Sir Oswald Mosley, sixth baronet of his line,[2] suddenly looked
us straight in the face, as if for a moment he were trying to make
us feel the 'unforgettable' magnetism of his eyes; then his lips
opened in a cordial and fascinating smile. There's no doubt about
it; at sixty-six Sir Oswald has lost none of his powers of persuasion,
even if his gestures are a trifle less impetuous, his moustache à la
D'Artagnan a little grizzled and his body, which once was sheathed
in a tight-fitting pullover and riding-breeches, has now grown
stouter. Looking at him, we could not help reflecting that Filippo
Anfuso was not so far wrong when he swore that there exists on
this planet of ours a biological species that is unmistakably
Fascist. At the very first glance you could see that Mosley was
Fascist by instinct and by temperament rather than in his ideas.
He had the great good fortune to be born an English Fascist,
and that in itself has saved him from following to the bitter end
the adventurous and tragic paths of the other *'condottieri'* of the
1930s. However much he may have tried to make himself look
formidable by wearing impressive uniforms, by his fiery oratory
and his noble attitudes, he has always been influenced by his sur-
roundings, borne down by the weight of tradition or made to look

ridiculous when he was pelted with tomatoes. And if today, after changing his political creed for the fourth time, Sir Oswald Mosley can still pose as an ardent advocate of a united Europe, it is thanks to the fact that he was born in London and not in Predappio.

'It's wrong to call me a right-winger,' he said in the course of our interview. 'I have never been a man of the Right. My party is exactly in the centre of the political fronts, and my best collaborators are ex-Communists.' Not only does Mosley object to being considered a Fascist and a man of the Right, but he also repudiates the insinuation that he is an opportunist. How, then, are we to classify this man, who in the course of forty years was first a Conservative, then went over to Labour, later became a Fascist and now claims to be a believer in the idea of a 'third force' Europe?

He entered parliament when he was just over twenty-three. The Conservatives adopted him as a candidate because he had been educated at Winchester and Sandhurst, because of his record during the First World War, when he served in the 16th Lancers and later as a pilot in the Royal Flying Corps. But Mosley soon grew tired of the Conservative Party's 'lack of dynamism', its predilection for 'trivial, boring, mediocre' things; he went over to the Labour Party. But even the moderate British brand of Socialism failed to satisfy him, even when he became Chancellor of the Duchy of Lancaster in 1929. His opinion of parties is still negative; he maintains that they subordinate the interests of the country to their own or that of their class, and this in the end is bound to lead to a crisis and to the break-up of the British Empire. Obsessed by these ideas he resigned his ministerial post, left the Labour Party, and as an act of defiance to all the old parties he called the one he founded the 'New Party', which was not Fascist, but already showed leanings towards Fascist principles and dynamic action. The electorate showed no enthusiasm whatsoever for this quick-change artist Mosley. He was beaten at the polls and never went back to parliament; moreover, he found himself alone, abandoned even by the little group of Labour M.P.s who had followed him in his adventurous career.

This isolation induced him to found another party, not of equals, but of followers, who would take their orders from one leader, in accordance with the best traditions of Fascism. Thus on 1st October 1932 Sir Oswald Mosley became the leader of the British Union of Fascists, which at first had only 10,000 members but was described by the Italian Press of those days as having $1\frac{1}{2}$ million.[3]

Since he firmly believed that he would one day come to power, Mosley hastened to publish his *Mein Kampf*, which he called *The Greater Britain*, and in which he predicted the coming of a Corporative State with 'every man working not for his own victory, but for that of his side', while the executive took over virtually all the functions of parliament. In April 1933, after adopting the fasces and black shirts as his symbols, he went to Rome to have a talk with Mussolini and visit the Fascist 'Tenth Anniversary Exhibition'. On his return to London he wrote in *Blackshirt* that Fascism was 'the greatest creed that Western civilization has ever given to the world' and that 'it is destined to become the universal movement of the Twentieth Century'; it was only because he wanted to avoid minimizing his own work that he added: 'In each country Fascism will have its own methods and characteristics.'[4]

For years Mosley wasted his undeniable gifts as an orator[5] in transposing into a Britannic key the themes of Nazi and Fascist propaganda. The British public, more tolerant than any other, forgave him for his attacks on the Jews, the violence of his stewards at the Olympia meeting, the punitive expeditions organized by the Fascist Defence Force and the provocative parades of Blackshirts. They even forgave him for writing an article in which he condemned the British government's decision to declare war on Germany.[6] But when he persisted in describing the war as a manœuvre organized by Jewish financiers, the authorities lost patience, and Mosley and his wife were imprisoned, while 900 of his followers were interned in the Isle of Man. He was released in 1943 on the grounds that he was suffering from phlebitis.

Mosley's Europe

'Yes, I used to be a Fascist,' Sir Oswald went on to say, 'but I defy anyone to point out one single occasion in my political career when I supported aggression. I have always been against violence and on the side of the underdog.' He denies that he ever received financial support from Mussolini; he denies ever having treated his adversaries with brutality or having organized intimidatory marches through quarters of London where the population was mainly Jewish. For that matter he hardly needs to exonerate himself. The confusion that reigned after the war was as helpful to Mosley as it was to so many Continental Fascists. In fact he found that the situation was even more propitious than it had been in 1932, since Churchill, like himself, was not averse to the idea of a preventive war against Russia. On 7 February 1948 Mosley accordingly decided to found yet another party, which he called the Union Movement, this being all the more urgent because some of his ex-followers had started crypto-Fascist movements like A. K. Chesterton's League of Empire Loyalists, over which Mosley could exercise no control.[7]

But although Mosley did his best to pose as the leader of the Anti-Comintern and as a staunch supporter of European unity, his new party attracted only 5,000 members. Disappointed with this response, Mosley sold his country house in Wiltshire and moved to Ireland, with the apparent intention of withdrawing from politics for good. But in 1953 he re-appeared in London and stood as a candidate at the borough elections, being greeted by his few admirers with the strains of *Lili Marlene*. Exploiting once more the anti-Jewish prejudices of certain sections of the public, he polled only 10 per cent of the votes in one of the Stepney wards, after which he again disappeared. When he surfaced once again on the occasion of the 1959 general election, his quick-change act seemed to be definitely a thing of the past—or so he himself asserted.[8] 'We have decided,' he said, 'to stop gangsterism in our party'; and he therefore condemned all violence, maintaining that he was no longer an anti-Semite and that he was interested in only one thing— Europe. Worried by the slowness of the campaign for a united Europe, he tried to force the pace by convening a congress of neo-Fascist movements, which met in Venice on 4 March 1952, the aim being the creation of a 'European National Party'. Such a party was in fact created, but only on paper, since the *Movimento Sociale Italiano* continued to call itself the MSI, and the *Reichspartei*, *Jeune Europe* and Mosley's own Union Movement retained their old names, despite the fact that the document creating the new party bore the signatures of Giovanni Lanfré, Count Alvise Loredan, von Thadden, Jean Thiriart and Oswald Mosley.

What exactly is Mosley's Europe? First of all, it is a Europe of revenge, a 'third block' stretching 'from Brest to Bucharest', after ridding itself (no one quite knows how) of both American and Russian troops, after reunifying the two Germanys, 'reconquering the lost German territories', 'giving Italy breathing-space' and putting an end to the 'political and military power of the United Nations'. This Europe, which will approximately have the frontiers conceived by Hitler, will have a 'common government as regards foreign policy, defence, economic policy, finances and scientific research', it will set up a 'prices and incomes' mechanism to ensure social justice everywhere, and will create a 'system of production and consumption independent of usury and capitalism, of anarchy and Communism'.

'But if we want to realize this Europe,' Sir Oswald explained in the course of our interview in Paris, 'we haven't a moment to lose, because the hour of the clash with Communism is imminent. Only if we are strong and free from all obligations can we dictate our own conditions to the two *blocs* which are beleaguering us.'

Mosley has foreseen everything. Europe will give up trying to defend Asia and will leave that to Soviet Russia; the United States will be allowed to keep its protectorate over South America and Europe will be given that part of Africa which is still inhabited by Whites. 'We can't go on giving territories away,' he explained. 'I don't think anyone will accuse us of lack of generosity if we keep a third of Africa for ourselves and leave the rest to the Africans.' This, one must admit, is a great concession, for in his latest book, *Europe: Faith and Plan*, Mosley recognized, not without some bitterness, that if it had not been for the propaganda following the war and the consequent strengthening of world Communism, the old colonialism might have lasted for another hundred years. Incidentally, Mosley's generosity is not altogether disinterested. His plan for the partition of Africa envisaged the enforcement of a kind of 'Monroe doctrine', which would stop any penetration into Africa on the part of Russia. 'Any African State that might yield to the blandishments of Russia would be surrounded by a *cordon sanitaire* and told to think it over.' He corrected himself at once: 'Of course, these African countries would be completely independent. In fact they could establish an all-black Commonwealth among themselves. Because, if I may say so, it's sheer hypocrisy to keep the new African States in our Commonwealth. We must give them their liberty and leave them to themselves; then the slums of London will be emptied and there will be no more of those detestable mixed marriages.' Mosley fixed his steely eyes upon us and added:

If they then tell us to get out of the whole of Africa, we must say that we have not the slightest intention of doing so, any more than the Americans would be willing to leave their continent to the Redskins. Europe can't be separated from Africa. Only with

Africa can we be independent of the two *blocs* and avoid being controlled by high finance, and finally create a State of producers.[9]

Today, however, this man who one critical night a quarter of a century ago hoped to be summoned to Buckingham Palace and asked to form a government that would start peace negotiations with Hitler and Mussolini, has lost all his appeal; every time he tries to harangue a crowd he is attacked and heckled, and he has seen his activists reduced to a paltry 1,500 and his supporters to ten or fifteen thousand.[10] Now he finds a following (and only a meagre one at that) only in certain quarters of London or in the smaller industrial towns (e.g. Middlesbrough) where there has been an influx of coloured immigrants over the last few years—Negroes, Jamaicans and Pakistanis. In such places, racial tension is high, and both the Conservatives and the Labour Party have been induced to amend the laws governing public meetings. 'Any legal measure tending to limit the freedom of speech, for moral or social reasons, must be carefully watched by democrats,' says the Labour Minister Denis Healey; 'but in a democratic society Fascism and racialism produce the same kinds of problems as blasphemy and obscenity—of which in a certain sense they are examples. It would thus seem inevitable that they must be treated in the same way.'[11]

For the last twenty years Mosley has been trying to win back the reputation he enjoyed as a young man, when they used to call him the *chevalier sans peur ni reproche*, when he advocated the nationalization of the banks and described himself as a 'left-wing Socialist'. In an attempt to dissipate the last doubts he even wrote a book calley *Mosley, Right or Wrong?*, in which he answered no fewer than 316 questions. But the Europe he now envisages is no better than the Europe that Hitler tried to build. Amidst pan-European slogans and the profession of the noblest ideas we can still discern racialism, anti-Semitism and all the old Nazi ideas, together with hatred of the progress made by the 'Third World' [Russia], contempt for the Nuremberg verdict, admiration for Franco and Salazar (who 'are desperately trying to save their countries from anarchy and Communism'), the claim that Hitler's massacres were no worse than the acts of terrorism committed by the Stern Gang, approval of South Africa's apartheid policy and an obsession with the idea that 'we must preserve the race as we preserve our families'.

Nevertheless, he does not lack admirers in Britain, even outside right-wing circles. Colin Wilson, that most illustrious representative of the 'angry young men', wrote in *Twentieth Century* that Mosley was by far the most intelligent politician he had ever met, and he is not the only one to think so. As Bruce Renton has pointed out:

> Mosley is a strange phenomenon. British politicians recognize his merits; the papers publish favourable reviews of his books; and nobody protests unless he starts one of his 'marches on Trafalgar Square'. Then they all protest, not because they are anti-Fascists, but because they have a feeling that Mosley is anti-British. It is this nationalistic feeling, rather than the political or ideological aspect, that would seem to be at the root of the 'Mosley peril'—a feeling that he might himself make more acute as the tension between the white and coloured populations grows in every country in the world as well as in Britain.[12]

The 'idiot friends'

During our interview in Paris, as soon as Sir Oswald had finished outlining his plan for the future ordering of the world, we asked him what he thought of the leaders of the British National Party and the National Socialist Movement, the two pro-Nazi competitors of the Union Movement. Mosley's reply was prompt and scathing: 'They are idiot friends. They keep on forming and dissolving parties, more to annoy me than for any other reason. I have already taken legal proceedings against them three times. They are admirers of Hitler, racialists, fanatics and anti-Semites.' Noticing our surprise, he added:

> I know what you want to say; that I, too, used to be an anti-Semite. True, but I had no quarrel with Jews as a whole, only with those who dragged my country into the war and in 1956 into the Suez venture. I have never approved of Hitler or of his extermination camps. I've been a soldier, and I can't understand how anyone can kill unarmed people.

Much younger than Mosley and far more radical in his ideas, Colin Jordan, the leader of the National Socialist Movement, has revived all the Nazi paraphernalia, from brown shirts to riding-breeches, from leather belt to swastika armlets, from the *Horst Wessel Lied to Soldatenleben*, from *Sieg Heil!* to *Juden 'raus!*[13] He demands the expulsion of Jews and coloureds from Britain, he wants to replace parliamentary government by an authoritarian and racialist State;[14] he is even grateful to Arminius because, by destroying the legions of Varus, he preserved the purity of the

Nordic races; he talks as if Hitler were his spiritual adviser, and
he would like to do away with the United Nations and install a
'World National Socialist Order of Aryan Nations'.

Jordan's misfortunes date from 1st July 1962, but at the same
time they brought him notoriety. On the morning of that day,
having paid the regulation fee, he mounted the rostrum in Trafalgar
Square and, protected by dozens of policemen, began his speech
by declaring that Hitler's war was a just one and that world Jewry
was the real enemy of the British people.

> You cannot destroy a deeply rooted idea like National Social-
> ism . . . You can persecute it. You can ban its books, its songs and
> its symbols; you can do anything you like, but it will live in the
> minds of men. Our opponents are doing their best to destroy
> National Socialism, but the fact that we are here today proves that
> they have failed . . . Hitler was right![15]

The British are accustomed to listening to all kinds of nonsense in
Trafalgar Square, but Jordan's speech was too much for them.
The orator was accordingly pelted with tomatoes and pennies and
the police had some difficulty in rescuing him. Charged with
inciting racial hatred and forming a semi-military organization
called 'Spearhead',[16] Jordan appeared in court together with his
lieutenants John Tyndall, Denis Pirie and Roland Kerr-Ritchie, and
was sentenced to nine months' imprisonment. But before he went
to prison he had the consolation of meeting the late leader of the
American Nazi Party, Lincoln Rockwell, with whose help he
founded a new neo-Nazi International, the 'World Union of
National Socialists' (WUNS), the aim of which is 'the total destruction of the traitorous Jewish and Communist groups, and of subversion'. At a Gloucestershire farm near the 'Valley of Death and
Tombs', where British neo-Nazis are secretly trained, Rockwell
swore allegiance to his new chief saying that he placed himself
under the orders of Colin Jordan. From now on he was leader of
all the Nazis in the world and it was understood that he would
obey him. Which, however, did not prevent him, a few months
later while Jordan was still in prison, from proclaiming himself
'international commander' of the Nazi movement.

On 31 May 1963 Colin Jordan was released from Wormwood
Scrubs, full of bellicose intentions. First of all he wrote an article
for the *National Socialist* entitled 'From prison to victory'; then he
filled the whole of the journal's front page with a large photograph
of Hitler, beneath which were the captions 'Hitler was right!' and

'His spirit lives on!'[17] In the next issue he published a photo of Rudolf Hess and demanded his release, while his lieutenant, Tyndall, ended an article on the 'spirit and mission of the SS' by declaring that 'the SS-man has been our model; an SS-State is now our aim.'[18] During the ensuing months Jordan inundated Germany with leaflets and posters bearing photos of Hitler. He then decided to take a wife and his choice fell on a lady of 'Norman-Viking stock', Françoise, niece of the famous couturier Dior, who, while Jordan was in prison, had become engaged to his henchman John Tyndall. The wedding took place in London on 6 October 1963 at the headquarters of the National Socialist Movement in Princedale Road, Notting Hill, to the accompaniment of rites which were more grotesque than pagan. Before a table covered with a Nazi flag the couple swore that they were 'of Aryan race and free from hereditary taints', after which they made incisions in their fingers in order that their blood might mingle and a drop fall on the first page of *Mein Kampf*; finally Colin Jordan exclaimed: 'We declare this marriage valid.' This was followed by toasts, Nazi salutes and the singing of the *'Horst Wessel Lied'*. Three months later, however, Françoise, disappointed in her husband, absconded to Paris, pursued by the British leader. Eventually the couple were reconciled and in No 7 of *The National Socialist* Françoise even indulged in self-criticism. The consequences of all this, however, had to be borne by the British Nazi party, whose membership dwindled still further.[19] It suffered an even greater decline in June 1965, when a branch of the Ku-Klux-Klan was founded in Britain.

Averse to sensational enterprises and more moderate in his outlook is the leader of the British National Party, Andrew Fountaine,[20] who, however, cannot claim to be a model of consistency, since in 1935 he fought in Abyssinia against Mussolini's Blackshirts and a year later was in Spain fighting for Franco. According to Fountaine, Britain is on the brink of a precipice and no longer knows what patriotism means, because the government consists of political traitors, because the Church, the Boy Scouts and the House of Commons have a higher percentage of homosexuals than any other community, British women are unable to find beds in hospitals where they can give birth to children because all the beds are already occupied by West Indian women, and finally, because it is Washington that gives orders to the admirals of the Royal Navy.[21] Like Mosley in the 1930s Fountaine wishes to save Britain from 'catastrophe', but the only remedy he can think of is to attack the

200,000 coloured immigrants who have settled in Britain, and also the Jews, whom he accuses of controlling the army and the economy and owning half of London. But the British National Party does not confine itself to attacking Jews, Negroes and Jamaicans in accordance with the best traditions of British racialism. From an article by John Bean,[22] editor of the party's journal, *Combat*, we learn that the Sicilians are a mixture of Mediterranean, Asiatic and Negro races and that it is really intolerable that Britain should be expected to offer them hospitality.[23] The article would not have surprised us (there is plenty of rubbish of this sort in the masses of neo-Fascist literature we have looked through), if the British National Party had not joined one of the Internationals which claim to be fighting for a free, proud and wonderful Europe. A Europe—as John Bean himself informs us in his article—in which Sicilians would have the same status that Himmler and Rosenberg assigned to coolies.

13 Greece and South Vietnam

The 'anti-Communist crusade'

The Cold War was undoubtedly one of the main factors that contributed to the resurgence, in Europe, Asia and the two Americas, of Fascist or para-Fascist movements. The division of the world into two *blocs*, the anti-Communist campaign launched by the 'free world', the psychological mobilization of the masses against the 'Red Peril'—all these things provided the extreme right-wingers, who until then had been overawed by the apocalyptic Nuremberg verdict, with unexpected support and an ideal opportunity to resume their propaganda and even to boast that they had been the very first to enter the lists in the struggle against Communism. As we have already seen, the theory that the Fascist International was reconstituted and acquired new strength thanks to the sums deposited in Swiss and Spanish banks towards the end of the Second World War by the Nazi secret services, is not without some foundation (even when it is shorn of some of its more picturesque details), but it cannot by itself explain the extent of the Fascist revival in more than sixty countries. We are bound to admit that the anti-Communist crusade, with its florescence of very prosperous and active 'committees' and 'leagues', had a far greater influence than the 'secret Nazi funds', since it resulted in the birth of Fascist groups in countries which had hitherto been immune or in the resuscitation of forces which it was believed had been extinguished.

Another feature of the Cold War was the emergence along the demarcation line between the two worlds, and in particular at those points where friction was greatest, of authoritarian régimes, which were welcomed or openly backed up by the United States, no matter what administration was in the White House. In the South Korea of Syngman Rhee, the Turkey of Adnan Menderes, the South Vietnam of Ngo Dinh Diem and the Greece of Karamanlis, anti-Communism appeared to be the most suitable and heaven-sent vehicle for the installation of dictatorships supported by the conservative elements. Among the dictatorships which flourished beneath the banner of anti-Communism two were of a markedly Fascist character—those of Ngo Dinh Diem and of Karamanlis. But whereas in Greece the dictatorship represented a return of already existing forces, which in the 1930s had supported the pro-Fascist régime of Metaxas and collaborated with the Nazi occupation forces during the war, in South Vietnam in the mid-fifties an entirely new type of Fascism appeared, which took the name of 'personalism' and, against the background of a civil war, revealed all its reactionary nature and a hitherto unknown predilection for violence. In the following pages we shall deal with these two authoritarian régimes, which were typical products of the Cold War.

The Karamanlis era

The first skirmishes of the Cold War took place during the meetings of the Council of Foreign Ministers at the 1946 conference in Paris, but the first big clash between the two *blocs* was the Greek civil war in 1947, that is to say some time before Churchill's Fulton speech and the launching of the Marshall Plan. When the 'Truman doctrine' was announced on 12 March 1947, the United States undertook to support all the free peoples in resisting subjugation by armed minorities or by pressure from outside, and they accordingly offered Greece all the financial and military aid she might need to suppress the Communist revolt led by Markos Vafiades. This was Washington's first open act of defiance to Moscow, and America's economic and military intervention resulted in the rout of Markos's army on 16 October 1949. Greece thus managed to remain in the Western camp, but the condition of the country was so disastrous that she was no longer able to maintain a political equilibrium or to re-establish democratic institutions on the basis of nation-wide reconciliation. The years of the civil war brought to the surface all the most extreme Rightist elements, Fascist terrorists and collaborators, whose return and utilization in the anti-Communist crusade enabled them to make demands amounting to blackmail, to take as much revenge as they liked and to create their own militias.

The Greece that Konstantinos Karamanlis inherited in 1955 from Marshal Papagos, the victor in the civil war, after twenty-seven cabinets had fallen, was a cowed and divided nation, ready to accept a dictatorship. The economic Right was in power, supported by the monarchy, the army, the police and the anti-

Communist militia (TEA), while the men of the Left were in exile or in prison, and the remaining democratic and progressive forces were subjected to violence and restriction of their propaganda. Karamanlis, however, like all other modern autocrats, did not need to stage a spectacular 'march on Athens' in order to install a powerful régime; during his six years in power all he had to do was to undermine the 1952 constitution gradually and to govern in accordance with the emergency laws promulgated during the civil war or the Fascist decrees of Metaxas, keeping his opponents in prison and preventing any general reconciliation, and, whenever necessary, making use of the gendarmerie and the TEA to prevent the opposition from conducting any sort of electoral campaign. Having first taken these precautions, Karamanlis could afford to 'give democracy a free hand' and even allow the *Eirini Demokratia Amnisteia* (EDA), which had replaced the outlawed Communist Party, to participate in elections.

Behind the convenient screen of powerless democratic institutions Karamanlis's *Ethniki Rizopastikì Enosis* (ERE) set up a régime which, owing to the methods it used, was soon being openly accused of being Fascist. 'Every citizen', Michel Legris tells us in his analysis of one of the most odious aspects of this police régime,

> is obliged to exhibit a 'certificate of loyalty' on every possible occasion, whether he wants a job, a passport or merely a driving licence. Without this 'open sesame' (which testifies that the holder is a nationalist and therefore an opponent of Communism) there is, generally speaking, no possibility of earning one's living.[1]

Card-indexed and watched in this way, a Greek citizen finds himself at every moment liable to the penalties laid down by emergency regulations dating from the days of Metaxas (Law 375) or the civil war (Law 509). These measures prescribe forced residence for an unlimited period; terms of imprisonment for anyone who publishes information about banned parties (i.e. the Communist Party); and loss of citizenship for Greeks living abroad who indulge, or have indulged, in anti-Greek activities (this being intended to prevent the return home of the 200,000 exiles of the civil war). When, under pressure from Britain and America, Karamanlis decided on 30 July 1962 to abrogate the emergency laws, the democratic opposition revealed that Decree No 4234 of 1962 still contained provisions the effect of which was to retain all the penalties envisaged by the old emergency laws.[2]

The gravest accusation against the Karamanlis party, however, concerned the procedure at elections. All parties were unanimous in denouncing the subterfuges, the violence, the direct and indirect pressure, the campaign of intimidation and the presentation of lists of candidates containing the names of persons who did not exist. For example, the October 1961 election was held in an atmosphere of violence and terror deliberately organized by the para-military bodies supporting the régime. According to Claude Julien:

> The discontent in the centre and left-wing opposition is all the greater because, contrary to the procedure adopted at previous elections, the emergency laws were not suspended. As a result of these laws, in the eleven northern departments [where 45 per cent of the population live] meetings were prohibited unless special permission had been obtained from the police. Moreover, every kind of publication, including posters and propaganda leaflets, was subject to censorship. Lastly, a simple order from the police was sufficient to authorize the deportation without trial of any citizen. Thus seven candidates were deported to the island of Ayíos Evstrátios and two others were sent for trial by court-martial. Fifteen others were beaten up by 'special groups' and had to be admitted to hospital, while there were cases of candidates being 'worked on' at police-stations.[3]

In many ways Greece under Karamanlis reminds us of Italy in the years preceding the 'March on Rome'. Para-military organizations were able to carry on their terroristic activities unmolested, and often under the protection of the gendarmerie or even at its instigation. The anti-Communist militia, formed during the civil war and never disbanded, was trained by army officers and, as ex-Premier Papandreou said, 'carried out criminal assaults in broad daylight'.[4] Under the Karamanlis régime secret societies flourished which by their extreme nationalism and their choice of exotic names remind us of the patriotic societies in Japan. Thus we hear of bands of terrorists known as the 'Black Gloves' and the 'Pin Group', whose members could be recognized by the fact that they wore a pinhead, red or yellow according to their rank. Other groups did not need to camouflage themselves in this way, since they sported the emblems of societies which were recognized or even financed by the government. Among these were the 'Union of Combatants and Victims of the Resistance in Northern Greece', whose president was Xénophon Iozmas, a former Minister in the collaborationist government of 1944, and the 'Union of those who took part in the fight against Communism'. The government also had its own 'auxiliary anti-Communist forces', such as the TEA (National Security Battalions), the IDEA (a secret organization operating among the regular armed forces) and the OAAEE ('Organization of Invisible Defenders of the Greek People'). Even the young were infected by the nationalistic fever and were incorporated in the *Elpisophori* ('Young Hopefuls'), in the 'National and Social Youth Union', the 'Blue Phalange' or the 'Corps of Youthful Hope'.

The rehabilitation of collaborationists and the denigration of the Resistance were phenomena not confined to Greece, but in that country, as a result of the civil war, they assumed exceptional proportions. In government circles there was a noticeable tendency to consider that resistance to the Nazis had been a prelude to the revolt led by Markos Vafiades, and to condemn both as being forms of Communist sedition. This explains why, as late as 1962, out of ninety-one detainees held in the prison of Cetami on Crete, seventeen were ex-members of the ELAS who had been arrested after their return home from Dachau, Auschwitz and Buchenwald.[5] When the civil war ended in 1949, vengeance was wreaked not only on those Communist guerrillas who had not managed to escape abroad with the *andartès* of Markos, but against all members of the Resistance, who were imprisoned without trial or on charges that could not be proved, executed by gangs of neo-Fascist hired assassins, or left to die of hardship in concentration camps.

These camps, which according to Greek government sources were still holding 20,921 political detainees on 1st December 1949,[6] were not closed down until towards the end of 1962, but the 1,031 prisoners who at that time were still being held in the camp on Ayíos Evstrátios and in other camps were simply reclassified as common criminals and transferred to ordinary prisons.[7] In the summer of 1963, nineteen years after the liberation of Greece from the Nazis and fourteen after the end of the civil war, over 1,000 persons were still in prison—600 because of their activities during the Resistance, 470 for taking part in the civil war, and 70 on charges of 'espionage'. 'What Kadar did in Hungary after five years,' the French Socialist Deputy Deschizeaux told the 'Conference for a general amnesty for Greek political detainees and exiles', held in Paris on 23 and 24 March 1963, 'Karamanlis cannot refuse to do nineteen years after the end of the German occupation.'[8] But neither this appeal from Paris nor that made by Bertrand Russell led to the freeing even of a few dozen prisoners. It was only in the autumn of 1963 and after the fall of the Karamanlis régime that any amnesty on a large scale was proclaimed.

In a number of letters sent to international Resistance organizations the political detainees made their situation known and formulated their accusations against the Karamanlis régime. Seventy detainees suffering from tuberculosis wrote as follows from the prison of Amphissa:

> In this country, where not a single war criminal is still in prison, where a special law has been passed authorizing the murderer Merten to continue his neo-Nazi activities,[9] where sites have been set apart for the erection of monuments to the glory of the invaders in the very places where they carried out massacres and wholesale destruction . . . in this country members of the Resistance are still being persecuted with unprecedented ferocity. Not a single cross commemorating Resistance men who fell in battle has remained standing. Half a million Resistance members are registered in the police files, and this prevents them finding employment and supporting their families. Recently, to pacify public opinion at home and abroad, the authorities closed the concentration camp at Ai-Strati, but a few weeks later sixteen others were opened near isolated villages, and political detainees and ex-members of the Resistance were sent there. Lastly, after eighteen years, 1,300 political detainees are still in prison, most of them serving life sentences. Are the decisions that keep us in prison legal? No. Everyone in Greece knows that the crimes attributed to us were the fruit of lies and frame-ups. The trials that have taken place were held in exceptional circumstances, in the climate of a civil war. If one of us were to give way, renounce his ideas and deny that he took part in the Resistance, he would cease to be regarded as a criminal and be released at once. But we shall refuse to pay this price for our liberty![10]

And the detainees in Khalkis wrote:

> For eighteen years we have been dragged from one prison to another—eighteen years marked by hardships, exhaustion, blood and death. Our tragedy, that of our families and of the whole Greek people, began eighteen years ago and is still going on. From time to time diseases strike us down and put an end to our sufferings.[11]

On 24 December 1962, immediately after his release from prison, Manolis Glezos, the man who in 1941 had torn down the Nazi flag flying over the Acropolis, summed up the situation when he said:

> Only in Greece were the victors in the war against Fascism sent to prison, where they still remain, while war criminals and collabora-

tionists have been amnestied. The gravity of this injustice becomes even more evident when we remember that out of 16,000 sentences passed by the courts 14,000 were later quashed by higher tribunals, and thousands of militants who had in the meantime been executed were declared innocent after their deaths . . . The continuance of this state of affairs is intolerable. It is a slur on Greece, to use the term employed by Lord Russell in his message to the political detainees. It degrades our civilization and harms the prestige of our country by putting Greece on the same level as Fascist Spain or Portugal.[12]

The international campaign on behalf of the Greek political detainees, which was first brought to the attention of the public at the Paris conference and had its most sensational episode in the attack on Queen Friederike while she was in London,[13] embarrassed the Greek government and aroused the fury of the right-wing extremists, who decided to avenge this insult to their national honour. The victim designated was the EDA deputy Grigorios Lambrakis, a former Olympic Games champion and a well-known doctor, who tried to approach Queen Friederike in London and hand her a petition on behalf of the political detainees. A few weeks before the outrage, during a session of the Greek parliament, Lambrakis had received a first warning. Deputy Papadopoulos, son of the Greek 'Quisling' and a representative of neo-Fascist extremism, shouted: 'Lambrakis, you shall die!' A few days later, Rula Lambrakis, his wife, received a threatening telephone-call, and on 22 May, in Salonika, as Lambrakis was leaving a meeting of the 'League for Peace and Nuclear Disarmament', he was deliberately knocked down by a motorbike and sidecar driven by two right-wingers, Spyros Kotzomanis, a former collaborationist and a well-known terrorist, and Emanuellidis. Lambrakis was seriously injured and died a few days later.

The inquiry into this crime, which the police tried to stifle, but which was loudly demanded by the public, led to the arrest, not only of the two men directly responsible, but also of several high-ranking police officials, who were accused of abusing their powers and of complicity in the murder of Lambrakis. Another man who ended up in prison was the ex-Minister Xénophon Iozmas, who was allegedly the leader of the 'Pin Group' which had been entrusted with the task of removing the progressive Deputy. (The two terrorists and thirty-six others implicated were not brought to trial in Salonika until February 1965.) The 'Lambrakis affair', which the opposition regarded as a second edition of the Matteotti murder,

K

compelled King Paul to break with Karamanlis and dismiss him. The sovereign, who took two years to make up his mind, staged his own version of the Italian 25 July, without, however, turning it into a melodrama, and by sacrificing Karamanlis, managed to save the monarchy *in extremis*. A few months later, on 3 November, a general election resulted in a decisive defeat for the party of Karamanlis and brought the 'centre union' back to power, under the leadership of an old Liberal, Georgios Papandreou. Karamanlis who, on the eve of the election, had said: 'If I don't win, Greece will be plunged into anarchy,' announced his intention to retire from politics and go abroad for several months. At the next election, in February 1964, Papandreou obtained more than 52 per cent of the votes cast, thus confirming the desire of the Greek people for a radical change in the country and allowing the new Liberal Premier —in the meantime Paul I had died and been succeeded by Constantine II—to guide the nation back into the path of democracy.

On 30 March 1964 the correspondent of *La Stampa*, Stefano Terra, telephoned to his paper in Turin and said: 'Tonight the postwar period will officially end in Greece when Premier Papandreou announces his government's intention to abolish the emergency laws.' And in fact, a month later 453 'politicals' were released and 'certificates of loyalty' and forced residence were abolished. In the following July, after the discovery of a plot to assassinate Papandreou and the irruption of 300 young Fascists into the parliament building, the government decided to disband all 'para-State organizations' of the extreme Right, of which there were eleven, three of them illegal. These measures, however, served merely to 'defascisticize' the country and did not cure its ills. As Marcello dell'Omodarme has aptly remarked:

> For the Greek people it was not enough that Papandreou should just keep the promises he had made before the election. Freeing political detainees who had been in prison ever since the civil war, abolishing the certificates of loyalty needed to obtain employment, disbanding the ERE action squads—all these things were essential if a democratic way of living was to be restored . . . But what the people really wanted above all was that they should be offered new prospects in the economic and social fields. For a government responsible for the country's destiny the problem is, how to find a policy which will put an end to unemployment and emigration— those chronic ills of Greece. But this will be possible only if the existing economic structure is overthrown, if the economic forces of which Karamanlis was the expression are rendered harmless.[14]

These forces, however, taking advantage of the lack of cohesion and hesitation shown by Papandreou's party, succeeded in forcing the old statesman to resign in the summer of 1965, and with the support of the young and ambitious King Constantine II they have brought back a coalition right-wing government, by means of what many have described as a veritable *coup d'état*.

The real *coup d'état*, however, was still to come. The political right wing was quite unable to check the growing discontent among the people as a whole, symptoms of this being the popularity—despite all his vacillations—of the old leader, Papandreou, and the increasing pressure exercised by the left-wing groups. In April 1967, fearing that the general election due to be held in May might result in a swing against the conservatives—and indirectly against the monarchy—a group of high-ranking officers hatched a plot which was put into execution on the 21st of that month.

After overthrowing the government, dissolving parliament and casting into prison all their known or potential adversaries, the military junta formed a puppet government which was approved by the King and virtually signified the abolition of all civil rights. The 'Prometheus plan'—as the plot was called—enabled the junta to seize power in Athens in twenty-four hours. Thousands of citizens were thrown into prison or sent to concentration camps. Special courts were set up to try the real or alleged adversaries of the new régime. The freedom of the Press was abolished and the junta forced the new government, under Constantine Kolias, to issue 'moralistic' decrees dealing with such trivial matters as the wearing of mini-skirts or long hair. A dictatorship on the lines of that of Metaxas was established. The military-Fascist type of government installed by General Patakos and Colonels Papadopoulos and Makarezos, who were the instigators of the plot, put the clock back in Greece by twenty-five years.

The Ngo family and 'personalism'

In South Vietnam, anti-Communism did not confine itself, as it did in Greece, to supporting a dictatorship, but started a civil war, and even went so far as to clamour for methods such as genocide and mass deportations—measures which had never been employed since the days of Nazi oppression. The man who undertook the task of leading this crusade in South-East Asia, after the defeat of the French at Dien Bien Phu and the division of Vietnam into two parts, was the Catholic Ngo Dinh Diem, whom the emissaries of Foster Dulles had discovered in an abbey at Bruges, which he had entered as a lay brother. On his anti-Communism, dating from 1952 (when, as Premier, he defeated Ho Chi Minh's first revolt) the Americans could rely implicitly, even to the point of inducing him to disregard the Geneva agreement which had stipulated the holding of a general election and the reunification of Vietnam. 'The agreement signed in Geneva', Ho Chi Minh, the Premier of North Vietnam, said recently,

> guaranteed the people's democratic rights; the patriots who had fought to free their country from French colonialism were not to be made the victims of reprisals; within two years of the signing of the agreement a general election on democratic lines was to be held, which would have resulted in a peaceful reunification of the country. Instead of which, at the direct instigation of the American government, Diem contemptuously disregarded the agreement he had signed, and this he was able to do only with the military and financial aid of the Americans; from 1955 on, Diem's supporters began exterminating the patriots who had taken part in the Resistance movement.[15]

The same conclusions were reached by an American scholar who certainly cannot be suspected of philo-Communism: 'The all-Indo-China elections which had been set for 1956 were never held. Diem's régime refused to take part on the grounds that the Communist north would never permit free voting. The matter was quietly dropped and Indo-China remained, like Korea, rigidly divided—Vietnam, nominally democratic, in the south, the Vietminh Republic, Communist, in the north.'[16]

Relying on the support of the United States, Diem managed in the space of two years to rid himself of all his rivals. First he dismissed the by now discredited Emperor Bao-Dai, after mobilizing public opinion against him and crushing him by means of a referendum. Then, with the assistance of the Military Aid Advisory Group, he succeeded in reorganizing the army, eliminating over-ambitious generals and reducing to impotence the little armies of the religious sects—*Cao-Dai* and *Hoa-Hao*, as well as the rival *Binh-Xuyên* gang. When he found himself alone, he proclaimed a republic, assumed the office of President (with full powers), held a general election, created a national assembly and granted a constitution to the country. 'On 26 October 1956, when I proclaimed the constitution, I realized the dream of a lifetime. Vietnam was at last a democratic country.'[17]

Diem seemed to be enamoured of the word 'democracy' and at the same time obsessed by it. It recurred again and again in his conversation, almost as often as that other habit of his of always saying *n'est-ce pas*. But he also took care to explain that he had not been content to accept just the democratic principles, but had enriched them with new additions and new interpretations. 'We are moralists, not legal experts. For us ethics always come before politics.' Diem's democracy, which in practice has shown itself to be the worst form of oppression, on the theoretical level is a strange, disconcerting mixture of concepts based on the Gospels, Greek logic, the Vedas, the Upanishads and the Vietnamese civic virtues— *thanh* (loyalty) and *tin* (honesty). From this blend of Western and Eastern morals Diem (or rather his brother Nhu, who is the family theoretician) extracted a doubtful doctrine called 'personalism', not to be confused—or at least so the spiritual heirs of Emmanuel Mounier will hope—with the doctrine of the same name excogitated by the founder of *Esprit*;[18] from which, nevertheless, it draws its inspiration.

'Personalism does not exclude personal liberty; in fact it maintains that man is free by divine grace,' Diem explained. 'But as regards political liberties, these must follow and not precede the moral regeneration of the citizen. So long as the citizen is not ready for democracy, it is the State's duty to safeguard his political liberties.' And since, for Diem, the citizens of Vietnam were not yet mature, he felt that it was quite right to deny them any liberty. In fact, although Diem allowed his country to have a certain number of democratic institutions, was outwardly obsequious to the constitution and was continually using the word 'democracy', he was by instinct an autocrat, remained aloof from the masses and, despite certain modernistic theories of his, was still an old mandarin governing by divine investiture, in accordance with the ancient Confucian code.

For ten years, down to the day of his assassination, Diem wanted to see everything, to check every detail and make every decision himself. Since he regarded his Ministers merely as spokesmen, every matter had to be brought to his table; no military operation, however unimportant, could be carried out without his consent. As for the five parties which send Deputies to the Assembly, in practice there are only two—the *Phong Trao Cach Mang Quec Gia* (National Revolutionary Movement), founded by Diem himself, and the *Can Lao Nhan Vi* (Labour and Personalism), run by his brother

Nhu. In a naïve attempt to camouflage these subterfuges, Diem ex-cogitated others, even allowing a self-styled Socialist Party to be formed, whose Deputies were nominated by the President himself! For this reason, and in view of his other disconcerting conceptions of democracy, Diem's particular brand was rechristened 'diemocracy'.

Although Ngo Dinh Diem talked of democracy and explained that 'the French Revolution was a bourgeois one, but ours is definitely a people's revolution', in reality he restored the power of the old feudal nobility and tried to fill the ideological void of the ruling party with the abstract and confused messages of 'personalism', and above all he endeavoured to concentrate all power in the hands of his own family circle. He appointed as his 'political adviser' his brother Ngo Dinh Nhu, who besides being the 'brain' of the family was head of the secret police and through his own followers could control the whole of the region round Saigon. Another brother, Ngo Dinh Can, was given central Vietnam as his sphere of influence, while the least known, Ngo Dinh Luyén, was sent as ambassador to London. Yet another brother, Ngo Dinh Tuc, who was archbishop of Hué, controlled the rank and file of the Catholics.[19] This team of brothers holding sway over Vietnam was in turn dominated by the most complex and controversial figure in the family group, Madame Nhu, wife of the founder of 'personalism'. As a parliamentary Deputy and president of the 'Vietnamese Women's Solidarity Movement', Madame Nhu brought about a veritable revolution in the country's way of life by persuading the Assembly to prohibit divorce (which could be granted only by presidential decree), polygamy, concubinage, the 'taxi-girls' (who were re-educated and sent to fight the Communists), dance-halls, beauty contests, boxing and even sentimental songs, which were alleged to be 'indecent, harmful to the national spirit and detrimental to the morale of those who were fighting against Communism'. But what the Vietnamese had against Madame Nhu was not this revolution, but the sinister influence she had over Diem and the intolerance and hatred she stirred up with her narrow-minded, hysterical ideas.

As far back as 1955, little more than a year after the Ngo family had risen to power, a French journalist wrote that 'the authoritarian methods practised in Vietnam are clearly akin to the most orthodox type of Fascism'.[20] Combining the intimidation technique of a McCarthy with the inquisitorial methods of a Torquemada, Diem took advantage of the anti-Communist crusade to persecute all those who were against him and tried to destroy all opposition by organizing the biggest 'witch-hunt' of our times. Emergency regulations were put into force; special tribunals sat permanently; accompanied by mobile guillotines, courts-martial were moved from one district to another; people were imprisoned or killed for trifling offences under Law 10/59, promulgated in the hope of exterminating the Viet-Cong. If we want to form an idea of the prevailing atmosphere of hatred and suspicion, we need only read this item of news from a Saigon newspaper: 'Pham Van Diem, who practises traditional medicine, was arrested for carrying a fountain-pen made in China. One month's imprisonment.'[21] Referring to the Communist adversaries, another paper incited its readers to commit murder: 'They must be beheaded or shot, killed like mad dogs.'[22] And such sentiments were echoed by the *Gauleiter* of Central Vietnam, Ngo Dinh Can, when he said: 'My hand will never weary of killing Communists. Each of you must offer the life of a Red to our country. I shall offer thousands.' In a climate of this sort, which encouraged denunciations and spying, 30,000 opponents finished up in concentration camps. In the camp at Phuloi, in 1959, 1,000 detainees died of a mysterious food-poisoning; and Diem refused to allow the International Red Cross to hold an inquiry.

In the early 1960s there was no mistaking the fact that 'Diemism' was heading straight for the gas-chambers of Himmler. Faced with this prospect, the opposition, after attempts to overthrow Diem by legal means in 1954 and 1959, decided to resort to force, and on 20 December 1960 a National Liberation Front was formed which included Communists, Socialists, peasants with no definite political views, members of the *Cao-Dai* and *Hoa-Hao* Buddhist sects and intellectuals who had escaped falling into the hands of Diem's police. This heterogeneous opposition party finally accepted the leadership of the Communists (who had acquired valuable experience while fighting the French from 1945 to 1954), but in substance it remained a national, non-party opposition fighting to re-establish a 'democratic and neutral government' in Saigon. In the first year of guerrilla warfare it gained control of a quarter of the territory of South Vietnam.[23]

In reply, Diem increased the strength of his army and auxiliary forces,[24] while Nhu created his 'special units' of police and his wife the 'para-military women's movement'.[25] But the half-million men whom Diem threw into the furnace of the civil war did not succeed in defeating the tens of thousands of Viet-Cong guerrillas. The partisans were favoured, not only by the nature of the terrain—marshland or jungle—but also by the psychological errors made by the Nationalists. In the combat zones Diem's troops behaved as if they were an invading army. They burned forests and crops with napalm, bombed villages from the air, imposed a curfew, conscripted the inhabitants for forced labour and arrested thousands of people as suspects. This 'scorched earth' policy was just what the Viet-Cong needed, since it won them the sympathy and support of the rural population, which in South Vietnam represents 80 per cent of the whole.

The 'pacification plan'

To ward off this new danger, Ngo Dinh Diem agreed to launch a 'pacification plan' evolved by Professor Eugene Staley, an American who was a strategist as well as an economist. The plan, which was put into execution in the early months of 1962, provided for the grouping of the scattered population in the areas affected by the fighting into 1,000 'strategic villages', while 16,000 other Vietnamese villages were to be protected by field-works manned by 'self-defence' groups and equipped with radio transmitters, so as to cut the Viet-Cong off from the peasants and deprive them of their sources of supplies and information. The plan was not a new one, since it had already been successfully tried out in Malaysia and Algeria. The only novelty lay in its monstrous proportions. In an attempt to portray its author, the Australian journalist Wilfred G. Burchett wrote:

> Staley himself is almost the personification of the central figure in Graham Greene's famous book, *The Quiet American* . . . An economist who likes to pass for a 'Liberal', he emerged on the South Vietnamese scene with missionary-like fervor to 'save the country from communism'. With clinical efficiency he set to work to draw up a plan which a Hitler or an Eichmann would have been proud to dream up.[26]

And in fact 9 million peasants were torn from their fields and transferred to concentration camps which were hypocritically known by the idyllic names of 'prosperity zones' and 'agrovilles'. The National Liberation Front, although by destroying a dozen of these 'strategic villages' it speedily proved that they were by no means a 'Siegfried Line', accused Diem of employing Nazi methods in deporting whole populations and of trying to transform the country into one huge concentration camp, a complex which the peasants were forced to erect with their own hands.

One of the authors of the present volume was able to visit several of these villages, and he feels bound to say that the National Liberation Front's accusations were not altogether unjustified.

Not only did they remind us immediately of the *camps d'héberge-ment* built by the French in Algeria for the same purpose—to separate the inhabitants from the warriors of the National Liberation Front—but in them we found the same barbed-wire entanglements and the same atmosphere; and the government officials gave us the same explanations: 'The villages are to be used only temporarily for defence purposes; their real purpose is to give the peasants social training and educate them to community life.' All this, as in Algeria, behind barbed wire, ramparts planted with bamboo stakes and watch-towers.

The villages we were allowed to visit lay to the north of Saigon, in the famous 'Zone D', the scene of innumerable ambushes. Our jeep was in fact preceded by two others full of soldiers from a barracks on the outskirts of the capital. The surrounding country-side is flat, the crops being rice, vegetables and sugar-cane, and it is intersected by canals. The road of red earth looks rather like a racing-track, and it could easily be mined. And in fact every day one or two vehicles are blown up.

The first 'strategic village' we came to was called An Phu Dông. Inside its fortified perimeter were 3,000 peasants, some of them labourers (earning the equivalent of about half-a-crown a day, often paid in kind), while others were small landowners (the richest owned about thirty acres). The village had a history. During the struggle against the French it had been the headquarters of the Viet-Minh; it was here that the first clandestine newspaper was printed and from here the first radio messages to the country were broadcast. When Vietnam was partitioned at the seventeenth parallel in 1954, the Viet-Minh guerrillas withdrew towards Hanoi after burning the village that had been their most celebrated hideout. An Phu Dông had since been rebuilt and on the top of the iron roof of the little market was a portrait in colours of President Ngo Dinh Diem.

The commander of the 'Civil Guards' showed us the platoon of young men who were doing their turn of guard duty. Then the government official in charge of An Phu Dông and six other villages invited us into the only brick house in the village for the usual 'briefing'. Everything had been arranged before our arrival— notice-boards with diagrams, a plan of fortifications, iced Coca-Cola, fruit from the local orchards, and perfumed towels with which to wipe away the perspiration. The alliance between the Americans and the Vietnamese made itself felt in this mixture of customs and methods. An Phu Dông is, of course, a model village, the one which is always shown to Western journalists, American Congress-men or Senators, or investigating commissions. And yet, to bring it to its present state of efficiency took only three months, the operation being divided into ten stages which the official proceeded to explain with the aid of maps, diagrams and a pointer. We shall examine this scheme in detail because it was one of the most incredible (and tragic) stories we had ever heard.

The first stage was a meeting between the villagers and the government official. It was an awkward encounter, because the peasants were suspicious, or even hostile, and it was the functionary's task to convince them that the Viet-Cong were all murderers against whom they must defend themselves, that they must build roads, dig trenches and ditches, fill sandbags and, lastly, take it in turns to mount guard. The second stage was the carrying-out of these orders, and here many difficulties arose, though the presence of detach-ments from the army and the 'Civil Guard' was usually enough to convince even the most refractory. Once the fortifications had been finished, the inhabitants were informed of the government's plans for fighting the Viet-Cong. The programme could also be studied on a poster stuck up in the centre of the village. It included rules and suggestions as to how to report the presence of Viet-Cong, the technique of killing them, the rewards that would be paid, and the ethical aspect of the struggle.

The fourth and fifth stages concerned the division of the village into sectors; the classification of the inhabitants as 'good' or 'bad' (the huts of those suspected of Communist sympathies or who had relatives among the Viet-Cong were marked in black on a map kept by the official); the selection of trustworthy elements; the num-bering of the houses; the taking of a census (each family was lined up outside its house and photographed); and the distribution of forms containing particulars of each member of the family, with the usual anti-Viet-Cong tirade on the back. When they had been thus counted, registered, numbered, photographed and classified, each peasant was given a badge bearing his name, the number of his house, the number and sex of each member of his family, and the sector of the village in which he lived. The badge was a blue disc resembling those worn by American soldiers above their shirt-pockets, but full of numbers, letters and details.

At this point the village began to be 'strategic'. The sixth stage envisaged semi-military training with real rifles. The seventh con-sisted of an exchange of views with 'teams' from neighbouring villages. The eighth, of real military training, with false alarms and sham attacks. During the ninth stage, a radio station began to function, broadcasting selected programmes for six hours every day within a radius of three miles. The tenth stage was reserved for making improvements in the village.

When the official finally laid aside his pointer, he was anxious to show us how the village functioned in actual practice. He rang a bell, and a few moments later a strange noise could be heard that seemed to come from every direction, from near at hand as well as from far away. Later, we found that it was the noise made by beating a bamboo cane with a piece of wood, and we noticed that this task was entrusted to the old. Sitting at the doors of their huts, they went on beating their bamboos for an hour, with a patience and resignation that brought a lump into our throats, while the young men ran to the ramparts bristling with bamboo stakes or to the strongpoints made of sandbags. The beaming functionary insisted on showing us all the security arrangements, the miles and miles of defences, the ditches intersecting the fields, the booby-traps full of spikes to catch the Viet-Cong, rows of little boys who presented arms with bamboo canes, and girls who knew how to strip a rifle and put it together again with their eyes blindfolded. And all the time the maddening noise of the bamboos beaten with sticks went on and on.

This was a 'strategic village'. We visited seven of them. 1,700 had been built already. 1,500 were under construction. By the end of 1963 it was expected that 17,000 would have been finished. On that day the whole of South Vietnam would be a labyrinth of trenches, ditches, ramparts, booby-traps and barbed wire—a labyrinth in which 13 million Vietnamese would mount guard all day long, while an impressive propaganda machine would go on reminding them that 'every one of you must offer the life of one Viet-Cong to the country'.[27]

Even in Russia in the days of Stalin it would have been impossible to find a universe of concentration camps of such huge proportions. Although there were delays in the execution of the programme, 8,600 'strategic villages' had been completed by the end of 1963 and the number of peasants behind barbed wire undergoing 'community re-education' had risen to $10\frac{1}{2}$ millions.[28] The Americans of the 'Military Assistance Command', whose numbers rose from 3,000 to 190,000 between 1960 and 1966,[29] seem unable to perceive the sinister, anti-democratic and purely Nazi aspect of this operation; on the contrary they complain that the barrier is inadequate. In violation of the Geneva agreement, the members of the American Commission do not limit their activities to the training of Vietnamese and anti-partisan units, to placing every type of weapon and air transport at their disposal, but themselves take part in the fighting; 'South Vietnam . . . has become a testing ground for new United States Army guerrilla tactics designed for fighting in tropical jungles';[30] they 'teach Vietnamese fliers how to spray Communist-held areas with a chemical that turns the rice fields yellow, killing any crop being grown in rebel strongholds'.[31]

Jules Roy criticizes the behaviour of the Americans in this 'crusade' very severely:

> America's material and moral aid to Diem is just one aspect of her fight against the Communist *bloc*, and no account is taken of the injustice and suffering it brings with it for the poorest classes, or of the rot that has set in among the middle and upper class.[32]

In the United States a few voices are raised against this 'dirty war', but they are the voices of isolated individuals. 'It is most disturbing,' we read in Senator Mike Mansfield's report, 'to find that after 7 years of the Republic, South Vietnam appears less, not more stable than it was at the outset, that it appears more removed from, rather than closer to, the achievement of popularly responsible and responsive government.'[33] A group of intellectuals sent a letter to President Kennedy in which, among other things, we read:

> The truth is that in South Vietnam, ten thousand miles away from the United States, our army, in order to support an open and brutal dictatorship, that of President Diem, is waging, with more than twelve thousand officers and men, a war that has never been declared and has never received the approval of the United States Congress; moreover, it is a 'dirty and cruel' war, as *The Nation* of 19 January 1963 calls it, as dirty and cruel as the war waged by France in Algeria, and one which has profoundly shocked the consciences of Americans.

From time to time, as a result of these attacks, American public opinion was shaken and Diem's last hour seemed to have come, but, as Henri Amoroux points out: 'At the height of the storm, when the plotters were rubbing their hands and Diem was tottering, some American general or prelate would descend from an aeroplane and the next day Diem would be on his feet again. Since he can always rely on American support, he is indestructible.'[34] Kennedy succeeded Eisenhower at the White House, but America's defensive policy remained unchanged until the *coup d'état* in November 1963—'There is no alternative to Ngo Dinh Diem.'

Consequently, Diem remained in power for almost ten years, while the civil war became more bitter every day and the police régime paralysed the whole life of the country. Between 1955 and 1961, according to information supplied by the National Liberation Front, 75,000 of Diem's adversaries were killed, 270,000 were in 900 prisons and concentration camps, and another $\frac{1}{2}$ million had been arrested and subjected to torture.[35] 'What struck me in particular,' a German doctor, Erich Wulff, reported on his return from Vietnam,

> was the terror inspired by the police. In the psychiatric hospital of the Faculty in Hué, political prisoners were continually being brought before me who had been driven to the verge of insanity by prolonged solitary confinement in cells. On such occasions I noted that all the detainees, without exception, had been beaten and tortured. Some of them had spent two years in prison without being charged or tried. Nine times out of ten they were illiterate peasants who did not even know why they had been arrested. Some important personage, whom they had perhaps criticized one day among themselves, had taken his revenge by accusing them of being Communists.[36]

The persecution of the Buddhists

In the Spring of 1963 Diem started a new campaign, this time against the Buddhists, who, as regards religion, represent the majority of the inhabitants. According to Erich Wulff:[37]

> It all began on Wednesday 8 May, the birthday of Buddha, the equivalent of December 25 for Christians . . . At Hué, the religious capital of the Buddhists of Indo-China, I saw machine-guns open fire on the crowds and killing children. I also saw troops using poison gas to attack students demonstrating near a pagoda.

The hunt for Buddhists was carried out by Ngo Dinh Nhu's 'special units'[38] and lasted throughout the summer, among its many unforgettable episodes being the suicide of Thich Quang Duc who, together with other monks, burned himself alive as a protest against these attacks. The *New York Times* rightly observed that this was not a religious war: 'The Diem-Nhu government is at odds with the Buddhists, not because they are Buddhists, but because they represent a separate social force and potentially a separate political force of a kind the Saigon government finds inimical.'[39]

Diem's isolation was now greater than ever, and his only support came from the fanatical security forces under the command of his brother Nhu. After the tragic summer of 1963 one of his former Ministers, Ho Thong Ming, described the Diem régime as follows:

> Behind the façade, sordid truths lie hidden—corruption, denunciations, stagnation and the negation of all democracy. We must remember that under Syngman Rhee ninety opposition Deputies sat in the parliament at Seoul, whereas Diem will not tolerate a single

one in Saigon! . . . One after the other, he has got rid of Bao-Dai, of the sects, of the French, of the internal opposition, of the Buddhists and even of the Vietnamese themselves, and now he finds himself in difficulties with the Americans.[40]

But once again the Americans took everything lying down and failed to react. The presidential election was too close to allow Kennedy to make any drastic change in American policy in Vietnam and thus provide his adversaries, who were already criticizing him for showing weakness in his dealings with the Soviet *bloc*, with other weapons. Consequently, while admitting that Diem had 'gotten out of touch with the people' and that the persecution of the Buddhists was 'very unwise', Kennedy confirmed that the United States intended to go on helping South Vietnam.[41]

Once again the course of political events saved Diem, but now the criticisms, ever more fierce, began to come from his own followers. Tran Van Chuong, father of Madame Nhu and a former ambassador to the United Nations, declared over the American radio:

> We have had Louis XIV, then Napoleon, Hitler, Stalin, Mussolini, all of them more or less efficient dictators because they knew how to delegate authority. On the contrary, the Diem brothers refuse to delegate any of their powers and are peculiarly inefficient. The Diem régime is totalitarian, unpopular and stupid.

Asked what he thought of his daughter, he replied: 'She is the real head of the government, the real commander of the army, the real ruler of all Vietnam.'[42]

Across the sinister Vietnamese stage, littered with ruins and strewn with corpses, amidst praying crowds and monks killing themselves in the 'lotus position', Madame Nhu, whom the American press during the summer of 1963 christened Lucretia Borgia-Nhu, strolled nonchalantly, wrapped in her famous silk robes, her forehead fringed by her jet-black hair, her eyes too hard to be beautiful—always ready with a retort, argumentative, and evil.

Sister-in-law of the dictator Diem and wife of the inventor of 'personalism', she infected both these men with her intolerance and showed that she wielded far more power than Evita Perón had ever done in the Argentina of the *descamisados*. She was more powerful and far less lovable than the blonde and slender Evita. One episode alone will suffice. On 27 February 1962, when two rebel AD-6 Skyriders attacked the presidential palace with bombs and rockets, they concentrated on the wing occupied by Madame

Nhu, who, however, emerged unscathed, except for a few slight scratches. But hatred of the 'First Lady' had reached such a pitch that many months after this incident there were people in Saigon who were still ready to swear that the real Madame Nhu had died amidst the ruins of the palace, and that the woman who later appeared in public was her double.

Of this hatred she was perfectly well aware. Replying to a journalist, Madame Nhu admitted that her role had been approximately the same as Evita Perón's but added: 'Evita was loved, but I am not.' The Buddhists could not love her, because she was responsible for their being persecuted. Nor could the Catholics, after they had had a chance to judge her views on religion by her cynical remark that 'if the God of the Christians really exists, I can use my certificate of baptism as a passport to Paradise'.[43] Regarding the Catholicism of Madame Nhu (and of her husband and brother-in-law) certain reservations are justifiable. As Jean Lacouture remarked, 'it is closer to the Catholicism of a Torquemada than to that of Pope John XXIII, and she would not have the slightest objection to lighting the pyres herself, if her enemies had not saved her the trouble by throwing themselves on to them first.'[44] Hers is a religion from which piety has been banished, and replaced by fanaticism. Asked what she thought of the suicides in the Buddhist pagodas, she could only express her scorn for the monks for using imported petrol and making a 'barbecue'.[45]

The excesses committed by the Ngo family at length compelled the United States to look for an alternative. But the solution they chose, which amounted to replacing Diem by another 'strong man', offers little hope of success, for the war in South Vietnam is one of those wars that can never be won. 'There is only one real solution,' wrote Tibor Mende, 'and that is to admit that the war in South Vietnam can be settled on a political basis and to adopt that solution, which presupposes the removal of its principal adversaries—the Diem family.'[46] This was the solution proposed by the Geneva conference in 1954—the reunification of the two Vietnams after a general election to be held under UN supervision. But when he heard what was being proposed, Diem lost his temper. 'I could never accept that. One cannot commit suicide over questions of procedure. Don't forget: South Vietnam is an island in the ocean of Communism, an island that might easily be submerged.'[47]

While the fortunes of the mandarin Ngo Dinh Diem were setting in a bloodstained sky, Nhu and his wife were threatening to transform Saigon into a heap of rubble, beneath which they dreamt of burying their enemies as well as their false friends, the Viet-Cong as well as the Americans. They seemed to be fascinated by the Wagnerian end of Hitler in the Chancellery bunker while the whole of Berlin was burning, and South Vietnam entered upon the twenty-fourth year of uninterrupted war with black—the colour of mourning, of despair and of the treacherous night—as its dominating colour. It was the colour of the short tunics worn by the peasants as they bent over the gleaming water in the rice-fields, the colour of the battle-dress worn by the warriors of the Viet-Cong and of the uniforms of the 'Civil Guards' who were defending 'strategic villages', and it was the colour of Nhu's SS. All the actors in this bloody civil war chose black, not as a symbol of defiance or to show their contempt for death—which is a romantic foible peculiar to European Fascism—but in order to render the struggle grimmer and make every ambush more deadly. Clad in these theatrical, existentialist boiler-suits, they waged their secret and nocturnal war in a country of rice-paddies and swamps, of forests and mountains and dense tropical jungle. A country without roads which provided an ideal background for guerrilla warfare, a country which knows better than any other in South-East Asia what round-ups, starvation and death mean. A country of peasants who have learned to accept the calamities of war as if they were in the natural order of things; an unfortunate country given over to the Cold War, whose inhabitants are doomed to extermination. And yet Nguyen Kien still believes that all is not yet lost:

> We cannot help feeling a thrill of pride when we see our own countrymen displaying determination and heroism, and moreover, such intelligence, in this long struggle against powerful enemies; when we see how our little, unarmed nation has offered stout resistance to French colonialism, to Japanese Fascism, to British troops and to the colonial might of the United States.[48]

Diem falls, but the war goes on

The hopes of Nguyen Kien seemed to be coming true on 1 November 1963, when tanks surrounded the presidential palace and began to shell it. Inside were Ngo Dinh Diem and his brother Nhu, with a few hundred soldiers of the presidential guard. Abandoned to their fate by the Americans, who suspected them of having started negotiations with Ho Chi Minh's government,[49] the Ngo brothers could no longer rely on Colonel Le Quang Tung's 'special units', which had been sent to the front only a few days before as a result of American pressure. During the night, after seven hours of fighting, Diem and his brother slipped out of the palace and took refuge in the church of St Francis Xavier, in the Chinese quarter of Cholon. But a few hours later the rebels arrived with an armoured car and in the course of the afternoon, in circumstances which are still far from clear, they were killed. Madame Nhu, who escaped the same fate simply because she was abroad at the time, accused the Americans of supporting the rebels, adding that Judas got thirty pieces of silver for betraying Jesus Christ, but the Ngo brothers were sold for a handful of small change. Such was the epitaph of the Diem dictatorship, which had lasted nine years and five months.

In the days immediately following this *coup d'état*, the most conspicuous symbol of the Diem régime, the Trung sisters' statue, was demolished, the dance-halls which had been closed by order of Madame Nhu reopened their doors, and the *Gauleiter* of Central Vietnam, Ngo Dinh Can, was arrested and shot in the following May. But that was all. There had been no real revolution, merely the replacement of Diem by another 'strong man', Duong Van Minh. To a journalist who asked him why he had included in his government a number of military and civilian personages who had compromised themselves during the Diem régime, the 'great' Minh candidly replied: 'We all belonged to the old régime; there can be no doubt about that.'[50] In fact, except for the removal of the Ngo brothers, nothing had changed. The strategic villages remained where they were, Nhu's policemen took the oath of allegiance to the new régime, the men of the 'special units' were brought back from the front and handed over to the army, and the prisons remained as full as ever; while the ideological leadership of the anti-Communist crusade was entrusted to the *Dai-Viet* ultra-Nationalist party, which was certainly no less extreme in its views.

Meanwhile, 'pacification', in other words the war, went on. And when General Duong Van Minh began to show neutralist and francophile tendencies, he was replaced, after a bloodless *coup* on 30 January 1964, by General Nguyen Khan, the man who had saved Diem from the rebel paratroopers in November 1960, a man whom the Americans trusted and one of those who maintained that the war must be carried into North Vietnam, beyond the seventeenth parallel. To intensify the struggle against the Viet-Cong, Khan called up 50,000 more men and ordered the mobilization of the entire civilian population, in order 'to employ all the active forces of the nation and allow every citizen to participate, directly or indirectly, in the struggle against the Communists'.[51] Under this new military dictatorship the last hope of avoiding the horrors of civil war faded away. The campaign against the Viet-Cong was extended to include neutralists and all those who were clamouring for peace. An American, Helen Lamb, accused her country of not even trying to find a peaceable solution and wrote that a cruiser armed with missiles, the *Providence*, had been sent up the river to Saigon

> to quell the rising tide of neutralist feeling. As if this show of American force could undermine Saigon's longing for peace! Now since the ruling dictator equates advocacy of neutralism with treason, neutralism again has no voice in Saigon. But it has many silent followers.[52]

Cowed by the mandarin Diem's inquisition, decimated by famine and guerrilla warfare, silenced by a Fascist military dictatorship, lost to democracy perhaps for many decades to come, the people of South Vietnam spent the last days of 1964 digging air-raid shelters and preparing for total war.

In 1965 and 1966 the dimensions of the conflict in Vietnam assumed such proportions that they became a major factor in the crisis in international relations. On the battlefield itself the partisans and the North Vietnamese on the one side and the Americans with their South Vietnamese supporters on the other are now waging war on a full scale, using poison-gas, resorting to bombardment from the air (recently extended to North Vietnam as well) and fighting pitched battles on the ground.[53] The nature of this conflict and the danger it represents to world peace have led to diplomatic action in all parts of the world with a view to finding a solution to the problem. Parallel with this diplomatic activity, there is also a widespread feeling in the United States, and especially among intellectuals, that something must be done soon to terminate the American military involvement in South Vietnam.

14 Japan

The patriotic murderers

The Japanese extremists' favourite weapon is the dagger. When committing acts of terrorism they may also use pistols, hand-grenades, or even sticks of dynamite, but they are convinced that no weapon is more suitable for inflicting 'divine punishment' than a *Samurai* dagger. They were convinced of this in the 1930s and they still are today, after losing a war, after the dropping of atomic bombs on Hiroshima and Nagasaki, after a long period of military occupation followed by a gradual revival and an industrial boom. During the 1930s they used to stab Liberal ministers who 'were obstructing the path of the gods', the path leading to the conquest of the world. After the war they used their daggers without distinction against Communists and Socialists, Liberal Democrats and pacifists, persuaded that they were now surrounded by traitors and defeatists, by enemies of their country.

The long list of outrages began in January 1947, the perpetrators being members of the *Shinei Taishū Tō* (New and Powerful Masses Party). Convinced that Kikunami Katsumi, a Communist member of the Diet and a prominent trade-union leader, was one of the men chiefly responsible for the difficulties besetting Japan, they called upon him at his lodgings and exhorted him to use his influence to call off a strike he was planning, and when they met with a refusal, they dealt him a severe wound in the forehead with a dagger. In July 1948, a few days after the attempt on the life of the Italian Communist leader, Palmiro Togliatti, a youthful member of the *Nihon Hankyō Remmei* (Japan Anti-Communist League) tried to assassinate Tokuda Kyūichi, the secretary-general of the Japanese Communist Party, by throwing a stick of dynamite at the platform from which he was speaking at the Saga town hall. Though he was hit by thirty splinters Tokuda survived both this and a second attempt a year later. On 21 September 1954 the designated victim was Yoshida Shigeru, the Conservative Premier, guilty, in the eyes of the extremists, of wanting to go to Washington to compromise

Japan's independence still further. But the hired assassin, Maruyama Toshiyuki, head of the Kōbe branch of the *Dai Nihon Seisan Tō* (Great Japan Production Party), was arrested before he had time to use his dagger. In June 1960, the Socialist leader Jotaro Kawakami was severely wounded by a seventeen-year-old boy named Seizaburo Toma, and four months later another student, Otoya Yamaguchi, 'punished' the secretary-general of the Socialist Party, Inejiro Asanuma.

It was only after this latter crime, which took place in a Tokyo theatre in the presence of 3,000 spectators and was also seen on television by 10 million viewers, that the public at large learned that the ultra-nationalists had returned to the attack in Japan. A photograph taken at the very moment when the student was plunging his dagger into the belly of the corpulent Asanuma appeared in newspapers all over the world. In this photo Otoya has his eyes half closed and is gripping the dagger with both hands; Asanuma is doubled up and his glasses are slipping off his nose. It was a sensational snapshot which no one could ever forget. People asked who this Otoya Yamaguchi was and they found it difficult to believe that fanatics of his type still existed.

Otoya was a boy of seventeen, of below average height, emaciated and short-sighted. At the moment of the crime he was wearing the black, gold-buttoned uniform of a university student, but he had neglected his studies in order to have more time for politics. He was the *oyabun*, or head, of a group of right-wing extremists, and he had previously been arrested nine times by the police for hooliganism and beating up trade-unionists, pacifists or left-wing students (*Zengakuren*). He had been an active member of the *Dai Nihon Aikoku Tō* (Great Japan Patriots' Party) headed by the fanatical Akao Bin, and of the 'Anti-Communist League for the Freedom of Asia', run by a former member of the Japanese Gestapo, Toshio Nakto. On 12 October 1960 he was attending a meeting in one of Tokyo's largest theatres, at which, among other orators, the Conservative Premier Hayato Ikeda, and his most formidable opponent, the Socialist Inejiro Asanuma, were to speak. It was only a month before the general election and political feeling was running fairly high. Otoya sat in one of the front rows with Akao Bin and about thirty young extremists. These neo-Fascists were not there just by chance—on the contrary everything had been carefully planned beforehand. Suddenly some of the 'patriots' jumped on to the stage and began throwing anti-Socialist leaflets into the stalls. None of the sixty plain-clothes policemen attempted to stop them. Otoya took advantage of the general confusion, slipped on to the stage and plunged his weapon three times into Asanuma's belly. It was a *Samurai* dagger ten inches long.

As Asanuma lay dying on the floor, Akao Bin seized the microphone and began to abuse the Socialists and the *Zengakuren*, alleging that they were responsible for all acts of violence. At length the police arrived and cleared the theatre, but later, once the inquiry was over, everyone carefully avoided any talk about a plot and no one tried to find out who were the instigators of the crime. True to the traditions of political assassins, Otoya Yamaguchi took all the blame for what he had done, explaining his motive as follows: 'I killed Asanuma because he was a traitor and wanted to hand Japan over to the Communists.' Then, for fear lest he might be forced to say more, he hanged himself in his cell. As for Akao Bin, he was stopped by the police, interrogated and released at once. Yet there can be no doubt that he was Otoya's *oyabun*, a man who made a profession of turning out super-patriots, modelled on the lines of the many famous assassins of the 1930s, like Sagoya Tomeo, Inoue Nisshō and Kita Ikki. But it is also clear that Akao Bin must in his turn have been commissioned by somebody else, by someone who had no desire for the matter to be brought before a court and had enough influence to prevent this. In fact, once the actual perpetrator of the murder was dead, the Asanuma file was pigeon-holed.

From 1960 on the extremists, disappointed by the policy of the Conservative government, which they thought too moderate and conciliatory, and unpatriotic, abandoned their campaign against the men of the Left and, as they had done in the 1930s, tried to get rid of the men in power. Even the pro-Fascist Premier Kishi Nobusuke, who favoured the policy of rearmament and restoration advocated by the extreme nationalists, was attacked. On 14 July 1961 he narrowly escaped being stabbed by the leader of the *Taika Kai* (Great Reform Society), the sixty-year-old Taisuke Aramaki. On 7 February 1963 it was the turn of his successor, Premier Hayato Ikeda. Three members of the *Kōkoku Dōshikai* (Rising Nation Comrades' Party) decided to kill him because he maintained 'friendly relations with Communist countries like China', but they were arrested in the train between Osaka and the capital. On 17 July 1963 two extremists set fire to the house of the Minister Kōno Ichirō. And on 5 November of the same year Premier Ikeda narrowly escaped being killed. An election meeting in Kuriyama had just ended when a young man rushed out of the crowd and tried to hand a petition to Ikeda, but the police, who were suspicious of such petitioners, managed to stop him and the petition fell to the ground together with a ten-inch dagger. On a sheet of paper were the words 'divine punishment', the traditional formula of right-wing terrorists. The would-be assassin was a young man of twenty-four called Takao Ishimoto, who belonged to the semi-military sect of the *Sōka Gakkai* (Value-Creating Academy), which with its 13 million adherents was the most curious and at the same time disturbing phenomenon of these post-war years. Later Ishimoto confessed to the police that he wanted to kill Ikeda because he was 'too fond of the Communists', and accusation that seems absurd when we remember the efforts made by Ikeda's party to persuade the Diet to amend the constitution on more conservative and anti-Communist lines. It does, however, show the lengths to which the Japanese neo-Fascists of the 1960s are prepared to go—those worthy successors of the men who thirty years before had been responsible for the downfall of the country's precarious Liberal structure and had handed Japan over to the militarists.

This was not the last outrage in the series. On 24 March 1964 a nineteen-year-old youth named Kowa Shoitani, who was unemployed and half blind, entered the courtyard of the United States Embassy in Tokyo and with a dagger seriously wounded the ambassador, Edwin Reischauer, who was just getting into his car. After trying unsuccessfully to make the police believe that he was mad, Kowa Shoitani told them that he wanted to punish the ambassador for the crimes committed by the Americans in Japan—for example, the death-sentence passed on General Tōjō and the 'decline in public morality', which according to this young terrorist was a direct consequence of the American occupation.

MacArthur's reforms

When we consider the energy with which, immediately after Japan's surrender, the 'Proconsul' MacArthur tackled the ambitious project of reforming Japanese society, it is difficult to understand how such a powerful and extreme right wing can have come into being. Convinced that they could introduce democracy like any other article 'made in USA', the American experts who landed in Tokyo in the late summer of 1945 set to work at once, with an enthusiasm as admirable as it was naïve, to destroy the huge pyramidal structure with, as its apex, an Emperor who had been defeated, but was still a god. To destroy this formidable *ziggurat*, they began nibbling away at its ideological foundations by prohibiting the teaching of any kind of militarist or ultra-nationalist creed in the schools, by censoring the history and geography books and suppressing the famous 'courses in morals' *(shūsin)*. The next target was Shinto, which as the State religion had been responsible for the ultra-nationalistic education received by the Japanese. Accordingly, Shinto was deprived of government support, and the circulation of the famous 'patriotic' texts was likewise forbidden. These included the *Kokutai no Hongi* (Fundamental Principles of the National Polity), the *Bushido* (*Samurai* code of behaviour) and the *Shimmin no Michi* (The Way of the Subject) and likewise forbidden was the use of expressions pertaining to the imperial ideology such as *Hakkō Ichiu* (The Eight Corners of the World under One Roof) and *Dai Tōa Sensō* (Great East Asia War). Thus, pending Washington's decision as to the Emperor's fate, he was invited to divest himself at least of his divine attributes. On New Year's Day 1946 Hirohito complied with this request and broadcast the following message:

> The ties between us and our people have always stood upon mutual trust and affection. They do not depend on mere legends and myths. They are not predicated on the false conception that the Emperor is divine and that the Japanese people are superior to other races and fated to rule the world.[1]

When ultra-nationalist publications had been prohibited, Shinto reduced to poverty, the Yasukuni shrine, where soldiers who had died in battle used to be deified, discredited and the Emperor forced to deny his own divine ancestry, the Americans began their task of rehabilitation by dissolving the ultra-nationalist organizations, banning extreme right-wingers from holding public offices, arresting and trying war criminals, and dismantling the military set-up and the Ministry for the Interior, which had been the most efficient organism of Japanese Fascism. The list of purgees comprised 210,287 persons (almost 50,000 of these being notorious right-wing extremists), and 900 were sentenced to death (the first on the list being General Tōjō). In addition, between February 1946 and December 1951 233 extremist movements were disbanded, and MacArthur's staff, animated by an ever more obvious fervour, proceeded to democratize the country by encouraging the growth of

trade unions, abolishing all restrictions on strikes, introducing
agrarian reforms and suppressing under the new civil code the
excesses of paternal authority and the majorat system. They also
split up the big industries controlled by the *zaibatsu*, abolished the
arbitrary powers of the police, extended the suffrage to women,
introduced a maximum eight-hour day in factories and, lastly,
drafted a new constitution, the first and ninth Articles of which
were particularly important. Under the first the Emperor divested
himself of all his powers and transferred them to the people;[2] under
Article 9 Japan forswore war for ever and undertook that 'land, sea
and air forces, as well as other war potential will never be maintained'.

The dismantling of Japan's old politico-economic structure was
obviously fraught with many difficulties, but it soon won the
approval and support of the intelligentsia and of the urban working
class. Had it been completed, it might have made the restoration
advocated by conservative and reactionary elements more difficult.
The first to perceive that the sweeping reforms imposed by the
Americans were threatening the very foundations of the country
were the extremist groups, whose slogans had been buried beneath
the rubble of the old State edifice and who had lost the traditional
support of the bureaucratic oligarchy, the army and the mighty
zaibatsu. They had managed to survive the *gyokusai* (glorious
defeat), but now they found themselves isolated to such an extent
that in time they seemed doomed to disappear.

Perhaps because it had never managed to become a party of the
masses, as it had in Italy and Germany, Fascism in Japan had
suffered less from defeat than in those countries. Generals like
Anami, Sugiyama and Onishi had chosen the honourable way out
and committed *hara-kiri*, thus rejoining in the hereafter the 2 million
soldiers whose lives had been fruitlessly sacrificed in the war; but
the theoreticians of Japanese Fascism, the super-patriots and the
men who murdered for the sake of their country decided that it
would be better to go on living and content themselves with sending
a few dozens of their disciples to split their bellies before the gates
of the imperial palace.[3] As Masao Maruyama has pointed out:

> It is ironical to note that the vast majority of officers of the
> armed services and their supporters, the rightist group leaders, who
> had boasted of 'dying for the cause of the nation', holding that 'life
> should be regarded [as] lighter than a feather, if given for the
> sake of the Emperor' etc., facing the greatest disgrace wrought

upon their traditional symbol, should *not* have chosen the way of death.[4]

A little later, however, amidst the flood of reforms, they found themselves in an embarrassing position, and some of these groups went into voluntary liquidation, while others sought to avoid the dangers of the purge by 'adopting "democratic" names and slogans, thinking thus both to hoodwink the Occupation and to curry favour with the general public'.[5] Thus, to quote a few examples, the *Kokusai Taishū Tō* (National Essence Mass Party), founded at Osaka in 1931, became the *Zenkoku Kinrōsha Dōmei* (National League of Working People), the *Aikoku Sha* (Patriots' Society) adopted the generic name of *Shin Nihon Tō* (New Japan Party), and the *Kodama Kikan* (Kodama Agency) was turned into the *Nihon Kokumin Tō* (Japan National Party). This trick, however, did not work for long and the extremist groups soon found themselves on the list of banned organizations.

Conversely, the reassuring presence of the occupation forces galvanized the Japanese democrats, who had hitherto been unable to express their opinions freely. A few months after the end of the war Daisetsu Suzuki was able not only to demolish the legend of the suicide-squad of air-pilots, but also to present it as a consequence of mistakes made by the High Command:

> They tried to overcome this lack [of scientific knowledge] by means of spiritual and physical forces which developed into the *kamikaze* idea. The unscientific mentality of Japanese military men was shared by the rest of the nation. Tactics of this kind, which were intended to restore balance, were destined to end in suicide. Far from being a reason for pride, they will remain a blot on the Japanese people's history.[6]

These violent attacks on revered myths and ideologies which only a short time before no one would have dared to discuss, coupled with the 'persecution' to which they were subjected by the occupying power, persuaded many extremists to disband their organizations and convert them into more modest enterprises whose activities were limited to the specifically social and economic sectors. Some of the groups even migrated to the rural areas, where the wave of reforms had caused less harm, where respect for the Emperor was still unimpaired, and the seeds of nationalism could thus fall on more fertile ground. As soon as they came out of prison or had been removed from the army by the purge, men like Tachibana Kōsaburō, Mikami Taku, Katō Kanji, Sugawara Hyoji and Ishiwara Kanji[7] devoted their energies to building rural villages, increasing agricultural production, and founding schools where, in addition to agriculture, those precepts were taught which in the 1930s had helped to turn out numbers of super-patriots ready for any sacrifice. While awaiting better days, some of them organized terrorist bands bearing innocent labels such as *Shinshū Nōjō* (Divine Land Farm) or *Kinō Kumiai* (Back-to-the-Land Union).[8] Other groups remained in the cities and devoted themselves to all kinds of activities, such as organizing business undertakings, associations for helping returning soldiers and societies whose aim was the inculcation of respect for the Shinto temples. Among these the most widely known was the *Fuji Kadō Kai* (Peerless Poetry Association), whose task it was to exploit poetry as a vehicle for perpetuating the worship of the gods and respect for the Emperor.

While the pre-war extremist groups were thus struggling to survive by assuming with more or less success the strangest disguises, new organisms were created, whose leaders (at all events in the early days) apparently had no connexion with the movements, cliques and conspiracies of the 1930s. The Trojan horse of all such groups was anti-Communism, a new and reliable excuse which enabled them to carry on their activities with a show of legality, and even to help the Conservative government to repress the left-wing parties, whenever strikes or demonstrations took place. They also supported the policy of rearmament and did not disdain to provide the American occupation authorities with information about the activities of the Communists. Among these groups, which were anti-Communist because it suited their purpose, were several which hoped to become big parties and had the same aims and characteristics as the pre-war Nazi and Fascist movements (a people's revolution, aversion to capitalism, and racial discrimination). Those which attracted a certain amount of support were the *Kyūkoku Seinen Remmei* (National Salvation Youth League), founded by the Conservative Orita Masanobu; the *Nihon Kakumei Kikuhata Dōshikai* (Japan Revolutionary Chrysanthemum Flag Comrades' Association), founded by Fukushima Seishi; the *Daiwa Tō* (Great Conciliation Party), which demanded among other things the expulsion of all Koreans and Chinese, the restitution to Japan of Okinawa, the Kurile Islands and even Formosa, and the creation, at United Nations' expense, of a 5 million-strong Japanese army to defend the whole of Asia; the *Nihon Hankyō Remmei* (Japan Anti-Communist League), which immediately distinguished itself by organizing attempts on the lives of left-wing leaders; and the *Shinei Taishū Tō* (New and Powerful Masses Party), which specialized in blackmail, unofficial police work and black-marketeering.

Despite all their efforts to exploit the racial prejudices of the masses against the Koreans and the other minorities, and the use of slogans extolling peace, democracy, the people's rights and Socialism, these movements were unable to rid themselves of many anachronistic elements and failed in their attempts to gain popular support. The masses soon identified them—and quite rightly—with the groups responsible for the loss of the war and the subsequent phase of shortages, one of the reasons being that, once the rigours of the purge had become a thing of the past, the nominal heads of such organizations were replaced by men who had just come out of prison and bore the all too well known names of prewar extremists. Despite these disadvantages, however, the bad times for right-wing extremists were fast drawing to a close. The Cold War, the fighting in Korea and the sudden reversal of American policy regarding rearmament put a definite stop to the programme of reforms and changed the whole situation in Japan.

The 'Reverse Course'

The benevolent notion of reforming Japanese society and making Japan 'the Switzerland of the Far East' was bound to remain a blissful dream. To start with, the programme of reforms was far too advanced. As Nathaniel Peffer points out,

> When American businessmen began to appear in Tokyo, what they saw smacked of New Dealism, of 'creeping Socialism'. Why sanction in Japan under American auspices what they deemed dangerous heresy at home? And why, moreover, build up the power of labor in Japan to equal power with ownership, when they considered this an invitation to revolution at home? Slowly but surely American policy in Japan conformed to the beliefs of the most influential classes at home.[9]

Another motive underlying the change of American policy was the advent of the Cold War and the victory of Mao Tse-tung in China. The Americans believed that 'the struggle between the Soviet Union and the United States had reduced the importance of the effort to change Japanese society, and that it was of greater significance to rebuild Japan as a useful base for American power and to reduce the strain on American resources'.[10] Consequently they made an abrupt change of course and tried to transform the 'Switzerland of the Far East' into the 'most formidable bulwark against Communism in Asia'.

This was a far quicker and easier operation than its predecessor, because it was supported by the Conservative government in Japan, which asked for nothing better than a return to the old structure of the State. In the months following the outbreak of the Korean War, 201,000 Fascists and ultra-nationalist purgees were allowed to return to their former posts, and at the same time a new purge began, this time directed against Communists. In July 1950, in flagrant violation of Article 9 of the constitution, General MacArthur authorized Japan to reconstitute her army,[11] and a few months later John Foster Dulles, as one of the conditions of the Security Pact, obliged Japan to cede to the United States 261 naval and air bases. This violation of the constitution on the part of the Americans encouraged the Japanese government to follow the same line, and in fact, while on the one hand they yielded to American pressure, in compensation they were able to abolish or water down the reforms imposed by the Americans.

This 'reverse course' adopted by the United States enabled the conservative elements in the government once again to centralize the police, which thus regained the sinister powers it had had before the war; to abolish the anti-monopoly laws and put the *zaibatsu* on their feet again;[12] to reorganize the heavy industries (which worked at full pressure during the Korean War); to restrict the right to strike and suppress the committees which had been set up to democratize education; to persuade the Diet to pass a 'law for the prevention of subversive activities', not unlike the 'law for the preservation of order' introduced before the war by the military-Fascist government; and even to restore full civil rights to former members of General Tōjō's cabinet, thus enabling the former Minister for Industry, Kishi, to become Premier and remain in power until popular indignation compelled him to resign on 23 June 1960.[13] Although the left-wing parties tried—and are still trying—to stop the abrogation of the democratic constitution, the Conservatives impaired its efficacy day by day, while Emperor Hirohito, in open defiance of Article 20, rendered homage to the shrines at Isé and Yasukuni, thus encouraging the masses to return to the old religious and patriotic traditions. The number of daily visitors to the Yasukuni shrine fell to a few dozen in 1946, but by 1952 it had risen to 5 million a year, and a few years later the 'War Museum' was reopened, where the crowds were able to rekindle their patriotic feelings by reading the exalted prose, exhibited in show-cases, of the pilots of the suicide-squad or by contemplating bloodstained uniforms, pierced helmets and sharp *Samurai* swords.

About this time, *kendō* and *jūdō*, which had previously been banned by the occupation authorities as manifestations of militarism, again became fashionable. Patriotic songs and military marches also became popular once more, and among the best-selling gramophone records were 'Our Gallant Soldiers' and 'The Hills of Manchuria'. The flag of the Rising Sun, symbol of Japanese imperialism, flew again on all public buildings. In 1954 the film that attracted the biggest audiences was *Nihon Yaburezu* ('Japan was not defeated'). A 'Commission for the Revision of the Constitution', consisting of scholars known to be loyal to the Crown, began to insist that Hirohito should enhance his prestige by becoming 'Head of the State', instead of being just a 'symbol of the State', and that he should once again be head of Shintoism, now that this form of ancestor-worship had been restored to the dignity of a State religion. In 1958 right-wing extremists staged a repetition of the Italian Fascists' macabre exploit at Musocco, raiding the crematorium of the American cemetery and removing the ashes of General Tōjō and six other war criminals who had been hanged with him.[14] Moreover, an investigation revealed that, especially in the rural districts, the dangerous beliefs and preconceptions that had driven Japan to war and defeat were flourishing more vigorously than ever.[15] The officers of the new army resorted once again to the old, inhuman methods of training, with the result that during a twenty-four-hour march, later described as the 'march of death', two soldiers died from exhaustion (an inquiry revealed that they had been prodded and beaten with bamboo canes). The Minister of Education, Matsunaga Tō, denounced the attempts of the occupation authorities to 'weaken the Japanese race' and decided to reintroduce 'courses in morals' in order to make the younger generation more patriotic.[16] And lastly, in this atmosphere of renascent exaltation there was a revival of patriotic-religious sects like the *Sōka Gakkai*, of which, since it has recently become important, we shall speak later.

Imposed by decree and undermined by vested interests, Japanese democracy, with the passage of time and the recurrence of such episodes, became an increasingly fragile barrier against the offensive of the Conservatives, who, in order to distract attention, flourished the noble banner of tradition.

The rehabilitation of the 'patriots'

Encouraged by the Conservatives in their own government as well as by the Americans, 'rehabilitated and free to enter politics',[17] the right-wing extremists began to re-form their groups without any attempt at concealment, and by 1951 540 such groups already existed. Three years later the number of ultra-nationalist organizations had risen to 750, and by 1956 the police had listed over 1,000 in their records, with a total membership of about 100,000. Of these 'more than 600 were marked as "dangerous" and about 30 were under special surveillance'.[18] About the same time, Asazo Nagamatsu, who is an authority on the subject, calculated that there were about 3,000 such groups with a total membership of half a million. Among their leaders and financial backers we find all the best-known names in pre-war extremism: men like Akao Bin, Inoue, Nisshō, Okawa Shūmei, Kodama Yoshio, Tsukui Tatsuo and Kuhara Fusanosuke. They had all just come out of prison, after preaching subversion and political assassination for thirty years and organizing most of the 'incidents' of the 1930s. They were resolute, fanatical men with good connexions in the world of finance, prepared to go to any lengths and ready to make all sorts of opportunist political deals.

In fact, whereas the Fascism of the 1930s had been uncompromisingly anti-democratic and anti-West, neo-Fascism pretended to be pro-American and in its propaganda it used slogans borrowed from the democratic parties, attacked feudalism, talked about the rights of man and elaborated schemes smacking of Socialism. All its hatred and its old violence were used to promote the most extreme forms of anti-Communism, since this was the card which had enabled it to re-enter the arena and gave it a certain air of 'respectability'. But although in its programmes it used the terminology of the democratic parties, the underlying tone was suspect and the trick could easily be spotted. Anti-Communism was merely a pretext. Anti-Fascism, led by the men of thirty years before, retained all of its characteristics intact. And as they gradually grew stronger, the anti-Communist factions entered into alliances with the anti-American secret societies, while the racialists exploited the hatred felt for the Koreans (just as Nazism had exploited anti-Semitism), the more religious-minded sects condemned the materialism of the West and the ultra-nationalists sought to restore the

Empire and the divine powers of the Tenno and Japan's role as the leading nation in Asia.[19]

A detailed study of this phenomenon would fill several volumes. Even Ivan Morris, author of the most exhaustive book on Japanese right-wing extremism, had to draw the line somewhere. We shall therefore confine ourselves to mentioning only those 'noble societies' which became the subjects of controversy or succeeded in putting their plans into execution. A prominent place must undoubtedly be given to the Japanese Anti-Communist League, which in 1951 came under the control of the fanatical Akao Bin and changed its name to *Dai Nihon Aikoku Tō* (Great Japan Patriots' Party), achieving, if not the first place as regards making converts, at least the fame of having provoked most incidents.[20] A briefer existence, on the other hand, was the lot of the new offshoots of the former *Shizan Juku* (Purple Mountain Institute), such as the *Shin Nihon Kokumin Dōmei* (New Life Japan People's League), which welcomed the most notorious pre-war terrorists into its ranks and tried to enrol recruits for Chiang Kai-shek's army, and the *Yachihoko Sha* (Myriad Weapons Society), which demanded the integral restoration of the Emperor's powers and described the trial of General Tōjō as a 'cannibalistic rite'. Another party which made its reappearance under the leadership of Kawakami Toshiji was the *Dai Nihon Seisan Tō* (Great Japan Production Party) which strove to destroy all Bolshevik influence and unite all the peoples of Asia. Then there was the *Kyōwa Tō* (Harmony Party), whose aim was a Japan neither capitalist nor Communist, but with the Emperor still the supreme head of affairs. Definitely Nazi in its opinions was the *Kokka-Shakaishugi Rōdō Tō* (National Socialist Workers' Party), which under the leadership of Higo Tōru became known for its savage attacks on the Americans. The Korean crisis in its turn resulted in the formation of two anti-Communist factions —the *Kokudo Bōei Kenkyūkai* (National Territory Defence Research Association) and the *Sokoku Bōei Dōshikai* (Fatherland Defence Comrades' Association).

When, however, we examine the composition of these groups, we find that their members were all professional agitators and terrorists, Fascists, nationalists and well-known Conservatives, men who in any case belonged to the pre-war generation. A return to the old customs, the complete restoration of the Shōwa régime, the rehabilitation of Shinto, protection against the Red Peril—these were all themes offering little attraction to the younger generation,

who during the years of occupation had been able to form some
idea, confused though it might be, of the concepts of democracy
and were often fascinated by the left-wing movements, especially
by the aggressive *Zengakuren* student organization, which conducted campaigns against Fascism and in defence of the constitution. But while it is true that in 1951, when visiting the university
of Kyoto, Emperor Hirohito was greeted by students carrying
banners with such devices as 'Not Welcome!', 'No More Wars!' and
'No more Deification of the Emperor!', it is also true that from
that time on reactionary ideas penetrated into scholastic circles,
that teachers with progressive ideas were dismissed as 'undesirables',
that thousands of others had to learn to keep their mouths shut
when 'reports on character' were introduced, that a methodical
revision of textbooks was undertaken and that the 'courses in
morals' were launched once more—all these things being symptoms
of extreme nationalism, in other words of Fascism.

It was at this juncture that the first right-wing youth movements
made their appearance, marked from the beginning by virulent
anti-Communism, hatred for pacifism and a delirious kind of
patriotism. Side by side with moderate groups like the 'New Japan
Student League', semi-military 'corps' sprang up which attracted
the more fanatical elements and revived all the oaths, the boss-
follower system *(oyabun-kobun)*, the techniques and slogans of
pre-war days, when similar 'corps' had been the shock-troops of
Japanese Fascism. The *Junkoku Seinen Tai* (National Martyrs
Youth Corps) had tens of thousands of members, who wore dark-
blue uniforms, shouted unmistakably Nazi slogans and sang an
anthem the fourth stanza of which runs as follows:

> Confusion reigns in the land!
> The red traitors are striving to devour us,
> While the money-mad plutocrats prance about.
> Is there no one to sustain our country?
>
> Firm as iron are we—
> Young men of the National Martyrs Youth Corps![21]

In the practical sphere this corps organized attacks in the streets
on the *Zengakuren* and members of similar left-wing trade unions,
and demanded the expulsion from Japan of all Koreans, the
banning of the Communist party, the penalization of the greedy
zaibatsu, and the adoption of a firm policy which would restore to
Japan her position as the leading country in Asia.

The *Gokoku Seinen Tai* (National Protection Youth Corps) had fewer members (who wore khaki uniforms), but it had the sinister reputation of being the youth movement of the fanatical *Gokoku Dan*, which from 1954 on counted among its leaders Inoue Nisshō, the most formidable instigator of assassinations during the 1930s, Sagoya Tomeo, who distinguished himself in 1930 by killing Premier Hamaguchi Yūkō at the main railway station in Tokyo, and Konuma Tadashi, who in 1932 had murdered the Finance Minister Inoue Junnosuke. Fortunately, despite the example set by their leaders, the young men of the *Gokoku Seinen Tai* became more famous for the way they financed themselves by means of blackmail and intimidation than for any acts of political terrorism they committed. The Tokyo police, who are notoriously easy-going when they have to deal with right-wing extremists, gave them the following testimonial: 'The National Protection Youth Corps, which purports to be a patriotic rightist organization, is a vicious gang of hoodlums reeking [*sic!*] crime and violence in the name of patriotism.'[22]

Akao Bin

A visit to Akao Bin's headquarters will give us a better idea of how these young super-patriots live, how they are indoctrinated and trained in the use of violence. The head office of the *Dai Nihon Aikoku Tō* is in Tokyo, in the old Asakusa quarter, and consists of a few wooden huts standing inside the walls of a burnt-out Shinto temple. One hut is used as a dormitory, one as a canteen and another for meetings, while one is reserved for the *oyabun* himself, Akao Bin. Above the tops of the corrugated-iron roofs the skeleton of the shattered temple can be seen.

Seated on a mat, thin and erect, with his gleaming yellowish skull and two enormous pouches beneath his eyes, the man who for nearly half a century has been teaching the younger generation the virtues of political violence motions to us to sit down on a mat in front of him. From behind his shoulders the eyes of Buddha, Christ, Mohammed and Confucius stare down upon us. There was also a large photo of the student Otoya Yamaguchi, murderer of the Socialist leader Asanuma. The room was filled with the heavy odour of fish soup, and reminded us at one moment of an antiquary's shop, at another of a temple. The walls of the hut were covered with religious pictures and lined with shelves full of statuettes and scrolls containing ideograms. In one corner was an ancient spinet, painted black; in the opposite corner was a bundle of fencing swords. On a shelf were a dozen or so helmets, painted white, together with cudgels, ironshod clubs and brass knuckledusters. Through one door we could look into the kitchen; through another into a corner of the gymnasium, where some young men in boiler-suits were practising *sūmō* and *jūdō*.

'I returned to political life in 1951,' Akao Bin began, 'after six years of imprisonment and exile. I found Japan changed, subdued and subservient to democratic methods. But this, I think, is only an interlude, a period of preparation. I am not a democrat; I am a Fascist—a Fascist of the Italian type. My aim is a *coup d'état*, and there is going to be a *coup d'état!*'[23]

Akao Bin is a lawyer in his early sixties, and for the last forty years he had been a political agitator by profession. At first he was an anarchist, after that a Socialist, and then, in the early 1930s, he discovered Fascism, a doctrine which he found congenial. After this he founded the *Dai Nihon Kōdō Kai* (Great Japan Imperial Way Association). In 1951, immediately after his 'rehabilitation', he started the *Dai Nihon Aikoku Tō* (Great Japan Patriots' Party), and in the following year, with the unofficial support of the former Conservative Premier Ashida Hitoshi, he founded the *Saigumbi Sokushin Remmei* (League for the Acceleration of Rearmament). But politics were not enough, and 'as an antidote to the confusion of the times' he presented Japan with a new form of Shintoism. He has undoubtedly been the most active of all the extremist leaders. His youthful disciples, trained in accordance with the principles of 'pure patriotism', are to be found everywhere. At Haneda Airport, thanking Foster Dulles for allowing Japan to rearm. In the Diet, protesting against the agreement with Moscow. On the streets, fighting with the *Zengakuren*, who are against nuclear tests. Outside the Sōhyō offices, throwing stones at trade unionists. Generally they go about in squads of thirty each; on special occasions by the hundreds.

For many years Akao Bin was pro-American and proud of having shaken hands with Foster Dulles, but today he has revised his ideas considerably. 'Asia,' he told us, 'is crumbling before the advance of Communism, because of the stupidity of the Americans and the impracticability of their ideas. Liberalism cannot stop Communism in a disturbed part of the world like this. To stop it we shall have to resort to Fascism again.' He knocked once or twice with his bony knuckles and two young men came running in with a large map. It was a map of Asia in 1942, when the Japanese Empire was in its heyday. The areas marked in red stretched from the frontiers of India to the Gilbert Islands, from Manchuria to Java. Akao Bin looked at the map with an air of satisfaction and said:

If Japan could once again become the leader of Asia and instil National Socialist ideas, I am sure that Moscow and Peking would shelve their plans of conquest. But the Americans don't trust us; they dole out arms to us and in the meantime Communism is winning hand over hand. Would you like an example? Eisenhower had to cancel his visit to Japan, but Gagarin was received here with all the honours. Remember what I am telling you. If Japan goes Communist, the whole of Asia is done for.

For a moment he remained silent, gazing at the map of the Japanese Empire with his large, wild eyes. Then he made a gesture of annoyance and said:

We have committed a whole series of unpardonable errors, and do you know why? In 1940 the Japanese let the soldiers do the thinking, instead of the theoreticians of Fascism, and they could not see who their real enemies were. Why were we so foolish as to attack the United States, when our declared enemy was Communism? We ought to have attacked Russia in 1941, while the Germans were advancing on Stalingrad. Instead of which we signed a non-aggression pact with Moscow, and with that we threw away any chance we had of winning the war.

With another gesture of irritation he dismissed the young men with the map of his imperial dreams. 'We shan't make the same mistake again,' he said.

When the day of the *coup d'état* comes, we shall have the military on our side, but it will be we who will make the decisions—we politicians. I can tell you in confidence that we are on the eve of great events. Here in Japan we are reliving the years before the advent of Hitler and Mussolini. Don't be too impressed by the moderate speeches in the Diet or by the show of strength that the trade unions and the left-wing parties are making. Everything is on the point of collapse, if it has not already collapsed. Only the façade is still standing. Because Japan has never been democratic and never will be. Japan is nationalistic, Fascist, Shintoist, imperialist. Japan is Japan.

Akao Bin took his left foot in his hands. It was covered with a much-worn striped sock, and he gazed at it ecstatically and stroked it, beneath the childish eyes, veiled by thick glasses, of the picture of the murderer of Asanuma. When we asked him a question, he gave a start, but he had not heard what we said and resumed the thread of his previous discourse. 'I am convinced that, faced with the Communist menace, the whole of Asia will become Fascist, and in the end she will find a great leader, another Hitler. And I am likewise sure that God in his providence has already caused this leader to be born among us and has endowed him with the character of a new Mohammed, a leader who combines the gifts of a man of action with the spiritual gifts of a prophet.' There was a brief pause, after which he added: 'In Japan that leader is myself. But I am still surrounded by incomprehension. They still depict me as an extremist, and I suffer, as Jesus Christ must have suffered, when I see that my people do not understand me. I suffer, and moreover I am compelled to live in the direst poverty.'

The jacket he was wearing, his threadbare shirt and his tie which looked like a piece of string, certainly did not give the impression of affluence, but outside in the yard stood three new trucks, with 'Gagarin, go home!' scrawled on their sides. Who had paid for those trucks? Who provided for the thirty young men who took turns at Akao Bin's headquarters? Who was financing the movement's monthly, the *Patriotic Review*? The Fascist leader made no reply to these questions; he digressed, denied receiving any subsidies, accused the Press, 'which is all Red', of boycotting him and reducing him to starvation. As soon as he could, he sheered away from this embarrassing topic and returned to the theme of his party's plans. 'We shall have,' he said, 'a society of the National Socialist type, with the Tenno at its centre. It will condemn the excesses both of Communism and of capitalism and will be profoundly religious, drawing its inspiration from Shintoism, Jesus Christ, Buddha, Confucius and Mohammed. Like the Communists, we have chosen red as our symbol, but our red is that of the glorious flag of the Rising Sun.'

After the death of Asanuma, Akao Bin enjoyed a brief moment of popularity and rose to the top of the scale in the list of extremist *oyabuns*, but at the 1960 election he was no more successful than he had been in the past and did not obtain enough votes to ensure him a seat in the Diet. Like Jesus Christ, he was grieved by this lack of understanding, all the more so because he perceived that his 'factory of heroes' was bringing him very little money. When his sorrows become too much for him, this manufacturer of heroes seats himself at the spinet, summons his young men, and together they sing songs like 'Our Gallant Soldiers' and 'The Hills of Manchuria', beneath the somewhat ironical gaze of the protomartyr, Otoya Yamaguchi.

Before he left to keep an urgent appointment, Akao Bin insisted on our spending some time with his young men, 'the last real patriots in Japan'. Despite their rather forbidding appearance, the patriots were quite ready to talk. They were students who had interrupted their studies, unemployed workmen, ex-soldiers or small artisans whose businesses had failed. From what they told us we could see that they were either malcontents, exhibitionists or fanatics. Most of them came from the provinces, and though they felt the fascination of the great city, they hated its ostentatious wealth and its lax morals and they despised the selfishness of the workmen and their political ideas, which were 'untraditional'. Conversely, they like discipline, obligations, duties, and the loyalty demanded by the ancient and more recent codes of behaviour, such as *Bushido*, the *Kōdō* and the *Kokutai no Hongi*, which uphold the dogma of the Emperor's infallibility and stress the responsibility of the group rather than that of the individual, self-discipline and the exaltation of frugality, respect for teachers and the glorification of warriors. They are willing to accept a hard and Spartan life as part of the doctrine of passive obedience which was so skilfully exploited by Japanese militarism during the 1930s as being 'the foundation of national greatness'.

During the year they spend under Akao Bin's roof they never drink wine and never go near a woman. 'Rise with the sun' is the first commandment in their decalogue. 'Hasten to sweep the floor' is the second. 'Kneel with your face towards the Imperial Palace and say a long prayer' is what the third enjoins. 'Obey the will of the Emperor at every hour of the day' is the fourth. Even if they wanted to escape carrying out their duties, they could hardly do so, for the walls of the huts are covered with exhortations to fulfil them. Then comes the time when they go down to the gymnasium and by practising *sumō*, *kendō* or *jūdō* try to keep their weight down to the ideal level of 150 pounds. After breakfast at seven o'clock the members disperse, some take one of the trucks and make a propaganda tour, while others go to school or to work. In the evening they meet again for a frugal meal, after which they play *go* or *shōgi*, or sing songs round the spinet. At nine o'clock sharp the lights are turned out and silence reigns in the precincts of the Shinto temple. Only Akao Bin is entitled to infringe this cloistral rule.

The search for unity

The chief weakness of the Japanese extreme Right has been its failure to form a united front. Plenty of attempts have been made, especially by the more consistent and active groups, but with little success. The first efforts date from November 1951, when Fukuda Soken, editor of the first anti-Communist journal to appear in Japan after the war (the *Bōkyō Shimbun*), sponsored a meeting of 150 representatives of the extreme Right. Shortly afterwards, Akao Bin took an active part in organizing the *Zen-Nihon Aikokusha Dantai Kyōgikai* (All-Japan Council of Patriotic Societies), but not until May 1954, after conferences in Mito and Osaka, was the *Kyūkoku Kokumin Sōrengō* (National Salvation People's General Federation) formed, which has so far been the extreme Right's chief unifying force.

The various groups which joined the *Sōrengō* reached complete agreement on certain fundamental aims, such as the need for rearmament, the destruction of the Communist Party and its allies, and the restoration of full powers to the Mikado. But from the operational standpoint the front existed only on paper, since none of the groups was prepared to sacrifice its own identity, its own leader or its own methods. During the discussions, the conflict between 'pure nationalists' and 'National Socialists' cropped up once again—the very factor that had prevented unification in the 1930s—and there was considerable friction between the old and the new generations. It is, in fact, significant, that the famous extremist Inoue Nisshō ended his autobiography by appealing, not to the masses, but to himself. Although he was one of the pillars of the *Sōrengō*, Nisshō obviously did not believe in large parties, preferring to rely on the daggers of the super-patriots which were sure to reach their targets and on his own talents as consummate conspirator. 'The time for strength has come,' he wrote; 'in terms of Shinto, this is a time not for the jewel and the mirror, but for the sword . . . Now Japan is free from the occupation and I, too, have had my liberty restored. Now things will begin to happen! I am fully conscious of my own nature as a child of revolution. When I observe conditions in Japan and in the world, I feel confident that there is still a final service for me to perform.'[24]

Collaboration between the extreme Right and the militarist parties also proved difficult and yielded scant fruits. Although each of these two forces clamoured for full-scale rearmament, reproached the trade unions for their 'unpatriotic attitude' and the younger generation for its 'selfishness', and though they both wanted to restore the Emperor's powers, their alliance was one of convenience rather than of mutual sympathy. The Japanese extremists could not forget that in the 1930s, after they had opened the way for the army with their daggers, they had been pushed aside, discredited or even brought before the courts. Conversely, the *gambatsu* thought that these nationalists by profession were all fanatics, visionaries or opportunists. It should, however, be added that, despite the absence of any mutual esteem and the fact that they were virtually rivals, collaboration between these two tendencies has increased during these last years of slow but systematic restoration.

It was the 'reverse course' that helped the right-wing extremists and brought the militarists to the fore again. The gravity of this policy cannot be denied when we remember that in Japan it was the army that was mainly responsible for the excesses of the last war (and for the defeat itself), and not the one-party system, as was the case in Germany and Italy. The rehabilitation, by April 1952, of 116,753 regular officers out of a total of 122,235 who were 'purged', enabled all military men up to the rank of colonel to join the new army, which two years later had a percentage of 'compromised' officers as high as 24·4, while in the navy the percentage was nearly 80. When they found themselves banned from serving in the new army, many senior officers decided to try their luck in the Diet—for example, Ugaki Kazushige, Tsuji Masanobu, Mazaki Katsuji, Hoshina Zenshirō and Matsumura Shūitsu—and were elected with big majorities. Others, like Colonel Hattori Takushirō, founded 'institutes', which under cover of doing research into the last war in reality fanned the flames of revenge, supported in this task by the big ex-Servicemen's associations, such as the *Nihon Gōyū Remmei* (Japan Native-Friend League), and pro-rearmament societies like the *Butoku Kai* (Martial Virtues Association) and the *Nihon Aikyō Remmei* (Japan Fatherland League), all headed by former generals or admirals who had compromised themselves under the imperial régime.

Although the new Japanese army is as strong as it was in 1931 on the eve of the invasion of Manchuria, and has a far greater fighting potential, for the time being it is controlled by civilians, who do not seem inclined to hand over the command to the military, even when their aspirations are more or less identical. This control by civilians, particularly noticeable in the sphere of moral guidance of the 'citizens in uniform', annoys old fire-eaters like the former admiral Hasegawa Kiyoshi. 'Under our constitution,' he once said, 'it is impossible for the armed forces to have the proper spirit. The men today are treated like civilians. They can't act like soldiers and sailors. No one wants to die. But soldiers and sailors must die for their country in an emergency.'[25] Not only do they not want to die, but it would seem that they have also lost all taste for politics and conspiracies. In 1962, when a group of officers, financed by a big industrialist and (it is whispered) by the military Junta in South Korea, tried to seize power, the army merely stood by and the plot was a dismal failure.

Despite its failure to form a united front and establish firmer links with militarist circles, the Japanese extreme Right shows plenty of vitality and aggressive spirit. Even the Chief of Police, Akira Natano, felt bound to admit this after the unsuccessful *coup d'état* in 1962. 'The Left talks a lot,' he said, 'but the Right acts.' It acted, as we have seen, either in its own interests or on behalf of third parties, and was willing to undertake the humblest tasks. Its field of action may seem to have been limited, but this was due to the fact that much of its programme was realized by the Conservative government, which from 1946 on, except for one brief interlude of a few months, was in power all the time. Anxious to lead Japan back to traditional ways and to restore the old discipline and moral code, the Liberal Democrats soon showed that they were more reactionary than the Conservatives, especially as regards the importance they attached to factions such as those headed by the war-criminal Kishi and ultra-nationalists like Satō Eisaku and Ishi. Rearmament, the reconstitution of the monopolistic groups, the control of education, the restoration of certain powers to the police, and the reintroduction of certain festivals and ceremonies having a nationalistic character, were among the 'conquests' achieved by the Conservative government in defiance of the democratic constitution. Proof of this was given by the Minister of Education, Kiyose Ichirō, when he boldly declared in the Diet that Constitution Day (3 May) was 'not a day of glory, but of national humiliation',[26] while the Liberal Democrats adopted for propaganda purposes a song which ran as follows:

> So long as this Constitution rules,
> Unconditional surrender is our lot.
> 'Save Mac's Constitution,'
> The General's lackeys cry.
> But the star of our homeland will rise again,
> And so will the spirit of our country.[27]

The Sōka Gakkai

'. . . If the Conservatives are able to retain control without the help of the ultra-nationalists, it will be probably impossible for the new "secret societies" to attain the status of their pre-war predecessors.'[28] In these few words Hugh Borton aptly describes the arbitrary powers assumed by the Conservatives and the servile attitude of the extreme right wing, and it remained true as far as events down to 1959 were concerned. In other words, until the appearance (or perhaps we ought to call it reappearance) of the *Sōka Gakkai* which (although students of the subject do not include it among the definitely extreme movements), began to assert itself, thanks to its messianic and ultra-nationalist background, as the most authentic expression of Japanese neo-Fascism. We must remember that the *Sōka Gakkai* has not been relegated to the fringe areas like the other 'sects' or 'secret societies', but has held seats in Parliament since 1959 and has been steadily gaining ground, with the result that it is now the third largest political organization in the country after the Conservatives and Socialists.

Founded in 1930 by two primary-school teachers, Tsunesaburo Makiguchi and Josei Toda, the *Sōka Gakkai* (Value-Creating Academy) was in its early years a purely religious movement, just like the other sects drawing their inspiration from the doctrines of the Buddhist priest Nichiren. It quarrelled with the State religion—Shintoism—and with the Emperor who was its supreme head, and it was banned in 1942 by General Tōjō's militarist government. A year later all the members of its headquarters staff were sent to prison 'for insulting the Emperor and attempting to disturb the public peace'. As a result of the bad treatment and privations to which he was subjected, Makiguchi died on 18 November 1944 in a cell of the Sugamo prison, while Josei Toda was released a month before the Japanese surrender and was able to get his party on its feet again with the aid of an ambitious slogan—'If during the next seven years we do not succeed in getting 750,000 families to join our association, you need not worry about my funeral; you can just scatter my ashes in Tokyo Bay.' This goal was achieved in 1957, after which the rate of growth increased even more rapidly, so that in May 1964 the *Sōka Gakkai* could boast that it had 13 million adherents and predict that by 1967 36 million Japanese would own a copy of the *Gohonzon*, a book of maxims by Nichiren which was presented to every new convert.

What do the Japanese of the 'transistor age' find in the doctrines of this 'Value-Creating Academy' which draws its inspiration from a Buddhist reformer who lived 700 years ago? Surrounding itself with an aura of mystery, the *Sōka Gakkai* sets out not only to alleviate the sufferings of the Japanese people by preaching the philosophy of the *Nammyokorenge-kyo* (supreme mystic law of the lotus), but also to spread the same gospel among the other unhappy peoples of the world 'oppressed by Marxism, democracy and false and inferior religions'.[29] Naïve, but at the same time dangerous, it appeals to all, whether they are Japanese or not, to the oppressed and depressed, to the weary and the poor, to the sick and to those whose lives have been failures, offering to each one of them the comforts of the 'only true religion in the world', the only one that can solve every spiritual and material problem.

In other words it intends to fill the 'moral vacuum' which it maintains has been created in Japan by the introduction of democratic reforms at American instigation—reforms which are foreign to Japanese tradition. At the same time it returns to the nationalist-Fascist theme of the 1930s, the *Hakkō Ichiu* ('the eight corners of the world under one roof') and promises the Japanese that if they follow the doctrines of Nichiren they will become masters of the world, as they unsuccessfully tried to become during the last, sanguinary, war. The claim that it is universal is, in fact, one of the outstanding features of this mystical neo-Fascism, which wants to destroy all other 'false and outdated religions' and all other 'putrescent ideologies', in order to achieve its supreme aim of dominating the whole world.

The *Sōka Gakkai* exploits the bewilderment of the masses, especially in the country districts; it encourages their deep-seated affection for the old national discipline; it revives the repressed ambitions of millions of office-workers who still remember the days of great victories, of the Empire and the 'sphere of co-prosperity' as the best and most glorious in their lives; and it fans the hatred they have for everything foreign. In the Diet, its representatives attack the Conservatives for thinking only of the population's material needs, and at the same time they attack the Left, accusing it of atheism and defeatism, and announce that what Japan needs is spiritual guidance and a discipline which the existing political parties are unable to provide and only the *Sōka Gakkai* can offer. Officially it claims to be a religious movement and it deliberately nominates candidates only for seats in the Senate, in which it has fifteen seats, maintaining that the Lower Chamber is too 'political' and too 'unspiritual'. This, however, is merely part of a wait-and-see policy, which serves to conceal the real power of the association during its period of maximum growth. In May 1964 it announced that in future it would also nominate candidates for the Lower House and did actually put up thirty-two. Its claim to be purely a religious body is in any case absurd. Not only has it always expressed its opinions clearly on matters of home policy, taking the side of the anti-Communist and anti-working-class factions, but it has even criticized the Conservative government's handling of foreign policy, insisting on firmer and more energetic measures being taken to secure the return of the Ryukyu archipelago (including Okinawa) to Japan, as well as the Kurile and Bonin Islands, while it also supports a *rapprochement* to those Asiatic peoples who are 'more willing to listen to the Buddhist teachings of Nichiren'. In November 1964 the *Sōka Gakkai* took a decisive step and founded the *Komeitō* (Honest Government Party), the leadership of which was entrusted to Koji Harashima. But since the Japanese constitution prohibits political activities on the part of religious bodies, the *Sōka Gakkai* announced that the *Komeitō* was to be considered as an organization completely independent of the Buddhist sect, thus resorting to yet another expedient in order to camouflage its startling expansion.

Despite its mysticism, which is nothing new, its complexes, its tedious liturgical ceremonies and its veneration of one of Nichiren's teeth, which is preserved in the temple at Taisekiji where it glitters like a pearl, at least 80,000 Japanese join the *Sōka Gakkai* every month and a vast campaign of proselytism is being carried out in all the countries of Asia as well as among the Japanese living in the United States and in the Latin American republics. The technique of conversion definitely smacks of intimidation and terrorism. 'If you are converted, you will enjoy good health, prosperity and happiness. Try it and you will see.' That is what the missionaries in search of proselytes say. 'If you refuse, you risk a catastrophe.' The first thing a convert is called upon to do is to destroy the altars or images pertaining to his former religion. Subsequently he is initiated in the Nichiren sect's shrine situated nearest to his home, and during this ceremony he is presented with a copy of the *Gohonzon*, which he is told to venerate and keep in his home on a special altar known as a *butsudan*.

From then on he becomes part and parcel of an organization with a typically militarist structure and is expected to 'contribute personally' to the propagation of the movement's ideas by arranging 'neighbourhood meetings' in his home after he has finished work, during which he must try to obtain new converts by reading passages from the *Gosho*, Nichiren's 'collected works'. As soon as the sect has gained a footing in a quarter or village, the enrolment of the population begins, in accordance with the former Nazi system of 'blocks'. Fifteen families form a 'squad'; six squads make a 'company'; ten companies, a 'district'; thirty districts, a 'region'; and a given number of regions constitutes a 'chapter-general', answerable directly to the headquarters in Tokyo, where the president (or commander-in-chief) has the last say. The *Sōka Gakkai* also runs a youth movement, which is modelled on the *Hitler-Jugend* and the Fascist *Gioventù Italiana del Littorio*; a university section; a research section; a cultural section; an 'advisory' section, and a control section. Subscriptions and the sale of altars and other objects bring in an annual income which in 1963, for example, amounted to $8\frac{1}{2}$ million dollars. And lastly, once a year the *Sōka Gakkai* organizes a national congress, which is attended by tens of thousands of members and ends with a mass rally in the Tokyo stadium and a parade of members of the youth movement, who march past the platform on which the president and commander-in-chief, Daisaku Ikeda, is standing.

Daisaku Ikeda is thirty-five years old and became head of the movement on 3 May 1960, after the death of Josei Toda. Before that he had been a member of the youth movement. He has emphasized the association's militaristic tendencies and encouraged *shakubuku* (compulsory conversion). He told the correspondent of an American magazine that he intended to 'destroy the corrupt elements in Japanese politics, who ignore the individual and think only of their own interests'. When asked for his opinion on other religions, he replied: '*Sōka Gakkai* leaders and I, myself, have thoroughly studied and researched all the religions of the world. We found them all to be wanting in one way or another . . . false, too mystical, obsolete.'[30] Despite the society's remarkable success and the suspicion that many Conservative and even Socialist members of the Diet have secretly joined it, the *Sōka Gakkai* has many enemies and the democratic Japanese newspapers describe it as Fascist, militaristic, fanatical, sacrilegious, ultra-nationalist, dangerous, intolerant and aggressive. The vice-chancellor of the Risshō University, Shobun Kubota, was particularly severe in his judgement:

> The principle of Buddhism is restraint of men's desires as regards sex, gluttony, riches and ambition, but the *Sōka Gakkai* promises to satisfy all these desires. It exploits the weaknesses of mankind as a vehicle for its own expansion. It has the same characteristics as Nazism and is, in short, a corrupt form of Buddhism.[31]

As long ago as 1958 Morris described it as 'a form of anti-leftist nationalism that could exert a very important influence, especially in a period of economic crisis',[32] while Michael Edwardes thought that its political aims were obscure, but that it had a conservative tendency and might represent an unwelcome element in Japanese political life.[33] Until a short time ago, the *Sōka Gakkai* was of interest only to specialists, but recently it has become known to the European and American public thanks to certain television programmes which have stressed the Fascist and nationalistic tendencies of this 'Value-Creating Academy'. And on the eve of the Japanese general election in the autumn of 1963 *Le Monde* devoted part of a leading article to it:

> Interest will also be concentrated on the number of votes the extremist parties obtain—not only the Communists of the Left, but also a curious right-wing organization which for the last two years has been very active, the *Sōka Gakkai*. This is a Buddhist sect and at the same time a party, a kind of politico-religious Poujadism. Its success shows that despite the country's prosperity, areas of discontent and frustration still exist which, if no remedy can be found, might become propitious soil for the rebirth of a Japanese neo-Fascism.[34]

This is all the more likely because democracy, which was imposed upon Japan by decree in 1945, has been unable to take root in soil still permeated by authoritarianism. 'In spite of defeat, occupation, political and social reforms, and technological progress,' Hessell Tiltman wrote,

> Japan will continue to be a distinctive, racially conscious, traditionalist society . . . The Japanese are again flocking to Shinto shrines on festival days. Paternalism continues to be the predominant note in industry . . . Loss of 'face' is still a fate to be avoided at all costs. Neither the new freedoms nor ten years of double-dyed democracy has changed the intricate and intimate social patterns and fundamental thought-processes . . . The Japanese continue to be unrepentantly Japanese.[35]

A serious crisis which Japan might well find it impossible to avoid in the course of the 1960s, combined with the pressure exerted by the old reactionary forces and the new pseudo-spiritual and traditionalist movements, might drive her into new authoritarian experiments, and this time Fascism might assume a new aspect, less violent and less aggressive than in the past—for example, the mystical aspect of the *Sōka Gakkai*. That Buddhist sect which has managed to transform itself into a large party (something that no other extreme right-wing party has ever succeeded in doing, either before or after the Second World War) and, on the occasion of the elections for the Senate in 1962, sent its supporters to the polls marching in military formation. A sect which, under the pretext of filling with its own gospel the spiritual voids typical of all post-war periods, is really seeking to drag Japan back to the medieval tyranny of the 'code of behaviour' propounded by the Tokugawa Shoguns.[36]

15   The United States of America

The Dallas 'incident'

We do not know who first coined the expression 'Dallas, the city of hate'. It certainly caught on and is still used by people all over the world when they discuss John F. Kennedy's assassination, while the Texan city feels that the words are now indelibly branded on its flesh. The first to resent this were the 238 members of the Dallas Citizens' Council,[1] who have ruled the city since 1937 by pulling invisible strings behind the scenes. Bankers, industrialists, oil and insurance magnates (there is not a single intellectual among them, not one lawyer or doctor), for the last twenty-five years they have managed to control all the corridors of power, to preserve the city's good name and to spread the legend that, although the inhabitants may be forceful or even brutal, they are nevertheless loyal and honest. But the 'incident' on 22 November 1963 inflicted what may perhaps prove to be irreparable harm on this, the richest city of the South West. Accusations have been levelled, not only against its police, its judiciary and information services, but even against its climate (which is described as deadly) and its people (who are said to be crazy and intolerant extremists).

Once the storm had blown over, the leading men in Dallas tried in various ways to restore the city's image. Stanley Marcus, owner of what is commonly known as 'the millionaire's emporium' (where you can buy the most expensive and curious things, from a two-seater submarine to a Chinese junk), thought that the best way would be to appeal to the Texans to be tolerant, and his message filled half a page in the city's two dailies. In the course of it he said: 'This community has suffered from a spirit of absolutism in recent years . . . The rejection of this spirit of "absolutism" and the acceptance *and* insistence by *all* citizens of differing points of view seem to us to be essential for the future health of our community.'[2] Other citizens, overcoming the dislike they had always felt for Kennedy, suggested erecting a monument to him, or at least a tablet on the spot where he was killed, but they immediately encountered the opposition of the city's 238 guardians, who expressed their willingness to bear the whole cost of the memorial, but wanted it to be erected in Washington, not in Dallas. Accustomed to solving every problem with money, they would have been ready to build a temple of solid gold, provided it was as far away as possible from Dallas, where the Kennedys had never been very welcome.

These, so far as we know, were the only steps taken by Dallas to placate the wrath of the nation. On the other hand the attitude which led to Dallas being called 'the city of hate' has not changed in the slightest. Dallas is still the Mecca of dyed-in-the-wool conservative preachers like Billy James Hargis and exponents of the near-Fascist John Birch Society like Senator John Rousselot. The retired General Edwin Walker still flies the American flag upside-down to remind his fellow-citizens that the White House is still full of Communists. Haroldson Lafayette Hunt, the richest man in the world, is still called the 'Angel of the Right' and still finances the ultra-conservative movements. In the streets and in the theatres accusations are still being levelled against America's more liberal-minded men, together with demands for the dismissal of Chief Justice Earl Warren, for the eviction of the United Nations from New York, for the severing of diplomatic relations with the Soviet Union and, in the words of Barry Goldwater, for the waging of a struggle 'not for peace, but for total victory'—in other words for a preventive war. Certain Protestant ministers have even gone so far as to maintain in their sermons that the murder of Kennedy, deplorable though it may have been, was an act of God, because Kennedy was a Catholic President.[3]

Although Dallas remains a dangerous hotbed of hatred and the stronghold of the Radical Right, there are many people who believe that it is wrong to lay the whole blame for the tragic end of the thirty-fifth President of the United States on this proud and prosperous 'Frontier City'. Among them is the illustrious historian Henry Steele Commager, who tried to discover the real causes of the violence which from time to time crops up in American society and gives rise to misgivings. 'No, the causes of our sickness,' he wrote, 'are not to be found in the history of the frontier, or even of slavery. They must be sought rather in our society as a whole, and not in a particular section or group.'[4] For Commager the present wave of violence must be ascribed to the long practice of war, the indiscriminate bombing of German and Japanese cities, the nuclear tests, the psychosis of the Cold War, the vanity, arrogance and feeling of superiority that Americans display in their dealings with other peoples, the cruel myths (e.g. the extermination of the Red Indians) which Hollywood has been cultivating for three generations. Thus, for the author of *The American Mind* it was not Dallas that killed the man of the 'New Frontier', but the violence which is subtly undermining the whole country.

The famous columnist Walter Lippmann is of a different opinion.

> What happened in Dallas could, to be sure, have happened in another city. But it must be said that the murder of the President was not the first act of political violence in that city but one in a series. The man who is now the President of the United States was manhandled by his fellow-Texans. The man who represents the United States at the United Nations was spat upon. In this atmosphere of political violence lived the President's murderer.[5]

Dallas, in fact, had begun to interest the journalists about a dozen years before, when it offered full moral and financial support to Senator Joe McCarthy, who was organizing the biggest 'witch-hunt' America had ever seen. When the myth of the 'Grand Inquisitor' crumbled, Dallas undertook to support the John Birch Society, which had inherited the legacy of the Senator for Wisconsin, to resuscitate the Ku-Klux-Klan, to finance the 'National Indignation Convention' which was bringing pressure to bear on Congress to stop all aid to Tito, the 'Texans for America' who wanted to lynch the Chief Justice, the racist 'Texas Aryans' and dozens of other extremist organizations. It was at Dallas—as Lippmann reminded his readers—that Lyndon Johnson had been insulted and struck three years before. And it was from Dallas that General Edwin Walker began his march on Oxford in the hope of stopping integration in the schools. It was in Dallas that the shops owned by Jews were daubed with swastikas in April 1963. It was in Dallas that Madame Nhu received a triumphal welcome. And once again, it was in Dallas that Adlai Stevenson had been assaulted by bands of extremists carrying placards with 'Death to the United Nations' written upon them.

It is therefore not surprising that on 22 November 1963, the day of John Kennedy's visit to Dallas, the city was deluged with handbills bearing the portrait of the President (full-face and profile, as in the files of criminals), with the heading 'Wanted for Treason'.[6] It is not surprising that the ultra-conservative *Dallas Morning News* should have sold a whole page to the extreme right-wing 'American Fact-finding Committee', which filled it with insults and threats to Kennedy. Nor is it surprising that the children in the Dallas schools clapped when they heard that the President had been killed. Hatred had slowly and inexorably taken possession of the whole city. Hatred for the man who was leading Americans towards a new frontier, towards a goal which meant greater social justice, equality between the races and the abolition of privileges. 'Why are you crying, Mommy?' said a little girl in Dallas on that tragic 22 November, showing in what an atmosphere of tension she had been brought up. 'Why are you crying when you and Daddy always said you hated him?'[7]

It was a hatred that lasted even after Kennedy's death, because it was a hatred that intended to destroy a whole policy of renewal. The hatred of the provincial, isolationist, racialist, fundamentalist and reactionary America for the more liberal America which, as Kennedy intended to say in the speech he never made in Dallas, must 'practice what it preaches about equal rights and social justice'. A hatred that was cultivated, exalted and given a blessing, as is shown by this passage from a letter published by the *Houston Chronicle*: 'Yes, there is a deep, burning hatred in Dallas, and I pray to God that it may continue and spread throughout the entire nation until the Communist malignancy which is threatening all of our lives is completely destroyed.'[8] For the Dallas extremists this malignancy was everywhere; it had already invaded the White House, the Supreme Court, the halls of Congress and the Palace of the United Nations, and the preacher Fred Schwarz prophesied that within ten years it would have covered the whole of the American continent and stifled all liberty.

It was a hatred bordering on frenzy, and often fanned by lying propaganda. A hatred that could have armed the hand of Lee Oswald or perhaps of some other man—the name of the assassin is of no importance in the framework of the story. 'It may well be,' Pierre and Renée Gosset wrote,

> that a conspiracy will be revealed. But the climate we found in Dallas is more deadly than any conspiracy. If it was written in the book of destiny that John Fitzgerald Kennedy would die by an assassin's hand, it was quite logical that it should have happened here. A psychoanalyst would say that in the recesses of its heart Dallas had already killed him.[9]

Dallas—where reactionaries are called conservatives, conservatives are deemed to be moderates, moderates are mistaken for liberals, and the real liberals are described as progressives and therefore suspected of being Communists—thus threw a new light, with its 'incident', on the problem of the American Radical Right, which for the last forty years has been trying by every possible means—from intolerance to racialism, from contempt for democratic institutions to plans for the introduction of emergency regulations—to halt America, to drag her back to the 1920s, to the days before the New Deal.

The offensive of the Radical Right

Never since the days of McCarthyism has right-wing conservatism made such rapid and striking progress in the United States as during the last few years. According to a document published by the American Federation of Labor and Congress of Industrial Organizations, there exists a real 'threat from the Radical Right' which is trying in every possible way to 'subvert the Constitution of the United States'. Like every other American phenomenon, there is no secrecy about it. A list of American extremist movements appears in a reference-book published in Los Angeles, called the *First National Directory of Rightist Groups*, which anyone can buy. From it we learn that the number of groups has doubled since 1952 and there are now more than 2,000 of them, including neo-Fascist, racialist, segregationist and semi-military movements.

According to Professor Alan F. Westin of Columbia University in 1961 alone this subversive front received from industrialists (and in particular from the Texan oil-magnates) contributions equivalent to about 6,000 million Italian lire, though other students of the American Right put the figure even higher. On the basis of such data many observers think that the Radical Right is today far better organized and more influential than it was in the days of McCarthyism or in the ten years of fierce opposition to the reforms of the New Deal. Peter Edson, the columnist of the Scripps-Howard chain, goes so far as to say that 37 per cent (162) of the members of the House of Representatives and 25 per cent (25) of the Senators today support the theories of the Radical Right.

The first signs of a revival appeared in 1958, and the progress of the Radical Right became more rapid after the advent of John F. Kennedy, the presentation of his programme of reforms and the change in the attitude of the United States towards the Soviet Union in its painstaking quest for peace. From that time on the 'respectable

Right', which had always pretended that it would have nothing to do with the 'lunatic fringe', broke with tradition and entered the lists, encouraging the Radical Right and financing its shady activities. The reconstitution of the right-wing front has also been helped once again by the distrust of everything new and of any extension of America's involvement in international affairs. Once again the mainsprings of extremist sentiment have been isolationism, an exaggerated nationalism (invariably accompanied by hatred of Europe), ethnical prejudices, religious and atavistic phobias, the fundamentalist revolt against modernism, dislike for trade unionism and the progressive ideas of intellectuals, and the centralization policy adopted by the Federal government.

In the United States, Rightist campaigns have hitherto always coincided with periods of economic depression, delicate moments in international relations or outbreaks of racial violence. But during the last forty years the reactionary movements have chosen other pretexts and set themselves other aims, manœuvring their forces in accordance with the demands of the situation.[10] In the 1920s the ideology of the Radical Right was exenophobic, and stress was consequently laid on ethnical and religious questions. Those were the days when Thomas E. Watson inveighed against Catholics and Negroes and wrote the same kind of incitements to violence that brought the editor of *Der Stürmer*, Julius Streicher, to the gallows in Nuremberg.[11] They were the days when Edward Y. Clarke was reorganizing the second Ku-Klux-Klan and in the name of the purest Americanism was urging his 5 million hooded disciples to defend America with fiery crosses, with kidnappings, the whip and the rope, and with tar and feathers.

After the big slump, the 1930s produced even more extremist movements, led by Messiahs and demagogues of every description. On 31 January 1933, the day after Hitler seized power, William Dudley Pelley founded the Legion of American Silvershirts, explaining that he had a mission to save America, 'as Mussolini and his Blackshirts saved Italy and Hitler and his Brownshirts saved Germany'.[12] In the same way, George E. Deatherage, 'Honourable Grand Commander of the Knights of the White Camellia', tried to unite all the Christian (i.e. anti-Semitic) groups into one organization with a fiery swastika as its emblem. They were the years during which Huey P. Long, Governor of Louisiana, launched the slogan 'Every man a King' and an emphatically 'populist' programme the sole aim of which was to open the way to the White House for himself. As Leopold Kohr says, Long was a figure as hateful as Hitler and had the same totalitarian aspirations as the German dictator.[13] They were the days when the Reverend Gerald B. Winrod made frequent visits to Germany in the hope of finding support for his anti-Semitic and anti-Catholic ideas; when the 'Sentinels of the American Republic', behind the screen of an ardent and patriotic anti-Communism, were conducting their campaign against trade unions, social reform and other New Deal measures, just as the more moderate but more powerful American Liberty League was doing.[14] They were the days when, from his church of the 'Little Flower' at Royal Oak in Michigan, Father Charles E. Coughlin spoke over the radio to $3\frac{1}{2}$ million listeners, for the most part workmen, labourers and unemployed, urging them, in language padded with patriotic, moralistic and socialistic slogans, to rise against the Wall Street bankers, the Jews and the intellectuals. Often described as a kind of proletarian Fascism, Coughlinism, as Francis Biddle points out, 'followed the same tactics of violent anti-Semitism popularized by Hitler's Brownshirts',[15] sided with Franco during the Spanish civil war, supported the Axis Powers and, even after Pearl Harbor, maintained that an international conspiracy of Jews was preparing to hand America over to Communism.[16]

The 1940s, partially monopolized by the Second World War, did not witness the birth of any Rightist movements worth mentioning. Joe McCarthy did not appear upon the scene until the early 1950s, after the *coup d'état* in Prague, the Berlin blockade, the war in Korea and the leakage of atomic secrets from the United States had created an atmosphere peculiarly suitable for the launching of any kind of 'crusade'. All that was necessary was to dig out the old themes of isolationism, and exploit the discontent and fears of the working classes and the urge towards conformism among the new immigrants. For four years, with the aid of repressive laws and by adopting the same weapons of intimidation as Goebbels, McCarthy poisoned the atmosphere in the United States, denouncing thousands of people as 'bad security risks', urging his followers to neutralize the more progressive elements in the country and describing as 'dogs to be brought down' the 25,000 members of the American Communist Party. 'According to a Gallup poll, in 1954 50 per cent of the American people approved and 29 per cent disapproved of McCarthyism, with 21 per cent expressing no opinion.' Commenting on these startling figures, Hans J. Morgenthau wrote: 'It will not do to minimize McCarthyism as a temporary aberration . . . in truth the American people were no more victimized by McCarthy than were the German people by Hitler; both followed their tempters with abandon.'[17]

The last stage of the Rightist campaign is still in progress and, as we have already said, it became more pronounced in the early 1960s, after Kennedy had been elected President and had defined the aims of his 'New Frontier'. This is the last desperate effort of a coalition made up of heterogeneous elements, which we shall examine in the following pages, and although it gives grounds for apprehension, appeals to sordid interests, exaggerates the dangers and creates an atmosphere of collective hysteria, it has not succeeded in producing any shifting of opinion sufficient to make the formation of a new party possible—that third party for which the American Right has always longed. 'It is relatively easy to build a new extremist movement in this country,' says Seymour Martin Lipset, 'but it is difficult if not impossible to build a party.'[18] For the simple reason that it is impossible to unify the 2,000 Rightist groups, whose leaders are notoriously incompetent and continually quarrelling among themselves, while the bulk of their supporters come from different social levels, with different interests and aims.

Although he was aware of the weakness of the American Radical Right, Fred J. Cooke ended a long study of American extremism with these words:

> Let us be clear about this: the face of America that emerges from the portrait of the Radical Right in 1962 is *not* the face of fascism as we have known it in Europe. But unmistakably it is a face bearing the marks of a sickness that could develop into fascism. The denigration of democracy, the demand for conformity and the attempt to outlaw the heretic, a patriotism pitched at the level of chauvinism, the faith that military might, rather than diplomacy, can assure our international goals—these are the marks of the illness.[19]

The man on horseback

For forty years the American Right has been waiting for a Messiah. For forty years it has been looking for a man with all the qualifications needed in a 'saviour of the country'; he must be strong, he must be full of faith, and he must lead the nation mounted upon a white horse. The American Right, which made fun of Roosevelt's wheel-chair and accused Kennedy of governing from the tricycle of his daughter Caroline, thought that it had found the 'man on a white horse' in the person of the demagogue Huey Long, later in Senator Robert Taft, then in the 'Proconsul' Douglas MacArthur, and finally in the Grand Inquisitor, Joe McCarthy. But all these intrepid horsemen were thrown off before they had even started their triumphal cavalcade.

Despite these crushing reverses, the Radical Right has not given up hope. In the last few years it has turned its eyes on another man, the Republican Senator Barry Goldwater of Arizona, who, in its opinion, possesses all the talents of the previous idols rolled into one. Goldwater, who was nominated as Republican candidate for the White House in the summer of 1964 by the Los Angeles Convention, is a man just over fifty, tall, athletic, a first-rate pilot of jet-aircraft, a former Major-General in the Air Force Reserve, a writer of books and a columnist, and a good speaker and business-man. To him the American journalists applied adjectives such as sensational, remarkable, bold, energetic, jet-propelled; or con-versely, barefaced, hysterical, mad and apocalyptic. He is a man whom the conservatives in the northern States like, and the old reactionaries of the Deep South like him, too. A convinced con-servative and an uncompromising man, who told the Senate in 1957 that he was 'happy to note today that the word "modern" has disappeared from the language of the Republican Party'.[20]

His world, in fact, looks back to the past. At times it has seemed as though his ambition was to restore the America of the 1920s, before the reforms of the New Deal came into force; or perhaps even to bring back the America of 1911, before Wilson and Federal taxes; or even the America of 1898, before the days of Theodore Roosevelt. Barry Goldwater is, in fact, the interpreter of the policy of those who do not love the modern America and, as a counterblast to Kennedy's 'New Frontier', he offers them an older frontier, one which will please the little ordinary men of the Far and Middle West, the new rich of the South who feel that they are threatened by the fiscal policy of the Federal State, and a few groups of military men who would like to keep the civilians under their thumb. Using an apt metaphor, *The Nation* wrote that if Kennedy and Goldwater reached the final of the United States presidential stakes, it would be a contest between the twentieth and the nine-teenth century, between two worlds, between two diametrically opposed conceptions.

This new hero of Protestant America's conservatism and

puritanism is—note the paradox—the grandson of a Jewish haber-
dasher who migrated from a little Polish ghetto to California about
the middle of the last century. Big Mike Goldwasser was a restless
man, who loved novelty and adventure. When, in 1860, people
began talking about Arizona and its gold-mines, he set out in his
wagon towards the Colorado, while desultory fighting was still
going on between the Apache Indians and the pioneers. In the
course of a few years Big Mike opened a chain of stores between
Prescott and Yuma, and by the time he settled definitely in Phoenix,
he was believed to be the wealthiest trader in Arizona. When Barry
opened his eyes for the first time in 1909, the Goldwassers had
americanized their name by changing it to Goldwater; they had
become Protestants and the family fortune had grown considerably.
Barry, however, showed little inclination for the trade of his forefathers, and it was not until after the death of his father that he
decided to take an interest in the chain of stores. In the meantime
he had spent four years in a military academy in Virginia and had
piloted every type of aircraft. On the outbreak of war he joined
the Air Force, distinguished himself in ferrying heavy bombers to
Britain and was demobilized in 1945 with the rank of Colonel.

On his return to Phoenix he gave a good account of himself as
a municipal councillor, cleared the gambling dens out of the city
and in 1952, thanks to the support he received from local businessmen, he was elected Senator for Arizona. On reaching Washington
he immediately teamed up with the witch-hunter Joe McCarthy
and scandalized his own party by voting against the appointment of
Charles Bohlen as ambassador to Moscow. This revolt against
Republican directives, which marked the beginning of his controversy with Eisenhower, damaged his reputation in the capital, but
not in Phoenix, where his popularity grew as he expounded his
extreme conservative views. These views he summarized in 1960
in a book entitled *The Conscience of a Conservative*, which in a
very short time sold 100,000 copies. Nevertheless, in that same year,
only one American in every hundred had ever heard of him.[21]

His popularity received a sudden boost when, after Kennedy had
been installed in the White House, he launched a systematic and
unusually violent campaign against Democratic policy, predicting
that it would lead America to disaster. As regards foreign policy, his
starting-points were that 'an abject fear of death is penetrating into
the American conscience' and that 'it will not be long before a
universal Communist Empire covers the whole world'. Goldwater

attacked the conciliatory policy of the United States, the thaw and the suspension of nuclear tests; on the other hand, he was in favour of invading Cuba and sending Chiang Kai-shek's troops to land in China, of the rearmament of Germany and the use of nuclear weapons against the rebels in Vietnam. He also announced that if he were to be elected President in 1964, he would sever diplomatic relations with the Soviet Union and leave the United Nations, 'that foreign power which decides things for Americans'. Instead of a policy of compromise and appeasement, he would support an aggressive and dynamic strategy, encouraging the peoples behind the Iron Curtain to revolt and starting military operations against the more vulnerable Communist régimes. This would allow him to achieve, not peace, but a total victory over international Communism.

These ideas were approved by certain army circles, by industrialists who had made huge fortunes by supplying war materials, and also by the extremist movements, including the John Birch Society. But Goldwater's views on domestic matters also brought him popularity. The new rich liked him because of his determined attacks on interference by the Federal authorities in matters of taxation, agriculture and education. The businessmen liked him because he had said that the trade-union leader Walter Reuther was 'a greater danger than the Russian sputniks'. The racialists of the South liked him when he declared that the Supreme Court had violated the constitution by imposing integration in the schools. Conservatives liked him when he preached that America's troubles were all the fault of the Democrats who had established a 'Welfare State'.[22]

His popularity became so great that by 1962 he had become the mascot of the American Radical Right, and in the following year his candidature for the presidency was seriously considered even by the moderate and 'respectable' right wing. Goldwater threw himself into the struggle unsparingly, touring the United States with his 'Bonanza', writing three articles every week for a chain of newspapers and continually intervening even in marginal questions of American policy. By the summer of 1963 he had already outdistanced all the other Republican candidates like Rockefeller and Nixon, and when America was shaken by the march of 300,000 Negroes on Washington, he was looked upon as the most suitable candidate whom the Republicans could put up against Kennedy.

The assassination of Kennedy did not help Goldwater's camin his popularity, as if those three shots fired in Dallas had found a profound echo in the public conscience and had made those who were indulging the demon of violence think again. Goldwater tried to regain some of the lost ground by moderating the tone of his speeches, retracting some of his statements and quarrelling with Robert Welch, the founder of the John Birch Society.[23] But by now it was far too late to abandon his old supporters and adopt a more moderate line. All the more so because the most famous columnists in America—headed by Republicans like Joseph Alsop and Walter Lippmann—were beginning to point out the contradictions in his policy, his irritating habit of over-simplifying the most complicated problems, and the dangerous anachronisms contained in his conservative 'philosophy'. In the *Washington Post* Lippmann made himself almost brutally clear: 'Goldwater . . . is a radical reactionary who would . . . dismantle the modern state. His political philosophy does not have its roots in the conservative tradition but in the crude and primitive capitalism of the Manchester school. It is the philosophy not of the conservators of one social order but of the newly rich on the make.'[24] Some writers even went so far as to say that Goldwater had the economic ideas of a Poujade, the military ideas of a MacArthur and the cynicism of Machiavelli's Prince. And while the more liberal Americans denounced his extremism and his low intellectual level, the neo-Fascists of the John Birch Society complained that he was too moderate. Disappointed and resentful, they saw that this 'half-Jew', although he might be the most 'Americanist' candidate available, was not their man, not their 'man on a white horse', not their Messiah.[25]

It would nevertheless be wrong to think that the 'Goldwater appeal' was destined to lose all its force. Just as it would be wrong to think that Goldwater's career is over simply because he was badly beaten at the presidential election on 3 November 1964. Despite a defeat unprecedented in American history, the Senator for Arizona has not disappeared from political life, and he can find consolation in the fact that 24 million Americans voted for him and must consequently be assumed to share his opinions. The heir of McCarthy in his ability to utter anathemas and to create an apocalyptic atmosphere, Barry Goldwater is still the staunchest defender of the 'Old Frontier' and of a petty-minded, conservative America, a man who detests all novelties, new international involvements and new social responsibilities. At Independence Day parades, this American hero who can pilot a jet-aircraft mourns the passing of nineteenth-century society and still evokes wild applause when, as he does every year, he appears in the streets of Phoenix mounted on a magnificent Indian steed, with a big cowboy's hat on his head and the broad smile of a man who knows how to captivate a crowd and bend it to his will.

The John Birch Society

It may well be that the American Radical Right had nothing whatever to do with the murder of President Kennedy, at all events as regards the material execution of the crime. This, at least, is what emerges from the pages of the 'Warren Report', published on 27 September 1964—a report which in many respects is unsatisfactory. But the Right could not conceal its own gratification, and it made another blunder when it tried to exploit the regrettable incident in Dallas by making people believe that Kennedy was killed by a Communist.

If we examine the attitude of the most important among the extremist organizations, the John Birch Society, we are left with the definite impression that after 22 November 1963 it hoped there would be chaos in America, or a sudden atomic war with the Soviet Union, or at the very least that it would be possible to stir up trouble in the American political world. Twenty-three days after the murder in Dallas, the John Birch Society rented a whole page in the leading New York daily in order to warn the country against the danger of a Communist conspiracy and, with an imperious 'the time has come to invite every red-blooded American to react as such'.[26] Two months later, in its own monthly bulletin, it maintained that the Dallas tragedy was merely a settling of accounts between accomplices; that the Communist Oswald had killed the Communist Kennedy, because the latter, whose job it was to subvert and sabotage the American defences, had not succeeded in achieving this objective by 1963, the date fixed by World Communism for the actual conquest of the United States. Since Kennedy had thus become a negative political element, Oswald had removed him.

These ridiculous accusations against the man of the 'New Frontier' need not surprise us. Ever since the day of its foundation the John Birch Society had shown a tendency to believe that every American citizen was a more or less conscious agent of the Kremlin. When we glance through the Society's copious literature, mainly inspired by its founder, Robert Welch, we learn that Kennedy was an amoral individual whose sole aim was the installation of a popular democracy in the United States; that Eisenhower, like Truman and before him Roosevelt, was a dedicated, conscious agent of the Communist conspiracy; and that the former head of the Central Intelligence Agency, Allen Dulles, was the most protected and untouchable supporter of Communism in Washington. In the list of agents and traitors we also find the names of General Marshall, John Foster Dulles, Robert Kennedy, Adlai Stevenson, Eleonor Roosevelt, Nehru and Nasser, whereas Willy Brandt is only a 'comsymp' (fellow-traveller), Chief Justice Earl Warren is a Socialist and a hypocrite, and Nelson Rockefeller is trying to make the United States part of a World Socialist State. Still according to Welch, America is 50–70 per cent under Communist control, and Europe, except for Spain, Portugal and Eire, is in a state of even greater subjection.

The world of Robert Henry Winborne Welch is the same as Joe McCarthy's. A world in which no man is safe or free from the suspicion that he may be a traitor. 'I am an alarmist,' Welch himself admitted, 'and I hope to make you alarmists, too.'[27] In other words, men who know how to hate, whose only sustenance is conformism, fear and resentment, who embark on the crusade against the progressives with the same fanatical zeal that in the past led them to attack Jews, Negroes, Quakers and Catholics.

When Welch founded the John Birch Society at Indianapolis on 9 December 1958, he was well aware that times had changed, that to be accused of being a crypto-Communist does not mean the end of a man's political career, and that McCarthy had been a unique phenomenon. Consequently, before trying his luck, he decided to make his own organization a modern and efficient instrument equipped with ample funds and every possible means of propaganda. He failed to achieve his ambitious target of a million subscribers,[28] but he did manage to concentrate the public's attention on his own hysterical utterances and on the figure of the missionary-soldier John Birch, who had been killed in China by a patrol of Communist soldiers and was hailed by Welch as 'the first casualty of World War Three'.[29] He also gained the support of the leader of the Republican Right, Barry Goldwater, of an extremist general, Edwin Walker, of the notorious anti-Semite Merwin K. Hart, as well as of sundry admirals, senators, judges, publishers, industrialists, Protestant and Catholic prelates. One of these last,

Mark K. Carroll, Bishop of Wichita, remarked in a letter in reply
to a friend's description of the John Birch Society, that the twelve
guidelines behind the philosophy of the Society were the Ten
Commandments in updated language, and enclosed a cheque for
ten dollars. Carroll was not the only Catholic prelate to express his
sympathy with this neo-Fascist organization's aims. In a letter
dated 28 April 1960, which was subsequently published, the Archbishop of Boston, Cardinal Richard Cushing, expressed his opinion
of the Society by saying that he could not think of a more dedicated
anti-Communist than Robert Welch, and expressing his admiration
of the Society.[30]

Only four years after the founding of the society a Gallup poll
revealed that at least 10 million Americans found Welch's
'philosophy' interesting. This is not surprising, for the philosophy
of this former candy-manufacturer reflected the petty conservatism
of the provincial middle classes, whose aim, as Wright Mills
reminds us, 'is the destruction of the legislative achievements of
the New and Fair Deals'.[31] Welch, however, was clever in the way
he presented old ideas as something novel. Before entering politics
he had, in fact, been a commercial traveller; he even wrote a
manual on the behaviour of the perfect salesman *(The Road to
Salesmanship)* and therefore knew how to 'sell' the outworn themes
of Protestant fundamentalism, liberally spiced with anti-Communism, to the 100,000 members of his Society, as if they were
sensational novelties. Interpreting, for example, the isolationist
hankerings of a certain sector of American public opinion, and
exploiting the fears caused by the atomic psychosis, Welch found it
easy to denounce the United Nations, the 'futile and costly North
Atlantic Treaty', and even the World Health Organization and
every other body providing aid to foreign countries, as seditious
and Communistic. To attract the racialists of the South he even
maintained that the campaign for racial equality meant nothing
less than the creation of a 'Negro Soviet Republic' in the South.

Welch's 'philosophy' may be found in the 180 pages of his *Blue
Book* (variously described as a Bible, as the American *Mein
Kampf* and as a modernized version of the 'Protocols of the Learned
Elders of Zion') and in his booklet *The Politician*, which reveals
to an even greater degree the authoritarian and anti-democratic
leanings of its author. Glancing through these texts we come across
little Machiavellianisms like, 'The achievement of concrete results

requires the use of every means, no matter how low and petty';
or historical judgments such as, 'Hitler is preferable to Stalin. After
every mass execution, Hitler's conscience tormented him. But not
Stalin's. Hitler was immoral, Stalin amoral, that is to say worse.'
The men he admired were few in number—Chiang Kai-shek,
Franco, Salazar, Batista, Trujillo, the colonels of the OAS—all
men of the same type, who agreed with him in thinking that it was
time to have done with democracy because it was 'a demagogic
weapon and a perennial swindle'.

Another proof of the society's extremism is provided by the fact
that among Welch's closest collaborators was the Austrian-born
William S. Schlamm, who achieved notoriety in 1960 when he
went to Europe to preach on the society's behalf (some say that
he was sent by the Pentagon) the necessity of a preventive war
against the Soviet Union. In the course of a lecture given in
Cologne, Schlamm went so far as to say that America could easily
sacrifice 700 million people to defend the West and its territorial
aspirations in Eastern Europe. This infuriated the German
Social Democrats and Liberals so much that they asked their
government to expel him, thereby showing that with his extremism
Schlamm even surpassed the local neo-Nazis. In any case Schlamm's
words would not appear to have fallen on deaf ears, for at the
height of his campaign the *Bundeswehr* asked to be equipped with
tactical atomic weapons, in a memorandum which revealed the
impatience of the German generals at the control exercised over
them by the civil authorities.

The success of the John Birch Society, especially in California
and the Deep South, was partly due to the aura of secrecy surrounding it, at all events in its early days, and partly to the fact
that it gave the leaders of the provincial middle class a chance to
rise above the new rich and pose an an élite. They formed a kind
of aristocracy divided up into cells, which Welch ruled like a dictator, all discussion being forbidden and nobody being allowed to
hold an opinion differing from his. When Bryton Barron, a former
functionary in the State Department, made up his mind to quit the
society, he explained that he could no longer stand it because the
policy of having to agree with the chief's decisions had proved disastrous in other circumstances.[32] For years Welch tried to defend
himself against the accusation that he acted like a 'little Hitler' and
maintained that the absolute control he exercised over the society

was necessary in order to prevent Communist infiltration. But from 1962 on, after he had been attacked by Barry Goldwater and by the leader of the right-wing intelligentsia, William F. Buckley, Welch was forced to give up some of his powers, and when in the following year he was elected honorary president of the society, his influence declined still more.

The gradual elimination of Robert Welch did not change either the aims or the methods of this extremist society. It still carried on its hate campaigns against the United Nations, against Earl Warren (guilty of having dealt a mortal blow to racial segregation with his famous verdict in 1954), and against shopkeepers who sold articles imported from Communist countries. Its latest campaign was an attempt to stop children from collecting money for poor children in other parts of the world under the auspices of the UNICEF, an organism of the United Nations.

In 1963 the John Birch Society showed its desire to imitate the Fascists by organizing an armed unit, known as the RAF, but a later and more serious development was the infiltration of Birchites into local government and the two big parties. The reason why Kennedy undertook the journey to the South from which he never returned was that a Democratic Senator, Gale McGee, had invited him to go and see for himself the harm the extremists were causing with their skilful infiltration.[33]

Professor Alan F. Westin of Columbia University places the John Birch Society midway between the 'hate right' (represented by Rockwell's neo-Nazis) and the 'semi-respectable right' (which includes the White Citizens' Councils in the South and the Daughters of the American Revolution).[34] On the other hand Dr Samuel B. Gould thinks that the society is definitely 'a neo-Fascist group resorting to the most advanced Hitlerian techniques'.[35] In the course of a television interview on 23 November 1961, when he was asked for his opinion on Robert Welch's movement, ex-President Eisenhower replied that he did not think the United States needed 'superpatriots'. Five days before, in Los Angeles, Kennedy had said: 'They look suspiciously at their neighbours and their leaders. They call for "a man on horseback" because they do not trust the people. They find treason in our finest churches, in our highest court and even in the treatment of our water.' Two years later, in the speech he was to have delivered in Dallas, Kennedy did not forget to mention the Birchites; 'There will always be dissident voices heard

in the land, expressing opposition without alternatives, finding
fault but never favor, perceiving gloom on every side and seeking
influence without responsibility.'

This was the last, severe but polite warning that John Kennedy
gave to the society of hatred and hysteria. Three months later a
Birchite, Redilo P. Oliver, wrote the following epitaph on the man
of the 'New Frontier':

> If the international vermin succeed in completing their occupation
> of our country, Americans will remember Kennedy while they live,
> and will curse him as they face the firing squads or toil in a
> brutish degradation that leaves no hope for anything but a speedy
> death.[36]

Only when we read such words as these can we assess the price
that America is paying for its freedom of thought, speech and
association.

The anti-Communist 'crusades'

1961, the year of the Cuban crisis, the Berlin Wall, guerrilla warfare
in Laos and the last dramatic clash between the United States and
the Soviet Union over the question of nuclear tests, was a year
of encouraging successes for the American Radical Right. The
intensification of the Cold War had created an atmosphere of
doubt, uncertainty and excitement which pervaded the whole
nation—a climate that lent itself to exploitation by the extremist
organizations. 'If you can't go and fight in Cuba or Laos,' ran
one of the most popular appeals launched by the ultra-conserva-
tives, 'try at least to fight those who are living around you.' The
television screens were occupied more and more frequently by
Billy Hargis, Fred Schwarz, Clarence Manion, Dan Smoot and
Cleon Skousen, who in apocalyptic tones predicted the imminent
end of Christianity and Western civilization and proclaimed
crusades against the 'Red Dragon'. 'Do you want to be free to
celebrate Christmas in the future?' was one of the items in a ques-
tionnaire distributed in millions of copies by the former Protestant
preacher Fred Schwarz, and in their replies people made all kinds
of suggestions as to the best way to fight Communism.

The hysteria of the McCarthy years was recreated thanks to a
cleverly co-ordinated plan; that climate of apprehension and suspicion which Raymond Fosdick had described twelve years before

as being extremely dangerous. 'In our concern over what Communism may do to democracy,' he wrote, 'we have overlooked the danger of what we ourselves may do to democracy under the stimulus of fear.'[37] But those who were exploiting the fear of Communism had no qualms whatever as to whether, by so doing, they might harm democracy; for them Communism, whether at home or abroad, was just a pretext, and their real enemy was democracy. 'Behind the screen of anti-Communism,' *Time Magazine*, which cannot be suspected of having left-wing tendencies, wrote on 8 December 1961, 'many right-wing extremists are pursuing their own private aims and serving their own interests, which range from a policy of respectable conservatism to segregation, isolationism, higher tariffs and the abolition of income-tax.'

Once again the fear of Communism was exploited by the right-wing extremists and by those who financed them in order to make things difficult for the country's liberal legislators. Once again, those who were not 'patriots', were promptly deemed to be 'comsymps'. Once again, in the battle against evolution and in the name of Americanism, the old weapons of fundamentalism were brought into play—intolerance, apocalyptic predictions, a delight in mystification and a Manichaean way of thinking. The oil-magnates of Texas and many industrialists in the Far and Middle West, who in 1950 had supported McCarthy, now found a more profitable use for their money by subsidizing 'Christian crusades' and anti-Communist schools, putting their faith in men who in a way were incredible and in the course of time revealed their true nature, which was that of fanatics and swindlers.

Let us pause for a moment to consider three men who achieved notoriety even outside the United States—the former Reverends Fred C. Schwarz and Billy James Hargis, and the founder of the 'Minutemen', Robert Bolivar DePugh. Of these three, Fred Schwarz was the most successful, and this not only because today he can claim to be 'the most closely watched man in America', but also because over the last few years he has managed to make a huge fortune after starting from nothing. In 1953, when he arrived in California from his native Brisbane, he had only ten dollars in his pocket. Schwarz however, in addition to being a doctor and a preacher, was also a good psychologist, and he saw at once that the climate of the country was propitious, that the provincial masses were bewildered and gullible, and that a righteons crusade against evil was the best thing in which to invest his ten dollars. He was

M

not mistaken. Today the annual turnover of his 'Christian Anti-Communism Crusade' is in the region of one million dollars.

Schwarz began his crusade at Long Beach, where he set out to teach the Americans the truth about Communism and to initiate them into the mysteries of historical materialism. But as soon as he began to receive financial backing from the Allen Bradley Company of Milwaukee and from someone in the Schick Safety Razor Company, the tone of his lectures became less didactic and more aggressive. Adopting the apocalyptic style of Father Coughlin, this former Australian preacher announced :

> I believe that he [Khrushchev] has chosen San Francisco as 'headquarters of the World Communist Dictatorship'[38] and that local Communists have stated that if they ever got into power, they would 'put to death a mere fifty million people'.[39]

After informing the public of the scourges in store for them, Schwarz harangued them in sermons in the course of which he exploited all the old techniques of revivalism. 'Christians, awake! The enemy is at the gates. Don the armour of the Christian and give battle. With culture, evangelism and devotion we shall combat the Communist enemy and, if need be, offer our lives for this noble cause.' At other times he would terrify his listeners with detailed descriptions of the Communist invasion and the subsequent massacres. 'When they come for you, as they have for many others, and on a dark night, in a dank cellar, they take a wide-bore revolver with a soft-nose bullet, and they place it at the nape of your neck . . .'[40]

With this macabre repertory Schwarz toured the United States, addressing crowds of sometimes more than 15,000 people, giving lectures to army personnel, selling copies of his book entitled *You Can Trust the Communists*, receiving donations and, in California alone, persuading forty-one mayors to organize 'anti-Communism weeks'. Two priests, John Simmons and Brooks Walker, who on the evening of 1 February 1962 had the courage to denounce the fanaticism of this ex-preacher, had their houses blown up the same night. This episode at last aroused the Californian Democrats from their torpor. In a series of articles for the *San Francisco Chronicle*, a journalist named Randebough revealed the sources of Schwarz's funds (among these being a firm which supplied military equipment and was notoriously opposed to the policy of co-existence), while 290 university professors, ministers of the various Churches and judges declared in a statement to the press that the extremist views expressed by Schwarz were a danger to the education of the young. The John Birch Society promptly came to the Australian's defence, but the only effect of this support was to weaken Schwarz's position, and when, in 1962, he decided to transfer his crusade to New York, he suffered his first setback and failed to fill even half of Madison Square Garden.

So much for Fred Schwarz. And the life-story of Billy James Hargis is more or less the same. In 1955 he began his crusade by travelling to Europe, where he organized the launching of half a million balloons which carried as many Bibles to the far side of the Iron Curtain. On his return to Tulsa in Oklahoma he had acquired sufficient fame to enable him to start his 'Christian Crusade',[41] which a few years later was also receiving donations at the rate of $1 million a year. In temperament and style, however, there was a vast difference between Schwarz and the corpulent Hargis. Whereas the Australian was at pains to give his movement at least an appearance of middle-class respectability, Hargis deliberately resorted to tub-thumping, made no secret of the fact that he was one of the leading figures in the John Birch Society, and delivered frontal attacks on the Democratic administration, the New Deal, the United Nations, Chief Justice Warren and all the other *bêtes noires* of the Radical Right. Thanks to the support of the Texas oil-men, he was able to make use of 140 radio and 24 television transmitters, over which he broadcast his messages to 46 States, never omitting to show his business acumen by stressing the fact that 'the Christian Crusade is the best equipped anti-Communist organization in America to do the titanic job of retrieving [*sic*] our college and high school students to paths of a sound, decent, sane Christian-Americanism'.[42] For that matter, anyone who attended one of his conventions could easily see that his outstanding characteristic was typical of a shopkeeper. In the intervals between the delegates' speeches Hargis used to harangue the audience, brandishing a copy of his own book *(Communist America—Must it be?)* and shouting: 'There's 15 chapters, 200 pages, and they're four for a dollar.' Or else he would say: 'The Christian Crusade hotel is now open at the foot of Pike's Peak. Now it's just two for six dollars a day, and children under twelve are free.'[43]

While Schwarz and Hargis believed in radio and television crusades, Robert Bolivar DePugh put all his faith in his own gun. In 1960, claiming that under the constitution every citizen has the right to possess weapons, the proprietor of the Biolab Corporation of Narbonne (Missouri) formed a small private army—the army of the 'Minutemen'—which a year later had a strength of 25,000 warriors, divided into 3,000 groups scattered all over American territory.[44] What urged these men to hoard arms and ammunition, to build anti-atomic shelters, provide themselves with gas-masks and train in the Californian desert or in the swamps of Illinois, was the conviction that all Congressmen were Communists (even if they did not know it) and on the day of the invasion the American defence system would not work. On that day—or so they maintained—the survival of America would depend entirely on the numbers and the fighting skill of the Minutemen. But despite all the appeals they published in numerous papers—'Put the real power in the hands of civil defence; put yourself and your gun at the service of a free America. For further details write "Minutemen", 613 East Alton, Independence'—the goal of 1 million guerrillas by 1963 was not achieved. And the neo-Fascists of the John Birch Society were very unkind to DePugh's super-patriots: 'They're idiots; there are better ways of doing things.'

That former Disciple of Christ, Billy James Hargis, had for a long time been worried by this dispersal of the Radical Right's forces. On 21 March 1962, after prolonged negotiations, Hargis at last managed to assemble the representatives of a hundred extremist organizations in Washington and to form a united front which took the somewhat pretentious name of 'Brotherhood of the Saviours of the Country'. In its reports on this first congress of American *ultras*, the Democratic press had no difficulty in proving what for that matter had long been suspected, namely that there was a close connexion between the 'Christian Crusades' and the anti-Semite, neo-Fascist, racialist and militarist groups. It was a front that speculated on the fear of Communism, exploited the more ingenuous forms of patriotism, and raised the banner of a not very clearly defined Christianity. When we listen to a phonograph-recording of the 'Hymns and Sayings of Billy Hargis' (on sale at $4·95), we are tempted not to take it very seriously. This, however, would be a mistake. It would merely show that we were forgetting all those ultra-conservative elements who, despite all the clowning, are pulling the strings of a plot against democracy, and also forgetting all the hate which, through a thousand visible or invisible channels, is being injected into the body of the American nation.[45]

The neo-Nazis

Since November 1958 the biggest Nazi flag that has ever flown over American territory has been hoisted every morning on the roof of a two-story yellow house—928 North Randolph Street, Arlington, Virginia. At first this ceremony offended the susceptibilities of quite a few citizens, most of them men who had fought in Europe, where they had seen too many swastikas. But besides the flag, what irritated the people of Arlington was an ominous notice reading: 'Headquarters of the American Nazi Party. No admittance. Trespassers will be prosecuted or shot.' A committee of protest was formed and a charge was brought against the owner of the house, a former major in the Naval Air Force, George Lincoln Rockwell, but the flag and the notice remained where they were. 'It is not a crime,' Judge Catterall decreed, 'to call yourself a Nazi; criminality stems from acts and not words.'[46]

Banned and hated in Europe, the swastika has found legal hospitality in America, though its situation is precarious. American law, which in the 1930s tolerated all the Nazi movements that sprouted among the German community (e.g. Walter Knappe's Teutonia group and Fritz Kuhn's German-American Bund), has made no effort since the last war to dissolve parties and movements drawing their inspiration from Nazi doctrines. The fact that judges intend to carry respect for the Bill of Rights to extreme limits does not, however, mean that they have tender feelings for American Nazis. As soon as they infringe the law, they are punished severely. Consequently, the number of people in the United States today who prefer to 'live dangerously' is very small. If we believe what their leaders say, there are tens of thousands of them. According to the police, not more than 5,000.[47]

The first post-war Nazi movement, the National Renaissance Party, was formed in January 1949. It was under the leadership of James H. Madole, who established his party headquarters in Yorkville, that part of Manhattan which is inhabited mainly by Germans and between 1937 and 1941 witnessed the parades of the 'Bund Boys' and the ominous fluttering of their standards. Madole promptly announced his programme. 'What Hitler did in Europe,' he wrote in his *Bulletin*, 'the National Renaissance Party intends to do in America.' In short, it would fight for the abolition of the parliamentary system in favour of government by an élite; it would

defend the Aryan race against contamination by deporting the coloured race; and lastly, by eliminating the Jews, it would put an
end to Communism. Pending the realization of this formidable
plan, James Madole, who was invariably surrounded by a score
of guards wearing the uniforms of Hitler's SA, confined his activities to skirmishes with isolated groups of Jews or Negroes, and
several times found himself in trouble with the police for disorderly
conduct or illegal possession of weapons. Finally, in 1963, after
a meeting interrupted by the throwing of numerous rotten eggs, he
was obliged to give up the swastika and adopt the new and less
compromising symbol of Sir Oswald Mosley's Fascist movement—
lightning in a circle.[48]

More active and with a larger following is the American Nazi
Party, which is said to have three or four thousand adherents,
mostly in Arlington, Chicago, Los Angeles, New York and Boston.
It was founded by George Lincoln Rockwell, who after the arrest
in London of Colin Jordan, the 'World Führer', claimed the right to
call himself 'Acting World Führer of National Socialism'. Rockwell,
a little over forty when he was murdered on 25 August 1967, was
tall, athletic, with a lock of rebellious hair which was continually
falling over his forehead. Both his father and mother were
on the stage, and he himself was a clever imitator of Hitler, assuming the same rigid poses and the same glowering expression,
and mouthing broken English as if he were a German.

Rockwell's programme was far more extreme than Madole's and
can only be described as a product of hatred and irrationality.
In the 1930s, while attempting to define the position occupied by
American Nazis, Franklin D. Roosevelt quoted the apt expression
'lunatic fringe'. Like Pelley, Deatherage and Coughlin thirty years
ago, Rockwell belonged to this lunatic fringe, which steadfastly
asserts the necessity of genocide, gas-chambers, deportations and
eugenetic controls. Speaking in 1962 to the students of Hunter College, Seth D. Ryan, one of Rockwell's lieutenants, frankly declared
that his party 'favoured execution in the gas-chamber of all whom
it considered "Communists", a class in which he included President
Kennedy'.[49] And this is how Rockwell intended to solve the Negro
problem: 'When we come to power we'll appropriate 50 billion
dollars to build a modern industrial nation in Africa, and offer
$10,000 to every Negro family willing to migrate there . . . Negroes
who stayed here would be rigidly segregated.'[50] With the Jews he
was even more ruthless; those who want to leave will have their

property confiscated; those who decide to remain will be sterilized. And lastly, in keeping with his motto, 'For race and nation', Rockwell thought that it would be impossible to tolerate the presence of defectives and abnormals in his ideal world, and he consequently envisaged the setting-up of a national eugenetics commission, which would take steps to sterilize the hopelessly insane and all those who were biologically dangerous. Up to this point Rockwell was merely following in the footsteps of Hitler. His personal contribution was a very modest one; he said that he would do his best to put women back in the kitchen and to encourage the re-establishment of paternal authority, thus interpreting the aspirations of certain conservative and anti-feminist circles in America.

Unlike James Madole, who spent most of his time writing anti-Jewish pamphlets, Rockwell was a man of action and an indefatigable organizer. From his headquarters in Virginia—a State which in his opinion was the 'last bulwark of a free America'—he was ever ready to set out in his yellow motor-bus bearing the inscription 'We do hate'. Full of young men in khaki uniforms with swastika armlets, this 'hate bus' appeared in February 1962 in the streets of Philadelphia, where the film *Exodus* was being shown for the first time. On 29 September of that same year it went to Birmingham (Alabama), and this time it was the Negro leader Martin Luther King who was the target. As an alternative to these warlike outings, Jewish cemeteries were desecrated. These were obviously deeds, not words, but Judge Catterall apparently ignored them.

Emboldened by the notoriety he acquired after his expulsion from Britain, where he had attended a neo-Nazi international congress in August 1962, Rockwell intensified his provocative campaign and tried to establish contact with other extremist groups, in particular with Elijah Muhammad's Black Muslims.[51] He also sent telegrams expressing his solidarity to General Edwin Walker, who organized the resistance to Federal troops in Oxford. When the Negro organizations decided to march on Washington, Rockwell announced that he would do his best to stop them by organizing a counter-demonstration. 'It is necessary,' he said, 'to teach these revolutionary Negroes a lesson, for they are openly threatening to stab the Republic in its heart.'[52] Boarding his 'hate bus', Rockwell travelled all over Virginia in the hope of recruiting 10,000 volunteers, but when 28 August came and Washington was invaded by the biggest crowd of Negroes America had ever seen, the little Führer from Arlington could find only twenty volunteers--too few to enable him to organize a counter-march. Not only that, but half-way there, at Emporia, Rockwell had to spend a few days in prison for inciting the Whites to use violence against the Negroes.

He was not discouraged by this setback. He spent the last months of 1963 organizing a fitting welcome for Madame Nhu, with placards reading: 'Grill all the Reds' and 'We love Madame Nhu.' A few days later he had leaflets dropped from a plane over Toronto, proclaiming: 'Hitler was right; Communism is Jewish.' On 28 November, six days after the murder of Kennedy, Rockwell's followers paraded in front of the White House, bearing posters inscribed with peremptory demands to 'invade Cuba at once' and 'destroy the red Cuban rats'.[53] In between, besides taking care that a candle was always kept burning in front of a portrait of Hitler, Rockwell indoctrinated his youthful disciples and wrote letters to prominent Jews bearing a swastika as postmark, together with one of his two slogans—'*Juden 'raus*' or 'Bring back Auschwitz'.[54]

Lastly, among the minor neo-Nazi groups we must mention the National States' Rights Party, which has its headquarters in Birmingham (Alabama), where it publishes a monthly magazine called *The Thunderbolt*, maintains contact with Scandinavian neo-Nazi groups and numbers among its members Matt Koehl, Mayward Orlando Nelson and John Kasper, who write savage articles attacking the Jews and Catholics. The Birmingham group gained special distinction during the summer of 1963 by the way it opposed racial integration.[55]

Although these extremist groups have a negligible following in the United States and are generally not taken seriously, they are under the constant supervision of the Federal Bureau of Investigation, more especially since it was discovered that some of the neo-Nazi groups had established contacts with Rumanian, Czechoslovak, Hungarian and Yugoslav refugees whose pasts were not all they should have been. Despite the severity of the American immigration laws, even a man like the former *Ustaše* Minister for the Interior, Andrija Artukovic, who was accused of having massacred 200,000 people—among them 1,293 children, old people and Rabbis —managed to find a refuge in the United States in 1949.[56] Shortly before his death Kennedy had agreed to consider a request made by the Yugoslav authorities for the extradition of Artukovic, who in the meantime had been contributing to *Ustaše* publications like *Danica* and *Nasanada*, published in Chicago, had granted interviews, appeared on television and passed himself off as a respectable exponent of anti-Communism.

Among others who found a safe refuge in America at about the same time were a large number of Hungarian Fascists, who founded a Hungarian paper in New York called *Szabad Magyarszag* (Free Hungarians), which continually extols Nazism, publishes libellous statements about the Jewish community in America and accuses the United States of extorting money from the Bonn government by blackmail. In 1962, after discovering that this paper was exercising a harmful influence on Hungarian refugees, the American authorities decided to prevent it from circulating, though they did not actually suppress it. The most remarkable case, however, was that of the Rumanian Viorel Trifa, a former commander of the 'Iron Guard'. At the end of the war, when he was accused of having taken part in a pogrom in Bucharest in January 1941, Trifa managed to flee the country and reach Italy, whence in 1950 he went to the United States. Here, although he was denounced by the World Jewish Congress and by the Rumanian Orthodox Church, Trifa contrived to get himself appointed bishop of a somewhat obscure sect, the Rumanian Episcopal Orthodox Church. Thus disguised, the former commander of the 'Iron Guard' had the audacity, one day in 1955, to go to Washington and recite the inaugural prayers at a session of the Senate in the Capitol.[57]

The racialists

Late at night on 20 June 1964 the telephone rang in the newsroom of the *Baton Rouge Sunday Advocate*. The sub-editor on duty lifted the receiver and heard a truculent voice say: 'If you still have any doubts about the revival of the Ku-Klux-Klan, come out and see the burning crosses.' That night, on the outskirts of Baton Rouge and at four other places in Louisiana, 150 crosses were set alight, and in front of each a Klansman clad in his medieval white robes with a cross above his heart recited the ritual formula: 'The Bible teaches that the Negro is inferior to us Anglo-Saxons. The Jews are inferior, too. God is a segregationist.'

This tragic masquerade, a nightly occurrence in one or other of the Southern States, is usually the prelude to a punitive expedition against the Negroes who are fighting for integration, and is only one of the methods employed to intimidate the coloured community and remind them to 'keep their place'. 'Negroes in this country,' writes James Baldwin, '. . . are taught really to despise themselves from the moment their eyes open on the world.'[58] The sooner they learn that they are second-class citizens, the sooner they will rid themselves of their illusions. They must be taught at once that they will have to spend their lives in racial ghettoes, that the most menial and worst-paid tasks will be reserved for them, that they will be the last to be taken on and the first to be sacked, that their wages will be only half those paid to white men, that their children will be inadequately educated and that, especially in the South, justice will never be on their side.[59]

Among all the contradictions that beset American society, the Negro problem is undoubtedly the oldest and gravest. No one can fail to notice the difference between the America which elsewhere is fighting to establish the principles of liberty and equality, and the America that seems incapable of applying these principles at home. There have, it is true, been changes in the last few years. In 1954 a judgement of the Supreme Court struck a shrewd blow at segregation, and since then the Federal government has been doing its best to obtain for the 20 million American Negroes, if not 'real equality', at least 'equality in the eyes of the law'. This has put an end to lynchings (of which there were about 4,000 between 1882 and 1951), but it has not yet been possible to stop violence. On the contrary, it can be said that racial homicide, which in the old days was a kind of secret and complicated rite, has adapted itself to the times and become more systematic, effective and frequent. A rifle-shot, often fired from behind a man's back, has replaced the cord, the whip and tar, while dynamite is used for more important 'operations'. With such weapons, between April and September 1963, twelve Negroes and one white man were killed, the latter being a postman named William Moore, who in Alabama courageously undertook a one-man protest march against racial discrimination.

Although today it has lost much of its prestige, the most stubborn adversary of racial equality is the Ku-Klux-Klan, which has often been believed to be extinct but has invariably cropped up once again, full of hatred and violence, whenever the Negroes have been granted some concession. Today, however, the burning crosses, the white hoods, the hymn of 'The Old Rugged Cross', the titles born by the complex hierarchy (Imperial Wizard, Dragon, Titan, Cyclops etc.) no longer have the same gruesome appeal that they had forty years ago, when there were 5 million Klansmen, 50,000 of whom could march with impunity through the streets of Washington or oppose the Catholic Al Smith's candidature for the presidency, shouting their slogan: 'Keep the Pope out of the White House'. Today their numbers are down to not more than 70,000, and only in Alabama do they exercise a certain amount of political influence thanks to the presence in Tuscaloosa of Robert Marvin Shelton, who since 1961 has held the title of Imperial Wizard of the United States Klans, Knights of the Ku-Klux-Klan.

A former employee in a rubber factory, Robert Shelton rose to the highest rank in this secret society thanks to his reputation for intolerance, bigotry and extremism. True to the traditions of the society, now more than a hundred years old, Shelton hates Negroes, Jews, Catholics, Indians and the Federal government, and used to maintain that he was fighting to prevent the constitutional régime from falling under 'the dictatorship of the Kennedys'. Speaking at Spartanburg in South Carolina in August 1963, with a huge cross blazing behind his back, he said: 'The integrationalist movement draws its inspiration from Communism and its aim is the installation of a world government and the creation of a new race of half-breeds.'[60] One month before, the 'Grand Dragon' of Georgia, Calvin Craig had said:

> The Negroes will not be satisfied until we have openly declared a racial war. By that I don't mean that we shall resort to violence. But if the State cannot protect its citizens, we ourselves shall ensure that they are protected. The Whites have been betrayed, and in Georgia most of them are ready to take up arms.[61]

Ever since the Klansmen discovered that 80 per cent of the psychiatrists in the Southern States were Jews, they have imagined that the Society for Mental Hygiene and the psycho-pathological research centres are part of the most monstrous conspiracy ever organized in the United States, and in some States they have even managed to stop all research in this sector. They accused the Jews of 'wanting to brainwash the Americans', and even of setting up a secret hospital in a remote part of Alaska where many Whites were subjected to lobotomy and turned into Communist robots or passive instruments of racial integration. Although these hate campaigns met with a certain amount of success, the revival of the Ku-Klux-Klan has been on a very modest scale, its financial potential has been much reduced, and its new members are drawn only from the lowest and poorest sectors of the white population. And one day in January 1958 the fame of its invincibility and ruthless efficiency was brusquely shattered when some Lumbec Indians who were attacked by Klansmen at Maxton in North Carolina routed them with a few rifle-shots.[62] Nevertheless, in 1964 and 1965 a certain increase in the criminal activities of the Klan became noticeable, and this alarmed the American government. An investigation conducted by a German newspaper revealed that 2,000 American soldiers stationed in Germany were members of the Klan. In the United States the sect's violent racial campaign culminated in the murder of a female member of the racial equality movement, Viola Liuzzo, who was killed in March 1965. The Alabama court which tried the culprits acquitted them, perhaps indicating the extent of the Klan's ramifications. After this episode the government ordered a public inquiry. Almost at the moment when this was due to begin, the 'Grand Dragon' of the Klan, Daniel Burros, whose activities and Jewish origin had been revealed by the *New York Times*, committed suicide. Since then the campaign against the Ku-Klux-Klan has undermined its position to such an extent that a further revival will hardly be possible.

While the Ku-Klux-Klan was thus engaged in a desperate struggle for survival, with the outdated practices of its primitive rites as its only weapons, it was gradually supplanted, from 1955 onwards, by the outwardly respectable White Citizens' Councils, which today control many local administrations and political organizations, whether Republican or Democrat.[63] The emergence of these White Citizens' Councils was followed by the adoption of new and more modern methods of carrying on the struggle (for example, economic pressure applied to Negroes and progressive Whites), and showed that the Radical Right, which in the past had recruited its members mainly from the lower classes or the impoverished and despairing lower middle class, was now finding adherents in the upper strata of the middle class. These were 'respectable' professional and business men, who had little use for burning crosses and preferred more efficacious and anonymous methods of intimidation. They distrusted all progressive measures and thought that the only way to cover up their own activities was to attack the central government, accusing it of interfering in the internal affairs of the various States and thus prejudicing their juridical and moral autonomy, while at the same time they opposed integration simply because they had not the slightest intention of foregoing their own privileges.

In the course of this campaign, which they vainly seek to ennoble by interspersing it with legal dissertations, the White Citizens' Councils make use of trusted men who owe their high positions to the support they have received from the Councils themselves—men like the governor of Mississippi, Ross Barnett; the governor of Arkansas, Orwal Faubus; and George Wallace of Alabama. On 16 July 1963 the last-named told the Senate that he was opposed to John Kennedy's anti-racist laws and that a President who backed a law like the civil rights law ought to be removed from public life. Shortly before, his colleague Ross Barnett had said that they would not drink of the cup of genocide and there was not a single case in history of the white race surviving racial integration. And while governors Wallace, Faubus, Barnett and Patterson were campaigning on the highest levels, and the Senator for Georgia, Richard Russell, was employing the filibuster technique to obstruct the passage of the anti-racist laws, on the lower levels the White Citizens' Councils did not disdain to resort to violence (by using the forces of law and order in the various States) or to come to terms with the more extreme groups of the 'lunatic fringe' in order to get rid of their most troublesome adversaries. Thus, despite all their efforts to appear respectable, the members of the White Citizens' Councils frequently found themselves on the same side of the fence as the Knights of the Ku-Klux-Klan, Lincoln Rockwell's neo-Nazis, General Walker's Birchites, DePugh's Minutemen, and the 'Christian Crusaders' led by Fred Schwarz and Billy Hargis.

'The majority of white people in the United States have literally no idea of the violence with which Negroes in the South are treated daily—nay, hourly. This violence is deliberate, conscious, condoned by the authorities.'[64] These words were written by Robert F. Williams, the first Negro who ever dared to form an armed body in America to defend the Negroes of Monroe, North Carolina, from the attacks of the Ku-Klux-Klan and the Minutemen.[65] Today Williams is an exile in Cuba and his desperate gesture has found no imitators. But how long will the Negro masses, who today are adopting Gandhi's tactics of non-violence as suggested by moderate leaders like Martin Luther King, Roy Wilkins and James Farmer, remain patient? How long will they put up with the humiliation of segregation, terrorist attacks on their homes and churches, the truncheons and hoses of the police, and the bites of tracker-dogs? How long will they be able to resist the appeals of Elijah Muhammad, whose answer to white racialism is a Negro racialism which even hopes for the extermination of the white race (by a vengeful Negro God)?

For the Negro writer James Baldwin, we are on the eve of great events. His standpoint is halfway between the 'legalitarians' like Martin Luther King and extremists like Elijah Muhammad, and he is the spokesman of those who still hope for a peaceful solution, though time is now running short. Baldwin warns us that, if a solution cannot be found very soon, the Biblical prophecy which a slave turned into a melancholy song may well come true:

> God sent Noah the rainbow sign,
> No more water, the fire next time!

While James Baldwin still hopes that 'thoughtful' Whites and Negroes will find a way to end the racial nightmare and 'change the history of the world', Elijah Muhammad foresees only a clash between the two races, and has even found a name and a date for the great battle that will decide to which of the two races this planet Earth belongs.

The Black Muslims

The 'Battle of Armageddon' will begin on an unspecified day in the year 1970, and the first continent to disappear will be North America. Immediately after that the apocalyptic machine, which will be shaped like a wheel and have a diameter of half a mile, will fly over all the countries inhabited by white men and destroy them with bombs, poison-gas, fire, hail and earthquakes. Thus, after 6,000 years of domination, the race of 'Caucasian demons' will vanish from the face of the earth, and with them their false religion, Christianity. The world will then be inhabited exclusively by Afro-Asians and peace and justice will at last reign for ever.

This prophecy contains, in a synthesized form, all the doctrine of Elijah Muhammad, the Negro from Sandersville who since 1934 has described himself as 'the guide, the master and the spiritual head of the Nation of Islam in the West'. When it suits him, Muhammad declares that his prophecy will soon come true, and at other times he relegates it to the realm of eschatology, but it reveals all the elements that have made the Black Muslims the most dangerous of all the movements that have sprung up in the United States over the last decades. It is remarkable for its messianic nationalism, its extreme racialism and its rejection of everything pertaining to the white race (from its religion to its culture). It believes that the Battle of Armageddon—in other words the extermination of the white race—is the only remedy for the tribulations of American Negroes. It is on account of this uncompromising hatred that the Black Muslims have been described as the inevitable reaction to the Ku-Klux-Klan and the other segregationist movements.

For that matter America has already experienced other explosions of Negro racialism. As long ago as 1920, after proclaiming himself (in New York) as provisional president of Africa, the Jamaican Marcus Garvey tried to unite all Negroes under one flag and demanded 'not law, but force; not justice, but power'. Countering white racialism with a rabid Negro racialism, Garvey founded a Church of his own (in which the Angels were black and Satan was white), suggested the creation of a Black House in opposition to the White House, formed a para-military 'Universal African Legion', and even expressed his approval of the Ku-Klux-Klan, which he claimed was useful because it encouraged Negro nationalism. Later, Garvey was frequently compared with Hitler on account of his torrent-like rhetoric and his ability to arouse the most primitive emotions of the masses. He himself frankly admitted that his doctrine was based on racial Fascism:

> We were the first Fascists. We had disciplined men, women and children in training for the liberation of Africa. The black masses knew that in this extreme nationalism lay their only hope and readily supported it. Mussolini copied fascism from me but the Negro reactionaries sabotaged it.[66]

Elijah Muhammad is rightly acknowledged to be the heir of Garvey. But whereas the 'Black Moses' predicted a return of the American Negroes to the promised land, i.e. Africa, Muhammad has decided to found his 'Nation of Islam' on United States territory. 'Give us three, four, or more States . . .' he declared in Washington in 1959. 'Give us what we ask them for, for the next twenty twenty-five years, until we are able to go for ourselves.'[67] According to Muhammad, the land and aid over a period of twenty-five years would be but a trifling compensation for four centuries of exploitation of the Negroes. Accordingly, as time went on, he raised his bid to include one-seventh of United States territory and was fond of saying that it is impossible to share with wolves, that integration was only a white man's stratagem to avoid punishment and annihilation, and that the only possible solution was the creation of a 'Negro Republic', rigorously separated from that of the Whites.

If we want to understand Muhammad's fierce hatred of the white race as summed up in his slogan 'Separation or Death', we must study his previous career and take note of certain episodes which undoubtedly had an influence on his character. For example, when he was only eleven years old, he was present at the lynching of a young Negro accused of having violated a white girl. While the Negro was being hanged and riddled with bullets, the little Elijah made a vow: 'I swear that if I grow up and find a way to avenge him and our people, I will do it.' Twenty years later, in Detroit, he made a practice of attending all the meetings at which the Muslim 'prophet' Noble Drew Ali preached Negro supremacy, describing America as being merely an 'extension of Africa' and maintaining that the Christian religion was harming the Negroes. But the decisive encounter of his life occurred in 1930, when he met another Muslim 'prophet', W. D. Fard, who claimed that he had arrived in America straight from Mecca in order to redeem the Negro people. Four years later Fard suddenly disappeared and Elijah Muhammad, who in the meantime had become his right-hand man, took over the leadership of the Black Muslim movement, which had now become a concentration of all the anti-White resentment of Garvey, Noble Drew Ali and the other pioneers of American Negro nationalism.

After establishing the headquarters of his sect in Chicago, Muhammad appealed to the poorer urban Negroes, who were living in squalid ghettoes and hated both the Whites and the rising Negro middle class who were inclined to adopt a more conciliatory attitude. Having conferred upon himself the title of 'messenger of Allah' and using messianic language, Muhammad endeavoured to rid the Negroes of their inferiority complex by reversing all the theories of the white racialists. Thus he maintained that Negroes were stronger and more virile than Whites, that a Negro's brain weighed one and a half ounces more than a white man's, and that they were kind and generous, whereas the Whites were to be compared with Satan because they had invented gas-chambers and atomic bombs and had reduced the Negroes to slavery, 'holding a gun and a Bible in one hand and a bottle of gin in the other'.[68]

Muhammad did his best to convince the Negroes he was indoctrinating that it was no good trying to negotiate with white men or coming to terms with them, no matter whether they were the worst types of racialists or sincere Liberals. 'You say, "We are already free. Abraham Lincoln freed us." That is not the kind of freedom I speak of. Abraham Lincoln was not your friend . . . He was not your friend any more than George Washington.'[69] No white man, Elijah Muhammad insisted, however progressive he might be, could be a friend of the Negroes, and no white government could help the Negroes to escape from their inferno. 'It is really inconceivable,' the Messenger of Allah observed ironically, 'that the American government—mistress of the seas, lord of the air, conqueror of outer space, squire of the land and prowler of the deep bottoms of the oceans—should be unable to defend us from assault, rape and murder on the streets of these cement jungles.'[70] Consequently, he concluded, the Negroes should never trust the Whites, not even when they swore that they were animated by the best intentions.

> They are not come to this hour because they love us nor is integration a sign that they are sorry for their sins. The blunt fact is our oppressors see fire coming. They see the handwriting on the wall and know what it means. They would have you believe that the days ahead hold glory for the Christian world.
> My beloved, I, Elijah Muhammad, who must speak if it kills me and who will die rather than lie, tell you this: I know tomorrow, I know the end of it all. Tomorrow is not heaven for the Christian world; tomorrow is hell for the Christian world . . .'[71]

This prophetical, violent, anti-Christian and anti-White language caught the imagination of the Negro proletariat in the great Northern cities. In twenty years the Black Muslims increased their numbers from a mere 8,000 to 100,000, and then, in the brief space of only two years, from 100,000 to 200,000. Today no one knows how many there are, but they are certainly very numerous, even if they have not achieved the goal of 5 million which they forecast for 1964. According to *Time* (10 August 1959) there are 70,000 Black Muslims; according to *Sepia* (November 1959) 200,000. The *U.S. News World Report* (9 November 1959) estimated the figure as being anything between 10,000 and 70,000. Muhammad, who is a tireless organizer, has founded branches of his movement in more than 100 American cities; he has brought the number of 'temples' up to fifty, and anticipating the day of 'separation', he has urged the Black Muslims to create an economy of their own, no longer dependent on that of the Whites or of the 'collaborationist' Negroes. To this end the sect has opened shops, restaurants, supermarkets and small factories, and it is rapidly transforming itself into an economic force, which will be in a position to publish its own newspapers, found universities and schools, and create an 'Islamic Center' in Chicago, the estimated cost of which will be nearly 200 million dollars.[72]

But Muhammad devotes most of his attention to the education of the 'new Negro', to freeing him from all his complexes, stripping him of the last remnants of white culture, making him strong, disciplined, proud, self-reliant and ready for the 'Battle of Armageddon', no matter whether this turns out to be a real battle or only a metaphor. To achieve these results the 'Messenger of Allah' makes the Black Muslims celebrate rites and swear oaths, he imposes an austere way of life, places them under the orders of 'captains', and to those whom he recruits from among the 'Fruits of Islam' he entrusts the defence of the sect, of its members and their poverty. In thirty years Muhammad has thus given his movement the structure of a secret, military society. A society which is ready to defend itself, but also to take the offensive. 'We must return to the Mosaic law of an eye for an eye, a tooth for a tooth. What does it matter if ten million of us die? There will still be seven million left, and they will live to enjoy justice and liberty.'[73]

Although Muhammad has recently modified some of his ideas, adopting a less aggressive attitude to Christianity and denying that he is preaching the doctrine of racial hatred, the Federal Bureau of Investigation keeps a close watch on the activities of the Black Muslims, and students of the problem call the movement 'the Negro version of the Radical Right'.[74] In fact, even if we admit that its inspiration is dynamic and genuine, and that its protest is the silent protest of at least three-quarters of the American Negroes, the fact remains that its underlying ideology is grotesque and dangerous and contains much that is undoubtedly irrational. Speaking to the members of the Negro National Bar Association, Senator Kenneth B. Keating said: 'A very disturbing development has been the emergence of a new hate group in the United States, which calls itself Moslem and whose leader preaches a cult of racialism for Negroes and extreme anti-Semitism.'[75] Similar accusations have been made against the Black Muslims by leading Muhammadans and by Negro organizations which adopt more democratic methods in their fight against segregation.

The Black Muslims' latest paradoxical exploit was their pact with the neo-Nazis of the American Nazi Party, which reminds us of the close alliance, forty years ago, between Marcus Garvey and E. S. Cox of the Ku-Klux-Klan. Lincoln Rockwell was frequently a guest at meetings of Negro extremists and he has said that he considers Elijah Muhammad to be 'one of the greatest men in the world'.[76] The Black Muslims also expressed their approval of Verwoerd, who introduced apartheid in South Africa, and of Governor Wallace of Alabama, for the support he gave to segregation. Conversely, the Texan oil-magnates and the John Birch Society have never attempted to hide their sympathy for this Negro extremist movement. Malcolm X, who ranked immediately below Elijah Muhammad in the sect's hierarchy, claimed that there was 'a perfect identity of views' between the Black Muslims and the neo-Nazis because they were both fighting for a complete separation of the two races.[77] At the time of the Negro 'march on Washington' these two radical movements confirmed that they were allies by adopting the same hostile attitude to 'moderate' Negroes and alleging that the march had been financed and organized by the Federal government itself. They also agreed in expressing their satisfaction after the assassination of President Kennedy, though when Malcolm X was rash enough to say so at a meeting of 700 Black Muslims, Elijah Muhammad announced that his chief lieutenant had been temporarily suspended.

Seizing the chance offered by this incident—though the real reason was the long-standing rivalry between him and Elijah Muhammad—Malcolm X left the Black Muslims and founded an even more extreme movement. '1964 threatens to be the most explosive year America has ever witnessed,' he said at one of the first meetings of this new Black Nationalists Party in Cleveland . . . 'and now we have the type of black man on the scene in America today . . . who just doesn't intend to turn the other cheek any longer.'[78] It is not yet possible to judge what the prospects of this new movement are, one reason being that Malcolm X was murdered in Harlem on 25 February 1965, but his call to meet violence with violence may well cause a crisis in the movement led by the Messenger of Allah, who has hitherto been content to preach racial hatred without resorting to direct action. In May 1964, after the defection of Malcolm X, a still more extremist group calling itself the Blood Brothers was formed, which is said to be a heretical offshoot of the Black Muslims. The new group, which is said to recruit its mem-

bers from among the 'Fruits of Islam', specializes in armed assaults
on Whites, and in particular on Jews. The Blood Brothers were
accused of being responsible for four murders committed in New
York during the early months of 1964.

In many respects the Black Muslims and their recent offshoots
can be viewed as mere caricatures of a revolution, but the fact that
they are irrational and often grotesque does not imply that they
will remain within their present limits. As James Baldwin said in
the course of an interview:

> The desperation that led the Black Muslims to demand an
> autonomous State is felt by practically all Negroes. Of course, there
> will never be a Negro Republic; first of all, they have no real
> programme. But if President Kennedy's proposed laws should
> happen to be rejected by the Senate, they might become far more
> important than they are at present.[79]

On that day the 'Trial' of the white man which a Boston Black
Muslim, Gene Walcott, turned into a play that was greeted with
wild enthusiasm by Negro audiences,[80] might assume a more
sinister meaning and be the prelude to that 'Battle of Armageddon'
which the more cautious Elijah Muhammad prefers for the moment
to relegate to the regions of eschatology, whereas the younger and
more pugnacious Malcolm X would probably have rejected its
mystical aspect and made it a real battle to be fought among the
cotton plantations of the South and in the streets of the northern
cities. It must not be forgotten that the trial of the white man—at
all events on the stage—invariably ends with a verdict of guilty and
a demand for the death-penalty. And according to Gene Walcott
the case for the prosecution is overwhelming:

> I accuse the white man of being the biggest liar on earth. I
> accuse the white man of being the biggest drunkard on earth. I
> accuse the white man of being the biggest eater of pork on earth,
> although the Bible forbids him to eat it. I accuse the white man
> of being the biggest gambler on earth. Gentlemen of the jury, I
> accuse the white man of being the biggest murderer on earth. I
> accuse the white man of being the biggest warmonger on earth. I
> accuse the white man of being the biggest adulterer on earth. I
> accuse the white man of being the biggest thief on earth. I
> accuse the white man of being the biggest hypocrite on earth. I
> accuse the white man of being the biggest sower of discord on
> earth . . .

The 'Warlords'

For General Edwin A. Walker the civil war between North and South did not end on 9 April 1865. In front of his house in Dallas he still flies the Confederate flag and he behaves as if he were still at war with Washington. The military court of inquiry held to investigate his activities found that he was an 'eccentric'. After the riots in Oxford some people even called him a 'madman'. But Walker is neither an eccentric nor a madman. He is just a re-actionary general, of a type that can be found in any army. A general who is afraid of peace and dreams of a preventive war. A general who thinks that he ought to enter the 'button room' and put an end to the policy of appeasement. In other words a warlord. And in the United States he is certainly not an isolated case, though fortunately he is an extreme one. He is the most radical exponent of that military élite which ever since the last war has been trying to gain more and more power and, contrary to all the rules of law, tradition and common sense, claims that it ought to have political control of the country.

A much-decorated veteran of the Second World War and the Korean campaign, and considered to have been one of the best fighting generals, Walker was the man whom President Eisenhower chose in 1957 when he decided to send Federal troops to restore order in Little Rock. That at that time Walker was still a loyal and responsible officer is proved by the speech he made to the students in that little town torn by racial conflicts. 'The United States,' Walker warned them, 'is a nation under law and not under men . . . we are all subject to all the laws, whether we approve of them personally or not . . . there can be no exceptions.'[81] But it seems as if the embittered climate of Arkansas, under the governorship of Faubus, infected him. In May 1959 he joined the John Birch Society, thus contravening the laws he had extolled only two years before. His connexion with this neo-Fascist organization was not dis-covered, however, until two years later when, as commander of the 24th infantry division stationed in Germany, he continually spread propaganda against the Federal government among his troops and allowed extreme right-wing publications to circulate. Summoned before a court of inquiry and transferred to another post, Walker chose to resign his commission, justifying his action in these defiant words:

It will be my purpose now, as a civilian, to attempt to do what I have found it no longer possible to do in uniform. War has been declared. Every man is a soldier. I think of the words of the Marine General to his men: 'We are surrounded. We must not let them get away.'[82]

These arrogant words, couched in the style of a Buck Rogers comic strip, were soon to be followed by deeds. Walker was seen at Rightist meetings in the company of the ex-Reverend Billy James Hargis and the former candy-manufacturer Robert Welch. On 24 October 1963 when Adlai Stevenson was assaulted as he was leaving a theatre in Dallas after having just said: 'It becomes increasingly difficult, therefore, to understand the logic of these super-patriots . . . who decry every attempt at negotiation and conciliation and offer no alternative save weapons that will destroy friend and foe alike,' Walker's comment was: 'Adlai got what he deserved. I am ashamed of those citizens of Dallas who have not the courage to say what they mean.' Two days later in Jackson, in a speech to 250 members of the White Citizens' Councils, Walker repeated his usual charges—that the State Department was full of Communists, that the Soviet Union received copies of all United States military plans, and that Congress was virtually 'a prisoner of the United Nations'. And he ended his speech with a veiled threat: 'The Kennedys have liquidated the government of the United States . . . Unless we oppose the United Nations, there will not be a President of the United States again.'[83] Less than a month later, somebody did 'liquidate' the most obnoxious of the Kennedys—and in Dallas, too. On that occasion Walker made no comment, but a week later he broke his silence and accused Lee Oswald of having been the author of an attack on himself seven months earlier. Curiously enough, this 'revelation' was published for the first time by a Munich neo-Nazi journal—the *National-Zeitung und Deutsche Soldaten-Zeitung.*

Many things had contributed to make Edwin A. Walker an extreme case. Not the least of these was the grave decision taken by Eisenhower in 1958, at one of the most critical moments of the Cold War, to allow army officers to act as secret agents and spread anti-Communist propaganda among soldiers and civilians. This order was countermanded by McNamara a few years later, but Walker maintained that it justified his actions.

The mobilization of the 24th Infantry Division cold war effort was superseded by authority from a 1958 directive of the National

Security Council, the top advisory board to the President, which called for the mobilization of all arms of government, civilian, diplomatic, military—in the cold war. My efforts became the rationale for my relief.[84]

Undoubtedly Walker went too far in following the directives of the National Security Council, but it cannot be denied that the suggestion that he should play a political role and try to influence the opinions of his soldiers came originally from the Department of Defence. For that matter, Eisenhower, in his farewell address to the nation on 17 January 1961, admitted that he had made a mistake and warned his successor against the danger of giving too much power to the army:

> This conjunction of an immense military establishment and a large arms industry is new in the American experience. The total influence—economic, political, even spiritual—is felt in every city, in every State House, every office of the Federal government . . . We must never let the weight of this combination endanger our liberties or democratic processes.

The army's role in the State and in American society has, in fact, increased to an unprecedented degree since the last war. The Pentagon, with its budget totalling millions of dollars, has become the biggest purchasing agency in the world and is consequently in a position to affect the whole of American life. The alliance between the big business economy and the military bureaucracy began during the war and continued during the following two decades, producing that enormous apparatus known as the military-industrial-technological complex. In their efforts to consolidate this new oligarchy and make it easier to obtain orders for the supply of war materials, big industries like the General Dynamic, Boeing, Lockheed, North American Aviation and Remington Rand have given employment to 1,400 retired officers, some of these being well-known figures like MacArthur, Ridgway, Wedemeyer, Kirk and Bedell Smith.[85] Military influence has played a decisive role in the scientific world and when scientists were needed to produce nuclear weapons and missiles this led to what Wright Mills calls the 'militarization of science'.[86] Even the field of education has been unable to escape military control. With the institution of courses for officer cadets and compulsory 'security screening' for students and professors, the American scholastic system is becoming a barracks, a huge factory turning out conformists and yes-men.

With so much power behind them, it was not difficult to foresee that one day the 'warlords' would try to influence the country's policy and even to force the hands of civilians. We know all too well how MacArthur did his best to extend the Korean War;[87] how Admirals Radford and Carney tried to persuade Eisenhower to resort to armed intervention in China and atomic reprisals against the Viet-Minh; how Norstad wanted France and Germany to be supplied with atomic weapons. So far, however, the civil power has been able to neutralize these attempts on the part of over-ambitious officers. But although their increasing and sinister influence is generally acknowledged, it has not been possible to deprive them of their latest privilege, that of influencing public opinion. The military have taken advantage of this to launch a huge programme of 'public orientation', spending tens of millions of dollars and employing thousands of propagandists, some in uniform and some not, many of whom have revealed their right-wing, reactionary tendencies and, together with the extremists of the Radical Right, have criticized the government's policy, clamouring for 'global militancy' and a preventive war.

This collusion between the military and the Radical Right was exposed in June 1961 in a report to the Defence Secretary, McNamara. The author of this memorandum, the Democratic Senator William J. Fulbright, cited eleven cases of seminars or public meetings in which high-ranking officers took part and exponents of the Radical Right also spoke. 'Running through all of them,' Senator Fulbright revealed,

> is a central theme that the primary, if not exclusive, danger to this country is internal Communist infiltration . . . the thesis of the nature of the Communist threat often is developed by equating social legislation with socialism, and the latter with communism. Much of the administration's domestic legislative program, including continuation of the graduated income-tax, expansion of social security . . . Federal aid to education, etc. . . . . would be characterized as steps toward Communism.

At Fort Smith, Fayetteville, Little Rock, Pittsburgh, Pensacola, Houston and dozens of other places, high-ranking officers sat on the platform with extremists like Billy Hargis, Fred Schwarz and George Benson, approving everything they said. 'Perhaps it is far-fetched,' Senator Fulbright says, 'to call the revolt of the French generals an example of the ultimate danger. Nevertheless, military officers, French or American, have some common characteristics arising from their profession and there are numerous military "fingers on the trigger" throughout the world.'[88] Fulbright's apprehensions—which later, after the unsuccessful landing in Cuba and the spread of 'shelter-mania',[89] were also shared by President Kennedy—were not altogether unjustified. It may be true that the plant of American militarism has very shallow roots, but as things are at present, the alliance between the military bureaucrats and big industry seems to be growing stronger rather than the contrary. If we add to this alliance (which has virtually compelled American capitalism to continue its wartime economic policy) the tendency among many members of the military élite to support the theories of the Radical Right, then the problem of United States militarism is revealed in all its gravity, and only general disarmament—which is highly improbable—can save the United States from becoming 'a garrison State', as Eisenhower himself feared.[90]

To us the destiny of the American Radical Right seems to be closely bound up with the international situation. If this should remain stable, the wave of extremism that characterized the early 1960s and culminated in the murder of President Kennedy might come to a stop and recede, as was the case with the hysterical type of McCarthyism in 1954. If, on the other hand, it were to get worse, then the partisans of 'immediate action', who are to be found among the Birchites and in the army, among diehard conservatives and executives of the armaments industry, might try to get the upper hand. 'It is not necessary to insult the right wing in our country by calling it fascist,' wrote John Weiss; 'it is, however, necessary to say that an intense social crisis, or a series of "defeats" in American foreign policy, might well put them in a mood to accept totalitarianism as a possible way out.'[91] Moreover, the American Radical Right must be judged, not by its present composition, the number of its adherents or of the Senators and Deputies it sends to Congress, but by its function as a catalyser of all the active and latent reactionary forces in the country, by its determination to encourage religious and racial intolerance, its hatred of progress, its fear of new ideas and its contempt for culture and intelligence.

But although bigotry and intolerance have deep roots in the United States, although loyalty is often identified with conformism and the periodical orgies of witch-hunting often remind us of what happened in Nazi Germany, the fact remains that, as Francis Biddle, a former Attorney General, has pointed out, 'we have never accepted them, or anything like them, as did the Nazis, who welcomed the persecutions, and encouraged the violence as an integral "ideal" of the new "revolutionary" state policy.'[92] However powerful they may be, the Rightist movements have never been able to halt the peculiar process of American democracy; and they have achieved only partial and ephemeral successes at moments of crisis. Their periodical aggressiveness has been restrained by the instinctive distrust all Americans feel for authoritarian solutions, by the peculiar structure of the American constitutional system, the division of power, the protection of the law, freedom of speech and the common sense of the majority. For example, just when McCarthyism was at its height, a 'Fund for the Republic' was launched, which had as its specific aim the defence and diffusion of the principles contained in the Declaration of Independence, the Constitution and the Bill of Rights. On that occasion, the task of reminding Americans of their devotion to the secular traditions of constitutional liberty was successfully fulfilled. We must, however, add that in a country where the military-industrial-technological complex is growing ever stronger and its ambitions greater with every day the Cold War lasts, the barriers raised against subversion are today being subjected to a heavier strain, and for the more thoughtful, sensitive Americans it is becoming harder to believe with Herman Melville that they can remain the only bearers of the 'ark of liberty in the world'.

16   Latin America

The 'avengers' of Eichmann

On 31 May 1962, after a trial that had lasted eight months and focused the attention of the whole world on the *Beit Haam* in Jerusalem, *Obersturmbannführer* Adolf Eichmann was hanged in the Israeli prison at Ramle. A few days after the ashes of this man who had 'crossed the line dividing human beings from wild beasts' had been scattered over the waters of the Mediterranean, a Jewish girl student, Graciela Narcisa Sirota, was kidnapped in the streets of Buenos Aires by four *niños bien*, who took her to an empty flat and branded a swastika on her right breast. A day or two later, another Jewish student, Riccardo D'Alessandro, was subjected to the same treatment. 'Vengeance' for the execution of Colonel Eichmann was not confined to these two episodes. Plastic bombs exploded in a number of synagogues, many shops owned by Jews were sacked, and a bomb wrecked the premises of an Israeli travel agency. The anti-Semitic campaign assumed such proportions that the Minister of the Interior, Carlos Adrogue, appeared on television to appeal for order, promising that the perpetrators of the outrages would be punished and accusing the extreme right wing of being responsible for them. 'The critical period through which the Republic is passing has been aggravated by the outrages committed by these legatees of Hitlerism. The attacks on our Jewish compatriots, on their synagogues, institutions, shops and homes, are a disgrace to Argentina and cannot be tolerated.'[1]

This 'vendetta' was not confined to Argentina, where Eichmann had lived for many years under a false name and where he had been kidnapped by agents of the Israeli 'Section 06'. In the capital of the neighbouring Republic of Uruguay groups of neo-Nazis shelled a Jewish restaurant with a bazooka, threw 'Molotov cocktails' into a Jewish school and, after beating them up, branded Dr Maximo Handel Blanc and another young Jew. Likewise in Montevideo, a girl named Soledad Barret, daughter of the Paraguayan dictator Alfred Stroessner's most stubborn adversary, was kidnapped by several 'young Hitlerites', who, when she refused to shout 'Long live Hitler! Long live the OAS! Death to Fidel!' incised swastikas on her legs with a knife and then threw her out of a moving car. About thirty other Jews were beaten up, branded or disfigured with vitriol. When the police failed to intervene, 20,000 young people paraded on the esplanade in front of the University of Montevideo to show their solidarity with these victims of racial hatred. 'This is the twenty-ninth attack made by Uruguayan Nazis,' said one of the speakers, 'and so far the police and the authorities have done nothing. But we of the *Mesa Coordenatora Antifascista* intend to make the Fascists stop disfiguring the faces of Jewish women and scarring the legs of our girls.' Racialist demonstrations also took place in Bolivia and Peru between June and December 1962, and despite the lack of zeal shown by the South American police forces in discovering and punishing the culprits, it became clear that the responsibility lay with the neo-Fascist International, which seemed to have found in Latin America a more favourable theatre for its operations than in Europe.

This may be true, the reason being that the ground had been carefully prepared. We have already shown how, ever since the 1930s, the 'Houses of Fascist Culture', the 'Hispano-American Institutes' and above all Rosenberg's APA (the organization which kept a watch on the activities of Germans living abroad) had launched an intensive campaign the aim of which was the diffusion of totalitarian and racialist ideas in the Latin American countries, especially in those where there were large and well-established Italian and German colonies. The German communities were at the same time under the control of the *Auslands-Organisation* headed by Rudolf Hess. This campaign lasted for more than ten years and resulted in the formation of an efficient 'fifth column', which was particularly useful to the Axis Powers during the Second World War, and also, in every part of the continent, became the moving force behind the various *pronunciamientos, cuartelazos,* Caudillist movements and para-Fascist régimes. In Brazil, the Greenshirts of the integralist Plinio Salgado made their appearance as long ago as 1933 and were later absorbed by Getulio Vargas's *Estado Novo*. In Bolivia, where the German military mission under Colonel Kundt and Captain Ernst Röhm (who later became Hitler's right-hand man) had made a deep impression, Gualberto Villaroel seized power, he being, like Juan Perón, a typical product of the pro-Nazi military 'lodges' which Röhm had set up all over

South America.[2] Sympathy for the Fascist ideologies even survived the total collapse of the Axis Powers, as is proved by the success achieved in Colombia by the Fascist, terrorist régime under Laureano Gómez and by Perón's *justicialismo* in Argentina, and by the rise to power of military *golpistas* (trained in the same Nazi-Fascist school as Perón) like Pérez Jiménez in Venezuela and Manuel Odria in Peru.

Berlin considered this part of the world to be such fertile soil that almost all the Nazis who escaped capture after the German surrender were sent to Latin America by the ODESSA organization. Argentina probably received the largest quota, since it offered a safe refuge to criminals like Adolf Eichmann, responsible for the 'final solution' of the Jewish problem; the diplomat Karl Klingenfuss; the former Slovak Foreign Minister Ferdinand Durčansky, responsible for the death of 50,000 Czechoslovak Jews; the diplomat Franz Rademacher, whose escape to Argentina was described by the Buenos Aires Nazi journal *German Honor* as 'an extraordinary feat of rescue from the clutches of the Jewish jackals';[3] the *Luftwaffe* General Adolf Galland; the leader of the *Ustaše*, Ante Pavelich, and thousands of other Italian, Rumanian, Slovak, Croat and Hungarian Fascists.[4] These fugitives could easily be concealed and absorbed by those sectors of the European communities which formed the 'fifth column' and had not been the victims of reprisals at the end of the war. 'Argentina,' wrote *Eco del Mundo* towards the end of 1947,

> is still the most convenient hiding-place for Nazis who plotted and are still plotting to achieve world supremacy for Germany. Nearly a hundred thousand German Nazi sympathizers are still circulating freely and undisturbed in the country. Of these sixty thousand were members of the Nazi Party, while twenty thousand belonged to German 'sports clubs' or societies which, as the Allies discovered after the war, were really clandestine Nazi groups. Today the German-Argentine 'Union Club' has more than a hundred branches in strategic positions and on a war footing. At least four other Argentine organizations are still as active as they were in the days of Hitler.[5]

Thousands of others found refuge in Brazil, Venezuela, Chile, Paraguay,[6] Cuba, Colombia and Peru, where they swelled the ranks of existing extremist groups and often became expert advisers to the dictators who have succeeded one another in South America during the post-war years. This clandestine influx of Nazis assumed such proportions and revealed such a perfect organization that for a time it was even believed that Hitler and Eva Braun had escaped to Argentina in a submarine. In any case the arrival of these escapees led to a considerable increase in the number of 'punitive expeditions' against Jews. To quote only one example, at Bogotá in 1946 gangs of young men in uniform and wearing Nazi emblems wrecked most of the shops owned by Jews. In 1950 in the Colombian city of Medellín (headquarters of the neo-Fascist *Joven América*) a requiem mass was celebrated in memory of the Nazi war criminals hanged by the Allies and was attended by young men wearing swastika armlets. In Brazil, in 1958, a man was arrested during an anti-Semitic demonstration who turned out to be one of those responsible for the massacre in the Riga ghetto. About the same time periodicals expressing Fascist or anti-Jewish views began to appear, like *Der Weg* and *Azul y Bianco* in Argentina, *La Escoba* in Uruguay, *Die Brücke* and *Europan* in Brazil.

Poverty and Pronunciamientos

The seeds of hate fell on a continent which was progressing very slowly, afflicted by all the ills, and where social injustice went to incredible lengths. The Colombian scholar Oscar Delgado tells us that 110,000 big landowners (owning an average of 10,000 acres each) monopolize the arable land in Latin America (over 1,000 million acres), while tens of millions of peasants have nothing but a tiny patch of land and live under indescribably wretched conditions. In an attempt to give a convincing and succinct picture of the prevailing poverty Alfred Sauvy wrote:

> Take the average income of a Frenchman, already inadequate as we all know; halve it and you have the average income of an Argentinian; halve that again and you have the income of a Brazilian. That will give some idea of the low standard of living down there. But halve the income of a Brazilian and you get that of an Ecuadorian, and if you halve it for the fourth time you have the income of a Bolivian. And we must not forget that the average income lies halfway between the richest and the poorest. Behind these figures there is sheer misery.[7]

Inevitably, wherever the average income is lowest and the peasants live in the direst poverty, the government is authoritarian, and the dictators, if they do not become absolute masters of the country's economy (like the Somoza family in Nicaragua) empty the State coffers before they are replaced by still stronger men.

Fulgencio Batista left Cuba with the equivalent of 40 million pounds; when Pérez Jiménez was forced to flee from Venezuela, his 'savings' amounted to about 80 million pounds; and as for the 'liberator' of the Dominican Republic, Rafael Léonidas Trujillo, it is calculated that by the time he died he had accumulated a fortune of about 330 million pounds. This kind of 'Caudillism' is a veritable scourge which has no parallel in other continents and is older than Fascism, to which it is nevertheless akin in the way it defends the interests of oligarchies, in its one-party system, its contempt for the opposition, its police régime, its resort to torture, its physical removal of adversaries and its habit of forming pretorian guards (the most famous of these being the *tonton-macoutes* responsible for the personal safety of the Negro dictator of Haiti, François Duvalier, who on 3 April 1964 proclaimed himself president for life).[8]

These dictatorships have always received (and some of them are still receiving it) the direct or indirect support of the United States, who since the days of the Monroe doctrine have had a kind of protectorate over Central and South America. Under pressure from military circles and in order to defend American investments in the twenty Latin American republics, Washington has always supported, and sometimes, as a result of CIA intrigues, even imposed or created, the Fascist military dictatorships of Anastasio Somoza in Nicaragua, Castillo Armas in Guatemala, Rafael Trujillo in the Dominican Republic, Rojas Pinilla in Colombia, Remón in Panama and Batista in Cuba. In Guatemala, in 1954, in order to overthrow the progressive régime of Arbenz Guzman, whose projected agrarian reforms would have been contrary to the interests of the American United Fruit Company, the CIA under Allen Dulles even organized a small army of mercenaries who managed to oust the Guzman régime and restore a dictatorship. Seven years later, though less successfully, the CIA staged a repetition of this operation by landing 2,000 guerrillas near Havana at the Bay of Pigs, after training them at secret base-camps in Nicaragua and Guatemala.

Even today, after most of these tyrants have been overthrown by popular revolts, Washington is still supporting a number of dictators (Stroessner in Paraguay, Duvalier in Haiti etc.), though since the appearance on the scene of Fidel Castro they prefer to support more reputable and mildly progressive men, in the vain hope of steering Latin America towards a 'protected democracy' rather than towards the insurrectional methods favoured by Ché Guevara. But this trend towards a 'new look' (typified by the confidence placed in leaders of the 'reform trend' and by the launching of the *Alianza para Progreso*) may have come too late in a continent ravaged by guerrilla warfare, where a struggle without quarter is being waged between the various secret organizations and oppression is tending to increase rather than decrease, against the background of the Manichaean conflict between East and West. More often than not this ideological conflict serves as an excuse for the traditional guardians of public order and conservatism, who are, of course, the military. During 1963 four 'reformist' governments backed by the United States were overthrown by military *pronunciamientos*[9] after a press campaign which accused the four deposed presidents of having failed to suppress the Castroists and Communists.

Except in Uruguay and Costa Rica, the armed forces of the Latin American Republics have played the part of protectors of the interests of the big landowners and capitalists, and consequently, like the German SA, the Fascist action squads and the Falangists, they are regarded as oppressors by the working classes and the peasantry. This exclusive role played by the military caste as supporters of reaction fulfilling the functions of a gendarmerie whose duty it is to suppress the lower orders explains why Latin America has produced only two popular Fascist movements, Perón's in Argentina and the Vargas régime in Brazil. And it also explains why these two movements, with the support of the poorest classes, created a type of Fascism which, as Seymour Martin Lipset says, can be called 'leftist'.[10] A Fascism which is essentially progressive and almost a forerunner of Castroism, and which has gone much further towards the left than the respective *Caudillos* intended.

From Vargas to Perón

Before dealing with the neo-Fascist movements still active in Latin America at the present time, we therefore feel that we must say a few words about 'Getulism' and 'Peronism' which, although they were to a certain extent subservient to the traditional oligarchies, were not in any sense forerunners of existing extremist right-wing groups like the military *golpistas*.

'Of all the decisions made by Vargas, probably none had greater implications than his determination to bring the working groups into the political arena . . .'[11] That decision was made in 1938, and it was the first time anything of the sort had happened in the Latin America of big landowners and agrarians. Getulio Vargas, who had previously relied on Plinio Salgado's 'Greenshirts' as well as on the Communists led by Luis Prestes, eventually outlawed both these movements and set up a popular and vaguely corporative dictatorship (the *Estado Novo*), as remote from Mussolini's 'Caesarism' as it was from Salazar's 'professorialism'. Appealing to the bewildered and not yet politically-minded masses, who crowded into the big urban centres which were rapidly becoming industrialized, Vargas secured their support by introducing a programme of reforms which would have benefited them. But his was a doctrine of intentions, the doctrine of a dreamer. Nevertheless, when he was deposed by the military in 1945, there was a kind of popular rising, known as *queremismo* because the populace was fond of shouting *'Queremos Getulio!'* ('We want Getulio!'). The bewildered masses, who for the first time had been granted social safeguards such as a minimum wage and an eight-hour day, were incapable of judging the régime as a whole or of identifying its obnoxious aspects, and they remembered only its advantages (enjoyed only by the working classes in the big cities) and its good intentions.

The same could be said of the Perón legend. As soon as he came to power, Colonel Perón followed the example set by Vargas, basing his tactics on the support of the working-class masses, who until then had been the victims of despotic masters (or at the best, of paternalism), and he won them over with his attempt to introduce social democracy into Argentina. He introduced a certain number of legislative measures which—at all events during the first years of his régime—undoubtedly helped to raise the standard of living and wages, allowed more time for leisure and gave the workers in the cities a sense of social security, while with his 'Peons' statute' he tried to help the agricultural labourers and tenant-farmers at the expense of the big landowners. When he finally succeeded in gaining control of the trade unions and extending their activities by making them instruments of collective bargaining supported by the State, he laid the foundations of Peronism and gave it some hope of surviving even after the fall of his régime.

This programme, which might easily be taken for that of a Labour Party with extremely radical intentions, inevitably won the approval

N

of the masses, who in the meantime had found in the leader's wife, Evita Perón, a kind of impassioned inspirer and protectress.[12] But Peronism, although it benefited the workers, had many features reminiscent of Fascist authoritarianism—its contempt for parliamentary procedure, a strong dose of nationalism, the idea of the Corporative State and its exaltation of the leader's presidential functions. Juan Perón, who had served as military attaché in Rome during the imperialistic phase of Fascism, had been much influenced by its ideas, but when he published the 'twenty principles' of his political doctrine, which he called 'justicialism', he took care to make his standpoint clear. 'We shall create a kind of Fascism, but we shall carefully avoid making the mistakes Mussolini made.' He was also at pains to stress his doctrine's universal character, explaining that 'justicialism' was 'a term halfway between spirituality and materialism, a new word which, born in Argentina, will conquer the world by reviving hope'. In reality, once the woolly thinking was removed, there was nothing new in this doctrine. It was a kind of *Caudillismo* (in Buenos Aires it drew its inspiration in particular from the Argentinian dictator Juan Manuel Rosas) mixed up with totalitarianism of the Mussolini type.

Peronism undoubtedly gained the support of the poorest classes, but the few successes it achieved proved far too costly. On 16 September 1955 the 'people's colonel' was deposed by the army, after the State had been brought to the verge of bankruptcy. But the *descamisados* refused to admit his mistakes, his compromises and mystifications, and for years continued to scrawl on the walls of factories *Perón eterno, Perón volverá!* ('Perón for ever, Perón will return!'), while the Peronist leaders preserved their influence within the trade unions, and even made the Argentinian Trade Union Council the only body capable of offering effective resistance to the army.

Perón failed because he was an improviser and a demagogue, but he undoubtedly roused the masses in his country, releasing quantities of pent-up energy and reviving a whole series of unfulfilled hopes. The governments which occupied the Casa Rosada after his eclipse always had to reckon with his followers, who represented about 25 per cent of the electorate and were reluctant to join the traditional parties.[13] In particular, it was generally assumed that the Left would denounce Perón's mistakes and try to attract the *descamisados* by promising to stage a real revolution. But the unexpected persistence of the Perón legend compelled the leaders of the Communist and Castroist left wing to try to come to terms with the Peronist electorate in 1962, without worrying unduly about their Fascist tendencies. On 29 May 1963, the exiled President Arturo Frondizi appealed to the 'intransigent radicals' to form a united front with the Peronists, giving, among other reasons, this:

> In Argentina there will never be peace, development and justice, not to mention real liberty and rights, without the participation of 'justicialism' on an equal footing with the other democratic movements. 'Justicialism' represents the majority of the working class and it is a movement with deep national and Christian roots, symbolizing—for the workers in particular—social justice and economic independence, the two causes which inspired the political activities of President Juan Domingo Perón. Whatever mistakes and aberrations occurred in the integral application of such principles, the oligarchy, when it tries to wipe out 'justicialism' completely, is merely showing that its aim is, not to find ways of remedying those errors and aberrations, but to destroy the profound significance which 'justicialism' had, and still has, for the workers of Argentina. It should therefore be made quite clear that every manœuvre, every attempt, every compromise tending to isolate us from 'justicialism', or to isolate it from the affairs of the nation, will plunge the country into anarchy.[14]

The Spanish historian Salvador de Madariaga, however, disagrees with this opinion and maintains to this day that 'the Peronist movement, frankly Fascist in its form and in its methods, is a living menace to the peace and stability of the whole system'.[15]

Faced with opposition from the right-wing parties and the army and assiduously wooed by the Left, the 'justicialist' movement is still—twenty-four years after its first appearance on the political scene and twelve years after the fall of Perón—the most important factor in Argentinian public life, and in 1962 alone it provoked five military revolts. The masses who are still under its influence and still believe in Perón's populist ideas, might be ready to join in other experiments, but they might equally well decide to return to democracy.[16] It is certain, however, that there can be no such return until Argentina makes those drastic social changes which are so urgently needed, and so long as the army, whether 'red' or 'blue', continues to play an important role in the political life of the nation.

Except in Argentina, where the masses are still hesitating between Perón's populism and the lure of Castroism, Latin America is following the Cuban experiment with much sympathy, and in many quarters Castroism is considered to be the only cure for the continent's chronic ills. Consequently there have been outbreaks of guerrilla warfare in several Central American republics, as well as in Paraguay, Ecuador, Venezuela, Colombia and Peru, while a 'peasant league' has made its appearance in the north-east of Brazil. Francisco Julião in Brazil, Hugo Blanco in Peru, William Aranguren in Colombia and Marco Antonio Yonsoza in Guatemala are all trying to emulate Castro. Ernesto Ché Guevara's manual of guerrilla warfare seems to have replaced every other textbook.

Rejected by the masses, even in its milder, populist and Latin-American version, Fascism in the 1960s has become the hope of the extreme right wing, which hopes that it will be able to counter Castroism (or at all events the reforms put forward by the *Alianza para Progreso*) by organizing guerrilla warfare on its own account. An example of this new policy is provided by Brazil, where during the last few years armed *capangas* organized by the landowners have been active in suppressing the peasants, while Carlos Lacerda, governor of the State of Guanabara, makes similar use of the *quadrilhas* (action-squads) forming part of his *Milicia Anticomunista*.[17] In March 1964, when President João Goulart had a law passed by the Brazilian parliament for the expropriation of uncultivated land and invited the peasants to take over such land, 200 big landowners in the State of Goiaz dispatched 'commandos' to fight the peasants, while in São Paulo some army generals overthrew the Goulart government on 1 April of that year, thus paving the way for the *coup* which men of the Right like Governors Magalhaes Pinto, Carlos Lacerda and Adhemar de Barros had been preparing for a long time. 'In Latin American parlance,' said *The Nation*, commenting on this 'constitutional revolution',

> the 'Gorilas' represent the coalition of wealthy oligarchs and military leaders who periodically stage 'bogus revolutions' under the banner of anti-communism in order to stay the forces of reform. The recent overthrow of the Brazilian government is a classical 'Gorila' movement.[18]

Goulart was accused of being a fellow-traveller and of wanting to expropriate the big landowners, whereas in reality, although at least 200 projects for agrarian reforms were lying in the archives of the parliament buildings in Brasilia, he had only authorized the expropriation of waste land, which was only a timid prelude to a reform. When Goulart fell, a reactionary military government under General Humberto Castello Branco had 8,000 people arrested in one week (among them being the leader of the 'Peasant Leagues'. Francisco Julião), suspended 40 Deputies and deprived another 100 citizens of their civil rights, including the last three presidents of Brazil. 'The forces of renewal in Brazil,' said *The Nation* by way of consolation, 'cannot always be contained by military movements.'

The 'Tacuara'

An even graver sympton of a Fascist revival in Latin America was the proliferation of ultra-patriotic and racialist organizations like the *Tacuara*, the *Guardia Restauradora Nacionalista*, the *Unión Cívica Nacionalista*, the *Nuevo Orden Hispano-Americano*, the *Frente Nacional-Socialista Argentino* in Argentina, the *Legión Boliviana Social-Nacionalista*, the *Frente Estudiantil Nacionalista* in Uruguay, the *Movimiento Avanzado Nacional* in Colombia, the *Movimiento de Acción Nacional* in Venezuela, the *Frente Patriota* in Mexico, the *Acción Revolucionaria Nacional* in Ecuador, and the various branches of the neo-Fascist *Joven América*, which drew their inspiration from, and were in close contact with, Jean Thiriart's *Jeune Europe*. The chief centres of the *Joven América* movement were Buenos Aires, Montevideo and, in Colombia, Bogotá and Medellín.

Of these the most active were the Argentinian organizations and the best-known was the *Tacuara* ('The Spear'), which after the execution of Eichmann in 1962 launched the biggest anti-Semitic campaign Argentina had ever known. Founded in 1930 by a student named Juan Queralta, it adopted as its emblems the Andean condor (stylized so that it looked like a Prussian eagle) and the red star of the dictator Juan Manuel Rosas. Today it describes itself officially as a Falangist movement whose aim is to set up a Fascist Corporative State in Argentina. In reality, the 'national syndicalists' of the *Tacuara* are more interested in the myths and methods of the Nazis than they are in Don José Antonio Primo de Rivera's vague ideology. Their battle-cry is *Heil Tacuara!*, to which in 1962 they added *Patriotismo sí, judíos no!* They are believed to have been responsible for the branding of swastikas on the bodies of Jews.

The head office of the *Tacuara* is in Buenos Aires, at 415 Avenida Tucumán, and consists of a few untidy rooms, in which the stuffy atmosphere reminds one of a Fascist 'den' during the heroic years of the movement. Here in 1963 one could find the two leaders of the *Tacuara*, José Baxter[19] and Alberto Ezcurra Uriburu, the latter being a great-grandson of the dictator Rosas and son of General José F. Uriburu, who during his two years of office in the early 1930s tried to turn Argentina into a Corporative State under a Fascist élite. When asked about his movement's aims, Alberto Ezcurra Uriburu replied:

> We shall defend our country as a unified whole; we shall defend the Catholic values against Marxist-Jewish-Liberal-Masonic-capitalistic materialism. We are not anti-Semites with racialist aims, but we are enemies of Jewry. In Argentina the Jews are the servants of Israeli imperialism, and they have shown what they are by violating our national sovereignty when they arrested Adolf Eichmann In this struggle we have much in common with Nasser.[20]

The real motives of their hatred were, however, somewhat different. The affront to Argentina's national dignity was only a pretext. As an organ of the big agrarian capitalists the *Tacuara* tried to convince the poorer classes, who were infuriated by the scandulous affluence of the old ruling class, that the real bloodsuckers, the real starvers of the people, were the 475,000 Jews living in the country. This was the technique that the Nazis had used in Germany in 1933, but in Buenos Aires, although in the summer of 1963 the walls were still covered with inscriptions such as 'Jews are traitors!' and 'Jews to the gas-chambers!', the masses did not fall into the trap, and all hopes of a pogrom vanished. Similarly, the attempt made by the *Tacuara* to identify the Jews with the Castroists also failed.

This neo-Fascist organization has about 3,000 members, who are more prominent than those of any other group when it comes to fights with the Communists and Castroists or at the 'oceanic' rallies staged by the Peronist party. They receive military training from former SS officers who have found a refuge in Argentina, while their shock troops are trained in camps set up on the estates of the big traditionalist families. That the *Tacuara* draws its inspiration from Nazism and is in touch with the 'Black International' received a further proof when it was discovered at the beginning of 1961, after an attempt to blow up a synagogue at Johannesburg, that this Argentinian extremist organization had ramifications on the other side of the Atlantic, in South Africa, where the racial situation affords ideal opportunities for anti-Semitism.[21] On account of its anti-Zionist attitude, the *Tacuara* is also viewed with favour by the rulers of the Arab States. At the United Nations, the Saudi Arabia delegate, Ahmada Shukiary, was rash enough to say so, and this evoked an indignant protest from the president of a Jewish association:

> Never in the history of the United Nations has a delegate had the audacity to make such an outrageous suggestion as that made by Mr Ahmada Shukiary, when he recommended that the *Tacuara* should be taken under the wing of the UN.

Less aggressive than the *Tacuara,* but equally Nazi in its ideas, is the *Guardia Restauradora Nacionalista,* which counts among its members many sons of big landowners and military 'Gorilas'. Ultra-nationalist, anti-Communist and anti-Semitic, the *Guardia Restauradora* places its hopes in the advent of a general who will know how to establish a conservative dictatorship and will force the crowds who in recent years have flocked to the cities, where they fall an easy prey to Castroism, to return to the land. Run by the twenty-two-year-old Juan Carlos Coria, the *Guardia* has a theoretician—a chaplain of the *Santa Casa de Ejercicios* named Julio Meinvielle, who on several occasions has been rebuked by his Catholic superiors for the anti-Semitic tone of his works (see, in particular, his *El Judío en el misterio de la Historia*).[22] Nor must we forget to mention, among the Argentinian racialist movements, the group of pseudo-intellectuals headed by Marcello Sánchez Secondo, which until 1961 published the periodical *Azul y blanco* (banned by Arturo Frondizi because it preached racial hatred), and now prints the bi-weekly *Segunda República*.[23] And finally, on 1st June 1964, under the auspices of what was vaguely described as the 'Argentinian National Party', Adolf Eichmann's son held a press conference in Buenos Aires, in the course of which he said: 'My father fought for all those who are threatened by international Jewry and Zionism.' On that occasion the youthful Horst Eichmann was wearing a swastika armlet.

This brief excursion among the dictatorships and neo-Nazi movements in Latin America shows clearly enough that the struggle between the proletarian masses and the forces of conservatism is only just beginning and that action squads have not got beyond the experimental stage. It would be wrong to attach too much importance to the 'rescue plan' put forward by the United States at Punta del Este, since the *Alianza para Progreso,* three years after its foundation, seems to be paying no attention to the restoration and strengthening of democracy in the Latin American republics, while its programme of reforms has likewise been a failure.[24] 'The only defect in this magnificent plan,' Paul Sweezy and Leo Hubermann wrote in 1961, when discussing what the American press had already christened the 'Alliance without progress',

> is that it will never work. And the reason why it will not work is that neither the oligarchies governing Latin America nor the United States government have the slightest intention of promoting, or even only permitting, the reforms which are absolutely essential if there is to be any satisfactory development south of the Rio Grande.[25]

And we do not believe that the decision taken by the United States to station anti-guerrilla forces in Panama and elsewhere can help democracy or enable the peoples of Central and South America to achieve what they call their 'second independence'—a real, effective independence. Direct intervention by the United States would only intensify the struggle between the forces of conservatism and those of revolution, and would transform the Latin-American continent into one great theatre of civil war.

17 South Africa

The Nazi precedents

'Let us waste no more time in futile lamentations and nauseating excuses,' says Frantz Fanon at the end of his *Les Damnés de la Terre*. 'Let us get away from this Europe which never stops talking about man, though it kills him wherever it finds him, at the corner of every street and in every corner of the world.' With these words the Algerian Fanon is not asking his readers to get away from Europe because of the crimes she has committed in the past (100 million Africans sold as slaves, the bloody campaigns of conquest, forced labour, segregation), but because of the crimes she is still committing today in her last African citadels by using violence and fraud, and may still commit tomorrow thanks to her influence alone and her skill in corrupting. Fanon's distrust of Europe is complete, so complete that he rejects her thirty centuries of experiments and conquests. He hopes that Africa will create 'not an imitation which would be nothing but a caricature', but an entirely new society and a new humanism. When we think of the methods employed by the Whites in South Africa, Rhodesia and Angola, in order to safeguard their privileges, we must admit that his distrust is justified. 'Europe's farewell gift to us,' an African writer told us in Johannesburg, 'has been Fascism. In Algeria she resuscitated the SS. In South Africa, the concentration camps. Where is she going to build the gas-chambers?'

In Africa, the last days of colonialism did, in fact, coincide with a desperate attempt to solve the knotty problem of the co-existence of Whites and Africans by imposing régimes based on violence and intolerance, just like the Fascist dictatorships. The classic example of this is the white community in South Africa, which in the 1960s is still trying to stop the natural growth of African nationalism by adopting an ultra-nationalistic policy which can have no future and which spreads a doctrine of hatred and destruction.

The Boers, in particular, who during the years of the Great Trek displayed an incredible will to survive and are now determined to preserve at all costs the identity of *het Volk*, reacted to the *swart gevaar* (black peril) with a decision and a programme that can be understood only if we bear in mind that the Afrikaners still believe in predestination and have a messianic conviction that, as a people, they have been entrusted with a special mission. Boer nationalism, which made its first appearance in 1912, when the Bible was translated into Afrikaans, received its definite confirmation in 1961, when the Boers gained a decisive victory over the more liberal-minded British element, which led to the proclamation of the Republic and the country's exit from the Commonwealth. This nationalism is a compound of racialism bordering on fanaticism and a desire for power and political supremacy *(baaskap)* that knows no material or moral limits and is charismatically sure that it cannot possibly be wrong. In the programme of the secret *Broederbond*, which ever since 1918 has played a decisive role in the development of *Afrikanerdom*, we read that the Boers are determined that the British element shall remain a minority, while their other rivals, the Coloureds, are to be kept in check by means of laws that reduce segregation to a system.[1]

During the 1930s the success of Nazism in Germany convinced the more aggressive and race-minded Boers that the teachings of *Mein Kampf* could also find application in South Africa, and that the moment for action was at hand. There thus arose, on soil that could hardly have been more fertile, the *Ossewa Brandwag*, which represents—as its *Kommandant-Generaal*, J. F. Van Rensburg, has explained—'the defence of Afrikaner nationalism against parliamentarism. The *Ossewa Brandwag* is not an imitation. It is a movement that has taken different names in different countries. In Italy it is called Fascism; in Germany, National Socialism; in Spain, Falangism; in South Africa, *Ossewa Brandwag*.' This movement reached its zenith in 1940, when it had more than 400,000 adherents and organized its *Stormjaers*—shock troops who distinguished themselves by committing numerous acts of sabotage and assaulting Jews or soldiers leaving for Europe to fight against the Nazis. Towards the end of the 1930s other Nazi or anti-Semitic movements made their appearance, among them being Louis Weichardt's 'Greyshirts', the *Boerenasie* led by Manie Maritz, and the South African Gentile National Socialist Movement under a certain Johannes von Strauss von Moltke, whose aim was 'to destroy the perversive influence of the Jews in economics, culture, religion, ethics and statecraft, and to re-establish European Aryan control in South Africa for the welfare of the Christian peoples'.[2] At a time when the country was already at war with Hitler's Germany, the former Minister Oswald Pirow defied the authorities and founded a movement called *Nuwe Oord*, of which seventeen members of parliament were members, though only for a short time.

Almost all the leaders of the Nationalist Party, which is at present in power and must therefore bear the responsibility for the policy of apartheid, either belonged to one of these Nazi movements or else expressed approval of them, including the late Premier Verwoerd who, when he was editor of *Die Transvaler*, for years conducted anti-Jewish and pro-Nazi campaigns.[3] Edwin S. Munger has compiled an interesting anthology of racialist and anti-Semitic invectives, bearing the signatures of the men chiefly responsible for apartheid—Malan, Strijdom, Louw, Erasmus and Dönges.[4]

The victories achieved by Hitler during the first two years of the war strengthened all the Nazi-inspired movements, and even the ministers of the Dutch Reformed Church (which later supported apartheid) made no attempt to conceal their feelings and refused to baptize the children of men who had gone to Europe to fight on the side of the Allies. One of them, the Reverend Jan Vorster (brother of the present Prime Minister), told a session of the Synod that 'Hitler's *Mein Kampf* points the way to greatness and can serve as an example for South Africa. Hitler has given the Germans a vocation and a fanaticism which will enable them to stand up to anyone.' Premier Smuts, who was pro-British and an interventionist, was obliged to send the more exuberant preachers to concentration camps. After the defeat of Hitler, anti-Semitism was temporarily relegated to the attic, while the pro-Nazis of the 'Greyshirt', *Nuwe Oord* and *Ossewa Brandwag* movements were absorbed into the Nationalist Party, which had by now imposed itself upon the country as the only patriotic party and had appropriated the hegemonic methods and programmes of the Nazi movements.[5]

The Nationalists in power

In 1948 the Boers finally succeeded in coming to power and proceeded to indulge in an orgy of racialism that can only be compared with the hysteria prevalent in Germany during the 1930s. At the inauguration of the Pharaonic monument commemorating the Voortrekkers, the epic of the Boer pioneers and the victory of the 'chosen people' over the accursed Africans, Premier Malan addressed a quarter of a million Afrikaners who had assembled at the foot of the sacred hill, dressed in 'trekker' costume, and he ended his speech by shouting:

> Back to your people; back to the highest ideals of your people; back to the pledge which has been entrusted to you for safekeeping; back to the altar of the people on which you must lay your sacrifice; back to the sanctity and inviolability of family life; back to the Christian way of life; back to the Christian faith; back to your Church; back to your God![6]

Malan's appeal did not fall on deaf ears. In the rest of the continent the Africans were beginning to formulate their demands, but the Afrikaners were leaving their villages and flocking to the city, the great capital and seat of power which hitherto had been controlled by the British element. English-speaking functionaries were gradually replaced and the civil service passed into the hands of the Boer racialists, who made Afrikaans the official language, hoisted the *Vierkleur* instead of the Union Jack, sang 'Die Stem van Suid-Afrika' instead of 'God save the Queen' and substituted German uniforms for those of the British army. The white opposition was reduced to impotence, while the black majority was immured in ghettoes under the apartheid laws. To complete this gigantic operation, they promulgated iniquitous and immoral laws, installed a police régime, and even falsified history. As John Coleman de Graft-Johnson points out, the racialist historians of South Africa's Witwatersrand University, with their distortion of historical facts, even managed to lay the foundations of a new *Herrenvolk* theory, worse than any propounded by Hitler, a theory which, if literally interpreted, makes the Negro a foreigner, an intruder, a new arrival in Africa.[7]

In 1958, when racial tension reached its highest point, because the plan for total segregation was about to come into force, Hendrik Frensch Verwoerd became Prime Minister. He was an anti-Semite and a great admirer of Hitler, whose theories and triumphs he had extolled in the columns of *Die Transvaler*. At the same time important posts were given to pro-Nazis who had been members of the *Ossewa Brandwag*, and these men set up the biggest concentration camp the world has ever known (hypocritically justified on religious, ethical and legal grounds). This was a camp for 13 million Africans, 'Coloureds' and Indians, which with its meticulous planning surpassed even the gigantic structure set up by Himmler to accommodate whole populations.

As soon as parliament had codified the segregation laws, the plan for the separation of the *'uitlanders'* from the chosen people was put into execution.[8] For four legislatures in succession there was a Boer majority, and parliament seemed to be doing nothing but turning out racialist laws. By 1962, after the passing of the Population Registration Act, the Mixed Marriages Act, the Group Areas Act, the various Pass Laws, the Job Reservation Act, the Suppression of Communism Act, the Public Safety Act and the Bantu Education Act, the Africans had been deprived of all their possessions and rights, including that of being still able to consider themselves human beings. As we have written elsewhere:

They cannot vote, they cannot choose their jobs or change them. They cannot specialize or try to improve their position. They cannot own anything, not even a plot of barren land in the 'reserves'. They cannot eat in the same restaurants or go to the same theatres or places of amusement as the Whites. They cannot share the same beaches, sit on the same seats, use the same lifts, the same buses or the same trains. They cannot marry white women, or have any social contacts with them. They are not allowed to enter railway stations, post offices or banks by the doors through which the Whites pass. They cannot go to the same schools or universities, or use the same libraries. They cannot offer their blood to a white man, and if they are doctors they can perform post-mortems only on Negroes. They cannot live in the white men's cities, and even in their own townships they can only rent houses. If they go into domestic service in the cities, they cannot take their families with them. If their wives visit them without first obtaining permission, they may be charged with trespass or with having unlawful sexual intercourse. If they are absent without leave, even for one night, they may lose their right to live in the city. They cannot take part in politics, because their parties have been outlawed. If, despite this, they dare to do so, they are classified as agitators and intimidators and believed to be Communists, even when they are not. They can be arrested and imprisoned without trial. They can be searched without a warrant, and if they are found without their passes, they are liable to a fine, or to be sent to a labour camp. And lastly, when they die, they are buried in a cemetery for Negroes only, even if they have worshipped the same God as the Whites and had greater faith in Him.[9]

The forcible removal of millions of Africans, the destruction by Nazi methods of townships like Sophiatown and Windermere, the restrictions as to residence placed on the more moderate elements, the massacres at Sharpeville and Cato Manor, the suicides of Africans and Coloureds who prefer to die rather than abandon their homes, the daily arrests of thousands of Negroes and their dispatch to prison-factories, were just episodes accompanied by energetic though isolated protests from a handful of progressive Whites, while the majority, whether they were Boers or of British extraction, either approved or said nothing. Ronald Segal was exiled on account of his opposition to the racialist government in Pretoria and he warns us that the complacent attitude of South African Whites is disagreeably reminiscent of that of the Germans who watched without protesting the hunting down of Jews during the *Kristallnacht*. And in one of the last numbers of *Africa South* he wrote:

> As the German at the window was guilty of the death of the Jew and all the deaths that followed, of Belsen and Oradour-sur-Glane, so are we guilty also. For what is done is done because we let it be done. Surely, it is we, even we, who by our silence and our quiet bodies are destroying the shacks of Windermere and the living and the not yet living that they guard.[10]

But Segal's forebodings do not even scratch the surface of Verwoerd's moral world. Whereas Hitler believed in the stars and occultism, Verwoerd asserted that he was in touch with God, and consequently infallible. Commenting on his appointment as Premier, he said: 'I believe that the will of God was revealed in the ballot.'[11] 'It is as God has willed,' he said after South Africa had left the Commonwealth.[12] And when David Beresford Pratt fired his revolver and wounded him, though not fatally, he told those who ran to assist him that God had caused the would-be assassin's hand to tremble. This messianic certitude could lead a man to do anything, and that was what alarmed democrats like Segal, who are keenly aware of the danger of a head-on clash between the white and the coloured communities. But although the two main organizations of the United Nations adopted about thirty resolutions condemning racialist methods in South Africa,[13] Verwoerd refused to stop apartheid, and it was only in the hope of deceiving world public opinion that he created, on the map, little African States called Bantustans, which in reality were just another hoax.[14] On 6 September 1966 Verwoerd was murdered by a messenger in the parliament building, but his successors have reaffirmed their belief in the soundness of the apartheid policy.

The reaction of the Africans

Since they cannot retaliate by legal means, because the two largest African parties—the African National Congress and the Pan-

Africanist Congress—were dissolved in 1960 after the Sharpeville massacre, the Africans have now decided to go underground and use direct action. This, after having tried for years to halt the monstrous mechanism of segregation by means of strikes, the boycotting of goods, civil disobedience and all the other devices of Gandhi's *Satyagraha*, or non-violence. And after having witnessed the failure of all the efforts made by the United Nations to convince the ruling white community to restore to 13 million Africans, Indians and Coloureds their dignity as men wronged by a Nazi-type legislation.

For years the President of the African National Congress, Albert Luthuli, has been seeking to oppose this desperate policy by all the means in his power, relying on *hamba kahle* (slow progress, step by step). Sticking to his principles, he has resigned himself to being an impotent spectator of the serious split in his own party —a split which in 1959 led to the formation of the Pan-Africanist Congress, a radical movement which wants to counter white racialism with black racialism. During our secret meeting at Stanger, where he is under house arrest,[15] Luthuli told us quite frankly that he was afraid he would be ousted by younger and more hot-blooded men who were determined to extirpate the evil plant of apartheid by using force. Although he acknowledged that the Pretoria government's stubbornness left no room for any other solution but violence, he was reluctant to give his approval to these young men thirsting for action. 'A Christian should not react to violence with violence,' he kept on repeating, as he gazed out of the window at the colourless landscape.

We do not know what has happened since our meeting to make Luthuli change his opinion, hampered as he is by the responsibility of being the holder of a Nobel Prize for his efforts to keep peace. What we do know is that the first acts of sabotage, the first *coups de main*, were organized by the *Umkhonto we Sizwe* ('Spear of the Nation'),[16] which the African National Congress later claimed to have founded. What from the very beginning has distinguished the operations of this secret army is the choice of objectives to be destroyed, a choice which reveals deliberate planning and is not just left to the imagination of individuals or contaminated by xenophobic feelings. The favourite targets are police-stations, pylons, petrol-dumps, pipelines and railway junctions. During the summer of 1962, following the techniques used ten years earlier by *Cheesa-Cheesa* agitators, a hundred fires were started in Natal, which destroyed 1 million quintals of sugar-cane. During the whole of this period not a single white man was attacked, and it was not until 27 October 1962, when the Pretoria government threatened to enforce a law passed in May authorizing death-sentences for saboteurs, that the 'Spear of the Nation' wrote a letter to the *Golden City Post* warning the authorities that the law of retaliation would be applied for every death-sentence passed by the courts.

In April 1962, a few months after the emergence of the 'Spear of the Nation', the clandestine Pan-Africanist Congress began to show signs of activity,[17] and since that date the South African newspapers have had to devote space almost every day to the exploits of the *Poqo* (which in the Xhosa language means 'lone men'), using the same techniques and methods as the Mau-Mau whose guerrilla operations kept Kenya on the *qui vive* for many years. The activities of the 'Spear of the Nation' are obviously under the restraining influence of the more liberal-minded elements among the white population, but Potlako Leballo, the acting secretary-general of the Congress, from his hideout at Maseru in Basutoland, has been reluctantly compelled to admit that the *Poqo* do not even obey the orders of their own leaders. The *Poqo* reject the idea so dear to Luthuli of a multi-racial community and base their operations on a literal interpretation of the slogan 'Africa for the Africans'.[18] Their methods thus envisage a war without quarter such as the Bantu writer Bloke Modisane predicted in 1959 when he wrote: 'Thousands of us are waiting . . . That will be it. We will gather in an appointed country and then go home to South Africa never to leave again. We will govern unless they kill us . . .'[19]

A Nazi legislation

The reaction of the racialist government to the new tactics adopted by the Africans was prompt and merciless. One might almost think that the conflagration started by the *Poqo* had been expected and desired. In any case it provided the Afrikaner majority with a pretext for introducing new anti-Liberal laws, just as the *Reichstag* fire had provided Hitler with an excuse to consolidate his dictatorship forty years before. As a South African Liberal, Patrick Duncan, has pointed out, the last two internal security laws have had the same effect as Hitler's Enabling Act in 1933. The Fascist nature of the Pretoria government is, in fact, emphasized by these emergency laws destined not only to make the segregation of the coloured races complete, but also to intimidate those members of the white community whose consciences rebel against the savagery of apartheid.

The Sabotage Bill, approved on 14 June 1962, punishes almost any type of offence against the racist government with penalties ranging from a minimum of five years' imprisonment to sentence of death. Commenting on this law, the International Commission of Jurists complained that it restricted the liberty of the individual to a greater extent than had been the case under the most pitiless dictatorships, whether of the Right or the Left.[20] But even this was not considered severe enough, and less than a year later, on 1st May 1963, the General Law Amendment Act was passed, providing for the detention of anti-racialists for a period of three months without the judiciary having any say in the matter. Like Salazar's PIDE, the 'Special Branch' is also allowed to prolong this period of detention for an indefinite time, while the Minister of Justice can alter any sentence into imprisonment for life. Finally, this law authorizes the banning of all existing organizations, the censorship of correspondence, the sentencing to death—should they return to the country—of exiles who have campaigned against apartheid, and the exercise of other drastic rights (special tribunals, emergency regulations, prohibited areas). Writing of this law on the eve of its approval, a Johannesburg Liberal newspaper said: 'After this can the Nationalists complain if South Africa is called a Police State?'[21] The same opinion was expressed by the International Commission of Jurists, which stated that this measure made South Africa 'now, more than ever, a Police State as regards laws and procedure'.

The man responsible for these laws, the former Minister of Justice and now Prime Minister, John Vorster, has all the necessary qualifications for his grim task. He was a general in the Nazi *Ossewa Brandwag*, and during the last war he was interned for two years in a camp at Koffiefontein, his internee number being 2229/42. On the strength of these two new laws Vorster hastened to ban the Congress of Democrats (the last refuge of European Liberals who still believe in a multi-racial South Africa) and to put under house arrest for a period of five years, without any trial or sentence, several hundred people who were known to be opposed to the segregation policy.[22] Availing himself of his power to commute sentences, he transferred the President of the Pan-Africanist Congress, Robert Sobukwe, who on 3 May 1963 had just finished serving a sentence of three years, to the penal settlement on Rubben Island, which is South Africa's Alcatraz. Referring to this episode in parliament, Vorster had no hesitation in saying that he would keep Sobukwe and other men in prison 'until the expiration of the earthly term of eternal life'. In the month of June it was Vorster again who, in a speech to the nation, gave a balance-sheet of one month's repression—3,245 *Poqos* arrested and 195 members of the Pan-Africanist Congress and African National Congress forced to leave the country. On 9 April 1963 six Africans were hanged in Pretoria, while the prison population had risen to the record figure of 67,700.[23] A new concentration camp was opened at Ficksburg on the borders of the Orange Free State, while in many places a curfew for Africans was introduced, from ten in the evening until four in the morning.

A protest against all this Fascist-type legislation was raised on 8 November 1962 by the African lawyer Nelson Mandela, one of Albert Luthuli's lieutenants. Transforming himself from the accused into the accuser, Mandela delivered in court a memorable *J'accuse*:

> I challenge the right of this Court to hear my case on two grounds:—Firstly, I challenge it on the ground that I will not be given a fair and proper trial. Secondly, I consider myself neither morally nor legally bound to obey laws made by a Parliament in which I am not represented . . . The white man makes all the laws; he charges us before his courts and accuses us and he sits in judgment over us. Whatever sentence Your Worship sees fit to impose on me for the crime for which I have been convicted before this Court, may it rest assured that when my sentence has been completed I will still be moved, as men are always moved, by their consciences. I will still be moved to dislike of the racial discrimination against my people when I come out from serving my sentence to take up again, as best I can, the struggle for the removal of these injustices until they are finally abolished once and for all.[24]

Nelson Mandela was sentenced to five years' imprisonment, and subsequently, after a second trial, in June 1964, to imprisonment for life. But such rigorous sentences could not daunt the coloured population. An Indian accused of sabotage, for which he might have been sentenced to death, had the courage to tell the Supreme Court: 'I have believed in passive resistance all my life, but this policy has got us nowhere. I decided to take part in the blowing up of the railway toolshed because it is the only form left to me of retaliating and protesting against the harsh methods of the government.'[25]

Changes in the laws of penal procedure permitting confessions made to the police to be used as evidence, paved the way for still more flagrant violence and trickery. 'Recently,' wrote a British expert on African affairs, Colin Legum, after a visit to South Africa,

> the courts stayed the execution of three men on the grounds that confessions had been extorted from them by the application of electric currents to their heads, which were swathed in damp blankets. Allegations of this Algerian type of police methods are heard more and more in the courts.[26]

Realizing that a racial war was now raging in the country, the Pretoria government introduced compulsory military service, doubling the strength of the army and increasing that of the 'Citizen Force'. At the same time it raised the allocation of funds for defence purposes to 157 million rand,[27] gave orders for 206 commando groups to be raised, to act as auxiliaries to the regular army, and signed a contract with the Anglo-American Corporation for the construction of three munitions factories.[28] One episode will suffice to give an idea of the growing tension in South Africa since 1962. In March 1963, after the discovery of a *Poqo* arsenal in Pretoria, the military authorities called out armoured cars and commandos because they were afraid there was going to be a veritable revolt. Panic, which the War Minister Fouché increased by continually issuing 'bulletins', spread to the white population. Settlers were advised to keep their guns within reach, and in almost every town 'pistol courses' were organized for women. One firm offered tear-gas sprayers for sale at 7·9 rands each, containing, according to the 'instructions for use', 'enough to keep a large number of people at bay if necessary'. Profiting by the atmosphere of panic, one of Hitler's former experts achieved a brief notoriety by teaching women how to use a special tear-gas pistol to put 'Negro aggressors' out of action. In the little town of Krugersdorp a man named Robert Roodt even organized a 'Home Guard', which gave military training to practically the whole of the white population.

Thus the Whites, like the Africans, began to organize extremist groups which could not be controlled by the authorities, like the Ku-Klux-Klan commandos who attacked the houses of white supporters of integration, or threw 'Molotov cocktails' into bars frequented by Negroes. In Durban, as in the days of the *Ossewa Brandwag's Stormjaers*, swastikas and anti-Jewish slogans were daubed on the walls. Amidst all this confusion and excitement, a former welter-weight champion named Wilhelm Albrecht Muser, without anyone attempting to stop him, founded an 'Adolf Hitler Debate Union' the aim of which was to prove that Hitler was an honourable man and that the German extermination camps had never existed. These debates were financed by industrialists and began and ended with the Nazi salute.[29] Another extremist, Peter Solomon Richard Willers, told the magazine *Drum* that he was chairman of the 'South African Nazi Party', that he was ready to assassinate the Ghanaian leader Kwame Nkrumah, and that he was on friendly terms with three Nazi war criminals who had found a refuge in South Africa and for whom he had the same respect as he had for the memory of Adolf Eichmann, whom he described as a 'real soldier'.

In view of the threatening situation and the number of people who condemned segregation on moral grounds, it might have been thought that the Verwoerd government would have definitely decided to abandon its plans for apartheid and have tried to reach a compromise.[30] On the contrary, we are told by no less an authority than the Anglican Bishop of Cape Town, Joost de Blank, that the determination of those opposed to all contacts between the two races became greater than ever.[31] The threat of civil war apparently convinced the men in power that the rhythm of the apartheid plan ought to be accelerated. During 1963 the government decided upon a large resettlement programme: 2,000 Africans were moved from their homes in Besterspruit; the African population of Western Cape Province was resettled and the territory became a white and Coloured area; 60,000 people of Indian and Pakistani descent were moved from the Transvaal, together with the people of Indian, Pakistani and Coloured descent living in the East Rand and Cape Peninsula. It is estimated that this move involved 10,000 Indians from Cape Peninsula alone.[32] The non-white population was forcibly removed from areas inhabited by Whites, where they had carried on their activities for several decades, and sent to 'locations' or 'reserves', these being bleak and barren zones which out of regard for the United Nations were given the high-sounding name of 'Bantustans'. 'By the year 2000,' the advocates of segregation maintained, 'Whites and non-Whites will at last be living in separate areas and South Africa will be nothing less than an earthly paradise.' What astonishes us in such statements is not so much their hypocritical tone, but the sublime confidence felt by the men in power that they would be able to keep the situation under control for the next thirty odd years, and this at a time when an 'Algerian atmosphere' was prevalent throughout the country. The attitude of the Dutch Reformed Church (responsible for bringing God and the Holy Scriptures into the apartheid scandal) is extremely disconcerting. Pretending to ignore the racial struggle, it reserved all its indignation for farmers who were using rockets to produce rain by artificial means. 'You are defying the will of God,' the preachers thundered. 'It is as if with your rockets you were poking your fingers into God's eyes!'[33] We might be back in the days of the persecution of Galileo or of the witch-hunts in Salem.

Day after day, shielded by a régime which was democratic only in name and in its meaningless institutions, and with the blessing of a Church which was teaching hatred instead of compassion, the Afrikaner ruling class perfected its system of domination and repression, without any interference from international bodies in an attempt to prevent Africa from being turned into an inferno— which would have involved actual intervention and not just the affirmation of principles.[34] Neither side lacked weapons, and their hatred was mutual. Each side tried to find allies, the Whites looking to Salazar and Rhodesia,[35] the Africans to the newly independent countries.[36] In his exaltation, which was a compound of racial pride and the same spurious mysticism that inspired the actions of Salazar, Verwoerd prepared to repel the onslaught, not only of the Africans in his own country, but of the whole continent, affirming that the assailants would have to face 'a nation with its back to the wall and ready to defend itself'.

'If the West were to lose South Africa,' Verwoerd said on 2 September 1963, 'the strategic and military balance of power would be altered to its disadvantage. We must therefore resist at all costs, until the West recovers its senses.'[37] At a time when the Whites had 'lost all sense of initiative', Verwoerd was thus claiming the merit of being the only white politician who had not yielded to the pressure and aspirations of the Negroes. During a meeting at Smithfield, he referred ironically to the regrettable decline of European influence in Africa, and the whole tone of his speech was sinister rather than arrogant. 'It may well be,' he said, 'that South Africa is destined to be the country which will provide Whites all over the world with a new source of inspiration.'[38] And in April 1964, after announcing that South Africa was now able to produce all kinds of weapons on its own account, he gave the West a final warning:

I can assure the Western nations that South Africa will use all her economic power if the attack takes the form of an economic

blockade, and that all her men and women are ready to fight if
it should come to violence. I am giving them this warning because
I do not wish to leave any doubts about a question which for us
is one of life or death.[39]

When we remember the disproportion between the forces of
repression and the weakness of the clandestine African army, we
are bound to admit that, as Colin Legum has pointed out, the
immediate prospect is that victory will be on the side of the counter-
revolution and that South Africa is destined to become more and
more Fascist.[40] In this respect the death of Verwoerd has made
no difference and it would even seem that the situation might grow
worse. In his introduction to Brian Bunting's *The Rise of the South
African Reich* Ronald Segal tells us that 'the parallel with the
German Reich grows every day more evident', and that the 'frontier of terror' was crossed by South Africa with the passing of
the General Law Amendment Act in May 1963. 'The new law,' he
says, 'has outlawed law itself.'[41] Hundreds of people have already
been sent to prison under this measure, which allows the police to
arrest any person suspected of 'subversion' and to keep him in
prison without any charge or proceedings for a period of ninety
days, which can be prolonged indefinitely. Against this law, which
can only be compared with the repressive legislation of totalitarian
States, sixty South African doctors and psychiatrists have protested, drawing attention to the fact that 'nothing can justify the
physical and mental suffering inflicted on persons who have not
been found guilty by a court of law'.[42]

'Once again,' we were told by an Indian doctor, Dr Naicker, in
his Durban home, 'the world, in its selfishness and indolence, has
allowed the canker of Nazi violence to spread. Will it repeat this
error by continuing to underestimate what is happening in South
Africa? Will it abandon us to our fate?' In February 1963 he was
ordered to leave his home and move to the quarter set apart for
Indians. Naicker, who is President of the South African Indian
Congress, refused to comply with the order. 'I have lived in this
house for twenty-five years and I am not going to leave it. I prefer
to go to prison rather than yield to racialist laws.'[43] It would not
be Naicker's first experience of life in a South African prison. Like
the two men whose portraits hang in his surgery—Gandhi and
Luthuli.[44]

18   Africa

The lure of Fascism

In Africa the lure of Fascism is nothing new. In fact, it can be said that, although it originally came from abroad, it is as old as African nationalism. In the 1930s, when Mussolini was posing as the 'protector of Islam', he did all he could to induce the Egyptian middle class to break the alliance with Britain and to win over the more extreme nationalist groups. A similar, and more successful, campaign was launched by Hitler, who became the idol of the young Egyptian ultra-nationalists after the publication of *Mein Kampf*. The Nazi party congress in Nuremberg in 1936 was attended by a large number of delegates from Cairo, headed by Ahmed Hussein, the leader of the *Misr al-Fatât* (Young Egypt) party's Greenshirts, and by Fathi Radouan and Nour Eddine Tarraf of the New National Party. No representatives of the powerful Muslim Brotherhood attended this conference, but they sided with the Greenshirts during the anti-British riots in January and February 1942, when Rommel and his *Afrika-Korps* were only fifty miles away from Alexandria and their battle-cry was *Ila'l—amân ya Rommel* ('Come on Rommel!').[1] Gamal Abdel Nasser was likewise in touch with Rommel, as we are told by one of his closest collaborators, Colonel Anouar el-Sadâte, author of *Revolt on the Nile*. According to Sadâte, 'We made contact with the German head-quarters in Libya and we acted in complete harmony with them.'[2]

Thanks to the zeal and anti-Semitic propaganda of the Grand Mufti of Jerusalem, Amin el Hussein,[3] it was also possible to raise an SS division consisting entirely of Arabs from Egypt, Palestine, Algeria, Syria and Iraq, which fought on the Russian front. The success of Nazism in Cairo was not, however, an isolated episode. Tunisian nationalism was influenced, though to a lesser degree, by the Axis Powers. Although he minimizes the part played by Habib Bourguiba, who in fact expressed himself rather vaguely in the speech broadcast by Radio Bari after he had been liberated by Axis troops in France,[4] Roger Le Tourneau admits that in the Destour there was a current favourable to Nazism among those who had been attracted by Hitler's attitude to Jews, by his flattery of the Arabs, and by the efficiency of German organization and the good behaviour of German troops in Tunisia—a trend that was particularly noticeable among young intellectuals.[5]

The complete collapse of Fascism in Europe at first discouraged the incipient African nationalist movements and made them reluctant to follow any authoritarian or anti-democratic trend. But where the seeds had taken root, as they had in Egypt, they soon bore fruit and, strangely enough, even in places where they had not previously been sown. This is a recent phenomenon dating only from the early 1960s and it is consequently only in the developing stage and may prove to be ephemeral. Nevertheless, it would be futile to ignore the fact that, since they achieved independence, almost all the African States have rejected the European models and the precepts of Western democracy. They have adopted a highly centralized one-party system; they have disbanded and persecuted the opposition parties, which they consider to be disruptive and anti-national forces. The transition is rapid from the two-party to the one-party system, and sometimes to a one-man system; in order to distract public opinion from internal problems, they encourage imperialistic campaigns to the detriment of neighbouring countries; they restrict political rights, introduce forced residence, set up concentration camps and reveal xenophobic tendencies. 'This trend,' writes Pierre Alexandre, 'which combines the exploitation of political and racial myths with Marxist formulas, often distorted and emptied of their original significance, is inevitably an unpleasant reminder of certain features of German National Socialism.'[6] To which Romain Rainero adds: 'The next few years will tell us which of these two trends is going to prevail in the Dark Continent—a dictatorship of the "enlightened absolutism" type, or dictatorship *tout court*. At the present time the two trends often co-exist precariously in any given State.'[7]

Nevertheless, we must beware of jumping to conclusions; otherwise, as Gwendolen M. Carter points out in her study of African one-party systems, we may render 'a disservice to them [the Africans] and ourselves'.[8] The choice of one national party, the adoption of certain typically Fascist methods and the installation of authoritarian régimes might well prove to be only transitory phenomena in the last and difficult phase of decolonization. At the moment, however, the danger of Fascism undoubtedly exists in

Africa, and it is something rather more than a yielding to temptation. In the following pages we shall try to identify the causes and the special features of this phenomenon.

The Sphinx of the Nile

First of all, let us consider the most serious and flagrant example, that of Egypt. Even before Nasser seized power in 1952, Cairo—like Madrid and Buenos Aires—had become a safe hideout for badly compromised Nazis. Here they enjoyed the protection of the Grand Mufti of Jerusalem, Haj Amin el Hussein, and they soon obtained jobs as expert advisers to the police and army, or established contact with the 'free officers' belonging to right-wing movements. In January 1952 the German and Swiss newspapers reported a curious meeting in Cairo between former SS officers and high-ranking Nazi functionaries, and later hinted that this meeting had had some connexion with the anti-British riots in July of the following year, which led to the fall of King Farouk.

Exactly what role the Germans played in this business it is impossible to say,[9] but it is known that the fires in the city and the *coup d'état* on 23 July 1953 were the work of extreme right-wing nationalists. In the former we can detect the hand of Ahmed Hussein's Greenshirts and the Muslim Brotherhood; in the latter, that of the 'free officers', whose leaders at the time of the revolt, according to Professor P. J. Vatikiotis, were (or had been) members of the above-mentioned pro-Nazi movements.[10] Nasser himself had been a member of the 'Young Egypt' organization for two years,[11] and he did not forget this when, as Minister for the Interior, he had to decide the fate of his former teacher, the fanatical Ahmed Hussein, who was charged with being responsible for the fires in Cairo. Hussein was, in fact, released and the inquiry was shelved.[12] After visiting Egypt the Socialist Gilles Martinet said:

> In the realization of this revolution from the top, the Eygptian leaders have given their régime certain features curiously reminiscent of Fascism. The hieratical eagle in the centre of the black, white and red flag of the old imperial Germany; the Mussolinian extravagance of the claim that the departure of the British was the result of a great military victory, to be celebrated with huge processions parading through the streets; the national guard which reminds us of the Fascist militia and is led by corpulent hierarchs— all these things make the Egypt of today look rather like the

Germany and Italy of yesterday. But we must avoid superficial comparisons. It is not a Fascist party that is in power, it is the army.[13]

What Martinet seems to forget is that it is an army led by men trained in a xenophobic Nazi school, who have never attempted to conceal their predilection for Fascist authoritarian régimes, the only kind of movement—in their opinion—which can provide the driving force needed for a nationalist revolution.

Whatever the outcome of the Nasser régime may be, the origins of the Egyptian revolution reflect beliefs and sympathies such as these. The attachment of these 'free officers' to tradition and the current reactionary ideologies of the *Misr al-Fatât* and the Muslim Brotherhood find clear expression in that miniature *Mein Kampf* written by Nasser and entitled *The Philosophy of Revolution*.[14] In his study of Egyptian 'military society', Anouar Abdel-Malek maintains that Nasser had no right to describe the insurrection on 23 July 1952 as a revolution;[15] it was just a *coup d'état*, a *putsch* organized by 'free officers' who knew how best to exploit the general discontent, but, once they were in power, found that they had no ideological basis and no political programme except an exaggerated patriotism tinged with National Socialism. Nasser never succeeded in filling this gap, despite all the pretentious announcements of programmes, the constitution of a one-party 'democratic, socialist and co-operative' system and the launching of a 'National Action Charter'.[16] It was destined to remain a régime of military men surrounded by technocrats, after vain appeals had been made to the intellectuals, the only men who might have been able to provide Nasser's revolution with an ideological foundation.

Empiricism and opportunism were thus the only norms followed by this Egyptian 'military society' and the first ten years of Nasser's rule were nothing but an uninterrupted sequence of contradictory acts, sudden decisions and emotional reactions, instead of calculated and coherent action. Only a month after the *coup d'état*, which had put an end to the feudal monarchy, the 'revolutionary' army that claimed to be defending the people arrested a number of trade unionists at Kafr el Dawwâr, and after a summary trial they were hanged. A month later, the Council of the Revolution introduced an agrarian reform bill—Law No 178—and seemed to be well on the way towards a programme of social renewal. But when we come to strike a balance ten years later, we find that this reform was a very modest one and by no means revolutionary; the big landowners were paid too much compensation and only a tiny fraction of the land went to the peasants; and finally, the State expropriated the rest of the land and, practically speaking, merely replaced the landowners in exploiting the labourers.[17]

It soon became clear that Nasser's was indeed a strange 'revolution', for it first attacked the Right and crushed the ultranationalist Muslim Brotherhood, after which it turned its attention to the Centre and Left, sending Communists, Socialists, Liberals and Constitutionalists to concentration camps. At one moment it supported the nationalist middle class, and at the next it turned against it. It accepted the help of left-wingers during the Suez crisis, and then sent them to the 'cemetery of the living' at Abu Zaabal.[18] It put an end to the semi-colonial system, but at the same time disbanded political parties and imposed restrictions on liberty. It built up an industrial economy, but banned the class struggle. It tried to free itself from the influence of the parties that had brought it to power, but continued to suppress the working classes. It built schools at the rate of one every two days, but lowered the general standard of education; it pretended to be helping the workers, but in reality it suppressed their trade unions. It preached anti-imperialism while adopting a policy that was decidedly imperialistic towards the neighbouring Arab and African States, camouflaging this policy as pan-Arabism.[19]

These contradictions were produced by a 'military society' which had no ideology, but claimed that it had the right to remain the arbiter of the situation for an unspecified period. A 'society' that groped its way or deviated abruptly to the right or left, according to whether Nasser was being subjected to the influence of Bandung or the Kremlin, whether he was about to meet Tito or Nehru, or whether he had just received a rebuff from Moscow or Washington, whether he was vying with the Syrian *Baat* or whether his plans for expansion had gone wrong. Opportunism and ruthlessness were among the outstanding features of the Nasser régime. The *Rais* had no qualms about offering hospitality to Nazi fugitives from Germany or Austria and giving them jobs in the police, the army and the broadcasting service.[20] Professor Johann von Leers, who had been Goebbels's closest collaborator, became Nasser's adviser on anti-Jewish propaganda;[21] when he found himself in financial difficulties, Nasser consulted Hjalmar Schacht, the former president of the Reichsbank; he denied that Hitler had massacred 6 million Jews[22] and employed German experts on missiles and aeronautics, so that he might be able to produce the most lethal weapons[23] on his own account; he mobilized the younger generation against *al istirmar* (imperialism) in order to save them from other temptations, and he did his best to persuade them that elections, political parties and Western democracy were merely instruments 'for the preservation of capitalism, feudalism, corruption and social and economic exploitation'.[24]

The most ridiculous claim made by this 'military society' was, however, that it could produce Socialism without Socialists, or even by persecuting them. It is true that Nasser changed the name of his solitary party from 'National Union' to 'Arab Socialist Union', but this did not alter the character of this Socialism imposed from the top. 'The men in power,' Abdel-Malek wrote,

> have no ideological roots in Socialism. They appropriate ideas and formulas of the Socialist type only in order to attract the masses, who are deeply hostile to dictatorships, and then use them as cover for what is really State planning and State control. You cannot have Socialism if you intern the men of the Left, nor can you have a classless society if you prevent the real and historical representatives of Egyptian Socialism from taking any part in it, from expressing their opinions, or even just existing.[25]

Another Arab scholar, Hassan Riad, is of the same opinion:

> The term 'Socialism' cannot possibly be used to describe the Nasser régime, despite all outward appearances and official proclamations such as the latest 'national charter'. It is quite true that under Nasserism the banks, the insurance companies, big industrial concerns and both home and foreign trade have been nationalized, but does that give it the right to call itself 'Socialist'? . . . It is common knowledge that State control by itself is not Socialism.

Consequently, Riad prefers to call Nasserism a 'reactionary and pro-Fascist régime' rather than a 'military society', or else 'ultra-static Pharaonic rule'.[26] Nasser's mose eminent spokesman, Hassanein Heykal, rebuts these accusations by pointing out that the 'Arab Socialist Union' cannot be compared with the Communist system or with Fascist ideology, because the party does not just represent the interests of the proletariat alone or of capitalism alone.[27] A claim of this sort is highly questionable, because events have shown that the army and civil service, with the help of the nationalistic *bourgeoisie*, have managed to create a new social category, which knows how to defend its own privileges against both the feudal elements and the huge mass of peasants and workmen, who have not benefited in any way from the revolution. Avraham Ben-Tsur on the other hand, maintains that 'President Nasser uses "Socialist" terminology to camouflage an economic and social policy which in reality is the same thing as capitalism.'[28] And in fact the nationalization measures have affected only the foreign or religious minorities (Copts, Jews, Greeks, Lebanese and Italians), and have spared the Egyptian private capitalists, who are classified as 'non-exploiters'. Discussing this, Marcel Colombe points out:

> One might object that Socialism of this sort is merely a kind of levy, a means of filling the State coffers, which are invariably empty as the result of an ambitious policy that was far beyond the country's means. It might also be said that by despoiling foreigners and 'intruders' in the way it does, the régime shows that it is xenophobic and pro-Islam rather than Socialist in the true sense of the term.[29]

This 'Socialism' which undoubtedly has many affinities with Nazism in its expansionist and racialist tendencies, has been warmly praised by a well-known Nazi propagandist, Wilhelm Landing:

> Nasser's ideology is destined to give its name to an epoch; it is an example pointing the way to be followed in the future . . . The Egyptian railways are models of punctuality . . . A new type of Egyptian has emerged who, while faithfully serving his President, lives in the hope of better things to come and ennobles his personality . . . This is a new type of Socialism, vigorous and popular.[30]

That, incidentally, was not the only tribute paid by the Fascist International to Nasser in the course of the last few years. Johann von Leers thought that Nasser was 'superior to Hitler, because Hitler wanted to do everything in his lifetime, whereas Nasser has been taught by his religion to do things gradually and to dedicate not only his own lifetime, but also that of his successors to the cause'.[31] Even Maurice Bardèche felt it incumbent upon him to pay tribute to Nasserism when he said:

> Nassar and his friends have discovered that the whole of Fascist mysticism is to be found in Islam, which is their past and, in the wider and more comprehensive sense of the term, their culture—that is to say, not only their source of inspiration, but something that conforms very closely with their nature and their instincts . . . Although it is just as inimitable as Hitler's Germanism, Nasser's crusade is, like National Socialism, confined to the men of one nation.

But its geographical situation and the moment of its emergence endow it with the greatest significance. Of all the Fascist mysticisms it is probable the one which will leave the deepest mark on history on account of its enduring consequences.[32]

Although Anouar Abdel-Malek perceives the danger of a lapse into Fascism and admits that the 'trend towards autocracy is increasing' rather than the contrary, that in Egypt 'progress is measured by the rate at which liberty is restricted' and that 'the paralysis of the social dialectic is complete',[33] he feels obliged to conclude his study on an optimistic note, pointing out that, after all, Egypt has regained her independence and her dignity, has improved her economic potential, encourages co-operation in agriculture, has witnessed the birth of a new social category, has chosen to follow an anti-imperialist and neutralist foreign policy and now seems to be well on the way towards Socialism, even if her methods may not be altogether orthodox and if she makes many mistakes and encounters many obstacles. He places his hopes in a steady advance towards Socialism, thanks to the hidden influence of the banned left-wing parties, and also because Nasserism contains certain positive elements, such as increasing co-operation with the Socialist nations, sound planning, the elimination of all the relics of feudalism, and the gradual transition from a reactionary to a progressive type of authoritarianism. He is confident that the technicians to whom the régime is obliged to entrust increasingly important functions, will succeed in undermining the authority of the military cadres; that the working class will become strong enough to offer effective opposition to the excessively brutal methods of the State; and that the peasants will finally awake from their thousand-year-old slumbers. But how many years will it take before this process of evolution can begin to bear fruit?

In 1961, immediately after the secession of Syria and the fiasco of the United Arab Republic, Nasser announced that his régime would be 'democratized' and that 'individual power' would have to give way to 'collective government', thus giving his listeners to understand that the military-Fascist régime would be replaced by a society governed by freely-elected bodies.[34] And in fact, three years after this announcement the country seemed to be on its way back to normal, when the new constitutional law came into force and a 'National Assembly' was convened on 26 March 1964. That, of course, does not imply that the Nasser régime can now be called 'democratic'. 'It would be wrong to believe,' Hassanein Heykal himself admits 'that with the election of a National Assembly we have achieved a definitive form of true democracy. For that we need a democratic government. And only the "Socialist Union" could provide a government and an assembly of that sort.'[35] As for Nasser himself, he confessed to the editor of *The Sunday Times* that it would take ten years before Egypt could once again enjoy a parliamentary system.[36] It must, however, be admitted that although Nasser with the aid of the one-party system, the army and the police, still holds the country firmly in his grip, a certain process of liberalization was inaugurated with the release of political detainees belonging to the two extremes (Communism and the Muslim Brotherhood), the abolition of martial law and of the state of emergency, and the suspension of the confiscation of property belonging to the members of the old ruling class.

But although these recent measures give reason to hope that the violent phase of Nasser's revolution is drawing to a close, Egyptian nationalism still gives grounds for apprehension and is still the unknown factor in Nasser's policy. Although Khrushchev made Nasser a 'Hero of the Soviet Union', in his speech at Aswan on 16 May 1964 he did not fail to stress that, while accepting the idea of Arab unity, he had not the slightest desire to see it realized under pressure from a racialist and messianic nationalism. 'My dear friends,' the former Russian Premier said on that occasion,

do you want me to tell you what I really think, or shall I say what I know would please all of you? What would have become of our revolution if Lenin, the great leader of our people, had said: 'Russians, unite against the whole world!; the Russians are the best people, they are the salt of the earth!'? In that case, what would the Ukranians have done? Or the White Russians? Or the Uzbeks and all the other peoples of our multi-national country? . . . My good friend Gamal Abdel Nasser is looking at me and thinking, 'What is Khrushchev driving at? What is he going to say next?' This is what I am going to say . . . Several orators have already spoken today and I have listened to their words. 'We Arabs, we Arabs, Arabs unite!' etcetera. When people assume this attitude, it would seem as if we Russians can have nothing in common with you Arabs and that we had better pack our bags and go home. We are not Arabs. Our master and leader Lenin told us to unite, too, but not on a nationalist basis, on the basis of work, of class! . . . In short that cry of 'Arabs unite!' needs clarification. Arab workers, Arab peasants, Arab intellectuals—all those who work must unite to fight for liberty and independence, for a new life, for their own rights, against those who exploit them. In a union of that kind there is room for the Russians, for the representatives of other nations, for all those who live by their own work, who are fighting for a better life, for liberty and for the welfare of the people.[37]

Nasser listened and did not seem too pleased with this lecture or with the way Khrushchev criticized Egyptian nationalism, which had been the mainspring of the revolution started by the 'free officers'. In a speech which he made four days later, however, he concealed his annoyance and tried to reassure his great benefactor by saying that 'Arab unity is not an appeal to racialist feeling' and that it was founded 'on liberty and Socialism'.[38] Hitherto, efforts have been made to achieve it by using violent, National Socialist methods, but we cannot for that reason exclude the possibility that Nasser may change his tactics. All we can do, then, is to await coming events. What is already certain is that Arab unity, to a greater extent than any other internal measure or reform, will be the decisive test that will enable us to judge the historical value of Nasserism.

Nkrumah the Redeemer

Patrice Lumumba said that Nkrumah was the 'Giant of Africa'. His admirers called him *Osagyefo*—the Redeemer—and depicted him holding the Tablets of Moses in his hand as they worshipped him: 'Lead us, kindly light, to the land of Canaan.' For some of his detractors he was 'the maddest visionary in Africa', the man who was pursuing a 'policy of the impossible'. For his adversaries he was a dictator, an African Mussolini, the vainest and most ambitious man that the 'Third World' had hitherto produced. For the former colonial powers, who left Africa by the front entrance and re-entered it immediately afterwards through the back door, he was a spoil-sport, the man who knew all the tricks of neo-colonialism and rejected the insidious plan for a Euro-Africa in favour of a united and really independent Africa. And as soon as Ghana was threatened by a serious economic crisis, they hastened to cut the ground away from beneath his feet, with the result that General Ankrah had no trouble in deposing him on 24 February 1966.

Which of all these descriptions comes nearest to the truth? Which is the most accurate portrait of Francis Nwia Kofie Kwame Nkrumah, the 'founder' and first president-monarch of Ghana? Strange though it may seem, there is a kernel of truth in all of them, and each one serves to complete the portrait of this puzzling man. Kwame Nkrumah is, in fact, at one and the same time a giant and a mad visionary, a lucid exposer of decolonization, a conceited dictator, a redeemer and an oppressor. Nkrumah is a typical representative of the proud new Africa but also of all its contradictions, its limitations and errors. His admirers never tired of telling us that Nkrumah was Africa and Africa was Nkrumah, and for once in a while they were not very far short of the truth.

Of all the epithets that have been used to describe him, the one that fits him best is certainly the term 'visionary'. He was, however, a visionary who had the good fortune to see many of his dreams come true. As long ago as 1951 he was dreaming of liberating Ghana, and suddenly one day the British threw open the gates of his prison and appointed him Prime Minister. In 1958 he summoned the leaders of the first eight independent African States to Accra and prophesied that the 1960s would witness the liberation of the whole continent. And at Addis Ababa in May 1963 he was surrounded by thirty-one heads of African States, four times as many as in 1958. But at Addis Ababa, convinced that the surrender of the last white strongholds was a foregone conclusion, he tackled an entirely new problem, which perplexed his listeners. It was the problem of the political and economic unification of the whole continent and he proceeded to expound his ideas in a speech which was certainly the most ambitious and coherent discourse ever heard in the 'Africa Hall', even if parts of it might be considered chimerical and premature. Ten years ahead of his colleagues, as he invariably was, Nkrumah denounced the intrigues of the neo-colonialist powers, who were doing their utmost to keep control of the African economy; he warned his listeners of the danger that Africa might become another Balkans and ended his speech by declaring that the only way to avoid being eternal client-States, eternal 'milch-cows of the Western world', was to give Africa a central government and one parliament, which could exploit all the vast resources of the continent, and create a common market, a central bank, a unified army and a joint diplomatic service which would speak in the names of all the peoples dwelling between Algiers and Cape Town.

A sceptical smile hovered on the lips of the heads of African States, while the foreign observers were frankly amused. In their reports to the Western chancelleries they said that that ubiquitous wet-blanket Nkrumah had traced a magnificent outline of unification in the air, but that this time the 'Messiah' stood alone. And in fact

o

the African summit conference was a victory of the moderate over the revolutionary Africa, and in discussing Nkrumah's plan it approved only the desire for unification, taking good care not to lay down any programmes or schemes. But barely four months after the thirty-two heads of African States had agreed to create a supranational organization, which was to be the embryo of a future unification, the forces of neo-colonialism, just as Nkrumah had predicted, launched a counter-attack and tried to water down the decisions taken at Addis Ababa, to get men they trusted appointed to the general secretariat and to compensate themselves for the loss of their last colonies by opening up new markets and thus making fresh profits. These manœuvres, sponsored in particular by French and United States diplomats, were a confirmation of the fact that the Messiah of Accra had been right once again and that his urgent appeals for immediate unification had been neither gratuitous nor premature.

On his return from Addis Ababa, where he had found himself alone, Nkrumah turned his attention to home affairs, which since 1961 had been going from bad to worse. He had been the favourite pupil of Padmore and Du Bois, but although he had contrived to make Accra the 'Mecca of pan-Africanism' and a centre for all the most revolutionary elements in the continent, he had been less successful as a statesman and as the leader of his own country. Respected by the rest of Africa (even if no one followed his advice), when reduced to the proportions of absolute sovereign of an African 'province' he revealed all his limitations. In Addis Ababa he had played the role of a Cassandra, but in Accra he never knew what would happen from one day to the next, and he could never foresee the next moves of an opposition which made violent attacks on him, or prevent attempts being made on his life. After 1962, when a state of emergency was declared, Nkrumah hardly ever appeared in public and never left the capital. There he divided his time between Flagstaff House, his official headquarters, and Christiansborg Castle, where he lived with his Egyptian wife and his young children. And wherever he went, the security measures were on a vast scale, like those taken to protect the lives of South American dictators.

Nkrumah attributed all his troubles to the opposition's 'anti-national manœuvres', which in his *Africa Must Unite* he described as 'violently destructive'.[39] Some of the blame for the state of affairs must certainly be attributed to the opposition, which had hired assassins in its ranks as well as martyrs, but as John Hatch rightly remarks, 'The tragedy of the situation was that the government, on its part, showed signs of identifying opposition with treason.'[40] Following this criterion, Nkrumah, during the nine years of his reign, either sent his opponents to prison or compelled them to leave the country, and in this way he managed to rid himself not only of the leaders of the parliamentary opposition,[41] but also of some of his best ministers and collaborators as well—men like K. A. Gbedemah, Tawia Adamafio and Ako Adjei. When we remember that Ghana has only 7 million inhabitants, the number of exiles—over 7,000—is startling. Commenting from his exile in London on the arrest of the Ministers Adamafio, Adjei and Kofie Crabbe,[42] Gbedemah, himself a former Finance Minister, said that Nkrumah had turned Ghana into 'a police State and a totalitarian régime', adding: 'I challenge Dr Nkrumah to tell the world what tribunal, whether ordinary or special, sent these men to the cells reserved for criminals condemned to death.'[43]

Kwame Nkrumah's authoritarianism was an old idea of his, and not merely an expedient due to circumstances or the particular needs of a tribal society. When he was living in the United States during the 1930s, his favourite author was the Negro racialist Marcus Garvey, famous because he had once said that Mussolini had copied Fascism from him. In his autobiography Nkrumah wrote: 'I think that of all the literature that I studied, the book that did more than any other to fire my enthusiasm was *Philosophy and Opinions of Marcus Garvey* published in 1923.'[44] Other books which influenced him were the writings and biographies of Napoleon, Lenin, Gandhi, Hitler and Mussolini. From the last-named, Nkrumah, after his rise to power, borrowed a lot of cheap demagogy and stock phrases such as 'Who is not with Ghana is against Ghana' and 'The unity of Africa must be achieved and we are going to achieve it'.

'If we want to compare him with someone else,' we have written elsewhere,

> we cannot do better than compare him with Mussolini. On account of his origin, and the way he boasted about it; the way he captivated crowds, carried them with him and sent them into raptures by using phrases which, when we consider them coolly, are merely specimens of empty rhetoric; the way he loved to display his culture, which in reality was only superficial and muddled; his romantic dreams of a rosy future and his certainty that he was 'the man chosen by Providence'; his claim to be a Socialist, whereas in reality he was an authoritarian; his cult of personality and physical strength; and

lastly, his deliberate vulgarity and affectation of simplicity, which in the early days won considerable popularity for Mussolini, too.[45]

But above all he borrowed from the Fascist dictators the technique of mobilizing the masses by creating a party militia (Workers' Brigades), a youth organization (Young Pioneers), party schools and groups of spies camouflaged as activists (Party Vanguard Activists), together with all the other ancillary bodies which form the natural foundations of any authoritarian régime. Once he had organized the masses, Nkrumah decreed that the party—his own party—and the nation were one and the same thing. Consequently, the adversaries of his régime became the enemies of Ghana and automatically liable to the penalties prescibed by the repression laws. Though it remained parliamentary in form until the end of 1963, practically speaking Ghana had been a totalitarian State for years, with Nkrumah holding all the power in his own hands. He was, in fact, President of the Republic, head of the government, commander-in-chief of the army, life-president and secretary-general of the Convention People's Party, which was the party in power and, from 1st February 1964 on, the only party in the country.[46] He appointed and dismissed Ministers as and when he liked, dissolved the National Assembly whenever he thought fit, since he considered it as being 'a mere instrument of his policy';[47] and lastly, by means of the Preventive Detention Act he was able to neutralize his opponents by imprisoning them for five years (the maximum term was subsequently raised to twenty years), while by resorting to the Criminal Procedure Act he could even have them sentenced to death.

Nkrumah denied that such things were the equivalent of a dictatorship. In his *Africa Must Unite* he declared that it had not been his intention to free his country from colonialism and then replace this by an African tyranny,[48] and in defending his own actions he pointed out that he had never confirmed death-sentences and that his régime had the full support of the Ghanaian people, whereas the opposition was becoming more and more isolated as time went on. In reality the opposition was not isolated, but persecuted to such an extent that it virtually ceased to exist. This was emphasized in the Ghanaian parliament on 6 June 1962 by one of the few surviving members of the United Party, S. D. Dombo, when he said:

> Anyone who attempts to organize it [the United Party] is branded as being subversive, and is charged and arrested. Even belonging

to that party is considered to be an act of subversion. But as far as I am concerned, the United Party is not dead! All our members may be detained, but the United Party is not dead. Give us the chance; grant us permits to organize rallies, and see whether or not people support our cause. But you have restricted our activities; you have tied our hands; and how do you expect us to organize?[49]

Even if we accept the theory advanced by some Africanists who consider Nkrumah to have been a dictator by necessity, we certainly cannot claim that he was a modest dictator. On the contrary, he was undoubtedly the least modest man in Africa. Equally puerile is the assertion made by some of his admirers that the sacred, mythical aura with which he deliberately surrounded himself was an indispensable weapon in an African country still faithful to the old tradition of obeying only men who posed as gods and claimed to be endowed with messianic and charismatic faculties.[50] Nkrumah introduced into his dictatorship a cult of personality which was undoubtedly more complex and fanciful than that of Mussolini, Hitler, or even Stalin—a cult which revealed all his cultural and political pragmatism. In Accra alone he was represented by a bronze statue weighing three tons and his name glittered in red and blue letters against the night sky above Kwame Nkrumah Square, the starting-point of a Nkrumah Road and a Nkrumah Avenue. His face appeared on coins flaunting the proud inscription *Civitatis Ghanaiensis Conditor*; on postage-stamps, side by side with that of Abraham Lincoln; in portraits which were displayed in every shop-window, in taxis, in Ghana Airways planes and in the ships of the Black Star Line; on the clothes, scarves and handbags of housewives and on the hats and ties of men. His arrival at the Parliament House was greeted by the blowing of horns, the roll of drums and a salute of twenty-one guns; he was continually being compared with Confucius, Mohammed, Napoleon, Washington and St Francis of Assisi; and the house in which he was born at Nkroful was turned into a national museum, which it was hoped would serve as 'a Mecca for African statesmen'.[51] The newspapers conferred upon him titles such as Messiah, Man of Providence, Founder, the African Simon Bolivar, Lion, Kindly Light, Good Shepherd, *Osagyefo* (Redeemer), *Katamanto* ('he who never lies'), *Kukuduruni* ('the Brave'), *Nufenu* ('strongest of all men'), *Uyeadieyie* ('man of glorious deeds') and *Kasapreko* ('he who speaks once and for all').[52]

The former Minister Adamafio, whose admiration for Nkrumah

did not save him from being tried for high treason in the summer of 1963, composed a poem a few years ago which he called 'Portrait of the *Osagyefo* Dr Nkrumah', containing, among other things, this magnificent passage:

> Kwame Nkrumah is our father, teacher, our brother, our friend; indeed our very lives, for without him we would no doubt have existed, but we would never have lived.[53]

The boys of the Ghana Young Pioneers movement shouted slogans such as 'Nkrumah is our Messiah', 'Nkrumah is always right', 'Nkrumah will never die'.[54] Two Anglican bishops, Richard Rose-veare and Cecil Patterson, ventured to express their doubts as to this last claim, and the 'Redeemer' promptly turned them out of the country. In fact, Nkrumah encouraged these forms of idolatry among the young, allowing his name to be substituted for that of God in imitations of Methodist hymns and of the Catholic Credo, and he even gave instructions that every morning in the schools the pupils should raise their arms and take an oath: 'I swear on my honour to be faithful to Ghana and to the founder of the national ideal, Kwame Nkrumah, to serve him with all my might and all my heart . . . So help me God!'[55] And the whole nation was ordered to recite the following prayer:

> Arise, O men of Ghana,
> For in Africa we have found
> The man we have long awaited,
> A new Moses,
> Who will guide us to the Promised Land
> Of glory and beatitude.
> Hail him, this man,
> He is the *Osagyefo*.[56]

Frantz Fanon would call all this 'a caricature and at the same time an obscene parody' of European Fascism, but Nkrumah did his best to turn it into a ritual indispensable for the mobilization of the masses, though it did not give the results he had hoped. On the contrary, towards the end of 1961, while Nkrumah was taking a holiday on the shores of the Black Sea as the guest of Khrushchev, the life of Ghana was paralysed by a general strike. This time it had not been organized by the opposition, but by the trade unions, which were one of the mainstays of the régime. Emboldened by the prevailing discontent, the opposition also raised its head and tried to obtain by violence what it had failed to obtain in the course of parliamentary debates. The attempts on the *Osag-*

yefo's life,[57] the frequent strikes and the economic difficulties caused by the wasting of money on prestige projects, seemed at the end of 1962 to be harbingers of the end of Nkrumahism. But once again Fortune came to the assistance of the 'Redeemer', who gradually retrieved his position by making use of demagogic methods, by punishing the most corrupt among his Ministers and functionaries, and by promoting Ghana to the rank of a 'popular democracy' in order to placate the 'left wing' of his party.

These grave episodes in 1962 taught Nkrumah more than one lesson. Although he proclaimed a state of emergency, he tried to come to terms with the opposition and freed several hundred political prisoners, among them Joe Appiah and Joseph Danquah (the latter was subsequently sent back to prison and died as the result of ill-treatment). Then he set about giving his régime a more clearly defined ideology. In the spring of 1964, with the publication of his *Consciencism*,[58] Nkrumah felt that he had at last, after many attempts, found the most suitable formula for African politics. He discovered it by re-reading Marx and Lenin and subjecting their views to a revision. He denied, for example, that the class struggle was a necessary premiss to the achievement of Socialism, and also rejected the Chinese theory that revolution was an indispensable prelude to the creation of a Socialist society. On the other hand, he insisted that the transition from African communal life to Socialism could also be effected in gradual stages.

Like other African leaders, Nkrumah ran up against great financial difficulties, made many mistakes, contradicted himself and turned to other solutions, all of which resulted in his being accused of behaving like a Fascist dictator or of preparing Africa for the penetration of international Communism. But despite all appearances to the contrary, it would be wrong to classify Nkrumah's authoritarianism as a typical right-wing trend, first because of the long struggle waged by the leader of the Convention People's Party against feudalism and the reactionaries, and secondly because the policy he followed in Ghana after 1957 was anti-capitalistic, neutralist and anti-imperialist. Nevertheless his régime might well be compared with some of the stronger populist movements, among which it is customary to include Peronism.

The American writer George W. Shepherd has pointed out that some 'Western circles have tended to idealize Ghana and, when all their expectations were not realized, to attack it'.[59] In his more recent writings Nkrumah claims that such an attitude is unfair and that Ghana could not be expected to achieve in less than ten years what it had taken Europe centuries to do. Nkrumah therefore pleaded for time and a closer study of his work, which would take due account of all the difficulties the African continent has had to overcome in this phase of decolonization.

But no such respite was to be granted. On 24 February 1966, while he was in a plane on his way to Peking, a military junta deposed him. Kwame Nkrumah, however, was not the type of man to submit without a struggle, as several other African heads of State did towards the end of 1965 and at the beginning of 1966. A few days later, in fact, he was in Guinea, where President Sékou Touré, acting in accordance with an old pact concluded between the two countries, symbolically made way for him, thus providing Nkrumah with a chance to set about organizing his return to Ghana (which, however, is highly improbable). What will be the outcome of this, it is not yet possible to say, but the fact remains that he foresaw what the future of Africa would be, and his urgent appeals for unity were extremely reasonable. His ideas about decolonization may be right, but his loud denunciations met with no response, and his attitude has probably done more to divide Africa than to unite her. Deprived of power by one of those plots which he himself knew how to weave so well, he will certainly never become the George Washington of Africa; but there can be no doubt that his 'vision' will be an important factor in the resurgence of the Dark Continent.

Democracy and the one-party system

The examples of Egypt and Ghana teach us that in the Africa of today the terms 'Socialism' and 'democracy' are frequently misinterpreted, and this misinterpretation is sometimes due to muddle-headedness, sometimes to bad faith and to a desire to deceive. Nevertheless, we should be doing a grave injustice to the new African élites if we were to infer from this that they have ceased to take any interest in the welfare of their countries and have given up trying, by dint of study, discussion and argument, to direct them along new paths, 'suited to the reality of Africa'. From Dakar to Abidjan, from Casablanca to Moshi, from Accra to Dar-es-Salaam, and from Cotonou to Addis Ababa, the passage of delegations never ceases. Meetings are sometimes at summit level, sometimes on the Foreign Minister level, and at other times just talks between men of culture. Africa has never known so many congresses, conferences and seminars, all held within the last few years—the years of independence, liberty and pride.

This almost frantic haste, the result of justifiable apprehension, to make up for lost time, emerges from a very significant passage in a paper read by Ernest Boka of the Ivory Coast, at a seminar held at Abidjan in January 1962:

> The destiny of Africa is at stake, and we have a feeling that these are decisive hours, fraught with both anxiety and joy. We feel that this is a historic moment, such as has perhaps never been experienced before, when anything might happen—either a rapid recession or a sudden leap forward, a lingering death or a laborious progress amidst lulls and snares. Never have we been faced with such grave problems all at the same time. But among all these problems there is one that we must settle right now, not because it is the most important, but because everything else will depend on how we solve it. And that is the problem of democracy.[60]

Having, in fact, freed herself from colonialism, Africa now has to choose which way she shall go, after comparing, analysing and considering all the doctrines that have been tried out in other parts of the world. Will Africa choose a completely original solution, discarding the experiments and theories of the older Europe as a result of that *négritude* which Jean-Paul Sartre called 'anti-racialist racialism'? Judging by the first theoretical formulations, it would seem that she will not. One might, however, speak, at all events at the present moment, of a (somewhat chaotic) medley of black-African and European ideas. For the poet and President of Senegal, Léopold Sédar Senghor, 'it is not a question of destroying colonialism, we have to go beyond it', drawing on those elements in African experiments and European contributions which still hold good in order to build a Socialist society in Africa. It must, however, be borne in mind that the African political world, when it uses the terms 'Socialism', 'democracy' and 'Communism', modifies their meaning by placing the adjective 'African' before them, which makes their political significance even vaguer. Senghor's Socialism, which to begin with differs from Nkrumah's or Nasser's, has its roots in African communal life rather than in the theories of Marx; and although it accepts some of the latter's conclusions, it does so only because they were subsequently modified by Teilhard de Chardin who, according to Senghor, created a harmonious synthesis between 'scientific Socialism' and religious faith.

o*

In Senghor's view, the African road to Socialism passes through Marx and Hegel, but it 'accepts only their positive values', such as the philosophy of humanism, the economic theory, the dialectic method and planning, and it rejects their atheism and the class struggle. From the French Socialist idealists like Saint-Simon and Proudhon it borrows federalism, mutual assistance and co-operation. From the African side it takes the communal tradition ('a less Cartesian kind of Socialism than the European form') and the cultural and religious values. This synthesis of theories and values should enable the new African élites to install democratic régimes in a continent which, owing to its political and intellectual backwardness, and the almost complete absence of class distinctions, seems to be averse to the very conception of democracy. Senghor, however, warns us that this democracy must be *strong*, in order to avoid 'on the one hand a Fascist dictatorship and on the other an unstable government, such as we witnessed in France during the Third and Fourth Republics'. Hence the necessity, according to Senghor, of certain limitations to the powers of trade unions and to the right to criticize claimed by the opposition parties, who are often 'in the service of the foreigner'.[61]

Ernest Boka, whom we mentioned above, seems to be rather less optimistic and asks 'whether and to what extent a democratic régime is suitable for Africa'. Although he admits that all the African States have given themselves constitutions starting with a short preamble defining public liberties and affirming their adhesion to the declarations of 1789 in France and of 1948 in all countries, Boka thinks that in Africa democracy will have to overcome at least three obstacles. 'For the sake of brevity,' he says, 'we will call them the paradox, the one-party system, and the dearth of intellectual and moral standards.' To Ernest Boka it seems paradoxical and presumptuous when African States that have only just achieved independence (and in which an 'enlightened *bourgeoisie*' such as has been the mainstay of European democracy for a hundred years simply does not exist) try to set up democratic régimes within a very short time, more especially at a moment when 'the Western democracies, which seemed to be the most solid, are beginning to ask what their future is to be and some people even maintain that democracy is outdated'. He also maintains that the multi-party system (which in Western countries is a synonym of democracy) is unsuitable for African society, which has no rigid class distinctions or 'historical memories which might create an abyss between groups of individuals'. In Boka's opinion the one-party system thus becomes inevitable, and this period of transition undoubtedly involves a risk of dictatorships. The third obstacle African democracy has to face is the African's intolerance and lack of civic spirit—defects which can be remedied only by better education.

Thus we have on the one hand Léopold Sédar Senghor who has confidence in his own plan for introducing democracy, and on the other Ernest Boka who doubts whether this is feasible, though he adds that 'the obstacles to democracy are not insurmountable'.[62]

Despite the danger mentioned by Ernest Boka, the moment they had achieved independence almost all the African States rejected the multi-party system and installed one-party régimes, which in some cases soon became dictatorships. 'By now,' says Romain Rainero, 'almost all these leaders of anti-colonial fronts have become the supreme and only rulers of their countries. The transition to dictatorships is everywhere imminent, and we have striking examples of what can already be called dictatorships.'[63] The explanation which the President of Guinea, Sékou Touré, gives of this process, is disconcertingly frank. Whereas in 1959 he defended himself against accusations that he was trying to establish a dictatorship,[64] today, on the contrary, he frankly admits it, adding this justification:

> Among the different forms of dictatorship established by the various régimes—personal, economic or financial, parliamentary or popular—we have chosen this last-named method of wielding power because it is the only one which, in every single case, is suited to the present condition and spirit of African society, the only one that can, without grave upheavals, enable us to make progress. The predominance of the party in the nation's life provides a guarantee against any loss of sovereignty on the part of the people. It is a guarantee provided by control from below.[65]

Dictatorship is thus admitted without any reservations. And even without any feeling of shame. 'The criteria of democracy have been safeguarded as regards internal affairs,' says the Mali Minister for the Interior, Madéira Kéita,

> thanks to the freedom of discussion, discipline, and democratic elections, not only to leading posts in the party, but also to legislative and administrative organisms such as the provincial assemblies and village councils.[66]

The President of the Niger Republic, Hamami Diori, likewise claims that democracy is safeguarded because of the dialectical relationships within the one party. 'Should there be any disagree-

Fascism Today

ment as to doctrine,' hes ays, 'it can be freely expressed inside the party, and need not result in a splitting-up into several parties.' This defence of the one-party system is based on two fundamental concepts—the necessity of ensuring the maximum efficiency in the government's efforts directed towards a rapid development of the country, and the idea that any opposition is futile (and also danger-ous and in the case of underdeveloped countries nothing less than a luxury. Nevertheless, as we shall see, the actual facts deprive these theories of their ideal content and show that in some respects they are merely alibis.

The Socialist alibi

The history of Africa during the last six years shows that, instead of speeding up the development of the new countries, the one-party system is tending in many cases to become an instrument of social domination. As for the presidential régime which all these countries adopted as eagerly as they did the one-party system, it has all the characteristics of an absolute monarchy and reduces the constitu-tion to the status of a *pro-forma* document. René Dumont, one of the leading experts on decolonization, gives a decidedly negative account of the first round of African experiments. He has made a special study of the former French territories, and he reports an ominous increase in the powers of the police, systematic persecution of opposition parties, corruption in the civil services and a tendency to protect the interests of the former colonial powers, since many of these countries have not succeeded in freeing themselves com-pletely from the 'colonial pact'. He criticizes the excessive expendi-ture on useless and spectacular projects (e.g. President Tubman's residence in Liberia, which cost the equivalent of $6\frac{1}{2}$ million pounds and Houphouët-Boigny's palace, which cost 4 million, and on embassies abroad, and also the high salaries paid to members of parliament. 'And above all, we cannot talk of Socialism when a member of parliament, after a month or two of "work" in an air-conditioned room has earned as much as a peasant woman earns in a whole lifetime spent beneath the scorching rays of the sun.' Dumont is an expert on agrarian problems and nobody is in a better position to judge the disadvantages under which Africa labours, these being her climate, the one-crop system imposed by the colonialists, the scourge of tribal leadership, and so on. Never-theless, Africa is far from being an accursed country. According to Dumont, the élites are to blame for the poor start that has been made, since they have been content to pay lip-service to Socialism while taking good care not to make any sacrifices themselves. In many of these countries, he says, Socialism serves merely as an alibi. In reality none of the essential problems has been tackled; on the contrary, corruption is rampant and a grasping caste of bureaucrats has arisen; to which one must add discrimination against the rural population, on such a scale that some peasants in the former French Congo are beginning to say that 'independence is not for them, but only for the people in the big towns'.

In his book, Dumont feels reluctantly compelled to express his doubts about this 'African-type Socialism' and to insist that if the élites responsible for this state of affairs do not distinguish themselves in the future by their honesty, devotion, austerity and willingness to make sacrifices, as well as by a technical ability which cannot be made up for by zeal and revolutionary talk, Africa is bound to relapse into a Latin American stagnation and 'will be irresistibly propelled down the perilous slopes of Fascism and Stalinism, or at all events of a police reign of terror such as has already made its appearance here and there'.[67] Frantz Fanon's diagnosis is much the same as Dumont's. They both believe that aid from abroad with a view to bolstering the new African élites (who in many cases are still men who owe their appointments to the former colonial powers) will serve only to drive them towards neo-colonialism and Fascist-type dictatorships. This process might well be accelerated if the Western powers were to present Africa with one last poisoned gift—military aid. 'In that case,' Fanon warns us, 'the former colonial power could exercise an indirect control through the middle class whom it supports and through a national army trained by its experts, which would dominate and overawe the populace.'[68]

The new scourges

Africa, then, has achieved her independence, but it cannot yet be said that she has become free. Most of the thirty-seven countries that shook off the yoke of colonialism between 1957 and 1965 have chosen the one-party system and are now living under dictatorial régimes. The others, although they have preserved their democratic institutions, have virtually emptied them of their content and made their constitutions a mere matter of form.

The effects of this evolution towards authoritarianism have quickly become evident. Since 1960 Africa has figured in the newspapers as prominently as South America. Hardly a week passes without our reading of plots against governments, political assassinations, arrests and legal proceedings against opposition parties, of régimes being overthrown and of attempts to expand by annexing neighbouring territories. Sometimes the plots are real, but more often than not they are deliberately exaggerated by the régime in power in order to provide an excuse for suppressing the opposition. Trials are invariably on a gigantic scale and the procedure is often unorthodox; the penalties are always severe—imprisonment for life, or death. 'It is not only in Spain,' we read in the Algerian weekly *Révolution Africaine*,

> that the execution squads are today shooting down freedom of thought. That is happening in several African countries, too, but there is a mistaken, incomprehensible reluctance to admit the fact . . . To the name of Grimau must be added those of the thirteen men sentenced to death on the Ivory Coast. We must do our best to save them from death.[69]

In April 1963, in fact, at Yamoussoukro, the village where Houphouët-Boigny, the President of the Ivory Coast, was born, a trial was held *in camera*, the charge being conspiracy against the State, and thirteen men were sentenced to death, seven to imprisonment for life, and thirty-four others to terms of detention. 'Though it would not be decisive,' E. R. Braundi wrote when commenting on this secret trial and the inadequacy of the proofs, 'a reprieve for the men sentenced at Yamoussoukro would be a real achievement in this campaign, which has now become a necessity, against the fascistization of Africa.'[70]

Plots and the resulting trials are always more frequent in countries where the party in power is still the *parti de l'administration*, or where the one-party system has been imposed by violence and fraud. This is the case in Chad, in the Niger Republic, in Cameroon and in Congo-Brazzaville, where in early 1963 big trials were heard *in camera*, the accused being given no proper chance of defending themselves. The more powerful régimes defend themselves desperately against subversion and try to terrorize their adversaries by inflicting increasingly severe sentences. In Ghana, during the first months of 1963, there were five death-sentences; in Tunisia, thirteen (of which only ten were carried out); in Mali, three (subsequently commuted to imprisonment for life); and on the Ivory

Coast, the thirteen we have already mentioned. The year 1964 began with the trial in Rabat, which ended with eleven death sentences.

Occasionally, the conspirators are successful, for example in Togo, where they killed President Sylvanus Olimpio. The Lomé *pronunciamiento* was of the South American type, swift and deadly, and it worried the leaders of other African countries, who at the Ouagadougou conference discussed the best ways of protecting their powerful governments from the anger of the people. The same problem was on the agenda at the summit conference in Addis Ababa, where it was unanimously agreed to add to the famous 'charter' a clause 'condemning without reservations political assassinations and all subversive activities organized by neighbouring States or any other country'.[71]

Generally speaking, the populace take no part in these conspiracies and they do not rejoice if they fail. They are simply mute spectators of the clashes and quarrels among the élites, but they are gradually acquiring a greater consciousness of their rights, of the wrongs they suffer and of the very meagre portion which is their lot. in Brazzaville, from being spectators they suddenly became actors. For them 13 August 1963 was a memorable day, for it marked the triumph of the masses over a strong government and created an extremely valuable precedent. A general strike called by the unions brought about the fall of the dictator Fulbert Youlou, a friend of Tshombe and an admirer of Salazar, and this on the very day when he intended to assume full powers and introduce the one-party system. Fulbert Youlou was a priest who had been suspended *a divinis* and who had once distinguished himself by drawing a pistol during a parliamentary sitting in order to overawe one of his adversaries. He provided what is perhaps the worst example of how the ideals of independence can be betrayed, and of abject obsequiousness to the interests of the neo-colonialist powers. His recklessness was such that he even appointed as his chief of police an ex-convict named Charles Delarue, who had been a Gestapo agent and was an expert in suppressing revolts and concocting false accusations against trade unionists. As Ernest Milcent points out, the rising in Brazzaville revealed 'the fragility of African régimes when they become dictatorships, ignore the everyday problems of the populace and seem to be opposing African unity'.[72]

The fall of Fulbert Youlou caused renewed alarm among the 'strong men' of Africa. Fearing that their opponents would be

encouraged by the success of the Brazzaville rising, they yielded
to the psychosis of conspiracies and engaged in a race against
time with their adversaries which led to more arrests, trials and
sentences. One month after the popular revolt in Brazzaville Houphouët-Boigny rid himself of his last opponents on the Ivory Coast,
while in the Chad François Tombalaye had some of his adversaries
arrested after incidents which resulted in twenty people being killed.
In Dahomey the insurgents deposed the President, Hubert Maga,
and the same thing might have happened in Gaboon, if French
troops had not intervened and restored the discredited Léon M'ba
to his pedestal. The wind from Brazzaville, however, is still blowing, and it is probable that some of the more corrupt among the
other dictatorships will eventually fall.

Even the mild Socialism of Léopold Sédar Senghor did not
escape criticism, and it was sorely tried by an attempted *coup
d'état*, on which the subsequent trial in Dakar did not throw
complete light. This incident enabled the poet of *Hosties Noires* to
rid himself once and for all of his rival Mamadou Dia[73] with his
progressive Socialism, and to install a presidential régime, after
vaunting his right to put *une seule tête sous un seul bonnet*. This
swing towards the right of the political axis (in the course of the
operation Senghor had the support of the privileged classes, of the
French community and the Muslim notables) gave grounds for
thinking that Senghor's 'Socialism' owed more to the example of
authoritarianism set by De Gaulle than it did to the theories of
Socialist writers and the promptings of Teilhard de Chardin, since
Senghor had previously been one of De Gaulle's ministers and
private advisers. The peculiar type of Socialism evolved by the
nationalistic African middle class, which, when it is not merely
an alibi, amounts to nothing more than a kind of arithmetic of
economic development, would seem to confirm the Algerian Frantz
Fanon's thesis regarding the futility of the middle-class phase in
underdeveloped countries. 'Once this caste has been crushed,
devoured by its own contradictions, we shall find that nothing has
happened since independence, that we have to start again from
zero.'[74]

The man who decided to omit the 'middle-class phase' altogether
and introduce a Socialist régime, was Ahmed Ben Bella, the
Algerian leader, but his attempt was ruined by all the friction
between nationalistic aspirations, partial fidelity to Islamic tradition,
and the flaws in a Socialist project which had no coherent pro-

gramme and no well-organized party to carry it out, and from the very start it revealed all the defects that made it so impracticable. In particular, Ben Bella's policy contained a dose of empiricism, and this meant that the National Liberation Front's operations were subject to dangerous oscillations, to which was added the failure to reconcile the contradictory trends which emerged within the party after the achievement of independence. Ben Bella's original slogan, 'Revolution without prisons', came to grief when he tried to suppress his opponents in Kabylia and the Aurès.[75] A *coup de main* organized by a group of army officers under Colonel Houaki Boumedienne in July 1965 not only deprived Ben Bella of the leadership by arresting him, but would seem to have started a new trend, in which Socialist watchwords have lost most of their force and the typical ingredients of Nasserism are becoming increasingly evident.

The situation appears to be similar in Morocco, one of the few African countries in which the multi-party system has official approval and one-party rule is, in fact, forbidden under Article 3 of the constitution. Behind the screen of democratic institutions the young King Hassan II is trying to govern the country with the help of a servile 'King's party', and he has introduced a kind of 'hereditary Gaullism'. Commenting on the mass arrests in early 1963 of leading members of the *Union Nationale des Forces Populaires* and the *Istiqlal*, the *New York Times* remarked that these dictatorial moves on the part of the youthful sovereign had led to the removal, and sometimes to the arrest, of men who had helped Hassan's father to free the country from the yoke of colonialism.[76] And the organ of the *Union Marocaine du Travail* has denounced the violence to which 'opponents of the Royal Palace' are subjected, remarking bitterly that 'torture has become a new factor in the Moroccan situation'.[77] Under Hassan II's rule military reactionaries play a preponderating role and they naturally prefer to resort to drastic liquidation of their adversaries. A striking proof of this was the murder, in October 1965, of the opposition leader Ahmed Ben Barka, which is alleged to have been the work of the Minister for the Interior, General Oufkir, who with the connivance of certain police functionaries laid a trap for Ben Barka in Paris.

The situation in all the thirty-seven independent African States was already tense, and it was further complicated during 1965 by the intervention on a large scale of army officers. The politicians, alarmed by the appearance of these new rivals, tried to win them over by showering them with decorations and money. In this way another privileged class was added to that of the bureaucrats, and it soon became conscious of its strength. At moments of crisis the military men acted as arbitrators, seizing power whenever the civilians were unable to find a solution. In the brief space of four months there was a kind of chain-reaction, and the military deposed the presidents of the Congo, Dahomey, the Central African Republic, the Upper Volta, Nigeria and Ghana. By now they have perfected their technique and are as efficient as the South American *golpistas*.

Intolerance, authoritarianism, hero-worship and extreme nationalism are thus phenomena which can be clearly discerned in the Africa of today. But the list of scourges does not end there. As Romain Rainero points out:

> With the aid of pan-African activists and by unearthing alleged anti-national plots the African governments have often tried to solve their internal problems by introducing a phase of imperialism into their policies, at the expense of other African States.[78]

Examples of this trend are not lacking. Morocco lays claim to Mauritania and the Tindouf area in Algeria; Ghana has its eyes on Togo; Tunisia wants a strip of land in the Algerian Sahara; Egypt has been trying for years to annex the Sudan; Somalia would like to take over Ogaden from Ethiopia and the Northern Frontier District from Kenya; while Nigeria covets the neighbouring Cameroon. And they do not always confine themselves to words, as is proved by the disputes between Algeria and Morocco in late 1963 and between Somalia and Ethiopia in April 1964.

Lastly, during this phase of developing African authoritarianism, we must note the tendency of the middle classes in some countries to support reactionary trends both at home and abroad, their aim being to prevent the working classes from acquiring more power. Things have reached such a point that, when a government feels that it is being attacked and can no longer trust the army and the police, it creates, as the Ivory Coast government did, a party militia, with the same functions that were formerly fulfilled by the SA in Germany and the MVSN in Italy.[79] In Katanga, where African aspirations coincided with the interests of the big international trusts, we have even witnessed the creation of militias comprising white mercenaries, most of these being ex-members of the OAS or of the Belgian, South African and Rhodesian extreme right wings. And we have also seen American, British and French supporters of

Tshombe rushing to help the tottering Katanga Republic—men who were known to be connected with organizations such as the John Birch Society.[80]

But where all the scourges we have mentioned are to be found together is in Cameroon, where the independence achieved in 1960 has had no effect whatever on the internal situation. The *Union des Populations Camerounaises*, which in 1955 was the only organized party in the country, today claims to represent the majority of the population and is the only party in Africa still waging an armed battle against the forces of neo-colonialism, after fighting in the past against the French occupation forces. For the last nine years these activists of the UPC have been living in the wilds, in the swamps, forests and mountains of Bamileké, Mungo, Sanaga and Wouri, sharing with the inhabitants of those regions famine and the fear of reprisals. With the most rudimentary weapons they try to resist a campaign of repression which for some unexplained reason the rest of the world continues to ignore, but which is pitiless.

What has inspired these partisans to keep on fighting for years? Perhaps as Félix Moumié says, the conviction that 'there has never been a case in history of a national revolt being stamped out by a foreign army'. Because, despite the granting of independence, France is still waging war in Cameroon, maintaining that this is the only way to stop Communism from gaining a footing in Africa. Nothing could be more false than this accusation which France brings against the UPC—the same accusation that she invariably levels against all her adversaries. When we were in Douala a few years ago, the Catholic Bishop Thomas Mongo, talked to us about the first leader of the UPC, and said: 'A year before he was murdered, I visited Un Nyobé in the jungle. We talked for hours and hours, and to me he seemed to be a good Christian and a sincere patriot. He told me that he had accepted help from the French Communists and the countries behind the Iron Curtain because he could not find anyone else to help him, and that he was prepared to renounce these alliances the moment Cameroon became free.'[81] But it suits the French to talk about 'Communist subversion' because it provides them with an excellent excuse, justifying their presence in Cameroon and the support they give to the 'crusade'. In reality, their aim is the complete destruction of the only popular national movement that is opposed to the use of military bases by foreign powers and to the exploitation of the country's enormous resources.

To save appearances, the French have left the task of repression to Ahmadou Ahidjo's government, one of those puppet régimes that could never exist if it did not receive support from Paris. But in reality at the beginning of 1964 the gendarmerie was still under the command of Lieutenant-Colonel Aurousseau, the army was trained and led by officers and N.C.O.s who took their orders from General Briand, while all air raids started from the airfield at Bouar, which was under the command of Colonel Bigeard, an officer who had made himself all too well known in Algeria with his experiments in counter-revolutionary warfare. To these forces must be added detachments of the Foreign Legion transferred from Algeria to Cameroon after the signing of the Évian agreement; African troops of the old *Communauté Française* recruited in Chad, the Upper Volta, Senegal and Mauritania; and finally the 'self-defence' squads, commandos and militias of Ahidjo's own party. In all about 100,000 men, enough to enable the Ahidjo government to keep the revolt down and the French to keep their hold over the country's economy and the air bases at Koundem, Koutaba and Douala.

But although Ahidjo had at his disposal the biggest mercenary army in Africa, although he had dissolved all the other parties and trade unions and had stifled all liberty with his emergency laws of May 1959, May 1960 and March 1962, he has not yet succeeded in repressing the revolt of the UPC. Today Cameroon offers the same picture of desolation and death as South Vietnam or Algeria during the 1950s. Tens of thousands of patriots have been tortured and sent to the concentration camps at Yoko, Mokolo and Edea. Hundreds of thousands of peasants have been forcibly removed from the areas affected by the revolt and interned in 'fortified villages' which are exact replicas of the *villages de régroupement* in Algeria and the *hameaux stratégiques* in Indo-China. On 24 April 1960, after clashes between patriots and gendarmes in the 'Congo' quarter at Douala, the whole area was surrounded by troops, sprayed with petrol from helicopters and then set on fire while the population were still inside. On 25 January 1962, the prefect of Wouri, Guillaume Nseke, ordered 105 political prisoners to be put in a sealed truck and sent to the concentration camp at Mokolo. When the truck stopped at Yaoundé it was found that thirteen of the occupants had died of suffocation, while twelve others died a few hours later in hospital. As soon as this became known, Archbishop Zoa denounced the outrage in a pastoral letter which was read in every church in Cameroon. Since he did not dare to expel the Archbishop, Ahidjo deported Abbé Fertin, who had defied the authorities by publishing the pastoral letter in the Catholic periodical *L'Effort du Caméroun*. On 1st May 1963 the department of Ndé was declared a prohibited area, and 50,000 peasants were compelled to abandon their fields and their possessions.

The above are just three episodes chosen from among a thousand. Three episodes in a drama the full story of which will never be known, as happened in Algeria and as will happen in South Vietnam. But what makes the situation in Cameroon even more serious is that, under the complacent eyes of the French, President Ahmadou Ahidjo has been able to set up an authentic Fascist dictatorship, a dictatorship which is the product, not only of a climate of violence, but of a deliberate plan organized by the leaders of the only party in accordance with Nazi theories and using Nazi methods. As we write these lines, we have before us a photostat copy of a top secret document of 144 pages, dealing with the leading functionaries in Ahidjo's party. The document bears the title *Premier Stage de formation des Responsables de l'Union Camérounaise* and it contains a report on an ideological debate which took place in Yaoundé between 1st and 6 August 1961. The most disconcerting passage is that which concerns the part played by Samuel Kame, the man responsible for the organization of the *Union Camérounaise*. After discussing whether membership of the only party in Cameroon ought to be open to all or confined to an élite, Kame analyses the structure and tactics of the Communist parties and finally concludes that the best model would be Fascism. On page 102 of this document we read:

The German National Socialist Party would sometimes decide, for example, to hold a meeting in some town that was completely dominated by the Socialists and Communists. The members of the action squad would arrive in a special train, form up at the station and march through the streets, a procedure which inevitably led to violent clashes. In the end a small group would manage to hold the meeting, and this always made a deep impression on German public opinion, which felt that these men could establish order when they wanted to. That is exactly what we need here. We must be ready to use our militia to compensate for the weakness of our police forces.

On page 107 Kame is even more explicit:

In a situation like our own, it is essential that we should organize militias consisting of young people of both sexes. In such matters we need have no hesitation in copying Fascist methods—squads, sections, companies, battalions, regiments and divisions. Such units, according to their numbers, must correspond to groups of houses, parts of quarters, whole quarters and groups of quarters, no matter whether we are dealing with towns or villages. These militias must be in a position to mobilize rapidly.

What Kame proposes is an exact replica of the Nazi *Sturmabteilungen*. Defeated in Europe, Goebbels, Rosenberg and Himmler are being taken as models in Cameroon. And side by side with them we find the theoreticians of counter-revolutionary warfare, the French torturers who learned their trade in Indo-China and Algeria. As he showed us his back covered with scars, a UPC activist who had found asylum in Ghana said:

The first time they arrested and tortured me because they said I was conspiring against France; the second time, because I was fighting against the Ahidjo régime imposed by France. On both occasions, before and after independence, the men who tortured me were Frenchmen; they tied me to a bar and beat me for nine days without stopping. You know what I mean—the torture they call the *balançoire* . . . After that, can I say that my country is free and really independent?[82]

The future of Africa

The forces of the European extreme right wing naturally take a favourable view of the establishment of so many petty dictatorships in Africa, since they can be easily controlled and persuaded to collaborate with the neo-colonialist powers in exchange for aid and protection. With rare exceptions, we are bound to conclude that the choice of the one-party and presidential system—which means that the power remains in the hands of an élite—has been an advantage as far as this new 'colonial pact' is concerned. But even in countries where a dictatorship has been installed in order to defend the anti-colonial revolution, there is a danger that it might remain in power for a very long time, together with all its odious repressive measures. 'Even if we admit that a dictatorship is necessary during the stage of preparation or transition,' says Luigi Salvatorelli,

it should at least be acknowledged as being a dictatorship, and there should be a movement towards, and a beginning of, real liberty and democracy. But there is nothing of the kind. Here we have a deliberate codification, an exaltation of the one-party principle and of individual despotism, in other words of 'duce-ism'.[83]

Frantz Fanon gives a different explanation of this phenomenon.

> Just as the middle class in any country shuns the constructive phase and plunges straight into enjoyment of its possessions, so, on the institutional level, it discards the parliamentary phase in favour of a dictatorship of the National Socialist type. Today we find that this Fascism in miniature, which in Latin America has been victorious for half a century, is a dialectical consequence of the semi-colonial States of the independence period.[84]

Aldo Garosci is equally pessimistic.

> For the second time in the course of a few months accusations of 'Fascism' have been levelled against the new National Socialist régimes which have sprung up in Africa . . . In these fringe areas, 'Socialism', 'Communism' and 'Fascism', which elsewhere are separated by a host of traditions and sociological factors, are perilously close to one another. Where there is no real working-class movement, but only a mass of peasants and urban workers controlled by charismatic groups or leaders of middle-class origin, where autarchy, the one-party system and the effort towards industrialization are based on the well-defined privileges of groups who blackmail and manœuvre the technicians, the forces of production and the intellectual élites, can we really speak of Socialism or Communism, or of a national or popular democracy, or should we not just call it Fascism?[85]

Can Africa avoid the fate of Latin America with its *pronunciamientos* and military dictatorships? Can she not find some way of avoiding the bitter experience of Fascist régimes? Which road must she follow if she wishes to achieve the real liberty that independence has not given her? The right road, that of unity, the solution that might enable her to avoid the dangers of balkanization and the lure of Fascism, was clearly indicated at the summit conferences in Addis Ababa and Cairo. But will the Africans be able to do what the Europeans failed to do after the last war, despite all the solemn promises that were made? And will the neo-colonial powers allow her to do it, if they continue to look upon Africa as a field for exploitation? Basil Davidson, who perhaps knows Africa better than any other man, foresees a hard struggle:

> The 1950s presided over the struggle for political emancipation. The 1960s and maybe the 1970s will preside over an even greater struggle for the fruits of political emancipation—for that new and unified society without which the peoples of Africa cannot independently survive or prosper.[86]

19 Conclusions

Our lengthy survey of right-wing extremism's words and deeds during the last fifty years is now at an end, and we must try to draw a few conclusions from this panorama of which we have traced only the rough outlines. Fascism and Nazism are still with us. Régimes and organizations inspired by them, or using the methods they have made all too famous, are still operating in all the five continents. This may seem anachronistic and inconceivable, but it is a fact. To us in the 1960s their ideas, from the point of view of logic and common sense, may seem to be few in number, unoriginal and above all cabalistic. To the pseudo-scientific elucubrations and political programmes of what we may call their 'classical' period their disciples have been unable to add anything that can be termed novel; their ideology and the framework of their programmes remain substantially the same as they were when the preceding generation created them, together with their dogmas, their ritual and, in short, their incurable irrationality. *The Protocols of the Learned Elders of Zion*, *The Myth of the Twentieth Century*, *Mein Kampf*, the *Doctrine of Fascism*, the *General Plan for the Reconstruction of Japan*, remain on the bookshelves of neo-Fascists and neo-Nazis, as if they were the Pentateuch and the Gospels of a mythology the immutable Olympus of which is thronged with a cohort of sinister prophets whose ideas have all been proved to be wrong, and of condottieri who have lost every battle they ever fought. Certain phenomena unpleasantly reminiscent of Nazi-Fascism—for example, anti-Semitism—seem to fall on fertile soil even in countries which were in the forefront of the battle against the régimes of Hitler and Mussolini and which are the complete negation of them. Take, for example, the Soviet Union, where, as we read in the October 1964 bulletin of the *Alliance Mondiale Antiraciste*, books are being published bearing titles such as *Le Judaïsme sans fards* and *Judaïsme et Sionisme contemporains*. This, however, does not mean that there are neo-Nazis in the Soviet Union, but it does show the incredible persistence of such ideas in a country where the Nazi ideology is rejected and vigorously combated.

The vocabulary of the followers of Mussolini and Hitler is still in current use, and these people still speak a language which is incomprehensible to rational minds. Into this lumber-room full of intentions, mystical notions and sophisms, not a breath of novelty can penetrate. For both Fascists and Nazis, fidelity to the forms and content of their own extravaganzas still has the integral force of an ecstatic rapture, and it never seems to occur to them that the techniques of presentation and inculcation have changed in the course of the last twenty years. When they want people to believe that they are meditating on the past, they start from an uncritical acceptance of certain postulates that were once fundamental and end up by affirming that these postulates will remain valid for all time, with the result that if we try to follow the meanderings of their impossible manner of reasoning, we simply lose the thread.

The spectacular process of conservative reaction that Europe has witnessed since the brief flame of the war of liberation died away has enabled the standard-bearers of these ill-omened ideas to re-emerge into the broad daylight of political life, at first with circumspection and later with an increasing arrogance. In Germany the serried ranks of Nazism are on the march once more, voluble and aggressive, and accepting without question all the heritage of Hitler. Not a comma has been changed, not a single note of thoughtfulness or repentance is to be heard in the ranks of the Nazi chorus which is again striking up the old tunes. Twenty years after the collapse of the Third Reich thousands of criminals who were responsible for the extermination of 6 million Jews and the ravaging of two-thirds of Europe are on the point of receiving full absolution for the crimes they committed, which in most cases have remained unpunished because during these twenty years West Germany has deliberately shielded them, providing them with hiding-places and enabling them to lead tranquil *bourgeois* lives, when she has not given them high-ranking posts in order to make use of their 'qualities' as faithful servants of the State. Nazism is still flourishing in the very bosom of the *Bundesrepublik*, and Nazis occupy the most important offices, displaying an arrogance born of the conviction that the democracy of Adenauer and Erhard intends to make use of their services and safeguard their ideals.[1]

Italian neo-Fascism is once more taking advantage of its own ambivalence. The opportunism of the Mussolini type has emerged in a new version with the MSI, under the leadership of a few minor exponents of the defunct Fascist régime flanked by 'nostalgics' representing various shades of opinion. It is trying to propagate Fascist ideas in conservative, anti-Communist and 'United Europe' circles, to whom it offers a not altogether disinterested assistance in the hope of becoming the last bulwark of such ideas.

Whenever it seems advisable, this neo-Fascism as propounded by the MSI assumes a democratic and parliamentary guise, striving to acquire a middle-class respectability and steering a careful course midway between the Monarchists and Liberals on the one hand and the *bourgeois* elements of the Christian Democratic Party on the other. Once they had chosen to follow this course, the first thing the leaders of the MSI had to do was, obviously, to get rid of the embarrassing elements forming their own extreme right wing. These latter, as the result of a kind of historical nemesis, had once again to experience all the bitterness of representing the shattered remnants of the 'revolutionary' aspirations which had been betrayed by those who occupied the leading posts during the post-war revival, and of being subordinated to a strategy of compromise within the broader framework of the conservative right wing. The 'leftism' still seething in this sector of neo-Fascism has provided grounds for some curious hypotheses, one of them being that it might give birth to something which in reality is anti-Fascist, owing to the fact that these elements, sooner or later, will tend to gravitate towards Socialism and Communism. This hypothesis is, however, without foundation, except as regards the rejection by this Fascist 'Left' of liberalism and capitalism, which they interpret in the broader sense as being expressions of oppression and exploitation. This is not enough to justify the belief that the confusion of ideas and intellectual anarchy which have distinguished 'left-wing' Fascism from the very beginning will soon be overcome; or to lead us to suppose that this revolt based on 'bradyseism' and abstract aspirations implies the acquisition of a political consciousness that can be defined in terms of class. Approaches made by Fascist 'left-wingers' to the working-class parties obviously amount to nothing more than personal revolts—even when they involve several individuals or organized groups—against certain tendencies of which they do not approve. To transform this into more general terms of principles, we should have to presuppose a new ideological 'synthesis', which it is difficult to conceive unless we follow the procedure adopted by Fascists when they are concocting some kind of improvisation. Especially among those members of the younger generation who are attracted by Fascist 'leftism' (which they interpret as an organic and fascinating scheme to demolish antiquated structures, abolish privileges and do away with the hypocrisy of a middle-class society), there may very well be a growing and genuine desire to find a revolutionary remedy without passing through the conventional stages of the class struggle, but their inability to solve all the contradictions in which they are involved might equally well persuade them to adopt a reactionary ideology as the best means of bringing about a renewal.

For example, Italian neo-Fascism includes among its aspirations, shared by both the right and the left wing of the movement, the question of 'national appeasement', to achieve which it is conducting a continual campaign, posing as the anxious and distressed promoter of a conciliation which twenty years after the civil war ought—so the Fascists say—to be the normal desire of all Italians. Here, too, the Fascists change their tune according to the requirements of circumstances; sometimes they harp on the theme of victimization; at other times they stress the equity and justice of ideas in which they sincerely believe, and they never tire of talking about 'patriotic' brotherliness. Nonetheless, the 'appeasement' which the Fascists propound in their guise of martyrs of democracy, is just a ridiculous pretext. The Republic has already gone so far in this direction as to grant Fascists the right to criticize it and to defame the struggle that gave birth to it. Not only that, but it has quashed the legal proceedings against those responsible for the establishment of the Salò régime and has turned them into a farcical 'purge' that has led to nothing, or—even worse—to the reintegration of Fascists and the placing of *Repubblichini* on an equal footing with partisans. Then again, political 'appeasement' has become just one of those 'unanimistic' expedients to which—ever since nationalism has been nationalism—the Right invariably resorts when it wants to use emotional appeals for an ambiguous unity in order to mobilize public opinion and direct it towards its own reactionary aims. On the moral and political plane, the identification of the ideal values and responsibilities of anti-Fascism with the motives of Fascism is impossible unless we are prepared to admit that irreconcilable antitheses can be identified.

And lastly, 'appeasement', when interpreted as meaning forgetting the past, involves wiping out something which cannot be wiped out except by those who—if such people exist—think that the vicissitudes of human life in a civilized society are not interrelated and have no bearing on one another, that they are the inevitable conse-

quences of the accidents of nature—which would bring us to the
threshold of insanity. Republican democracy in Italy, conceived as
being a prototype which has been tested in the workshops of post-
war reconstruction, has been far-seeing, indulgent, and often passive
—sometimes as the result of somewhat obscure calculations—in the
way it has dealt with the remnants of Fascism. They are allowed to
deny publicly that reality which has made it possible for them to
emerge once more; they can claim the right to avail themselves of
principles and guarantees of which they deprived the Italian people
over a period of twenty years; they can move about freely in a
country which, in order to win back from them its dignity as a
civilized nation, fought for two years in the Resistance movement
and filled the Fascist prisons with men who testified to this aspira-
tion. For this reason it can hardly be said that the Fascists have
been victimized, and their whining appeals for appeasement cannot
be considered as anything but a well-worn political expedient.

The ancillary forces

The violent outbursts which nowadays are the last resort of the greedy
supporters of colonialism have provided the Nazis and Fascists
with more than one chance to intervene, and at the same time to
become the advocates of atrocious reprisals against insurgent
peoples and extremist movements in the home country. The French
OAS and its Belgian ramifications were the protagonists of a campaign waged with the aid of plastic bombs, torture and premeditated
murder, their exploits being on the industrial scale compared with
the artisan methods of the *Cagoule*. Every time the extremist movements took advantage of the political situation, they occupied a
prominent place in the columns of the newspapers, but these
sporadic outbreaks of Nazism and Fascism always coincided with—
and were the direct result of—the presence within the traditional
economic and political right wing of authoritarian trends which
were determined to swing the political axis towards the right. The
MSI and the Fascist action-squads played leading roles in July
1960, when Tambroni, a former leader of the Christian Democrat
'left wing', egged on by the most retrograde elements in Italian
capitalism, tried to give the government's policy a rightward twist,
thus providing the Fascists with an opportunity to try their luck
in the streets of an Italian city. Popular reaction shattered this

extremist adventure; Tambroni was obliged to resign and the neo-Fascists relapsed immediately into isolation, adopted a more cautious policy and withdrew their *arditi* from the streets, where they had been roughly handled by the anti-Fascists. The ruthless campaign in Algeria, in waging which the conservative Right had the support of moderates, Social Democrats and, to a certain extent, even of Communists, made it possible for the OAS and the galaxy of para-Fascist organizations which flourished under the Fourth Republic to terrorize half of Europe and, with the aid of rebellious generals, to pave the way for a Gaullist *coup d'état*. Nevertheless, when De Gaulle and his supporters showed that they were determined to settle the problems of the colonial war and the political issue in France within the framework of neo-colonial and neo-capitalist policy, the subversive organizations found themselves unable to carry on with their Fascist venture, and Salan's conspiracy collapsed suddenly and, one might almost say, ignominiously.

In Greece, which for years had been under the quasi-Caesarism of Karamanlis, the pro-Fascist right wing enjoyed a revival and a prosperity reminiscent of the Metaxas era, but at the same time left-wing opposition grew stronger. In November 1963 Karamanlis was compelled to resign and the general election in the following spring was a triumph for the adversaries of Fascism, which vanished from the political scene like snow melting beneath the rays of the sun. It sought refuge under the wing of a democracy which it had itself done its best to destroy, and remained silent, without making even one courageous gesture of revolt.

Greek Fascism regained some of its power in the spring of 1967 after a *coup d'état* organized by a group of extreme right-wing colonels. This was the culmination of two years' work, during which the monarchy and the conservative elements prepared the stage for the advent of an authoritarian régime. But once again democracy succumbed to a coalition of the two traditional protagonists of reaction in Greece—the monarchy and the army. Organized Fascism had to be content with a subsidiary role.

In short, the fact remains that Nazi-Fascism, except on specific occasions when political conservatism and capitalist reaction give it scope for action and accept the aid of its subversive forces, is reduced to playing the role of a minority, dangerous because of the criminal methods to which it resorts in the course of the political struggle, but incapable of devising any plan for seizing power. It remains a reservoir of support for reactionary authoritarianism, but

it will never become the autonomous *avant-garde* of any type of
dictatorship which may try to establish itself independently of the
curve of intentions and complicity along which authoritarianism
proceeds. Lacking the support of that coalition of interests and
will-power represented by the economic pressure-groups and the
hegemonic classes which are their expression in the political field,
the Fascist 'revolutionaries' will continue to lie low and listen to
the rabid monologues of their leaders.

Fascism, nationalism and the one-party system

In current publications we frequently come across passages describing the one-party régimes which have sprung up during the last
ten years as experiments in Fascism or radical nationalism. To us
it seems that an *a priori* classification of this sort is quite wrong and
we have been at pains not to fall into the same error. Normally,
European conservatives and other 'right-thinking' people express
their scandalized—and hypocritical—astonishment when they learn
that the liberation movements of colonial peoples have given birth
to one-party régimes, and that the nationalistic element in such
movements is often strong, with a marked tendency towards
authoritarianism. If they were more self-critical than they are and if
they gave due consideration to the concrete factors of the historical
process, they would find a more satisfactory explanation of such
things in the very history of colonialism.

Centuries of domination by Western 'civilization' have relegated
hundreds of thousands of men to a position of inferior beings, more
or less closely subjected to exploitation by the occupying powers,
but having no say whatsoever in the control of their own destinies
or in the government of their country. Where colonial policy, instead
of being purely repressive, took the form of paternal guidance, the
aim of the governing powers was the creation of a native ruling
class whose members would become parasites and auxiliaries of
white power; or else they tolerated the emergence of a strictly
limited, local *bourgeoisie* which also tended to become parasitical,
fundamentally conservative, and nationalistic with authoritarian
leanings. The armies have frequently sponsored political tendencies born out of this process. In any case, in the underdeveloped
Asian, African and Latin American countries nationalist movements could more easily emerge in this way, simply because no
other possibility existed, or at all events none that offered any hope

of success. The evolution towards national independence, and the violent break with the colonial powers needed to achieve it, were in most cases due to such elements who, once they had achieved their aim, translated into terms of authoritarian power the nationalistic sentiments of which they considered themselves to be the trustees and quite logically confused them with the interests of the class to which they themselves belonged.

On the other hand, even in countries where the liberation movements were led by elements more representative of the popular will, because the revolt, or the achievement of independence by peaceful means, had its roots in certain native political traditions, the question of multi-party régimes and democratic government on European lines could hardly arise, or at all events would have been impracticable or dangerous. It is impossible to start a representative system from zero. To countries where the masses have no traditions of political activity, where an actual majority of the inhabitants are illiterates or semi-illiterates, plunged in a misery going back to the darkness of time and engaged in a daily struggle for physical survival, the customary formulas of our political system can offer nothing but meaningless rules and snares, or even a perilous source of anarchy. The parameters by which the institutions of traditional democracies are judged and political trends controlled, when applied in a context so different, for an infinity of reasons, from the world in which Liberal democracy developed, may cause incalculable harm and result in grave errors. Moreover, there are countries in which the progress towards national independence coincided with the victory of a political *avant-garde*, determined to achieve its aims without the process of *bourgeois* democracy, of which even the objective pre-requisites did not exist, because there was no middle class of the modern type. In such countries the search for a Socialist solution to the problem of power could not first pass through the pretence of a preliminary stage of the traditional democratic type; more frequently it opted for the one-party system, regardless of all the lack of stability, the deviations and disadvantages due to the objective incapacity or subjective inexperience of the protagonists of such a trend. All this does nothing to alter the fact that in one-party régimes—and in some of them to a very marked degree—authoritarian and extreme nationalist trends frequently emerged, some of a definitely Fascist or National Socialist type. Egypt under Nasser and Kwame Nkrumah's presidential régime in Ghana are in many respects replicas of systems of which we have unpleasant memories; the former, as we have already pointed out, has been contaminated by Nazi attitudes and sympathies, as well as by the actual presence of Nazis, while the latter, owing to the 'Caesarism' of its leader and the fact that it was a régime which openly declared that it would not tolerate any opposition or internal discussion, was more like an African version of Fascism.

The traditions of Arab nationalism were of such a kind that these authoritarian and 'populist' components, combined with a readiness to accept National Socialist doctrine, received an added stimulus from a particular interpretation of the Islamic gospel transposed into the political key. According to the version put forward by certain pan-Arab nationalist circles, Islam has a mission to liberate and unite all the Arab peoples, and the political implications of this theory are obvious. The Koran is alleged to contain a social doctrine based on principles which can be applied in the national and popular sphere, together with a strong dose of ethico-religious norms which can provide precepts for the behaviour both of individuals and of the nation as a whole within the framework of the State. At the same time there are other political trends based on Islamic precepts which reject any interpretation of Islam in the nationalistic sense, and in fact, for some Arab Socialists, the teachings of the Koran provide inspiration for a type of Socialism which is in keeping with the cultural, spiritual and material traditions of the Mediterranean world.

Generally speaking, changing conditions and the presence of so many contradictory factors in the evolution of these countries make it difficult to attach European labels to the ideal and political forces underlying them, and when we are discussing them we cannot employ the conventional political terms. The thorny path along which they are advancing presents new obstacles every day, and the ruling classes have to deal with problems of such vast proportions that they are bound to modify their views, change their plans and doctrinal formulas, and revise their original programmes. The demarcation line between democracy and authoritarianism, generic populism and revolutionary Socialism, extreme nationalism and enlightened patriotism, cannot be discerned at a first glance, and most certainly cannot be categorically laid down. Even more hazardous is any attempt to predict the future of the régimes already in power, since it cannot be excluded that they may not be radically transformed, even while they are actually in control of the affairs of State.

A revelation for the colonels

During the fighting in Indo-China and Algeria, the military extremists made a startling discovery—ideological warfare. Amidst the stirring vicissitudes of guerrilla operations which they were incapable of controlling and which for them were a humiliating experience, despite the overwhelming superiority of forces and equipment at their disposal, they discovered a new technique for extending military operations to the social sphere. The men who placed it at their disposal were their adversaries, who in their turn had borrowed it from the theoreticians and realizers of a great epic of warfare on a nationwide scale—Mao Tse-tung's Chinese revolution. What was the lesson they learned? They learned that in any war of liberation, the leaders of the national army must, if they want to achieve rapid and lasting successes, first create a favourable atmosphere and undertake a psychological campaign in order to win over to their side the population involved in the war. In other words, a prime necessity for every insurrectional movement is to combine actual military operations with the work of convincing the civilians, which can only be done by explaining, patiently and in great detail, the practical and ideal motives which link the aims of the insurrection with the normal aspirations and needs of the masses affected by the events. In this way an atmosphere of collaboration is created between the fighting men and the rest of the population, war becomes a catalysing agent for the energies of all, and even the poorest classes receive the message of emancipation and collaborate wholeheartedly with the military and political forces responsible for the war. The revolutionaries must find a way to present a programme involving at least some participation of civilians in the conduct of affairs, and they must then hand over to the civilians the responsibility for forming 'cells' in the new social and political organism which the forward march of the liberators gradually makes it possible to set up in the form of marginal institutions of the future State.

Naturally, in the minds of the Marxist theoreticians who invented it 'ideological warfare' was a technical corollary of an ideological process, in the course of which popular revolts would occur and lay the foundations of a Socialist State, provided that the 'military' and 'political' motives could be coordinated in such a way that they would appear to be the logical

P

consequence of the movements. The colonels who sympathized with—or were members of—the OAS, once this subtle psychological process had been revealed to them (in their case it might well be called a *chinoiserie*), made plans to take it over *en bloc* and to use it as an instrument of their colonial policy, in the name of which they were carrying out 'scorched earth' operations with the aid of napalm, tanks and electrodes applied to the testicles of prisoners. 'Psychological warfare' thus became the rage among the officers of the French army's general staff, who relinquished the prerogative of calling themselves the 'silent service'. The colonels plunged headlong into the labyrinth of ideology, applied sociology and mass psychology. In Kabylia and in the provinces of Constantine and Oran, where their troops had come up against the stubborn resistance of the partisans and the solidarity of the civil population, they recruited the necessary cadres of officers trained in 'psychological' and 'welfare' duties and then proceeded to introduce the practices borrowed from left-wing doctrine and revised to meet the demands of a war which was anything but 'left-wing'. The results, however, were on a very modest scale and confined to a few local areas, however much enthusiasm they might put into their work and despite all the means at their disposal. They were unable to understand why this revolutionary manual which they had studied so carefully and adapted to meet their requirements, did not, in their hands, produce the same effects as in Indo-China, or when used by the National Liberation Front. The majority of the population remained deaf to the appeals of the 'psychological service'; collaborationism made no converts, and the efforts made by the specialists to persuade the natives that the French soldiers were the bearers of a new gospel were wasted amidst the hostile indifference of those who were supposed to listen to it. Although it was a failure, the formulas of 'psychological warfare' as interpreted by the colonels, retained all their fascination for the military extremists. In fact they provided men like Argoud, Trinquier and Challe, and the young officers just commissioned from Saint-Cyr, with an ideological framework which amplified and replenished the stale notions of Fascist nationalism, giving them a veneer of 'social welfare' closely bound up with the role of the army, and thus ennobling and integrating its authoritarian schemes with 'modern' political postulates. It has been said that the 'ideological war' provided the military men for the first time with an 'ideology of their own' complete in all its parts, and suitable for establishing an overall relationship between the colonels and the popular way of thinking, without passing through the mediation of politicians.

It is easy to see the risks involved in this unusual method which, by jumbling up ideological values, gave the general staffs of armies an opportunity to assume the role of 'emancipators' by using a revolutionary technique for reactionary purposes. But the experiments carried out on the Indo-Chinese and Algerian guinea-pigs ended in a complete fiasco, though the idea of a 'social doctrine for the army' still fascinated those strategists who for years had never managed to win a victory, as well as newly-fledged officers who were anxious to revive the prestige of a profession which was no longer treated with the same unquestioning respect as in the past. A feeling of frustration and of being *déclassé* played an important part in fostering notions of the Fascist type, or at all events of an authoritarian type, among the right-wing extremists. The anti-Republican conspiracies hatched in the ranks of the French army during the last dozen years have drawn sustenance from a situation in which the generals attributed the blame for their reverses to the flabbiness and 'treachery' of politicians. In Germany, this phenomenon was the crux of the nationalist and anti-Weimar reaction which eventually led to the Hitler régime; and it can be discerned today, with the same somatic features, in the resurgence of German militarism, which attributes to unspecified circumstances and to the interference of Nazi leaders in the conduct of the last war the sequence of reverses suffered in Africa, Russia, Normandy and elsewhere.

The future of totalitarianism

We already know the questions that are on our readers' lips, now that we have reached the end of our study. Do Fascism and Nazism constitute a danger at the present time? In their present form, as variants of the extreme right wing, have they any chance of coming to power again? Before giving our own replies to these questions, we think that it will be useful to quote the opinions of politicians and journalists whose political views differ and to whom we put those very questions.[2] 'Fascism definitely disappeared at the end of the last war, after the demoniacal death of Hitler,' Giorgio La Pira assured us.

> Yes, Fascism, like the war, is a thing of the past. It has vanished because we have entered upon a period in which it will be impossible to wage wars, and Fascism lived on war alone. Of course, relics

Fascism Today

of Fascism still exist, but they are poisons which time will gradually eliminate. Franco is finished, and no longer counts for anything. In France, the OAS would have been eliminated long ago, if the Socialists had known what role they ought to play. In Italy, the Fascists are part of a phase that is over, and they have no tomorrow. They are old men and fools, their breasts still covered with medals. They are dead men.[3]

Emilio Lussu, a Socialist Deputy, does not share his Catholic colleague's optimism. 'Don't let us deceive ourselves,' he warned us:

> Fascism is still very much alive, as an extremist trend among the middle classes. The OAS was the latest proof of that. And here in Italy, Tambroni's experiment. I told De Gasperi one day that if the world were to split into two halves, all the Fascists would be in one half, and the anti-Fascists in the other. And De Gasperi raised his arms to heaven and admitted that my hypothesis was correct.

The Socialist Deputy Vittorio Foa, secretary-general of the Italian General Federation of Labour, thought, on the contrary, that there were limits to what Fascism could do. 'Anyway,' he said, 'Fascism cannot represent a grave danger today, simply because it is unable to provide an alternative. Nowadays the right-wingers have other ideas.' Senator Ferruccio Parri, the ex-Premier and Resistance leader, stressed that Fascism can assume disguises. 'The more responsible Fascists,' he pointed out, 'are well aware that the old ideas are no longer acceptable, and they even try to disown them and proclaim their devotion to democracy and constitutional methods. They want to show that Fascism is a "potentialized" party of values, just as thirty-five years ago they tried to pass it off as "potentialized Liberalism".' Asked what he thought about the prospects of a Fascist International in Europe, Parri replied:

> I don't believe that any such organization really exists on a serious basis, with the ability to carry out a co-ordinated policy on the international plane. Nevertheless, I think that the situation in all countries is very like what it is in Italy. In other words, there is still a potential reservoir of rancour, nostalgia, arrogance and national prejudice, which are natural sources of reactionary trends and, given favourable circumstances, might very easily find ways to co-ordinate their policies, which at the moment are not easy to identify.[4]

Ignazio Silone, a prominent anti-Fascist, emphasized that in Italy there are people who are 'dissatisfied with the régime established by the republican constitution', but who do not dare to oppose it openly and 'prefer to try to achieve their own conservative aims within its framework'. He thinks that the MSI are 'a collection of elderly nostalgics and immature young men' of no particular importance, who merely try to make themselves a nuisance to the Christian Democrats and Liberals. He denied the existence of 'a real Fascist International, because Fascism is exaggerated nationalism'. Though he added that 'obviously there is a feeling of solidarity between the right-wing régimes and movements in the various countries', and concluded by saying:

> The types of Fascism evolved in Italy, Germany and elsewhere after the First World War are in my opinion things of the past, though the conditions that made their success possible have obviously not vanished completely. Mass civilizations, bureaucratic control of public life, centralization, the decline of interest in politics among the younger generation, etc., are all aspects of a situation which might, in certain circumstances, lead to the re-emergence of Fascist-type régimes. In my book *La scuola dei dittatori*, I think that I have made it clear that a régime of the really Fascist type might manage to assert itself if it were to adopt as its slogan 'Down with Fascism!' The only remedy I can see is to fight against the spirit of obsequiousness wherever it appears, beginning, of course, with one's own party or trade union.

Achille Marazza, a Christian Democrat Deputy and former leader of the Committee of Liberation in Northern Italy, doubted whether any 'new' type of Fascism would emerge, but thought that Fascism *tout court* still survives in Italian public life, which according to him 'is contaminated by the poisons of authoritarianism, overweening ambition, corruption, fraud etc., all of which are typical of Fascism. But I am not so pessimistic,' he went on, 'as to believe that any MSI policy could provide an alternative, nor so optimistic as to think that one of the right-wing movements (which one?) can be considered as a kind of weapon held in reserve (for what?).' Though he is sceptical regarding Fascism's prospects as an international force, Marazza thinks that a study of the world situation does not justify our thinking that it is finished as 'a means of achieving power'.

Senator General Raffaele Cadorna, former commander-in-chief of the *Corpo di Volontari della Libertà*, said he never believed that Fascism was a system:

> It was a dictatorship based on the prestige of one man, to such an extent that it collapsed as soon as the prestige of that man began to decline.

'Modern dictatorships,' he went on, 'are a form of popular reaction to hardship, a kind of patent medicine administered to nations which, for historical, geographical or fortuitous reasons (e.g. a war) are unable to develop along peaceful, democratic lines.' According to Cadorna:

> Fascism, Nazism, the Caesarism of De Gaulle, like Russian or Chinese Communism, have a nationalistic foundation, and the same applies to the new régimes in the Middle East and Africa, where dictatorships—for that is what they really are—have to keep one eye on Moscow and the other on Washington.

For Cadorna, the MSI is a composite party, in which 'certain elements confine themselves to nostalgic longings, while others are tending towards liberalism with the accent on patriotism'. The marked divergence of opinions between the elements 'calling themselves Fascists' make it impossible, according to Cadorna, to take a Fascist International seriously; and finally, he thinks that in Italy democracy might be exposed to the dangers of attempts to install dictatorships only if 'the medley of parties, the instability and effeteness of governments, were to prove incapable of ruling the country at a time like this, which is one of natural development'. And his last words were: 'The example of France ought to teach us a lesson.'

The writer Primo Levi, a survivor of the extermination camps, thinks that Fascism still exists 'in various forms, some of them anything but "new".' He maintains that it exists

> as a psychological background, as an original element, in many strata of the Italian middle class, in the judiciary, in the civil service, and also as a kind of superiority complex. Among the younger generation it survives in strangely decadent and irrational forms. It is still very much alive in Italian official quarters (social assistance offices, the tendency to use demagogic language, lack of co-operation between functionaries and the public).

According to Levi the MSI 'has no real political significance and today is merely a "reserve weapon of the right wing", though if the European situation were to change, it might easily become more virulent'. As for the Fascist International, Levi thinks that it exists, but that it is not a very stable 'edifice', which, he says, is not surprising, because

> the lives of such nationalistic movements in, say, two neighbouring countries are inevitably brief; moreover it would seem that internal quarrels, the inevitability and even the desirability of war are things

which are firmly rooted in all Fascist ideologies. Consequently a Fascist International has little hope of being successful today, unless it can regain the confidence of the far more powerful 'International' of the economic right wing.

Riccardo Bauer, the president of the *Società Umanitaria*, describes Fascism as

> a non-liberal and anti-democratic conception of the relationship between the State and the citizen, the genesis and development of a political will, of the powers and functions of the majority as well as of minorities, and of the relationship between the legislative and the executive power and that of the law . . . based on a theory of negative discrimination which denies that all men are equal and is consequently bound to degenerate into nationalism, imperialism and racialism, and to resort to the one-party system under the leadership of a heaven-sent dictator.

'This conception of the essential relationships in political life,' he continued, 'is still alive and tending more or less to produce a dialectic in which the concepts of authority and liberty assume various attitudes, sometimes leading to a dramatic clash which, on the historical plane, may prove to be fruitful.' Bauer accordingly believes it to be only natural that, despite the collapse of Fascist institutions,

> Fascism has not entirely disappeared and still remains latent in the minds of the multitude who do not know how to draw the necessary conclusions from facts which have taken place before their eyes, of those who through mental inertia or habit have no desire to rack their brains after having grown accustomed for years to an obedience which was comfortable and advantageous, and lastly of those who under the Fascist régime accumulated fortunes which weathered the collapse and to which they still cling greedily.

Bauer therefore thinks that what we have to fear is not so much the existence of more or less open Fascist movements and trends, but the persistence of a

> Fascist mentality, conformist and essentially authoritarian, among far too many men whom the semi-revolution that was the outcome of the Resistance movement, thanks to clerical—and therefore pseudo-democratic—influence, has allowed to continue their careers, and who still retain the senile habits they acquired under Fascism.

In his opinion, the MSI and its youth organizations might be utilized as 'a shock remedy by blind and frightened conservatives, ready to pay desperadoes to enter the fray'. 'Remember 1921 and

1922,' he said, 'when squads of hooligans were raised by landowners and industrialists, in order to carry out punitive expeditions
with the aid of the police.' Consequently, according to Bauer, 'Fascism has had its day, but . . . it still exists as a residue and a trend,
and it might explode in a thousand different ways'. And he ended
by saying that the neo-Fascist movements are tending towards an
international alliance, because Fascism was not an exclusively
Italian phenomenon,

> as was shown by German Nazism and by the France of Pétain, and
> is now being shown by the France of De Gaulle, by the persistence
> of Nazism in the German administration and among the younger
> generation; in Austria, too, and by the shameful vitality of the
> Franco and Salazar régimes, by the tolerance with which they are
> viewed by too many people in every country, and—why shouldn't
> we say it?—by the still unchecked racialism of the United States,
> etc.

A definition of Fascism as 'a perennial state of mind' and therefore nothing 'new', was given by the Socialist Senator Pietro Caleffi,
another survivor of the concentration camps. Like Levi and many
others, he thinks that the MSI is 'the reserve of the right and semi-
right wing'. 'This we have been able to see during the last few
years,' he said, 'when the biggest party in Italy, most of whose
members were undoubtedly democrats, made use of the MSI to
keep itself in power, even when this led to disputes with the other
democratic parties.' According to Caleffi, we ought not to talk
of a 'Fascist International', but only of 'tentative approaches made
by the reactionary forces of Europe, who have found no suitable
means of expansion'. In short, the Socialist Senator thinks that
'Fascism as we knew it is a thing of the past; it might suddenly
reappear in other forms, if crises were to occur in democratic
countries, especially in an acute crisis such as war, supposing the
existing institutions were to collapse without being immediately
replaced by other institutions and forms of co-existence which
from the democratic point of view were more perfect'.

Carlo Donat-Cattin, a leading Christian Democrat, observed that
since Fascism is 'violence as the means and end of all political
activity', and since the myth of violence invariably attracts 'pressure-
groups or would-be pressure-groups who have not got reason, justice
and respect for the individual on their side', it is only natural that
Fascism should still attract a certain number of people in the Italy
of the 1960s. 'But,' he hastened to add,

we are not now living in the year 1922. Today the vested interests which might resort to the use of violence know no frontiers. The limit imposed by pre-war Fascist nationalism is a traditional and formal survival, but it can do nothing to check the feeling of solidarity among nations which is continually growing stronger. The Fascists in one country are anxious to get in touch with the Fascists in others, and that is the natural order of things. The outlook for Fascism is not intrinsic, but closely bound up with the weakness and corruption of democratic institutions and morals.

Now let us hear what the French have to say. 'I am not in the least convinced,' Georges Montaron, the editor of *Témoignage Chrétien*, told us,

> that Fascism is finished. For the simple reason that nationalism is by no means dead. If we fail in our attempt to create a united Europe, there will inevitably be a return to Fascism and nationalism. Without Europe, Italy will become Communist, France will have a Franco-type régime, and Germany will return to Nazism. A big crisis is imminent. In France we are already in the midst of it. As for Italy, if she does not turn her democracy into a modern instrument, she will end up by experiencing the same crisis as we did in 1958. For Italy, the only solution is a trend towards the left.

Jean-Marie Domenach, the editor of *Esprit*, thinks that the economic boom of the past few years has made the danger of Fascism more remote, and that if it ever appears again, it will be during a period of marked recession. 'In order to assert itself,' he said,

> Fascism has always needed poverty, it has always taken advantage of times of crisis. Of course, Fascism is something more than that—love of adventure, the desire to return to nature, a reaction against the monotony of life. But nowadays society offers excellent antidotes for things of that sort.

Pierre Stibbe, who is a Socialist, does not believe in the existence of any Fascist International, or in a Europe whose future existence 'will be dependent on the political and economic forces that dominate it. Should Europe become reactionary, anti-democratic and anti-working-class,' he said,

> Fascism will rise again from its ashes; but if, on the contrary, the workers, the trade unions and the forces of democracy in all the countries of Europe succeed in uniting and rescuing the new Europe from the domination of trusts and cartels, then there will be no room for Fascism. It was the product of the failure of Liberal capitalism, both in the beginning and at its zenith, to solve its own contradictions, to overcome its own crisis by the classical methods of free competition and parliamentary action. The danger

of Fascism will be eliminated only if capitalism either disappears or adapts itself to the needs of the modern world by resorting to state planning and a larger measure of state control, with the result that economic crises will become less frequent and less violent. Nevertheless, there is nothing to prevent the present prosperity of Western Europe, which seems to be forearmed against any renewal of the Fascist offensive, from being called into question, in the near or distant future, owing to some new factor which will give Fascism another chance.

In Belgium, Georges Dewamme, secretary-general of the Belgian resistance association, *Front de l'Indépendance*, stressed the point that 'Fascism, simply because it has no doctrine and lives on violence alone, cannot appear twice in the same guise. It is a mistake,' he maintains,

> to try to give a strict definition of it. The OAS may not have had all the characteristics of Fascism, but it was nonetheless Fascism. The Germany of men like Heusinger, Speidel and Strauss may not be the Germany of 1936, but we Belgians are still afraid of her. The *Spiegel* affair confirmed our fears.

These were the last specific statements we were able to obtain. In Germany people talk in whispers and the words 'Fascism' and 'Nazism' are uttered with reluctance and reservations. Or else they appear in a disconcertingly naïve context. 'No, I most certainly do not believe in any influence of the Nazi right wing,' Kron Brandeburg, the Bonn Social Democrat spokesman told us. 'The younger generation is deaf to its appeals. The young want television sets and cars; they want to travel. What could they gain from a war of revenge? What could they take away from other peoples that they do not already possess?' We found the same perplexing optimism in Austria, when we asked Otto Kranzlmayr, the Under-Secretary of State whom we mentioned in our chapter on that country, for his opinion. He wound up with a kind of judgement of Solomon: 'The more we can make people believe that democracy is alive and that certain advantages are guaranteed and respected, the more ground Fascism will lose.'

Here we must stop. The opinions we have quoted reflect ideas based on different ideological assumptions, on different interpretations of the historical and political reality and, presumably, on different degrees of perspicacity. A common denominator in several of the men we interviewed was the tendency to attribute the residues of Fascism and Nazism to the persistence of nostalgic states of mind, to the absence of any profound and unshakable faith in democracy and to a tendency to prefer authoritarian solutions whenever democracy seems to be faltering and tolerates corruption in public life accompanied by a decline in the sense of responsibility. For varying reasons hardly any of the men we interviewed thought that the 'classical' forms of Fascism and Nazism still have any importance as alternative forms of government; most of them, however, were convinced that, given 'certain conditions', there might be a 'return' of Fascism or Nazism in an unforeseeable form, which would, however, be easily identifiable because of its resemblance to the prototypes. To us it seemed that only a few of these opinions revealed any awareness of the fact that, although right-wing solutions of the older type are hypothetically possible, the reactionary elements in general are tending—as Vittorio Foa succinctly put it—to move other pawns. This is also our own conclusion.

The alarm caused by the presence of numerous and aggressive bands of 'nostalgics', who are still pining for the days of Benito Mussolini and Adolf Hitler, is not altogether groundless. Their numbers are often by no means negligible; they meet with sympathy and solidarity in many sectors of public opinion, especially among the middle classes; they broadcast slogans and incitements to violence which find an ominous echo in the consciences of too many members of the younger generation. But the explanations we have given, which coincide with the opinions of most of the men we interviewed, would seem to show that the neo-Fascists and neo-Nazis are only subordinate elements of more homogeneous forces which are the real depositaries of any violent reactionary movement. These forces can be identified in certain sectors of the economic and political right wing, among the military and bureaucratic castes, and in Catholic integralism. A coalition of all these elements might well provide a starting-point for a type of authoritarianism in which the Fascist and Nazi militias would discover their proper function, and they might not only achieve the distinction of being the armed elements in a plot, but also play the coveted role of more or less subsidiary political figures. There are, however, many signs that in the ranks of the anti-democratic and fundamentally absolutist front there are today, especially in the more advanced countries, tendencies whose aim is the achievement of complete control of the State, that is to say a concrete dictatorship of one class, to achieve which they would resort to tactics which Pierre Stibbe described as being one of the things which will bring about the disappearance of Fascism, i.e., State planning and State control, not for the purpose of changing the balance of society to the advantage of democracy and Socialism, but in order to stabilize a system at present dominated by oligopolies and thus achieve a symbiosis of the ruling political class, the management of State affairs and the solving of all social and economic problems. In such an event Fascism, as a means of seizing power by violence and 'solving the crisis and the contradictions of capitalism', would in all probability cease to be a nuisance or a danger. Tendencies in that direction can already be discerned at this very moment, after only a cursory examination of the development of oligopolistic capitalism during a phase involving a marked acceleration of the process of national and supra-national concentration. Once the 'protected democracies' and 'affluent societies' (in which, as we have pointed out, the traditional institutions of democracy can survive, though their dimensions will be reduced and they will be deprived of their truly democratic content) have been given a definite shape, then the modern form of authoritarian Rightism could carry to the extremes the technique of an absolutism 'on internal lines', which would certainly have no use for the schemings, the banality and brutality of old-style Fascism, but would repudiate them as worthless and outdated instruments of a one-class dictatorship.

It is not our task to delve further into this question. Others, we believe, will explore the forms that such a system might assume, the significance and proportions that a new type of absolutism combined with the mechanism of neo-capitalism might achieve. We have merely tried to draw attention to the problem, since it forms part of the question as to whether the heirs of Hitler and Mussolini still have cards up their sleeves which would enable them to win the rubber. Perhaps they have, but in any case the ultimate result will depend on the stronger partner, who must know when to throw in his hand and make a fresh bid; and above all he will need a new pack and will have to play his cards better.

Notes

Chapter One: What is Fascism?

1 BENEDETTO CROCE, *Pagine Politiche*, Bari, Giuseppe Laterza & Figli, 1945, viii, p. 51.
2 BENEDETTO CROCE, *Storia d'Italia dal 1871 al 1915*, vol. II, Bari, Giuseppe Laterza & Figli, 1929, p. 252.
3 *Cf.* SALVATORELLI, '*Lineamenti del Nazionalfascismo*', in *Antologia della Rivoluzione Liberale*, ed. by Nino Valeri, Turin, Francesco De Silva, 1948, pp. 377 ff., and in the same volume, '*Risposta di Salvatorelli ai critici di Nazionalfascismo*', pp. 423–431, and '*Ansaldo: il Fascismo come odio piccolo-borghese*', by GIOVANNI ANSALDO, pp. 345-362.
   Among Gobetti's writings, see esp.: PIERO GOBETTI, *La Rivoluzione Liberale*, Turin, Einaudi Editore, 1948, and in it '*Liberismo e operai*', pp. 49–51; '*I torti della teoria liberale*', pp. 62–68; and '*Libro quarto—Il fascismo*', pp. 183–193.
4 ENZO COLLOTTI, *La Germania nazista*, Turin, Giulio Einaudi Editore, 1962, p. 16.
5 DANIEL GUÉRIN, *Fascismo e gran capitale*, Milan, Schwarz Editore, 1956, pp. 18 ff.
6 *Ibid.*, pp. 295–297.
7 PAOLO ALATRI, *Le origini del fascismo*, Rome, Editori Riuniti, 1962, p. 34.
8 *Ibid.*, p. 21.
9 *Ibid.*, p. 21.
10 ENZO COLLOTTI, *op. cit.*, p. 18.
11 *Ibid.*, p. 17.
12 *Ibid.*, pp. 17–18.
13 JEAN TOUCHARD, *Storia del pensiero politico*, Rome, Edizioni di Comunità, 1963, p. 92.

Chapter Two: The 'Dark Valley' Years

1 J. PLUMYÈNE and R. LASIERRA, *Les fascismes français 1923–63*, Paris, Éditions du Seuil, 1963, p. 15.
2 ALDO GAROSCI gave a brilliant description of this in his *Storia della Francia moderna (1870–1946)*, Turin, Einaudi Editore, 1947.
3 ASVERO GRAVELLI, *Verso l'Internazionale fascista*, Rome, Nuova Europa, Libreria Editrice, 1932, X.
4 The 'Lapua' movement took its name from the little village of Lapua, where, on 1st December 1929, a number of farmers from

449

Eastern Bothnia formed an anti-Communist association and passed a resolution deploring the freedom of the Press and the activities of the Communists in Finland.

5   J. WULLUS-RUDIGER, *En marge de la politique belge—1914–1956*, Brussels, Éditions Berger-Levrault, 1957, p. 229.

6   *Ibid.*, p. 229.

7   J. A. PRIMO DE RIVERA, '*Le basi del falangismo spagnolo*', in *Quaderni dei C.A.U.R.*, No. 3, series edited by Eugenio Coselschi, Florence, Beltrami Editore, 1938, XIV, p. 31.

8   *Ibid.*, p. 32.

9   *Ibid.*, p. 31.

10   ANTONIO FERRO, '*Salazar, il Portogallo e il suo capo*', in the collection *Sprazzi dell'idea fascista sul mondo*, Rome, Sindacato Italiano Arti Grafiche, 1934, XII, p. 8.

11   *Ibid.*, p. 112.

12   O. SALAZAR, *Discorso del 23 novembre 1932*, in A. FERRO, *op. cit.*, p. 237.

13   *Ibid.*, pp. 237 ff.

14   GALEAZZO CIANO, *Diarto 1939–43*, Milan, Rizzoli, 1963, Vol. I, p. 29.

15   K. S. KAROL, *La Polonia da Pilsudski a Gomulka*, Bari, Edizioni Laterza, 1959, p. 41.

16   A. GRAVELLI, *op. cit.*, p. 185.

17   G. CIANO, *op. cit.*

18   An interesting specimen of Catholic apologetics is the biography of Engelbert Dollfuss by BARTOLO GALLETTO, *Vita di Dollfuss*, Rome, Casa Editrice A.V.E., 1935, XIX, edited with a preface by the titular bishop of Ela, Monsignor Luigi Hudal.

19   A. GRAVELLI, *op. cit.*, says that when, in 1931, the *Heimwehren* attempted a completely unsuccessful *putsch* in Styria, they received 150,000 Schilling from the 'German nationalists', i.e. the Nazis.

20   WILLIAM L. SHIRER, *The Rise and Fall of the Third Reich*, London, Secker & Warburg; New York, Simon & Schuster, 1962, p. 332.

21   GIORGIO GALLI, *I colonnelli della guerra rivoluzionaria*, Bologna, Società Editrice Il Mulino, 1962, p. 65.

22   *Ibid.*, p. 66.

23   MARCEL NIEDERGAND, *Les 20 Amériques Latines*, Paris, Plon, 1962, p. 243.

24   RICHARD STORRY, *A History of Modern Japan*, London, Penguin Books, 1961, p. 182.

25   *Cf.* H. CHASSAGUE, *Le Japon contre le monde*, Paris, Éditions Sociales Internationales, 1938. In our opinion this book by Chassague is the best contribution hitherto made by Marxist historiography to the analysis of Japanese history.

26   Quoted by H. CHASSAGUE, *op. cit.*, p. 106.

27   RICHARD STORRY, *op. cit.*, p. 172.

28   H. CHASSAGUE, *op. cit.*, p. 229.

29   *Ibid.* The text of the memorandum was published for the first time in Europe by the French review *Internationale Communiste*,

in its special number for December 1931, p. 1754. CHASSAGUE, *op. cit.*, p. 229, quotes an interesting passage from the book by SUGIMURA, Japanese ambassador in Paris in 1937, on international diplomacy. The Japanese diplomat states that '. . . the final aim of Japanese policy is to act as guide and leader of the Coloured races and to give them direct aid in their development . . . That is why Japan must have a very strong navy and army, not merely for purposes of self-defence.'

30 RICHARD STORRY, *op. cit.*, p. 173.
31 *Ibid.*, p. 172.
32 H. CHASSAGUE, *op. cit.*, p. 126.
33 *Ibid.*, p. 253.
34 RICHARD STORRY, *op. cit.*, p. 200.
35 RABINDRANATH TAGORE, *Nationalism*, London, Macmillan, 1921, pp. 42–43.

Chapter Three: The 'New Order' Myth

1 MAURICE BARDÈCHE, *Qu'est-ce que le fascisme?*, Paris, Les Sept Couleurs, n.d., p. 79.
2 *Ibid.*, p. 94.
3 LUIGI SALVATORELLI, *Nazionalfascismo*, Turin, Gobetti, 1923, pp. 21–23.
4 *Cf.* ENZO COLLOTTI, *La Germania nazista*, Turin, Giulio Einaudi Editore, 1962, p. 247.
5 *Cf.* WALTER HOFER, *Le National-Socialisme par les textes*, Paris, Plon, 1963, p. 178.
6 E. COLLOTTI, *op. cit.*, p. 247.
7 *Cf.* FRANJO TUDMAN, *'The Independent State of Croatia as an Instrument of the Policy of the Occupation Powers in Yugoslavia, and the People's Liberation Movement in Croatia from 1941 to 1945'*, in *Les Systèmes d'occupation en Yougoslavie*, 1941–45, Rapports au Congrès sur l'Histoire de la Résistance européenne à Karlovy Vary, les 2–4 septembre 1963, Belgrade 1963, pp. 135–192.
8 M. BARDÈCHE, *op. cit.*, p. 77.
9 J. PLUMYÈNE and R. LASIERRA, *Les fascismes français 1962–63*, Paris, Éditions du Seuil, 1963, p. 155.
10 *Ibid.*
11 ROBERT ARON, *Histoire de Vichy*, Paris, Fayard, 1954, p. 213.
12 J. PLUMYÈNE and R. LASIERRA, *op. cit.*, p. 150.
13 *Giovane Europa, Rivista dei Combattenti della Gioventù Universitaria d'Europa*, No. 3, 1942, article entitled *'Il capitalismo e il suo superamento'*, pp. 9–15.
14 *Giovane Europa, Organo del Combattentismo Universitario Europeo*, No. 4, 1943, article entitled *'Le aurore della vittoria'*, pp. 19–22.
15 *Giovane Europa*, No. 12, 1942, article entitled *'Come sorge un movimento politico'*, pp. 10–15.

16   *Giovane Europa*, No. 4, 1942, article entitled *'Europa'*, pp. 54–55.
17   *Giovane Europa*, No. 4, 1943, article entitled *'All' Europa'*, pp. 11–14.
18   *Ibid.*, p. 14.
19   RICHARD STORRY, *A History of Modern Japan*, London, Penguin Books, 1961, p. 229.
20   FREDERICK WILLIAM DEAKIN, *Storia della Repubblica di Salò*, Turin, Giulio Einaudi Editore, 1963, p. viii (introduction to Italian edition of work quoted below).
21   FREDERICK WILLIAM DEAKIN, *The Brutal Friendship: Mussolini, Hitler, and the Fall of Italian Fascism*, New York, Harper & Bros., London, Weidenfeld & Nicolson, 1962, p. 666.
22   GIOACCHINO VOLPE, *Storia del movimento fascista*, Istituto per gli Studi di Politica Internazionale, 1939, XVII, p. 35.
23   *Cf.* FRANCO CATALANO, *L'Italia dalla dittatura alla democrazia, 1919–1948*, Milan, Lerici Editore, 1962, p. 20.
24   *Cf.* LUIGI SALVATORELLI, *Storia d'Italia nel periodo fascista*, Turin, Giulio Einaudi, 1962, p. 56.
25   A. TASCA, *Nascita e avvento del fascismo*, Florence, La Nuova Italia, 1950, p. 250.
26   G. VOLPE, *op. cit.*, p. 63.
27   G. VOLPE, *op. cit.*, pp. 170–171.
28   PAOLO ALATRI, *Le origini del fascismo*, Rome, Editori Riuniti, pp. 21–2.
29   ATTILIO TAMARO, *Venti anni di storia, 1922–1943*, vol. II, p. 428.
30   PAOLO ALATRI, *op. cit.*, p. 20.
31   RUGGERO ZANGRANDI, *Il lungo viaggio attraverso il fascismo*, Milan, Feltrinelli Editore, 1962, p. 45.
32   *Ibid.*, p. 43.
33   *Ibid.*, p. 50.
34   *Ibid.*, p. 51.
35   An account, in our opinion reliable, of Guido Pallotta's odyssey is given by DAVIDE LAJOLO, *Il voltagabbana*, Milan, Casa Editrice Il Saggiatore, 1963.
36   F. W. DEAKIN, *The Brutal Friendship*, *op. cit.*, p. 673.
37   Communiqué issued by the *Agenzia Stefani* on 14 February 1945, quoted by GIACOMO PERTICONE, *La Repubblica di Salò*, Rome, Edizioni Leonardo, 1947, p. 252, note 1.
38   F. W. DEAKIN, *The Brutal Friendship*, *op. cit.*, p. 784.
39   Quoted by G. PERTICONE, *op. cit.*, pp. 288–289.
40   *Ibid.*, pp. 293–294, note 2.
41   *Ibid.*, p. 296.

Chapter Four: The 'Internationals'

1   Most of the information in the first part of this chapter is based on a letter dated 23 October 1963 from Simon Wiesenthal to

the Austrian Minister of the Interior, and on an interview which Wiesenthal granted to Angelo Del Boca at Turin on 22 May 1964.

2 For further information on the HIAG, see the following chapter, 'Germany'.

3 *Washington Post*, 6 May 1956.

4 At the end of the war the *Waffen-SS* consisted of forty divisions and 594,000 men. By 1st October 1944 its losses in the field amounted to 320,000 men. Among the foreign units we would mention the following: the French *Charlemagne* division, the Flemish *Langemark*, the Walloon *Wallonie*, the Dutch *Landstorm Nederland*, the Albanian *Skanderbeg*, the Muslim *Handschar* and the Croat *Kama* division. In addition to these there were three Cossack divisions, one Hungarian cavalry division, one Italian division, some Caucasian and Turkestan regiments, an Indian legion, two Rumanian battalions, one Bulgarian and one Norwegian battalion, and the 13th *Bosnische-Herzegovinische SS Gebirgsdivision*, formed at Sarajevo in 1943, in which a number of Arab volunteers served, including the Algerian Mohammed Said, alias Colonel Si Nasser, who later became a Minister in Ben Bella's government. According to the neo-Nazi periodical *Wiking-Ruf* (June 1957), the number of foreigners who served in the SS was as follows: 6,000 Danes, 10,000 Norwegians, 75,000 Dutchmen, 25,000 Flemings, 15,000 Walloons, 22,000 Frenchmen. The Amsterdam Rijksinstituut puts the number of Dutchmen at 25,000.

5 Among the HIAG's foreign branches are the HINAG (Holland), *Edelweiss* (Austria), *Dansk Frontkämpfer Førbund* (Denmark), *Veljesapu* (Finland), *Helpsorganisajonen for Kriegskadede* (Norway). Other groups exist in Belgium, Spain, Argentina, South Africa and Australia.

6 MAURICE BARDÈCHE, *Qu'est-ce que le fascisme?*, p. 98.

7 *Ibid.*, pp. 105–114.

8 *Ibid.*, p. 120.

9 Sweden had the good fortune not to experience the horrors of Nazism and, perhaps for this very reason, has played a notable part in the resurgence of extremist movements after the war. In addition to Per Engdahl's group, mention must be made of Göran A. Oredsson's *Nordiska Rikspartiet*, Sven A. Lundehäll's *Sveriges Nationella Förbund*, which publishes a weekly called *Fria Ord*, the publishing houses controlled by the anti-Semite Einar Aberg and by Carl F. Carlberg (died 1962), the latter firm being one of the joint owners of the review *Nation-Europa*, published at Coburg in West Germany. In May 1965 a considerable stir was caused in Stockholm by the arrest of Björn Lundahl, leader of the armed bands known as 'Viking Detachments', who planned to 'overthrow the present system controlled by the democratic bureaucracy and Zionist circles'. Lundahl, a former 'Grand Dragon' of the Ku-Klux-Klan, had threatened to murder some of the leading figures of the Jewish community in Sweden.

10 In 1962, the executive of the 'European Social Movement' seems to have consisted of Per Engdahl (Sweden), Maurice Bardèche (France), Ernesto Massi (Italy), Wilhelm Landing (Austria), Karl Dillen (Belgium) and Hermann Schimmel (Germany). Sir Oswald Mosley is no longer a member.

11 Quoted in *I quaderni neri della destra rivoluzionaria*, Turin, March 1963, p. 45.

12 *Ibid.*, p. 46.

13 From the resolution passed at the Zürich congress, September 1951.

14 *Ordine Nuovo*, Rome, March-April 1964, p. 50.

15 The NOE held its congresses at Zürich (1951), Paris (1952), Hanover (1954), Lausanne (1956), Milan (1958), Lausanne (1960), Lausanne (1962).

16 For further information on Thiriart's International see the chapters on Belgium and France.

17 The complete text of the manifesto is given in *La Révolution Nationale Européenne*, Brussels, Éditions Jeune Europe, n.d.

18 MAURICE BARDÈCHE, *op. cit.*, p. 116.

19 The dispute between the Italian and Austrian sections over the Alto Adige question began a year before the schism. In November 1962, a circular issued by *Giovane Nazione* (as the Italian section was called) states that: 'In the last number of *Junges Europa* (Austria) there is a paragraph stating that *Giovane Nazione* was in agreement with *Légion Europa*, which advocated the creation of an independent State in the Alto Adige. We are at a loss to understand how our Austrian comrades could have believed that we would ever accept such a proposal, all the more so since we explicitly declared in Bulletin No. 16 (July 1962) of the Milan Federation, in an article written in German and Italian, that we rejected this suggestion as absurd and impracticable. Our standpoint on the Alto Adige question was, and still is, that anyone putting forward such a proposal is playing Moscow's game by looking for any pretext that would serve to shatter the already fragile solidarity of Europe.'

20 In its heyday *Jeune Europe* had the following branches: *Jeune Europe*, Boîte Postale No. 9, Chaussée de Charleroi 33, Brussels 6 (Belgium); *Joven Europa*, Calle Mayor 1, Estudio No. 1, Madrid (Spain); *Junges Europa*, Postamt Wien 8 (Wederthorgasse), Postfach (Austria); *Junges Europa*, K. Kohl, Hindenburgstrasse 28, Langenhagen Han. (Germany); *Giovane Nazione*, Casella Postale 1056, Milan (Italy); *Ordine Nuovo*, Via di Pietra 84, Rome (Italy); *Centro Quaderni Neri*, Casella Postale 332, Turin (Italy); *Young Europe*, c/o Dingley James, 44 Lewis Buildings, Lisgar Terrace, London W.14 (England); *Jong Europa*, Tijmon Balk Eyssoniusstraat 15, Groningen (Holland); *Young Europe/Jong Europa*, Postbus 172, Kempton Park, Transvaal (South Africa); *Europan/ZS*, Caixa Postal 10624, *São Paolo* (Brazil);

Fiatal Europa, Ratz, Apartado 12113, Centro Narino, Bogotà (Colombia); *Jovem Europa*, Apartado 1283, Lisbon (Portugal); *Ataque*, Apartado de Correos 2352, Lisbon (Portugal); *SAC*, Pat Walsh, C.P. 551, Station B, Ottawa (Canada); *Joven América*, José Luis Menini, Casilla de Correro Central 3302, Buenos Aires (Argentina); *Joven América*, Ignacio Arismendi Posada, Carrera 66, No. 43/46, Medellín (Colombia); *Joven América*, Pablo de Idoyaga, Dr. Magested 1585, Montevideo (Uruguay); *Unga Europa*, Vera Lindhom, P.O. Box 2149, Stockholm (Sweden); *Europa Tanara* (Rumanians in exile), Lerchenauerstrasse 14, Munich (Germany); *Runebevoegelsen*, Postfach 7, Copenhagen (Denmark); *Jeune Europe*, R. Gueissaz, 66 Avenue d'Echallens, Lausanne (Switzerland); *Joven América*, Ricardo Montufar, head of the *Brigade Abden Calderón* (Ecuador). *Jeune Europe* also keeps in touch with the Bulgarian, Slovak and Ukrainian refugees who have their headquarters in Germany, the United States and South America.

21 For further information see the chapter on Great Britain.

22 On Colin Jordan see the chapter on Great Britain.

23 According to the British periodical *The National Socialist*, at the beginning of 1964 the WUNS had the following sections: The National Socialist Movement (Britain); The American Nazi Party (USA); the *Partido Nacional-socialista Chileno* (Chile); *Danmarks National Socialistike Arbejder* (Denmark); West European Federation' (France); *Frente Nacional Socialista Argentino* (Argentina); National Socialist Party of Australia (Australia).

24 Among the leaders of these *revanchiste* organizations we find, for example, the Slovene Ferdinand Durčansky, the Hungarian Fascists and former generals Zákó Andras and Kisbarnaki Farkas Ferenc, the Rumanian Ion A. Emilian, the former Bulgarian Secretary of State Dimitri Valcek and the former Hungarian Secretary of State Alföldi Geza.

25 The twenty-six *Ustaše* who attacked the offices of the Yugoslav Trade Mission at Bad Godesberg were tried in Bonn between March and June 1964 and sentenced to terms of imprisonment ranging from three to fifteen years. The organizer of the group, a Catholic priest named Raphael Medic Skoko, who had formerly been Pavelich's confessor and chaplain to his brigades, was sentenced to four years. The terroristic organization known as the Brotherhood of Croat Crusaders, to which the twenty-six *Ustaše* belonged, was dissolved by the Bonn government, but dozens of others like the United Croats Association, the Croat Democratic Committee, the Friends of the Drina and the Croat Social Service, almost all of them with headquarters in Munich, were allowed to continue their activities undisturbed, since they were registered as 'cultural' or 'humanitarian' societies.

26 *Frankfurter Rundschau*, 7 October 1962.

Chapter Five: Germany

1 From the Report of the Ministry for the Interior of the German Federal Republic, Bonn, March 1962.

2 According to the Hamburg newspaper *Die Andere Seite*, 10 October 1957: 'Out of 519 deputies in the new parliament about 25 per cent were members of the National Socialist Party or of one of its branches at the time of the Third Reich.' Even in East Germany Nazis are to be found in the political world. According to the 'free jurists' committee of enquiry', among the 433 official candidates for seats in the *Volkskammer* at the October 1963 election, there were 42 Nazis. In the previous chamber there had been 54.

3 *Cf. Critica*, 1944, Nos. V–VI; later included in *Pagine Politiche*, Bari, Laterza, 1945, p. 16.

4 According to the American State Department, down to May 1949 inclusive 9,600 persons had been sent to labour camps and 569,000 had been fined; restrictions regarding employment had been imposed on 134,000; 28,500 had had property confiscated and 23,000 had been banned from public offices. From a report issued by the Bonn Ministry of Justice in April 1961, we learn that between 1945 and 1960 2,027 Nazi criminals were tried and sentenced by the West German courts. From 1958 on, after the opening of the Research Centre for the investigation of Nazi crimes in Ludwigsburg, other proceedings were begun. (Incidentally, the head of this Centre, Erwin Schüle, had himself been connected with the Nazi party.) The Allied military tribunals sentenced 794 persons to death, but only 400 of these sentences were carried out.

5 Founded in the autumn of 1949, the SRP was declared unconstitutional by the Karlsruhe tribunal on 15 July 1952 and subsequently banned.

6 In Hitler's political testament Werner Naumann was appointed successor to Goebbels as Minister for Propaganda. On 14 January 1953 he was arrested by the British occupation authorities, together with six other Nazi officials accused of conspiring to overthrow the Bonn parliamentary régime. When the case was handed over to the German authorities, they pigeonholed Naumann's file without taking any proceedings. On this mysterious plot see ALISTAIR HORNE, *Return to Power*, New York, Praeger, 1956.

7 *Reichsruf*, 17 June 1959.

8 *Deutsche Soldaten-Zeitung*, No. 17, 1959. [General Kappler and Major Reder are the only two Nazi war criminals still in an Italian prison.]

9 Quoted by Jacques Hiver in an article which appeared in *France-Observateur* on 7 January 1960.

10 JOHN DORNBERG, *Schizophrenic Germany*, New York, Macmillan, 1961, p. 110.

11 If we are to believe Priester's records, there are 800 Nazi organizations in Germany. This figure, however, is undoubtedly an exaggeration. Or else it includes regional branches of the various parties and clubs which sometimes have only two or three members.

12 The extreme Right's principal weeklies and monthlies are the following: *Nation Europa, Der Reichsruf, Wikingruf, Der Sudeten-deutsche, Der Ring, Deutscher Aufbruch, Die Deutsche Freiheit, Der Freiwillige, Der Stahlhelm, Der Notweg, Deutsche Stimmen, Deutschlandbrief, Deutsche Gemeinschaft, Der Volksbote, Junger Beobachter, Nordische Zeitung, Alte Kameraden, Freie Nation, Deutsche Hochschullehrerzeitung, Deutscher Studentenanzeiger, Deutsche Wochenzeitung, Das Volk, Fanal, Trommler.* The following have now ceased publication: *Der Quell, Der Weg, Die Anklage.* Of the above, *Nation Europa* has for many years been considered to be the most authoritative organ of European neo-Fascism. Among its more illustrious collaborators are Sir Oswald Mosley, Einar Aberg and Maurice Bardèche. The extreme Right controls about forty publishing firms.

13 *Cf. Résistance Unie*, No. 6/7, June–July 1966, article entitled 'Eighteen months of the NPD—on the threshold of power'.

14 *La Voix Internationale de la Résistance*, No. 109, March 1967.

15 JOHN DORNBERG, *op. cit.*, p. 113.

16 Published each year by the Schild Verlag, Munich.

17 In the official proceedings of the Nuremberg international military tribunal (vol. XXIII, p. 549), we read that: 'It is impossible to name a single SS unit that did not have a share in these criminal activities. The *Allgemeine SS* played an active part in the persecution of the Jews, and served as a recruiting depot for concentration camp guards. Units of the *Waffen-SS* were directly involved in murders of prisoners of war and atrocities committed in the occupied countries. They supplied personnel for the *Einsatzgruppen* and took over control of the camp guards after the incorporation of the *SS-Totenkopf*, which had previously carried out these functions. Units of SS police were also used to commit atrocities in the occupied territories and exterminate the Jews. The central organization of the SS controlled the activities of these various formations and was responsible for special operations such as experiments on human beings and the "final solution of the Jewish question".' An excellent study of the role played by the SS under the Nazi régime can be found in JACQUES DELARUE, *Histoire de la Gestapo*, Paris, Fayard, 1962.

18 85 per cent of former Nazis are drawing pensions for services rendered to the Nazi régime, while a million victims of Nazi terrorism are still awaiting compensation for their sufferings.

19 *Der Freiwillige*, No. 10, October 1959.

20 *Nürnberger Zeitung*, 7 June 1960.

21 *Der Spiegel*, 5 November 1952.

22 *Deutsche Soldaten-Zeitung*, No. 12, December 1956.

23 T. H. TETENS, *The New Germany and the Old Nazis*, New York, Random House; London, Secker & Warburg, 1962, p. 143.

24 The largest of the *Landsmannschaften* is the *Sudetendeutsche* with 350,000 members, which has its headquarters in Munich. Enjoying the protection of the Federal Minister Seebohm, it attracts bigger crowds to its meetings than any other *revanchiste* organization and, as Sergio Segre writes in the special number of *Nuovi Argomenti* dealing with the German right wing (November 1960–February 1961, p. 306), it can be considered 'on the ideological plane' as the 'continuation of Konrad Henlein's *Sudetendeutsche Partei*, which formed the spearhead of Hitlerism in Czechoslovakia before 1938'.

25 Among the more important are the *Deutsche Jugend des Ostens*, the *Sudetendeutsche Jugend* and the *Turnerschaft*, the last-named being a sports and gymnastics club.

26 The leading periodicals of the *Landsmannschaften* are the *Sudetendeutsche Zeitung*, *Ost-West Kurier*, *Der Westpreusse*, *Unser Danzig*, *Das Ostpreussenblatt* and *Pommersche Zeitung*.

27 In the *Sudetendeutsche* alone we find the following Nazis occupying leading posts: Rudolf Lodgman von Auen (died 1962), founder of the 'Movement for a Greater Germany'; Leo Schubert, organizer of the Nazi movement among Sudeten Germans and a former *SS-Standartenführer*; the war criminal Franz Karmasin, ex-Secretary of State Monsignor Tiso's 'Quisling' government; the former *SS-Sturmbannführer* Paul Illing; Frank Seiboth, a one-time exponent of Nazism in the Sudetenland; Ernst Frank, brother of the 'Protector' of Bohemia and Moravia, SS General Karl Hermann Frank, who was executed in 1945; Franz Hoeller, former organizer of Nazi propaganda among the Sudeten Germans; and hundreds of lesser Nazis.

28 *Das ABC des Deutschen Militarismus*, Frankfurt, VVN, 1959, p. 28.

29 *Passauer Neue Presse*, 23 March 1953.

30 *Berliner Zeitung*, 3 June 1957.

31 *Neue Zürcher Zeitung*, 26 January 1952.

32 Seebohm is now dead.

33 Quoted in *Résistance Unie*, No. 6/7, Vienna, June–July 1964.

34 *Relazioni Internazionali*, No. 14, 4 April 1964, pp. 538–539.

35 Known as 'the bureaucrat of death', Hans Globke was sentenced to life imprisonment *in absentia* by an East Berlin tribunal on 23 June 1963, for 'grave crimes against humanity'. Shortly before, taking advantage of the changeover from Adenauer to Erhard, he had resigned his office. On the charges against Globke see REINHARD M. STRECKER, *Dr. Hans Globke*, Hamburg, Rütten & Löning, 1961. Globke was succeeded by Ludger Westrick, who had been one of Goering's collaborators in building up the German

Air Force and former chairman or director of twenty-seven companies during the Hitler régime.

36 In May 1960 he was dismissed as the result of a campaign launched against him by the German Democratic Republic and later carried on by democratic elements in West Germany.

37 See FLORIMOND BONTÉ, *Le dossier Heusinger*, Paris, Éditions Sociales, 1962, and *cf.* the same author's *Le militarisme allemand et la France*, Paris, Éditions Sociales, 1961.

38 T. H. TETENS, *op. cit.*, p. 45.

39 *Die Welt der Arbeit*, 9 October 1959.

40 *Frankfurter Rundschau*, 27 February 1963.

41 BRIAN CONNELL, *A Watcher on the Rhine*, New York, William Morrow & Co., 1957, pp. 119–120.

42 *Le Monde*, 23 March 1963.

43 *L'Express*, 14 September 1961.

44 *Deutsche Zeitung*, 7 March 1960.

45 *Washington Post*, 19 September 1954.

46 Quoted in *Résistance Unie*, No. 8/9, Vienna 1962.

47 *Frankfurter Rundschau*, 22 August 1960.

48 *L'Express*, 14 September 1961, article by Robert Jungk. Between 1961 and 1964 the *Bundeswehr* became still more powerful. Bonn was in fact authorized to build submarines displacing up to 1,000 tons, and in February 1963, after an interval of eighteen years, the construction of German-designed tanks was resumed. In 1964 Minister von Hassel also organized the 'Territorial Defence Force', which was not under NATO control.

49 Quoted in *The Congressional Record*, 15 April 1963.

50 *Economist*, 3 November 1962.

51 *Christian Science Monitor*, 10 November 1962.

52 *New York Times*, 13 November 1962.

53 Excluded from the government as a result of the '*Spiegel* affair' Strauss retired in December 1962 to his Bavarian domain, where he slowly prepared the way for a return to power by exploiting the discontent rampant among the ex-prisoners of war and by seeking to ally himself with ex-Chancellor Adenauer. In 1964 he tried to rally some of the right-wing and nationalist movements round the CDU, the party of which he is chairman. Strauss became the standard-bearer of the trend known as 'German Gaullism' and sided with Adenauer against Chancellor Erhard, who was timidly attempting to lead Germany back to a more realistic policy.

54 *The Times*, 12 November 1962.

55 JOHN DORNBERG, *op. cit.*, p. 281.

56 *Rheinischer Merkur*, 5 April 1953, quoted by TETENS, *op. cit.*, p. 255.

57 HEINZ ABOSCH, *La Germania senza miracolo*, Milan, Mondadori, 1963, p. 277.

58   Quoted by ABOSCH, *op. cit.*, p. 238.
59   Passages quoted by DORNBERG, *op. cit.*, pp. 277–278.
60   *Corriere della Sera*, 21 March 1963.
61   Since its foundation in 1946, the VVN has systematically de-
     nounced the resurgence of the Nazi peril in a series of publications
     which we have consulted in the course of our studies. Among
     many others we would mention *In Sachen Demokratie (Weissbuch
     über die militaristische und nazistische Gefahr in der Bundes-
     republik)*, Frankfurt/Main, 1960; *Die unbewältigte Gegenwart*,
     Frankfurt, 1962; *Das ABC des deutschen Militarismus*, 1959; and
     Die Waffen-SS: ein vierter Wehrmachtsteil? On five occasions the
     Federal authorities have tried to dissolve this anti-Fascist organiza-
     tion, accusing it of being inspired by the Communists (as if the
     Catholic Josef Rossaint, Father Weber and Pastor Niemöller, who
     are members of the committee, were Communists!), but they
     have never succeeded in getting rid of it, because every time the
     VVN was summoned before a court, it turned out that the judge
     was a Nazi and the case was remanded.
62   KARL JASPERS, *Freiheit und Wiedervereinigung*, Munich, R. Piper,
     1960. Our quotations are from the French translation, *Liberté et
     Réunification*, Paris, Gallimard, 1962.
63   Quoted by KARL JASPERS, *op. cit.*, p. 207.

Chapter Six: Italy

1   MARCELLA and MAURIZIO FERRARA, *Cronache di vita italiana 1944–
     1958*, Rome, Editori Riuniti, 1960, p. 24.
2   *Ibid.*, pp. 84–85.
3   *Cf.* FRANCO CATALANO, *L'Italia dalla dittatura alla democrazia*,
     Milan, Lerici Editore, 1962, pp. 647–648.
4   *Ibid.*, p. 655.
5   *Ibid.*, p. 657.
6   *Ibid.*, p. 630.
7   *Ibid.*
8   *Ibid.*
9   *Cf.* '*I giovani leoni del MSI*' in *Il Dialogo, Rivista di Lavoro
     Culturale*, No. 6/7, September 1962–April 1963, p. 171 (3).
10   *Ibid.*
11   *Cf.* MARIO GIOVANA, '*Il neofascismo in Italia*' in *Occidente, Rivista
     Bimestrale di Studi Politici*, ninth year, No. 6, November–December
     1953, p. 439.
12   Mario Bracci, Minister for Foreign Trade in the first De Gasperi
     Cabinet, explains the underlying principles of the amnesty law

and discusses the debate within the cabinet on Togliatti's project, in an article entitled '*Come nacque l'amnistia*', published in *Il Ponte*, 3rd year, No. 11/12, November–December 1947 (special number dealing with *La crisi della Resistenza*), pp. 1090–1107. In this article Bracci states that the number of political detainees released on 31 July 1946 under Articles 1 and 2 (offences involving sentences of not more than five years and offences committed after the Liberation) was 7061, of whom 153 were partisans, 4127 Fascists and 802 miscellaneous; under Article 3 (measures against Fascism) 2979. 'The number of persons sentenced for political offences who benefited by the amnesty,' writes Bracci, 'was 2202. The maximum number of persons under detention for political offences in the period before the amnesty was about 11,800. On 31 July 1947 the number of persons awaiting trial for political offences was 2157; 1361 had already been charged with political offences, but not yet tried, and 1396 had already been sentenced. The eighteen special assize courts,' Bracci says in conclusion, 'worked very quickly; between 1 January 1946 and 31 July 1947, out of a total of 37,800 denunciations, the investigation of 37,335 cases was completed and 8,800 trials before the courts took place' (pp. 1105–1106).

13 MARCELLA and MAURIZIO FERRARA, *op. cit.*, p. 182.
14 *Cf.* the article by M. GIOVANA quoted above, in *Occidente*, p. 443.
15 MARCELLA and MAURIZIO FERRARA, *op. cit.*, pp. 304–305.
16 *Ibid.*
17 *Ibid.*, pp. 306–307.
18 *Ibid.*
19 *Ibid.*, p. 345.
20 On the Scelba law see note 3 to the last chapter of the present volume.
21 *Cf.* the article by M. GIOVANA, *cit.*, p. 448.
22 *Meridiano d'Italia*, No. 43, 5th year, 29 October 1950.
23 *Avanti Ardito!*, 1 March 1950.
24 *Asso di Bastoni*, 19 November 1950.
25 *Cf.* M. GIOVANA, *Art. cit.*, p. 447.
26 *Cf.* GIUSEPPE MAYDA, '*Inchiesta sul neo-fascismo in Italia*', No. 5, in *Resistenza*, No. 2, 18th year, February 1964.
27 From an interview granted to Angelo Del Boca in Rome, October 1962, on condition that the speaker's name would not be published.
28 The journalists Renzo Renzi and Guido Aristarco were arrested in September 1953, the former for having written and the latter for having published in the review *Cinema Nuovo* a film scenario entitled *L'Armata s'agapo* adapted from the novel of the same name (*Armata s'agapo*, i.e. Army of Love, was the nickname given by the Greeks to the Italian forces of occupation, implying that Italian solders were very efficient when it came to dealings with the opposite sex). Six months after the publication of the scenario the military authorities claimed that it was a libel on

the armed forces, and denounced the two journalists, who were tried and sentenced. The episode caused a scandal in Italy, one of the reasons being that the military authorities insisted that the case should be heard before a military court, on the grounds that the accused were citizens still liable to military service and therefore came under its jurisdiction.

29 Regina Coeli is the Roman gaol for prisoners awaiting trial. Arrested persons can be kept in custody at police-stations for seven days without being charged; after the expiration of seven days they must be either released, or charged and sent to Regina Coeli.

30 *Cf.* M. GIOVANA, *art. cit.*, p. 451 (8).

31 *Cf.* M. and M. FERRARA, *op. cit.*, p. 418.

32 'U.O.', *È tornato Zampanò*, in *Il Ponte*, 9th year, No. 3, March 1955, p. 289.

33 *Cf.* 'Minority report of Senators Sansone and Secchia on the bill introduced by Senator Parri: Dissolution of the Italian Social Movement in accordance with the provisions of the first paragraph of the twelfth provisional and final article of the Constitution (1125–A)', Rome, Tipografia del Senato, p. 7.

34 *Cf.* M. GIOVANA, *art. cit.*, p. 445 (9).

35 *Cf.* GIUSEPPE MAYDA, *art. cit.*, in *Resistenza*.

36 See the episodes mentioned in the 'appendices' to the above-quoted 'minority report' on the Parri bill providing for the dissolution of the MSI.

37 Interesting, as regards the quarrel between the MSI and *Giovane Nazione*, is the episode which Fred Borth, leader of *Junges Europa* mentioned to the authors of the present volume when they met in Vienna. *Cf.* above, pp. 89 and 208.

38 On the events of July and August 1960, see, *inter alia, La Nuova Resistenza*, supplement to Nos. 7 and 8 of the review *Rinascita*, July–August 1960.

39 Statement made to Angelo Del Boca in Rome, October 1962.

40 *Cf.* DENNIS EISENBERG, *L'Internazionale Nera—Fascisti e nazisti oggi nel mondo*, Milan, Sugar Editore, 1964, p. 107. Eisenberg's book is very summary and inexact in quoting names, episodes and dates, and also in quoting passages from neo-Fascist and neo-Nazi articles and manifestos. It should therefore be treated with due reservation.

41 *Cf.* LUCA BERNARDELLI, *'Inchiesta sul neofascismo'*, No. 2, in *Resistenza*, 17th year, No. 6, June 1963.

42 Leaflets containing similar statements were distributed in several Italian cities. The periodical *Patria indipendente, Quindicinale della Resistenza e degli ex combattenti*, printed a photographic reproduction of one such leaflet distributed in Brescia by the *Associazione Studentesca Giovane Nazione*, modelled on the Roman leaflet and ending with the words: 'We reverently lower the imaginary colours of our mourning legions in homage to the

sacrifice made by this new martyr. Adolf Eichmann, we will remember you!'

43 On the relations between the leaders of the OAS and the Italian neo-Fascists see, *inter alia*, '*Il plastico è arrivato in Italia*', in *Vie Nuove*, 1 March 1962; '*A Milano Soustelle è di casa*', in *Vie Nuove*, 15 March 1962; and the article by Lino Ronga entitled '*Ancora forte l'OAS in Italia*', in the political weekly *Il Punto*.

44 An original copy of this leaflet is in the possession of the authors. In the special number of *Europa Combattente* for October–November 1963, the neo-Nazis of *Giovane Nazione* disowned the producers of the leaflet, which they described as 'horrifying' and attributed to people who wished to throw discredit on the 'struggle for Europe'. The editors of the journal stated that they had made enquiries and ascertained that the headquarters of 'The Circle' was in Ireland under the direction of 'a Jewish Communist who is apparently of Italian origin and an honorary member of the SS. Herr Himmler,' the writer continues, 'would turn in his grave!' (article entitled *Il Nazismo*). Now, apart from the fact that the contents of the leaflet do not differ in any way from the usual style adopted by the neo-Nazis of *Europa Combattente* and deal with the same subject-matter, it seems highly improbable that an Italian branch of an Irish organization run by a Jewish Communist could have existed. The *démenti* of the journal's editors would thus seem to be a rather absurd excuse invented in the hope of forestalling investigations by the police. And in fact the writers of the article in which the existence of the Irish organization is revealed refer to the interrogation of 'one of their local managers' by the Special Branch of the Turin police in connexion with the text of this leaflet.

45 *Aristocrazia—Foglio di azione politica diretta da Augusto Pastore*, Novara, December 1962; article entitled '*Un capo per ogni epoca—Il nostro simbolo*', by Augusto Pastore.

46 *Europa Combattente—Organo di Giovane Nazione*, special number, July–August 1963, article entitled '*Angola—Europa*'.

47 *Ibid.*, article entitled '*Spezzare la colonizzazione del dollaro*'.

48 *Europa Combattente*, October–November 1963, article entitled '*Boicottare i prodotti americani—Cibo USA=Cancro*'.

49 *Europa Combattente*, May–June 1964, article entitled '*Un trucco contro l'Europa—la decolonizzazione*'.

50 *Europa Combattente*, October–November 1963, article entitled '*Perchè vogliamo l'Europa*'.

51 *Ibid.*, article entitled '*La preghiera di un Europeo*'.

52 *Ibid.*, article entitled '*La "stella del giorno"—il nazismo*'.

53 *Europa Combattente*, February 1964, article entitled '*Rivoluzione*'.

54 *Europa Combattente*, July–August 1963, article entitled '*Finirà il caos?*'

55 *Ibid.*

56 There exist, for example, a 'Centre for political, economic and

social studies' at Trieste; a 'Research Centre' for pro-Fascist Catholic integralists in Turin, founded by some students who organize ideological debates and undertake research work; a 'National Publishing Centre' in Rome, which specializes in the publishing of works glorifying or commemorating Fascism and its experiments in colonization; also in Rome, a 'National Institute for the Study of Political Economy', which according to the 'nostalgics' is a kind of 'high school' for the cadres of the MSI and other neo-Fascist organizations; a 'Centre for National Social Studies' in Milan, with interests mainly in the economic field, and a journal called *Continuità* which appears at irregular intervals.

57 *Cf*. D. EISENBERG, *op. cit.*, p. 103.

58 *I Quaderni Neri*, 1st year, No. 2/3, October 1963, pp. 7–8.

59 On 12 May 1964 the Turin assize court sentenced Salvatore Francia to nineteen months' imprisonment and a fine of 270,000 lire for glorifying Fascism, defamation of the Resistance movement and libelling the former commander of the fifth Piedmontese Partisan Zone, Benvenuto Revelli (alias Nuto). Francia was also sentenced to be deprived of his electoral rights for five years, and the publication of *I Quaderni Neri* was forbidden for a year. In November of the same year Francia had to face similar charges before the tribunal of Cuneo, following a denunciation by the former partisan leader Dr Benedetto Dalmastro, and this time he was sentenced to eight months' imprisonment, the sentence being suspended. In both cases Francia was found guilty of libel because he had published, first in his magazine and later in leaflets, fantastic accusations against the two former partisan leaders, to whom he attributed crimes against members of their own formations. See *'Finalmente una condanna contro i "Quaderni Neri"'* in *Resistenza*, 18th year, No. 5, May 1964.

60 See article entitled *'Giovane Europa'*, in *Europa Combattente*, February 1964.

61 At Novara, on 29 April 1963, Emilio Gay assaulted Fanfani while he was addressing a meeting. This young 'nostalgic', leader of the Turin group of *Giovane Europa*, was tried and sentenced on 16 November 1963 to eight months' imprisonment, the sentence being suspended.

62 *Cf*. *'I giovani leoni del MSI'*, in *Il Dialogo op. cit.*, p. 170.

63 SANDRO COVA, *'Se guarda bene la mia mascella vede che son fascista'*, in *Il Giorno*, 24 October 1962.

64 In July 1963, another neo-Fascist leader, Giacomo Lalli, founder of the *Fronte della rinascita nazionale*, who had been a candidate at the general election held in that year, was the subject of a judicial enquiry because he became involved in a big building scandal in Milan, where he had founded a housing co-operative and was said to have embezzled huge sums (according to some reports 250 million lire) in order to finance his election campaign.

Lalli, who led a life of luxury, was said to have drawn 2 million lire a month for his personal expenses.

65 *Cf.* SALVO MAZZOLINI, '*Troppo personali i fondi di Michelini*', in *L'Espresso*, 23 June 1963.

66 *Cf.* '*La Relazione dell'on. Michelini al VII Congresso del MSI*' in *Il Secolo d'Italia*, 3 August 1963.

67 *Cf.* the above-quoted number of *I Quaderni Neri*.

68 Statement made by Salvatore Francia to the authors of the present volume in July 1964.

69 *Cf.* '*Sospette riserve su un trionfo contrastato—Vita della "Piccola Europa"*,' weekly column by 'C. A.' in *Il Secolo d'Italia*, 3 February 1963.

70 Statement made by Salvatore Francia to the authors of the present volume in July 1964.

71 *Cf. Pietro Nenni ci parla di Segni e di Togliatti*, interview with the Socialist leader in *La Gazzetta del Popolo* of Turin, 19 August 1964.

Chapter Seven: France

1 *La Parisienne*, special number dedicated to *La Droite*, October 1956, p. 558.

2 *Jeune Nation*, 19 July–1st August 1958, from an article by Pierre Sidos.

3 *La Sentinelle*, March 1952.

4 J. R. TOURNOUX, *L'Histoire Secrète*, Paris, Plon, 1962, p. 256.

5 From a circular issued by the *Front National Français* (FNF).

6 PIERRE FOUGEYROLLAS, *La conscience politique dans la France contemporaine*, Paris, Denoel, 1963, p. 118.

7 RENÉ RÉMOND, *La droite en France*, Paris, Aubier, 1963, p. 278.

8 Later, in 1947, they obtained permission to publish a periodical called *Les Aspects de la France*.

9 SAINT-LOUP, *Les Volontaires*, Paris, Presses de la Cité, 1963.

10 MAURICE BARDÈCHE, *Nuremberg ou La terre promise*, Paris, Les Sept Couleurs, 1948, p. 146.

11 MAURICE BARDÈCHE, *Qu'est-ce que le fascisme?*, p. 14.

12 *Ibid.*, pp. 88–89.

13 *Ibid.*, pp. 164–165.

14 *Ibid.*, p. 194.

15 *Ibid.*, pp. 194–195.

16 *Jeune Nation*, July 1958.

17 *Le Monde*, 16 February 1964. *Jeune Nation* was dissolved by order of the authorities on 15 May 1958, and the Sidos brothers then founded the *Parti Nationaliste*, which in turn was suppressed by the Gaullist régime on 12 February 1959, only six days after its foundation. During the campaign for the presidential election in 1965 François Sidos worked for the *comités de soutien* organized by the *Europe-Action* movement to support the candidate of the

extreme right wing, Tixier-Vignancour; at that time his brother Pierre was leader of a new ultra-nationalist group called *Occident*, while Jacques was serving a ten-year sentence of imprisonment.

18 *France-Observateur*, 31 January 1957.

19 CHARLES DE GAULLE, *Le fil de l'épée*, Paris, Union Générale d'Éditions, 1962, p. 158.

20 CHARLES DE GAULLE, *Mémoires*, Paris, Plon, Vol. 1, p. 74.

21 Quoted by PAUL-MARIE DE LA GORCE, *De Gaulle entre deux mondes*, Paris, Fayard, 1964, p. 393.

22 *Occidente*, Turin, November–December 1953, p. 398.

23 *L'Humanité*, 14 February 1950.

24 PIERRE POUJADE, *J'ai choisi le combat*, Saint-Céré, Société Générale des Éditions et des Publications, 1955, p. 116.

25 *Fraternité Française*, March 1955.

26 *Fraternité Française*, 12 November 1955.

27 *Rivarol*, 12 January 1956.

28 *Fidélité*, February 1956.

29 STANLEY HOFFMANN, *Le Mouvement Poujade*, Paris, Armand Colin, 1956, pp. 387–388.

30 In November 1963, after a long silence, Poujade reappeared and founded a new party, the *Union et Fraternité Française*. The Saint-Céré bookseller hoped to obtain support among the refugees from Algeria, especially from the small farmers and middle class. The 800,000 refugees from Algeria have formed two large associations, the *Ranfranon* and the *Anfanoma*, headed by Colonels Thomazo and Trinquier and by the former deputy Le Pen.

31 Quoted by PIERRE VIDAL-NAQUET, *Lo Stato della tortura*, Bari, Laterza, 1963, p. 36.

32 *Ibid.*, p. 196.

33 The best known among the works on *Action Psychologique* is ROGER TRINQUIER's *La guerre moderne*, Paris, Plon, 1961.

34 In Algeria Georges Sauge was in contact with the integralist movement *Cité Catholique*, which publishes a review called *Verbe*.

35 PAUL-MARIE DE LA GORCE, *op. cit.*, p. 536.

36 *Ibid.*, p. 569.

37 *Le Monde*, 15 November 1960.

38 Quoted by PIERRE VIDAL-NAQUET, *op. cit.*, p. 101.

39 *Le Monde*, 27 October 1960.

40 Quoted by JACQUES FAUVET and JEAN PLANCHAIS, *La fronde des généraux*, Paris, Arthaud, 1961.

41 J. PLUMYÈNE and R. LASIERRA, *Les fascismes français 1923–63*, Paris, Éditions du Seuil, 1963, p. 291.

42 J. R. TOURNOUX, *op. cit.*, p. 35.

43 *Résistance Unie*, February 1962.

44 *France Presse-Action*, published by the CNR and OAS, 21 October 1962.

45 This and the following statements by Domenach, Montaron and Stibbe, were made to A. Del Boca in Paris in October 1962.
46 *Témoignage Chrétien*, 9 March 1962.
47 On right-wing and military plots in Algeria and on the origins and operations of the OAS, see the following: MERRY and SERGE BROMBERGER, *Les treize complots du 13 mai*, Paris, Fayard, 1959; M. and S. BROMBERGER, G. ELGEY, J. E. CHAUVEL, *Barricades et Colonels*, Paris, Presses Universitaires de France, 1960; J. A. FAUCHER, *Les barricades d'Alger*, Paris, Presses Universitaires de France, 1960; ROBERT BUCHARD, *Organisation Armée Secrète*, Paris, Albin Michel, 1963; ANNE LOESCH, *La valise et le cercueil*, Paris, Plon, 1963; MARIE ELBE, *Et à l'heure de notre mort*, Paris, Éditions Presses de la Cité, 1963; J. J. SUSINI, *Histoire de l'OAS*, Paris, Table Ronde, 1964; MORLAND, BARANGÈ and MARTINEZ, *Histoire de l'Organisation de l'Armée Secrète*, Paris, Julliard, 1964; id., *OAS parle*, Paris, Julliard, 1964 (the five last-named books contain statements by persons who belonged to, or sympathized with the OAS).
48 *Le Monde*, 12 February 1963.
49 *Le Monde*, 6 March 1963.
50 *France-Observateur*, 22 May 1958.
51 *L'Express*, 29 April 1964.
52 The statements by Montaron, Domenach and Stibbe were made in the course of interviews in Paris in October 1962.
53 *Combat*, 26 October 1962.
54 *Combat*, 24 October 1962.
55 *Quaderni Piacentini*, No. 15, March–April 1964.
56 On the night of 17–18 July 1963, as part of his campaign against the workers—which was severely criticized by, among others, the Bishops of Metz, Nancy and Verdun on 1st May 1963— De Gaulle had a bill approved by Parliament which made it obligatory for employees of public and private enterprises to give five days' notice of their intention to strike. All the French trade-union organizations considered this law to be an infringement of the liberty to strike, since it made lightning and go-slow strikes virtually impossible.
57 *Le Monde*, 2 February 1964.
58 CHARLES BECQUET, *L'ethnie française d'Europe*, Paris, Éditions Latines, 1963.
59 From a speech made on television, 31 December 1962; *cf. Le Monde*, 2 January 1963.
60 *L'Express*, 12 September 1963.
61 *Le Monde*, 5 July 1964.
62 *Le Monde*, 29 March 1964. On De Gaulle and Gaullism the following works may be profitably consulted: EUGÈNE MANNONI, *Moi, Général de Gaulle*, Paris, Éditions du Seuil, 1964; PAUL-MARIE DE LA GORCE, *De Gaulle entre deux mondes*, Paris, Fayard, 1964; J. F. LE CALONNEC, *La France et 'Moi'*, Paris,

Bibliothèque de l'homme d'action, 1962; ARTHUR CLENDENIN
ROBERTSON, *La doctrine du Général de Gaulle*, Paris, Fayard, 1959;
PIERRE VIANSSON-PONTÉ, *Les Gaullistes, Rituel et Annuaire*, Paris,
Éditions du Seuil, 1963; JACQUES DAUER, MICHEL RODET, *Les
orphelins du gaullisme*, Paris, Julliard, 1962; CYRUS SULZBERGER,
En observant De Gaulle, Paris, Plon, 1962; RENÉ COURTIN, *L'Europe
de l'Atlantique à l'Oural*, Paris, L'Esprit Nouveau, 1963; ROGER
MASSIP, *De Gaulle et l'Europe*, Paris, Flammarion, 1963; JACQUES
DUCLOS, *Gaullisme, technocratie, corporatisme*, Paris, Éditions
Sociales, 1963; HENRI CLAUDE, *Gaullisme et grand capital*, Paris,
Éditions Sociales, 1961; SAVERIO TUTINO, *Gollismo e lotta
operaia*, Turin, Einaudi, 1964; UGO RONFANI, *Perchè De Gaulle*,
Bari, Laterza, 1965.

Chapter Eight: Austria

1   This and the following statements are extracts from a conversation
between Angelo Del Boca and Fred Borth, in Vienna on
7 November 1962.

2   Episode reported by *Nation Europa*, 25 August 1961.

3   Quoted in *Résistance Unie*, No. 12, December 1962.

4   *Ibid.*

5   The *Europafront* was supported by Luc Pauwels, Peter Janssen,
Fred Rossaert (Flanders); Tijmon Balk (Holland); Demilov
(Rumania, representing the refugees from Eastern Europe); and
Werner Krause (Austria). *Cf.* the chapters in the present volume
on Belgium and on the Fascist Internationals.

6   *Nation Europa*, 1st September 1961. Similar statements can be
found in the journals run by Borth, *Der Angriff* and *Junges
Europa*.

7   A glance at the ÖKB's publications shows, for example, that the
SS, 'since they went everywhere and held the whole world at
bay, cannot have been composed of idiots'; that 'the Second World
War was certainly not planned in Berlin, but in London and
Washington, with Poland fulfilling a minor provocative function';
that Austria's neutrality is 'of value only to Communist propaganda
and World Bolshevism'; and that all progressives are 'intellec-
tualoids who dirty everything that for a German is honourable'.

8   The BHJ formed part of a larger organization (the ANJÖ) and
maintained close contacts with kindred German bodies; its leader
was the well-known extremist Konrad Windisch, editor of a
periodical called *Der Trommler*; Windisch has on several occasions
been arrested on account of his subversive activities and the
anti-Semitic propaganda he has carried on.

9   The *Olympia* student association was dissolved in November 1961,
after the authorities had discovered that some of its youthful
members had taken part in terrorist activities in the Alto Adige.

Shortly afterwards, however, the legal proceedings against these terrorists were shelved.

10 The *Landsmannschaften der Volksdeutschen* includes the follow- ing refugee organizations: *Donauschwaben, Sudetendeutsche, Siebenbürger Sachsen, Karpatendeutsche, Baltendeutsche, Gott- scheeren, Deutsche der Bukowina,* and the *Deutsche* from that part of Styria which was formerly Austrian and now belongs to Yugoslavia.

11 In April 1964 the FPÖ, in collaboration with the *Kameradschaft 4* (an association of former SS-men) started a campaign for the release of the Austrian Major Walter Reder, who was responsible for the massacre at Marzabotto and is now serving a sentence of life imprisonment at Gaeta.

12 Hans Wagner was formerly a Sudeten Deputy in the Prague parliament; he edited the Nazi journal *Wegwarte* until it ceased publication on 30 May 1960.

13 Sentenced to death in 1948 and subsequently released, Theodor Soucek later founded the SORBE, which advocates 'European neutralism' and 'social racialism'; he also edited the 'New European Order's' German language monthly *Europaruf*; in February 1963 he went bankrupt and fled to Spain.

14 Statement made to A. Del Boca in Vienna, 6 November 1962. According to information received on 4 September 1964 from Simon Wiesenthal, during the last year of the war Gredler belonged to the Resistance movement. Wiesenthal also stated that most of the other FPÖ deputies were former Nazis or SS officers.

15 Extract from the proceedings of the World Conference in Florence (20–23 November 1959) organized by the *Federazione Inter- nazionale dei Resistenti,* p. 73.

16 *Cf.* DENNIS EISENBERG, *L'Internazionale Nera—Fascisti e nazisti oggi nel mondo,* Milan, Sugar Editore, 1964, p. 87.

17 At a cabinet meeting, the Socialist Minister of the Interior, Afritsch, stated that among the ex-Servicemen present were pro- fessional agitators like Fred Borth and Norbert Burger.

18 Those two speeches were made at Innsbruck on 20 June 1959.

19 Brought to trial in Vienna in December 1965, the former head of the Flemish SS was acquitted and immediately released. In a comment on this incredible verdict which appeared in the *Volksgazet,* the vice-president of the Belgian Socialist Party, Jos Van Eynde, said: 'The jury which acquitted Verbelen insulted the tombs of thousands of our fellow-countrymen who during the five years of the Nazi occupation paid with their lives for their loyalty to Belgium.'

20 This was the case with Franz Murer, Joseph Hoblinger, Franz Razesberger and Joseph Slavik, all of whom were accused of massacring Jews. According to Simon Wiesenthal, the man who discovered the hideouts of Adolf Eichmann, Erich Rajakovic and hundreds of other Nazis, about 1,500 war criminals are hiding

under false names in Austria. In February 1964 Wiesenthal handed to the Austrian Minister of Justice, Broda, a file on the criminal activities of fourteen Austrian citizens who had been trained at the 'murder school' in the castle of Hartheim near Linz. This school functioned from 1941 to 1944.

21 After the rejection of this motion the *Berg Isel Bund* came under the control of extremists like Kranebitter, Oberhammer and Widmoser. The *Berg Isel Bund* was founded at Innsbruck in 1954 by the university professor Franz Gschnitzer and Dr Eduard Widmoser; its membership soon rose to 40,000. Another association which demands the annexation of the Alto Adige to Austria is the *Notring für Südtirol*, headed by Alphons Gasser.

22 According to what Josef Kerschbaumer said on 16 December 1963 during the trial of the Alto Adige terrorists, the BAS was founded in 1959 'to put the question on an international basis'. After Kerschbaumer's arrest, the leadership of the BAS passed into the hands of Georg Klotz, Alois Amplatz and Professor Günther Andergassen; the last-named was arrested in Venice on 6 April 1964. In order to show the falsity of the statement that the activists of the BAS were merely 'respectable' patriots, we give below some names of BAS members (or men who have worked for the BAS) who have been in contact with neo-Nazi groups: Norbert Burger (generally recognized as the brain of the organization; has always maintained contacts with Austrian and German neo-Nazi groups); Herbert Kuehn (before blowing up the cloakroom at the railway station in Verona on 20 September 1962 worked for the OAS in Paris, where he placed a bomb in a cinema; arrested and tried in East Berlin for dynamite outrages); Joachim Lothar Dunkel, Ulrich Becher, Hartmund Müller (arrested while they were trying to smuggle large quantities of dynamite into Italy; formerly belonged to the German extreme right-wing organization, *Bund der vaterländischen Jugend*); Ottokar Destaller (a former Nazi, implicated in the Austrian risings in 1936 and 1938); Otto Pietermeier (entered the SS as a volunteer at the age of sixteen; at the Milan trial said that if the Africans, 'who are on a lower level than we are', were given independence, then the South Tyrolese had all the more right to demand it); Günther Schweinberger (member of the pan-German *Olympia* society); Peter Kiensberger and Gottfried Höfner (both members of the *Bund Heimattreuer Jugend*).

23 This statement was made by Burger in March 1963 to the Viennese weekly *Wochenpresse*. Statements of the same sort were also reported by the authoritative Swiss daily *Neue Zürcher Zeitung*, in the summer of 1961.

24 Burger was granted political asylum in West Germany thanks to the personal intervention of the Minister for the Interior, Hermann Höcherl.

25 From the report on the trial in the Turin *La Stampa*, 18 December 1963.

26 The *Kulturwerk* published a review called *Südtirol in Wort und Bild*, edited by Eduard Widmoser, one of the leaders of the *Berg Isel Bund*. As early as 1961 the Frankfurt/Main *Neue Kommentare* denounced the subversive activities of the *Kulturwerk* in a special issue bearing the significant title 'Sudetenland 1938, South Tyrol 1961—The same methods, the same men. The same aims?' On the guerrilla warfare in the Alto Adige, see GIANNI BIANCO, *La guerra dei tralicci*, Rovereto, Manfrini Ed., 1963.

27 At Munich, in 1964, at a meeting organized by the Christian Social Union, a resolution was passed demanding self-determination for the Alto Adige and the intervention 'on human and Germanic grounds' of the Bonn government, which was asked to bring pressure to bear on Rome regarding the acceptance of the claims of the South Tyrolese. During the meeting, Professor Franz Klüber of the university of Regensburg, author of an article entitled 'The legal and theologo-moral grounds for active resistance in the South Tyrolese struggle', repeated that a resort to violence in the Alto Adige was perfectly legitimate. ·

28 Statement made to A. Del Boca in Vienna, 5 November 1962.

Chapter Nine: Belgium

1 MICHEL GÉORIS-REITSHOF, *Extrême droite et néo-fascisme en Belgique*, Brussels, Pierre de Meyere Éditeur, 1962, pp. 24–26. This little book by a young Belgian journalist, who is a Socialist, gives an admirably accurate account of the development of extreme right-wing movements in Belgium, and is also one of the few publications we know of containing a complete list of such movements in any one country.

2 In addition to those mentioned, there are other small groups details of which will be found in Géoris-Reitshof's book and also in a list published in the March number of *La Voix Internationale de la Résistance*, p. 16. In the same issue there is a brief report on neo-Fascist and neo-Nazi movements in all countries.

3 *Nation Belgique*, 2nd year, No. 56, 11 August 1961, editorial.

4 *Ibid*.

5 *Nation Belgique*, 2nd year, No. 59, 1 September 1961; article entitled *'Un seul slogan—Compropriété'*, by 'Clavaroc' (pseudonym of H. Moreau).

6 *Cf.* HENRI MOREAU, *Votre avenir—Pour un vrai socialisme dégagé de Marx*, Brussels, Collection 'L'Occident Communautaire', 1962.

7 M. GÉORIS-REITSHOF, *op. cit.*, p. 63.

8 *Cf.* Chapter 4, above, 'The Nazis think of the future'.

9 The text of the 'Manifesto to the European Nation' is in *Jeune Europe*, 3rd year, No. 98, 1st June 1962.

10   *Nation Belgique*, No. 56, 11 August 1961.

11   M. GÉORIS-REITSHOF, *op. cit.*, p. 63.

12   *Cf.* above, Chapter 4. Among the exponents of European neo-Nazism who are probably in contact with Thiriart and his organization there is also Paul Van Tienen, a bookseller in The Hague, a former Waffen-SS officer and chairman of the 'military intellectual club' for Dutch neo-Nazis. Van Tienen founded the *Archives*, an association which distributes books on Nazism. This Dutch bookseller attended the meetings at Malmö and Venice, and is considered to be one of the leading figures among the 'nostalgics'. But he has few followers and their activities are limited to the distribution of works exalting Hitler's 'New Order'. On Van Tienen and Dutch neo-Nazism see the article entitled *'Dossier Nero—Il nazista gross-europeo'*, in *Vie Nuove*, 12 April 1962.

13   *Cf.* *'Dossier sul Fascismo Europeo—L'Internazionale Nera'*, in *Vie Nuove*, 12 April 1962.

14   *Jeune Europe* paid particular attention to this agitation. See, in No. 185, 29 May 1964, the article entitled *'La deuxième grève médicale sera ultradure'*. Under the title *'Belgium's Medical Poujadiste'*, the *Sunday Times* of 12 April 1964 had hard things to say about the Fascist character of the agitation among the doctors as a result of pressure from the extreme right wing.

15   *Cf. Jeune Europe*, No. 185, 29 May 1964, article entitled *'Du marxisme au délit de droit commun ou du sermon au bâton'*, by J. Thiriart.

16   *Cf. Jeune Europe*, No. 184, 22 May 1964; No. 186, 5–12 June 1964; No. 189, 17–24 July 1964.

17   *Cf. Jeune Europe*, No. 188, 3–10 July 1964, article entitled *'La vérité sur Goldwater'*.

18   H. MOREAU, *op. cit.*, pp. 123–124.

Chapter Ten: Spain

1   Statement made to Angelo Del Boca in Turin, December 1963.

2   From Franco's speech to the second Trade Union Congress in Madrid, as reported in *Le Monde*, 13 March 1962.

3   JESÚS LÓPEZ PACHECO, *Pongo la mano sobre España*, Rome, Ed. Rapporti Europei, 1961, p. 52.

4   *Joven Europa*, circular No. 6, 1962.

5   On Ridruejo's conversion, see the interesting autobiographical passages in his *Escrito en España*, Buenos Aires, Losada, 1962.

6   DIONISIO RIDRUEJO, *op. cit.*, p. 121. See also STANLEY G. PAYNE, *Falange, a History of Spanish Fascism*, Stanford (Calif.), Stanford University Press/London, Oxford University Press, 1962, p. 200.

7   SALVADOR DE MADARIAGA, *Spain*, London, Jonathan Cape, 1947, p. 394.

8 RAMÓN SERRANO SUÑER, *Entre Endaya y Gibraltar*, Mexico City, Epesa Mexicana, 1947, p. 366.

9 DIONISIO RIDRUEJO, *op. cit.*, p. 78.

10 In a book published in 1957, entitled *Hacia una meta institucional*, Madrid, Ediciones del Movimiento, JOSÉ LUIS ARRESE states that 'the real Falange occupies about 5 per cent of the leading posts in Spain'. The following are said to be Falangists: 2 out of 16 Ministers; 1 out of 17 under-secretaries; 8 out of 102 directors-general; 18 out of 50 civil governors; 8 out of 50 presidents of provincial administrations; 65 out of 151 members of the national council of the Falange; 137 out of 575 deputies in the *Cortes*; 133 out of 738 provincial deputies; 766 out of 9,155 mayors; 2,226 out of 55,960 municipal councillors.

11 According to certain Socialist sources (Zugazagoitia and Llopis) quoted by PAYNE, *op. cit.*, pp. 97–98, on the eve of the 1936 elections José Antonio was in touch with Indalecio Prieto concerning an amalgamation of the Falange and the more moderate wing of the Socialist Party. José Antonio is said to have offered the leadership of this 'Socialist Falange' to Prieto and to have expressed his willingness to accept a subordinate post. This statement is not confirmed by any other source, but in view of the many contradictions in José Antonio's way of thinking it may well be true. Ridruejo (*op. cit.*, p. 13) says that 'José Antonio never had the histrionic confidence of the Fascist leaders and seemed to be always adopting a critical attitude towards himself, looking for something he could not find'.

12 JOSÉ LUIS ARRESE, *op. cit.*, pp. 191–192.

13 Quoted by STANLEY G. PAYNE, *op. cit.*, pp. 251–256.

14 PAYNE, *op. cit.*, p. 256.

15 *Es Así*, Madrid, No. 1, January 1963.

16 *Es Así*, Madrid, No. 2, March 1963.

17 *Es Así*, Madrid, No. 3, July 1963.

18 From a speech made in Madrid on 9 March 1963. Reprinted in *Relazioni Internazionali*, 25 March 1963, pp. 387–389.

19 The letter is dated 30 October. *Le Monde* quotes passages from it in its issue for 8 November 1963.

20 In 1945, after the collapse of the Axis powers, Arrese published a booklet entitled *El Estado Totalitario en el pensamiento de José Antonio*; speaking of the Falange leader's refusal to go to Montreux in 1934 to attend the Fascist International's congress, Arrese tries to make out that Falangism had never drawn its inspiration from Nazism or Fascism. Subsequently, the authors of official books on Falangism, from Manuel Fraga Iribarne (*Comment est gouvernée l'Espagne*, Madrid, 1952) to José Solís Ruiz (*Nueva convivencia española*, Madrid, SIPS, 1959), invariably denied the existence of Fascist ideas in the *Movimiento*.

21 These statements were made by Ridruejo to Angelo Del Boca in the course of conversation, on 11 January 1961 in Madrid.

22 Extract from a letter dispatched on 30 May 1960 to the four bishops of the Basque lands.

23 PAYNE, *op. cit.*, p. 200.

24 From *L'Espagne et la Primauté du Droit*, published by the International Commission of Jurists, Geneva, 1962, p. 80. This document, which in itself is sufficient to brand the Franco régime, should—according to information we received in Madrid in 1961— have also included a section on the tortures inflicted in Spanish prisons. We do not know why the Commission of Jurists decided not to publish documents which would have helped to make the 'white book' more complete.

25 On the evolution of Fascism, see the chapter entitled *Grandezza e decadenza dei plebei*, in *Fascismo e gran capitale* by DANIEL GUÉRIN, Milan, Schwarz Editore, 1956, pp. 136–163.

26 In a speech which he made at Vichy on 15 May 1957, the then Minister of Education, Gabriel Arias Salgado, tried to explain the difference between *Caudillaje* and a dictatorship: 'They are two different political situations, because the essentially temporary character of a dictatorship is not to be found in *Caudillaje*, which must obviously continue for a long time. . . . The *raison d'être* of a dictatorship depends on the existence of a constitutional system which will continue and is only suspended for the time being; it is not an objective, precise and limited risk due to circumstances . . . whereas *Caudillaje* is generated by a chain of historical events leading to political chaos and by the liquidation of the past. . . . Either tacitly or openly, we expect *Caudillaje* to create a new historical, juridical and political order. . . . A dictatorship is transitory, *Caudillaje* is fundamental.'

27 The most recent attempt to define the 'organic democracy' of the Franco régime was made by the *Caudillo* himself, when he addressed the National Council of the *Movimiento* on 9 March 1963. *Cf. Relazioni Internazionali*, 23 March 1963, pp. 387–389.

28 ANGELO DEL BOCA, *L'altra Spagna*, Milan, Bompiani, 1961, p. 43.

29 Although it has reaped many benefits during the last twenty years, the Spanish Church is today divided in its attitude towards the Franco régime. Several members of the Catholic hierarchy— among them the Primate himself, Plá y Deniel—favour a liberalization of the régime and have even given their support to the workers of the HOAC *(Hermandades Obreras de Acción Católica)* and the JOC *(Juventud Obrera Católica)* who are insistent in their demands for trade unions completely independent of the State. On the other hand, prelates whose ideas are closer to those of Cardinals Ottaviani and Bea are fervent supporters of Franco. The conflict between the two trends became even more evident as a result of the interview granted by the mitred Abbot of Montserrat, Monsignor Aurelio Escarré, to a correspondent of *Le Monde* (14 November 1963). The Abbot criticized the Franco régime sharply, affirming that in its policy it did not follow the

Catholic principles which it claimed to be supporting, and he even went so far as to make statements like the following: 'The victors, including the Church, which was compelled to take their side, have done nothing towards putting an end to this distinction between victors and vanquished'; 'the absence of all social justice is frightening'; 'taking them as a whole, our politicians are not Christians'. The task of replying to Escarré was undertaken by the Abbot of Valle de los Caídos, Justo Pérez de Urbel, a member of the Council of the *Movimiento* and a deputy in the *Cortes*. After describing the Abbot of Montserrat as a 'busybody', he said that he was adopting a disgraceful attitude towards a government 'which is upholding the faith of Spaniards, supporting the Church and working for peace' (*cf. Le Monde*, 10 December 1963). A little more than a year later, in March 1965, Monsignor Escarré was obliged to leave Spain and seek refuge in Italy.

30 Nothing worthy of note has yet been written about the *Opus Dei*, which 'left-wing' Catholics prefer to call the *Opus Diaboli* or 'white freemasonry' on account of its extreme integralist views. In the course of the three decades of its existence it has transformed itself from a secular institution into the biggest economic pressure-group that Spain has known in modern times. If we want to obtain an idea of the spiritual and material aims of this *Sociedad Sacerdotal de Santa Cruz y del Opus Dei*, however, we need only read the disconcerting book written by its founder, Monsignor José Maria Escrivá de Balaguer, entitled *Camino*.

31 One of Franco's latest statements about the question of his successor occurs in the course of an interview granted to a correspondent of *Le Figaro* (16 December 1963): 'Our system of succession, based on the promulgation of a law which made Spain a kingdom, was ratified by a crushing majority on the occasion of the 1947 referendum. This system offers, not only a solution, but also an alternative; either a prince of the blood can assume the crown, or else a regency can be established in accordance with the provisions of this law, if the interests of the country require it. In this way we are not obliged to break away from the traditional system, which is a characteristic feature of our country's history, or to resort to republicanism, which on two occasions has already brought discredit on our country and caused its ruin.'

32 That Franco is deceiving both the monarchists and the Falangists is definitely proved by the fact that, practically speaking, he has already nominated as his 'successor' a general, the former commander of the 'Blue Division', Muñoz Grandes. His appointment as Vice-Premier on 11 July 1963 shows that Franco intends that Spain shall remain under a military dictatorship. In fact, as long ago as 1936—as PAYNE (*op. cit.*, p. 148) mentions—one of Franco's collaborators, Colonel Castejón, said: 'My personal opinion is that for a long time in Spain's future the delicate and pre-eminent

role of being the just, balanced, serene and imperative arbiter of public affairs is reserved for the Army.' In early 1964, no fewer than seven ministries were under military control. We must therefore accept with reservations the promise Franco made in April 1964 that he would liberalize the régime and that, first of all, he would share with others the offices he now holds.

33 HERBERT RUTLEDGE SOUTHWORTH, *El Mito de la Cruzada de Franco*, Paris, Ruedo Ibérico, 1963, p. 180.

34 JUAN GOYTISOLO, *Spagna 1963*, in *Il Giorno*, 31 March 1963.

35 A source quoted by PAYNE (*op. cit.*, p. 242), but not confirmed, states that between these two dates 192,684 people were killed. This figure, like all others referring to the number of dead on either side during the civil war, must be considered as a gross exaggeration.

36 ELENA DE LA SOUCHÈRE, *Explication de l'Espagne*, Paris, Grasset, 1962, p. 221.

37 Quoted in *L'Espagne et la Primauté du Droit*, *op. cit.*, p. 64.

38 The most exhaustive work on Spanish opposition to Franco and on the excesses committed by his régime between 1945 and 1964 is *España hoy*, edited by Ignacio Fernández de Castro and José Martínez, Paris, Ruedo Ibérico, 1963. See also LUIS RAMÍREZ, *Nuestros primeros veintecinco años*, Paris, Ruedo Ibérico, 1964.

39 *Le Figaro Littéraire*, 4 May 1963.

40 *Le Monde*, 26 April 1963.

41 *L'Express*, 25 April 1963.

42 *Le Monde*, 24 April 1963.

43 Among the more notable refugees we will mention Léon Degrelle, head of the Belgian Rexists, Ante Pavelich, leader of the *Ustaše* (died in Madrid in 1959), Horia Sima, commander of the Rumanian Iron Guard, and a number of former Nazi officers of the 'Condor Legion' which destroyed Guernica. To these must be added the dictators Juan Perón and Fulgencio Batista; still later arrivals were the French extremists who tried to seize control of Algeria (Salan, Gardy, Gardes, Lagaillarde, Susini, Ronda, Perez, Laquière, to mention only a few names). That Madrid has offered hospitality to Nazis, Fascists and right-wing extremists is admitted by Colonel Argoud in a letter he wrote to Godard on 6 September 1961, published by *L'Express* on 12 October of the same year: 'In view of its geographical position and the international situation, Madrid is the only capital possible.' Otto Skorzeny, who has made Madrid one of the main bases for his neo-Nazi activities, is of the same opinion.

44 Extract from the oath which judges have to take in accordance with the law of 25 July 1956.

Chapter Eleven: Portugal

1 The four big landowners are Fosser de Andrade, Santos Jorge, The Duke of Cadaval and the Duke of Palmela. Elsewhere in the

country the same acreage is divided up among 54,000 small proprietors. The information can be found in the *Registro Predial*, the Portuguese register of landed property.

2   The rate of infant mortality is 88.6 per 1,000, higher than in some African countries, e.g. Senegal (67.5). Tuberculosis, with 54 deaths per 100,000 inhabitants is also a scourge, followed by diphtheria, tetanus, typhoid, and pellagra, the last-named being almost unknown in the rest of Europe. Other statistics show how backward the country is. For every 1,000 inhabitants there are 12 cars, 67 radios and 5 television sets. The consumption of meat per head of population is 5 centigrammes a day; on an average a Portuguese goes to the cinema 3 times a year, to the theatre once every 11 years, and to a concert once every 383 years; in 1959 5 films were produced.

3   Most of the biographies of Salazar are hagiographies and therefore completely unreliable. Among the principal ones we will mention: ANTONIO FERRO, *Salazar*, Paris, Grasset, 1939; PAUL SÉRANT, *Salazar et son temps*, Paris, Éditions des Sept Couleurs, 1961; HENRI MASSIS, *Salazar face à face*, Paris, Éditions de la Palatine, 1961; CHRISTINE GARNIER, *Vacances avec Salazar*, Paris, Grasset, 1952.

4   Previous attempts had failed. In 1949 General Norton de Matos withdrew his candidature because he maintained that the wishes of the people had not been respected. For the same reason the mathematician Rui Luis Gomes and Admiral Quintão Meireles withdrew in 1951.

5   P. FRYER and P. MCGOWAN, *Oldest Ally*, London, Dennis Dobson Books, 1961. We are indebted to this book for much valuable information.

6   The influx of foreign capital into Portugal has been on a larger scale than in any other European country. Banks, telephones, telegraph and transport services, insurance, factories, mines, electric power stations and a number of commercial firms are controlled by foreign financial groups, in many cases British.

7   Anti-Fascist demonstrations became particularly frequent after 1 May 1963, and resulted in numerous arrests.

8   It is also said that Mussolini lent several functionaries of the Italian OVRA to Salazar. For their services they received from President Carmona the medal of the Order of Christ, the second highest Portuguese decoration.

9   Until the end of the Second World War the 'Greenshirts' used the Fascist salute. Today they have adopted a modified form of it. As in Spain, there are only a few neo-Fascist groups in Portugal, since Salazar holds a kind of monopoly. There is, however, the Portuguese section of the *Nouvel Ordre Européen* International, *Ordem Nova*, headed by Zarco Ferreira. Jacques Ploncard d'Assac, a disciple of Maurras who runs Radio Portugal's programme *The Voice of the West*, is connected with this group. Here is an example of what Ploncard d'Assac thinks

Q*

about the decline of colonialism: 'The peoples of the overseas countries accepted the guardianship of the West. They did not seriously think of getting rid of it, and the wisest among them today mourn the passing of the empires and realize the futility of so-called independence. Like the inhabitants of the home countries they have been the victims of destructive political systems, of ideologies based on false premises which have proved incapable of defending either natives or Europeans against the occult powers of Plutocracy and Subversion. We must rebuild Europe instead of destroying her Empires. These latter will be re-formed when the real Revolution of the twentieth century has liberated the West from Plutocracy and Communism, those two faces of the same Materialism.' (From the March-April number of *Ordine Nuovo*, Rome, 1964, p. 15.)

10 For the activities of the PIDE, we have used, among other sources, the 'report' submitted by Portuguese anti-Fascists to the committee of the 'Congress of the Partisans of Peace' (Stockholm, 1961). The report is reprinted in *Dossier sul Porto-gallo*, edited by Dante Bellamio, Milan, Edizioni Avanti!, 1963.

11 DANTE BELLAMIO, *op. cit.*, p. 58.

12 ANTONIO FERRO, *Salazar*, Paris, Grasset.

13 Previous insurrections had been suppressed. At São Tomé in 1953 1,000 Africans were killed because they protested against forced labour. At Bissao, in Guinea, on 3 August 1959, several dozen Negroes were killed during a strike and hundreds of others were deported to the island of Galinhas.

14 ANDERS EHNMARK and PER WÄSTBERG, *Angola and Mozambique*, London, Pall Mall Press, 1963, pp. 117–118.

15 The *palmatória* or *baramatola* is a kind of table-tennis racket with five holes in it. When the palms of a man's hands are violently beaten with it, the pain is excruciating owing to the suction of air through the holes. The punishment is part of the daily routine and can be ordered by the *chefe de posto*. In the words of a native song: 'The Portuguese beat us on our hands, on our own and on our women's.'

16 On 5 March 1962, a commission of three jurists whom the ILO had appointed to investigate conditions in Portuguese Africa reported that although Salazar's government was trying to abolish forced labour, the Diamond Company of Angola was still 'recruiting labour through its functionaries and native chiefs, using methods which involved coercion and sometimes amounting to forced labour'.

17 From an article by H. GALVÃO, reprinted in *Africa Speaks*, edited by James Duffy and Robert A. Manners, Princeton (New Jersey), Van Nostrand, 1961, p. 173.

18 The British control the coal-mines at Maotize in Mozambique, as well as the production of tea and cotton; Krupp has coal and iron interests in Angola; the Anglo-American 'Diamang' has a

monopoly of diamonds; the Gulf Oil and Petrofina companies are exploiting the oil recently found in Angola and Mozambique. The annual profit-rate of these companies fluctuates between 20 per cent and 45 per cent.

19 ANDERS EHNMARK and PER WÄSTBERG, *op. cit.*, p. 19.
20 In 1962 he was elected honorary president of the MPLA, one of the two largest independence movements in Angola.
21 In 1963 the Afro-Asiatics launched an anti-Portuguese offensive through the UN and other international organizations. At the 'summit' conference in Addis Ababa thirty-two independent African States decided to boycott Portugal and South Africa and break off diplomatic relations with these two racialist countries. After being repeatedly asked by the Security Council to stop repressive action in the Portuguese colonies and to prepare them for independence, Salazar made the following statement in the course of a speech on 12 August 1963: 'People abroad are loudly demanding independence for Angola, but Angola is a Portuguese creation and could not exist without Portugal. The national conscience rooted in that province is not an Angolan national conscience, but Portuguese. There are no Angolans; there are only Portuguese of Angola. What I have just said applies to Mozambique as well.'

Chapter Twelve: Great Britain

1 This and the following statements were made by Sir Oswald Mosley to Angelo del Boca in the course of an interview in Paris on 22 October 1962.
2 Unlike Hitler, who was the son of a minor Customs official, and Mussolini, who was the son of a blacksmith, Mosley comes of a family of the landed aristocracy established in Lancashire for four hundred years. Moreover, he married into his own class. His first wife was Lady Cynthia Curzon, daughter of the Foreign Secretary, and the King and Queen were among the guests at their wedding. Two years after Lady Cynthia's death, Mosley married, in 1934, the Hon. Diana Freeman-Mitford, daughter of Lord Redesdale and sister of Unity. Mosley's second marriage took place privately in Berlin and among the guests were those new aristocrats of the Third Reich, Dr and Frau Goebbels.
3 *Cf.*, for example, the article by c. m. FRANZERO in the *Giornale d'Italia*, 15 April 1933.
4 Mosley's programme provided for a one-party system (that party would obviously have been the BUF); a government which would not be answerable to parliament, but would ask for the approval of the nation once every five years, by means of a plebiscite; a

House of Commons on corporative lines; and a Senate of deserving citizens to replace the House of Lords.

5　COLIN CROSS, *The Fascists in Britain*, London, Barrie & Rockliff, 1961; New York, St. Martin's Press, 1963, p. 97, quotes what Churchill's son Randolph said of Mosley in 1934: 'There is no doubt that Sir Oswald Mosley is today the most accomplished speaker in the country. His eloquence has often been compared to that of the leaders of Fascism in other countries. Personally I find him more attractive than any of them. He does not thunder like Mussolini. He has most in common with Dr Goebbels. Both possess a voice with a real ring of conviction which carries a thrill to the audience.'

6　Nevertheless, about this time Mosley was very careful. In a message to British Fascists which appeared in *Action* he wrote: 'Our country is involved in war. Therefore I ask you to do nothing to injure our country or to help any other power.' Only one passage was deleted from the message by the censor: 'This war is no quarrel of the British people; this war is a quarrel of Jewish finance.'

7　To be precise, the first British Fascist to resume his activities after the last war was the well-known anti-Semite Arnold Leese, who until his death in 1956 published the monthly *Gothic Ripples* (Anti-Jewish Information Bureau, Guildford, Surrey).

8　At the general election in 1959, in North Kensington, Mosley polled 2,821 votes, 8 per cent of the total votes cast.

9　The quotations, other than those from the interview, are taken from Mosley's two books, *Mosley, Right or Wrong?*, London, Lion Books, 1961, and *Europe: Faith and Plan*, London, Euphorion Books, 1958. Other books by Mosley include *The Greater Britain* (1932), *One Hundred Questions Answered* (1936), *Tomorrow We Live* (1938), *My Answer* (1946) and *The Alternative* (1948).

10　Figures given by MICHAEL HAMLYN, *Sunday Times*, 17 May 1964.

11　In *Il Punto*, 15 August 1962.

12　*Il Punto*, 30 August 1962.

13　Colin Jordan's political career began in 1950 when he started the Birmingham Nationalist Club. After moving to London he founded the White Defence League, which played a leading part in skirmishes with West Indian immigrants. In 1960 Jordan and his group joined forces with Andrew Fountaine's British National Party, but Jordan was expelled a year later on account of his extremism.

14　See John Tyndall's booklet entitled *The Authoritarian State, a National Socialist publication*, London, 1962.

15　*The National Socialist*, No. 6, 1964.

16　When they searched the premises of the National Socialist Movement the police found several tins of a liquid weedkiller which could be transformed into a powerful explosive by adding a little sugar. On one of these tins the word 'weedkiller' had been altered to 'Jewkiller'.

17 *The National Socialist*, No. 4, May 1963.

18 *The National Socialist*, No. 5, August 1963.

19 The National Socialist Movement claimed to have 1,000 members, but according to Michael Hamlyn (see above, Note 10) it consisted only of 50 activists and 200 sympathizers. The NSM was responsible for the founding in France of a section of the WUNS, which was discovered in the summer of 1964 and dissolved after the arrest of its leader, Yves Jeanne. Although the French section of the WUNS never had more than 40 members, it was extremely active and maintained contacts with neo-Nazi groups in fourteen countries. In May 1964, a month before the group was dissolved, Yves Jeanne decided to change the section's name to the more significant one of *Front National Aryen*. In the course of its investigations, the *Sûreté* found that many of the members had physical defects or were moral degenerates, and that the neo-Nazi leaders of the group exploited their exceptional aggressiveness, due to a feeling of inferiority. A typical case is that of a man who was the twenty-two-year-old illegitimate son of a German soldier who had served with the occupation forces in France and was later killed. Since childhood he had been humiliated because other children called him a *Boche* and he told the investigating authorities that he had so much wrath pent up inside him that he decided to become a Nazi in order to take his revenge on the cruel French provincials.

20 Fountaine, a wealthy landowner from Norfolk, began his political career in the ranks of the Conservative Party and was nearly elected to Parliament. Later, however, he was asked to resign from the party on account of his extremist views. The British National Party claims to have about 1,000 members and about 2,000 sympathizers.

21 *Twentieth Century*, Spring 1963, pp. 27–32.

22 John Bean, a chemical engineer, founded the National Labour Party and later joined Fountaine's British National Party, becoming its technical expert.

23 *Combat*, No. 17, May–June 1962.

Chapter Thirteen: Greece and South Vietnam

1 *Le Monde*, 11 July 1963. On the restrictions on the freedom of the Press, *cf. The Economist*, 21 March 1963, which reported that during the first two months of that year five Athens papers had been penalized simply for criticizing the government. For a more exhaustive study of Greece under Karamanlis, see the special number of *La Nouvelle Critique*, July–August 1963, edited by André Gisselbrecht.

2 On this point, see the article entitled *'Disagio in Grecia per l'affare Lambrakis'*, in *Relazioni internazionali*, 8 June 1963, pp. 714–715.

3 *Le Monde*, 28 October 1961.

4 *Le Monde*, 28 October 1961. After 1945 these militias replaced the Fascist groups known as *X*, *Kités* and *EMA*. Until the day when they were disbanded they consisted chiefly of peasants.

5 As reported in an article in *L'Express*, 16 May 1963.

6 The figures are quoted in a letter written by the Greek embassy in Paris to the editor of *Le Monde* (16 March 1963).

7 According to the Athens paper *Afghi* on 1st June 1963 the political detainees were distributed among the various prisons as follows: Averoff, 30 men and 9 women; Ayios Pavlos, 15; Aigina, 370; Lefcada, 30; Khalkis, 51; Sotiria, 29; Amphissa, 78; Trikkala, 106; Heptapyrgos, 46; Itzedin, 80; Halicarnassus, 180. This makes a total of 1,045 detainees, slightly more than the figure given by the Karamanlis government.

8 *Le Monde*, 26 March 1963.

9 Released in 1960, *Kriegsverwaltungsrat* Dr Merten was the last Nazi war criminal to be held in a Greek prison. As head of the military administration in the Salonika-Aegean theatre of war, he made arrangements with Adolf Eichmann and his assistants Wisliceny and Günther for the deportation to Auschwitz of 50,000 Jews from Salonika. This was stated by Wisliceny when he was interrogated in Nuremberg on 3 January 1946 (the text of his evidence can be found in *Le Dossier Eichmann*, Paris, Buchet-Chastel, 1960, pp. 206–210).

10 Extracts from a letter sent to the FIR *(Fédération Internationale des Résistants)* in Vienna and reprinted in the Federation's French-language bulletin, No. 2, 30 January 1963. The letter also refers to political offenders in forced residence, who are said to have numbered about 4,000 at that time.

11 *Ibid.*, Bulletin No. 4, 29 March 1963.

12 Reported in *Rinascita*, 1 June 1963.

13 A daughter of the Duke of Brunswick and a granddaughter of Kaiser Wilhelm II, Friederike was brought up in Germany and has never made a secret of her sympathy for Nazism. But photographs of her in the uniform of the *Hitler-Jugend* caused less stir than her virulent anti-Communism, which for many years made all attempts at national reconciliation impossible.

14 *Cf. Il filo rosso*, November 1963, pp. 19–20.

15 From an interview granted by Ho Chi Minh and published in *Mondo Nuovo*, 9 June 1963. It is worth recording that it was Ho Chi Minh himself who, by an act of clemency, saved Diem's life; in 1945, Diem had been arrested and sentenced to death for collaborating first with the French and later with the Japanese.

16 NATHANIEL PEFFER, *The Far East,* Ann Arbor, University of Michigan Press, 1958, p. 479. Peffer, who is Professor of Inter-

national Law at Columbia University, worked for some time as an adviser to the State Department.

17 This and the following statements in quotation marks are extracts from an interview granted by Ngo Dinh Diem to Angelo Del Boca and published in the *Gazzetta del Popolo*, 29 May 1962.

18 In a letter to *Le Monde* (25 August 1963) the editor of *Esprit*, Jean-Marie Domenach, wrote: 'With regard to current events in South Vietnam, "personalism" has been mentioned as the official doctrine of Ngo Dinh Diem, his family and his State. I would like to make it clear that this "personalism" is quite different from the doctrine with which Emmanuel Mounier's name is connected. The "personalism" to which *Esprit* is continually referring takes a layman's view and wants to be on the side of the poor; in any case it respects the personal dignity of every individual, whatever his religion may be.' It is understandable that Domenach was indignant when Nhu tried to fill the ideological void of his régime by using the name of a movement which is one of the most significant expressions of contemporary Catholic thought. Moreover, at the 'Centre' for the propagation of 'personalism', which all officers and functionaries of the régime have to attend, teaching is confined to generic anti-Communism and criticism of all other religions (except Catholicism) and little attention is paid to Mounier's theories, though his terminology is borrowed, which only adds to the general confusion of ideas.

19 In South Vietnam the Catholics represent about 10 per cent of the population (against 80 per cent Buddhists), but many of them come from the North and were persuaded to join in the great exodus (in 1954) by the apocalyptical predictions of Catholic priests, who spread the rumour, among others, that the Virgin Mary had left North Vietnam and that anyone who wanted to regain her favour must move to the South. According to the review *Informations Catholiques Internationales* of 15 December 1961, 676,384 Vietnamese Catholics proceeded by forced marches to South Vietnam, guided by a ship with an illuminated Madonna on board. When they came into contact with the Diem régime, this religious minority adopted an almost mystical attitude of resistance to the 'red peril'. During the last few years of Diem's régime, however, many Catholics, even if they had received favours from him, deserted his cause. 'The favouritism shown by Diem to Catholics,' we are told by Georges Montaron, editor of *Témoignage Chrétien*, 'was an attempt to undermine the rights, independence and freedom of the Church. His reactionary policy and clericalism were a greater help to Communism than Ho Chi Minh's propaganda.'

20 *Les Marchés Coloniaux*, 15 December 1955.

21 *Tu-do*, Saigon, 22 May 1959.

22 *Cachmang quocgia*, Saigon, 14 July 1959.

23 According to Michel Bosquet, in *L'Express*, 29 August 1963:

'Among the leaders of the Vietnamese opposition whom I have met in Paris, even the most anti-Communist (those of the Vietnamese Democratic League) believe that 90 per cent of the inhabitants support the National Liberation Front (FLN), of which the Viet-Cong is the armed advance-guard and which includes both nationalists and Communists.' Besides the FLN there are other opposition movements with varying shades of opinion, many of whose members have sought refuge in France, Japan or Cambodia.

24   On 1 October 1963 the strength of the regular army was 210,000 men; of the militia *(Baoandoan)*, 110,000; of the rural 'Civil Guards' *(Dan ve)*, 100,000; of the police, 90,000, making an overall total of 510,000 men.

25   In the summer of 1963 the 'special units' consisted of 6 battalions, while 3,000 women were members of the Women's Movement.

26   WILFRED G. BURCHETT, *The Furtive War. The United States in Vietnam and Laos*, New York, International Publishers, 1963, p. 66.

27   *La Gazzetta del Popolo*, 25 May 1962, article by Angelo Del Boca entitled *'Mille villaggi simili a lager per intrappolare i Viet-Cong'*.

28   Figures given by *Time Magazine*, 18 October 1963.

29   According to the 1954 Geneva agreement, the strength of the United States Military Mission was not to exceed 863 men. But on 1 February 1966 the American expeditionary force numbered over 190,000 men, backed by a military set-up equal to, if not larger than, that employed during the war in Korea.

30   *New York Times*, 22 March 1951.

31   *Newsweek*, 27 November 1961. In March 1963, General Giap, Commander-in-Chief of the North Vietnamese People's Army, sent a protest note to the president of the International Control Commission, in which, *inter alia*, he said: 'Many people have died; others have been blinded or have suffered burns. Many head of cattle have also been lost, and thousands of acres of rice, other crops and fruit-trees have been destroyed.'

32   Fernand Gigon (in *Il Giorno*, 7 September 1963) explained the reasons, other than political, which keep the Americans in Vietnam. 'The Americans are spending $1\frac{1}{2}$ million dollars every day in South Vietnam. This enormous mass of money serves to keep the country going and prevent it from collapsing beneath the burden of the war. But this figure of $1\frac{1}{2}$ million needs to be examined more closely. Out of this huge sum, 1,200,000 dollars, if not more, go back to the United States at once. In short, this $1\frac{1}{2}$ million is an administrative item rather than a daily reality. For example, if a helicopter is shot down by the Viet-Cong, it is invoiced to the Vietnamese government at 300,000 dollars. If a tank is blown up, it is debited at the rate of anything up to $1\frac{1}{2}$ million dollars. All the

profits on the supply of arms and munitions go to American industry and to the American economy.'

33 From the Report to the Senate Foreign Relations Committee. April 1963.

34 *Croix sur l'Indochine*, p. 19.

35 Other sources give different figures. For example, Erich Wulff speaks of 150,000 internees, of whom 80,000 are non-Communists. Certain Hanoi sources give the number of killed between 1954 and 1963 as 156,000 and the number of detainees as 370,000. Wilfred Burchett, *op. cit.*, quotes a statement by Nguyen Van Nieu, secretary-general of the FLN, containing the following figures: 105,000 killed between 1955 and 1963, and 350,000 internees at the end of 1963, in 874 prisons and concentration camps.

36 Quoted by Michel Bosquet, in *L'Express*, 29 August 1963.

37 *The Observer*, 18 August 1963.

38 According to the *New York Times*, 7 September 1963, the attack on the Buddhist pagodas was carried out by troops under Colonel Le Quang Tung. The same paper reported that the CIA was contributing 250,000 dollars a month to the upkeep of Nhu's 'special units'.

39 *New York Times*, 9 August 1963.

40 *Le Monde*, 19 September 1963.

41 During an interview granted to the Columbia Broadcasting System's television network on 2 September 1963.

42 From an interview broadcast by Radio New York Worldwide (11 October 1963). Some newspapers claimed that Madame Nhu was the fourth richest woman in the world.

43 *Paris-Match*, 31 August 1963, article by Michel Clerc.

44 *Le Monde*, 24 August 1963.

45 *The Sunday Times*, 25 August 1963, article by Brian Crozier.

46 *Jeune Afrique*, 5–12 March 1962.

47 From Angelo Del Boca's interview with Diem, *cf.* Note 17.

48 NGUYEN KIEN, *Le Sud-Vietnam depuis Dien-Bien-Phu*, Paris, F. Maspéro, 1963, p. 306.

49 In *Le Monde*, 5 December 1963, Jean Lacouture wrote: 'It was an article by Joseph Alsop, which appeared in the *New York Herald-Tribune*, that sounded the alarm. It mentioned statements by Nhu and facts tending to show that with the help of the French ambassador in Saigon, M. Lalouette, and his colleague in Hanoi, M. de Buzon, negotiations had actually been started between Ho Chi Minh's government and that of Diem, through Manelli, the Polish representative on the International Control Commission.' These 'facts', however, would appear to have little foundation and may have been merely a pretext for removing the Ngo brothers, whose presence had now become an embarrassment.

50 *Le Monde*, 7 November 1963.

51 *Le Monde*, 7 April 1964. On 11 June 1965, after various *coups d'état*, General Nguyen Cao Ky took over the government.

52 HELEN B. LAMB, *The Tragedy of Vietnam*, New York, Basic Pamphlet 17, 1964, p. 40.

53 According to American sources, Viet-Cong losses were 26,500 in 1962, 25,000 in 1963, 21,200 in 1964 and 35,382 in 1965. The South Vietnamese government forces are said to have lost 13,000 men in 1962, 21,000 in 1963, 29,500 in 1964 and 42,088 in 1965. As for the Americans they had 618 casualties between 1961 and 1963 (106 killed, 501 wounded and 11 missing), 136 killed and 1,022 wounded in 1964, and 1,275 killed, 5,466 wounded and 137 missing in 1965. In this latter year they lost 275 planes and 76 helicopters. It should also be noted that in 1964 72,000 men deserted from the Saigon army, while in 1965 the number of deserters was over 90,000.

Chapter Fourteen: Japan

1 Quoted in *Political Reorientation of Japan*, edited by Supreme Commander Allied Powers, Washington, USGPO, 1949, p. 470.

2 Until the day of the surrender Hirohito bore the titles of *Kotei* (King-Emperor), *Tenno* (King of Heaven) and *Mikado* (Honourable Door). He was sacred and inviolable, invested with the sovereign power, supreme commander of the army, and high priest of Shintoism. On 3 May 1947, when the new constitution came into force, Hirohito was divested of all his powers, including even those normally granted to other constitutional monarchs. The 'Son of the Sun Goddess Amaterasu' became merely the 'symbol of the State and of the unity of the people'.

3 On 13 August 1945, twelve members of the *Meirō Kai* (Bright Sunshine Association) committed ceremonial *seppuku* together with their leader Hibi Waichi. On 24 August fourteen adherents of the *Daitō Juku* (Great East Institute), including their leader Kageyama Shōhei, took their own lives.

4 MASAO MARUYAMA, *Nationalism in Post-War Japan*, Conference Paper, 11th Institute of Pacific Relations Conference, Lucknow, 1950, p. 8.

5 IVAN MORRIS, *Nationalism and the Right Wing in Japan*, London, Oxford University Press, 1960, p. 42.

6 *Sekai*, Tokyo, March 1946. According to Jiro Horikoshi, the famous designer of the Japanese 'Zero' fighter-aircraft, in *kamikaze* operations 2,530 pilots of the Naval Air Service and about the same number of Army Air Force pilots lost their lives. On this subject, see: MASATAKE OKUMIYA and JIRO HORIKOSHI, *Zero*, New York, Ballantine Books, 1957.

7 *Cf.* MORRIS, *op. cit.*, pp. 44–55.

8 An excellent analysis of the activities of these groups can be found in: R. P. DORE, *Land Reform in Japan*, London, Oxford University Press, 1959, pp. 391–404.

9 NATHANIEL PEFFER, *The Far East*, Ann Arbor, University of Michigan Press, 1958, p. 508.

10 W. REITZEL, *United States Foreign Policy, 1945–55*, Washington, Brookings Institution, 1956, p. 173.

11 In ten years the strength of the Japanese army rose from 75,000 to 242,000, while the Air Force was equipped with 1,100 jet aircraft, the Navy with 203 vessels and the missiles units with 4 Nike-Ajax stations.

12 The *Mitsui*, the *Mitsubishi* and the *Sumitomo*, which had controlled a considerable part of the Japanese economy during the war and for this reason had been broken up into hundreds of small firms in 1945, were rapidly re-formed, and though not all of their former directors were retained, their structure remained practically the same as before the war. The *Mitsui*, for example, today controls 400 firms (ranging from chemical factories to shipyards, from mines to steelworks, from textile to foodstuff firms), is financed by its own banks and seils its own products through the *Mitsui Bussan*, which is the biggest commercial undertaking in Japan.

13 Since the war Kishi has spent seven years in Sugamo prison (Tokyo), because in 1941 he had been Minister of Commerce and Industry in the Tōjō Cabinet.

14 Seven years later, in 1965, Hideki Tōjō was rehabilitated in school textbooks, in which he was described as a paternal politician, understanding and generous; attempts were also made to exonerate him from all responsibility for the Pacific War, by shifting the blame on to the Americans.

15 According to DORE, *op. cit.*, pp. 483–484, 55 per cent of the people questioned were convinced that 'Japan is still the land of the gods'; 81 per cent were certain the leadership in Asia would fall to Japan and not to China or India; 85 per cent were against political parties and favoured one movement 'representing the entire nation'; 51 per cent were convinced that the aims of the last war were justified, and 85 per cent hoped that the last American soldiers would soon leave Japan.

16 *Mainichi Shimbun*, 5 August 1957.

17 H. BORTON, W. J. JORDEN, P. F. LANGER, J. B. COHEN, D. KEENE, M. WILBUR, *Japan between East and West*, New York, Harper, 1957, p. 37.

18 IVAN MORRIS, *op. cit.*, p. 201.

19 ANGELO DEL BOCA, *Occhio Giapponese*, Novara, Istituto Geografico De Agostini, 1963, pp. 218–219.

20 See our interview with Akao Bin, pp. 309–314.

21 Quoted by IVAN MORRIS, *op. cit.*, p. 334.

22 *Asahi Evening News*, 11 June 1957.

23 This and the following statements were made to Angelo Del Boca in Tokyo on 29 May 1962.

24 INOUE NISSHŌ, *Hitori Issatsu*, Tokyo, 1953, p. 397.

25 *Japan Times*, 31 July 1956.
26 IVAN MORRIS, *op. cit.*, p. 21.
27 Quoted by the Tokyo magazine *Sekai*, June 1957, p. 69. 'Mac' is, of course, General MacArthur.
28 *Japan between East and West*, *op. cit.*, p. 39.
29 'There are many religions in this world. For example, the two branches of Christianity, Protestantism and Catholicism, the various Buddhist sects, Islam, Hinduism and other groups too numerous to mention. We are accustomed to hearing about all these religions, and it can be said that they can be classified as important or negligible, profound or superficial, according to the faith which they instil in their followers. In reality not one of them has achieved valid results in the absolute sense; the world is losing its faith. Hence the need for the work of the supreme religion, Nichiren Buddhism.' (From a *Sōka Gakkai* propaganda booklet by Richard Okamoto.)
30 From an article by Richard Okamoto, 'Japan: The Booming Economy has found a New Religion with 10,000,000 Adherents bent on dominating the World', *Look*, 10 September 1963.
31 *Ibid.*
32 IVAN MORRIS, *op. cit.*, p. 141.
33 MICHAEL EDWARDES, *Asia in the Balance*, London, Penguin Books, 1962, p. 68.
34 *Le Monde*, 25 October 1963.
35 *The Guardian*, 29 May 1962.
36 All passages in inverted commas for which there is no reference in the notes are from propaganda publications of the *Sōka Gakkai*.

Chapter Fifteen: The United States

1 Not to be confused with the racialist White Citizens' Council to be found in every Southern city.
2 Stanley Marcus, *Dallas Morning News*, 1 January 1964.
3 Episode mentioned by Saul Friedman in *The Nation*, New York, 3 February 1964.
4 Article entitled *'How Explain Our Illness?'* in *The Washington Post*, 1 December 1963.
5 Article entitled *'Today and Tomorrow: Murder most foul'*, in *The Washington Post*, 26 November 1963. Professor Reece McGee is of the same opinion: 'I believe that—except in Mississippi—the probability of such a danger is greater in the State of Texas, and this on account of five factors which are either characteristic of that State or particularly acute there. These are: 1) the absolutist nature of the local way of thinking; 2) the institutionalization of personal violence; 3) the number of firearms and the habit of carrying them; 4) the political respectability of the Radical Right; 5) the non-existence, officially, of a Radical Left.' From *The Nation*, 21 December 1963.

6 The actual text of the handbill ran as follows: 'This man is wanted for treasonous activities against the United States: 1) Betraying the Constitution (which he swore to uphold): He is turning the sovereignty of the United States over to the Communist controlled United Nations. He is betraying our friends (Cuba, Katanga, Portugal) and befriended our enemies (Russia, Yugoslavia, Poland). 2) He has been wrong on innumerable issues affecting the security of the United States (United Nations—Berlin Wall—Missile removal—Cuba—Wheat deals—Test Ban Treaty, etc.). 3) He has been lax in enforcing Communist Registration laws. 4) He has given support and encouragement to Communist inspired racial riots. 5) He has illegally invaded a sovereign State with Federal troops. 6) He has consistently appointed anti-Christians to Federal office: upholds the Supreme Court in its Anti-Christian rulings. Aliens and known Communists abound in Federal offices. 7) He has been caught in fantastic LIES to the American people (including personal ones like his previous marriage and divorce).'

7 *The Economist*, 30 November 1963.

8 Sam Freedman, *'Tussle in Texas'*, *The Nation*, 3 February 1964, pp. 114–117. 'I am sure,' writes the above-mentioned Professor McGee, 'that in Texas many people, sincerely, if perhaps unconsciously, associated John Kennedy with Sin (and his religion probably contributed to this), and it is impossible to reach compromises with Sin or find any solutions except destruction.'

9 *L'Express*, 12 December 1963. On the political situation in Texas, see JOHN BRAINBRIDGE, *The Super-Americans*, New York, Doubleday, 1961, and CAREL ESTES THOMETZ, *The Decision-Makers*, Dallas, Southern Methodist University Press, 1963.

10 On extremist movements in the second half of the nineteenth century, such as The American Party, The Know-Nothings and The American Protective Association, see GUSTAVUS MYERS, *History of Bigotry in the United States*, New York, Random House, 1943.

11 *Cf.* the periodicals edited by Watson, *People's Party Paper* and *Watson's Magazine*.

12 GEORGE WOLFSKILL, *The Revolt of the Conservatives*, Boston, Houghton Mifflin Co., 1962, p. 84. Other organizations also drew their inspiration from Nazi ideology, e.g. the National Blue Shirts, Minute Men, Sons of Loyalty, Khaki Shirts, Black Shirts, White Shirts, etc.

13 LEOPOLD KOHR, *The Breakdown of Nations*, London, Routledge & Kegan Paul, 1957.

14 For the whole story of the American Liberty League, see GEORGE WOLFSKILL, *op. cit.*

15 FRANCIS BIDDLE, *The Fear of Freedom*, New York, Doubleday, 1951, p. 79.

16 See CHARLES E. COUGHLIN, *Am I an Anti-Semite?*, Detroit, 1939, and *Why leave our own?*, Detroit, 1939.

17 HANS J. MORGENTHAU, *The Purpose of American Politics*, New York, Alfred A. Knopf, 1960. On McCarthy, see RICHARD H. ROVERE, *Senator McCarthy*, New York, Harcourt, Brace, 1959.

18 DANIEL BELL, *The Radical Right*, New York, Anchor Books, Doubleday, 1964, p. 446.

19 F. J. COOKE, 'The Road to Fascism', in *The Nation*, special number on American extremism, 30 June 1962, pp. 565–606 (Part V).

20 EDWARD CAIN, *They'd rather be Right*, New York, Macmillan, 1963, p. 91.

21 For further details on Goldwater's life, see his biography by STEPHEN SHADEGG, *Barry Goldwater, Freedom is his Flight Plan*, New York, Macfadden, 1963, which, however, is the work of an admirer, like EDWIN MCDOVELL's *Barry Goldwater, Portrait of an Arizonan*, Chicago, Henry Regnery Co., 1964. For the other side of the medal, see FRED J. COOKE, *Barry Goldwater, Extremist of the Right*, New York, Grove Press, 1964, and ARTHUR FROMMER, *Goldwater from A to Z*, New York, Pocket Books, 1964.

22 Goldwater has expounded his views in *The Conscience of a Conservative* and in *Why not Victory?*, New York, McGraw-Hill Book Co., 1962.

23 Despite his controversy with Welch, Goldwater has never rejected the John Birch Society; according to *Newsweek*, 20 May 1963, he once said: 'I know it contains some damn fine people.'

24 WALTER LIPPMANN, 'Today and Tomorrow: The Goldwater Challenge', in the *Washington Post*, 7 January 1964.

25 For Welch he is 'a politician', and therefore a man who cannot be trusted.

26 *New York Times*, 15 December 1963.

27 Quoted by EDWARD CAIN, *op. cit.*, p. 76.

28 According to some writers, the John Birch Society has between 60,000 and 100,000 members; according to others, not more than 16,000. In 1963 it spent 2 million dollars on publicizing its 'message' in the United States.

29 Captain John Morrison Birch was killed in a little Chinese village called Huang-Ko, while collecting information in the Tsingtao region, which was under Communist control.

30 These letters were reprinted by RICHARD VAHAN in *The Truth about the John Birch Society*, New York, Macfadden, 1962, pp. 92–93. Subsequently, as we are told by RICHARD DUDMAN, *Men of the Far Right*, New York, Pyramid Books, 1962, pp. 77–78, Cardinal Cushing tried to justify himself by explaining that he had only met Welch once before he wrote the letter in question and knew nothing about the activities of his society.

31 C. WRIGHT MILLS, *The Power Elite*, New York, Oxford University Press, 1956, p. 36.

32 *Cf.* RICHARD VAHAN, *op. cit.*, p. 38.

33 According to a Gallup poll, in February 1962 8 per cent of Americans approved of the John Birch Society, 43 per cent were against it and 49 per cent had no opinion. An analysis of this poll can be found in DANIEL BELL, *op. cit.*, pp. 421–439. In view of the increasing activity and aggressiveness of the John Birch Society, about a hundred prominent figures in the political, cultural, financial and religious sectors decided to found a 'National Council for Civic Responsibility', the aim of which was to give the American public a critical insight into the activities of the John Birch Society and other extremist organizations. At one of his first Press conferences (*cf. New York Times*, 18 October 1964) the president of the new organization, Arthur Larson, mentioned that 'the groups of the Radical Right are today spending twenty million dollars a year to cover the cost of—among other things—seven thousand weekly appearances on radio and television in fifty States'. The same figures are quoted in the excellent study by ARNOLD FORSTER and BENJAMIN R. EPSTEIN, *Danger on the Right*, New York, Random House, 1964.

34 See the excellent essay by ALAN F. WESTIN, *The John Birch Society: 'Radical Right' and 'Extreme Left' in the Political Context of Post World War II (1962)*, in DANIEL BELL, *op. cit.*, pp. 239–268.

35 Quoted by RICHARD VAHAN, *op. cit.*, p. 108.

36 REDILO P. OLIVER, *'Marxmanship in Dallas'*, *American Opinion*, February 1964.

37 RAYMOND FOSDICK, *'We Must Not Be Afraid of Change'*, *New York Times Magazine*, 3 April 1949.

38 ARNOLD FORSTER and BENJAMIN R. EPSTEIN, *Danger on the Right*, New York, Random House, 1960, p. 56.

39 FRED SCHWARZ, *The Mind, Heart and Soul of Communism*, 1958, p. 22.

40 Quoted by DANIEL BELL, *op. cit.*, p. 10.

41 Hargis is also president of an anti-Communist league calling itself 'We, the People'.

42 Quoted by EDWARD CAIN, *op. cit.*, p. 214.

43 *Time*, 17 August 1962.

44 The name given to the groups varies from one part of the country to another. In Illinois they are called the 'Illinois Internal Security Force'; at San Diego in California, the 'Loyal Order of Mountain Men'.

45 A complete list of American Rightist movements in which the prevailing trend is anti-Communist would fill dozens of pages. Those listed below are among the most important: National Indignation Convention, Liberty Lobby, Survival USA, Crusade for Americanism, Texans for America, Stay American, Americans for Constitutional Action, Dallas Patriotic Council, Project Alert, American Coalition of Patriotic Societies, Cardinal Mindszenty Foundation, Freedom in Action, Intercollegiate Society of Individualists, American Council of Christian Laymen, Catholic

Freedom Foundation, Daughters of the American Revolution, and the American Legion. Although they have failed to achieve the same notoriety as Hargis and Schwarz, the following 'super-patriots' have become fairly well known: W. Cleon Skousen (a former FBI agent who runs the 'All-American Society'); Mr and Mrs Kent and Phoebe Courtney (joint founders of the 'Conservative Society of America'); Frank McGehee (of the 'National Indignation Convention'); George S. Benson, president of Harding College, Searcy, Arkansas; Wayne Poucher (whose radio programme, *Life Line*, is financed by Hunt, the Texas millionaire); D. B. Lewis, Dan Smoot, Clarence Manion, the Reverend Carl McIntyre and Willis Stone.

46 *New York Herald-Tribune*, 31 March 1961.
47 By way of comparison, in 1939 the *Bund* alone had 8,300 members.
48 The National Renaissance Party has contacts with Einar Aberg's racialist group in Sweden and with the American anti-Semitic movements. In Madole's periodicals we read that Hitler was 'Europe's George Washington'; that Negroes and Jews were 'responsible for the degeneration of our beautiful country'; that Anne Frank's diary was 'an apocryphal work the aim of which was to make people believe that the Germans really exterminated the Jews'; and that the reparations pact between Germany and Israel was 'the biggest swindle in history'.
49 *New York Times*, 12 April 1962.
50 Statement made to Louis Cassels of the UPI and reprinted in the *Rocky Mountain News*, Denver, Colorado, 11 January 1962.
51 See below, pp. 354–360.
52 Quoted from *Le Monde*, 21 August 1963.
53 Rockwell's many activities were discussed on American television on 18 January 1964, in the 'Court of Reason' programme sponsored by the National Educational Television. Rockwell was also the editor of the fortnightly *Rockwell Report*, of the bi-monthly *The Stormtrooper*, and manager of a publishing house which specializes in Nazi literature. He was murdered in Arlington, Virginia, on 25 August 1967.
54 The American Nazi Party maintains contact with the European Nazi movements, with the Australian National Socialist Movement led by Donald A. Lindsay and Arthur Smith, and with the Canadian League.
55 In 1963 Matt Koehl became a member of the American Nazi Party, and Rockwell made him editor of the *National Socialist World*, which appeared once every four months and was the first periodical to be published by the World Union of National Socialists (WUNS). Among American neo-Nazi and anti-Semitic groups we must mention Merwin K. Hart's National Economic Council, the Christian Education Society founded by Conde McGinley (died 1963), William J. O'Brien's Loyal American Group, Macfarland's Nationalist Action League, the Young

Americans for Freedom and the Christian Nationalist Crusade under the leadership of Gerald L. K. Smith, which publishes, among other literature, the monthly *The Cross and the Flag*, having a circulation of 27,000 copies. Among the most widely read anti-Semitic publications is the Christian Education Society's *Common Sense* (98,000 copies).

56 According to the February 1964 number of *The Realist*, Artukovic entered the United States on 16 July 1948 under the assumed name of Alois Anic. He is also said to have been sentenced to death in France for complicity in the assassination of King Alexander I of Yugoslavia and the French Minister Louis Barthou.

57 Episode mentioned by Philippe Ben in *Le Monde*, 22 April 1962.

58 JAMES BALDWIN, *The Fire Next Time*, New York, Dial Press, 1963, p. 39.

59 On the Negro problem in America, see: ARNOLD ROSE, *The Negro in America*, New York, Harper & Brothers, 1948; E. FRANKLIN FRAZIER, *Black Bourgeoisie*, Glencoe (Illinois), Free Press, 1957; JAMES Q. WILSON, *Negro Politics: The Search for Leadership*, Glencoe, Free Press, 1960; JOHN HOPE FRANKLIN, *From Slavery to Freedom*, New York, Alfred A. Knopf, 1958; EDMUND AUSTIN, *The Black Challenge*, New York, Vantage Press, 1958.

60 Quoted from *Le Monde*, 20 August 1963.

61 Quoted from *Le Monde*, 11 July 1963.

62 During the 1930s the Ku-Klux-Klan kept in touch with the German-American Bund; nowadays it has contacts with the racialist groups in Scandinavia, Australia and South Africa. On the Klan, see: JOHN MOFFAT MECKLIN, *A Study of the American Mind*, New York, Harcourt Brace, 1924.

63 The first White Citizens' Councils appeared in 1955, in Mississippi and Georgia. The theoretician of the movement is said to be Judge Tom P. Brady, author of an anti-Negro book entitled *Black Monday*.

64 ROBERT F. WILLIAMS, *Negroes with Guns*, New York, Marzani & Munsell, 1962, p. 41.

65 Speaking of the attack on racialists which took place on 27 August 1961, Williams (*op. cit.*, p. 41) says: 'Some of the five thousand men recruited in Monroe to attack the Freedom Riders were members of the Fascist Minutemen organization.'

66 Quoted by J. A. ROGER, *The World's Great Men of Color*, New York, Vol. 2, p. 602. On Garvey, see: EDMUND DAVID CRONON, *Black Moses: The Story of Marcus Garvey and the Universal Negro Improvement Association*, Madison, University of Wisconsin Press, 1957; and GEORGE PADMORE, *Panafricanisme ou Communisme*, Paris, Présence Africaine, pp. 97–113.

67 From a speech made in Washington on 31 May 1959, quoted in E. U. ESSIEN-UDOM, *Black Nationalism*, University of Chicago Press, 1963, p. 260.

68 'The Evils of Christianity', in *Los Angeles Herald-Dispatch*, 9 January 1960.
69 *Islamic News*, Chicago, 9 July 1959, p. 7.
70 *Islamic News*, Chicago, 6 July 1959, p. 2.
71 From an article by Muhammad published in *Islamic News*, Chicago, 6 July 1959, p. 7.
72 For detailed information on the organization, recruiting methods, religious rites and aims of the Black Muslims, see: E. U. ESSIEN-UDOM, *Black Nationalism*, Chicago, University of Chicago Press, 1962; and C. ERIC LINCOLN, *The Black Muslims in America*, Boston, Beacon Press, 1963.
73 *Chicago American*, 23 February 1960.
74 DANIEL BELL, *op. cit.*, p. 141.
75 *Pittsburgh Courier*, 29 August 1959.
76 Statement made during Rockwell's interview with Louis Cassels, mentioned above.
77 *New York Herald-Tribune*, 5 June 1963.
78 GEORGE BREITMAN, *Malcolm X Speaks*, New York, Grove Press, p. 25.
79 From an interview granted by Baldwin to Jacques Amalric; *cf. Le Monde*, 24 August 1963.
80 Gene Walcott, who now calls himself Louis X and is a minister of the Temple of Islam in Boston, in addition to *The Trial*, has written a satire on 'Americanized' Negroes entitled *Orgena*.
81 JOHN J. LINDSAY, *The Case of General Walker*, p. 245.
82 From Walker's report to the United States Senate in October 1961, as published in EDWIN A. WALKER, *Censorship and Survival*, New York, The Bookmailer Inc., 1961, pp. 17–18.
83 *New York Times*, 27 October 1963.
84 From Walker's report to the Senate, *op. cit.*, p. 24.
85 These facts and figures were put before the United States Senate; *cf. Congressional Quarterly*, 27 March 1961.
86 C. WRIGHT MILLS, *op. cit.*, p. 232.
87 After MacArthur's death in Washington on 5 April 1964, two American journalists, Jim Lucas and Bob Considine, published a report on an interview they had had with the General in January 1954, which they had undertaken not to publish until after his death. According to Considine's article in *Journal American*, MacArthur's plans were as follows: 'I could have won the Korean war in ten days at the most, with losses considerably below those suffered during the so-called armistice period, and this would have changed the course of history. First of all the enemy's Air Force would have been put out of action. I would have dropped from thirty to fifty atomic bombs on their air bases and other dumps scattered about in the neck of Manchuria. . . . After destroying the enemy's Air Force, I would have sent five hundred thousand of Chiang Kai-shek's troops into action, backed up by two divisions of U.S. Marines. . . .

You will ask what would have prevented the enemy from receiving any number of reinforcements from across the River Yalu. Well, my plan was that while the landing forces were proceeding south, a strip of territory five miles wide running from the Yellow Sea to the Sea of Japan was to be sprayed with radio-active cobalt. Cobalt is a material that costs very little, and its radio-activity lasts from sixty to 120 years. For at least sixty years it would have been impossible to invade North Korea by land. The enemy could not have marched through the radio-active zone. . . . We had it in our power to destroy the Chinese army and the military potential of Red China. Perhaps for ever. My plan was a sure one. But I was forbidden to put it into execution.'

88 From the *Memorandum submitted to the Department of Defense on Propaganda Activities of Military Personnel*, in *Congressional Record*, 2 August 1961, pp. 13436–13442. With regard to 'military fingers on the trigger', the American Security Council deserves a mention, an organization financed by over 3,000 industrialists which assists big firms in carrying out 'security checks' on employees and workmen and lists all those suspected of left-wing leanings. On the 'strategical committee' of this organization we find all the service officers who were opposed to distension, e.g. Admirals Radford, Stump, Ward and Ben Morcell, and Generals Wedemeyer and Almond.

89 On 'shelter-mania', which started as the result of an imprudent speech made by Kennedy on 25 July 1961 and was immediately exploited by warmongers and speculators, see: ARTHUR I. WASKON and STANLEY L. NEWMAN, *America in Hiding*, New York, Ballantine Books, 1962.

90 In two speeches (on 25 March and 6 April 1964) which had worldwide repercussions, Senator Fulbright stressed the fact that 'the officer class seem to be more interested in continuing the Cold War and obtaining more money for defense purposes than in finding solutions to world and national problems', and advocated a drastic revision of United States foreign policy which he said was based on the 'crusading spirit of the Cold War'.

91 JOHN WEISS, *'Fascism, Politics and War'*, in *New University Thought*, Detroit, September–October 1963, p. 45.

92 FRANCIS BIDDLE, *op. cit.*, p. 109.

Chapter Sixteen: Latin America

1 *Le Monde*, 7 July 1962.
2 He was killed on 21 July 1946, and, like Mussolini, strung up by the feet from the balcony of the presidential palace. It is said that a photograph of the scene in Piazzale Loreto in Milan, published in the Bolivian Press, impressed the people of La Paz

and prompted them to treat their own dictator in the same manner.

3 Quoted by T. H. TETENS, *The New Germany and the Old Nazis*, London, Secker & Warburg, 1962, p. 48.

4 After the fall of Perón in 1956, the more prominent Nazis left Argentina and found a safer refuge in countries like Spain and Egypt.

5 *Eco del Mundo*, December 1947.

6 Joseph Mengele, the executioner of Auschwitz, is living in Paraguay under the protection of Stroessner. On 27 November 1959 he was granted Paraguayan citizenship.

7 *L'Express*, 27 September 1962. On social and economic conditions in Latin America, see the interesting study by RENÉ DUMONT, *Terres Vivantes*, Paris, Plon, 1961.

8 On Latin-American dictatorships see: JESÚS DE GALINDEZ, *La Era de Trujillo—Un estudio casuístico de la dictatura hispano-americana*, Santiago del Cile, Editorial del Pacífico, 1956; A. HICKS, *Blood in the Streets, The Life and Rule of Trujillo*, New York, 1946.

9 Under the governments of Ydigoras Fuentes (Guatemala), Arosemena (Ecuador), Villeda Morales (Honduras) and Juan Bosch (Dominican Republic).

10 SEYMOUR MARTIN LIPSET, *Political Man—The Social Bases of Politics*, New York, Doubleday, 1960, and London, Heinemann, 1963. On Perón's régime see also: ROBERT J. ALEXANDER, *The Perón Era*, New York, Columbia University Press, 1951; GEORGE I. BLANKSTEIN, *Perón's Argentina*, Chicago, University of Chicago Press, 1953.

11 *Cf.* JOHN J. JOHNSON, *Political Change in Latin America—The Emergence of the Middle Sectors*, Stanford (Calif.), Stanford University Press, 1958, p. 167.

12 Evita was undoubtedly one of the most remarkable figures in contemporary history. Her early life was a hard one, and after she arrived in the Casa Rosada she devoted herself to works of charity, of which she practically held a monopoly, founding a huge social institute, the money for which came direct from the public treasury. Her death from cancer when she was only just over thirty served to enhance the legend of her life. At her funeral the crush was so great that eight people lost their lives and 3,000 were injured.

13 After the banning of their party in 1956, the Peronists obeyed instructions and left their voting-papers blank. At some elections, 30 per cent of the voting-papers have been blank.

14 *Relazioni Internazionali*, 15 June 1963, pp. 766–767.

15 SALVADOR DE MADARIAGA, *L'Amérique Latine entre l'Ours et l'Aigle*, Paris, Stock, 1962, p. 54.

16 The movements drawing their inspiration from 'justicialism' are the sixty-two trade union organizations and the following neo-

Peronist parties: *Unión Popular, Justicia Social, Bandera Blanca, Tres Banderas*, and *Movimiento Popular Neuquino* (the last four being only provincial bodies). In the Peronist *bloc* there are today three distinct trends: the 'hard core', which still acknowledges Perón as its leader and accepts his totalitarian ideas, the 'conciliatory' trend, and the 'legalists' who favour 'Peronism without Perón'. Neo-Peronist extremists and the *Tacuara* action squads were responsible for many acts of terrorism in 1963 and 1964. During the prolonged sojourn in Argentina of Perón's wife, Maria Esther, in late 1965 and early 1966, a new organization was set up in the hope of bringing the Peronist movement under the direction of one central body.

17 Carlos Lacerda is considered to be the most formidable controversialist in Brazil. He is also known as 'the presidential gravedigger', because he drove Getulio Vargas to commit suicide, forced Janio Quadros to resign and also brought about the fall of Goulart in April 1964. He is an extreme right-winger, a diehard conservative and a virulent anti-Communist. In 1963 the journal of the Labour Party, *Ultima Hora*, accused him of allowing the police to use typically Nazi methods in repressing strikes and even authorizing them to kill beggars instead of attempting to 'redeem' them.

18 *The Nation*, 13 April 1964.

19 During 1965 the leadership of the *Tacuara* was taken over by Patricio Errecalde Pueyreddon. In the course of a Press conference the new leader stated that his movement was 'well armed and well trained' and that it would wage 'total war on Zionism'. He also revealed that the former leader, José Baxter, had fled to Communist China, taking with him a sum amounting to £55,000.

20 From Luigi Galleano's interview with Alberto Ezcurra, published in *Resistenza*, 1 May 1963.

21 See the following chapter on South Africa.

22 When the American magazine *Look* described Meinvielle as the *éminence grise* of Argentinian Nazism, the pro-Franco *SP*, in its number for 15 December 1962, took up the cudgels on the priest's behalf, maintaining that he was 'one of the most distinguished Spanish-speaking Catholic essayists'.

23 There are dozens of other neo-Fascist or racialist groups operating in Bolivia *(Falange Boliviana)*, in Chile *(Acha* and the *Partido Nacional-Socialista Chileno* under the leadership of Heinz Pfeiffer-Richter), in Mexico (the 'National Union for Country and Race'), in Uruguay (the group of Czechoslovak Fascists who run the periodical *Europan*), etc., etc.

24 A White House spokesman, Pierre Salinger, speaking at Los Angeles on 21 May 1964, said that it was an open secret that the *Alianza* had not come up to President Kennedy's expectations and had done nothing to justify the enthusiasm with which its advent had been greeted.

25 PAUL M. SWEEZY and LEO HUBERMANN, *Teoria della politica estera americana*, Turin, Einaudi, 1963, p. 78.

Chapter Seventeen: South Africa

1 On the origins of Afrikaner nationalism, see GWENDOLEN M. CARTER, *The Politics of Inequality*, London, Thames & Hudson, 1959, and LEO MARQUAND, *The Peoples and Policies of South Africa*, Cape Town, Oxford University Press, 1960. For the history of South Africa in general, see C. W. DE KJEWIET, *An History of South Africa*, Oxford University Press, 1957, and the short but cogent essay by ALAN PATON, *Hope for South Africa*, London, Pall Mall Press, 1958.

2 Quoted by BRIAN BUNTING, *The Rise of the South African Reich*, London, Penguin Books, 1964, p. 63. It should also be remembered that during the last war General Smuts was obliged to send troops to the former German colony of South-West Africa, which today has been virtually annexed by South Africa, to suppress pro-Nazi activities. Excited young men used to gather round mythical fires, shouting *'Ein Reich, ein Volk, ein Führer'*, and some of them went to Europe to fight for Hitler.

3 In 1936, when the Nazi persecution of Jews was beginning, Verwoerd and five other professors from the University of Stellenbosch called on Premier Hertzog to protest against Jewish refugees from Germany being allowed to enter the South African Union. After the war, Verwoerd was accused by the Johannesburg *Star* of having systematically falsified news received during the war. He sued the paper for libel, but lost his case, Judge Mellin ruling that falsification had been proved and that Verwoerd had 'made his paper an instrument in the service of the Nazis'. In 1961 he wrote an editorial for the Coburg periodical *Nation Europa*, which is edited by the former SS General Arthur Ehrhard and is known to be one of the publications sponsored by international neo-Nazism.

4 EDWIN S. MUNGER, *African Field Reports,* Cape Town, C. Struik, 1961, pp. 485–502.

5 RONALD SEGAL, in his *Into Exile*, London, Jonathan Cape, 1963, p. 223, says that: 'The first meeting of the enlarged Senate in January 1956 was a gala occasion. One of the newcomers was Senator Louis Weichardt, former leader of the Greyshirt movement in South Africa. "The Greyshirts," he explained, "were liquidated for something far superior to take their place." This tribute, presumably, was directed at the Nationalist Party of which he had now become a respected spokesman. Another newcomer was Senator Jan Grobler, one-time member of the Nazi-type "New Order", started during the war years by Oswald Pirow.'

6 Quoted by RONALD SEGAL, *op. cit.*, p. 42.

7 JOHN COLEMAN DE GRAFT-JOHNSON, *African Glory. The Story of Vanished Negro Civilisation*, London, Watts & Co., 1954.

8 For a complete list of the segregation laws passed between 1911 and 1960, see K. L. ROSKAM, *Apartheid and Discrimination*, Leyden, A. W. Sijthoff, 1960, pp. 54–60. See also the more detailed *L'Afrique du Sud et la Primauté du Droit*, Geneva, 1961, published under the auspices of the International Commission of Jurists. On the use of violence by the police, see the documentary evidence in the book by PATRICK DUNCAN, *South Africa's Rule of Violence*, London, Methuen, 1964.

9 ANGELO DEL BOCA, *Apartheid: affanno e dolore*, Milan, Bompiani, 1962, pp. 18–19.

10 RONALD SEGAL, *op. cit.*, p. 168.

11 RONALD SEGAL, *African Profiles*, London, Penguin African Library, 1962, p. 21.

12 *Le Monde*, 22 March 1961.

13 See the UN documents S/5310 of 6 May 1963 and S/5246 of 16 September 1963, issued by the Special Committee appointed to examine the segregation policy of the Government of the South African Republic, under the chairmanship of the Guinean Diallo Telli.

14 Here are two opinions on the Bantustans. In an interview at Stanger on 6 December 1961, Albert John Luthuli said to Angelo Del Boca: 'I am sure the government knows that the Bantustans are impracticable, first because they involve sacrifices which the Whites are not prepared to make, and secondly because we are definitely against any attempt to balkanize South Africa, either politically or economically. Yet the government is continually talking about it, with the hidden and naïve intention of convincing the rest of the world that the much-abused South African racialists are in reality worried about the fate of the natives and are about to offer them democratic institutions, or even self-government.' Actually, the Pretoria government is only trying to gain time.' On page 11 of the UN document S/5310, we read: 'The creation of Bantustans, put forward by the government as a proof of its sincere desire to continue the policy of "separate development" is, in the opinion of this Committee, a measure tending to accentuate and intensify the existing inequality. . . . These decisions have increased the tension in the reserves and have been the cause of grave incidents, especially in Transkei.'

15 See our interview with John Luthuli in *Apartheid: affanno e dolore*, *op. cit.*, pp. 177–189.

16 On 16 December 1961, at the time when the first acts of sabotage were committed, leaflets were distributed revealing the anti-racial tendency in the *Umkhonto we Sizwe*. Among other statements, we read: 'The government's policy of force, repression and violence could not for long be countered by passive resistance alone. The choice is not ours; it has been made by the Nationalist

government, which has rejected every peaceful request for the granting of rights and liberties, answering each request by using force and still more force . . . In these operations, we are acting in the interests of the entire population of this country—black, coloured and white—whose future happiness cannot be achieved until the Nationalist government has been overthrown, and white supremacy abolished; only then will liberty and democracy triumph, will full national rights be granted, making all the peoples of this country equal.'

17 The earliest insurrectional movement was the 'Hill Movement', also known as the 'Congo Movement', which carried out its first operations in Transkei in December 1960. In May 1963 the APDUSA (African Peoples' Democratic Union of South Africa), a new secret organization, distributed leaflets in Durban appealing to Africans not to join the auxiliary police.

18 *Poqo* operations are, in fact, characterized by indiscriminate violence. During the night of 21 November 1962, after an unsuccessful attack on the police station at Mbekweni near Paarl, which cost the attackers five dead, *Poqo* members killed the first two Whites they came across, a girl and a young man. In Transkei, on 14 December, they attacked the house of the collaborationist chief Matanzima, but were repulsed and lost six men. In early January 1963 they put a bomb in the building in Durban where the racialist journal *Die Nataller* is printed, and nearly succeeded in blowing up petrol tanks containing half a million gallons. On 2 February, near Engcobo (Transkei) they attacked and killed five Whites who were standing beside their caravan. A few days later they surrounded the house of another collaborationist chief, Jonginamba Deliwe, and killed him. They were pursued by the local police and army units, and fighting went on for several days. Some of these exploits were deprecated by Potlako Leballo, because in some places the political organizers enlisted the help of witch-doctors. According to Leballo, the membership of the *Poqo* movement is about 150,000.

19 Quoted by LOUIS E. LOMAX in *The Reluctant African*, New York, Harpers, 1960, p. 14.

20 *Le Monde*, 20 June 1962.

21 *Rand Daily Mail*, Johannesburg, 24 April 1963.

22 A long list of names is given in the above-quoted UN document S/5310, pp. 12–19.

23 *The Observer*, 30 June 1963, reported that 129 persons (only two of them Whites) were executed in 1962, and that 17,576 prisoners had received 86,583 strokes of the cane.

24 *The Observer*, 18 November 1962.

25 *The Economist*, 18 May 1963.

26 *The Observer*, 5 May 1963.

27 According to Document S/5310: 'Expenditure for defence purposes rose from 44 million rand for the financial year 1960–61,

to 72 million in 1961–2 and 129 million in 1962–3. The estimated expenditure for 1963–4 was 157 million rand, that is to say four times as much as before the Sharpeville incident.' Expenditure on the police service rose from 36 million rand in 1960–61 to 47 million in 1963–64.

28 South Africa relies chiefly on Great Britain, the United States and France for her supplies of arms. Great Britain, which has investments in South Africa amounting to about £1,000 million, supplies armoured cars and Blackburn Buccaneer and Canberra aircraft. France supplies Mirage III and Fugas-Magister planes and Alouette helicopters. The Panhard company has also built an assembly-line for armoured vehicles, while the Société Le Carbone has built a missile factory. After the total embargo on the export of weapons to South Africa approved by the Security Council in August 1963, the United States and Britain agreed to stop the export of any weapons that might be used for purposes of repression, but they are still supplying those 'necessary for external defence'.

29 *Rand Daily Mail*, 24 April 1963.

30 The 'secret charter' drawn up by the Nationalists (which, however, they have no intention of using except as a last resource) offers the Africans 40 per cent of the territory. At present the Bantustans represent only 13 per cent of the area of South Africa. Verwoerd is said to have been against this concession.

31 *The Sunday Times*, 18 November 1962.

32 Document S/5310, pp. 9–10.

33 *Rand Daily Mail*, 1 March 1963.

34 Despite the embargo on the supply of weapons and the fact that the Secretary-General of the United Nations was asked to report to the Security Council on the situation in South Africa, some of the African countries thought that the twenty-eighth resolution against apartheid passed by the UN would be ineffective—and they were not altogether wrong. Subsequent resolutions have proved equally ineffective.

35 From 1961 on Verwoerd negotiated with Lisbon and Salisbury in the hope of concluding a mutual defence pact with the other white countries in Africa. During the rebellion in Katanga, Verwoerd, Salazar and Welensky openly supported Tshombe and his mercenaries and the *Union Minière*. In 1963 Verwoerd supplied arms and economic aid to Rhodesia, and promised the then Premier, Winston Field, that the South African army would intervene in the event of an emergency. A new strategic railway will shortly be opened between the two countries. In November 1965, Ian Smith's unilateral declaration of independence strengthened the 'white African' block, and segregation has now been extended to Salisbury—though perhaps only temporarily.

36 Among the resolutions passed on 24 May 1963 at the African summit conference in Addis Ababa, paragraphs 8, 9, 11, 12, 14

R

and 15 of the 'confidential' document are interesting, because they ask the thirty-two African countries represented at the conference: 1) to break off diplomatic relations with Portugal and South Africa; 2) to boycott their goods and forbid their aircraft and ships to make use of airfields and ports; 3) to set up a co-ordination centre in Dar-es-Salaam, which would finance and organize national liberation movements; 4) to grant asylum and give military training to nationals of countries not yet liberated; 5) to enrol volunteers. During 1963 most of these resolutions were put into effect.

37 *Le Monde*, 5 September 1963.
38 *Le Monde*, 20 August 1963.
39 *Le Monde*, 28 April 1964.
40 *The Observer*, 12 May 1963.
41 BRIAN BUNTING, *op. cit.*, pp. 9–11.
42 *Le Monde*, 18 December 1963.
43 *Rand Daily Mail*, 9 February 1963.
44 In May 1964 Albert Luthuli was informed that he would be kept under house arrest in Stanger for another five years.

Chapter Eighteen: Africa

1 *Cf.* ANOUAR ABDEL-MALEK, *Égypte, société militaire*, Paris, Éditions du Seuil, 1962, p. 31. On p. 47, Abdel-Malek states that pro-Fascist circles had great faith in General Aziz El-Masry, Chief of the General Staff, who was dismissed by the British in 1942 for collusion with the Axis Powers. MANFRED HALPERN, in his *The Politics of Social Change in the Middle East and North Africa* (Princeton University Press, 1963), gives a list of neo-Islamic totalitarian and Fascist movements active in the Middle East, including the Syrian National Socialist Party, the Iranian National Socialist Workers' Party *(Sumka)* and the *KhaKsar* and *Jama'-at-i-Islam* movements in Pakistan.

2 Quoted in *Prevent World War III*, New York, Summer 1963.

3 Amin el Hussein, who is the symbolical head of 'all the Palestines', was an active Nazi propagandist in Berlin and France, and later fled to Cairo, where he has been living since 1946.

4 Bourguiba included the 'Rome speech' in his volume of articles and speeches published under the title *La Tunisie et la France*, Paris, Julliard, 1954, pp. 182–184.

5 ROGER LE TOURNEAU, *Évolution politique de l'Afrique du Nord musulmane, 1920–1961*, Paris, Armand Colin, 1962, p. 100.

6 *Il Mulino*, Bologna, July–August 1962, p. 687; special number dedicated to African problems during the decolonization period.

7 ROMAIN RAINERO, *Il nuovo volto dell'Africa*. Florence, Sansoni. 1963, p. 175.

8 GWENDOLEN M. CARTER, *African One-Party States*, Ithaca (N.Y.), Cornell University Press, 1962, p. 2.

9 In its issue dated 25 August 1952, *Newsweek* said: 'There is no evidence that Germans initiated the *coup*. It is, however, known that the young officers who did the planning consulted the German advisers as to "tactics". Cairo reports attribute the smoothness of the operation to German advice. Also, the young officers are reported to have chosen General Neghib as their leader on German advice. Later, Neghib publicly praised the work of the German advisory group, thus giving it an official stamp.'

10 In his *The Egyptian Army in Politics*, University of Indiana Press, 1961, VATIKIOTIS examines the cultural formation and political views of twenty 'free officers' who played an important part in the 1952 *coup d'état* and states that Nasser, Abdel Hakim Amer and Kamal Heddin Hussein were member of the Muslim Brother-hood; that Hassan Ibrahim, Anouar el-Sadâte and Gamal Salem belonged to the pro-Nazi party headed by Ahmed Hussein; and that Hussein Zulfikar Sabry carried out acts of sabotage in connivance with Rommel's headquarters staff. The list given by VATIKIOTIS is, however, incomplete; the names of other well-known men should be added, e.g. Rachad Méhanna, Hussein El-Chaféi and Abdel Monein Abdel Rouf, who were likewise members of the Muslim Brotherhood. On the activities of these extremist right-wing movements, see JEAN and SIMONE LACOUTURE, *L'Égypte en mouvement*, Paris, Éditions du Seuil, 1956, pp. 100–181.

11 In the course of an interview granted to David Wynne-Morgan and published in *The Sunday Times* (17 and 24 June, 1 July 1962) under the title *'My Revolutionary Life, President Nasser's Own Story'*, the *Rais* said that in the two years following the Alexandria demonstration (1935), he had been a member of Ahmed Hussein's party, the *Misr al-Fatât*.

12 Ahmed Hussein was in the news again in 1936, when he published a kind of Egyptian *Mein Kampf* entitled *Imânì*. In the course of ten years his party changed its name three times; in 1935 it called itself the *Misr al-Fatât*, in 1940, the 'Islamic National Party', and in 1946 it became the 'Socialist Party'. The virulent hatred of Jews expressed in his newspaper, *Al Ichtirakya*, surpassed anything that appeared in the papers controlled by Goebbels.

13 *France-Observateur*, 28 June 1956.

14 Published for the first time in *Foreign Affairs* in 1954, this little book has since been translated into several languages under the auspices of the Egyptian Ministry of Information. We have used the Italian translation, published in Cairo by *Dar Al-Maaref*. In *Les Fascismes dans l'histoire* (Paris, Éditions du Cerf, 1959, pp. 41–42) HENRI LEMAÎTRE says of this work: 'In his book, the author of *The Philosophy of Revolution* (the Egyptian dictator's *Mein Kampf*) lays down principles and expounds theories which are in the purest style of Fascism and his xenophobia is National Socialist rather than Islamic. Nevertheless, the United Arab Republic, apart from the fact that it is only in its infancy, cannot serve as

a model, because its Fascism is mingled and confused with other elements.'

15 ANOUAR ABDEL-MALEK, *op. cit.*

16 On the 'charter', see the article by FIKRI MELEKA entitled *La direction collégiale assurera l'exercice démocratique de l'action populaire* in the September–October number of the Egyptian review *Le Scribe*.

17 In reality Nasser expropriated less land than a former Bey who was a member of the Senate had threatened to confiscate eight years before. Nor, as a result of his extravagant prestige policy, could he meet the demands of the workers, who were being paid wretched wages. With typical hypocrisy the Cairo journal *Al-Ahram* published on 30 February 1962 a government announcement—preceded by a pompous preamble maintaining that 'President Gamal Abdel Nasser is anxious to realize the aims of the Egyptian revolution'—saying that 11,000 jobs were available at a daily wage of 180 Egyptian mils (less than four shillings), which was the figure established ten years earlier as the minimum wage for a labourer.

18 After the campaigns of persecution culminating in the arrest of numerous Communists and progressives, in particular between 1954 and 1956 and from 1959 to 1962, several thousand members of the opposition were sent to the concentration camps at Abu Zaabal (Cairo), in the El Kharga oasis, at Kena (Upper Egypt) and in the Fayum. In *France-Observateur* (16 June 1955) Michel Barrat wrote: 'Nowadays the political prisoners are being sent right out into the desert, to the new camp at Siwa. Another camp has already been got ready further south, in the Kharga oasis. It can accommodate 7,000 prisoners. No water, no huts; only barbed wire beneath the rays of the sun. The prisons in Cairo and other large cities are so crowded, that "politicals" have had to be put with common criminals. And when they organized a protest strike, they were given fifty strokes of the whip.' Between 1959 and 1963, thirteen prisoners died under torture (electric shocks, water pumped into their stomachs, or beatings-up), and the Catholic review *Esprit* published a harrowing account of these atrocities. On 4 July 1963 Nasser, who had previously denied the existence of any such camps, told a representative of *Le Monde* that he had decided to do away with these concentration camps. 'Three-quarters of our prisoners have already been freed during the last few months, and before the end of the year there will not be a single political prisoner left in the whole of the United Arab Republic.' But another year passed before he fulfilled his promise. This he did just before Khrushchev arrived in Egypt, but at the same time he issued a decree giving him authority to send ex-inmates of concentration camps back to prison if circumstances made it necessary.

19 From the attempt to annex the Sudan in 1954 to the incorporation

of Syria in 1958, from the failure to re-form the United Arab Republic in 1963 to armed intervention in the Yemen, Nasser's policy has always been based on two guiding principles—expansion within the Arab world and penetration into Africa up the Nile valley. The broadcasts of the 'Voice of the Arabs' programme are the best proofs of Egypt's imperialistic aims.

20 As a matter of fact a certain number of Nazis reached Cairo before Nasser came to power. Between 1948 and 1951 King Farouk employed a number of German experts, among these being Wilhelm Voss—who during the war had been in charge of the supply of weapons to the armed forces and, according to *Der Spiegel* (26 October 1955), was warmly recommended by the West German government—General Wilhelm Fahrmbacher, Major-General Oscar Munzel, and the parachutist Colonel Gerhard Mertins. After he came to power, Nasser intensified the search for German experts, and during a debate on Middle East affairs on 3 May 1963 the Senator for Alaska, Ernest Gruening, produced a long list of names, including, among others, the following: the former *SS-Standartenführer* Baumann (known in Eygypt as Ali Ben Khader), who had had a share in the destruction of the Warsaw ghetto; Willy Berner (alias Ben Kashir), who had been one of the guards at the Mauthausen concentration camp; Lieutenant-Colonel Leopold Gleim (alias Al-Nasher), who was placed in charge of the United Arab Republic's security services; Erich Altern, formerly Gestapo Commissar for Jewish Affairs in Galicia; Heinrich Willermann (alias Naim Fahum), formerly SS medical officer at Dachau, who was placed in charge of the medical services in Egyptian concentration camps together with Hans Eisele, formerly chief medical officer at Buchenwald; *Obersturmbannführer* Bernard Bender (alias Ben Salem), who is now the head of Nasser's security police; *SS-Gruppenführer* Alois Moser (alias Hassan Yuleiman), in charge of the training of Nasser's youth movements; Joachim Däumling, former head of the Gestapo in Düsseldorf; *SS-Gruppenführer* Buble (alias Amman); Karl Luder, a former 'hierarch' in the *Hitler-Jugend*; SS-General Dirlewanger, who is now an adviser on guerrilla warfare.

21 Von Leers died in January 1965. Other Germans who, according to Senator Gruening, worked with him were Louis Heiden, a former head of the Nazi information service, who translated Hitler's *Mein Kampf* into Arabic, *SS-Führer* Daniel Perrit-Gentil, and Georges Dieudonné, alias Georges Oltremare, a former leader of the Swiss Nazi Party. According to a report submitted on 14 April 1965 to the *Union Internationale de la Résistance et de la Déportation* in Munich by a committee of experts, the Arab League offices in various parts of the world are supporting the chief neo-Nazi and anti-Semitic movements. The report states that Egyptian functionaries are said to be in contact with members of the *Tacuara*, the *Guardia Restauradora Nacionalista* and the American

Nazi Party, as well as with the movements led by Malcolm X and Colin Jordan. It is claimed that Cairo spent 23 million Marks on subsidies to movements in Germany alone.

22 On several occasions the Egyptian government has denied that the Nazis ever committed atrocities against the Jews. According to *Le Monde* (5 May 1962) an Egyptian Minister, Zulfikar Sabry, made the following statement in the Egyptian parliament: 'The Nazis never exterminated 6 million Jews, and not even 1 million. Hitler allowed Jews to emigrate against payment of a given sum. As for the poorer Jews, he sent them to camps so that he might be in a position to negotiate with the Zionist leaders and obtain the money and materials he needed to keep the war going.' In a volume published by the Egyptian Ministry of Information (*Eichmann dans le miroir d'Israel*, Cairo, Al Taawon, 1961, p. 12) we read: 'If it accepts Ben Gurion's demands, the West German government will continue to pay compensation, not to individual Jews, but to Israel, *because of the six million Jews who are supposed to have been victims of Hitler*' (italics ours).

23 Among the German experts on missiles who are working (or have worked) for Nasser, the German Press mentions the following: Eugen Sänger, director of the Research Institute in Stuttgart and one of the leading world authorities on spatial matters; Paul Goercke, Wolfgang Pilz and Hans Kleinwächter, who formerly worked for the Nazis at the Peenemünde experimental station; Heinz Krug and about a hundred other more or less well-known scientists. They were responsible for the construction of two missiles—the *El-Kahir* (with a range of about 350 miles) and *El-Safir* (range about 185 miles), which were built in the factories numbered 36, 135 and 333, at Heluan and Heliopolis on the outskirts of Cairo. In 1966 the United Arab Republic had from 800 to 1,000 of these missiles. The Egyptian aircraft industry owes its development to the celebrated designer of German fighter aircraft Willy Messerschmitt, and to the Austrian designer Ferdinand Brandner. According to *Der Spiegel* (8 May 1963), with the assistance of about 380 German and Austrian engineers and technicians these two produced various types of fighter aircraft, among them being one which was faster than the Mach. 2. Even after the revelations which appeared in newspapers all over the world, the Bonn government made no attempt to persuade German scientists to return home or to restrict the export of strategic materials to Egypt. In an interview with a representative of the London *Daily Express* (4 August 1963) Brandner himself said: 'We obtained all the equipment and materials for our laboratories from West Germany, Austria, Switzerland and the United States.' For its part, the government of the United Arab Republic has never denied the presence in Cairo of a small army of German scientists, and it has even tried to defend their reputations. In the columns of *Al-Ahram* (27 June 1964) Nasser's spokesman,

Hassanein Heykal, said that 'it is absurd to talk about their having worked for the Nazis, since they were merely doing their duty to their country. Anyway, if America and other powers make use of their services, why shouldn't Egypt do the same?' On the other hand we know less about their achievements in the fields of nuclear weapons and poison gas, of which there was some talk in the British Press in May 1964, especially in *The Guardian*.

24 From a speech made by Gamal Abdel Nasser on 26 November 1961.
25 ANOUAR ABDEL-MALEK, *op. cit.*, pp. 351–352.
26 *Partisans*, January–February 1963, pp. 42–58.
27 *Al-Ahram*, Cairo, 31 January 1963.
28 *Nouvelles Prospectives*, Tel Aviv, June–July 1963, p. 95. In an interview granted to Erich Rouleau (*Le Monde*, 20 March 1963), Michel Aflak, the theoretician of the Syrian *Baat*, maintained that Nasserism did not appeal to the 'people's organizations' and stressed the weaknesses of a purely military régime. In the ensuing controversy, due mainly to the failure to reconstitute the United Arab Republic, Nasser turned the tables on the *Baat* and described their policy as 'dictatorial and Fascist'.
29 *Orient*, Paris, fourth quarter 1961, p. 64. Similar accusations were also made by *The Economist*, 5 May 1962.
30 *Europa-Korrespondenz*, Vienna, January 1960.
31 Quoted by DENNIS EISENBERG, *Fascistes et Nazis d'aujourd'hui*, Paris, Albin Michel, p. 161.
32 MAURICE BARDÈCHE, *Qu'est-ce que le Fascisme?*, Paris, Les Sept Couleurs, n.d., pp. 128–129.
33 ANOUAR ABDEL-MALEK, *op. cit.*, pp. 364–365.
34 *Le Monde*, 26 September 1962.
35 *Le Monde*, 12 April 1964.
36 *The Sunday Times*, 1 February 1963.
37 *Relazioni Internazionali*, 30 May 1964, pp. 817–818.
38 *Progrès Égyptien*, 21 May 1964.
39 KWAME NKRUMAH, *Africa Must Unite*, London, Heinemann, 1963.
40 JOHN HATCH, *Africa Today and Tomorrow*, New York, Praeger, 1960, p. 47.
41 *Cf.* statements made by the opposition leaders Kofi Busia and Joseph B. Danquah, in *Africa aspetta il 1960*, by ANGELO DEL BOCA, Milan, Bompiani, 1959, pp. 169–174.
42 On 11 December 1963, after the acquittal of these three men for lack of evidence, Nkrumah decided to dismiss the Chief Justice, Sir Arku Korsah. Parliament was recalled and on 23 December it passed a law which virtually put all the power in the hands of the President of the Republic, who was given the right to quash verdicts of the special tribunal, if this was necessary 'in the interests of the security of the State'. This law was backdated to November 1961
43 *Le Monde*, 8 October 1962.

44 *The Autobiography of Kwame Nkrumah*, Edinburgh, Thomas Nelson & Sons, 1957, p. 45.

45 ANGELO DEL BOCA, *op. cit.*, p. 161.

46 The result of the referendum on the one-party system was as follows: 2,773,920 'for' and 2,452 'against', out of a total of 2,900,000 votes cast. In the days immediately preceding the general election—as we read in the *New York Herald-Tribune* for 25 January 1964—one of the government-controlled newspapers, the *Ghanaian Times*, stated that 'we have means of identifying all those who fail to vote or who do not put their ballot-papers in the right box'.

47 PHILIPPE DECRAENE, *Le Panafricanisme*, Paris, Presses Universitaires de France, 1959, p. 43.

48 KWAME NKRUMAH, *op. cit.*

49 *Cf.* the Ghanaian *Parliamentary Debates*, Vol. 27, No. 15, 6 June 1962, p. 556.

50 RICHARD WRIGHT, in *Écoute, homme blanc*, Paris, Calman-Lévy, 1959, p. 121, maintains that Nkrumah wanted power not for its own sake, but for that of his people, but this is in contradiction with Nkrumah's charismatic certainty that he was unique, indispensable and irreplaceable. 'This nation is my creation,' he told Gwendolen M. Carter (*Independence for Africa*, New York, Praeger, 1960, p. 134); 'if I should die there would be chaos.'

51 *Parliamentary Debates*, Accra, May 1961.

52 Titles mentioned by the Accra *Evening News*, quoted by SMITH HEMPSTONE, *The New Africa*, London, Faber & Faber, 1961, p. 484.

53 Quoted by DAVID E. APTER, *Ghana in Transition*, New York, Atheneum, 1963, p. 326.

54 *The Observer*, 4 September 1961.

55 *Le Monde*, 15 May 1963.

56 Special number of the *Star of Africa*, on the occasion of the *Osagyefo*'s fifty-fourth birthday, Accra, New Nation Publishing Company, 1963, p. 7.

57 Five attempts were made on Nkrumah's life. The first three resulted in 21 people being killed and 385 injured.

58 KWAME NKRUMAH, *Consciencism*, London, Heinemann, 1964.

59 GEORGE W. SHEPHERD, Jr., *The Politics of African Nationalism*, New York, Praeger, 1962, p. 87.

60 *La democrazia in Africa*, edited by ROMAIN RAINERO, Milan, Edizioni di Comunità, 1962, p. 59.

61 The quotations are from LÉOPOLD SÉDAR SENGHOR, *Politica Africana*, Rome, Edizioni Cinque Lune, 1962.

62 *La democrazia in Africa*, *op. cit.*, pp. 59–80.

63 *Ibid.*, p. 30.

64 *Cf.* the interview with Sékou Touré, in ANGELO DEL BOCA, *op. cit.*, p. 79.

65 Quoted by CHARLES-HENRI FAVROD, *L'Afrique seule*, Paris, Éditions du Seuil, 1961, p. 102.

66 From an interview granted to a representative of *Jeune Afrique*, April 1963.

67 The quotations are from the volume by RENÉ DUMONT, *L'Afrique est mal partie*, Paris, Éditions du Seuil, 1962.

68 FRANTZ FANON, *I dannati della terra*, Turin, Einaudi, 1962, p. 140.

69 *Révolution Africaine*, Algiers, April 1963.

70 *France-Observateur*, 18 April 1963.

71 'Charter of the Organization of African States and Madagascar', article 3, paragraph 5, Addis Ababa, 24 May 1963 (text in French).

72 ERNEST MILCENT, in *Témoignage Chrétien*, 25 August 1963.

73 On 13 May 1963 the former Premier Mamadou Dia was sentenced to imprisonment for life by the Senegal High Court of Justice. Extenuating circumstances were not admitted, and the sentence was surprisingly severe.

74 FRANTZ FANON, *op. cit.*, p. 141.

75 For favourable opinions on Ben Bella see: CLAUDE ESTIER, *Pour l'Algérie*, Paris, François Maspéro, 1964; DANIEL GUÉRIN, *L'Algérie qui se cherche*, Paris, Présence Africaine, 1964. Several works have been published by adversaries of Ben Bella, among them being: HOCINE AIT AHMED, *La guerre et l'après-guerre*, Paris, Les Éditions de Minuit, 1964, and MOHAMMED BOUDIAF, *Où va l'Algérie?*, Paris, Librairie de l'Étoile, 1964.

76 *New York Times*, 17 August 1963.

77 *Avant-Garde*, Rabat, 1 September 1963. On the counter-measures taken during the summer of 1963 and the proceedings against the UNFP leaders, see: *La vérité sur 'Le complot'*, in the French-language supplement to the Casablanca daily *At Tahrir*, November 1963; *Procès de l'UNFP*, report by Maître Nicolas Jacob; *Le Procès de Rabat*, document No. 3, Paris, 1964; *Bulletin du Comité d'étude sur la situation au Maroc, Numéro Spécial*, Paris, January 1964.

78 ROMAIN RAINERO, *op. cit.*, p. 117. See also MAMADOU DIA, *L'Économie Africaine*, Paris, Presses Universitaires de France, 1957, pp. 109–115.

79 *Cf. Le Monde*, 28 August 1963.

80 See the article entitled *La guerre des 'lobbies'* by ERICH ROULEAU, in *Le Monde*, 9 January 1962. The man who had been mainly responsible for the disintegration of the new Congolese State, Moise Tshombe, suddenly reappeared in Léopoldville during the summer of 1964, claiming that he had come back to bring about a 'national reconciliation'. When he failed to do this, as was only to be expected, he asked for foreign military aid to suppress a revolt organized by the supporters of Lumumba. Commenting on the arrival of the Americans in the Congo, the Dakar Catholic weekly *Afrique Nouvelle* (August 1964) remarked: 'Whenever

American "technicians" arrive, it means that the war will be prolonged and that the country will be divided up. Meanwhile, the Congo is in the same situation as Laos. It needs only one more step to make it like Vietnam and Korea.'

81 Statement made to Angelo Del Boca in Douala on 12 May 1959. Ruben Un Nyobé, the first president of the UPC, was killed in 1958 by machine-gun fire during an ambuscade. His successor, Dr Félix Moumié, died in Geneva after drinking a liquid containing thallium. He had been enticed there by a self-styled journalist named William Bechtel, who in reality was a counter-espionage agent.

82 For further information on the campaign of repression in Cameroon, see the 'UPC memorandum' sent to the heads of States and governments who were members of the African Unity Organization (23 August 1963).

83 *La Stampa*, 3 September 1963.

84 FRANTZ FANON, *op. cit.*, p. 138, and in the chapter entitled *Disavventure della coscienza nazionale, ibid.*, pp., 119–164.

85 *Le Monde*, 23 September 1963.

86 BASIL DAVIDSON, *Which Way Africa? The Search for a New Society*, London, Penguin African Library, 1964. p. 182. On the restriction of liberty among the African peoples, see also GIAMPAOLO CALCHI NOVATI, *L'Africa Nera non è indipendente*, Milan, Edizioni di Comunità, 1964.

Chapter Nineteen: Conclusions

1 The statutory limitation for all crimes committed by Nazis and collaborationists was due to expire in September 1964 in France and Belgium, on 8 May 1965 in Germany, and on 29 June 1965 in Austria. The basic concept of these prescription measures was, as is well known, that after twenty years a crime cannot be punished because 'no one would remember anything about it'. The associations of Resistance members and deportees, together with other anti-Fascist organizations, protested against the proposed prescription, maintaining that the very large number of Nazi war criminals who have not been punished is due, not to mere chance, but to the fact that no co-ordinated measures were taken in good time by most of the European governments in order to track down the culprits and bring them to trial. At the headquarters of the *Amitiés de la Résistance Belge* in Brussels, a Press conference was organized on 13 February 1964 by the *Union Internationale de la Résistance et de la Déportation* under the chairmanship of Albert Le Roye, president of the Belgian association, during which Hubert Halin, chairman of the 'Committee of Experts for the struggle against neo-Nazism', told the journalists that many men guilty of atrocious massacres during the war were

still at liberty in various European countries, and also in South America and Africa. Halin pointed out that the hospitality granted to these men, and the fact that in many cases no attempt to obtain their extradition had been made by the countries concerned, were an insult to the memory of those who had sacrificed their lives for the Resistance cause, and that a full-scale campaign should be launched in order to compel the governments concerned to suspend the prescription measures and in the meantime trace the criminals. A report on Hubert Halin's Press conference was published in the Resistance periodical *Risorgimento*, No. 3, Turin, 1964, pp. 56–58. In *La voix internationale de la Résistance* (No. 76, June 1964), edited by Halin and published in Brussels, we read that adherence to the original prescription date would have meant that 1,693 Belgians sentenced to death and 501 sentenced to life imprisonment, all *in absentia*, for crimes committed under the Nazi régime would have had their sentences quashed. The same periodical stated that in Poland and Israel legal measures had been taken to suspend the statutory limitation as regards war crimes. On 19 November 1964, the Belgian parliament approved, by a substantial majority, a law proroguing prescription for war crimes for another ten years. On 25 March 1965 the West German parliament passed a bill according to which the statutory limitation will still be twenty years, but starting from 1 January 1950. The bill also contains provisions defining the types of crimes which render the culprits still liable to prosecution.

2 The statements here reproduced were obtained by the authors of the present volume between September 1962 and March 1963.

3 In 1961 Senator Ferruccio Parri introduced a bill providing for the dissolution of the MSI, in accordance with the first paragraph of the 'Twelfth and Final Draft of the Constitution of the Italian Republic', which specifically forbids the 'reconstitution in whatsoever form of the dissolved Fascist Party'. Provision was made under Law No. 645 of 20 June 1952 for the enforcement of this paragraph of the constitution, but although the Fascist characteristics of the MSI were obvious, the law was not enforced. The senatorial committee appointed to examine Parri's bill rejected it in a majority report which maintained that the legislature had no authority to define the 'Fascist' nature of the MSI, and that investigation of the case and a decision as to the dissolution of the MSI must be left to the judiciary. In their minority report Senators Sansone and Secchia gave ample reasons for disagreeing with the decision of the majority, and these were discussed at a meeting organized in Florence by the Federal Committee of the Resistance and held on 2 July 1961, in order to clarify the provisions of the constitution as regards this matter. (The proceedings at this meeting can be read in *Un Adempimento Improrogabile*, edited by the *Comitato Promotore e del Consiglio Regionale Toscano della Resistenza*, Florence, 1961.) The meeting was

attended by prominent jurists, and a resolution approving Parri's bill was carried unanimously.

4   When interviewing these Italian politicians, writers and journalists regarding their ideas about Fascism today, we also asked them specifically whether they thought the MSI ought to be banned or not. General Raffaele Cadorna said that he did not think that a democratic régime should dissolve any party. 'Banning the MSI,' he said, 'would mean giving it publicity.' Ignazio Silone replied that 'it would be to the MSI's advantage to become a clandestine movement; so long as it is free, it can be kept in quarantine'. Deputy Marazza said that 'at one time' he had been in favour of applying 'Fascist laws and methods' to the MSI. 'If that had been done,' he added, 'it is obvious that the MSI could never even have been formed. But since we have chosen to use democratic methods even towards them, we must content ourselves with enforcing the laws for the defence of the State.' Primo Levi was in favour of banning the MSI. 'I don't know what the political consequences would be,' he said, 'but I would be willing to pay a pretty high price in order to get it banned. It seems to me that this is just a logical way of making a clean sweep, though none of the Christian Democrat governments has ventured to make it. The presence of the MSI in parliament and of their speakers at public meetings constitutes a political danger as well as a danger to morals, one of the reasons being the very low intellectual level of everything the neo-Fascists say and write.' According to Riccardo Bauer, any such action against the MSI would be futile and might produce unexpected results. 'The worst elements in the MSI,' he said, 'would remain if it were to become a clandestine movement. What is important is to take effective action against the exponents of neo-Fascism every time they infringe the law or commit acts of violence.' Senator Piero Caleffi thought that 'a democratic régime ought not to resort to methods typical of a dictatorship', and that in any case it would be better 'to keep the most violent and headstrong Fascists in a party of their own, rather than have them contaminating other parties'.

Index

530 *Index*